Thomas L. Thompson

The Historicity of the Patriarchal Narratives

Thomas L. Thompson

The Historicity of the Patriarchal Narratives

The Quest for the Historical Abraham

Walter de Gruyter · Berlin · New York
1974

Beiheft zur Zeitschrift für die alttestamentliche Wissenschaft
Herausgegeben von Georg Fohrer
133

ISBN 3 11 004096 4

Library of Congress Catalog Card Number: 72—76042

Printed in Germany
Satz und Druck: Walter de Gruyter & Co.

to

Professor D. Dr. Kurt Galling

Preface

The manuscript for the following study was written between May 1969 and June 1971. Since then some alterations and corrections have been made. The text, however, has been revised to include a discussion of the most recent literature only in those cases where this literature is seen to differ substantially from earlier publications.

Since this work attempts a synthetic treatment of the interdependent interpretations of historical materials scattered through several quite distinct academic fields, I am specially grateful for the advice and detailed criticism I have received from many people of greater experience than mine. In this respect, I want particularly to thank the following: Professor Dr. Hellmut Brunner, Professor Dr. Herbert Haag, Dr. Dorothy Irvin, Dr. John Landgraf, Professor Dr. Wolfgang Röllig, and Professor Dr. Hans Peter Rüger.

To Professor D. Dr. Kurt Galling, to whom this book is dedicated, I am permanently indebted, for his interest, his encouragement, and his constant support since my first semester in Tübingen in 1963.

I wish also to thank the Gressmann Stiftung for their generous financial aid in helping to meet the publication costs of this volume, and Professor D. Dr. Georg Fohrer for accepting this book as a Beiheft for the Zeitschrift für die alttestamentliche Wissenschaft.

Tübingen, October, 1973

Table of Contents

Chapter 1

Introduction

A. ARCHAEOLOGY OR BIBLICAL CRITICISM?

The present study is an attempt to review the central arguments that are currently held by biblical scholars in favor of the historicity of the patriarchs in Genesis. For reasons of time and space I have had to limit my study to the traditions in Genesis about Abraham, Isaac, and Jacob. Those arguments which attempt to relate Jacob to the Hyksos movement are either dependent upon the historicity of the Joseph traditions, or will be considered — without direct reference to the Hyksos — in Chapter 2, which deals with the names of the patriarchs. In regard to the historicity of the Joseph stories it is hardly too bold to say that few scholars would consider that it has been established independent of the widespread acceptance of the historicity of Gen 11 through 36. An examination of the literary structure of the individual traditions about Joseph and the three major patriarchs is outside the scope of this work. Nevertheless, the structures of Gen 11 10 ff. and Gen 14 will be considered, since their literary forms have direct significance for the question of historicity.

A treatment of the arguments for dating the patriarchs to the Amarna Period is here limited to a discussion of the relationship between Genesis and the Nuzi tablets. I hope to treat this question along with the literary relationships of the Genesis narratives in a reinvestigation of the "Homer and Bible" question at some future date. That the present study in no way supports this "alternative" dating will become clear in the following pages.

The thesis under review is generally accepted as proven, or at least as probable. There are, of course, many variations of the thesis, for not all authors who treat the subject accept the complete accuracy and relevance of every aspect of the historical analogue that has been constructed. Yet nearly all accept the general claim that the historicity of the biblical traditions about the patriarchs has been substantiated by the archaeological and historical research of the last half-century. Indeed, within the last ten years, the delineation of the "patriarchal period" as a real historical period has been commonly spoken of as one of the major achievements of biblical archaeology[1]. This opinion has become so commonplace that many recent works on Genesis and the patriarchs proceed on the assumption that this historicity has already been substantially proven and might serve as a basis for subsequent interpretation[2]. Even literary critical studies of individual traditions within Genesis now accept the basic historicity of Abraham, Isaac, and Jacob, and see the present ground of debate to lie not in the question of historicity itself, but in the dating of the "patriarchal period", whether it is to be found in the first half of the Second Millenium B. C. or during the Amarna Period[3].

Protests against this general tendency are not totally absent[4]. They have, however, either been directed against the more obvious abuses of certain biblical archaeologists, or have been of such a general nature that they serve only to cast some doubt on the complete conclusiveness of the thesis as now presented[5].

The results of my own investigations, if they are for the most part acceptable, seem sufficient to require a complete reappraisal of the current position on the historical character of the patriarchal narratives. These results support the minority position that the text of Genesis is not an historical document, but is rather

---

1 Cf., e. g., G. E. Wright, Modern Issues in Biblical Studies — History and the Patriarchs, ET 71 (1959/60), 292: "One of the remarkable results of archaeological research during the period between the two Wars was the sudden emergence of the Patriarchal Age of Biblical History as one which could be fitted within an actually discernible period in the history of Western Asia."

2 So, H. H. Rowley, Worship in Ancient Israel, 1967, 5—7; E. H. Maly, Genesis, Jerome Biblical Commentary 1968, 7: "With regard to the patriarchal history, the basic 'facts' included such items as the movements of the patriarchs, their occupations, their relations with their neighbors, and their marriages and deaths. There is every reason for the modern scientific historian to accept this basic family history, which served as the foundation for the author's religious history. The sciences of ancient Near Eastern history and especially of archaeology have shown that the underlying social, juridical, political, geographical, and religious conditons in Genesis are precisely those of the Second Millenium and could not have been invented by an author living in a much later period. Consequently, strictly on historical grounds, we can admit the existence of these seminomadic shepherds who originated, at least proximately, in Upper Mesopotamia, migrated to Canaan, lived out their lives much as described in Genesis, and at least some of whom descended into Egypt."

3 R. Kilian, Isaaks Opferung, SBS 44, 1970, 5. 9f.

4 E. g., J. J. Finkelstein, The Bible, Archaeology and History, Commentary 27 (1959), 341—349; W. Stählin, Auch darin hat die Bibel Recht, 1964.

5 Of particular interest is the very sharp but completely justified critique of Morton Smith, The Present State of Old Testament Studies, JBL 88 (1969), 19—35. See also, B. Mazar, The Historical Background of the Book of Genesis, JNES 28 (1969), 73—83.

a collection of literary traditions whose "historical background" and "Sitz im Leben" need to be sought at every stage of each tradition's development. As literary tradition, no part of Genesis can be assumed to be history unless its literary character can first be shown to be historiographical, at which point the usual norms of validation as to its veracity must still be applied[6].

Central to the argument for the historicity of the patriarchal narratives is the understanding that the historical value of Gen 11_{26}ff. is substantially supported by what we know of the movements of the Early West Semites in Mesopotamia of the Ur III and Old Babylonian Periods, in Egypt of the First Intermediate, and in Palestine during the archaeological period variously known as Intermediate EB-MB or Middle Bronze I. Largely because of the long established character of this interpretation there has been a tendency not only to see the patriarchal narratives in the light of this historical background — indeed as historical records themselves — but also to interpret the historical and archaeological information in the light of the biblical narratives, with a resulting harmonization that makes the hypothesis increasingly difficult to analyze; for such analysis demands not only an investigation of whether the biblical traditions really do presuppose the type of background that historical studies and archaeology offer, but it demands a new investigation of the historical and archaeological sources as well. Because of this, it seems necessary to insist on a methodology of writing the history of the ancient Near East which observes a careful distinction between the types of materials at hand, and which allows historical conclusions to be drawn only after each type of material has been independently examined. Thus, archaeological materials should not be dated or evaluated on the basis of written texts which are independent of these materials; so also written

---

[6] This view of the patriarchal narratives is not particularly new here, and is indebted to the work of H. Gunkel, Genesis, 1966[7]; see also his Jakob und Esau, PrJ 176 (1919), 339—362, and Jakob, RGG[2], III, 14—17; H. Greßmann, Sage und Geschichte in den Patriarchenerzählungen, ZAW 30 (1910), 1—34; Ursprung und Entwicklung der Joseph-Sage, Eucharisterion, Festschrift H. Gunkel, hrsg. von H. Schmidt, 1923, 1—55; and K. Galling, Die Erwählungstraditionen Israels, BZAW 48, 1928. "Die 'Wanderung' oder, wie man zu sagen pflegt, das Nomadentum dieses Patriarchen beruht also nicht auf irgendwelcher geschichtlichen Erinnerung, sondern ist eine künstliche Konstruktion der Sagensammler, um verschiedene Traditionen zusammenzuschweißen. Diese elementare Erkenntnis der Sagenforschung macht alle modernen Bestrebungen, die 'Wanderung Abrahams aus Ur in Chaldäa nach Hebron' mit Hilfe der Phantasie als lebendige Wirklichkeit zu gestalten, von vornherein als aussichtslos zunichte." (Greßmann, ZAW 30, 9f.). For a review of the research on the patriarchs since Wellhausen, see the admirable study of H. Weidmann, Die Patriarchen und ihre Religion, 1968.

documents should not be interpreted on the basis of archaeological hypotheses.

Regarding the question of historicity itself, it is important to point out that the argument for historicity is generally not based on literary, internal grounds (that the stories purport to be historical records); it is rather based on an argument from analogy: that the history of the early Second Millenium is so strikingly similar to the background of the patriarchal narratives that the conclusion, that they must correspond in fact, is seen as directly following. In other words, the ability to maintain the historicity of the patriarchal narratives depends on the cumulative weight of an analogy as well as the actual correspondence of the various factors drawn from different sources and types of sources which go to make up the historical analogue. This is particularly true of those arguments involved in what I would like to call the "Amorite Hypothesis" which is dealt with in the following six chapters of this dissertation, which arguments attempt to establish the historical probability or verisimilitude of the patriarchal narratives and serve as the foundation for most of the significant alternative and supporting arguments which have been proposed (discussed in chapters 8, 9 and 10), and without which these alternative reconstructions could not command significant adherence.

The major architect of the "Amorite Hypothesis" has been W. F. Albright, who, over the past fifty years, has developed a chain of evidence supporting a view of the history of the early Second Millenium which has dominated scholarly discussion about the background of the patriarchal narratives. The thesis has been most thoroughly developed in several works of Kathleen Kenyon, especially in the new Cambridge Ancient History and her Amorites and Canaanites[7]. It has achieved standard textbook acceptance in such influential works as G. E. Wright's Biblical Archaeology[8], J. Bright's History of Israel[9], and E. A. Speiser's Genesis[10]. Significant variations of this hypothesis are to be found in M. Noth's Geschichte Israels[11], in

---

[7] Posener, Bottéro and Kenyon, Syria and Palestine, c. 2160—1780, CAH, fasc. 29, 1965²; Amorites and Canaanites, 1966. For the numerous works of Albright over the last fifty years see Bibliography.

[8] G. E. Wright, Biblical Aracheology, 1957; see also his Westminster Historical Atlas to the Bible, 1957.

[9] J. Bright, History of Israel, 1959; see also his Early Israel in Recent History Writing, SBTh 19, 1956, and Modern Study of Old Testament Literature, in: Albright Festschrift, 13—31.

[10] E. A. Speiser, Genesis, Anchor Bible Commentrary, 1964.

[11] M. Noth, Geschichte Israels, 1954²; Der Beitrag der Archäologie zur Geschichte Israels, VTS (7 1960) 262—282; Die Ursprünge des alten Israel im Lichte neuer Quellen, 1961.

H. H. Rowley's From Joseph to Joshua[12], and in several widely publicized articles of Roland de Vaux[13].

Particularly important in the history of the development of this interpretation is the methodology used by Martin Noth (and to some extent by de Vaux). In his analysis of the formation of the biblical traditions by means of form criticism, Noth has sought to discover the "historical core" which reaches back to the origin of the traditions, rather than the historicity of the traditions as a whole. He finds this core in the migrations of the "Proto-Aramaeans" in the early Second Millenium. Although he has been led to reject the historicity of many of the traditions in their present form, his position is much closer to that of John Bright than is generally apparent[14]. What common ground there has been, however, has largely been ignored, and Noth's position grossly misconstrued as a result of the accusations of "nihilism" and "subjectivism" which have been made by Albright and several of Albright's students[15]. The very sharpness of these accusations, however, brings out very clearly the narrowness of the basis on which the Albright school has constructed its historical conclusions: the pseudo-objectivity which has distorted their otherwise admirable historical research.

While de Vaux[16] has given credence to Wright's claim that the reason for the discrepancy between the conclusions, e. g., of Noth and

[12] H. H. Rowley, From Joseph to Joshua, 1950; see also Recent Discoveries and the Patriarchal Age, BJRL 32 (1949/50), 44—79 (republished in: The Servant of the Lord, 1952, 271—305).

[13] R. de Vaux, Les Patriarches Hébreux et les Découvertes Modernes, RB 53 (1946), 321—348; 55 (1948), 321—347; 56 (1949), 5—36, which appeared in German as: Die hebräischen Patriarchen und die modernen Entdeckungen, 1959; and Les Patriarches Hébreux et l'Histoire, RB 72 (1965) 5—28, which appeared in German as: Die Patriarchenerzählungen und die Geschichte, SBS 3, 1965; and in two slightly different recensions in English: The Hebrew Patriarchs and History, ThD 12 (1964), 227—240, and Method in the Study of Early Hebrew History, in: The Bible and Modern Scholarship, ed. by J. Philip Hyatt, 1966, 15—29.

[14] As pointed out correctly by J. A. Soggin, Ancient Biblical Traditions and Modern Archaeological Discoveries, BA 23 (1960), 100, and partially affirmed by R. de Vaux in: The Bible and Modern Scholarship, 18f.

[15] W. F. Albright, in: The Israelite Conquest of Canaan in the Light of Archaeology, BASOR 74 (1939), 11—23, speaks of a "nihilistic attitude of Alt and Noth toward the early history of Israel". See also, Jethro, Hobab and Reuel in Early Hebrew Tradition, CBQ 25 (1963), 1, and especially History, Archaeology and Christian Humanism, 1964, 140f., where his criticism is transparently political. Albright has been most closely followed in this attack by G. E. Wright, particularly in the article, Archaeology and Old Testament Studies, JBL 77 (1958), 39—51.

[16] R. de Vaux, The Bible and Modern Scholarship, 19; see also J. Holt, The Patriarchs of Israel, 1964, 20.

Albright, is that Noth has based his study on internal (what Wright would call "subjective") form critical grounds, and that Albright has followed external (what Wright would call "objective" and "empirical") criteria[17], this picture by no means describes the real state of affairs, for Noth has not refused "completely to use archaeological data"[18], as anyone who is familiar with Noth's work knows[19]. Noth's primary objections to those who would grant historicity to most of the early biblical traditions have not been on the grounds of literary criticism, but rather on the basis of historical criticism: that the extra-biblical material was insufficient to affirm the claims that were being made[20].

Not only do Wright and Albright explicitly reject the necessity of investigating the biblical traditions by means of form criticism and the history of traditions, in favor of an "empirical methodology with its full employment of archaeological data as the only source of external criteria in reconstructing history from tradition"[21], but their

[17] G. E. Wright, JBL 77 (1958), 46.

[18] Ibid. 47f.; cf. also J. Bright, Early Israel, the chapter, "The School of Alt and Noth". In contrast, cf. Albright's memorial to Alt, JBL 75 (1956), 169!

[19] Noth's familiarity with and use of extra-biblical data becomes obvious by the sheer volume of his archaeological, topographical and linguistic studies, many of which are still today among the most important works on their subject; e. g.: Die israelitischen Personennamen im Rahmen der gemeinsemitischen Namengebung, BWANT 3. F. 10, 1928 (also see his article in ZDMG 81, 1927, 1—45); Zum Problem der "Ostkanaanäer", ZA 39 (1930), 213—222; Mari und Israel, eine Personennamenstudie, in: Alt Festschrift, 1953, 127—152; his topographic studies of Transjordan, esp.: Das Land Gilead als Siedlungsgebiet israelitischer Sippen, PJ 37 (1941), 50—101; Israelitische Stämme zwischen Ammon und Moab, ZAW 60 (1944), 11—57; Die Nachbarn der israelitischen Stämme im Ostjordanlande, ZDPV 68 (1959), 1—50; and Jabes-Gilead, Ein Beitrag zur Methode alttestamentlicher Topographie, ZDPV 69 (1953), 28—41; his important studies of the Execration Texts: Die syrisch-palästinische Bevölkerung des zweiten Jahrtausends v. Chr. im Lichte neuer Quellen, ZDPV 65 (1942), 9—67, as well as several studies of more general nature: see above note 11 as well as his as yet unsurpassed archaeological and historical textbook, Die Welt des Alten Testaments, 1962[4]. I only list here a selection of those works which have significance for the study of the patriarchal traditions; for further bibliography see especially the back issues of the PJ and ZDPV.

[20] Noth, VTS 7 (1959), 262f.; See also the very important critiques of K. Elliger, Review of G. E. Wright, Biblische Arachäologie, TLZ 84 (1959), 94—98, and G. von Rad, History and the Patriarchs, ET 72 (1960/61), 213—216; Offene Fragen im Umkreis einer Theologie des Alten Testaments, TLZ 88 (1963), 411.

[21] G. E. Wright, JBL 77 (1958), 46 (emphasis added). Also interesting is Albright's statement: "I am a resolute 'positivist' — but only in so far as positivism is the expression of the modern rational-scientific approach to physical and historical reality." History, Archaeology, and Christian Humanism, 140.

historical interpretation can make no claim to be objective, proceeding as it does from a methodology which distorts its data by a selectivity which is hardly representative, which ignores the enormous lack of data for the history of the early Second Millenium, and which wilfully establishes hypotheses on the basis of unexamined biblical texts, to be proven by such (for this period) meaningless mathematical criteria as the "balance of probability", which itself is established by the extremely undependable principles of analogy and harmonization. It is obvious that what is objective in archaeology are the potsherds, and in biblical criticism, the biblical manuscripts. What we seek for in historical interpretation is not objectivity but verifiability, and the primary test of our conclusions is not so much coherence as integrity, whether they correspond to and adequately explain the data given. Methodologies do not legitimately determine one's results; for methods must be so developed that they enable us to represent and give meaning to the data we examine; it is the facility of this process which validates whatever methods we decide to pursue. If we wish to communicate what insight we have into the meaning of historical and biblical data, then the relationship between the objectively given and our representation of it must be verifiable. Only then can we begin to speak about "historical fact". It is Noth's observation of the unreliability of Albright and Wright's historical interpretation which has brought upon him the charge of nihilism, but it is this very caution (and doubt about his own hypothesis as well) which shows him to have been more faithful to the historical task than his overzealous critics[22].

In this context of concern for historical verifiability, the now notorious remark of J. Wellhausen makes good methodological sense: "Freilich über die Patriarchen ist hier kein historisches Wissen zu gewinnen, sondern nur über die Zeit, in welcher die Erzählungen über sie im israelitischen Volke entstanden . . ."[23] The validity of this principle that the historical knowledge about the patriarchs is commensurate with the antiquity of the traditions about them is implicitly borne out even by the most vociferous critics of Wellhausen, as can be seen first of all by the attempt to see as relevant to a refutation of Wellhausen's reconstruction of biblical traditions, evidence from any period preceding the twelfth century B. C., that is, by an argument for the antiquity and commensurate credibility of the tradi-

---

[22] J. A. Soggin's defense of Noth (BA 23, 1960, 98), and his comparison of Noth's work to that of the 15th century Florentine L. Valla's exposure of the "Donation of Constantine" forgery is somewhat overextended, since Noth does not deny the historicity of Abraham, but only that it has been proven.

[23] J. Wellhausen, Prolegomena zur Geschichte Israels, 1905[6], 316.

tions, and, secondly, the related attempt to see the J, E and P sources of the documentary hypothesis as ultimately going back to one original tradition, which has its final source in the actual events. This original tradition, recognized by the common elements found in the three sources as understood by Wright, Albright, and Bright[24], enables them, for all practical purposes, to ignore the implications of the documentary hypothesis, and to speak of a basic historical tradition which has been passed on orally. Whatever then can be anchored to a period prior to the formation of Israel can be seen as part of this original patriarchal history[25].

The immediate difficulty of such a hypothesis, however attractive it may be, is that to attach this original tradition to real historical events of the early Second Millenium demands that some means of transmitting this tradition intact for over eight hundred years must be assumed[26]. Moreover, this hypothesis totally ignores the individual and independent character of most of Genesis' pericopes, as well as the increasing fragmentation of the sources that is observable the further back one goes in the history of the traditions. Those elements which bind the pericopes together, such as the promise motif, are demonstrably late[27].

On the other hand, the sheer mass of parallels, which have been claimed to exist between the patriarchal narratives and what is known of the early Second Millenium, seems to support the claim that only this early period can adequately serve as the milieu from which these traditions emerged, and therefore the means of transmission, though now lost, *must* have once existed, and that the fragmentation observable in our present texts must reflect the end result by which an original history became legend[28].

The major questions which we will review are: 1) the validity of the historical analogue to the traditions — the correctness of seeing the

---

24 G. E. Wright, ET (1960), 294; Albright, History, Archaeology, and Christian Humanism, 154; CBQ 25 (1963), 1—11; and J. Bright, History of Israel, 65.

25 Typical of many studies is the map shown on page 11 of H. M. Orlinsky's Ancient Israel, 1956, entitled: "The Near East in the Patriarchal Period", showing simultaneously sites which did not exist simultaneously: in Egypt, the Twelfth Dynasty Beni-Hasan and the Eighteenth Dynasty Tell el-Amarna, in Palestine, the Middle Bronze I Kadesh and Late Bronze Ugarit, and in Mesopotamia, Ur of the end of the Third Millenium and the Mittani Kingdom of the 16th—15th centuries!

26 G. von Rad, ET 72 (1960/61), 214. Still pertinent in this respect is the remark made long ago by Albright: "The long memory possessed by semi-civilized peoples for historical facts is a pious fiction of over zealous apologists." Historical and Mythical Elements in the Joseph Story, JBL 37 (1918), 113.

27 G. von Rad ibid. 213. See also below, Chapter 11.

28 Speiser, Genesis, xxvii—xliii.

proposed background of the patriarchal narratives in the Amorite migrations of the early Second Millenium or some comparable alternative, and 2) the verification offered this analogy by the parallels that have been found between the Nuzi customs and the reconstructed tradition. We will also examine the historiographical intent of some of the central biblical themes, particularly the migration theme, the chronologies and genealogies, and Genesis 14, in an attempt to show that in this quest for the historical Abraham, we are not dealing with a legitimate historical reconstruction which merely lacks verification; we are rather dealing with a search that is essentially misdirected. Not only has the historicity of Abraham not been proven, but it does not seem to be implied in the biblical narratives themselves. It is extremely important to keep the biblical view in the forefront of our discussion, for it is that which we are ultimately trying to understand. Our goal is the clarification of the narratives of Genesis and of the formation of those narratives. The question of historicity is so fundamental to an understanding of the early stages of this tradition, that, if these stages are not founded on historical events, our understanding of them can only begin with the recognition of that fact.

B. THE BIBLICAL CHRONOLOGIES FOR THE PATRIARCHAL PERIOD

Attempts to relate the biblical chronologies with an absolute dating scheme have a very long tradition. Modern methods[29] can be looked upon as continuing the efforts of the early Christian computers, especially Julius Africanus and Eusebius. English and American scholarship has been most directly influenced by the computations of the 17th century Archbishop James Ussher, whose chronologies were incorporated into the notes of the King James Bible[30].

These early attempts are particularly interesting, because most of the significant methodological principles that are now commonly used were already then highly developed. The existence of divergent chronological schemes within the Bible itself, which plague modern efforts to find the "original" behind the Masoretic, Samaritan, and

---

[29] See especially F. M. Th. de Liagre Böhl, Das Zeitalter Abrahams, AO 29 (1930), 20f.; H. H. Rowley, From Joseph to Joshua, 57—108; F. Rienecker, Lexikon zur Bibel, 1960, 19—22 and 159—162; S. J. de Vries, IDB II, 580—599; and J. Finegan, Handbook of Biblical Chronology, 1964, 193f.

[30] Especially his Veteris et Novi Testamenti and Chronologia Sacra, to be found in C. R. Elrington and J. H. Todd, The Whole Works of the Most Rev. James Ussher, 1847—1864, vols. 8—11.

Septuagint traditions[31], is even more apparent when the various reconstructions of early writers are compared[32].

Africanus seems to follow the LXX tradition for the most part (allowing 230 years between Adam and the birth of Seth), but he gives a date of 2262 A. M. (anno mundi) for the flood instead of the LXX's 2242 A. M., and 3277 A. M. instead of the LXX's 3387 A. M. for the migration of Abraham. It is, of course, possible that Africanus depends here on a tradition other than the LXX, but it seems far more likely that he is improving on or correcting the Septuagint tradition on the basis of extra-biblical "evidence". He apparently starts his calculation from the 250th Olympiad, the time of the close of his work, which he knows to be 192 years after the resurrection[33]. His correspondence with the biblical chronology is made on the basis of the tradition that the birth of Jesus occurred in the year 5500 A. M., a tradition also to be found in an Egyptian revision of the chronology of Hippolytus[34]. With this correspondence, he is able to move back to the reign of Cyrus the Great, which began in Olympiad 55, 1, and to calculate this date as 4943 A. M.[35]. Africanus is then able to give an absolute date to the Exodus which he believed to have occurred at the same time as the Greek flood, which, according to Greek legend, took place during the reign of Ogygos, the first king of Thebes. This event occurred 1020 years before the First Olympiad. Then, since there are 217 years from the First Olympiad to the reign of Cyrus, he could conclude that there were 1237 years between the Exodus and the return from the Exile (an event which Africanus identifies with the beginning of Cyrus' reign)[36]. This renders a date for the Exodus of 3707 A. M. — though this part of the calculation is not found in the extant fragments of Africanus' writings. Africanus then apparently returns to the LXX tradition for his date of Abraham's entrance into Canaan (3277 A. M.) which is 430 years before the Exodus[37]. The chronological scheme which he follows for the antediluvian patriarchs corresponds with that of the LXX, except that he has Lamech born in the 187th year of Methusaleh, as in the

---

31 For useful tables of these three schemes, cf. M. D. Johnson, Purpose of Biblical Chronologies, 1969, 262—264.

32 E. g., the system as found in the Book of Jubilees, or the three different systems reflected in the work of Josephus (ibid. 265); also compare the reconstructions of Africanus and Hippolytus of Rome (Finegan, Handbook, 146f.).

33 M. J. Routh, Reliquiae Sacrae II, 1846, 306; also see Finegan op. cit. 144.

34 Finegan ibid. 147.

35 For this cf. ibid. 144.

36 For the text of Africanus, see Routh 272f. Finegan's commentary (op. cit. 140—145) is not entirely dependable.

37 Corresponding to LXX, Ex 12 40.

Masoretic tradition, instead of the LXX's 167th year[38]. For the ages of the patriarchs after the flood, Africanus follows the LXX tradition throughout, except that he does not include the generation of Kenan (which is found in the LXX and in the Book of Jubilees but not in the Masoretic tradition). Thus the combined generations up to the migration of Abraham are calculated at 110 years less than the LXX total of 3387 A. M., rendering the needed date of 3277 A. M. for the journey of Abraham. The simplicity with which these adjustments were made by Africanus has the appearance of scholarly emendation; the sources for his emendation were found ready in the materials at hand: a combination of historical knowledge (the flood of Ogygos), and textual criticism (the variant traditions).

Eusebius' chronology is mostly derived from the LXX, giving 430 years for the time from Abraham's entry into Canaan to the Exodus. However, he gives 480 years (with the Masoretic text) instead of the LXX's 440 years for the time between the Exodus and the building of the temple. In his Canon he establishes a correspondence between the biblical stories and events contemporary to them, which he gathers from his knowledge of world history, beginning with the first year of Abraham and ending with the 289th Olympiad (379 A. D.). Except for the divergence already noted, he remains faithful to the LXX text, and seems more intent on correlating the past "historical" events than attempting any major reconstruction[39].

The system of Archbishop Ussher follows the Masoretic text for its pre-Abrahamic chronologies, and does not attempt any major reconstruction after the manner of Africanus, merely organizing the biblical texts according to the modern chronological scheme, giving the date of Adam at 4004 B. C. He follows the LXX tradition for the period between the migration of Abraham and the Exodus, and the Masoretic tradition for the period between the Exodus and Solomon's temple, giving a date of 1921 B. C. for the migration of Abraham (the same date which he gives for the death of Terah!).

Most modern commentators[40] generally attempt to place the biblicical traditions in their historical setting more or less in the manner of either Eusebius or Africanus. Some proceed by calculating the biblical chronology first of all on the basis of the biblical texts alone.

---

[38] Africanus' scheme from Adam to the Flood corresponds with Josephus (Ant. I. 3.4 and Ant. VIII. 3.1) except that Josephus' date of 1662 A. M. for the Flood corresponds with Africanus' birth of Noah as well as the LXX's date for Noah's birth in 1642 A. M. Josephus' date for the birth of Noah in 1656 (Ant. I. 3.9) and of Abraham in 2946 (Ant. I. 6.5) may well be related to the Masoretic tradition which dated the Flood to 1656 A. M. and Abraham's birth to 1946 A. M.

[39] Cf. R. Helm, Eusebius, 7. Band, Chronik des Hieronymus, 1956.

[40] See note 29 and the bibliography given by Rowley.

These calculations differ from one another depending on which biblical references and which versions are used. So, for example, the calculations could be based on 215 years for the time of the patriarchs themselves +430 years for the sojourn in Egypt (Ex 12 40f.), or + 400 years for the oppression (Gen 15 13); or the calculation could be made on the basis of the tradition found in the Samaritan Pentateuch, the LXX, and Gal 3 17, which gives 430 years for the time from Abraham's entrance into Canaan to the Exodus. For the period after the Exodus to the building of the temple, I Kings 6 1 gives 480 years (according to the LXX, 440 years). An alternative to this can be found in Judges and Kings where the Masoretic text gives us a total of 554 years + the period of Joshua and the elders + the reign of Saul; i. e., upwards of 600 years. The LXX gives 544 years + Joshua and the elders + Saul. Gal 13 18 gives 40 years for the wandering and 450 years from the Conquest to the time of Samuel. Depending upon what combinations are followed, one might allow from 870 to more than 1245 years between the migration of Abraham and the construction of the temple. Archbishop Ussher calculates a date of 1021 B. C. for Solomon's temple. To find the historical background for the patriarchal period by following this system, one need merely calculate the date of Abraham and other patriarchal events, and correlate them with the known history of the Near East. This is the methodology developed by Eusebius.

By far the majority of commentators, however, follow a method of calculation similar to that of Africanus, and attempt to adjust the biblical chronology at those points at which they "know" the traditions to be inaccurate. The most common adjustment is the change of the date for Solomon's temple to 967 B. C.[41]. The possibilities one then has are either to accept the biblical traditions for the earlier chronology, thus arriving at a date as low as 1622 B. C. for the entrance into Egypt[42], or to adjust the chronology further by dating the Exodus at some time in the thirteenth century[43]. This absolute date for the Exodus (the conquest is usually dated 40 years later as in the biblical tradition) is based on the discovery that several sites in Palestine were destroyed about this time, as well as on the well known hypothesis of Nelson Glueck that Southern Transjordan had not been occupied before the thirteenth century[44].

The biblical traditions are usually accepted, for the time earlier than the Exodus and dates for the migration of Abraham are usually

---

[41] Rienecker, Lexikon 160; P. Montet, Egypt and the Bible, 1968, 7. Böhl (Das Zeitalter) gives a date of 960 B. C.

[42] Montet ibid.

[43] For full discussion see H. H. Rowley op. cit. note 29.

[44] On this, see below ch. 9.

given either by adding 430 years with the LXX, 400 years with Gen 15 13, or 645 years with the Masoretic text. Others, however, finding this chronology far too high, and recognizing the artificial and undependable character of the high ages of the patriarchs, resort to the genealogical lists to discover how far back before the Exodus the patriarchal period should be placed. The patriarchal period itself is consequently reduced to the normal span of three generations. Gen 15 16 speaks of the period from the entrance into Egypt to the conquest as having lasted only four generations. Moreover, the genealogy of Perez the son of Judah, found in Ruth 4 18-22, makes David the tenth generation from Judah. Hezron, the second member of the genealogy, is among those who enter Egypt with Jacob; Nahson, from the fifth generation after Judah, belongs to the wilderness period. The stay in Egypt can be even further shortened by reference to Num 57 59. Yochebed, the daughter of Levi was born in Egypt, and was the mother of Moses. Thus Moses is separated from Abraham by no more than five generations[45], and the Exodus is separated from the time of David by no more than six generations[46].

Similar conclusions might be drawn from the genealogies for Issachar and Manasseh, where only four generations separate the sons of Jacob from the conquest. This time is even more abbreviated in the genealogies of Benjamin whose grandchildren are among the leaders of Joshua's army. A great deal of manipulation is needed, however, to make these genealogies correspond with each other, to say nothing about the considerations of source and form criticism. Nevertheless, they do offer opportunities to scholars for finding the background of the patriarchs in the historical events of the latter part of the Second Millenium as well as in earlier periods.

The major objection to all of these reconstructions is that they make no attempt to *understand* the biblical chronologies and genealogies. What they offer, rather, are alternatives to the biblical schemes, and their attempts to establish the "correct" biblical chronology destroy the biblical perspective and worldview which gives their data meaning. That Abraham lived 175 years has to be taken seriously, but it is nonsense from an historical critical perspective. These alternative chronological schemes, because they are alternatives to the biblical point of view, must be justified independent of the meaning which the traditions have. That is, if the biblical data are to be given the weight of historical facts which bear an absolute weight independent of their context within a specific chronological scheme, then validation of these reconstructions must be based on historical

[45] C. H. Gordon, The Patriarchal Narratives, JNES 13 (1954), 58.
[46] Böhl, Het Tijdperk der Aartsvaders, 1925, 16.

and archaeological criteria alone. As self-subsisting hypotheses the above reconstructions cannot even claim a priori plausibility.

The Meaning of the Masoretic Chronology: The variant chronological schemes of Josephus appear to be eclectic, largely but not entirely dependent on the LXX and the Masoretic traditions[47]. The system found in the Book of Jubilees is obviously based on a calculation which dates the conquest to the year 2450 A. M., with the result that the 50th Jubilee begins with the occupation of the promised land. The antediluvian chronology closely resembles that of the Samaritan Pentateuch, but the ages after the Flood seem to be unique. The Samaritan Pentateuch chronology shares features of both the Masoretic and the LXX traditions, and is closest to the LXX, with some peculiarities of its own; e. g., the age of Methusaleh and Lamech at the birth of their firstborn. Whether it has its own plan, or is simply eclectic is unknown. The original perspective of the LXX system remains elusive, and the best attempt so far to discover it seems to be that of Africanus. His emendations, though very slight, seem to be derived, however, from his own historical view of the past. The Masoretic system of the P chronology is highly complex and uses the symbolism of both ages and generations. There seems good reason to believe that this system is responsible for much of the material that is found in the P chronology.

The Masoretic system is a theological construction based on a chronological scheme of a Great Year of 4000 years, which is fulfilled at the rededication of the temple by the Maccabees in the year 4000 A. M.[48]. The saving events on which the system is based are the Edict of Cyrus, the construction of the temple by Solomon, the Exodus, the call of Abraham, the birth of Abraham, and the creation of Adam in the year 1. The known historical information on the basis of which the system begins is the length of time between the Edict of Cyrus in 538 B. C. and the rededication of the temple in 164 B. C. — a total of 374 years, the exact number of years necessary to complete the needed total of 4000 years. The pivotal date of the main structure is the dating of the Exodus in the year 2666 which represents 2/3 of the Great Year and 26 2/3 generations of 100 years from the time of Adam: Adam to Abraham = 20 generations, + Isaac, Jacob, Levi, Kohath, Amram, and Aharon = 26 + Eleazar, who belonged to the generation of the Exodus[49]. The 100 year generation scheme is explicit in Gen 15 13-16, and is related to the 40 year generation in the chronological data given to the lives of

---

[47] M. D. Johnson, Purpose of the Biblical Chronologies, 265.

[48] Ibid. 32 and table 262.

[49] Wellhausen, Prolegomena, 308.

some of the patriarchs. So: Abraham lives for 100 years in Canaan, and Isaac is born when Abraham is 100 years old. The combination with 40 appears when Isaac marries at the age of 40 and has his firstborn son Esau at the age of 60, who marries at 40 when Isaac is 100 years old. A multiple of 12 generations of 100 years is perhaps reflected in the time given between the birth of Abraham in 1946 A. M. and the building of Solomon's temple in the year 3146 A. M. A combination of 12 generations of 40 years, or a 480 year period is of prime importance to the basic Masoretic scheme which gives 480 years from the time of the Exodus to the building of the temple, then 430 years to the Exile and the destruction of the temple +50 years for the duration of the Exile = 480 years from the building of the first temple to the Edict of Cyrus and the reconstruction of the second temple. The 430 year period (from the building of the temple to its destruction) is then used again as one moves back from the Exodus to the entrance into Egypt. Half this amount (215 years) is then given for the period from the entrance into Egypt to the promise given to Abraham, which is broken down on the basis of the 40 and 100 year generation schemes already mentioned.

Figure 1:

Adam	1 A. M.	
Birth of Abraham	1946 A. M.	
Promise to Abraham	2021 A. M.	
Entrance into Egypt	2236 A. M.	
Exodus	2666 A. M.	
Solomon's temple	3146 A. M.	
Exile	3576 A. M.	
Edict of Cyrus	3626 A. M.	= 538 B. C.
Rededication	4000 A. M.	= 164 B. C.

That all of the chronological data used in the Masoretic text for the P chronology is original in this system cannot be claimed. The ages of the pre-Abrahamic patriarchs, as well as the dates given for the lives of the patriarchs from Abraham to Jacob seem to be adjusted rather than created. Although we must consider the possibilities of discovery as well as of creativity in the formation of this chronological plan, nevertheless all the data dependent on the 480—430—215 year scheme, as well as the date of the Exodus in the year 2666 A. M., and the date of the birth of Abraham in 1946 A. M. seem best explained within the Maccabean or post-Maccabean theological framework of the Great Year.

It does not appear that we can use any of the extant chronological systems to arrive at an absolute date for the patriarchal period.

They were not constructed from the point of view of the historical critical method, and it is methodologically unsound to treat them as if they were.

Nor are the genealogies useful for historical critical study. The worldview from which they arose was totally different. This discussion, however, will be left for Chapter 11.

> The final solution to the interpretive problem, when it comes, must . . . interpret (the text) in terms of its own thought world, a world far more accessible to the contemporary historian than to interpreters of past generations. And the final test of such a proposed solution must be the degree to which it preserves the continuity between text and milieu[50].

---

[50] J. S. Holladay Jr., The Day(s) the Moon Stood Still, JBL 87 (1968), 167.

Chapter 2

The Names of the Patriarchs and the "Patriarchal Period"

A. STATEMENT OF THE PROBLEM

The discussion about names similar to those of the patriarchs which have been found in extra-biblical sources is the most important single issue in the debate over historicity. While it cannot be said that the argument for historicity stands or falls on the argument about the names, the names have taken a central place in every detailed discussion of the topic[1]. Although all must agree that the names of the patriarchs are clearly not fabricated[2] but fit well into the common Near Eastern nomenclature, many conclude on the basis of this authenticity that the essential historicity of the narratives has been established[3]. It is only a short step further to assume that, if we can determine the period in which the names best fit, we can then affirm a probable date for the patriarchs. Here, however, the more usual approach has been to confirm an already presupposed date for the patriarchs on the grounds that similar or identical names could be found in extra-biblical records at "roughly" the same time. It is then this period that has been claimed as the period in which names of

---

[1] W. F. Albright, From the Stone Age to Christianity, 1946; The Archaeology of Palestine, 1949; Archaeology and the Religion of Israel, 1953; The Biblical Period from Abraham to Ezra, 1963; Yahweh and the Gods of Canaan, 1968; R. de Vaux, Les Patriarches Hébreux et les découvertes modernes, RB 53 (1946), 321—348; RB 55 (1948), 321—347; RB 56 (1949), 5—36; and Les Patriarches Hébreux et L'Histoire, RB 72 (1965), 5—28; G. E. Wright, Biblical Archaeology, 1962; J. Bright, History of Israel, 1959; A. Parrot, Abraham et son temps, 1962; J. Holt, The Patriarchs of Israel, 1964; H. H. Rowley, From Joseph to Joshua, 1948; Recent Discovery and the Patriarchal Age, BJRL 32 (1949/50), 44—79; H. Cazelles, Patriarches, DBS 7 (1961), 136ff.

[2] Analogously, J. J. Finkelstein (The Bible, Archaeology, and History, Commentary 27, 1959, 347) protests with justice that "never . . . was it ever suggested that the topographical or onomastic references in the Bible were wrong or fictitious even by the extreme exponents of the Higher Criticism, or for that matter, even in the 'exposés' of the Bible by modern atheists."

[3] N. Schneider, Patriarchennamen in zeitgenössischen Keilschriftsurkunden, Bb 33 (1952), 522; R. de Vaux, RB 72 (1965), 5—9; W. F. Albright, Archaeology of Palestine, 236. For a more cautious view see H. H. Rowley, BJRL 32 (1949/50), 45ff.

this sort are most likely to occur[4]; indeed, all other periods are thought to be unsuitable[5]. Two errors are involved in this argument: 1) the presupposition that the earliest known use of a name is the most probable period in which to date an undated occurrence of it[6], or the presupposition that someone bearing this name would have lived at the time of the earliest known occurrence of the name[7]. 2) indifference to many of those patriarchal type names occurring in periods that are not suggested as patriarchal periods. Those who placed the patriarchs in the first half of the Second Millenium have emphasized the material from this early period to the exclusion of other equally valuable material. Roland de Vaux, after discussing the evidence for the name of the city of Harran, that it occurs in the twentieth, nineteenth, and eighteenth centuries, and after having mentioned that it also exists in the thirteenth century, and a considerable time after that, asks: "Est-ce un hasard si elle est surtout attestée à la période que la Bible assigne aux patriarches?"[8] However, there was hardly a period in which Harran did not exist! It might be asked with as much justification: "Is it an accident that Harran is 'mostly' attested during the period in which the patriarchal traditions were formed, that is, during the period of Aramaean domination of that area in the early Iron Age?" De Vaux is seriously misleading here for another reason: a city is by no means more real because we have more references to it. A city does not attain "common" existence; it either does or does not exist. One certain reference to it is as much proof

[4] A. Mallon, Les Hébreux en Égypte, Orientalia 3, 1921, 49; G. E. Mendenhall, Mari, BA 11 (1948), 16; R. T. O'Callaghan, Aram Naharaim, Analecta Orientalia 26, 1948, 29; H. M. Orlinsky, Ancient Israel, 1956, 19; H. H. Rowley, BJRL 32 (1949/50), 73. On the other hand, de Vaux (Method in the Study of Early Hebrew History, The Bible in Modern Scholarship, ed. by J. Philip Hyatt, 1966, 26) points out that "the names parallel to those of the Bible are found in texts which cover the whole of the Second Millenium". This seems to contradict what he says in his 1946 article.

[5] F. M. Cross, Jr., The Priestly Tabernacle, BAR, 1961, 204; J. Bright, History of Israel, 70; also R. de Vaux (RB 72, 1965, 9; The Hebrew Patriarchs and History, Theology Digest 12, 1964, 229) who remarks that this type of proper name is extremely common among the "Amorites" of the early Second Millenium, but rare among the Canaanites and Phoenicians, failing to note that they are also extremely common among the Aramaeans and the Israelites of the First Millenium B. C.

[6] de Vaux ibid. W. F. Albright, From Abraham to Ezra, 2; M. Burrows, What Mean these Stones?, 1941, 259.

[7] J. W. Jack (The Date of the Exodus, 1925, 37n) gives an alternative to what is usually suggested, while in no way impugning the historicity of the patriarchs: "There is evidence that the two names (Jacob-el and Joseph-el) were in existence long before these patriarchs were born."

[8] RB 72 (1965), 9f.; Theology Digest 12 (1864), 230.

of its existence as a thousand references from the same period. Then too, we must wonder whether too much importance is being put on evidence simply because we have it. Do we have more evidence from the earlier period because more written texts have been discovered from that period (Mari, the Cappadocian texts, Nuzi, Alalakh, Taʿannek, Ugarit, Amarna, etc.), and also because more scholars have been looking for "patriarchal-type" names in these early texts than in later texts? A fourth century occurrence of the name of Abraham in South Mesopotamia would hardly create much excitement! How much has our evidence been determined by the understandable desire of the researchers to support their theses?

A much more remarkable example of this type of presentation is found in de Vaux's earlier statement: "on a vu qu'en dehors d'Israël les noms d'Abraham et de Jacob n'étaient attestés — et peu fréquemment — que dans la première moitié du IIe millénaire. Nous remontons ainsi aux origines même d'Israël, et ce fait seul est une présomption sérieuse en faveur de la tradition biblique"[9]. This is simply not correct. De Vaux, himself, tells us in the same article[10] that there is a "Jacob-el" place name in the list of Thutmosis III (ca. 1490—1436)!

The picture is even further confused by a lack of certainty about what can be proved by reference to this material. While most authors who see this material as significant for the historicity of the patriarchs are ostensibly relating the patriarchal type of name with similar types to determine when this kind of name would be most likely to occur, the names which are seen as significantly similar are those which are identical to the patriarchs' names. It is clearly not the authenticity of the names, but the patriarchs themselves that are being sought, in spite of all claims to the contrary. Thus, the name *Abam-rama*, even though identified as Akkadian[11], is seen as a more significant parallel than *Aḫ(i?)ram*, which has exactly the same form as Abram, and also occurs in the Old Testament. This, however, unaccountably seems to give it less, rather than more, significance.

R. de Vaux, for example, in commenting on the name *'brm*, which occurs in the Ugaritic texts, remarks with dismay that two people bore the name, one a Cypriot and the other an Egyptian[12]. Quite clearly, what is disturbing is the realization that what has been found is not evidence about the patriarchs themselves, but rather only about their names. The search for the authenticity of

---

[9] RB 53 (1946), 327.

[10] Ibid. 323.

[11] N. Schneider, Bb 33 (1952), 518.

[12] RB 72 (1965), 8: "il est curieux, et inquiétant . . ."

Abraham's name has become, at least for some, a quest for the historical Abraham. For, if authenticity alone were the goal, these Ugaritic names would demonstrate the widespread use and popularity of this name, proving without cavil (and, moreover, without doubts about orthography!) that the name Abram is authentic[13].

Though the evidence for the names has failed to produce a conclusive witness to the patriarchs themselves[14], this material has achieved, nevertheless (perhaps because of its sheer bulk), a prominent position in the development of arguments which purport to show the "essential" historicity of the narratives about the patriarchs, particularly Gen 11 10—12 4. The movement of the patriarch's family from Ur of the Chaldees to Ḫarran, and from there into Palestine, and finally to Egypt, is seen as paralleled by a remarkable series of coincidences gleaned from history: the incursion of groups of peoples with similar names into South Mesopotamia who are identified with the Amorites, the discovery of semi-nomadic groups further northwards at Mari, the discovery of "Benjaminites" near Ḫarran and/or a caravan center at Ḫarran, a possible connection of cultic interests between Ur and Ḫarran, and then, moving into Palestine, the discovery of similar names in the Execration Texts, which might be related to the archaeological evidence for a period of semi-nomadism in Palestine. Finally, in Egypt, we are given the choice between the *ʿ3mw* of the First Intermediate Period (Abraham) who are thought to be Amorites, since a group with a similar sounding name, the *amurrū*, show up in South Mesopotamia at "approximately" the same time, and the Hyksos (Jacob and Joseph), who are considered to be "Amorite-related" invaders of Egypt. It is the names of the patriarchs which seem to tie all of these "coincidences" together, enabling scholars to see the patriarchal narratives as an abbreviated form of the history of the Near East in the Second Millenium[15].

---

[13] de Vaux is not alone in this search for direct references to the patriarchs themselves: cf. Schneider, Bb 33 (1952), 518.

[14] H. H. Rowley, BJRL 32 (1949/50), 67.

[15] This interpretation is accepted by de Vaux (Theology Digest, 1964, 232; RB 72, 1965, 11—13) who connects this with a proposed "Amorite" movement and settlement during the early part of the Second Millenium: "Il est difficile de ne pas reconnaître dans cette situation un arrière-fond historique qui convient admirablement aux traditions concernant les Patriarches." (RB 72, 1965, 13). It is difficult to understand how the discovery of linguistically related groups in different geographic localities can so easily be interpreted as evidence for a movement of a people from one area to another. As the same type of interpretation occurs again in much of the discussion about *Ḫab/pirū* in the Near East, it will be useful to discuss this problem in the treatment of this thesis below in Chapters 3 to 5 and 8.

The proponents of this reconstruction offer it as a refutation and as a replacement of older interpretations which had considered the patriarchal narratives as unhistorical[16].

This search for historicity has led to a breakdown in the growing understanding, so well begun in the early part of this century, of the genealogies of Genesis as basically aetiological and of the individual names as eponymous. Indeed, names like those of Abraham, Isaac, Jacob, and Joseph are not so clearly eponymous. And, so it is assumed, if these are not, perhaps that the others appear to be is but groundless coincidence; perhaps, after all, the cities and tribes do take their names from Genesis' heroes. Commentaries continually reinforce the belief that there is a sharp division between Genesis 11 and Genesis 12; that in the one we are in the realm of legend, folklore, and mythology, and that with the latter we enter history. Many would draw this dividing line somewhat earlier, beginning what is historical with Gen 11 10, so that Terah, his family, and the "migration" from Ur to Ḫarran are included in the historical section[17].

It will be my contention throughout that this process of historicizing Genesis is a serious error in biblical interpretation, and, to the extent that it depends upon the evidence we have from Near Eastern nomenclature, totally unfounded. Some questions which must be asked of our evidence are: Do the names really demonstrate or make more probable the historicity of the patriarchs? Do they help to date the period in which the patriarchs belong? Do they support the thesis that the narratives of Genesis mirror the history of the Second Millenium, specifically the movements of the Amorites?

In what follows I do not treat all of the Biblical and extra-biblical names that are related to the names of the patriarchs, but rather limit myself to those names that have been brought into the debate about the historicity and the dating of the patriarchs, as well as to some which seem to be of use in placing this discussion in its proper context[18].

---

16 de Vaux, RB 72 (1965), 5; N. Schneider, Bb 33 (1952), 16; G. E. Wright, Biblical Archaeology, 17; B. Vawter, A Path through Genesis, 1956, 8. 15.

17 U. Cassuto, Commentary on Genesis, II 1964, 250; but see especially W. F. Albright, Contributions to Biblical Archaeology and Philology, JBL 43 (1924), 385.

18 For further information and bibliography on the names see: H. Ranke, Early Babylonian Personal Names, Babylonian Expedition of the University of Pennsylvania, Series D, vol. 3, 1905; K. Tallqvist, Neubabylonisches Namenbuch, Acta Societatis Scientiarum Fennicae, Tomus 32, 2, 1906; and, Assyrian Personal Names, Acta Societatis, Tomus 43, 1, 1918; A. T. Clay, Personal Names from Cuneiform Inscriptions of the Cassite Period, YOS 1 (1912); Th. Bauer, Die Ostkanaanäer, 1926; A. Gustavs, Die Personennamen in den Tontafeln von Tell-Taʿannek, ZDPV

B. THE NAMES IN CONTEXT: ABRAHAM

The name אברם or אברהם is unquestionably a West Semitic personal name[19], both because of its form and the elements from which it is constructed[20]. The form of the name is a sentence composed of a noun in the nominative as subject and a finite verb in the perfect tense as predicate, such as מלכירם, עמינדב, אלישמע, אליסף, etc; this is to be distinguished in form from those names in which the nominative element is last; e. g., נתנאל, בניהו, עזריהו, etc[21].

An alternate form of this name is אבירם, which has a *yōd* joining the two elements[22]. Martin Noth has shown clearly that in sentence names such as אבירם this letter has no significance whatever[23]. We find such names as אחאב alongside of אחיאב (Eleph.), but even more important are those examples where the same individual is given both forms: אבשלם and אבישלם (I Kings 15 2. 10 and II Chr 11 20. 21), אלפלט and אליפלט (II Sam 5 16 and I Chr 14 5). This phenomenon is

50 (1927), 1—18, and 51 (1928), 169—218; M. Noth, Gemeinsemitische Erscheinungen in der israelitischen Namengebung, ZDMG 81, N. F. 6 (1927); BWANT 10 1928; Mari und Israel. Eine Personennamenstudie, Festschrift A. Alt, 127—152; Remarks on the Sixth Volume of Mari Texts, JSS 1 (1956), 322—327; G. Ryckmans, Les noms propres sud-sémitiques, Bibliothèque du Muséon II, parts 1—3, 1934 bis 1935; A. Vincent, La Religion des Judéo-Araméens d'Eléphantine, 1937; J. J. Stamm, Die Akkadische Namengebung, MVÄG 44, 1939; R. de Langhe, Les Textes de Ras Shamra et leurs Rapports avec le Milieu Biblique de l'Ancien Testament, Dissertationes Lovanienses, Series II, Tomus 35, 1 & 2, 1945; D. J. Wiseman, The Alalakh Tablets, Occasional Publication of the British Institute of Archaeology at Ankara no. 2, 1953; H. B. Huffmon, Amorite Personal Names in the Mari Texts, 1965; G. Buccellati, The Amorites of the Ur III Period, 1966; F. Gröndahl, Die Personennamen der Texte aus Ugarit, 1967.

19 H. Greßmann (Sage und Geschichte in den Patriarchenerzählungen, ZAW 30, 1910, 2 n. 3) tried to explain this name as Akkadian; he is followed by N. Schneider, Bb 33 (1952), 518. On this point, see further below.

20 So M. Noth, BWANT 10, 1928, 20. 52. Noth gives us very essential methodological advice (3) when he reminds us that we should not compare single names with other single names only, but rather that names can only be understood in the larger context of related names.

21 For a thorough discussion of these forms see Noth, BWANT 10, 1928, 20f.

22 U. Cassuto, A Commentary on the Book of Genesis, vol. II, 1964, 267; C. H. Gordon, Ugarit and Minoan Crete, 1966, 150.

23 Noth, BWANT 10, 1928, 33f. De Vaux (RB 53, 1946, 327) denied any relationship between the names אברם and אבירם. In 1965, however, he speaks of the form אברם as a contraction of אבירם, comparing it with the forms אחאב and the Akkadian *Aḫiab*, and also אבנר and אבינר (Les Patriarches hébreux et l'histoire, RB 72, 1965, 8.) These examples are in no way demonstrative of de Vaux's contention, first because they are not the same type of name as אברם, and second, because it is impossible to demonstrate that the form אבירם is prior to אברם.

also found by comparing the Hebrew and Greek texts: אחאב and Αχιαβ (Jer 29 21), and: אלידד and Ελδαδ (Num 34 21)[24]. It is very difficult to understand the *yōd* as a first person suffix, since, in the basic form of this type of name the first element does not designate family relationship but is theophoric[25]. Indeed Noth argues that the elements אב and אח themselves are theophoric[26]. He shows that they are used in the same manner as other unequivocally theophoric elements are used. We find Cannanite בעלרם, alongside of אחרם, Israelite יהורם together with אברם, and אביסף with אליסף[27]. He also points to the comparable element עם which not only shows up in cuneiform with a theophoric determinative (*ᵈAmum-ešuḫ*), but also can be shown like אב to have been used in the same way as theophoric elements: עמידע, אבידע, אלידע, עמכרב, אבכרב, אחכרב, אלכרב, etc[28]. The elements אב, אח, and עם are among the most common elements of Semitic names.

The element רם is likewise one of the more common of the verbal elements that are used with theophoric subjects. The root of the verb is רום[29], and the name אברם can be translated "Father is exalted"[30].

It can be concluded from this comparison with biblical nomenclature that the name אברם, both in its form and its separate elements, is to be considered typical of early Hebrew names. Because of this typical character and the fact that it is a specifically West Semitic form of name, caution must be used in comparing it with names (even when the resemblance is striking) that are derived from other linguistic groups[31].

The alternative form used in Genesis: אברהם, needs further discussion. Gen 17 5 offers a derivation of the name by means of a word-play between הם and המון, interpreting אבר הם to mean "Chief of a

---

[24] For these and further examples both from the Old Testament and other sources, cf. Noth, BWANT, 10, 1928, 33f. and 237.

[25] Ibid. 68—70.

[26] Ibid. 69: "Als Subjekte sind aber אב und אח ohne Zweifel theophore Elemente." Also, see 'Mari und Israel, eine Personennamenstudie', Alt Festschrift, 143.

[27] Noth, BWANT, 10, 1928, 70.

[28] Ibid. 77.

[29] This becomes quite certain when we compare the names חירם, King of Tyre (II Sam 5 11) and חירום, an artisan from Tyre (I Kings 5 32). Cf. Noth, ZDMG 81 (1927), 28.

[30] L. Hicks, Abraham, IDB I 15. Brown, Driver, and Briggs (Hebrew and English Lexicon of the Old Testament, 1959, 4) translate this name "exalted father". This translation, however, does not recognize that רם is the predicate of the sentence name.

[31] L. Hicks, Abraham, 15.

multitude"[32]. For this meaning the tradition seeks an etymology in אב־המון גוים. This, however, is popular etymology. The linguistic etymological derivation seems rather to be רם from the root רום[33].

De Vaux, in commenting on this popular etymology, points out that, since the tradition clearly no longer understands the original meaning of the name, the name itself must be considered as very ancient[34]. That it is ancient can be demonstrated by early uses of this name, and names with the same form and similar elements, in extra-biblical sources. The converse of De Vaux's conclusion, however, is equally important: that the tradition (at least that dealing with the meaning of Abraham's name) is necessarily later than the earliest extant use of the name; i. e., that the earliest usage cannot be equated with the biblical usage. This is especially significant since, as Fichtner has shown[35], the etymologies of Genesis can hardly be considered late reconstructions, but belong among the early traditions of the Bible. They are, for example, found only in the narratives dealing with traditions about the time before the monarchy[36].

While the form אברהם is usually explained as a dialectical variant of אברם[37], it is not understood in Genesis as merely a variant form. In Gen 17 5 new meaning is given to the patriarch along with the new name. Consistently after 17 5 the patriarch is referred to as אברהם. Because of this consistency of use — though the ultimate origin of the difference in the forms is to be found in dialectical variations — the linguistic explanation does not give us a satisfactory understanding of this form as it is used in the Bible. To explain the variations on the grounds of such a difference in dialect alone would demand a division of the Genesis narratives which is not otherwise justifiable. Rather, it seems that the form אברהם is used throughout the narratives following Gen 17 5 specifically because of the aetiological etymology given there. This aetiology forms part of the general structure of the Genesis tradition as a whole; the subsequent use of the name Abraham is not original to each narrative segment. Thus

---

32 Brown et alii, loc. cit.

33 Contra Brown (ibid.); see below note 37.

34 de Vaux, Theology Digest, 229; RB 72 (1965), 8.

35 J. Fichtner, Die etymologische Ätiologie in den Namengebungen der geschichtlichen Bücher des alten Testaments, VT 6 (1956), 382f. 387. For general principles of interpretation, see F. M. Th. de Liagre Böhl, Volksetymologie en Woordspeling in de Genesis-Verhalen, MKAW Letterkunde 59A, 1925, 49—79.

36 The last occurrence seems to be in II Sam 12 25. Cf. J. Fichtner ibid. 387.

37 L. Hicks (Abraham 15) is in all probability correct in seeing אברהם as an Aramaic expansion or variant of אברם. Just as Aramaic רהט is equivalent to Hebrew רוץ, and בהת to בוש so רהם is an expansion of רום. See further on this below, note 106.

אברהם functions as a c u e n a m e[38], carrying in its meaning the Yahwistic promise that the patriarch will become a great nation.

To say that אברהם is used in Genesis as a cue name still recognizes that it is a real personal name, and that in some of our narratives it may perhaps have been original. It is, nevertheless, quite possible that this form had nothing to do with the earliest level of our narratives and that it was first introduced by J as an integrating factor of his theology of promise. This level of the tradition at least must be considered post-Davidic.

Many extra-biblical names similar to the name of the patriarch have often been brought forward as means for dating our earliest traditions about Abraham as part of the general effort to define more precisely the "patriarchal period". A discussion of each of them in the context of general ancient Near Eastern nomenclature, will show, I believe, not only that this effort has not succeeded, but that because of the nature of the chronological and geographical spread of Early West Semitic names, the effort must be completely given up. Ever since A. Ungnad discovered the name *A-ba-am-ra-ma* in a letter from Dilbat from the time of Ammisaduḳa in the Old Babylonian period[39], it has played a critical part in the discussions about the name אברם[40]. The name occurs in several texts[41] in three variant forms: *A-ba-am-ra-am*, *A-ba-am-ra-ma*, and *A-ba-ra-ma*[42]. The name was quickly identified by Greßmann with the biblical name אברם and seen as decisive proof that the name of the patriarch was a genuine Semitic personal name and not a divine name[43]. By 1926, however, Greßmann had changed his mind and rejected any relationship whatever between the two names[44]. Noth, in his work on Hebrew personal names, objected to the identification of these names on basically structural grounds[45].

38 This term I owe to Professor Arnold Williams who used it in a public lecture on Spenser given at the University of Detroit in the Fall of 1968.

39 A. Ungnad, Urkunden aus Dilbat, 7. Heft der vorderasiatischen Schriftdenkmäler, 1909, 59f. Ammisaduḳa, according to the low chronology, reigned from 1582—1561, not at the time of Hammurapi (1728—1686) as Greßmann (ZAW 30, 1910, 2) suggests.

40 So Albright as early as 1918 (Historical and Mythical Elements in the Joseph Story, JBL 37, 133).

41 Ungnad, Urkunden, 60, in texts 92, 97, 101, 102, 198.

42 Ibid. texts 198: 33,198: 27 and 92: 6,13 respectively. Cf. also A. Tallqvist, APN, 82 n. 5 and J. J. Stamm, AN, 103 and 292.

43 ZAW 30 (1910), 2f.

44 Review of Th. Bauer: Die Ostkanaanäer in ZAW 44 (1926), 301f.: "... die Namen Abam-rāma und אברם (haben) nichts miteinander zu tun."

45 Noth (BWANT 10, 1928, 52), at the completion of this book, is apparently not aware of Greßmann's earlier identification of the specifically Akkadian *A-ba-am-ra-am* with the just as clearly defined West Semitic אברם

In spite of this caution, since Greßmann's ZAW article of 1910, biblical scholars have generally accepted the identification of these two names in one manner or another[46], and this has been introduced into the standard textbook data[47]. Two different directions have been taken in the process of identification, agreeing only in that they both accept the identity of the names. One sees the name *A-ba-am-ra-am* as West Semitic and as equivalent to the name אברם[48]; the other sees the name אברם as Akkadian, identical with the Akkadian name *A-ba-am-ra-am*[49]! In fact, the names can have nothing to do with each other; they are totally unrelated, nothing more than homonyms.

In discussing the name *A-ba-am-ra-ma*[50], Albright rejects the translation given by Ungnad: "Er hat den Vater liebgewonnen" on the grounds that the stem רום "be high" (sic!) does not exist in Akkadian[51]! To reject Ungnad's Akkadian derivation[52] of the name for this reason is specious, since Ungnad does not understand the stem to be West Semitic רום but rather Akkadian *rḥm* "love, have mercy", an extremely common element of Akkadian names as well as some West Semitic names[53]. Albright translates the name *A-ba-am-ra-ma* as well as the name אברם: "He is exalted (or 'lofty') with respect to father," i. e., "of exalted lineage"[54]. This impossible translation totally ignores the structure of West Semitic names like אברם[55], which, as we have already seen, is a sentence composed of a noun in the nominative case, plus a verb in the perfect tense[56]. Albright

---

[46] Albright, JBL 37 (1918), 133 and n. 21, and again: The Names Shaddai and Abram, JBL 54 (1935), 194. 199 and 202. N. Schneider Bb 33 (1952), 516—522, and R. de Vaux, RB 53 (1946), 323.

[47] M. Burrows, What Mean These Stones?, 259; G. E. Wright, Biblical Archaeology, 42; U. Cassuto, Genesis II, 267; J. Holt, The Patriarchs of Israel, 1964, 82; G. A. Barton, Archaeology and the Bible, 344.

[48] Principally Albright; see above n. 46.

[49] Schneider loc. cit., see above n. 46. De Vaux (RB 53, 1946, 323) sees both as possible, but unaccountably continues to assert the relationship as certain; similarly: A. Parrot, Abraham et Son Temps, 1962, 33.

[50] Albright, JBL 54 (1935), sees this form as the "correct" one over against *A-ba-ra-ma* and *A-ba-am-ra-am*, because he sees in the former the loss of the mimation "due to dissimilation" (194), and in the latter form, he sees an Akkadianized form of a West Semitic "perfect stative" which in "North Canaanite" still had a vocalic ending (199).

[51] JBL 37 (1918), 133.

[52] Urkunden aus Dilbat 60.

[53] For example, biblical ירחמאל. Noth, BWANT 10 (1928), 187. 199. More recently, Huffmon, APNM, 261.

[54] JBL 37 (1918), 133 n. 21; JBL 54 (1935), 199.

[55] It is to be wondered how Albright would translate such names as מלכירם or אלרם.

[56] Cf. also: אחרם, אלרם, אליסף, etc. Albright's translation is clearly an attempt to join a normally intransitive verbal element (רום) with the quite clearly oblique case of *Abam* in the Akkadian name!

seems to gloss over the serious difficulty of the case ending in the first element of the name *A-ba-am-ra-am*[57]. The element אב of אברם is the subject of a sentence name, corresponding to such elements as אח and עם in West Semitic theophoric type names. Corresponding elements in Akkadian names are *abu-*, and *aḫu-*[58]. These are nominative elements and are found both with and without the mimation[59]: as in *Abum-bani, Aḫu-banû, Aḫum-kênum, Aḫu-na'id, Iddin-abu,* and *Iddin-aḫum*[60]. Names with the accusative case ending are regularly found in Akkadian: *Aḫam-arši, ᵈNN-aḫa-iddinam, Aḫam-nišu, ᵈEnlil-aḫam-iddinam*[61], and are a completely different type of name from those formed with the nominative. An exact equivalent in form to *A-ba-am-ra-ma* is to be found in the Akkadian name *Mu-tam-ra-ma*[62]! Cuneiform parallels to the name אברם are to be found in such forms as *Abi-ra-mu, Aḫi-ra-mu,* and *Aḫu-ram(?)-nu*[63], though, as we shall see, it is not always possible to distinguish in cuneiform between names from the West Semitic root רום and the common Semitic root *rḥm*.

N. Schneider, in contrast to Albright, understands the name *A-ba-am-ra-am* correctly, seeing the first element as an Akkadian accusative with mimation (The accusative is also found in one of the variants without the mimation) and translates, it "Er hat den Vater lieb"[64]. Unaccountably, however, he concludes, that, because of this, the name אברם is to be explained as Akkadian and as related to names of the third dynasty of Ur[65].

If Schneider were correct in saying that, since *A-ba-am-ra-am* is to be explained as Akkadian, so is אברם, the very basis of the analysis

---

57 De Vaux (RB 53, 1946, 323) in translating the name in this way: "Il est grand quant à son père, il est de bonne naissance," seems to agree with Albright.

58 M. Birot, Trois textes économiques de Mari (II), RA 47 (1953), 168.

59 Because of this I see no reason to prefer the form *A-ba-am-ra-ma* to *A-ba-ra-ma* as more "proper".

60 Stamm, MVÄG 44 (1939), 56.

61 Ibid. 44.

62 Ibid. 58. Stamm correctly translates this: "Liebet den Gatten."

63 Tallqvist, APN, 5. 17 and 19 respectively.

64 Bb 33 (1952), 518f.

65 Although Schneider is presenting his argument as a reason for rejecting interpretations that are critical of the historicity of the Genesis narratives, he appears to presuppose that historicity from the outset; as a result his argument tends to be somewhat circular. Since he has found the name *Na-ḫa-ru-um* as a personal name in the Ur III Period, and the name *A-ba-am-ra-am* from Dilbat of 350 to 400 years later, he concludes strangely that the name Abram (sic!) is a name of a citizen of Sumer and Akkad (Ibid. 517)! Joined to this peculiar chronology are two further "principles": (1) that since the names (of Nahor's family) are not Sumerian, they must be Akkadian, and (2) since these names are East Semitic, an explanation from West Semitic is to be excluded!

which he uses to arrive at this conclusion would be destroyed. It then would become totally impossible to distinguish one name from another within the Semitic families. For when we say that the name *A-ba-am-ra-am* is an Akkadian name, we say it because the *-am* of *Abam-* shows us that the first element of the name is the object of the verb and thus that the entire name is structurally distinct from the West Semitic אב(י)רם form which consists of a nominative plus verb. It is, of course, within the realm of possibility that under West Semitic influence the originally Akkadian name has been "shortened" so that it resembles the West Semitic form[66], but then the two different (?) names would be totally indistinguishable, which they are not[67]. Because of the similar formations of the verbs רום and *rḥm*, when we speak of a name being Akkadian or Early West Semitic, we are speaking primarily on the evidence of structure. אברם is different from *A-ba-am-ra-am*, in form, in the elements that make it up, and in its language.

In cuneiform texts it is extremely difficult, and at times impossible, to distinguish those names that are formed from West Semitic רום[68] from other elements having *rm* in them. This is true not only of the names which have the root *rḥm* "love" as in *A-ba-am-ra-am*[69], but also those formed from the verb *rmy*, "throw, strike, settle down"[70], and from the nouns *rīmu* "bull"[71], *rāmu* "grace"[72], as well as from those hypocoristic names whose third

---

[66] As, e. g., *Aḫi-ramu*, etc.!

[67] If the names were found in a context in which all names were consistently understood as either Akkadian or West Semitic, then a decision could be reached; however, the decision would not be based on structural grounds.

[68] *Ra-me-ilu, Ra-ma-ilu, Elu-ra-ma, Ra-ma-da (Ram-Adad?)*, Tallqvist, APN, 185f. Note the theophoric elements!

[69] Many names have this element with the meaning "have mercy", especially with theophoric elements, so: *Šamaš-ri-ma-an-ni, Ì-li-rí-me⁷-an-ni, Re-en-šu-ilu, Ili-riša-ri-ma, ᵈNabû-rema-šukun*, etc. Stamm, MVÄG 44 (1939), 167f. This is also found in the imperfect: *I-ri-man-ni-ili, Irēm-ši-ᵈGula*, etc. Ibid. 90. Also: *Ri-im-Addu, Ašur-ra-mi-im-šarri*, Tallqvist, NBN, 330. Related to these are also those names built from the element *narâmu* "Dear", such as *Na-ram-Addu*, and the hypocoristic forms *Na-ra-mu-um* and *ᶠNa-ra-am-tum*. (Ibid.)

[70] As in *La-ti-ra-me-e, Mu-ut-ra-me-e* (n. b.), *Su-mu-ra-me-e, Su-mu-ra-me-em* (Huffmon, APNM, 262f.). Also cf. the name רמי in the Aramaic inscriptions from Elephantine: A. Vincent, La Religion des Judéo-Araméens, 413.

[71] *Nabu-rim-ilani* (Tallqvist, APN, 157).

[72] *Ra-a-mu-ša-ilani-šu*; also note well *rîmu* in the name *Nabû-ri-mu-ú-a* (Tallqvist, NBN, 330). Other related elements are: *rîmûtu* "graciousness", as in *Rim-ut-bêl* and *Nabû-ri-mu-ᵖˡ·* and *rimênu* "merciful", as in *Ri-me-ni-Marduk, Sin-ri-me-ni* (ibid.).

radical is *r* as in *Ia-qa-rum,* (which is from *Iaqâru* plus mimation)[73]. Those that seem closest in form to the name אברם consist of a theophoric element in the nominative case plus perfect verb[74]. While recognizing that these names could be Akkadian, and without ignoring the ambiguities of the cuneiform names[75], so many parallels exist among the Early West Semitic names that we may be justified in speaking of them as Early West Semitic in form[76].

Names similar to אברם appear not only in the first half of the Second Millenium, but in nearly every period when we have names from West Semitic peoples. Beginning with those names that are formed in the imperfect of רום, we find at Mari several names such as *Ia-ri-im-^{d}Da-gan,* and *Ia-ri-im-ḫa-am-mu*[77] comparable to similar names found at Chagar Bazar[78], at Alalakh[79], and at Ugarit[80].

Names built from the perfect of רום are much more common as well as more clearly related to the structure of the name אברם. Here we find in the extra-biblical material much the same variations as in the biblical names. Hypocoristic forms in the perfect are found at Mari: *Ra-ma-tum, Ra-ma-nu-um,* built from *ram* with the hypocoristic endings *-atum* and *-anum*[81], comparable to the name *Rwm*

[73] M. Birot, RA 47 (1953), 164; also to be included here is *Ia-sarum* from *iašaru* + *m* (ibid.), and perhaps *Aḫ-e-rum* (Clay, PN, 50); but, on the other hand, might this correspond with אחירם? (Cf. M. Noth, ZDMG 81, 1927, 36); see further on this, H. Huffmon, APNM, 132.

[74] Huffmon ibid. 87.

[75] Ibid.: "The analysis of what may ... be called perfect verb forms involves much more uncertainty than the analysis of the imperfect, which is readily identifiable by form."

[76] This is not to imply that the early West Semites formed a linguistic unity. They did not. Cf. below Chapter 5. The bearers of this type of name in the earlier period are variously referred to as Ostkanaanäer by Th. Bauer and B. Landsberger, Proto-Aramaeans by Martin Noth, Amorites by Albright and Huffmon, Amurrites by A. Goetze and West Semites by I. J. Gelb. On the question of terminology see below Chapter 3.

[77] Huffmon, APNM, 262. Also compare the names *Ia-ri-im-li-im* and *Ia-ri-im-^{d}Addu* (Noth, Alt Festschrift, 143), as well as perhaps the partly damaged *Ia-ri-im* ... (ARM VII, 114.3; Huffmon APNM, 262).

[78] *Ia-ri-im-li-im,* C. J. Gadd, Tablets from Chagar Bazar and Tell Brak 1937—38, Iraq 7 (1940), 38, Pl. II, A. 968.3; also Huffmon, APNM, 262.

[79] *Ia-ri-im-mu,* and the very frequently occuring *Ia-ri-im-li-im.* Wiseman, The Alalakh Tablets, 136.

[80] *Ia-ri-(im)-mu, Bin-ia-ri-mi, Ia-ri-milku (= Yarim-milku), yrm, bn yrm, yrmʿl, yrmbʿl, yrmt* (F. Gröndahl, Die Personennamen der Texte aus Ugarit, 182).

[81] Huffmon, APNM, 262. The hypocoristic endings found with the Mari names are important in distinguishing these names from Biblical names. This will be particularly important for some of the historical conclusions to be drawn from this material. See further, below, Chapter 5.

found on a cylinder seal from Byblos[82], as well as the biblical hypocoristic name רם[83].

Among names that have the full sentence form, we find that most of the elements corresponding to אב are used also outside the Bible. So we have at Mari the name *Ì-lí-ra-am*[84] and perhaps *Ba-aḫ-li-ra-?*[85], which are to be compared with the names found at Ugarit: *Ilu(AN)-ra-mu, ilrm* and *bʿlrm*[86], at Taʿannek in Palestine: *ᵈEn-ra-am*[87], *E-lu-ra-ma*[88], as well as to the biblical י(ה)ורם[89].

The Biblical מלכירם[90] is to be compared to the seventh century Assyrian name *Mil-ki-i-ram-am*[91] and the near contemporary מלכירם found on a potsherd at Samaria[92].

We find the element עם in the name *Ḫa-mu-ra-ma* at Mari[93], in the Assyrian *Am-ra-mu*[94], and the biblical עמרם[95].

The element אח we find at Mari in the name *Aḫ-ra-am*[96], and at Ugarit, in the name *aḫrm*[97]. This is identical to the אחרם of the "Aḥiram" sarcophagus[98], and is also the same name as *A-ḫi-ra-mu*

---

82 See W. F. Albright, The Eighteenth Century Princes of Byblos and the Chronology of Middle Bronze, BASOR 176 (1964), 44f. Compare also the often recurring Egyptian name *rm* from New Kingdom texts (H. Ranke, Die Ägyptische Personennamen, Bd I, 1935, 222a).

83 Noth, BWANT, 10, 1928, 145.

84 Huffmon APNM, 25. 262.

85 Ibid. 174.

86 F. Gröndahl, Die Personennamen der Texte aus Ugarit, 116 and 182.

87 Tallqvist, APN, 161 (Taʿannek 1,18 and 7,6); Huffmon, APNM, 262; A. Gustavs, Die Personennamen in den Tontafeln von Tell Taʿannek, ZDPV 51 (1928), 186f.

88 (Taʿannek 7, R3) Huffmon Ibid., and Noth, BWANT 10 (1928), 88; A. Gustavs, ZDPV 51 (1928), 189f.

89 Noth, BWANT 10, 1928, 52.

90 Ibid. 118 and 145.

91 Variants: *Mil-ki-ra-me, Mil-ki-ra-mu* (Tallqvist, APN, 137).

92 Harvard Excavations at Samaria I, 264, nr. 64, and Noth, BWANT, 10, 1928, 118.

93 Huffmon, APNM, 88. 196f. and 262. The *-u* of the element *Ḫa-mu-*, as also in the name *E-lu-ra-ma*, is the nominative case ending. This is a very common characteristic of the early West Semitic names at Mari.

94 Dated by Tallqvist (APN 22) to 681 B. C.; see also KAT³ 483.

95 Noth, BWANT 10, 1928, esp. 16 and 33; also ZDMG 81 (1927), 31. The South Arabic name *ʿmrm* is to be derived from the root *ʿmr*. Cf. G. Ryckmans, Les Noms propres sud-sémitiques, Bibliothèque du Muséon 2, 1934, I, 167. 309. II, 109. W. W. Müller (Die Wurzeln Mediae und Tertiae Y/W im Altsüdarabischen, Dissertation, Tübingen, 1962, 57f.) finds no root רום "to be exalted" in Old South Arabic.

96 J. Bottéro and A. Finet, Repertoire Analytique des Tomes I à V, ARM XV, 1954, 141; Huffmon, APNM, 267; Noth, Alt Festschrift, 143.

97 F. Gröndahl, Die Personennamen der Texte aus Ugarit, 182. (Cf. also the name *šmrm*, Ibid.).

98 Albright (The Phoenician Inscriptions of the Tenth Century B. C. from Byblos, JAOS 67, 1947, 153—155) dates this inscription to the early tenth century. This was

from the seventh century Assyrian texts[99], as well as the Biblical אחירם[100]. We also have the name of the eighth century king of Tyre, *Ḫi-ru-um-mu*, whose name has been found in the Assyrian texts[101], which is to be related to the Biblical name of a man from Tyre חירום.

While the form **Ab-ram* itself has not been found in the Mari texts, it has been found frequently enough in other sources for West Semitic nomenclature. However, since many parallels have been claimed, like *A-ba-am-ra-am*, merely on the basis of similarity of consonants, some discussion of those parallels that have been put forward seems necessary.

The most regularly referred to of these names is that found in the Posener Execration Texts: *ibwrhni* prince of *šmwʿnw*[102]. This has been paralleled to the name אברהם with varying degrees of certainty[103]. The difficulties of demonstrating the parallel are great. The initial "element" *ibw-* is thought to be Semitic *ʾabu*. Some Semitic geographical and personal names with the element *ab-* or *abi-* are transcribed in Egyptian as *ib-*[104], and the *-w-* is understood as a nominative

accepted by H. Donner, Zur Formgeschichte der Aḥiram-Inschrift, WZL 3 (1953/54), 283, and KAI II 2, and now seems to be generally followed. On the other hand, R. Dussaud (L'origine de l'alphabet et son évolution première d'après les découvertes de Byblos, Syria 25, 1946—48, 36—52), has maintained a 13th century date for this inscription and is recently strongly supported by R. Hachmann, Das Königsgrab V von Jebeil (Byblos), Istanbuler Mitteilungen 17 (1967), 93—114. The name in the inscription is read: בנאחרם and לאחרם! Dussaud, Les Inscriptions Phéniciennes du Tombeau d'Ahiram, Roi de Byblos, Syria 5 (1924), 137. Dussaud's translation (136) "fils d'Aḥiram" and "pour Aḥiram" is apparently based on the Biblical אחירם. This shows quite concretely how insignificant the connecting vowel is. Noth (Alt Festschrift 143 n. 2) expressed some doubt that אחרם is composed of the elements אח and רם, and suggested that the name might possibly be an accusative of a word built from one stem. However, the name is given twice — not once as Noth assumed — and in neither case in the "accusative".

99 Variant forms of this name are *PAP-i-ra-me*, *PAP-ra-mu*, and, perhaps *Aḫu-ram(?)-nu* (Tallqvist, APN 17 and 19).

100 Num 26 28; cf. M. Noth, BWANT 10 (1928), 18. 65 n. 5. 70. 145; and ZDMG 81 (1927), 18.

101 Noth, ZDMG 81 (1927), 28; Tallqvist, APN, 88.

102 E 55; cf. L. H. Vincent, Les Pays Bibliques et L'Egypte à la fin de la XIIe Dynastie Égyptienne, Vivre et Penser, II (RB), 1942/3, 200f.; also, perhaps, E 56: *ibw . . . i*, prince of *qȝqȝm* (ibid. 201).

103 Ibid.; Albright, The Land of Damascus between 1850 and 1750 B. C., BASOR 83 (1941), 34, and, A Third Revision of the Early Chronology of Western Asia, BASOR 88 (1942), 32; J. A. Wilson, ANET, 328 and 329 n. 8; J. Bright, History of Israel, 70; A. Weiser, Abraham, RGG[3], 68; R. de Vaux, RB 53 (1946), 323 n. 5; RB 72 (1965), 8.

104 See on this especially G. Posener, Une liste de noms propres étrangers sur deux ostraca hiératiques du Nouvel Empire, Syria 18 (1937), 189: *ibšȝ* = *abî-šar(?)*; *ibšmw* = *abî-šemu*; and *ibj* = אבי.

ending similar to that found in so many of the names from Mari and Ta'annek[105]. The *r* causes no difficulty, and the *h* is thought to be attractively like the ה in אברהם[106]. The final *n* instead of the expected *m* is explained by reference to South Arabic[107]. Reference is also made to the South Arabic personal name *'brhn*[108].

This parallel is only successful if all of the arguments are both valid and relevant. However, recourse must be had not only to some peculiarities of Egyptian orthography, but to Akkadian, Ugaritic, and Arabic materials. It must be said that *ibwrhni* would be a very peculiar transliteration or "dissimilation"[109] of the name אברהם. Before this name is accepted as a parallel to the patriarch's name we should perhaps ask if it can be more easily explained on other grounds.

The name is strikingly similar to another name which has been associated with the name אברם, that of the fourteenth century king of Ugarit, *Ibiranu/i/a*, son of *A-mis-tam-ri*[110]. This name is found several times in Akkadian texts in two forms: most commonly with a theophoric element, as: *ᵈNinurta-i-pi-ra-ni*, *ᵈNusku-i-pir-an-ni*, and *ᵈSin-i-pi-ra-an-ni*[111]. These names are quite clearly Akkadian, not

---

105 As seen above, e. g., *Ḫa-mu-ra-ma* and *E-lu-ra-ma*.

106 de Vaux, in attempting to explain the different spellings *rm/rhm*, compares this to Ugaritic *bt* and *bht*, *'lht*, etc. (RB 72, 1965, 8). However, *bt* and *bht* are equivalent to בית, בתּים, Syriac: ܒܝܬܐ/ܒܬܐ, although nobody can explain either the Ugaritic *h* or the Hebrew/Syriac *dageš*. Ugaritic *ilht* is parallel, e. g., to Hebrew אמה, אמהות, Aramaic אב, אבהת, etc. In all these cases the stem of the noun is monosyllabic: *il*, *am*, *ab*, etc. A better interpretation might be suggested on the basis of Old South Arabic's written or "parasitical" *h*; i. e., an unetymological *h* that "auf einen ursprünglichen zweigipfligen Akzent zurückgeht", e. g., ũ > uʰu > uhu. (M. Höfner, Altsüdarabische Grammatik, 1943, 27f. For a fuller discussion, see N. Rhodokanakis, Studien zur Lexikographie und Grammatik des Altsüdarabischen, Bd I, 1915, 12—56). A good parallel to this is found in German: Ja, when stressed, often becomes Jéha. (For this discussion of *rm/rhm*, I am fully indebted to H. P. Rüger of Tübingen).

107 R. de Langhe (Les Textes de Ras Shamra-Ugarit, II 281) suggests that South Arabic *ḥrm* is also written *ḥrn*, but this seems questionable.

108 Albright, BASOR 83 (1941), 34 n. 13. See, however, G. Ryckmans, Les noms propres, I 254 and 278.

109 Albright, BASOR 83 (1941), 34.

110 Referred to by E. Weidner (Der Königspalast von Ugarit, AfO XVI, 1, 1952, 116) and published by J. Nougayrol, Le Palais Royal D'Ugarit III, Textes Accadiens et Hourrites MRS VI, 1955, where it appears four times in fragmented form (5. 168. and 196) and three times clearly readable (162. 166. and 168). Cf. Nougayrol's discussion on page 246. See also, F. Gröndahl, Die Personennamen der Texte aus Ugarit, 88.

111 Stamm MVÄG 44 (1939), 189; Clay, PN, 73b. 115a. and 125a respectively.

only in the order of the elements which is common to Akkadian names but unusual in West Semitic names[112], but also in the verb form, the Akkadian preterit, which should not be confused with the West Semitic imperfect[113].

We also have the Akkadian hypocoristic of this name in the form *I-pi-ra-an-ni*[114]! which demands that we understand the Ugaritic royal name, and perhaps *ibwrhni* as well, as a hypocoristic of *(ᵈX)-i-pi-ra-an-ni*: "(The God) has cared for me"[115].

More acceptable parallels to the name אברם have been cited, some of which are particularly interesting:

From Late Bronze Taʿannek we have the unfortunately damaged text with the name *A-bi-ra-* . . .[116].

From Ugarit we find names identical to those of the patriarch's. In the Akkadian texts from Ugarit we have the name *A-bi-ra-mu*[117]. In the alphabetic cuneiform, from texts discovered in 1954, we find the name born by two individuals[118], *abrm alšy* and *abrm mṣrm*, a Cypriot *abrm* and an Egyptian *abrm*[119]. That the names are born by individuals who seem possibly to be other than West Semites plays no role whatever in classifying the names as Early West Semitic, and as perfect parallels to the name אברם.

On a hieratic ostracon from the Louvre, dated to the end of the reign of Sesostris I or to the beginning of the reign of Rameses II (c. 1290), we find the name *íbrm*[120]. As Posener has clearly shown, the name should be transliterated אברם[121].

A much debated possible parallel comes from the reign of Shoshenk I (945—924 B. C.) found in an inscription on the outer

---

112 Huffmon, APNM, 76f.

113 Ibid. 16. On this further see below the discussion of the name יעקב.

114 Stamm, MVÄG 44 (1939), 189; Clay, PN, 90b.

115 Following Stamm (ibid.) in the translation, who renders the above name: (*ᵈX*) "hat mich versorgt".

116 (Taʿannek 12, 2) referred to by Böhl, Das Zeitalter Abrahams, AO 29 (1930), 54 n. 67; also see Tallqvist 5.

117 Nougayrol, (PRU III 240); F. Gröndahl, Die Personennamen der Texte aus Ugarit, 182.

118 This name has been correctly recognized by Ch. Virolleaud, Les nouvelles Tablettes Alphabétiques de Ras Shamra, Comptes Rendus, Académie des Inscriptions et Belles-Lettres, 1955, 79; C. H. Gordon, Ugaritic Textbook 2095:2.4; Ugarit and Minoan Crete 150; A. van den Born, Abraham, Bibellexikon, 13. De Vaux identified these names with the one given in the Akkadian texts (RB 72, 1965, 8).

119 Virolleaud ibid., and E. Vogt, Ugaritica, Bb 37 (1956), 387; also F. Gröndahl (182): *ibrm, abrm*.

120 Ostracon E 14354, Posener, Syria 18 (1937), 183—197.

121 Ibid. 189.

wall of the Karnak temple. The inscription gives a list of 156 captive towns from the Egyptian campaigns[122]. One of the places listed reads *pꜣḥwḳrw* + place determinative and then *ꜣbꜣrmʿ*[123]. Breasted, relating the first word to a proposed Hebrew or Aramaic חקל, which he understands to mean "fields", translates the place name: "Field of Abram"[124]. He derives the חקל from the Aramaic, citing the New Testament ʽΑκελδαμάχ which is normally translated "Field of Blood"[125]. An expression similar in meaning to what Breasted suggests in his translation occurs very frequently in biblical place names: such as, "Field of Moab"[126], and "Field of Zoan"[127], where the Hebrew word שדה is used[128]. Because *pꜣḥwḳrw* occurs compounded with the name *ꜣbꜣrmʿ*, and, moreover, since it occurs in the same way with at least seven other place names in these inscriptions, it is perhaps legitimate to suggest that, like שדה, it is to be understood as a compound of a place name. *ḥwḳrw* might also be equivalent to חקר: Hebrew חקרה; Aramaic חקרא, "city" or "citadel"[129].

It is not entirely clear that the second element of this name is Abram. Kyle, in 1911, pointed out that Breasted failed to transliterate the final ע, and that the name should be read *Abirama*[130]. It is not clear, however, that Kyle's quite valid correction is significant in our discussion of the name as a parallel to אברם, since the element *ram* in Early West Semitic names typically has the vocalic ending *-a (-rama)*[131].

It is possible that this inscription contains the name אברם as a place name, but this cannot be said (because of the ע) with complete

---

122 Breasted, The Earliest Occurrence of the Name of Abram, AJSL 21 (1904f.), 22.

123 The original text is conveniently found in ibid. 36. Breasted transliterates this: *Pꜣ-ḥw-ḳ-rw ʾ-bʾ-rʾ-m*.

124 Breasted (ibid.; AER IV, 352f.; and The "Field of Abram" in the Geographical List of Shoshenk I, JAOS 31, 1911, 290—295) is followed by W. Spiegelberg, Agyptologische Randglossen zum alten Testament, 1904, 14; J. Wilson, ANET, 242; G. E. Wright, Biblical Arachaeology, 148.

125 Breasted, JAOS 31 (1911), 290. This is rejected by de Vaux (RB 53, 1946, 323 n. 5).

126 Gen 36 35 I Chr 1 46. Cf. also שדי מואב in Ruth 1 1. 2. 6.

127 Ps 78 12. 43.

128 These are to be understood as compound place names, like בית שמש, and are not to be confused with the plural of שדה, sometimes used with place names meaning: "(the) fields of X".

129 So Böhl (Das Zeitalter Abrahams 34) translates the name "'Burg' oder 'Zitadelle' des Abraham". Cf. M. Jastrow, A Dictionary of the Targumim, I, 1903, 497b.

130 M. G. Kyle, The "Field of Abram" in the Geographical List of Shoshenq I, JAOS 31 (1911), 90. Kyle is wrong in his suggestion that Breasted did not have a correct copy, since Breasted published a photograph of the inscription in his AJSL article of 1904.

131 Huffmon, APNM, 90f. and 106.

confidence[132]. The existence of such a place name in tenth century Palestine could be important for biblical interpretation.

A final parallel to the name אברם might be mentioned from the late eighth and early seventh century Assyrian inscriptions. In these texts, a woman's name *ᶠAD-ra-mi*[133] appears and has caused some debate, having been transliterated in two different ways. Tallqvist reads it *ᶠAbi (AD)-ra-mi*[134], which would correspond with the Early West Semitic pattern of names built on the stem רום in the perfect. Stamm, however, transliterates the name *ᶠAba (AD)-ra-mi*, and insists that the name is not Aramaic but Akkadian[135], apparently to be paralleled to such names as *A-ba-am-ra-am*, with the *Aba-* understood as a direct object of a verb from the stem *rḥm*. This objection, though possible, does not seem justified, since we have clear Aramaic influence in this group of names, and also because the ideogram *AD* is generally to be read in the nominative as *Abi*, *Abu*, or *Ab*. The name could be transliterated into Hebrew script as אבירמי or simply as אברמי.

In concluding this section dealing with the name אברם it seems that we can already draw some general conclusions. The contention that the patriarchal names fit "only" or "best" into the first half of the Second Millenium[136] is, on the basis of the evidence for this name alone, clearly false. We have seen that names of the same type as אברם are found from the time of the Mari texts down through the Neo-Assyrian period, and that names directly parallel to אברם are found from the second half of the Second Millenium until long after the Genesis traditions had been formed[137].

The conclusion to be drawn from the names investigated so far is that the name אברם is a West Semitic name of quite common sort, and can be expected to appear wherever we find names from West Semitic peoples. A study of the name אברם in its proper context makes it quite clear that the discovery of related names and even

---

132 J. Simons, Egyptian Topographical Lists, 1937, 183, states that the translation: "The Field of Abraham" is no more acceptable than "The Field of Bulls", taking the meaning of the second word from אביר "bull". However, not only is this type of expression not found among place names in the Old Testament, but also no cognizance seems to be taken of the final ע in *ȝbȝrmʿ*. A letter-by-letter transliteration from the Egyptian into the Hebrew script would be אבארמע.

133 (Cf. *Abi-ra-mu*) On both these names, see Tallqvist, APN, 5, and Noth, ZDMG 81 (1927), 31.

134 Tallqvist ibid.

135 Stamm, MVÄG 44 (1939), 292.

136 For literature, see footnotes 4 and 5 above.

137 The names *A-ba-am-ra-am*, *I-bi-ra-na*, and probably *Ibwrhni*, as we have seen, are unrelated.

exact parallels can help in no way in dating the patriarchs or the "patriarchal period". The name is not to be dated to any specific period[138].

This conclusion is further supported by an examination of the other patriarchal names: Isaac, Israel and Jacob.

C. ISAAC, ISRAEL, AND JACOB

The name Israel on one hand and Isaac and Jacob on the other reflect two quite distinct, though related forms: The name "Israel" is a sentence name composed of a verbal element and the divine name El[139], while the names "Jacob" and "Isaac" are hypocoristic names formed from the verbal elements only. Isaac and Jacob are commonly spoken of as "shortened" or "abbreviated" forms of the original *יעקב־אל and *יצחק־אל[140]. This interpretation is based, of course, on the etymological structure and classification of these and similar names. But just such classification and analysis shows that the "full" forms of the names Isaac and Jacob are hypothetical, and forms such as *Jacob-ba'al* or *Jacob-'am* and the like might be chosen as well. Though the element אל- is found very early and very often it is by no means exclusively used. The elements בעל, אב, אח, etc., are also found in the early records[141]. There is

138 That we do not gain, from the knowledge that the name was commonly used as a personal name, anything towards the establishment of the traditions' historicity is only to be expected, since the use of wholly constructed names (like the cue names in the Book of Ruth) is a characteristic of only some fictitious writing. To show that the name David is a personal name in nineteenth century England does not really support the historicity of David Copperfield; it only shows us, whatever it is worth, that Dicken's hero bore a name which Dickens and his readers considered to be a real name. That Abraham's name, on the other hand, in its expanded form (אברהם) played an active part in the development of the Abraham tradition as a unit is also clear.

139 A very thorough discussion of this element is to be found in Noth, BWANT 10, 1928, 82—101.

140 We find this suggestion in e. g., Brown, Driver, and Briggs, Hebrew and English Lexicon of the Old Testament (reprint 1959), 785; R. de Vaux, RB 53 (1946), 323; H. Cazelles, Der Gott der Patriarchen, Bibel und Leben 2 (1961), 44; M. Haran, The Religion of the Patriarchs, Annual of the Swedish Theological Institute IV (1965), 346; van den Born, Jakob, Bibellexikon, 800.

141 The element יה(ו) on the other hand, seems relatively late, on the basis of Old Testament evidence. Although it is found with some of the oldest Old Testament personal names like יהושע and יהונתן (Noth, BWANT 10, 1928, 105f.), nevertheless, in contrast to the large number of ־אל, ־בעל, and ־עם place names, Yahweh place names are nearly nonexistent in the Old Testament and are found only in

nothing intrinsic in the form *יעקב־אל which makes it preferable for the hypothetical "original" of the name יעקב. Indeed, it is difficult to justify the implication that the theophoric forms are historically earlier than the hypocoristic forms. As we have seen in the discussion on the name אברם, hypocoristic forms appear in our earliest records. Moreover, the special hypocoristic endings like *-u(m)* and *-atu(m)* show that the difference in form between the hypocoristic and theophoric types cannot be simply explained by suggesting that the theophoric element has "fallen away". Rather, the hypocoristic is a variant form in its own right. Its dependence on the theophoric forms is a structural dependence only; i. e., the hypocoristic form presupposes a theophoric element in its meaning.

The Old Testament understanding of the names supports this interpretation that there is no reason to presuppose an earlier, original, theophoric form of the names Jacob and Isaac. In the traditions about the patriarchs, the play on the names which forms such an integral part of so many of our stories, consistently presupposes the hypocoristic forms. The biblical tradition always understands the name יצחק as: "he" or "she" "laughs", "mocks", "plays", or "fondles". Never is the name understood as *יצחק־אל[142]. In Gen 17 17 Abraham "laughs" (ויצחק); in 18 12 Sarah "laughs" (ותצחק) in disbelief; in 21 6 Sarah predicts that those who hear the news will "mock" (יצחק) her. In 21 9 Ishmael "plays" (מצחק) with Isaac and in 26 8 Isaac "fondles" (מצחק) Rebecca[143].

The Genesis stories understand the name יעקב in almost every possible way except *יעקב־אל: In Gen 25 26, as well as Hos 12 4, as

postexilic texts, and there very rarely: only ענניה (Neh 11 32) and בית יואב (I Chr 2 54). Cf. the name list of Borée (Die alten Ortsnamen Palästina 1930) especially 95f. (בעל names) and 99f. (אל and עם names); also 103. The name מריה of Gen 22 2 and II Chr 3 1 (and the aetiology of Gen 22 14a. 14b based on the name יהוה) is most likely a later form of a name that was originally without the theophoric element ־יה, as in the early reference to the place גבעת־המורה in Judges 7 1.

142 It is often pointed out in reference to this name that El, in the Ugaritic texts, is portrayed as laughing, which would give a context for such a name as **Isaac-el.* Cf. L. Hicks, Isaac, IDB II, 728—731; Stamm, Der Name Isaak, Festschrift A. Schädelin, 35. Stamm points to God laughing in the Old Testament as well: Ps 2 4 59 9 37 13 (ibid.).

143 Cf. H. E. Ryle, Isaac, HDB, 485; Stamm ibid. 33f.; R. de Vaux, RB 72 (1965), 9; J. Fichtner, Die Etymologische Ätiologie in den Namengebungen der geschichtlichen Bücher des alten Testaments, VT 6 (1956), 382f. In one passage at least an entire story plays on this understanding of the name (Gen 26 8ff.). In my opinion, this form of the name Isaac appears to be original, at least in the stories of Genesis, for these elaborate puns are not later additions to the stories or re-interpretations, but rather essential elements of the narrative.

related to "heel" (עקב): "he follows at the heel"; in Gen 27 36 25 26, and Jer 9 3 as "he (i. e., Jacob) overreaches" (עקב); in Jer 17 9 and the Jacob-Esau tradition, the name is understood as meaning "deceitful", or "insidious" (עקב); in Gen 30 40 it is related to the word עקד, "striped, streaked"[144].

With the puns on the name Israel, however, the interpretation is quite different. Both in Gen 32 28 and in Hos 12 5, the understanding of the name, though neither grammatically nor etymologically correct, presupposes the theophoric element in the wordplay[145]. On the other hand, in the hypocoristic name ישרון the Bible understands the meaning: Israel (not El) is righteous[146] in contrast to the "deceitful" Jacob. This name, like the names Jacob and Isaac, is understood to be without any theophoric element.

A hypocoristic name is not a name that has itself been shortened; rather, it is a short form, a variant, of the theophoric names constructed of both nominative and predicate elements. The hypocoristic is not to be understood as a type of "nickname", but rather as a different name, no more to be identified with the "fuller" forms than the name יהנתן is to be identified with אלנתן.

D. N. Freedman[147] claims, however, to have discovered the "original" form of Jacob in the יעקב אל of Deut 33 28. In 1948[148], he and F. M. Cross had emended this text to read: ישכן ישראל בטח בדד ען יעקב על ארץ דגן ותרש אף־שמו יערף טל and translated it: "Israel encamps in safety; securely apart dwells Jacob; upon a land of grain and wine, yea, his heavens drip down dew." The emendation was to change the אל ארץ to על ארץ so that it could read "upon" rather than "to" or "toward", which had made no sense. This brought the Masoretic text to correspond to the Samaritan Pentateuch and the sense of the Septuagint.

In 1963, however, Freedman proposed accepting the Masoretic text as the original and reading the word אל not as a preposition, but as the divine name, ־אל attached to the preceding יעקב. He, thereby, recovers "the original name of the patriarch . . . and resolve(s)

---

[144] Brown, Driver, and Briggs 784f.; van den Born, Jakob, 800; J. Fichtner 382f.; and F. M. Th. de Liagre Böhl, Volksetymologie en Woordspeling in de Genesis-Verhalen, MKAW, Letterkunde 59A, 1925, 68—70.

[145] For Hos 12 5, here, I am following Albright's reading (The Names of Israel and Judah, JBL 46, 1927, 158) וישר־אל מלכת: "And he prevented God (El) from going." (parentheses added) That this is not the "correct" etymology, that El is understood as object rather than as subject, is here beside the point.

[146] Further on this, see below.

[147] The Original Name of Jacob, IEJ 13 (1963), 125f.

[148] The Blessing of Moses, JBL 67, 196 and 210 n.

the grammatical difficulty as well"[149]. He thus renders the text: ישכן ישראל בטח בדד ען יעקב־אל ארץ דגן ותרש אפ שמו יערף־טל "Israel dwells in safety; By himself Jacob-el settles: (His is) a land of grain and must; his skies also drip with dew"[150]. This proposed emendation and translation (The emendation, it should be noted, does not affect the consonant text), though attractive, is impossible on two counts: First, the phrase ארץ דגן ותרש without the אל makes no sense whatever, and only by the arbitrary addition of "(His is)" can Freedman translate the text at all, but this addition cannot be understood from the Hebrew. Secondly, the Samaritan Pentateuch reads the preposition על and the Septuagint understands it as a preposition (ἐπὶ)! Freedman has hardly resolved a grammatical difficulty as he claims, but rather he has created not one but two serious difficulties in a text which previously had none, and for this reason his is hardly an acceptable reading. The text offers no difficulty and no emendation is needed. אל can and does mean "upon". The Bible does not know any difference between אל and על; and if we are to understand grammar on the basis of how Hebrew is used in the Old Testament, then we cannot differentiate the two forms. Sperber, in his examination of these two words, concludes:

> The particles אל and על are used promiscuously. Any differentiation in their meaning is without any foundation in the Bible, and must be considered as arbitrary. The practice adopted by commentators to amend the Bible text, even on the evidence of manuscript readings to the end that אל shall stand for "toward" and על "upon" or "against" works on the presupposition that these are the real meanings of these words[151].
>
> The Bible does not 'confuse' them, but uses them in the identical meaning, because they obviously are identical in their connotation[152].

He also points out that to accept such an emendation would demand a further 130 emendations in Ezekiel alone[153]; that is, we would have to rewrite the biblical text to fit our theory. As it is, Freedman's translation (not text) of 1948[154] stands as an acceptable translation both for the Masoretic and the Samaritan texts.

Little can be said about the name יצחק. It seems to be built from the imperfect, and is a typical occurrence of the hypocoristic form of a theophoric name like ישמעאל and is to be compared to

---

[149] IEJ 13 (1963), 126.

[150] Ibid. 125.

[151] A. Sperber, A Historical Grammar of Biblical Hebrew, 1966, 631.

[152] Ibid. 59.

[153] Ibid. 63.

[154] JBL 67, 196.

יבשם, ידבש, ישמא, etc. It appears in two forms: יצחק and ישחק. The root is either צחק, "to laugh", "to play", "to caress", or שחק which carries the meanings "to laugh at", i. e., "to deride", or "to play", "to jest" or "to make merry". There is little difference between these two roots, and the biblical puns on the name use the entire range of the meanings of both roots. Neither the name יצחק nor other names built on the same root are found elsewhere in the Bible or in other Near Eastern records[155]. Nevertheless, in form the name fits well with the Early West Semitic names that have been found throughout the Second and First Millenium, and which are so common in the early biblical texts.

The etymology of the name Israel is much more difficult. There is little agreement over the root. Brown, Driver, and Briggs suggest the root שׂרה "to persist, to contend"[156]. Koehler-Baumgartner suggests שׂרה "to fight"[157]. Noth relates the name to שׂריה and understands it to have been derived from משׂרה from שׂרא "to rule"[158]. Albright excludes the root שׂרה on theological grounds[159] and שׂרא on the grounds that no such word is known[160]. He chooses the verbal stem *yaśar* "to cut, saw", the meaning of which he derives from the Arabic *waśara* and the Ethiopic *šaráya* "to heal", though this meaning does not appear in Hebrew[161]. Sachsse suggests the root ישׁר "to be straight, upright"[162].

---

155 Noth, BWANT 10, 1928, 210f.; Alt Festschrift 143; R. de Vaux, RB 72 (1965), 8.

156 975, following G. Steindorff, Israel in einer altägyptischen Inschrift, ZAW 16 (1896), 331.

157 407, based on Gen 32 29. However, biblical etymologies are notoriously unetymological, as we have seen, for instance, with the name Abraham. Moreover this is not, as we shall see, the only biblical understanding of the name Israel.

158 BWANT 10 (1928), 191f. and 207—209.

159 JBL 46 (1927), 165. How Albright can maintain that the meaning "He contends with God" or the better "God contends" is not acceptable to Old Testament religious understanding is difficult to see, since clearly this meaning is not only acceptable but used in Hos 12 3! The theological difficulties are Albright's.

160 Ibid., but see Noth, BWANT 10, 1928, 192.

161 Albright ibid. 165—168.

162 Die Etymologie und älteste Aussprache des Namens ישראל, ZAW 34 (1914), 1—15. Sachsse's treatment is marred not only by his assumption that the Masoretic vocalization of the name is necessarily late (cf. the criticism of M. Noth, BWANT 10, 1928, 207), but also his assumption that there is a strict regularity in the Masoretic pronunciation, so that we can derive what must have been an original pronunciation from the patterns observed in the normal Masoretic pointing. For what it is worth, it might be noted that the Masoretic text reads צְלָפְחָד which corresponds with Sachsse's reconstruction יִשֲׁרְאֵל, but the Septuagint reads Σαλπααδ, which corresponds more to the form יִשְׂרָאֵל. Cf. Sperber, Hebrew based upon Greek and Latin Transliterations, HUCA 12/13 (1937/8), 106. G. A. Danell (Studies in the

On linguistic grounds any of these choices seems possible. That שׂ and שׁ coalesce and are often interchanged in biblical Hebrew is clear. The LXX transliterations make no differentiation whatever in the sounds[163]. Judges 12 6 (the Shibboleth/Sibboleth story) also suggests this[164], as does Jer 23 38, where we have a pun with the word משׂא (from the root נשׂא) and the verb נשׁה[165].

One observes a similar ambiguity in the nomenclature. The name שׂריה seems to be a theophoric name in the perfect tense from the root שׂרה or שׂרא[166], similar to the name חזקיה (from the root חזק). The name שׂרה or perhaps better שׂרי might be understood as a hypocoristic name in the perfect, like הזקי[167]. Here, the root seems to be שׂרה or שׂרא. יֵשֶׁר, on the other hand, seems to be a hypocoristic name in the perfect from ישׁר, and the name אֲחִישָׁר appears to be a theophoric name with a verb in the perfect tense from ישׁר[168]. The name יְשֻׁרוּן also seems to be derived from the root ישׁר (a hypocoristic

Name Israel in the Old Testament, 1946, 23) is far too uncritical in his acceptance of Sachsse's interpretation, and consequently his discussion adds little to the understanding of Sachsse's thesis.

Sachsse tries to establish rules for pointing based on the third radical of the verbal element, thereby allowing him to amend what does not correspond to his rule. Unfortunately no complete system seems to exist, for we find similar pointing in such names as יִזְרְעֶאל (contrast יִשְׁמָעֵאל!) and יִרְפְּאֵל, and in names like יִשְׁמַעְיָה and יִסְמַכְיָהוּ, though the third radical does not seem to be the cause. The Masoretic text, particularly with names, defies any complete systematization. The pointing for יִשְׂרָאֵל obviously corresponds with יִשְׁמָעֵאל. These are not, as Sachsse would have it, exceptions to his rule, but rather evidence that patterns, not rules, exist in the Masoretic system of pointing.

Nor can his appeal to the extra-biblical names help him at all, for, as Noth remarks (BWANT 10, 1928, 207 n.), Hebrew pronunciation can hardly be determined by these records. Sachsse tries to see in the Shalmaneser inscription's ^{mat}*Sir-ʾ-la-a-a* (p. 8) and Merneptah's inscription's *Ysyriȝr* (p. 9) a support for his hypothetical *יְשַׂרְאֵל. The root ישׁר (cf. Akkadian *ešēru*) has a wide range of meaning: "to be smooth', "tractable", "to please", "to suit", "to be liking", "to be just", "upright", "pious", and "the best of". Also God is ישׁר.

יֹשֶׁר means "straightness", יִשְׁרָה "uprightness", יְשֻׁרוּן "the upright", and שָׁרוֹן "plain", or "level country".

163 Sperber, Grammar, 230. 164 Noted by Danell 25.

165 Sperber, Grammar, 172.

166 W. Robertson Smith, Kinship and Marriage in Early Arabia, 1903, 34 n., but especially Noth, BWANT 10, 1928, 191f., who connects this with שָׂרָה.

167 For the variant spellings see especially Sperber, Grammar, 486. For the possible relationship of the name שרה to ישראל see W. Robertson Smith 34. Köhler-Baumgartner (929) give as the second meaning of שׂר: "notable people", "chief in a series", perhaps comparable to some of the extended meanings of ישׁר.

168 Etymologically equivalent to אחישר as Noth rightly understood (BWANT 10, 1928, 189.

form in the perfect plus the ending ־ן) after the manner of זְבוּלֻן. The name ישרון seems to be used as an alternate of ישראל in Deut 32 15 33 5 and 33 26. Deut 33 5 reads: "Thus Jahweh became king in ישרון, when the heads of the people were gathered, all the tribes of Israel together."

The name ישראל could either be a theophoric name with the verb in the imperfect from שׂרה or שׂרא, or, since the imperfect of ישר would normally be יִישַׁר[169], it is also possible that ישׂראל is a theophoric name with the verb in the perfect tense, similar to ידעיה and נתניה.

Names similar to ישׂראל have been found quite often in extra-biblical texts; but, here too, except for the clearly Akkadian names, there is some ambiguity in determining the root.

From Mari we have the West Semitic names *Ḫa-am-mi-e-sa-a[r?]*, and the hypocoristic form *Ya-sa-rum*[170]. From Alalakh we have *Ia-aš-šar-ḫu*[171] and *Ia-aš-ri-e-da*[172]. It is not entirely clear whether these names are to be understood as constructed from the imperfect form of the verb (and thus probably derived from שׂרא or שׂרה), or whether they are derived from the perfect and thus correspond to the Akkadian names built from the verb *išar* "to be fair, just"[173]. Corresponding to the West Semitic hypocoristic form *Ia-sa-rum*, we find the Akkadian name *I-ša-rum*[174]. Corresponding to the West Semitic theophoric names we find such forms as *I-sar-li-im*[175] and *I-šar-be-li*[176]. This suggests that the name *Iš-re-il*, found on a cylinder seal from the time of Narâm-Sin of Akkad is an Akkadian name from the root *išar*, and is not to be identified with West Semitic ישראל[177].

---

169 Köhler-Baumgartner 413f.

170 Huffmon, APNM, 212. The name *Ia-áš-ru-ka-an* does not apply, but comes from the Akkadian *šarāku*, "give, offer". Cf. M. Birot, Textes Économiques de Mari (III), RA 49 (1959), 16—19.

171 D. J. Wiseman, The Alalakh Tablets, Occasional Publications of the British Institute of Archaeology at Ankara, no. 2, 1953, 136 text 169.5.

172 Ibid. nos. 253.26, 256.22, and 267.7. For the theophoric element cf. *Ia-te-ri-(e)-da* (260.5 and 264.25, 29) and *I-li-e-da* (347.4) as well as *Zimri-eda* of the Amarna Letters.

173 Cf. Biblical ישׁר "to be upright"! The ambiguities of the שׂ and שׁ seem to be dialectical. So Steindorff points out that on the Israel Stele דמשק appears as *Ti-ms-ḳw*, though "normally" *s* = שׂ (Israel in einer altägyptischen Inschrift, ZAW 16, 1896, 331).

174 C. J. Gadd, Tablets from Chagar Bazar and Tell Brak 1937—38, Iraq 7 (1940), 39.

175 From Mari, Huffmon, APNM, 212.

176 From Chagar Bazar, Gadd, Iraq 7 (1940), 38; also Th. Bauer, Die Ostkanaanäer, 23.

177 J. W. Jack, The Date of the Exodus, 1925, 232 n. 3, and V. Scheil, Cylindres et Légendes Inédits, RA 13 (1916), 5f. Compare the Akkadian forms *Iš-ma-il*, *Iš-qu-il*, etc., Scheil 6.

At Ugarit we find the personal names *Yšril*[178], which corresponds to Hebrew ישראל. *Š* = both שׁ and שׂ[179] (cf. *Šd* = שדה, and *išb'l* = אשבעל).

The earliest possible reference to the biblical Israel occurs in the Merneptah Stele in the form: *Ysyriɜr*[180]. It occurs here with the designation of a tribe or group in a list of names of cities and regions in Palestine.

In considering the name Jacob we find a great deal of evidence, as it is one of the most common West Semitic names of the ancient Near East. It is found from Old Babylonian times to early post-Christian times.

The biblical name is clearly a hypocoristic imperfect from the root עקב and its meaning is either "May (the God X) protect", derived from the meaning of *'qb* in South Semitic[181], or perhaps better: "The (God X) is near," from the meaning of the root in Northwest Semitic (Hebrew, Ugaritic)[182].

The name יעקב shows us more than any of the other patriarchal names how clearly related these names are to the Early West Semitic nomenclature. M. Noth has gathered together the evidence from the later periods, and this can be stated in a few short sentences:

> Die Verwendung des Elements עקב in Personennamen (ist) bemerkenswert. Es begegnet verschiedentlich in palmyrenischen Namen, so in בעלעקב, עקבו, עקבי, עקיבא, und עתעקב; es findet sich in dem alten israelitischen Namen יעקב ... und ...

---

178 O. Eißfeldt, Neue Keilalphabetische Texte aus Ras Schamra-Ugarit, Sitzungsberichte der Deutschen Akademie der Wissenschaften zu Berlin, 1965, 28; Virolleaud, Le Palais Royal d'Ugarit, V 1965, n. 69.3, RS 18.49; F. Gröndahl, Die Personennamen der Texte aus Ugarit, 146; also see C. H. Gordon, Abraham of Ur, Driver Festschrift, 1963, 83f.; and H. Haag, Review of H. Seebass, Der Erzvater Israel, in ThQ 148 (1968), 107. Also the name *yšrd* (cf. Akk. *yašri-eda*): Gröndahl ibid.

179 Cf. Gordon, Ugaritic Textbook, 2069:3.

180 K. Galling, Textbuch zur Geschichte Israels, 1968², 39f.; Steindorff, ZAW (1896), 331.

181 For meaning cf. North Arabic *m'ḳabun* (Noth, BWANT 10, 1928, 177). G. Jacob's proposal to relate the name to the Arabic name for a bird: *ja'ḳūb*, "Steinhuhn" (G. Jacob, Der Name Jakob, Litterae Orientales 54, 1933, 16f., and van den Born, Jacob, 800) does not seem acceptable, mostly because it is an unparalleled and esoteric interpretation of what can be otherwise understood as coming from a root that is extremely common, and regularly and consistently found among those names which are most closely related to the early Hebrew names. It is not sufficient to be able to explain only one name, irrespective of its context; rather, the explanation must encompass not only that name, but also those names that seem to be related: such names as בעלעקב, נבועקב, etc.

182 So KAI no. 37 B1 (54f.); see further M. Dietrich and O. Loretz, Zur ugaritischen Lexikographie (I), BiOr 23 (1966), 131.

in den chronistischen Listen יעקבה[183] und עקוב; ebenso in Elephantine (ביתאלעקב נבועקב und עקוב) und Babylonien (*Aḳḳabbi-El*, עקביה, und עקוב); dazu kommen noch die südarabischen Namen עקב und עקבן[184].

To be added to this list are the עקב names from the recently discovered inscriptions from Hatra: *ʿqbʾ*[185], *ʿqwb*[186], *ʿqb*[187], *nšr-ʿqb*[188], *šmš-ʿqb*[189], and *ʿqb-šm*[190].

There are also a large number of similar names from Egypt and others from Mesopotamia of the Old Babylonian period[191]. In the Old Babylonian period they are particularly common and are found nearly everywhere that West Semitic names have been found. Because of the peculiarities and ambiguities of cuneiform writing, however, particularly with such consonants as ע and ק, the various forms in which the root appears should be carefully observed and individually evaluated.

By far the most commonly mentioned of these names in recent literature[192] is that found in Level I of Chagar Bazar, from the time of Iasmaḫ-Adad, son of Šamši-Adad I of Assyria, in the form *Ia-aḫ-qu-ub-AN*[193]. The form of the name is familiarly West Semitic, and since ע is often transliterated in cuneiform as *ḫ*[194], a transliteration

183 A variant form of the hypocoristic with the same meaning as יעקב.

184 Noth, BWANT 10, 1928, 45f. Perhaps also: אלעקב. Cf. G. Ryckmans, Les noms propres, I 224.

185 O. Krückmann, Die neuen Inschriften von Hatra, AfO 16, 1 (1952), 141—148, here, 141; no. 2 *smjʾ dj bt ʿqbʾ*, "*smjʾ*, the daughter of *ʿqbʾ*."

186 Ibid. nr. 16, p. 146.

187 Not *ʿqbʾ*; see footnote 50, p. 146, ibid.

188 *nšr-ʿqb br mrkʾdj*, "*nšr-ʿqb*, son of *mrkʾdj*", ibid. 147 nr. 23.2, 5.

189 Ibid. 142 and 146; no. 10a, 10c and 10d.

190 Ibid. 148 no. 27.4.

191 The following names are not discussed by Noth, who follows Bauer (Die Ostkanaanäer 70) too closely here. See Noth, BWANT 10, 1928, 46, and Alt Festschrift 152.

192 Referred to by, e. g., W. F. Albright, From the Stone Age to Christianity, 1946, 325f. n. 51, Northwest Semitic Names in a List of Egyptian Slaves from the Eighteenth Century B. C., JAOS 74 (1954), 231; R. de Vaux, RB 53 (1946), 324; R. T. O'Callaghan, Aram Naharaim, An Or 26 (1948), 28; H. H. Rowley, From Joseph to Joshua, 36 n. 3; G. E. Mendenhall, Mari, BA 11 (1948), 16 n.; J. Bright, History of Israel, 70 (who refers to the name simply as "Jacob"); Noth, Alt Festschrift, 142 n. 2; F. M. Cross, The Priestly Tabernacle, BAR, 1961, 204; H. Cazelles, Bibel und Leben 2 (1961), 44; van den Born, Jakob, 800 and Huffmon, APNM, 203.

193 Reported by C. J. Gadd, Iraq 7 (1940), 38, nos. 988, 989, and 995. See also: O. Loretz, von Soden Festschrift, AOAT 1, 218. 224; Texte aus Chagar Bazar und Tell Brak (Teil 1), AOAT 3 (1969), 21.

194 In Akkadian only ח and א are properly represented; ע sometimes appears as *ḫ* (so cuneiform ^{d}*ḫa-na-at* is used for West Semitic *ʿnt*, *ḫa-ab-du* for עבד and *Ḫa-am-mu* for עם), but, often as not, is simply not represented. Cf. Huffmon APNM, 14.

to West Semitic would render this name יעקבאל, similar to the name יעקב, but with the theophoric element אל־.

A name spelled in an identical manner has been found in the Old Babylonian cuneiform records excavated at Ḫarmal: *Ia-aḫ-qú (ku)-ub-AN*[195]. We find the same form: *Ia-aḫ-qú (ku)-ub-AN* in the records of Mananâ, king of Kish[196]. This form occurs three times here[197], along with the variant form *Ia-qú (ku)-ub-AN*[198] which occurs four times[199]. We find this second form in texts from Terqa on the Ḫabur from the time of Hammurapi: *Ia-qu-ub-AN*[200], as well as from other Old Babylonian texts from the time of Apil-Sin, Sinmuballit, and Hammurapi with the spelling: *Ia-qú (ku)-ub-AN*[201].

---

195 See S. D. Simmons, Early Old Babylonian Tablets from Ḫarmal and Elsewhere, JCS 14 (1960), 122, no. 100 line 21, and Huffmon, APNM, 203.

196 Who reigned about a century before Hammurapi; cf. D. N. Freedman, IEJ 13 (1963), 125 n.

197 M. Rutten, Un Lot du Lettres de Mananâ, RA 54 (1960), 77f., Tablet 11.27 and pp. 84f., Tablet 15.1 and 6. Also see Freedman ibid. and Huffmon APNM, 203.

198 Rutten ibid. 149.

199 There seems little doubt that the ע or *ḫ* is often left unexpressed before *q* in the cuneiform texts. We find such names as *Aq-ba-aḫu*, alongside of *Ḫa-aq-ba-a-ḫi-im*, *Aq-ba-an* and *Ḫa-aq-ba-an*, *Aq-bu-da-di* and *Ḫa-aq-bu-da-di*, *Aq-ba-ḫa-mu* and *Ḫa-aq-ba-ḫa-am-mu* or *Ḫa-aq-ba-ḫa-am-mú*. Cf. Huffmon, APNM, 36, and Noth, Alt Festschrift, 142 n. 2.

200 J. Nougayrol, Documents du Habur, Syria, 37 (1960), 206f., Tablet 206.4; also Huffmon, APNM, 203.

201 Th. Bauer, Die Ostkanaanäer, 27. 55, and Huffmon ibid. Bauer describes this: "Formell ostkanaanäisch, aber deutlich Nachbildung eines akkadischen *Ikun-pî-ilum*." (55). He is followed in this by Greßmann, Review of Th. Bauer, Die Ostkanaanäer, ZAW 44 (1926), 301f. This, however, was before the form *Ia-aḫ-qu-ub-AN* had been discovered at Chagar Bazar, and in 1953 Noth (Alt Festschrift 142 n. 2) takes exception to Bauer's thesis. But the ambiguities of this form should not be dismissed, for we do find the forms *I-ku-pi-pì-A-šur-Ašur* and *I-ku-pi-(ka)-ša* alongside of *I-ku-un-pi(ka)-^{d}Adad* (Stamm, MVÄG 44, 1939, 146f.). Moreover, we have the forms *I-ku-un-ba-li* from Alalakh as well as *Ia-ku-un-AN* from Ugarit (A. Goetze, Amurrite Names in Ur III and Early Isin Texts, JSS 4, 1959, 201), so that we must conclude that neither the consonants nor the vowels can give us a completely decisive answer in distinguishing, in many of our names, between the West Semitic root עקב "to protect" which is known from such names as יעקב and עקבבעל, etc., and the Akkadian elements *iḳun* and *iḳbi* "to announce" found in such unequivocal Akkadian names as *Šamaš-balāṭṣu-iqbi* (Tallqvist, APN, 209) or *Šarru-iqbi* (ibid. 217), and *^{f}I-ku-nu-bi(ka)-Adad* (ibid. 95).

The ambiguity is particularly great in such names as *Iq-bi-AN* (probably to be read *Iq-bi-ilu*) and *Ḫi-iq-ba-an* (Goetze JSS 4, 1959, 203) alongside of *Ḫa-aq-ba-an* and *Aq-ba-an* (Huffmon 36); also note *Aq-ba-a-ḫu-um*, *Ḫa-aq-ba-a-ḫi-im*, and *Iq-ba-a-ḫu-um* (ibid.). Perhaps we are to see those names that have both the *ḫ* and *qu* elements expressed, as constructed from the West Semitic

A cylinder seal, dated by Albright 1800—1600, gives us perhaps another form of the עקב names: *Ia-ak-ku-ub-e-da*. The second element is the same as that in the name *Zimri-eda*[202]. From the reign of Sinmuballit we have the hypocoristic form *Ia-ku-bi*[203] which, if the ע is understood, would be identical to our biblical hypocoristic יעקב[204]. From Ugarit we find the root עקב with the theophoric element בעל in the name *Ia-qub-baʿal*[205], and with the nominative element עבד in the name *Abdi-ia-qub-bu*[206].

The root עקב is also found in names formed from the perfect. From the excavation at Khafajah we find two names with the form *A-aḫ-qú(ku)-ub-AN*[207]. The variant *A-qú(ku)-un-AN* is also found here[208]. These names can easily be transliterated עקבאל. What is probably a hypocoristic of this form is found at Mari in the name *Ḫa-aq-ba-an*[209] which corresponds with the name עקבן from Elephantine[210]. Also probably to be included here are the theophoric forms *Ḫa-aq-ba-ḫa-am-mu-ú*[211] (particularly since the second element appears to be West Semitic), and possibly *Aq-ba-a-ḫu*, and others[212].

עקב; those with *qu* but not *ḫ*, or with *ḫ* but without the *u* of *qu* expressed, as probably West Semitic and those that have neither elements expressed as either of uncertain or Akkadian derivation.

202 Albright, Presidential Address: Palestine in the Earliest Historical Period, JPOS 15 (1935), 218 n.

203 Bauer, Die Ostkanaanäer, 27; Noth, Alt Festschrift, 142.

204 We also have the hypocoristic form *Ia-aq-bi-im* (Birot, Syria 35, 1958, col. IV, line 8, p. 11). Goetze (JSS 4, 1959, 203) suggests that we are dealing here with a different element, and rightly so if the suggestion offered above in note 201 is correct. The forms *Ia-ak-b(u?-ru)* from the reign of Ammisaduḳa and *Ia-ak-ba-ru-um* from the reign of Iluma-Ila (Bauer 27) are probably not hypocoristics built on the same root as יעקב since the normal hypocoristic endings are *-u(m)* and *-atu(m)* and at times *-an* (Huffmon, APNM, 132 and 137). The name *Ia-aḫ-bu-ú-um* (Huffmon 133) is missing the guttural *q*.

205 F. Gröndahl, Die Personennamen der Texte aus Ugarit, 111. 116.

206 Ibid. 112.

207 R. Harris, The Archive of the Sin Temple in Khafajah (Tutub), JCS 9 (1955), 107, Tablet 61.6 (Harris' transliteration 93), and 73, Tablet 12.3 (for transliteration 63).

208 Ibid. 114, Tablet 84r4 (transliteration, cf. 97, line 13).

209 M. Birot, Un Recensement des Femmes au Royaume de Mari, Syria 35 (1958), 12, col. 4, line 41. On hypocoristics, see Huffmon, APNM, 130—140, esp. 137. Cf. also *Aq-bu-ú* (Ranke, Early Babylonian Personal Names, Babylonian Expedition of the University of Pennsylvania, Series D, vol. 3, 1905, 67a).

210 Noth, BWANT 10 (1928), 46. 177.

211 Noth, Alt Festschrift, 132.

212 C. J. Gadd, Tablets from Chagar Bazar, Iraq 4 (1936), 185, fig. 2 A386.2. Gadd, however, misreads it (179) *Ak-ku-a-ḫu*, and consequently identifies it as Hurrian (182). The tablet is dated to the time of the First Babylonian dynasty by M. E. L. Mallowan, The Excavations at Tall Chagar Bazar and an Archaeological Survey

From Egypt we have several much-discussed names built from the root עקב. In a list of Egyptian slaves from the Middle Kingdom we find two names that appear to be hypocoristic forms built on the perfect of עקב[213]. Number 87 in the list reads: *ʿḳbtw*[214]. The ending *tw* probably represents the common hypocoristic ending *-atu*[215]. Number 37 from the same list reads *ʿḳbi,* constructed from the verbal element *ʿḳb* plus *i*[216].

The Egyptian scarabs from the Hyksos period offer us several names built on עקב in the imperfect. These names have been referred to regularly in the general literature[217]. By far the best treatment of these names is by S. Yeivin[218] who classifies the various names on

---

of the Habur Region, Second Campaign, 1936, Iraq 4 (1936), 92. On this name, as well as *Aq-ba-ḫu-um* (Harris, JCS 9, 1955, 109, no. 69r3), also found in tablets from the reigns of Apil-Sin, Hammurapi, and Šamšu-iluna (Th. Bauer, Die Ostkanaanäer, 11), *Aq-bu-da-da, Aq-bu-da-du-um* (Bauer 12), *Aq-bi-il* (ibid. 11), and the perhaps hypocoristic form *A-aq-bu-ú* (Harris 79, Tablet 28r1; also, cf. 94), see my remarks in note 201 above.

213 Albright, JAOS 74 (1954), 222—233; also referred to by J. Bright, History of Israel, 70.

214 Albright ibid. 230 and his discussion on 231.

215 This form is quite standard at Mari. Cf. Huffmon, APNM, 130—140.

216 The ending *i* is not specifically a hypocoristic ending, but it is found with many names (e. g., *A-bi-ra-mi*) without any apparent significance.

217 H. Greßmann, Sage und Geschichte in den Patriarchenerzählungen, ZAW 30 (1910), 7; C. F. Burney, Israel's Settlement in Canaan, The Biblical Tradition and its Historical Background, Schweich Lectures 1917, 1921, 89; W. Wolf, Der Stand der Hyksosfrage, ZDMG 83 (1929), 69; W. F. Albright, The Archaeology of Palestine and the Bible, 1932, 143; From the Stone Age to Christianity, 184—186; From Abraham to Ezra, 1963, 10; H. H. Rowley, From Joseph to Joshua, 35 and 64; R. de Vaux, RB 53 (1946), 324; H. R. Hall, The Ancient History of the Near East, 1960, 216f., and H. M. Orlinsky, Ancient Israel, 33.

218 S. Yeivin, Yaʿqobʾel, JEA 45 (1959), 16—18; also see A. Mallon, Les Hébreux en Egypte, Orientalia III, 1921, 43—49; and H. Stock, Studien zur Geschichte und Archaeologie der 13. bis 17. Dynastie Aegyptens, Äg F 12 (1942), 43—45. 67. and 263. The name on the Tell Beit Mirsim scarab (Albright, The Excavation of Tell Beit Mirsim, vol. II, The Bronze Age, in AASOR 17, 1936/37, Pl. 29, no. 2 and p. 44; JPOS 15, 1935, 227, and The Fourth Joint Campaign of Excavation at Tell Beit Mirsim, BASOR 47, 1932, 10, fig. 4), it should be noted, is hardly likely to be constructed from the root עקב. Albright reads the scarab: *zꜣ-rʿ ykb . . . dꜣ ʿnḫ.* The only radical common between this name and the patriarch's is the *b*. The *k*, which is a palatal, ought not to be confused with *ḳ*, which is a guttural. The scarab is also lacking the ʿ which is a strong consonant in Egyptian. Besides these two major discrepancies in the part that can be read, when it is noticed that the latter part of the name on the scarab is damaged, it can hardly be suggested with any confidence that it is related to יעקב. If it is Semitic at all, it should read: . . . יכב. A similar analysis seems to apply to the name *ykb-mw*, found at Buhen (II): Stock, Studien, 44.

the scarabs[219] according to seven types[220]: 1) *iiʿqbhr*, 2) *iiʿqphr*, 3) *iiʿpqhr*, 4) *iiqbhr*, 5) *iiʿqbʿr*, 6) *iikbʿr*, and 7) *iikbʿ*. This classification allows the possibility of clearer analysis[221]. The first three forms seem best understood as variant spellings for the name יעקבהד, the first element of which is identical to the biblical hypocoristic name יעקב. The theophoric element *hr*[222] = Semitic הד, that is, the Canaanite god Hadad[223] (Similarly, the Posener Execration texts' *smr-hr* = Ugaritic $\check{s}_2$*mr-hd*; cf. Mari *Zi-im-ri-*^{d}*Addu*)[224]. The fourth name, *iiqbhr*, could conceivably be built on the same *pattern* as the first three names and could be transcribed יקבהד. Number 5, *iiʿqbʿr* seems best explained as יעקבבעל[225] by assuming that a *b* has been omitted[226]. Numbers 6, and perhaps 7, have the final element בעל and a verbal form *iik* and should be translated "May Baʿal strike"[227]!

In the Hyksos scarabs discussed above two forms have the element עקב: יעקבהד and perhaps יעקבבעל. Both of these are good examples of the theophoric sentence name in the imperfect. However, the comparable form *יעקבאל occurs nowhere in the Egyptian records as a personal name[228].

---

219 Some of these are given by Mallon, Les Hébreux en Égypte, 43f., nos. 1—3, 7f., 10—13, and 27.

220 Yeivin, JEA 45 (1959), 16.

221 The analysis offered here varies somewhat from Yeivin's.

222 *Hr* is on no account to be transliterated אל which is regularly given in the hieroglyphs as *ir*, *ꜣr*, *iꜣr*, and *iꜣyr*; cf. E. Meyer, Der Stamm Jakob und die Entstehung der israelitischen Stämme, ZAW 6 (1886), 2; Sachsse, ZAW 34 (1914), 11. *Hr* forms in its own right a theophoric element; cf., the name *smꜣhr*.

223 Following O. Rössler in his discussion of early transcriptions of Semitic names: Das ältere ägyptische Umschreibungssystem für Fremdnamen und seine sprachwissenschaftlichen Lehren, Neue Afrikanische Studien 5 (1966), 221; W. F. Albright (From the Stone Age to Christianity 184) translates the name "May the mountain God protect", but such a divinity named הר is unknown. An Egyptian theophoric name is *ḥr*, "Horus", (as in *pšḥr*: Spiegelberg, Eine Vermutung über den Ursprung des Namens יהוה, ZDMG 53, 1899, 635, and in *ḥr nbw*: S. N. Horn, Scarabs and Scarab Impressions from Shechem II, JNES 25, 1966, 49). *ḥ*, however, is normally quite distinct from *h*. Moreover, the first element of this name *iiʿqbhr* is Semitic, which leads us to prefer the reading הד or הדד.

224 O. Rössler ibid.

225 Yeivin, JEA 45 (1959), 17f.

226 *bʿr* is the standard spelling for בעל; cf. E. Meyer, ZAW 6 (1886), 2.

227 The *k* is palatal, not *ḳ*; there is no ע nor any ב (Yeivin 17).

228 As commonly believed, usually transcribing *hr* by אל. Y. Elgavish (Chronique Archéologique: Shiqmona, RB 75, 1968, 417) reports the discovery of a scarab in a Middle Bronze II tomb with the name "Yaqob-el". Whether this scarab has been correctly read, or is similar to those already discussed, cannot be determined until the scarab is published.

This name does occur, however, in a list of place names in Palestine during the reign of Thutmosis III and again in the reign of Rameses II[229]. The place name in the Thutmosis III list found in the Temple of Ammon at Karnak reads: *Yʿḳbiꜣr*[230], which, transcribed, would read יעקבאל[231], a full theophoric name whose verbal element is the same as the biblical name יעקב, and whose nominal element is the god El.

The list of Rameses II is also found at the Karnak temple on the outside south wall. Number 9 of this list reads *Yʿḳbꜣr*[232]. Like the earlier reference this is to be transcribed יעקבאל[233].

---

229 The general discussions of this place name with the patriarch's name usually mention only the first reference, although some offer both. See J. W. Jack, The Date of the Exodus, 36 and 231; Meyer, ZAW 6 (1886), 1—11; A. Jirku, Die ägyptischen Listen palästinensischer und syrischer Ortsnamen, Klio. Beiträge zur alten Geschichte, N. F. 25 (1937), 15 and 38; G. A. Danell, Studies in the Name Israel, 43; H. Greßmann, Ursprung und Entwicklung der Joseph-Sage, Festschrift für H. Gunkel, Eucharisterion, I, 1923, 4; Studien zur Geschichte und Archaeologie 67; A. Mariette-Bey, Les Listes Géographiques des Pylônes de Karnak, 1875, 40; and S. Yeivin, JEA 45 (1959), 16.

G. E. Mendenhall, BA 11 (1948), 16n (reprinted but uncorrected in BAR II, 16n 20), gives a date of 1740 for the Thutmosis inscription, probably a printer's error for the 1470 given by Albright (A Third Revision of the Early Chronology of Western Asia, BASOR 88, 1942, 36n39), Mendenhall's source of information. Albright (ibid.) speaks of this town as having been named after the head of a clan who had lived in the immediately preceding centuries. But this is imaginary. There is no evidence for this at all.

H. R. Hall (The Ancient History of the Near East, 1960, 405) concludes from these names that "Jacobite Tribes" have already settled in Palestine. But it seems rather that in the Thutmosis list and in the Rameses list we are dealing with place names and not tribal names. In the Thutmosis list the name is found alongside of such well known sites as Qadesh, Megiddo, Damascus, Taʿannek, Akko, and Gerar (Meyer, ZAW 6, 1886, 1f.). It is, on the other hand, not absolutely certain that we are dealing with a city name, for other place names are also given, e. g., the Negev (Meyer 2) or, as in nr. 21: *śrwnꜣ*, the Plain of Sharon, as in Joshua 12 18 (Sethe, Urkunden der 18. Dynastie, III 1961, 782; A. Jirku, Aegyptische Listen, 8).

230 Sethe ibid. 785 no. 102a. Variants b and c give *yʿḳbimr*. The *m* is an obvious mistake for *ꜣ*.

231 As seen already, *iꜣr* is a standard Egyptian transliteration for אל. Hebrew ל is consistently transliterated *r* (*bʿr* is given for בעל). Similarly, no. 39 of the Karnak inscription reads *mšir*, which renders the Semitic משאל.

232 A. Jirku, Aegyptische Listen, 38.

233 It is quite possible that we are dealing with the same site. On the basis of the list of Rameses II, W. M. Müller places the name in the "westlichen Teil Mittel- oder Nordpalästinas". Cf. W. M. Müller, Die Palästinaliste Thutmosis III, MVÄG 12, 1, 1907, 27.

It should be noticed that in the Bible the name Jacob, outside of the patriarchal narratives, is generally used as a place name or a tribal name, rather than as a personal name.

The hypocoristic name יעקב could be related to *y'ḳbiꜣr* in a manner similar to the way ישרון is related to ישראל. Not only do we find a similar pattern in the use of the name Israel, but with the names of other great heroes too, such as the tradition about the great war hero and "mighty man of valor" in Judges 11 12 1-24 whose name was יפתח[234]. In Joshua 19 14. 27 we find the source of the eponym, the valley of יפתחאל which is the border of Zebulon, and in Jos 15 43 we find the city of יפתח. Also to be considered here is יבין of Joshua 11 1 and Judges 4 2. 7. 23: the "King of Hazor" and the "King of Canaan, who ruled in Hazor", in connection with the enemy city יבנה of II Chr 26 6 and the place name יבנאל of Jos 15 11 and 19 33[235]. Reference to these and like examples is particularly helpful, since no one would suggest that the city יבנאל was founded by יבין or that the city יפתח and the valley יפתחאל were respectively founded and owned by the hero יפתח as is done so often, for example, with the "patriarchal" cities of Gen 11.

The evidence of these names alone is not in itself sufficient to argue this thesis with any seriousness. This question can perhaps be better answered if we examine along with it the way in which the names of the other patriarchs of Genesis are used, particularly those which are considered in the tradition as being related to Abraham, Jacob, and Israel[236]. Such an examination, however, cannot be taken up here, but will be reserved for Chapter 11, where we will discuss the problem of the interpretation and the historiographical character of Gen 11 10—12 9. H. Gunkel's caution[237]: "Ein Generalschlüssel zu den Gestalten der Genesis ist also ihre Auffassung als Völker keineswegs", must be kept in mind, but, on the other hand, what is being dealt with here is not a "general key" to the problem of Genesis, but rather one very definite and explicit motivation for the genealogies and the names of the patriarchs. Though this may help little finally in the understanding of the various narratives about Abraham, Isaac, and Jacob (It is illegitimate, for example, to jump to the conclusion that the patriarchs are representatives of clans, and then to see their

---

234 Also mentioned in I Sam 12 11 as a great hero of the past.

235 Jos 11 1 ff., like Gen 14 and Jud 4f., is clearly a heroic tale. It should be noted that in both these examples, the place names have the theophoric -אל, but that the personal names like יעקב are hypocoristic.

236 This will be discussed further, in the context of the genealogies in Genesis, below in Chapter 11.

237 Genesis, 1966[7], LXXVI.

movements and actions as nothing more than tribal movements), it may help in understanding the historicity of Gen 11 10 ff., and perhaps something about the origins of the names of the three patriarchs about whom the narratives have been gathered.

Chapter 3

Mari and the Patriarchs

A. "LITTERA GESTA DOCET, QUID CREDAS ALLEGORIA . . ."

Although W. F. Albright describes the Genesis narratives as biographical[1], most scholars understand them as more indirectly mirroring historical events, as representing the actions of tribes rather than that of individuals, and see the travels of the patriarchs in these narratives, especially in Gen 11, as tribal movements or migrations. Consequently, to suggest that the patriarchs were in some way eponymous ancestors does not adequately resolve the contemporary debate over historicity. The central question about the historicity of the narratives is whether, from the standpoint of the First Millenium, they talk about any real past at all, if not of the patriarchs themselves, of the forerunners of Israel, and, if so, how far we can reconstruct that past. Almost all contemporary writers who would accept the historicity of our narratives admit that we have no direct evidence of the patriarchs themselves and that we are not likely to find any. Some, indeed, presuppose the eponymous function of the names of the patriarchs[2]. Moreover, those arguments which have as their conclusion the historicity of the patriarchs as individuals are established not on the claim of personal, but of ethnic or generic identity with specific groups of the Second Millenium B. C.; not on the basis of the discovery of the historical events of the lives of the patriarchs themselves, but on the basis of the discovery of similar events. Albright, for example, defends his thesis that Abraham was a Hapiru caravaneer of the early Second Millenium not so much by showing signs of Abraham's activities in what evidence we have of the caravan trade; rather, he attempts to show first, on the basis of the biblical texts, that Abraham, who is spoken of as a Hebrew in Gen 14, was in fact a caravaneer; secondly, that caravaneers in the Second Millenium were generally Hapiru, and that this Hapiru caravan trade was carried out particularly in the period in which Albright considers the Old Testament to have set Abra-

---

[1] The Biblical Period from Abraham to Ezra, 1963, 5; also implied in Yahweh and the Gods of Canaan, 1968, 56: "It is certain today that the Patriarchs were indeed human beings who were the heroes of stories handed down from the Patriarchal Age."

[2] Esp. Bright, History of Israel, 1959, 41—93.

ham; and thirdly, that these caravaneers visited the places with which Abraham is connected and performed the type of actions performed by Abraham. It is an attempt to establish a sufficiently strong chain of circumstantial evidence from which the probability of Abraham's individual historicity can be concluded[3].

A basically similar method is used, with more widely accepted results, to establish what is called the "essential historicity" of the narratives. This is a broad flexible term which allows for obvious inaccuracies, discrepancies, and anachronisms in the traditions, as well as for the possibility of variant traditions, though generally reducing these variants to a harmonized "original" event[4]. Its minimal understanding seems to demand that the traditions go back to a "patriarchal period" (though the exact extent of this period perhaps may not be determined), and that the traditions grow out of real historical events of that early time. It is what Bright means by "firmly anchored in history"[5].

This methodology reduces biblical criticism of Genesis to drawing out the "historical reality" from the metaphor of the biblical narrative. Gen 14 is seen as a historical record, in story form, of the destruction of MB I in Transjordan and the Negev. The covenant between Jacob and Laban is seen as a metaphorical representation of an historical boundary agreement between the Israelites and the Aramaeans. Hidden beneath the family history of Abraham journeying from Ur to Ḫarran and from there into Canaan, is the true history of major tribal migrations.

This lack of concern for literary form, i. e., for the intent, purpose, and function of the original traditions, has led to an overextension of the literary genre Stammessage, and assumes for narratives of this type an historical relevance which has yet to be clarified. The debate about historicity has been reduced to the question whether what the patriarchs do in Genesis is what the forerunners of Israel did in some analogous way.

The argument proceeds: If the patriarchs are to be seen as leaders of large tribal groups, then to show that tribal migrations of related linguistic peoples took place in a way reminiscent of the patriarchal movements demonstrates the historicity of these narratives and establishes for us the date of the patriarchal period. "Evidence" is what draws out and supports the analogy. "Enough evidence" is the accumulation of sufficient coincidence to bring about a judgment of historical "probability". Imperceptibly, historical research tends

[3] This thesis of Albright's will be treated in detail in Chapter 8. Here it is important only to draw out the general methodological principles.

[4] The flexibility of this position is well described in Bright's History 69.

[5] Ibid.

towards quantification in order to become "scientific". The quest is modest; argument is reduced to an accurate balancing of the facts and data for and against a given interpretation. If one "fact" is then balanced by a contrary "fact", or if the methodological presuppositions adopted by one scholar, are counterbalanced by the presuppositions of scholars of a different tradition, this quantitative evaluation, in its search for "objectivity", counsels that one can "believe or not, as one sees fit"[6].

The writing of history in this manner is no longer a question of either knowing an answer or establishing the various degrees of not knowing it. The various degrees of not knowing are added together and become "historical probability" which is even described as unquestionable and authentic[7]. Such a concept, however, is hardly legitimate, since, at least theoretically, historical possibilities are infinite. Rather, we have either adequate or inadequate evidence for believing that something happened, and the probability that an event occurred does not increase with the accumulation of inadequate evidence. Similarly, in scholarly discussion, the so-called "burden of proof" ought not be shifted from one side to the other of an argument. This burden always belongs to the one who attempts a synthetic interpretation of the historical data. The possibilities of interpretation are never limited to those that have been proposed. To use the term "evidence", meaning real historical evidence, is to assert that a given body of material, or a given text, is in fact related to the history which we wish to ascertain or clarify. It therefore is an absolute prerequisite to establish this relationship and to take seriously the methodological question raised by M. Noth concerning the study of the patriarchal narratives in his address to the International Congress for Old Testament Studies in 1959: "Es geht aber wissenschaftlich nicht darum, ob wir 'external evidence' brauchen, sondern ob wir 'external evidence' haben"[8].

This question is particularly important in discussing the alleged evidence from the early Second Millenium, particularly that related to the spread of the Early West Semitic names. In spite of a remarkable growth in historical knowledge about the entire Near East, and in

---

[6] This positivistic stand is taken both by Bright (ibid. 67) and by G. E. Wright, Modern Issues in Biblical Studies — History and the Patriarchs, ET 71 (1959/60), 294. Compare the dissenting remarks of K. Elliger, in his review of Wright's, Biblische Archaeologie, TLZ 84 (1959), 96, as well as those of M. Noth, Der Beitrag der Archäologie zur Geschichte Israels, VTS 7 (1959), 262f.: "Die geschichtliche Wirklichkeit ist nur eine gewesen; sie mit allen zu Gebote stehenden Mitteln zu erforschen, ist unsere Aufgabe."

[7] Bright, History, 69f.

[8] VTS 7 (1959), 271n.

spite of the great historical value of the Mari tablets and other related materials, we find that the present discussion about the patriarchs and their relationship to Mesopotamian history has changed very little over the past fifty years. In 1918, for instance, E. Kraeling interpreted "the migration of Terah" from Ur to Harran as a "great movement of the Suti from Chaldaea up the Euphrates"[9]. Today, the same interpretation is being given, but the Suti have been replaced by "Amorites" or "Benjaminites". Not that there is any greater probability that the patriarchs were related to these newcomers, but merely because, thanks especially to the Mari letters, we know a great deal more about these than we do about the Suti. Nor has accumulating "evidence" altered seriously Albright's analogy over the last 45 years, though it has changed somewhat according to the results of successive excavations and discoveries. In 1924 Albright constructed his interpretation on the basis of a proposed Aramaean migration from Paddan Aram (!) to Palestine and Egypt, with which he associated the Hebrew Abraham (Abram), the *Benê Ya'qob* and the Hyksos[10]. By 1935, as a result of his work on the Execration Texts, supported by his observations of a tomb painting found at Beni Hasan, he was able to interpret this new material as "evidence" that the Hebrew patriarchs entered Palestine from North Mesopotamia, not with the Hyksos, but during Middle Bronze I[11]. By the end of the decade, the Mari letters were "bringing striking support for the Israelite tradition, according to which their ancestors migrated to Canaan from the region of Ḫarrân"[12]. The information gained from these letters was so great that it was no longer possible to "doubt the substantial correctness of the Hebrew tradition which brought the family of Abraham from the land of Ḫarrân"[13]. The "Amorites and Proto-Aramaeans" now served as the analogue for the biblical traditions; and these biblical traditions themselves may perhaps be responsible for Albright's proposed migration of Amorites from North Mesopotamia to Palestine[14]. Within a decade, the process of analogy building was nearly complete, and the student of the Bible was told that every critical historical movement of the Second Millenium is either reflected in, or is directly useful for an under-

[9] E. Kraeling, Aram and Israel, 1918, 17; for the move to Palestine, cf. 31.

[10] Contributions to Biblical Archaeology and Philology, JBL 43 (1924), 393.

[11] Presidential Address: Palestine in the Earliest Historical Period, JPOS 15 (1935), 218—220.

[12] Review of the Two Sources of the Predeuteronomic Primeval History (JE) in Gen 1—11, JBL 57 (1938), 231.

[13] The Babylonian Matter in the Predeuteronomic Primeval History (JE) in Gen 1—11, JBL 58 (1939), 101.

[14] Ibid. 103.

standing of the patriarchal narratives[15]. Given this direction of his research, it is scarcely surprising that Albright concludes, on the basis of this overwhelming "evidence", that: "Abraham, Isaac, and Jacob no longer seem isolated figures, much less reflections of later Israelite history; they now appear as true children of their age, bearing the same names, moving about over the same territory, visiting the same towns (esp. Ḫarran and Naḫor), practicing the same customs as their contemporaries. In other words, the patriarchal narratives have a historical nucleus throughout"[16].

Since 1961 Albright has become more selective of his "evidence", without however giving any indications why he now feels that the previously indubitable evidence has become inadequate. The Amorite hypothesis and the conception of the patriarchs as semi-nomads give way to the new analogy built upon the hypothetical, but widespread, Ḫapiru caravan trade. The "evidence" is largely gleaned from the tablets from Cappadocia, Mari, Nuzi, and Amarna, the Execration Texts, the history of trade and commerce in the Near East, Middle Bronze I archaeology and exploration in Palestine and the Negev, as well as from the history of the domestication of the camel[17]. A phalanx of texts and historical materials is gathering in support of this thesis which is nearly as impressive as what supported the Amorite analogy.

I have emphasized the history of one man's thought, not with the purpose of criticizing Albright for changing his mind. Rather, because of the methodological limitations of this approach to history writing, such changes were necessary and are to be expected in the future as new material changes his "balance of probability". My intention is to point out that the methodology itself imposes a distortion not only on the interpretation of the biblical material, but also upon the growing historical knowledge in the light of which the biblical traditions are interpreted. Through increased historical under-

---

[15] W. F. Albright, The Archaeology of Palestine, 1949, 83; "The Middle Bronze Age corresponds to the Patriarchal Age of the Bible .... The Terachid movement from Ur to Harran and westward may have taken place in the 20th and 19th centuries, and Jacob's migration to Egypt may have fallen somewhere in the eighteenth or more likely the seventeenth century in connexion with the Hyksos movement." And on 206: "Nearly three centuries after the time of Jacob the Amarna tablets give us a picture which is in some respects like that of the Patriarchal Age in Genesis. In these documents the semi-nomadic ʿApiru appear as groups roving about the hill country, just as the Patriarchs are represented as doing in Genesis."

[16] Ibid. 236 (emphasis added).

[17] See especially Albright's, Abram the Hebrew. A New Archaeological Interpretation, BASOR 163 (1961), 36—54. A full review of this thesis is found in Yahweh and the Gods 47—95 and 232—234.

standing old distortions are exposed, and the proposed analogies constructed on the basis of such distortion must be altered or "improved" accordingly. Such distortion, however, is not necessary or excusable because of inescapable limitations inherent in all historical information; they are rather the direct result of the ungrounded assumption that these historical materials constitute evidence, of the conviction that there *is* a relationship between the history of the Second Millenium and the patriarchal narratives. Once such a relationship is presupposed, that the Amorites and the Ḫapiru, along with the Suti, are seen to have migrated from Ur to Ḫarran and from Ḫarran southwards, follows almost of necessity. Nor can it be surprising that those activities of the Ḫapiru which in some ways resemble semi-nomadism or the caravan trade, are seen as "characteristic" of them. If we assume a priori that they are related, how can there be an objection to interpreting the historical material in the light of the Bible as well as the Bible in the light of history[18]? One attraction of interpreting our texts in this way is that our parallels become more convincing, and what discrepancies there might be are significantly diminished.

Such inadequate methodology can only be corrected if, for purposes of analysis, and to establish criteria for our evidence, indeed to be able to determine whether there is any evidence at all, we first maintain a clear distinction between the biblical texts on one hand and the historical sources on the other. Not only must the sources be examined independently of each other, but no means should be excluded — even literary critical methods — to arrive at an understanding of the text which is consistent with its original purpose and intent; thus, the criteria for historical Anhaltspunkte are distinctly different when dealing with literary fiction than when examining chronicles or court records. Moreover, it is just as important to emphasize what is dissimilar as what is similar, and, to the extent that there are discrepancies, the parallel must be judged inadequate, and consequently any historical identification must be seen as unjustified.

[18] A now universally recognized example of such distortion would be A. H. Sayce's remark of seventy years ago: "Not long after Abraham's migration Hammurabi united Babylon under a single Kasdim (sic!) sovereign," (Ur of the Chaldees, ET 13, 1901/02, 65). This distortion that biblical concerns brought to the understanding of Babylonian history is clearly of the past, but the methodology is still used. It is questionable whether such distortion is justified even when — and this must be a perennial inadequacy — our historical information is limited.

B. "BENJAMIN" AT MARI[19]

The transliteration and translation of the name of a tribal group in the Mari tablets as *Bin-*(or *Benê*)*-ia-mi-na-a* by Georges Dossin[20] led many scholars to believe that historical knowledge concerning the formation of the Israelite tribe of Benjamin had been discovered[21].

The names of the people belonging to the Mari group were of the Early West Semitic type[22]. This seemed to strengthen the argument for identification with the Benjaminites of the Bible since many of the early Israelite names, patricularly those of the patriarchs, were known to be of this type also[23]. A third important factor in the identification was that the Mari group was found to have lived near Ḫarran and along the upper Baliḫ, as well as on the Middle Euphrates from Mari to the lower banks of the Ḫābūr[24], and again further West towards the coast[25]. This led Parrot[26] and Dussaud[27] to see in this displacement a possible historical counterpart of the biblical tradition of Abraham's journey from Ur to Palestine by way of Ḫarran. Schmökel maintains that the similarities are so great as to demand the assumption that the biblical tribe was a branch of the Mari group which broke off from the parent stem and came

---

19 In order to limit this discussion to what is directly pertinent to the evaluation of the proposed biblical parallel, a great deal of the information about the "Benjaminites" of Mari has had to be presupposed. The reader is referred to the excellent studies of J. R. Kupper, Les nomades en Mésopotamie au temps des rois de Mari, Bibliothèque de la Faculté de Philosophie et Lettres de l'Université de Liège, fasc. 142, 1957; I. J. Gelb, The Early History of the West Semitic Peoples, JCS 15 (1961), 27—47; H. Klengel, Benjaminiten und Hanäer zur Zeit der Könige von Mari (unpublished dissertation, Berlin, 1958); and the volumes of ARM.

20 Signaux Lumineux au Pays de Mari, RA 35 (1938), 178.

21 A rather complete collection of the various arguments on behalf of the identification has been made by M. Astour, Benê-iamina et Jéricho, Semitica 9 (1959), 5—20. The most judicious recent treatment critical of the identification is offered by M. Weippert, Die Landnahme der israelitischen Stämme in der neueren wissenschaftlichen Diskussion, 1967, 110—123.

22 Klengel, Benjaminiten, 29.

23 See above Chapter 2.

24 H. Klengel, Zu einigen Problemen des altvorderasiatischen Nomadentums, ArOr 30 (1962), 590.

25 I. e., Iamhad, Qatanum, and Amurru, cf. A. Parrot, Les Tablettes de Mari et l'Ancien Testament RHPR 30 (1950), 7.

26 Ibid. 6 and Abraham et son temps, 1962, 36—51.

27 La Pénétration des Arabes en Syrie avant l'Islam, Institut Francais d'Archéologie de Beyrouth, Bibliothèque archéologique et historique, Tome 59, 1955, 182.

southwards while the rest remained in Syria[28]. Thus the North-South leg of Abraham's journey is accounted for. W. von Soden, while pointing out that the evidence is as yet insufficient for proof, proposes as the best-grounded hypothesis:

Die Benjaminiten von Mesopotamien sind im 17. Jahrhundert oder später ganz oder teilweise nach Süden abgewandert und mit ihren Resten nach Palästina gelangt. Für solche Wanderungen von Beduinenstämmen fehlt es auch in der neuen Zeit nicht an Parallelen, und als Grund der Abwanderung könnte man den Einbruch der Churrier im 17. oder 16. Jahrhundert vermuten. Außerdem läßt sich dafür die biblische Überlieferung anführen, die Abraham aus Ḫarran, also genau aus dem Gebiet der alten Benjaminiten, nach Palästina kommen läßt[29].

Von Soden finds it impossible to believe that the similarity of names could be fortuitous, particularly since the names appear to be independent of their known locations, neither in reality living in the South. Moreover, they were both "Canaanite"[30]. In 1960 he reaffirmed his position, adding to the hypothesis the observation that a sub-tribe of the "Benjaminites" bore the name *Jariḫû*. It seemed possible that this was the origin of the name of the city Jericho[31]. M. Astour, devoting an entire article to this possibility, points out, however, the improbability that the name of the city Jericho was in existence during the Bronze Age as would need be assumed; in fact, our reference to the establishment of Jericho in I Kings 16 34 suggests a gap of some eight centuries that would have to be bridged[32]. When it is observed that the cult of the moon god was quite widespread and that the name of the biblical city is by no means unusual, a direct historical connection between the Mesopotamian tribe and the city of Jericho seems particularly unlikely. The general ethnic similarity of the two groups seems more than sufficient to explain the coincidence of the names[33].

The Mesopotamian origin of the tribe of Benjamin is hardly supported by the biblical tradition which sees Benjamin as the southern group of the Ephraim tribe and in the Stammessage

---

28 "Seine Herkunft ist hierbei im Hinblick auf die Abrahamerzählung (Gen 11 31 12 4 f.) immerhin bedeutsam." H. Schmökel, Alttestamentliches aus dem Briefarchiv von Mari, TLZ 75 (1950), 690.

29 Das altbabylonische Briefarchiv von Mari, WO 1 (1948), 197f., also see Kupper, Nomades, 81n1.

30 WO 1 (1948), 197.

31 Zur Einteilung der semitischen Sprachen, WZKM 56 (1960) 180n.

32 Semitica 9 (1959), 5—20.

33 Such as the Ḫapiru (sic!) names *Ardum* and *Abijau* which Astour (ibid. 11n) compares to the Hebrew *'Ard* of Gen 46 11 and *Abbiyya* of I Chr 7 8. But are these names closer to each other than Johan is to John or than Pierre is to Peter?

sees Benjamin as the one son of Jacob who was born in Palestine[34]. The thesis is proposed, however, as offering a correction to the biblical tradition, seeing in the identity of the names[35], and the similarity of the migrations of the Mari group to the Abraham tradition, sufficient justification for the reconstruction.

In Dossin's 1938 publications of the Mari tablets, two new groups of people were identified: the *DUMU.MEŠ-ia-mi-na* and the *DUMU.MEŠ-si-im-a-al*. Dossin read the signs *DUMU.MEŠ* as *Benê* and translated *Benê-ia-mi-n(a)* as "enfants du sud", and *Benê-si-im-a-al* as "enfants du nord"[36]. In another of the Mari letters he found the reading: *di-pa-ra-tim DUMU-ia-mi-na-a* (1.8) and *a-la-nu ka-lu-su-nu ša DUMU-ia-mi-na-a* (1.14), both lacking the plural determinative. This he then rendered *Bin-ia-mi-na-a* and translated"Benjaminites"[37]. The following year he defended this unusual reading and stressed its "exact" correspondence to the Hebrew name בן־ימין[38]. Here Dossin pointed out a number of personal names such as *Bi-nu-um, Bi-in-na-Ištar, Bi-na-ḫa-an-di-en, Bi-ni-ma-ra-as, Bi-ni-ia, Bi-na-am-mi,* and *Bi-in-na-rum*, arguing that they clearly demonstrated that the sign *DUMU* has to be read *Bin*, rather than, as would otherwise be normal in Akkadian texts, *māru*[39].

Dossin's argument, particularly that the name corresponded to the name Benjamin, received general acceptance from the scholarly world[40], and has been widely accepted[41]. In 1958, however, a new

---

34 H. H. Rowley, Recent Discoveries and the Patriarchal Age, BJRL 32 (1949/50); cited from; The Servant of the Lord, 1952, 292.

35 It should be noted that among the many scholars who would accept the identification of the names, some see no need to conclude a historical relationship: so W. F. Albright, JBL 58 (1939), 102; A. Pohl, Miszellen, Bb 20 (1939), 200; R. de Vaux, Les patriarches hébreux et les découvertes modernes, RB 53 (1946), 344, and Les patriarches hébreux et l'histoire, RB 72 (1965), 13; H. H. Rowley ibid., and Proceedings of the British Society of Old Testament Study, JBL 66 (1947), xxvii—xxxii; and H. Klengel, Benjaminiten, 43.

36 G. Dossin, Les archives épistolaires du Palais de Mari, Syria 19 (1938), 116 and 116n3.

37 RA 35 (1938), 178.

38 Benjaminites dans les textes de Mari, Mélanges Syriens offerts à Dussaud, 2, 1939, 981—996, esp. 982.

39 Ibid. 982. Compare the names in ARM V, 28: 13, *Bi-ni-im*; 28: 30, *Bi-nu-u[m]*; but contrast the name *Ba-an-nu-um* in Dossin, RA 35 (1938), 178, l. 3!

40 So Albright in JBL 58 (1939), 102: "The Hebrew tribal name *Benjamîn* already appears at Mari as *TUR.MEŠ-ya-mi-na*, i. e., probably, **Binû-yamîna*." In Yahweh and the Gods, Albright insists on the reading *banû*. (85).

41 E. g., by A. Parrot, RHPR 30 (1950), 5: "... l'on doit transcrire *TUR* par *benê* ou *bin*" and "Au singulier cela donne *Bin-ia-mi-na* correspondant exactement au nom hébreu *bin-yâmin*." In Abraham et son temps 45: "*Benê-iamina*." Klengel (Benjaminiten 16f.) reads the singular as *Bin-Ia-mi-na* and the plural *Binû-Iamina*.

text was published, which, if it did present the name of this group, gave the initial element in its syllabic form: *šanat Zi-im-ri-li-im* da_4-*wi-da-am ša Ma-ar-mi-i i-du-ku*[42]. Dossin was quick to point out that the second part of the name has many variant spellings: *ia-mi-na, ia-mi-na-a, ia-mi-ni, ia-mi-nim, ia-me-na,* and *ia-mi-i*[43]. Moreover, the name was found in such abbreviated forms as *DUMU.MEŠ-ia-mi* (24x's) and *DUMU.MEŠ-mi-i* (12x's)[44]. The considerable number of texts with *mi-i* show that the reading is not accidental[45]. Dossin concludes his remarks with the observation that, rather than seeing the proper reading as *mar(u)-ia-mi-na* which must assume an unlikely composite form deriving from both Akkadian and West Semitic, it is better to understand *ma-ar* as a translation of *DUMU* "son". Recognizing the implication of this, that *DUMU*, then if translatable as *māru*, could not be considered as part of the name itself, he suggests that the name should be translated not "Benjaminites", but Jaminites"[46].

H. Tadmor, arguing on different grounds, points out that West Semitic loan words at Mari were never rendered by logograms. Therefore, *DUMU.MEŠ* must be transliterated by the Akkadian *māru-*, and that the name of the tribe must have been *māru-iamia*. Moreover, geographic directions such as North, South, East, and West were normally rendered in the West Semitic forms rather than in the Akkadian; so: *sim'al, iamin, aqdam,* and *aḫar*[47]. H. Cazelles[48], in rejecting the arguments of Dossin and Tadmor, and insisting on the proper name Beney Yamina, on the grounds that *maru-iamina* would be a Mischform, ignores the pertinence of the actual reading we have: *ma-ar-mi-i,* and the implications this has in determining the relationship of *DUMU.MEŠ* with *ia-mi-na,* however it is read. Furthermore, he does not seem to understand the suggestion that Tadmor gives which does away with the difficulty of a Mischform on the grounds that the word *iamin* is the normal word used by the Akkadian speaking people of Mari for direction.

---

42 M. Burke, Un nouveau nom d'année du règne de Zimri-lim, RA 52 (1958), 57—59.

43 Mélanges Syriens 982n5.

44 A propos du nom des Benjaminites dans les "Archives de Mari", RA 52 (1958), 60—62, by G. Dossin.

45 M. Weippert establishes the certainty of the equation *ma-ar-mi-i* = *DUMU.MEŠ-mi-i* = *DUMU.MEŠ-ia-mi-na* by citing three variant year formulas for the reign of Zimrilim: *MU zi-im-ri-li-im da-aw-da-am ša ma-ar-mi-i (!) i-du-ku; MU zi-im-ri-li-im da-aw-da-am ša DUMU.MEŠ-mi-i (!) i-du-ku;* and *MU zi-im-ri-li-im da-aw-da-am ša DUMU.MEŠ-ya-mi-na (!) i-du-ku.* (Landnahme 111n2).

46 Dossin, RA 52 (1958), 61f.

47 Tadmor, Historical Implications of the Correct Rendering of Akkadian *dâku* JNES 17 (1958), 130n12.

48 H. Cazelles, Mari et l'Ancien Testament, RAI (XVe), 1967, 77f.

Noth's recommendation of an Early West Semitic form *banû* as a rendering of *DUMU*, on the basis of the personal names seems hardly justifiable[49]. This leaves the possibilities that the name of the group is either *maru-iamina* as suggested by Tadmor, or the term should be rendered "the people" or "the tribe of Iamina" as Dossin suggests, considering *DUMU*, not as part of the name, but as a word similar to the בן of Hebrew in בני שמשי. Since *iamin* is the normal word used for "south", that this is not a proper name at all, but a geographically descriptive term meaning "the southern people" or the "Southern Tribes", in contrast to the *DUMU.MEŠ-sim'al*, "the Northern Tribes", also becomes a distinct possibility. The solution seems to rest not on the way the term was pronounced, but on the functional meaning of each of its elements.

Gelb gives considerable evidence to show that *DUMU.MEŠ* ought to be read as a descriptive determinative; e. g., tribal names such as *Jawna-ḫamu* and *Ja'ilanum* are given both with and without a preceding *DUMU.MEŠ*[50]. That *DUMU.MEŠ* is sometimes used as a determinative and that the tribal name is not abbreviated is quite certain from ARM IV: 33[51] where we find *DUMU.MEŠ wi-i-la-nim* (l. 15) paralleled in another line (l. 5) by: *ṣa-ab wi-i-la-nim*: "The tribe of *Wîlânum*" and the "army of *Wîlânum*"! Consistency demands that *DUMU.MEŠ-iamina* be translated either as "the tribe of *Iamina*" or as "the southern tribe". Gelb shows that such consistency is justified since we have texts with the name given both separated from the determinative as in *DUMU.MEŠ-si-ma-al ù Ia-mi-in* (ARM I 60: 9), as well as one text without the determinative at all, reading simply *[I]a-[m]i-nu-um* (ARM I: 67: 7)[52].

The question whether the term *iamina* is a proper name or a descriptive term is more difficult: whether the texts are to be understood as referring to the "Yaminites", or to the "Southerners". While it is universally recognized that the original meaning of this term refers to some geographical location, some authors claim that, since the tribe is found northwest of Mari, they could not have received this name in Mesopotamia, but must have brought it with them; i. e., the term had already achieved the status of a proper

---

49 M. Noth, Die Ursprünge des alten Israel im Lichte neuer Quellen, Arbeitsgemeinschaft für Forschung des Landes Nordrhein-Westfalen, Geisteswissenschaften, Heft 94, 1961, 14. The form *Bunû* has at least equal claim as the Early West Semitic word for "son"; cf. M. Birot, Trois textes économiques de Mari (II), RA 47 (1953), 165.

50 Gelb, JCS 15 (1961), 38.

51 G. Dossin, Correspondance de Šamši-Addu et de ses Fils, 1951, 56f. ARM IV.

52 Gelb loc. cit., see note 54 above; Dossin, Correspondance de Šamši-Addu et de ses Fils, ARM I, 1950.

name[53]. This has the important historical consequence of seeing those groups referred to by the name as a tribe or some comparable group, and those tribes which are associated with this term as "sub-tribes".

The argument is inconclusive, however, for several reasons: (1) The many references to a similar group, the *DUMU.MEŠ-Sim'al*, give evidence not only that both names are to be understood as terms implying a geographical relationship[54], but, implicit in this, is that the terms take their meaning according to the relationship they have to each other! (2) There is no need to suppose that the terms, if they originated in North Mesopotamia, imply a reference to Mari. The one group may well have received the designation, "the Southern Tribes" in contrast to the other group "the Northern Tribes"[55]. (3) Of the four tribal groups which are mentioned among the "Southern Tribes"[56], the *Ubrabû*, the *Iaḫrurrû*, the *Iariḫû*, and the *Amnanû*[57], two of these are known as tribes which are also settled in Babylonia at the beginning of the Old Babylonian period: The *Amnanû* and the *Iaḫrurû* at Sippar. The *Amnanû* we find also settled near Larsa, and there is mention of the village of *Ubrabû* in the reign of Hammurapi[58]. Textual justification, however, for speaking of these groups outside of North Mesopotamia as "Benjaminites" as Kupper does[59], and as would be necessary if they are to be understood as subdivisions of one great tribe of Yaminites, is lacking.

Moreover, these groups can also be geographically fixed in North Mesopotamia. The *Ubrabû* are closely connected with another tribal group (not mentioned among the *DUMU.MEŠ-iamina*), the *Rabbû*, who live somewhere on the other side of the Euphrates[60]; the *Iaḫrurû* can perhaps be identified with the population of *Iaḫrur* which is someplace between the Middle Ḫabur and the Tigris[61]. The King of Tuttul, whose territory lies just northwest of the Baliḫ and Euphrates junction, is also referred to as the King of *Ma-at Am-na-ni-im*, "The

---

[53] W. von Soden, Das altbabylonische Briefarchiv von Mari, WO 1 (1948), 197. A similar argument is used in regard to the biblical Benjaminites.

[54] Kupper, Nomades, 81.

[55] The place name South Dakota, for instance, only makes sense in reference to North Dakota, as it is one of the northernmost states in the American union. So, too, there is a Southfield just north of the city of Detroit.

[56] This number should not be prematurely limited to four, cf. Klengel, Benjaminiten, 19.

[57] H. Klengel, Zu einigen Problemen des altvorderasiatischen Nomadentums, ArOr 30 (1962), 595.

[58] Kupper, Nomades, 75—77.

[59] Ibid.

[60] Klengel, Benjaminiten, 16f.

[61] Ibid. 18.

land of the *Amnanû*"[62]. The fourth tribe, the *Iariḫû*, is related to the territory of *Ia-ri-ḫi-i-KI*[63].

Rather than the name of a major tribal group which had spread throughout North Mesopotamia and Babylonia, the phrase *DUMU.-MEŠ-iamina* seems to be a term applying to the portions of several tribal groups that are located mainly in two areas: one stretching from Mari to Terqa and a short distance up the Ḫabur, and the other along the banks of the Baliḫ from the Euphrates to Ḫarran. Although the individual tribes have segments outside of this geographical area, it seems unlikely that the understanding of them as *DUMU.MEŠ-iamina* went beyond this circumscribed area[64]. It seems better to understand the term *iamina* as a specifically geographic term meaning "Southern", though often functioning in a manner similar to a proper name, referring to specific groups within a defined area. That other true tribal groups may have lived in this same territory and still maintained their individuality is likely; for those that did — such as some of the Ḫaneans — seemed to be much better known and more defined as an identifiable group in the Mari administration records than were the groups who fell under this general geographical term. A good parallel to this might be the term or "name" "Southerner" as used in the United States. Basically a geographically descriptive term, it nevertheless does not include all those who are native to the South. The term normally excludes, for example, all the various Indian tribes, and all Blacks. It is an amorphous term, but is regularly used with the intent of clarity.

The remainder of the argument[65] that the "Benjaminites" first settled in Babylonia[66], later moved northward to Ḫarran, and finally, in the wake of the Assyrian campaigns (Dussaud) or the Hurrian migrations (von Soden)[67], moved down to Palestine where they became the biblical Benjaminites, giving us something quite close to a historical parallel to the tradition of Gen 11, is not justified by the historical material that we have. While it seems certainly clear that the *Amnanû* and the *Iaḫrurû* are known quite early near Sippar and Uruk, and may perhaps be said to have settled in the South earlier than groups of the same name are found in the North, it is also true that we find these groups settled in Babylonia, where they have

[62] Ibid. 19.

[63] Ibid.

[64] For a very convenient map of the spread of the *DUMU.MEŠ-iamina*, see ibid. 73.

[65] As interpreted by von Soden, WO 1 (1948), 187—204; R. Dussaud, Une Traduction nouvelle de la Bible, Syria 35 (1958), 3f.; Kupper, Nomades, 77; and Parrot, Abraham et son Temps, 46.

[66] ". . . dans la région d'Ur" (!), Dussaud ibid., also cf. Parrot ibid.

[67] But see the remarks of Klengel, Benjaminiten, 43.

become part of the sedentary population[68]. Moreover, there exists no evidence of any movement of these people northwards; rather, what evidence we have sees them as having come from the northwest into the southeast[69]!

In considering the people near Mari, we find that not only are the people here also in the process of sedentarization rather than emigration, but both the evidence and the general opinion of scholarship is united in pointing to Jebel Bišri, and the North Arabian desert generally, as the most probable origin of these tribes[70], rather than Babylon[71]. Nor do we find satisfactory evidence of a westward movement from Mari; nor can it be supposed that they were settled all along the Euphrates and the banks of the Baliḫ as far as Ḫarran[72], from whence they then moved further westward to Iamḫad and Amurrū. If Bišri is taken as the general place of origin of these groups, and this seems quite likely, a careful study of the displacement map given by Klengel[73] shows that it is quite unlikely that such a large group, who do not show any signs of being strongly centralized, would have moved southeastwards towards the Mari region, then, turning back, travel along the Euphrates northwest to Ḫarran and, spreading further, leave the banks of the Baliḫ and cross the Euphrates moving towards Iamḫad, and finally turn southwestwards towards Amurrū! There are no known places occupied by this group along the Euphrates between Dit which is east of Bišri and Tuttul on the Baliḫ, directly north of Bišri, nor between the settlements along the Baliḫ and Iamḫad which is the western extension of the Bišri highlands, or Amurrū which is southwest of Bišri. It seems far more reasonable to suggest that these various settlements were populated by groups who moved out of the North Arabian desert into the various settled regions, independent of each other.

Evidence for a movement to the south into Palestine does not exist at all.

The following conclusions can be drawn: (1) The possibility of an historical movement of the *DUMU.MEŠ-iamina* from the area of Ur to Ḫarran and from there to Palestine mirrored in the tradition of Gen 11 must be excluded for historical reasons alone. (2) The way

---

68 Kupper, Nomades, 75ff.

69 Ibid. 78.

70 See esp. Kupper, Nomades, 47. 55. 63—65; Weippert, Landnahme, 112, and below in Chapter 4.

71 An origin common to both the South and the North Mesopotamian tribes would explain the coincidence of names; evidence for this is, unfortunately, lacking.

72 So Kupper 47.

73 Benjaminiten 73. The highlands of *Bišri* (Klengel: *Bisir*) should be shown further westward.

the term *DUMU.MEŠ-iamina* is used at Mari makes it impossible to identify it with the name Benjamin. For these reasons any attempt to identify the two groups is misleading. On the other hand the similarity of meaning in the term found at Mari with the etymology of the name Benjamin helps to clarify many of the ambiguities about the origin of the name of the biblical tribe[74]. The Mari name parallels the name Benjamin in a way comparable to the tribal name Teminite found in the Old Testament (the name of a tribe which lived in the north of Edom, but south of Israel)[75]. The names of West Semitic tribes and cities seem often to be derived from their geographical location; e. g., the Aramaic city of Sam'al (Zenjirli), the Transjordanian Arabic tribe of Benjamin, and the modern country of Yemen. One can never be justified in identifying groups with such names solely on the basis of nomenclature and a general ethnic similarity.

---

74 See further on this point K. Schunck, Benjamin, BZAW 86, 1963.

75 "Those of the South" or perhaps "the tribe of the Southwind"; Am 1 12 Jer 49 7. 20 and I Chr 1 45. The eponymous ancestor of this tribe is found in the biblical genealogies in I Chr 4 6. See recently: R. de Vaux, Téman, ville ou région d'Édom, RB 76 (1969), 379—385.

Chapter 4

The Early West Semites of Mesopotamia and the "Patriarchal Period"

A. THE "AMORITES" OF UR III AND MARI

There can be little doubt that the patriarchal type names are similar to many names which appear in the Old Babylonian and Ur III periods in Mesopotamia. Although parallels to the patriarchal names are found not only at this time, but, as we have seen, throughout the entire Second Millenium, and not only in Mesopotamia but throughout the Near East, as well as in the Old Testament in the early biblical period, and extensively in Assyrian, Aramaic, and Arabic texts from the time shortly before the Exile, nevertheless, the earliest ascertainable witnesses to this type of name, and consequently the earliest of those groups which might be considered linguistically related to the early Israelites, have taken on special importance in discussions about the patriarchs. More specifically, efforts have been made to discover what the biblical tradition has considered the history of the forefathers of the Israelites in the history of the earliest known West Semites: to place the migrations of the patriarchs from Mesopotamia into Canaan into the larger picture of Early West Semitic migrations.

The extensive work that has been done on the Early West Semitic names and the history of the Early West Semites over the past fifteen years allows the relevance of this history to the biblical traditions to be discussed with more clarity today than would have been possible earlier[1]. Early West Semitic names begin appearing in

[1] The major monographs to be cited are: D. O. Edzard, Die "Zweite Zwischenzeit" Babyloniens, 1957; J. R. Kupper, Les nomades en Mesopotamie au temps des rois de Mari, 1957; S. Moscati, I Predecessori d'Israele, 1956; also, The Semites in Ancient History, 1959; H. Klengel, Benjaminiten und Hanäer zur Zeit der Könige von Mari (unpublished Berlin dissertation, 1958); H. B. Huffmon, Amorite Personal Names in the Mari Texts, 1965; G. Buccellati, The Amorites of the Ur III Period, 1966; and F. Gröndahl, Die Personennamen der Texte aus Ugarit, 1967. For a correction and expansion of Buccellati's monograph, see C. Wilcke, Zur Geschichte der Amurriter in der Ur III Zeit, WO 5 (1969), 1—31. For bibliography and history of scholarship, see Buccellati 5—15, Huffmon 1—12, and for the earlier period, Th. Bauer, Die Ostkanaanäer, 1926, 82f.

the Near Eastern records towards the end of the Third Millenium. The most important sources come from Uruk and Drehem, Mari, Chagar Bazar, Alalakh, and the Diyala region, the Execration Texts and Ugarit.

The two most recent monographs on Early West Semitic onomastics in the Mesopotamian texts, those of Huffmon and Buccellati, both bypass the vigorously debated and historically important question of terminology. Huffmon chooses the term "Amorite" only because it is the traditional term. He intends no more by this term than to refer to the "(North)-west Semitic names in the Mari and the other Old Babylonian cuneiform sources"[2]. Consistent with his intention to allow his discussion to be affected only by linguistic concerns, he points out the danger of allowing historically weighted terms to determine the character of what should be a linguistic analysis:

> It has been a general practice in the collection of Amorite names to cite all names designated as *MAR.TU* ... Bauer[3], for example, included in his list names identified as *MAR.TU* but omitted obvious West Semitic names listed as Su-tu-ú. In the Mari texts such designations are rare; one can cite only the 35 members of *ga-yú A-mu-rum* ... but they are only one of the many groups of Ḫaneans, ... among whom Hurrian and Akkadian names are also found. Utilizing designations of offices one can add *Ma-ša-am, a DUB.SAR.MAR.TU* with the Akkadian name, "Twin Brother", and *[La]-wi-la-*^{d}*IM*, *Ma-li-ya*, and *Zi-im-ri-*^{d}*[I]m*, called *GAL.MAR.TU*, together with *Ya-ta-rum* and *A-li-im*, who are called *GAL.A-mu-ri-im*. But *Ma-li-ya* and *A-li-im* are not Amorite names. On the other hand, the *Sutū* names are all Amorite ... Moreover, the fact that *[Y]a-si-im-*^{d}*IM*, West Semitic, is called a Gutian, indicates decisively that such designations cannot be made the basis of the collection[4].

Buccellati, on the other hand, while equally eschewing discussion of the debate over terminology, gives a definition to his use of the term "Amorite" which includes not only the linguistic characteristics of the West Semitic names[5], but also those people referred to as *MAR.TU* in the Ur III texts, as well as their "language", to the extent that this can be determined from the nomenclature[6]. The basic unity of these various factors is implied in his definition of "Amorite", and the justification of this usage forms one of the major theses of his work. Unfortunately, the choice of materials on the basis of which his analysis proceeds is largely determined by the presupposition that if "linguistic continuity" (whether in reference to the people of Ur III designated as *MAR.TU* and the bearers of West

---

[2] APNM 6.

[3] Ostkanaanäer 3.

[4] Huffmon, APNM, 17. Only by including Appendix III (279f.) does he allow briefly his terminology to affect the selection of his material, since the Syrian territory Amurru is not significant for Huffmon's study of the West Semites.

[5] Amorites 12 no. 3.

[6] Ibid.

Semitic names of the same period, or both these groups and the bearers of West Semitic names of later periods) were shown, "historical continuity" becomes more plausible, with the inference (though guarded) that ethnic identity justifies the assumption of identity of historical tradition[7]. This presupposition, allowing him to consider West Semitic names as, by that very fact, related to the *MAR.TU* names, causes some distortion in his analysis of the onomastic materials, and has led him unjustifiably to imply that the majority of the *MAR.TU* names in the Ur III period were West Semitic[8].

In fact, most of the West Semitic names which are gathered from this period do not have *MAR.TU* determinatives. Moreover, when it is noticed that in such areas as Lagaš and Urnima most of the

---

[7] Ibid. 360ff.

[8] Ibid. So he begins chapter III (99ff.): "The following is a list of all personal names in Ur III texts which are followed by the qualification MAR.TU." (emphasis added). He divides a total of 309 names according to linguistic affiliation, giving the total number of names in each linguistic group as well as the percentage. His conclusion is that the preponderance of people referred to with the qualification *MAR.TU* bore West Semitic names. However, as Buccellati points out in his text but does not consider in his statistics, the vast majority of these names, particularly most of the West Semitic names, are not actually qualified by the term *MAR.TU*, but are only associated with names that are so qualified. Eleven names are included which are in no way associated with the *MAR.TU* qualification, simply because the names are West Semitic. By presupposing his conclusion, he has allowed significant distortion of his evidence. It is unfortunately on the basis of this distortion that most of the conclusions of his study are constructed. I append the following statistics giving first the number and percentages of names as presented by Buccellati, and then the actual number and percentage of these belonging to names qualified by *MAR.TU*:

Buccellati (100):

			MAR.TU Names	
Language	Abs. Number	Perc.	Abs. Number	Perc.
Sumerian	63	20.5%	46	32.17%
Akkadian	43	14.0%	18	12.58%
Akk./Amor.	28	9.2%	10	7.00%
Amorite	123	39.8%	31	21.68%
Amorite (?)[1]	—	—	12	8.39%
Unknown	51	16.5%	26	18.18%

[1] This classification I have added for those names which Buccellati classified as Amorite but was not sure of. They should be either classified separately or placed in the Akk./Amor. or Unknown classification.

The above charts show the deceptive character of statistical argument. On the basis of the first chart, it can be concluded that over half of the *MAR.TU* names of known linguistic affiliation are West Semitic. From the second chart, however, it could be argued that the overwhelming majority of the *MAR.TU* people bore Sumerian and Akkadian names!

MAR.TU people bear Akkadian and Sumerian names, and that hardly any bear West Semitic names[9], it is difficult to maintain that the terms "Amorite" *(MAR.TU)* and Early West Semitic can be used synonymously[10]. That the *MAR.TU* people are closely associated with the Early West Semitic and that many of the *MAR.TU* were influenced by the Early West Semites, has been clearly shown by Buccellati, but that they are to be identified, or that a common historical tradition is to be assumed for them, has not yet been proven.

Whether the Early West Semites can be treated as a unity is certainly the most important preliminary question in the debate over terminology. However, this has historical as well as linguistic implications. Historical identity — so that we can speak of the existence of a single unified people — is inadequately justified on the basis of linguistic evidence alone. Because a common origin and a common history has not yet been established for the various groups that appear in Mesopotania in the early Second Millenium, the legitimacy of using such a specific term as "Amorite", applicable to all people bearing West Semitic names, is questionable. The similarity of language is not the only basis of understanding these people; the linguistic identification is but one aspect, albeit the clearest, in the problem of the identification of the Early West Semitic people or peoples. If terminology must be sought that has only linguistic connotations (and this, apparently, must be the case — at least at present — since this is the only factor that all these disparate groups are known to have in common), then terminology must be chosen which does not carry with it other historical meaning. To call the West Semitic names of the early Second Millenium "Amorite" is to indicate a correlation between the names as a whole and the *MAR.TU* of the Ur III period, the inhabitants of the land of *Amurrū*, and the Amorites of the Old Testament[11]. Of course, it would

---

[9] Cf. ibid. 344. Nevertheless, that a significant portion of the people designated as *MAR.TU* who bear Akkadian or Sumerian names, were probably West Semitic must be assumed; for the West Semites were being absorbed into the older population where Akkadian and Sumerian names predominated. I. J. Gelb recently published a list of names from Tell Asmar which he dates about 40 years after the fall of Ur III. All but two of these names are West Semitic and are designated by the term *MAR.TU*. Cf. Gelb, An Old Babylonian List of Amorites, JAOS 88 (1968), 39—46. The possibility must also be considered that at least a few of those who bore West Semitic names were ethnically unrelated to the West Semites.

[10] Contra Gelb, The Early History of the West Semitic Peoples, JCS 15 (1961), 31f.; JAOS 88 (1968), 39—46.

[11] Cf. M. Noth: "Vor allem hat der Staat 'Amurru' der Amarnatafeln und der ägyptischen und hethitischen Texte mit dieser Herrenschicht gar nichts zu tun (keiner

hardly be objectionable and little confusion would result if the term "Amorite" were used to identify the language only[12], but then different terminology must be sought for the bearers of the names[13]. Such terminology as would bring together all of these groups in South Mesopotamia, North Mesopotamia, Syria, and Palestine in a time span of more than a millenium seems unlikely to appear[14]. This is particularly true since the Babylonians did not identify people so much according to race as according to geographical location and political and social structures. Religion, culture, and manner of living were what was decisive[15]. As Buccellati has convincingly argued, the individuals who were *MAR.TU* only continued to be *MAR.TU* as long as they continued to belong to a specific social and cultural grouping. Consequently, the city dwellers of the Far West are not included in the meaning *MAR.TU*[16]. At Mari, the "Akkadian" city dwellers and administration officials are seen over against the Ḫanean shepherds and villagers. The king of the "Akkadians and Ḫaneans", who is surely a member of the "Akkadian" population, bears a West Semitic name! It is seriously misleading to speak of "Amorite dynasties"; for ethnic history, however much it is useful to clarify problems of historical and cultural change, is a modern abstraction[17]. The spread of West Semitic names through

---

seiner uns bekannten Herrscher trägt einen Namen von dem oben besprochenen Typ), ebensowenig die Verwendung des Namens 'Amoriter' im Alten Testament." Die syrisch-palästinische Bevölkerung des zweiten Jahrtausends v. Chr. im Lichte neuer Quellen, ZDPV 65 (1942), 34, n 1.

12 A very general terminology would be needed for the language itself. Gelb's *Old, Middle,* and *New Amorite* (JCS 15, 1961, 47) is one attempt at this, but his identification of "New Amorite" with the Syrian territory of *Amurrū,* in contrast to Canaanite, Ugaritic, and Aramaic, is arbitrary.

13 Von Soden has correctly pointed out that it is unnecessary to justify the terminology on the basis of ancient usage. Zur Einteilung der semitischen Sprachen, WZKM 56 (1960), 180. On the other hand the term "Amorite" is particularly misleading for historical reasons. See on this further, S. Moscati, Israel's Predecessors: A Re-Examination of Certain Current Theories, JBR 24 (1956), 252, and I Predecessori, 125; Semites, 54—57; see also the remarks of Bauer (Ostkanaanäer, 2) who objects to the term, not only because it has borne completely independent connotations in the course of the Second Millenium, but also because it implies an ethnic unity for the Early West Semites.

14 A. Jepsen, Die "Hebräer" und ihr Recht, AfO 15 (1945/51), 62; M. Noth, Die Welt des Alten Testaments, 1962[4], 213.

15 So W. von Soden, Review of A. Borst: Der Turmbau von Babel, in BiOr 16 (1959), 131ff.

16 Buccellati, Amorites, 361.

17 M. Noth: "Unsachgemäß ist . . . die noch von manchen, z. B. von Albright, gebrauchte Bezeichnung 'Amoriter'; denn es existiert kein Beleg dafür, daß der alte

the ruling classes of Mesopotamia in the Old Babylonian period should not be interpreted as an "Amorite rise to power" or an "Amorite" coup d'état, so much as a witness to the thorough Akkadianization of many of the West Semites, so much so that among the "Akkadian" population "ethnic" Akkadians and "ethnic" West Semites can no longer be distinguished. *[Y]a-si-im^{d}IM*, the bearer of a West Semitic name[18], is, in fact, one of the Guti[19], and for this reason is probably not — though the possibility cannot be excluded — ethnically speaking, a West Semite. His name bears witness, rather, to the influence of the West Semites on the Guti.

The terminology to be sought needs to be able to bear historical weight commensurate with quite specific immigrations of many disparate groups into the cultivated lands of the Near East at the end of the Third and the entire first half of the Second Millenium. The term "Amorite" takes one element for the entire historical process, adding serious confusion to a historical period, when clarity and understanding depend on the ability to distinguish the *MAR.TU* people ("Amorites" if you will) from other West Semitic groups (Sutu are not Amurru!), as well as the ability to distinguish other ethnically and historically distinct groups. The term "West Semitic" seems to be without objection and has the advantage of being transparent; the term "Early West Semitic" seems better, as it distinguishes these groups from the later, better-known West Semitic languages and peoples. Other terminologies that have been suggested seem either to make as yet unfounded historical presuppositions, or otherwise seriously hinder historical interpretation. The term "Early West Semitic" also has generic possibilities and does not assume that the identical language be attributed to all these groups, but presupposes only those linguistic peculiarities which distinguish the Early West Semitic from East Semitic names[20]. The somewhat similar term

---

Name *Amurrū*/Amoriter jemals im II Jrt. v. Chr. speziell auf diese Herrenschicht angewandt worden sei" (emphasis added) ZDPV 65 (1942), 34. Moscati's objection to Noth (JBR 24, 1956, 250f.) on the basis of such titles as "King of the Land of Amurru" assumed by Hammurapi, misses the point, for such a title no more identifies Hammurapi as "Amorite" than the comparable Old Babylonian royal title "Chief of the land of Yamutbal" betrays the ethnic affiliation of the king.

[18] G. Dossin, Correspondance de Iasmaḫ-Addu, ARM V, 1952, 2: 11.

[19] Huffmon, APNM, 17.

[20] W. Moran's description of the Early West Semitic "language" as "an ancient and venerable uncle of both Canaanite and Aramaic" (The Hebrew Language in its Northwest Semitic Background, Albright Festschrift, 57) is perhaps too premature in its presupposition that we have a single language. The terminology that I have adopted is comparable (except for my distinction "Early") to H. Klengel's "Westsemiten" (Benjaminiten 34). It can also be compared with Aistleitner's "Altmeso-

"Northwest Semitic" might also be attributed to these names, if it is understood not to exclude South Arabic names from consideration[21].

Until clearly distinctive elements can be isolated from the possibly diverse structure of the Early West Semitic language, closer and more specific designations will have difficulty gaining adherence. B. Landsberger[22], starting from the observation that many of the *MAR.TU* bore clearly Akkadian names, found it necessary to distinguish the *MAR.TU* "Amorites" from the bearers of clearly West Semitic names whom he described as "Ostkanaanäer"[23]. He was careful to note, as T. Bauer is in following him, that the basis of this term is the demonstrable similarity of the names to the Canaanite language. The term "East-Canaanite" was chosen to avoid any implication of historical or ethnic relationship to the Canaanites[24]. Many scholars, however, objected to this terminology because "Canaanite" had traditionally been understood, not so much as a language in its own right, but as meaningful only in contrast to Aramaic[25]. In 1954, Landsberger attempted once more to give new

potamisches Westsemitisch", which term is however unfortunate, since, as Aistleitner himself points out, similar names are found outside of Mesopotamia. (Studien zur Frage der Sprachverwandtschaft des Ugaritischen I, AcOrHung. 7, 1957, 256f.).

[21] Cf. I. J. Gelb, JCS 15 (1961), 33 and 46; Bauer, Ostkanaanäer, 1; Jepsen, AfO 15 (1945/51), 63; Buccellati, Amorites, 125; but especially Albright, Review of Th. Bauer, Die Ostkanaanäer, AfO 3 (1926), 125, where he shows that the Early West Semitic names, in the use of sibilants, are closer to Arabic than to either Aramaic or Canaanite. M. Noth, on the other hand, objects to the term "West Semite" as too general; and because it has become quite clear that there were many different peoples in Syria and Palestine. (Die Ursprünge des alten Israel im Lichte neuer Quellen, 1961, 25). But, it is for this reason that a generic term is important. Moreover, it is not yet clear that the Early West Semites from Mari form a single linguistic group either.

[22] B. Landsberger, Über die Völker Vorderasiens im dritten Jahrtausend, ZA 35 (1924), 237f.

[23] Ibid. 238, in this, following E. Meyer, Geschichte des Altertums, vol I, 2, 1910³, § 396; cf. also Bauer, Ostkanaanäer, 83.

[24] Bauer, however, does argue for a common language and common origin of these people, who have come from the North Arabian desert and spread into the settled area from South Mesopotamia to the Mediterranean (Eine Überprüfung der "Amoriter" Frage, ZA 38, 1929, 152). In answer to Dhorme's criticism (Les Amorrhéens, RB 37, 1928, 63) that the names showed Arabic as well as Canaanite relationships, Bauer rightfully points out that in order to show a multiplicity of languages, one needs to show the same stem used in different linguistic forms (ZA 38, 166f., also 155f.).

[25] M. Noth, who had carefully distinguished some early forms of Hebrew names, which were similar to the Early West Semitic names, from later "Canaanite" names (Die israelitischen Personennamen im Rahmen der gemeinsemitischen

meaning to the term "Canaanite" by speaking of East and West Canaanite as two dialects of a single language[26]. The Ostkanaanäer, as represented by the Ḫaneans, he understands as a group distinct from the Westkanaanäer, who are represented by the *Kinaḫḫi* of the Phoenician Coast. He reserves the name *Amurrū* or "Amorite" for the *MAR.TU* people of the Ur III period whom he does not consider West Semitic[27]. Von Soden, for similar reasons, prefers the term "Kanaanäer" to "Amorite", but in order to distinguish them clearly from the Canaanite groups of the period after 1400 B. C., prefers the term "Frühkanaanäer"[28].

D. O. Edzard also uses the term "Kanaanäer", but means by it approximately what I have meant by the term "West Semite", including under it not only the "Ostkanaanäer", but also the Amurru and the settled people of Palestine and Syria including Ugarit; he, however, excludes the Aramaeans and the Arabs[29]. The difficulty with this term, as also with the term "Proto-Aramäer", is that, while Edzard recognizes a common denominator between the Early West Semitic names and the dialects of Palestine and Syria of the later period, he is unable to show that the names cannot be related also to other languages, particularly since we have the distinct possibility that the names discovered from the first half of the Second Millenium may give witness to a stage of West Semitic before the differentiation of the major linguistic clusters of Aramaic, Arabic, and Canaanite. If the analysis of the names is to be clarified beyond the generic specification "West Semitic", and the chronological specification "Early", it becomes necessary to concentrate on the divergent characteristics of the names. Ample evidence for historical, cultural, and social differentiation exists, and demands that we speak of

---

Namengebung, 1928, 27f. 43f.), argued that Bauer's evidence was insufficient (Zum Problem der "Ostkanaanäer", ZA 39, 1930, 213), particularly if Canaanite is understood as the language of the settled regions of Palestine known from the texts of Amarna and Ugarit, as well as Phoenician, Hebrew and Moabite, in contrast to Aramaean. Moscati understands Canaanite as "Whatever is not Aramaic" (Semites 98f.; JBR 24, 1956, 254) and is followed by Gelb (JCS 15, 1961, 33n19).

[26] Assyrische Königsliste und "Dunkles Zeitalter", JCS 8 (1954), 56n103.

[27] Ibid., see Huffmon's remarks, APNM, 4f.; see also, the criticism of Gelb's, JAOS 88 (1968), 46.

[28] WZKM 56 (1960), 189, and Jahwe, Er ist, Er erweist sich, WO 3 (1966), 178n1. This term is slightly different from Landsberger's "Ostkanaanäer" which is based on the supposition that both Ost- and West-kanaanäer entered the Fertile Crescent at approximately the same time, implying the connotation "Proto-Canaanite" for the "West-kanaanäer".

[29] Edzard, Zweite Zwischenzeit, 30n127. 42f.

many different groups, separated one from the other chronologically, geographically and culturally, as well as, perhaps, in place of origin. Moreover, many scholars see some evidence for linguistic differentiation already at the time of our earliest texts.

B. PROTO-ARAMAEANS

M. Noth's identification of these groups as "Proto-Aramaean"[30] is the most serious attempt to differentiate between some of the Early West Semitic groups, as well as to establish direct relationships between the Proto-Aramaeans and the patriarchs of the Bible. He observed that among the earliest biblical names, there are an overwhelmingly large number of names, like Israel and Jacob, which are constructed in the form: imperfect + nominative element or in the hypocoristic imperfect form[31]. He also noticed that these forms are almost entirely lacking in the period of the divided monarchy, the period of strongest Phoenician and Canaanite influence. Significantly, they reappear and become quite common again from the period shortly before the exile, and to the end of the Old Testament period become increasingly frequent, along with a growing influence of the Aramaeans on Israel[32]. In contrast, names built from the imperfect were exceedingly rare among the Phoenicians; yet, they were quite common among the Early West Semites[33].

Contrasting the "Canaanites" of Palestine and Syria to other Early West Semitic groups, such as those we meet in the Execration Texts[34], he suggests the probability that the Canaanite world was already an independent and well defined entity with its own linguistic peculiarities as early as the beginning of the Second Millenium[35]. He understood Hebrew as a hybrid language, constructed on the basis of the Early West Semitic language — still dominant in pre-monarchic Israel — which is gradually absorbed along with Israel into the Canaanite world. Since Aramaic names appear to follow the same structural patterns as the early Hebrew and Early West Semitic

30 Followed by J. Lewy, Zur Amoriterfrage, ZA 38 (1929), 243—272; K. Koch, Der Tod des Religionsstifters, Kerygma und Dogma 8 (1962), 108; J. Gibson, Light from Mari on the Patriarchs, JSS 7 (1962), 44—62; R. de Vaux, Les Patriarches hébreux et l'histoire, RB 72 (1965), 5—28.

31 Eighty-five names from the earliest lists. M. Noth, BWANT 10, 1928, 29, also 27f.

32 Ibid. 27—30.

33 Ibid., cf. also 43. This observation was subsequently strengthened by the discovery of the Mari Tablets.

34 M. Noth, Geschichte Israels, 1954², 117.

35 Zum Problem der "Ostkanaanäer", ZA 39 (1930), 214.

names, Noth concluded that the Early West Semitic type names were closer to the Aramaic than they were to the Hebrew/Canaanite[36]. It is largely on this basis that Noth first presented his term "Proto-aramäisch" for the Early West Semitic dialects, in constrast to the already hardened Canaanite dialects of Phoenicia. In my opinion, the strongest support for Noth's reconstruction is the parallel between the effects on Israelite nomenclature of the Aramaic-influenced late pre-exilic and post-exilic periods and the Early West Semitic characteristics of the pre-monarchic period names. The Early West Semites of the Old Babylonian period Noth sees as the earliest of several waves of immigrants who settled in the cultivated areas surrounding the Syrian-Arabian desert during the Second Millenium. It was to one of these immigrations that he saw the early Israelite tribes[37], as well as the Aramaeans, belonging[38]. Noth sees in the patriarchal traditions a possible connection between the Israelites and the immigrations of the early Second Millenium. The considerable time gap between this early period and the biblical period proper suggests to him, however, the probability of a connection rather with the Aramaean settlements[39].

The major weakness in Noth's reconstruction is his identification of the Early West Semites as "Proto-Aramaeans", and the closely associated hypothesis that in the Old Babylonian period they formed a distinct group from the already formed Canaanite groups of Palestine and Syria. The distinctness of the Early West Semitic names from the later Canaanite and Phoenician names is clear. However, that a differentiation existed at the beginning of the Second Millenium in Palestine and Syria, so that we can speak of the names from the Execration Texts as belonging to the Proto-Aramaeans, in contrast to other groups who are assumed to be Proto-Canaanites, is not clear from the records we have. On the other hand, Noth is correct in pointing out that the West Semitic language structure of early Palestine and Syria is not a unified whole. Distinctions are to be made, but it seems much more fruitful to establish our distinctions by comparison, as much as it is possible, of con-

---

36 Ibid. 216. A sketch presenting the interrelationships between the different West Semitic groups as understood by Noth can be found in BWANT 10, 1928, 55.

37 Much more than to the specifically Aramaean immigration; this seems to have been a major reason for his giving up for a time the term "Proto-Aramäer" for the Old Babylonian West Semites (ZDPV 65, 1942, 34f. n2), in addition to the hope that the Proto-Aramaeans would not be confused with the Aramaeans who are known only from the end of the Second Millenium.

38 Welt des AT 213; Mari und Israel. Eine Personennamenstudie, Alt Festschrift, 149f.

39 M. Noth, Geschichte Israels, 117f.; see also his more recent treatment in Ursprünge 32f.

temporary, or nearly contemporary, groups, since languages change and develop in the course of time and as a result of direct outside influences. The West Semitic dialects seem to differentiate themselves one from the other, not so much according to the place of origin of the people[40], as by the place of settlement, and the linguistic influences with which they come in contact[41]. Whether we can speak of Early West Semitic as "Proto-West Semitic" is, as yet, due to the lack of texts written in the language, impossible to ascertain[42]. It seems often to be related to newly arrived groups in the Fertile Crescent. It is, however, not limited to one period or to one area alone, but is found in South Mesopotamia of the Ur III and Old Babylonian periods and North Mesopotamia and East Syria during the Old Babylonian period. In Palestine and Syria it is found in the Execration Texts, in the texts from Alalakh, Ta'anach, Ugarit, Tell el-Amarna, as well as from the Old Testament. Once these groups settle they seem to be absorbed into the dominant cultures of the territories into which they came. In Mesopotamia, where the dominant culture is Sumero-Babylonian, these groups are soon totally indistinguishable from the earlier inhabitants, leaving some traces, however, particularly in the pantheon and perhaps the nomenclature of the common culture. In Palestine, the Phoenician coastal cities seem to be culturally ascendant, and the various West Semitic groups who entered adapted themselves to the emerging Canaanite language. Israel's earliest beginnings seem related to one of the later Early West Semitic immigrations, which brought many groups into Palestine and Transjordan, and subsequently under the influence of the established and culturally dominant Canaanites. Their individuality emerges in the process of settlement through political and economic consolidation, over against the city people on one hand, and the Ammonites, Moabites, and other like groups on the other. Political centralization and subsequent political hegemony over the cities leads to further and more complete absorption into the Canaanite world.

Politicization and territorial control came much more rapidly to the Aramaean settlers, and consequently they were dominated far less by the settled peoples and maintained a far greater linguistic independence. From the period shortly before the Exile, when Israel comes under the influence of the Aramaeans, many of the early name forms reappear in the Bible, but this does not justify the term "Proto-Aramaic" to designate the linguistic origin of Hebrew. Noth's

40 This may be because we know so little about the specific geographical origins of the different groups.

41 This is one of the major theses of S. Moscati's work; see especially, I Predecessori.

42 Cf. S. Moscati, Sulle origini degli Aramei, RSO 26 (1951), 16—22; I Predecessori; JBR 24 (1956), 245—254; and The Semites.

reaffirmation[43] of this term cannot be accepted, since, while the Aramaeans may well belong to the Early West Semitic groups, Edzard and Wagner have clearly shown that the Early West Semitic linguistic characteristics cannot be designated specifically as Aramaic. Edzard[44] argues mainly on the grounds of the inadequacy of Noth's evidence and the chronological distance between the Mari names and the period of the Aramaean settlements. He rightly points out that until more exact linguistic understanding of the personal names is at hand, such immediate solutions as Noth's remain impossible. M. Wagner[45] gives a direct critique of Noth's 1961 article by asking whether there is any equation that can be established between the known Aramaisms of Hebrew and the non-Akkadian elements of the Mari texts, mentioned by Noth as uniquely Aramaic, and concludes:

> Zusammenfassend ist festzustellen, daß sich von den 13 von M. Noth in besonders enge Verbindung mit dem Aramäischen gebrachten hebräischen Vokabeln nur deren 3 als den Aramäischen entnommene Lehnwörter erweisen. Das läßt den Schluß zu, daß zwischen den Aramaismen im Hebräischen und dem nichtakkadischen Sprachgut der Mari-Texte offenbar keine speziellen Beziehungen bestehen und die 'Proto-aramäer'-These von dieser Seite her nicht untermauert werden kann[46].

The assumption that has to be dispelled is that the Early West Semites can be spoken of as a single historical entity, when the only characteristics they have in common are a certain similarity in their names, and that most of them are apparently newcomers in the agricultural regions. Once we meet them in our records we find this supposed unity fragmented into many disparate and often antagonistic groups. Clearly, then, any term which is based on only one of these groups and used for all of them is inadequate and invalidates that term for its proper function. When we mean the Early West Semites generally, and use such terms as Amorites, Ḫaneans, Suteans, Aramaeans, Canaanites, or the like, it becomes extremely difficult to speak of these groups as historically distinct from each other; i. e., to speak of Ḫaneans who are not also "Yaminites".

---

[43] Ursprünge. Noth reasserts this terminology on the basis of a number of roots appearing in the Early West Semitic names which he explains as characteristically Aramaic.

[44] D. O. Edzard, Mari und Aramäer?, ZA 22 (1964), 142—149.

[45] M. Wagner, Beiträge zur Aramaismenfrage im alttestamentlichen Hebräisch, VTS 16 (1967), 355—371.

[46] Ibid. 365.

C. THE EARLY WEST SEMITIC "MIGRATION" FROM UR TO HARRAN

Evidence relating to the origins of the Early West Semitic groups is in most cases lacking; when we do have it, it is often vague or difficult to interpret.

The term *MAR.TU* (akk. *amurrū* "the West, Westerner") is a geographical term[47] which in the time of Sargon I was used for the furthest west of the four regions: Elam, Akkad, Subartu, and Amurrū. It is this western region which seems to be referred to in his campaign records as *KUR.MAR.TU.KI*[48]. In subsequent texts this term continues to carry the general meaning of "West" or "Westerner", without having the specific connotation of a proper name[49]. In the Mari records, it attains a more specific geographical delineation and seems to be located in the Far West, associated with such cities as Yamḫad, Qaṭna, and Hazor[50]. In the Amarna letters *Amurrū* refers to a specific political state founded by Abd-Aširta, which lasts about two centuries[51]. "The core of *Amurrū* lies in the area east of the Lebanon, bounded on the north by the kingdoms of Ugarit, Qaṭna, and Nuḫašši, on the east by those of Kadesh and Damascus, and on the south by the Egyptian possessions in Palestine"[52].

In none of the above senses does it have, however, an ethnic significance[53], and the rulers of the land *Amurrū* do not bear the type of West Semitic names which are borne by so many of the *MAR.TU* people of the Ur III period[54]. Goetze's suggestion[55] that the Mari reference to *ma-at A-mu-ri-im-KI*, "the land *Amurrū*" (i. e., the western region known from the later texts) is a reading for *KUR.MAR.TU* is unconvincing, not for orthographic reasons, but because the Akkadian *A-mu-ri-im-KI* is a specific place name, and cannot be translated "the land of the *Amurrū*", as would be necessary if it were equivalent to the *KUR.MAR.TU* of the Ur III texts. There also seems little likelihood on historical grounds that the

---

47 Moscati, I Predecessori, 125.

48 Bauer, Ostkanaanäer, 83f. Klengel, however, suggests that Šarkališarri's conquest over the "Amurrites" must refer to a defeat of the tribes from the Syrian-Arabian desert (Benjaminiten 35).

49 Moscati, Semites, 54; JBR 24 (1956), 250.

50 Huffmon, APNM, 280; A. Goetze, Review of J. R. Kupper, Les nomades, JSS 4 (1959), 143; A. Malamat, Northern Canaan and the Mari Texts, Glueck Festschrift, 165f.

51 Bauer, ZA 38 (1929), 148f., and Moscati, JBR 24 (1956), 251.

52 I. J. Gelb, JCS 15 (1961), 42.

53 B. Landsberger, ZA 35 (1924), 238; von Soden, WZKM 56 (1960), 181.

54 Bauer, Ostkanaanäer, 83; Moscati, I Predecessori, 125, and JBR 24 (1956), 251.

55 Goetze, JSS 4 (1959), 143.

MAR.TU people, and even less, the bearers of Early West Semitic names in general, came from the Phoenician coast[56].

Most scholars look to North Arabia for the place of origin of the Early West Semitic people. This is partly based on the hypothesis that all Semites originally came from Arabia, and it is supported by the generally recognized nomadic character of so many of the Early West Semitic name bearers[57]. What evidence we have from our texts also supports this, in that it is clear that some of the Early West Semites came from the Syrian-Arabian desert. A few clearly did not; and many other texts refer us to what may well be secondary places of origin. Nothing at all is known about the origin of most of the Early West Semites we meet in our texts.

An understanding of the term *KUR.MAR.TU* which appears in so many of our earliest texts associated with the Early West Semitic name bearers is essential if any sense is to be made of these early texts. It is not, as we have already pointed out, a territorial name[58]. The term *MAR.TU* seems to refer at times to a class of people[59], and at times to a tribal group[60]. The term *KUR.MAR.TU* seems best understood as referring to the territory in which *MAR.TU* lived. *KUR* seems best translated along with Edzard as "Land"[61], which may or may not refer to mountainous terrain[62]. It is clear

[56] Bauer, ZA 38 (1929), 148f. 151f. Moscati, Semites, 55, against Goetze ibid. 143f. 146. Goetze rests his argument on the existence of a "land Amurru" in the West in the Old Babylonian Period, but this is not really significant, since the lower Mesopotamian use of the term *MAR.TU* or *Amurrū* was never restricted to designate this territory only, but was also used for the generic "West" and "Westerner". When we add the observation that the names of the people of Syrian *Amurrū* are not of the same type, there seems little to support Goetze's argument.

[57] Especially Moscati, Semites, 29ff. 56; also Bauer, ZA 38 (1929), 145; Klengel, Benjaminiten, 35 and 44, Zu einigen Problemen des Altvorderasiatischen Nomadentums, ArOr 30 (1962), 592; Gelb, JCS 15 (1961), 36; see, however, his article in JAOS 88 (1968), esp. 43; Huffmon, APNM, 6; Buccellati, Amorites, 235f. J. M. Grintz, on the other hand, sees biblical support for an origin in Babylonia or Armenia! On the Original Home of the Semites, JNES 21 (1962), 186—189.

[58] Especially Buccellati, Amorites, 241f.: "The term *MAR.TU* never appears with the determinative *KI*, otherwise regular with geographical names. The lack of a writing *MAR.TU.KUR* is equally noteworthy, because the postposition of the word for 'mountain' occurs frequently in this period with truly geographical names."

[59] Edzard, Zweite Zwischenzeit, 38.

[60] Buccellati, Amorites, 241f.; Edzard ibid.

[61] Ibid. 31; but not necessarily synonymous with *ḫur sag* (n131): text C: Enmerkar, 141—146, *kur-MAR.TU*, "Das Land der *MAR.TU*."

[62] Klengel (Benjaminiten 55) argues that since, in the Mari texts, *mâtum* is normally written phonetically, *KUR* should be read *šadûm* "mountain". This usage, how-

from the Gudea inscriptions that some of the *MAR.TU* live in the mountains. Two mountains are mentioned: *Basalla* and *Tidanum*. *Tidanum* also occurs in the fourth regnal list of Šušuen, who built a defensive wall against the *MAR.TU*, referring to it as the *murîq Tidnum*[63]. Another text mentioning *MAR.TU* in connection with the mountains is from Isin, referred to by Buccellati: "... *ḫur-sag ki ša-ma-mu-um MAR.TU-še* ...", "(to the) mountain, the place of Šamamum, the *MAR.TU*"[64]. Buccellati's identification of this place with *ḫur-sag MAR.TU* (whether Tidanum or Basalla), and especially with the *KUR.MAR.TU* of the Drehem texts, is not justified. In the Drehem archives we have one text referring to animals belonging to *Nablānum*, a *MAR.TU*, which were put on a ship and directed towards *KUR.MAR.TU*. The man *Nablānum* is also otherwise connected with people from Mari. In another text *I-bi-iq-ri-e-ú* designated as a *MAR.TU*, belongs to a people or a place called *Ià-a-ma-tu*. This man is also connected with people from Mari and is said to go back to his city by boat (*uru-ne-ne-šè gin-ni-má-a ba-dé-DU*)[65]! While all of these texts could possibly refer to a *KUR.MAR.TU*, identical with the mountain Jebel Bišri (= *Basalla?*), it is by no means compelling. The Drehem texts do seem to show, however, that some of the *MAR.TU* were to be found upstream from Drehem, to have entered South Mesopotamia from the direction of Mari. We have no reason to consider any further place of origin than the Mari region itself, particularly since, as Buccellati himself has admirably shown, the *MAR.TU* of the Drehem texts are hardly to be confused with marauding Bedouin infiltrators, but rather appear as fully bureaucratized businessmen.

Some time ago Bauer and Landsberger tried to locate *KUR.-MAR.TU* on the basis of the titles born by Kudur-mabug, father of

---

ever, does not seem to hold for the earlier texts where "mountain" is normally rendered by *ḫur-sag*, also in conjunction with *MAR.TU*, so: Gudea Statue B VI 3—8: *ù-ma-núm ḫur-sag-me-nu-a-ta ba(11)-sal-la ḫur-sag-MAR.TU.ta-NA(4)-na im-ta-e-(11)* "Out of Umana, the mountains from Menua, out of Basalla the mountains of the *MAR.TU*, (Gudea) gathered stones." And Gudea Statue B VI 13—16: *ti-da-núm ḫur-sag-MAR.TU-ta šir-gal lagab-bé-a mi-ni-túm*: "Out of Tidanum the mountain of the *MAR.TU* marble was brought here in great blocks." (Texts from Edzard, Zweite Zwischenzeit, 31). Buccellati (Amorites 237) harmonizes our source material when he sees these texts as referring necessarily to J. Bišri. While it is possible that *Ba(11)-sal-la* may be a variant reading for Bišri, *Tidanum*, which occurs again in other texts connected with the *MAR.TU*, should be seen as a distinct place. See also on this question, C. Wilcke, WO 5 (1969), 1—31.

63 Edzard, Zweite Zwischenzeit, 33, texts c and d. Cf. also Bauer, Ostkanaanäer, 85.

64 Buccellati, Amorites, 239.

65 Ibid. 238.

Warad-Sin and Rim-Sin: *ad-da KUR.MAR.TU* and (interchangeable with) *ad-da E-mu-ut-ba-la*[66]; i. e., the "Father of the land of the Amurrū" or the "Father of Yamutbal". Bauer rightly points out that it is impossible to speak of *KUR.MAR.TU* as referring to the North Arabian desert, and that it must refer either to Yamutbal itself, or to a region immediately in the neighborhood. The term *KUR.MAR.TU* is not univocal in our texts, but means nothing more specific than the *MAR.TU* region, the place where *MAR.TU* live. When Kudur-mabug is called *ad-da KUR.MAR.TU*, it means that he rules also over the *MAR.TU* of Yamutbal in the East-Tigris region. In the same manner, Hammurapi is referred to as *ad-da KUR.MAR.TU* and as *lu-gal MAR.[TU]*. *KUR.MAR.TU* can then refer both to the regions of South Mesopotamia as well as to areas outside. On the other hand, references to *KUR.MAR.TU* in connection with the already settled groups of Early West Semites can hardly be used for determining the origins of these people[67]. For that, the eligible records seem to point to the mountainous regions already referred to, as well as to the place of origin of those *MAR.TU* who threatened the Sumerian cities[68]. There seems to be a general agreement that this destructive intrusion of *MAR.TU* came most directly from the East-Tigris region. That they ultimately came from the West or the Northwest should not be excluded[69].

Once the term *KUR.MAR.TU* is understood as equivocal, and is seen as referring to the various localities in which *MAR.TU* lived both within and outside of South Mesopotamia, the question about the place of origin of the *MAR.TU* people changes considerably. The question is no longer where *KUR.MAR.TU* is, but whether there is any region which presents itself as the homeland of the Early West Semites. The two mountain regions, *Basalla* and *Tidanum*, can probably be considered as primary, since they are clearly outside of South Mesopotamia. The region of Yamutbal and Mesopotamia in the direction of Mari are best presumed to be secondary areas of *MAR.TU* settlement.

While it is not certain that *Basalla* is to be identified with Jebel Bišri[70], the hilly region in North Arabia across the Euphrates and

---

66 Weidner, Die Könige von Assyrien, MVÄG 26 (1921), no. 2, 42f.; Bauer, Ostkanaanäer, 84f., and ZA 38 (1929), 147.

67 I. J. Gelb, JCS 15 (1961), 31f.

68 Cf. for instance the letter from Išbi-Erra to Ibbi-Suen, which shows Isin and Nippur being attacked preventing grain from reaching Ur. Th. Jacobsen, The Reign of Ibbi-suen, JCS 7 (1953), 39—41.

69 So, most recently, C. Wilcke, WO 5 (1969), 16.

70 The identification was first suggested by Böhl, Kanaanäer und Hebräer, BWAT 9, 1911, 34. Bauer's objection, however, still stands. Cf. Ostkanaanäer 85.

west of Mari towards Palmyra[71], there is independent evidence that Jebel Bišri was one major source both of the *MAR.TU* and other Early West Semitic groups. A regnal year of Šarkališarri, king of Akkad, refers to a campaign against the *MAR.TU* in *ba-sa-ar KUR*[72]. The place mentioned is probably the same as *Bi-[s]i-ir*, mentioned in one of the Mari texts where the "Yaminites" cross the river "in the direction of Bisir" *(a-na KUR Bi-[s]i-ir)*[73], which implies that the region was not far from the river, thus, probably Jebel Bišri[74]. The name Basar is spelled in Old Akkadian as *Bisuru*[75], and the mountain *Bi-ši-ir* or *Bi-eš-ri* is mentioned in the Assyrian texts[76].

From the Mari texts, we learn that the West Semitic group, the Ḫaneans, seems also to have come from across the Euphrates[77]. The *Ubrabû* and the *Rabbû* of these texts are probably to be located west of the Middle Euphrates[78]; the *Suti* also seem to belong to this region[79] along with the *Aḫlamu*[80]. From the Drehem texts a *MAR.TU* from the land of *Ià-a-ma-tu* is mentioned along with people from Mari[81].

Some texts point to areas outside the Syrian Arabian desert as well. A connection with the East might be seen in one text quoted by Buccellati which connects the *MAR.TU* with the city *Ki-maš*[82], which is in the neighborhood of modern Kirkuk. Early West Semitic influence in this region might also be concluded from the names of cities like *Simurrum and Šimānum*, which occur in the Ur III texts[83]. Amorites are also said to have come from the city *Dêr*, which is in the East-Tigris region[84]. A text from Ur mentions *MAR.TU* "of Sakkul-mada, to be identified with the Ebiḫ mountains"[85].

---

[71] J. Bišri reaches a short distance from the Euphrates all the way to Damascus and creates a grazing region across the northwest end of the Arabian Peninsula; to the south it is met by the Ḥamād and Wudjān; cf. H. Klengel, ArOr 30 (1962), 588.

[72] Edzard, Zweite Zwischenzeit, 33; Kupper, Nomades, 149f.; Klengel ibid. 590; Moscati, Semites, 52; Buccellati, Amorites, 236f.; Gelb, JCS 15 (1961), 29.

[73] G. Dossin, ARM V, 27: 26.

[74] See Kupper, Nomades, 47n2; Klengel, Benjaminiten, 55.

[75] Gelb, JCS 15 (1961), 31f.

[76] Buccellati, Amorites, 36; S. Smith, Early History of Assyria to 1000 B. C., History of Babylonia and Assyria, vol. 3, 1928, 98f.

[77] Klengel, Benjaminiten, 82f.

[78] Ibid. 17. [79] Edzard, Zweite Zwischenzeit, 108. [80] Moscati, Semites, 63f.

[81] Buccellati, Amorites, 238. This name occurs twice in the gentilic form *Ià-a-ma-ti-um*, which leads Buccellati to consider it a tribal name (242f.).

[82] Ibid. 94ff. But Buccellati suggests that *MAR.TU* is a scribal error for *Ḫu-mur-ti-KI*; see his comments on 247f.

[83] Ibid. 248. [84] Edzard, Zweite Zwischenzeit, 74.

[85] I. e., Jebel Ḥamrīn, (Buccellati, Amorites, 248) north of Baghdad, SSW of Kirkuk. Buccellati's further suggestions for eastern origins of some *MAR.TU* on the basis

The island of *Dilmun*, to the south of Mesopotamia in the Persian Gulf, is mentioned in the Drehem texts connected with the *MAR.TU*. I see little reason for Buccellati's scepticism concerning these texts[86]. Texts referring to "*MAR.TU* and diviners from *Dilmun*" and "the man of *Dilmun*" mentioned after one of the *MAR.TU*, the leather goods specified "for *Dilmun* and the *MAR.TU*", as well as the mention of *MAR.TU* engaged in transporting fish, support the *Dilmun* reference adequately. Furthermore, in the Tell Asmar text published by Gelb, one *MAR.TU* is derived *a-ab-ba-ta* ("from the sea"), which suggests a possible origin for him near the Persian Gulf[87].

In conclusion, what evidence we have for the homeland of the *MAR.TU* and other Early West Semitic groups points away from a single place of origin; from the time of our earliest records these people betray a disparate background. Any attempt to speak of them as a people, therefore, must either assume a unity prior to our records, or see a unity created after their entry into the fertile regions. However, these groups betray, once they come into contact with the Mesopotamian world, even greater divergency, which forces the historian to speak of many different groups whose only common ground is the general similarity of their names. This is seen not only on the basis of divergent status and function within the Mesopotamian economy, but also on the basis of tribal structure and the concepts of identity and distinction which the groups themselves possess.

We have already seen that in the Ur III texts the *MAR.TU* are understood as quite different kinds of people. This makes it difficult to accept the term *MAR.TU* as simply a tribal designation, though it is at times used along with other tribal names. While some continuity could possibly exist between the *MAR.TU* of *Tidanum* and *Basalla* and the *MAR.TU* who are involved in the destruction of the South Mesopotamian cities, it surely is necessary to see as distinct the Akkadian and Sumerian name bearing *MAR.TU* who are hardly distinguishable from the rest of the settled population[88]. So too, among the *MAR.TU* from Isin (whose names are mostly Early West Semitic) are found envoys of the king. In addition to leather goods purchased by these people are two chariots[89]. At Drehem, the *MAR.TU*, who bear predominantly West Semitic names, are engaged

of personal names, particularly the name *Qa-ad-ma-nu-um*, which he translates "Easterner", seems to me unconvincing; contrast the name *A-mu-ru-um*, "Westerner", 102.

86 Ibid. 249f.

87 I. J. Gelb, JAOS 88 (1968), 41. 43.

88 Buccellati, Amorites, 310—315.

89 Ibid. 302—310.

in the buying and selling of small cattle. They appear not as semi-nomadic shepherds, but as fully civilized traders, connected with Mari and other cities to the North[90]. Judging from the professions in which the *MAR.TU* were engaged, most of those whose names we find in the texts had little contact with semi-nomadism; they were envoys of the king; one was the mayor of Isin; they were bodyguards, soldiers, conveyors, lamentors, priests, brewers, weavers, farmers, fowlers, and janitors[91]. It must be supposed that the lives of these people were threatened as much as were the lives of the non-*MAR.TU* population by the semi-nomadic groups[92]. The overwhelming majority of the Early West Semitic names that we have in our records belong to people who were living with the non-West Semitic population and form a part of that culture. Except for a few general references to the attitudes of the agricultural and city people, information about the semi-nomadic groups is, typically, almost totally lacking. Surprisingly enough, however, most descriptions of the Early West Semites in modern scholarly literature are drawn from these few references[93].

In the later Mari records, the Early West Semites are often seen as large tribal groups in the process of sedentarization, but here too great differences are apparent, and historical continuity is only to be found within an individual group or tribe. The Ḫaneans, e. g., are more closely related to the administration of Mari, and live more in cities and villages than do the "Yaminites"[94]. Within the larger groups themselves many different ways of life are followed. Among the Ḫaneans we find semi-nomadic groups living in encampments *(nawû)*[95], but the Ḫaneans also live in cities *(ālānu)* and villages

---

[90] Ibid. 274—302.

[91] Ibid. 340; see also C. Wilcke, WO 5 (1969), 16f.

[92] For a discussion of these attacks by desert groups, cf. Th. Jacobsen, JCS 7 (1953), 36—47; Edzard, Zweite Zwischenzeit, 30—69, and C. Wilcke, Drei Phasen des Niedergangs des Reiches von Ur III, ZA 60 (1970), 54—69. For the chronology see Edzard op. cit. 17. Buccellati speaks of these barbaric *MAR.TU* as "Outer Amorites".

[93] M. Rowton, The Physical Environment and the Problem of the Nomads, RAI (XV[e]), 1967, 121: "We cannot as yet adduce formal proof that either Guteans, Amorites or Kassites were in fact tribal societies." Buccellati's conclusion that *MAR.TU* was used to refer to foreigners "Frequently, if not exclusively" (Amorites 232) is misleading in its intensity, since many of the *MAR.TU* were clearly as much at home as the rest of the population.

[94] Gelb, JCS 15 (1961), 38; Weippert, Die Landnahme der israelitischen Stämme in der neueren wissenschaftlichen Diskussion, 1967, 113—122; Kupper, Les Nomades, 12f.

[95] Gelb, JCS 15 (1961), 36.

(kaprātum)[96]. Some work in the service of the king of Mari, others in the army of Mari, others yet are in armed conflict with the Mari regime[97]. As was true in the Ur III period, the more thoroughly the West Semites are assimilated into the Mesopotamian culture, the less significant tribal bonds and relationships appear. The king of Mari himself bore a West Semitic name, but the West Semitic tribal groups who are still in the process of sedentarization are consistently referred to as foreigners. The West Semitic names of so many of the ruling class at Mari give witness to an already achieved complete sedentarization and "akkadianization" of many West Semites. The power on which the Mari dynasty itself is established is constructed on the basis of the indigenous social structure. A similar situation is found all across Mesopotamia. The first king bearing a West Semitic name is found in Larsa: Abisarê, who was followed by Sumuilu[98]. Sumuabum founded the first dynasty of Babylon at about the same time. Some of the rulers of Sippar, Kish, Marad, Eshnunna, and Kazallu bear West Semitic names[99]. The same type of name is found in the dynasties of Syria, also at Carchemish, Aleppo, and Qatna[100]. Quite clearly, the migration of Early West Semites into the settled regions all across Mesopotamia is not limited merely to the period of our texts, but followed a process of gradual sedentarization lasting several centuries. The disjointedness of this migration led to the gradual absorption of the new elements into the Sumero-Akkadian culture. Many different West Semitic groups were involved, sometimes joining together within Mesopotamia in loose federations like the "Yaminites". Others, like the *Yamutbal*[101] and the *Yaḫmutum*[102], settle in a single well-defined area and gradually gain control over the region. Still others distinguish themselves one from the other in different *gā'ûm* (Hebrew גוי), each led by a sheikh or chieftain[103]. In the records of Zimri-lim we have one list of 344 people to whom oil is rationed who are divided into thirteen different *gā'ûm*. We should probably understand these, along with Klengel, as "ethnic" or tribal entities[104]. In South Mesopotamia in the Old Babylonian period as

---

96 Weippert, Landnahme, 115.

97 Gelb, JCS 15 (1961), 37.

98 Klengel, Benjaminiten, 35f.

99 Gelb, JCS 15 (1961), 46; Klengel, Benjaminiten, 35f.

100 Moscati, Semites, 85.

101 Landsberger, ZA 35 (1924), 238; Huffmon, APNM, 175.

102 Buccellati, Amorites, 244f. 333.

103 Klengel, Benjaminiten, 24.

104 Ibid. 23f. M. Birot's explanation (Trois textes économiques de Mari, II, RA 47, 1953, 127) that the *ga'ûm* are specific territories in which the Ḫaneans were living seems to be contradicted by the summary given in column five, which concludes:

many as seven distinct West Semitic groups can be distinguished: *Yamutbal, Mutiabal, Numḫaya, Amnanum, Yaḫrurum, Ḫanû, Sutium,* and *Idamaras.*

While a certain continuity does exist in the type of names which the Early West Semites bore in the Ur III and Old Babylonian periods[105], and for this reason justification is perhaps lacking for speaking of two chronologically separate migrations of Early West Semites, nevertheless, considerable doubt has been expressed about speaking of a single West Semitic dialect either in Ur III alone or in the Old Babylonian period[106]. The recognition and differentiation of these dialects is yet to be achieved[107].

After even this brief sketch, it becomes clear that we cannot be justified, no matter what the linguistic affiliations are, in speaking of the Early West Semites in Ur III and the Old Babylonian period as a single unified group. Secondly, if movements and migrations can be seen, it is from the peripheral regions into the settled areas. No movement whatever is discernible which resembles a movement from Ur towards the northwest to Ḫarran. If a trend is to be noticed, it is in the opposite direction! Ur, rather than being the source of these migrations, is among the prizes sought. For Ḫarran, there is indeed evidence of a migration, but it comes from the South, from the banks of the Euphrates and ultimately from the Syrian Arabian desert, and moves northwards to Ḫarran. In no way does this resemble the traditions about the patriarchs in Genesis. Thirdly, we do not have what might be described as a general wandering of nomadic groups (among whom we can somehow imagine the family of Abraham); we have rather a picture of West Semitic immigrants.

Any efforts to support a historical relationship between the biblical patriarchs and the Early West Semites of the Ur III and Old Babylonian periods must be totally given up.

On the other hand, this material, particularly that from Mari, can play an extremely valuable role in biblical studies, as an analogue, if not to the patriarchal period, to the early settlement of Israel in Palestine; for it is our most complete source for understanding the

"Ḫaneans, resident at Mari." (M. Birot, Textes Économiques de Mari, III, RA 49, 1959, 18, col. V: 7—8). See further, A. Malamat, Aspects of Tribal Societies in Mari and Israel, RAI 15 (1967), 129—138.

105 Buccellati (Amorites 216) mentions that "There are 45 Ur III names that can be correlated to Old Babylonian names."

106 So Buccellati ibid. 188, also Bauer, Ostkanaanäer, 5; von Soden, WZKM 56 (1960), 185—191; and Dhorme, RB 37 (1928), 161; Gelb, on the other hand, argues for "only one West Semitic language" for Syria, Mesopotamia and Babylonia in the Old Babylonian period. JCS 15 (1961), 47; JAOS 88 (1968), 39f. 46.

107 W. von Soden, WZKM 56 (1960), 191.

process of sedentarization[108]. But to use this material as an analogy to the Bible is quite different from seeing it as historically related. It is important to distinguish comparative material which is directly historically relevant to our traditions from material which is analogous only — useful only as a crutch in analyzing historical problems such as the origin of Israel, where we have an inadequate understanding of the historical context[109]. Most of our sources for the historical background of the Old Testament come from the city cultures of Babylon, Syria and Egypt[110]. The texts from Mari, on the other hand, give us some understanding of a way of life which more completely resembles that of Early Israel before the monarchy[111].

These materials render sociological understanding, not historical verification.

---

[108] M. Weippert, Landnahme, 106. 110. G. E. Mendenhall, while he disagrees radically with Weippert about the origin of the Israelites, also uses the Mari material as no more than an analogue, useful for the reconstruction of, in some ways, a similar historical situation; cf. his review of Weippert's monograph in Bb 50 (1969), 433, as well as his article, The Hebrew Conquest of Palestine, BA 25 (1962), 66—87.

[109] Cf. A. Alt, Der Rhythmus der Geschichte Syriens und Palästinas im Altertum, Beiträge zur Arabistik, Semitistik, und Islamwissenschaft (1944), 284—306 (KS III, 1—19, esp. 13ff.), where seasonal nomadism at the end of the Second Millenium is discussed.

[110] Gibson, JSS 7 (1962), 46.

[111] In this respect, the sociological study of Rowton (RAI 15, 1967) showing the economic interdependence of tribal and village culture, can go a long way towards understanding much that is ambiguous about the end of the Late Bronze and Early Iron Ages in Palestine, as well as the Mari texts.

Chapter 5

The Early West Semites in Palestine and Syria

A. THE "PATRIARCHAL PERIOD"

The historical understanding of the Early West Semites in Palestine and Syria is severely limited, since so few written records from or about this region at this early period are extant[1]. The two major groups of texts which are useful for examining the Early West Semitic names and their place in the history of Palestine, the Execration Texts from Egypt and the cuneiform texts from Ugarit, are chronologically separated from each other by several centuries. Moreover, in the Ugaritic texts the bearers of West Semitic names appear as an already integrated part of the population, so that any discussion of their origin must remain almost totally speculative. Discussion about the origin of the people of the Execration Texts is even more forbidding, since we not only lack information about possible other groups in Palestine at this time, but we also lack adequate means for establishing the historical context in which these names should be studied. What discussion is possible is limited to the linguistic realm.

In spite of these limitations, many scholars have felt themselves justified, on the basis of the West Semitic movements in Mesopotamia, and especially on the basis of the archaeological discoveries in Palestine, in presenting a reconstructed history of an immigration of Early West Semitic peoples into Palestine during the period of transition between the Early and Middle Bronze Ages, usually dated between about 2300 and 1800 B. C. These Early West Semites are identified with the biblical Amorites who, as nomadic groups, are seen to enter Palestine during this period[2]. Since the biblical patriarchs

---

[1] S. Moscati, Semites in Ancient History, 1959, 80: "Direct historical sources do not make their appearance in Syria before the Second Millenium, and until the middle of that millenium they are extremely scarce. This fact has a fundamental effect on the reconstruction of Syrian history, and renders it much more uncertain and discontinuous than was the case for Mesopotamia." See his further remarks, 81ff.

[2] K. Kenyon, Amorites and Canaanites, 1966, 76: "... archaeology shows that the Amorites of the Bible arrived in Palestine c. 2300 B. C. as nomads and destroyers of a preexisting urban civilization." Also, Excavations at Jericho, 1954, PEQ 86 (1954), 45—63, here 58: "The newcomers (of the Intermediate Period) ... can with

had already been associated with semi-nomadic groups of Mesopotamia, thought of collectively as *amurrū*[3], what evidence that there was thought to be of nomadic life in Palestine at this time seemed striking corroboration and justification of the identification of the patriarchal movements with the movements of the Amorites in this early period[4]. Because of Albright's observation that this transitional period pottery culture was closely connected with North Mesopotamia[5], the emerging reconstruction of this historical period appeared quite adequate, supported as it was not only by archaeological finds and the "known" history of the Amorites in Mesopotamia, but also by the commonly accepted understanding of Abraham's "migration" from Mesopotamia in Gen 11[6]. That this was the "patriarchal period" — particularly the time of Abraham — was further bolstered by the claim that only during this period were the cities which are

---

a considerable degree of probability be identified as nomadic Amorites..." (Parentheses added). G. E. Wright (The Chronology of Palestinian Pottery in Middle Bronze I, BASOR 71, 1938, 34) also attributes the material culture of the EB IV/MB I Period to "an invasion of Amorite barbarians"; This is recently confirmed in his article, The Archaeology of Palestine from the Neolithic through the Middle Bronze Age, JAOS 91 (1971), 287—289. See also further G. E. Mendenhall, The Hebrew Conquest of Palestine, BA 25 (1962), 84; Y. Aharoni, Kadesh Barnea and Mount Sinai, in God's Wilderness, by B. Rothenberg, 1961, 115—189, here 123; G. E. Wright, Archaeology and Old Testament Studies, JBL 77 (1958), 43 and 46; E. Anati, Palestine Before the Hebrews, 1963; 364; H. Hahn, The Old Testament in Modern Research, 1966, 192; and especially, W. G. Dever, The Peoples of Palestine in the Middle Bronze Period, HThR 64 (1971), 197—226.

[3] See the remarks above in Chapters 3 and 4.

[4] On the nomadism of the patriarchal way of life cf. J. W. Flight, The Nomadic Idea and Ideal in the Old Testament, JBL 42 (1923), 158—224; for a list of biblical references see 159. For the identification of the patriarchs with the "Amorites" see note 2 above. K. Kenyon, in her Amorites and Canaanites (76) identifies the patriarchs with a Canaanite migration which she places at the very end of the EB IV/MB I Period. This is similar to the position of P. Lapp, The Dhahr Mirzbaneh Tombs, ASOR publication of the Jerusalem School: Archaeology, vol. 4, 1966, 114. This, in spite of the fact that Gen 12 6 places the entrance of Abraham into Palestine after the Canaanites were already there! For the importance which the nomadic characteristics of the EB IV/MB I Period have for the identification of the patriarchs with the Amorites, see recently K. Kenyon, Excavations in Jerusalem, 1965, PEQ 98 (1966), 74f.; for the identification with the patriarchs, cf. J. Bright, History of Israel, 1959, 72. On this entire question, see below Chapter 7.

[5] The Excavation of Tell Beit Mirsim IA: The Bronze Age Pottery of the Fourth Campaign, AASOR 13 (1933), 66f.

[6] This identification is expressed as certain by G. Mendenhall loc. cit. (see note 2) and by K. Kenyon, Amorites and Canaanites, 76. See also Albright, Palestine in the Earliest Historical Period, JPOS 15 (1935), 219.

mentioned in connection with Abraham in existence, and that only at this time was the "hill country inhabited and the coast deserted"[7].

The several sources for this complex hypothesis will have to be examined independently. Since we have already examined in the past chapters the Mesopotamian texts connected with the Early West Semitic names, it perhaps would be best, for the sake of clarity, to examine the Palestinian and Egyptian material by first taking a look at what we do and do not know about these people from the written sources.

B. THE LINGUISTIC MATERIAL FOR PALESTINE FROM THE EARLY SECOND MILLENIUM

On the basis of what linguistic evidence we have, it is impossible to show that the Early West Semites of Palestine ever came from North Mesopotamia. If the Palestinian Early West Semites had come from the North, then we should rightly expect to find a coherence between the linguistic structures of the South and the North and, where observable, a relationship of dependence of the South on the North. However, the linguistic material we have is far too limited and disjointed to suggest any such coherence. This fragmentary character of our material justifies only the vaguest and most indirect relationship between the Early West Semites of Palestine and those of North and South Mesopotamia. Because of this, the attempts to connect the patriarchs with hypothetical early Second Millenium West Semitic movements, whether as "Amorites" with Bright and Kenyon, or as "Proto-Aramaeans" with de Vaux and Noth, lack all support.

We have no linguistic evidence that the Early West Semites of Palestine, known from the Execration Texts[8] and a thirteenth dynasty list of Egyptian slaves[9], are newcomers or immigrants into

[7] B. Vawter, A Path through Genesis, 1965^2, 122. J. Bright's (History of Israel, 74) presentation of this argument is quite peculiar: "... so far as has been checked, the towns mentioned in the patriarchal stories — Shechem, Dothan, Bethel, and Jerusalem (sic!) — were actually in existence in the Middle Bronze Age. If the stories were late creations, this would have scarcely been the case."! (This will be discussed in detail in Chapter 8.)

[8] K. Sethe, Die Ächtung feindlicher Fürsten, Völker und Dinge auf altägyptischen Tongefäßscherben des mittleren Reiches, Abhandlungen der preußischen Akademie der Wissenschaften zu Berlin, 1926; G. Posener, Princes et Pays d'Asie et de Nubie, 1940; see also the newly discovered texts from Mirgissa in Northern Nubia: G. Posener, Les Textes d'envoûtement de Mirgissa, Syria 43 (1966), 277—287. For the dating of these texts see below, sections C and D of this chapter.

[9] W. F. Albright, Northwest Semitic Names in a List of Egyptian Slaves from the 18th Century B. C., JAOS 74 (1954), 222—233. The earliest occurrence of an Early West Semitic name belonging to a Palestinian seems to date from the reign

Palestine at the end of the Third or the beginning of the Second Millenium B. C. That the Execration Texts might rather give witness to an indigenous West Semitic population is suggested by the general West Semitic character of the geographic names as well as the personal names in the early part of the Second Millenium, in contrast, for instance, to the situation in Syria where the occurrence of non-Semitic and non-Hurrian geographic names side by side with Semitic and Hurrian personal names suggests an earlier non-Semitic, non-Hurrian population[10]. What must be admitted is that, in Palestine, "when the first historical sources appear, the Semites are already there"[11]. A positive argument for the existence of West Semites in Palestine as early as 3000 B. C. can be found in the West Semitic influence on the formation of the Egyptian language, both in its grammar (e. g.: 3rd pers. sing. *jnh* and plural *jnn*), as well as in the use of several basic West Semitic nouns (e. g.: *ʿ[j]n, mt, [j]d*), for which Egyptian did not have its own words[12]. From this very early time, we must assume a very strong influence of the West Semites on the settled regions.

It is also extremely difficult to maintain that the Early West Semitic names found in the Execration Texts can be understood as "Amorite", as names identical to those that have been found in the Mari texts. The inadequacies of Egyptian orthography make it impossible to distinguish the Mari *-ânu* from the Phoenician/Hebrew *-ônu*, or the Mari *â* from the Phoenician/Hebrew *ô*[13]. While one might

of Amenemes I: *Ia$_8$-ki-in-ilum*. Th. Pinches, A Cylinder Seal Inscribed in Hieroglyphic and Cuneiform in the Collection of the Earl of Carnarvon, JEA 7 (1921), 196; my reading follows W. von Soden, Zur Einteilung der semitischen Sprachen WZKM 56 (1960), 182f.

[10] I. J. Gelb, The Early History of the West Semitic Peoples, JCS 15 (1961), 27—47, for Syria, see 39f., for Palestine, 41.

[11] S. Moscati, Semites in Ancient History, 82. In a remarkably contradictory manner J. Bright brings out some of the confusion surrounding the discussion about the origin of these people (History of Israel 48f.). First he points out that the "newcomers", according to the personal names known from the Execration Texts, are "Amorites", but then he goes on to say that "these people brought to Palestine no fundamental ethnic change, for they were of the same general Northwest-Semitic stock as were the Canaanites". (!) With this declaration he betrays the fact that he has no justification for saying that these people are "newcomers", since only an ethnically distinct change in the population would show this. Moreover, it is immediately obvious that he has no reason to call one group "Amorites" and the other "Canaanites" or indeed to speak of two groups without the observation of some "fundamental ethnic change".

[12] Cf. on the West Semitic influence in early Egypt, I. E. S. Edwards, The Early Dynastic Period in Egypt, CAH², chapter XI, fascicle 25, 1964, 35f.

[13] Gelb, JCS 15 (1961), 40.

assume a chronological development to understand such distinctions as that between ḥ and ḫ in the Execration Texts and their identification in Hebrew as ḥ, the different use of sibilants in the Mari texts from that used in the Execration Texts at first only seems adequately understood as a difference in dialect[14]. The names of the Execration Texts have more affinities with the texts from Byblos, and to a certain extent, more with those from Alalakh than with the Mari names[15]. The picture is by no means so clear that historical conclusions can be drawn. In using the sibilants as criteria for differentiation by dialects, Albright noted that biblical שכם appears in the Amarna texts as *šakm(i)*, but in the earlier Egyptian texts as *ŚKMM*[16]. While the same manner of representing the sibilants was followed in a few other cases, with *s* representing *š* as it does in the Mari West Semitic names, for the most part, a quite distinct pattern was followed, which Albright refers to as "South Canaanite"[17], including in this designation primarily the Execration Texts and the Sinai inscriptions, but also the Byblos texts and most of the Pales-

---

14 Note, however, Gelb's caution, ibid. 40. 44.

15 H. B. Huffmon, Amorite Personal Names in the Mari Texts, 1965, 12 n. 67, against M. Noth (Die syrisch-palästinische Bevölkerung des zweiten Jahrtausends v. Chr. im Lichte neuer Quellen, ZDPV 65, 1942, 20f. 27) who sees not only all the personal names of the Execration Texts as identical in type, but also as identical to the West Semitic personal names from Mari. This identity in type, however, can only show that the names are all generally West Semitic; the linguistic study of these names is as yet insufficient to show dialectical variations within this general language grouping, and it is this kind of identification which is needed before we can speak of an identity of origin as Noth does. Gelb's remark here is important: "It is impossible at the present time to decide between two conclusions, one, that the language of the names in the Execration Texts preserves the characteristics of the older West Semitic language, namely Amorite, and the other, that it shows the innovating features of Canaanite." JCS 15 (1961), 39. Also see W. Moran, Mari Notes on the Execration Texts, Orientalia 26 (1957), 340. The difficulty seen by Noth (ZDPV 65, 27) in the element *ʿpr*, found in some of the personal names of the Execration Texts, but not however in the Mari texts, disappears completely with the observations of O. Rössler (Das ältere ägyptische Umschreibungssystem für Fremdnamen und seine sprachwissenschaftlichen Lehren, Neue afrikanische Studien, ed. by J. Lukas, Hamburger Beiträge zur Afrika-Kunde V, 1966, 218—229) who points out that *ʿpr* is the normal orthography used in older texts for the transcription of the Semitic word *ʿbd*, a West Semitic name element which is very common in the Mari correspondence and elsewhere.

16 W. F. Albright, The Egyptian Empire in Asia in the 21st Century B. C., JPOS 8 (1928), 233. 253; The North-Canaanite Poems of *Al'êyân Baʿal* and the "Gracious Gods", JPOS 14 (1934), 107f.

17 W. F. Albright, The Northwest-Semitic Tongues before 1000 B. C., Atti del XIX Congresso Internazionale degli Orientalisti, 1938, 449.

tinian texts from the Late Bronze Age[18]. On the strength of this divergence within the Egyptian texts, Albright suggested that there were two distinct Early West Semitic dialects[19] which he refers to as "South-" and "East-Canaanite" ("East-Canaanite" refers to the West Semitic names from Mari and the few Palestinian names which follow the same sibilant pattern). These "dialects" distinguish themselves according to the following table[20]:

Arabic *ṯ* is rendered in "S.Can." as *s* or *ṯ*, and in "E.Can." as *š*.
Arabic *ś* is rendered in "S.Can." and in "E.Can." as *s*.
Arabic *š* is rendered in "S.Can." as *š* but in "E.Can." as *s*.

If such a dialectical distinction is valid in the early Second Millenium in Palestine, it suggests that, if some of the Early West Semites were newcomers to Palestine, they did not come from Mari by way of Syria, but independently from the Arabian desert to the West. There is some objection, however, to the use of sibilants to establish variations in dialect. In only a few of our texts do we have a thoroughly consistent use of sibilants. In Mari, for instance, what would be represented in Arabic as *ṯ*, is given as *s* rather than the expected *š* in *sa-al-gu*$_5$[21]. The confusion of the sibilants at Alalakh is so great that Martin Noth's suggestion becomes attractive: that the variant use of the sibilants had perhaps best be explained as attempts of the scribes to grapple either with the peculiar sounds of foreign names as in the Execration Texts, or with familiar names in a writing

---

[18] Ibid. 448. This sibilant pattern is also followed in the cuneiform texts from Alalakh; so W. L. Moran, The Hebrew Language in its Northwest Semitic Background, Albright Festschrift, 67f. n29.

[19] The five dialects which Albright distinguished in 1938 (Atti del XIX Congresso 448) are too hypothetical to be useful. His "North Canaanite" (i. e., Ugaritic) is several centuries later than the Execration Texts (cf. esp., A. Goetze, Is Ugaritic a Canaanite Dialect?, Language 17, 1941, 127). Albright's "Proto-Hebrew" (derived from the Jerusalem Amarna tablets) suffers not only from a chronological distance from the Execration Texts but also from a severe lack of material, and his "proto-aramaic" (not the same as the Proto-aramäisch spoken of by Noth) does not exist at all.

[20] Albright has published two tables (Atti del XIX Congresso 448, and, The Early Alphabetic Inscriptions from Sinai and Their Decipherment, BASOR 110, 1948, 15n42), neither of which, however, is correct. In 1938, etymological *š* (that is, Arabic *š*) is given as *s* instead of *š* in South Canaanite, and as *š* instead of *s* in East Canaanite. In 1948, only the East Canaanite sibilant is corrected. There is also hopeless confusion introduced when, in 1938, he presents the South and North Arabic sibilants as distinct, but in 1948 he identifies them. W. Moran's listing of the sibilant variants in the Albright Festschrift (67n29) is correct.

[21] Moran ibid.

that was foreign as in so many of the groups of cuneiform texts[22]. The apparent patterns of sibilant use can easily be explained, since it is only to be expected that specific ways of handling the difficulties will be discovered and generally followed by various schools of scribes. When it is remembered that the Execration Texts are not always consistent in their use of *š*, sometimes rendering it as *s* and sometimes as *š*, and when it is noted that both *Lakis* and *Lakiš* appear in the Amarna Texts[23], and that this same double orthography[24] is found in the New Kingdom place names, the differentiation of the Early West Semitic language in Palestine into two distinct dialects as has been proposed by Albright, seems surely false.

While Albright's division of West Semitic between "Amorite" (understood as the Mari dialect) on one hand, and "Canaanite" (understood as primarily the Execration Texts, Ugarit, the Sinai Inscriptions, etc.) on the other, seems decidedly inadequate, the alternative sought by Goetze[25] in distinguishing between "Canaanite" (understood as Phoenician, Hebrew, and the "Canaanite" language underlying the Amarna letters) and "Amurrite" (i. e., Ugaritic, the Early West Semitic personal and place names largely gleaned from the Execration Texts and other Egyptian inscriptions, and the material in Mesopotamia from the Old Babylonian period) is hardly more acceptable. While Goetze adequately points out the serious differences that exist between Ugaritic and Canaanite[26], he fails to show a clear correlation between the Ugaritic Texts, the Execration Texts, and the Mesopotamian material. Of twelve points where there is evidence, Ugaritic corresponds with the Mesopotamian material in only seven cases. Of the other five points in question, only one (the assimilation of the nasal *-n*) can easily be understood as a chronological change within a single dialect[27]. Moreover, no serious attempt is made to show a positive correlation between the early Egyptian texts and the Mesopotamian material; the inadequacies of the Egyptian orthography, indeed, precludes any such positive correlation[28].

---

[22] M. Noth, ZDPV 65 (1942), 28.

[23] W. F. Albright, JPOS 8 (1928), 233.

[24] That a different orthography represents a different pronunciation as claimed by Albright (ibid.) has yet to be proven!

[25] A. Goetze, Language 17 (1941), 127—138, and his review of J. R. Kupper, Les Nomades en Mesopotamie au Temp des Rois de Mari, JSS 4 (1959), 142—147, and Amurrite Names in Ur III and Early Isin Texts, JSS 4 (1959), 193—203.

[26] Fourteen specific grammatical distinctions, many of which are quite fundamental: Language 17 (1941), 133.

[27] Ibid. 135f.

[28] I. J. Gelb, JCS 15 (1961), 39. For some specific differences, see M. Noth in ZDPV 65 (1942), 49.

The Ugaritic texts seem much more closely related to the later Palestinian languages than is generally the case with other Early West Semitic inscriptions[29]. Aistleitner, for instance, in his study of the linguistic relationship between Ugaritic and the Early West Semitic names, concludes that while they are clearly closely related, they are nevertheless to be sharply distinguished one from another, Ugaritic being much closer to Phoenician[30].

M. Noth in his 1942 article in ZDPV[31] reached much the same conclusion, showing first the differences between the Ugaritic and the Old Babylonian and Execration Texts[32], and subsequently the close similarities between the Ugaritic and the later Phoenician and Hebrew names. Still, the differences which Goetze has pointed out cannot be denied, and it does not seem justified to speak of a Canaanite language in the Second Millenium except in the most limited manner. It is important, rather, to stress the lack of linguistic unity in Palestine during the Second Millenium[33].

In spite of the inadequacy of our written records to give us even a general picture of the people of Palestine and their history during the early Second Millenium, some remarks — if only negative — do seem valid in the way of conclusion: The written materials do not witness to a major West Semitic migration into Palestine in the early Second Millenium, and argue against any such migration from North Mesopotamia. The Early West Semitic names from Mari are close to but not identical to the early Second Millenium names from Palestine[34]. This in itself precludes Northwest-Mesopotamia as the direct source of the Palestinian peoples. Moreover, the West Semitic of Palestine in the early Second Millenium is by no means unified, and attempts to divide them into two groups directly antece-

---

29 M. Noth ibid. 48f. and § 2; W. von Soden, WZKM 56 (1960), 178. 188.

30 J. Aistleitner, Studien zur Frage der Sprachverwandtschaft des Ugaritischen I, ActaOrHung. 7 (1957), 251—307, and II, ibid., 8 (1958), 51—98, here 90. It is doubtful that the term "Canaanite" can properly be used in this early period to include Ugaritic; indeed, in a list of workmen at Ugarit, one man is referred to as a "Canaanite", (A. F. Rainey, A Canaanite at Ugarit, IEJ 13, 1963, 43—45, and Ugarit and the Canaanite Again, IEJ 14, 1964, 101). This term apparently refers to the people of the Phoenician coast (S. Moscati, Israel's Predecessors: A Re-examination of Certain Current Theories, JBR 24, 1956, 247f.) and some Palestinian sites (Gelb, JCS 15, 1961, 42). Gelb, however, gives too much consideration to linguistic criteria, which in this early period are not clear, in distinguishing the geographical *Kinaḫna* from *Amurrū*.

31 Vol. 65, esp. 49—53.

32 Especially in regard to theophoric names; cf. 49—52.

33 A. Goetze, Review of Kupper, 145. This disunity is particularly apparent in the names found in the texts from Shechem (Cf. Noth, ZDPV 65, 1942, 66).

34 W. Moran, Albright Festschrift, 56.

dent to the later Amorites and Canaanites have been unsuccessful. In fact, if there is to be any clarity in the discussion about this early period, the use of such terms as "Canaanite" and "Amorite" has to be given up. The term "Canaanite" is not known until the Late Bronze Age[35], and the concept of Canaanite seems more derived from cultural, economic, and geographical grounds[36] than from any ethnic or linguistic unity. "Canaanite" as a linguistic or ethnic entity seems rather to be a derivative concept. Certainly the terms "Amorite" and "Amurrite" are not helpful in trying to understand this early period in Palestine. The term "Amurrite" in Palestine and Syria can only legitimately refer to the political entity *māt amurri* of the Amarna Period, which, as has long been recognized, has little to do with the Early West Semitic names[37]; nor can it be used legitimately for other areas of Palestine and Syria.

The Amorites of Genesis, on the other hand, do play a significant role in the history of Palestine, but much later than the period under discussion. According to the biblical narratives, their entrance into Palestine, into those regions in which they are met in the patriarchal narratives, follows the occupation of the Ammonites[38].

[35] *kinâḫḫi, kinâḫni*; M. C. Astour, The Origin of the Terms "Canaan", "Phoenician" and "Purple", JNES 24 (1965), 346; A. F. Rainey, IEJ 13 (1963), 43—45; 14 (1964), 101; S. Moscati, Sulla Storia del Nome Canaan. Studia Biblica et Orientalia 3 (1959), 268; I Predecessori d'Israele. Studi orientali publicati a cura della scuola orientale, IV 1956, 72; H. Haag, Die Archäologie im Dienste der Bibel. Seine Rede geschah zu mir, ed. by Fritz Leist, 1965, 164; A. van den Born, Kanaan. Bibel-lexikon, 914f. (for further literature).

[36] E. A. Speiser, Language 12 (1936), 121—126, and "Amorites and Canaanites", in: At the Dawn of Civilization. The World History of the Jewish People I, 1963, 163; S. Moscati, Israel's Predecessors. A Re-examination of Certain Current Theories, JBR 24 (1956), 247, and Semites in Ancient History, 83ff.

[37] Contra Gelb, JCS 15 (1961), who freely mixes the linguistic and geographical data of various chronological periods. See on the other hand, C. H. J. de Geus, De Amorieten in de Palestijnse Archeologie. Een Recente Theorie Kritisch Bezien, NThT 23 (1968/1969), 1—24, here 3. The use which J. van Seters (The Hyksos 1966) makes of the term "Amurrite" to speak of a common culture for almost the entire Near East lasting throughout the Middle Bronze Age mars an otherwise admirable analysis of the archaeological remains of Palestine during Middle Bronze II b—c.

[38] See especially, R. de Vaux, Les Hurrites de l'Histoire et les Horites de la Bible, RB 74 (1967), 502, and S. Moscati, JBR 24 (1956), 251 (with caution!). It is doubtful that the biblical name is derived from *māt amurri* (contra Moscati ibid. 252). The geographical location of the land of the Amorites is quite far from *māt amurri*. There is also a considerable chronological separation. The most important biblical references are: Judg 21 21-30 II Sam 21 2 Gen 14 13 Judg 11 22 1 34 ff. Jos 5 1, all of 12, and 24 8-15 Dtn 3 8 4 47 ff. and Num 21 18d ff. Cf. also the map of K. Kenyon, Amorites and Canaanites, 4.

C. THE EXECRATION TEXTS AND THEIR HISTORICAL SETTING

The major efforts to see the patriarchal stories as rooted in the historical events of the early Second Millenium, particularly as they are related to the historical identification of Gen 11 with some supposed movement of Early West Semites from Mesopotamia to Palestine, is supported by the historical reconstruction of a period in Palestine which is seen as analogous to the culture presupposed by these biblical stories. It involves the concurrence of the Early West Semitic names with a culture that is semi-nomadic in character moving toward sedentarization at a time that would be roughly contemporary with one of the several reconstructed biblical chronologies for Abraham. Such a period has been reconstructed by bringing together the Execration Texts with the transitional archaeological period EB IV/MB I[39], supported by the Egyptian records of the First Intermediate Period, the Story of Sinuhe, and the Egyptian tomb painting found at Beni Hasan.

Once a direct historical relationship between the people of the Execration Texts and the Early West Semites of Mesopotamia, and a mutual connection with Gen 11, is seen as unjustified, this argument for the historicity of the patriarchs is seen to rest on an historical analogy. So slender an argument, however, can only be maintained to the extent that the historical reconstruction on which the analogy is based can be upheld in detail. Because of this and also because we are dealing with an historical period in which information is so scarce that such widely separated events as, for example, the American War of Independence and the American Civil War, would appear, were they to have occurred in the early Second Millenium, as "roughly contemporary", the problems of chronology are extraordinarily crucial, and consequently the inadequacies of the chronological schemes which underlie the suggested historical pictures need to be pointed out.

The dating of the Execration Texts is of considerable importance for the completeness of the suggested analogy; for if these texts are seen as contemporary with EB IV/MB I, they can be used to interpret the archaeological remains of this period and to identify the people of this transitional period culture with "patriarchal type" names. Moreover, the Sethe Execration Texts have been understood by some to be considerably earlier than those published by Posener. This relative chronology is then used to support the interpretation, based

---

[39] Albright: EB IIIB and MB I; Kenyon: Intermediate EB—MB; P. Lapp: Intermediate Bronze I—II (more recently, EB IV/MB I); Glueck-Wright-Dever: EB IV and MB I; Oren, EB IV A/EB IV B; Tufnell: Caliciform Period; and Petrie: Copper Age. A clarification of the terminology can be found below in ch. 7.

on the archaeological finds, that we have at this period a nomadic culture in process of sedentarization[40].

When we examine the chronological evidence for the Execration Texts, and when we compare the content of the Sethe texts with that of the Posener texts, we find that there is no justification for separating them from each other by any considerable length of time. Secondly, there is no evidence that the people whose names appear in the Execration Texts are semi-nomadic, and there is considerable evidence to the contrary. Thirdly, the Execration Texts are separated from the transitional EB IV/MB I Period by nearly two centuries.

In 1926 K. Sethe published his study of 289 inscribed potsherds from the Berlin museum, 217 of which H. Schäfer had bought in Luxor in 1925[41]. The texts were written in Hieratic, inscribed on bowls found in a grave in western Thebes. Sethe interpreted these texts as lists of rebellious princes from Africa, Libya, Palestine and Syria, and Egypt, who threatened the inner security of Egypt. Although the palaeography seemed to suggest a date in the Twelfth Dynasty[42], the orthography and the language seemed to Sethe more closely related to Eleventh Dynasty and Old Kingdom texts. Because of this, he suggested a date towards the end of the Eleventh Dynasty (c. 2000 B. C.) as most probable[43]. This was further supported by his interpretation of the function of the Execration Texts, since it was far less likely that Egypt would have been so directly threatened by foreign rulers during the reigns of the powerful Twelfth Dynasty pharaohs; on the other hand, such a threat would be immediately understandable during the reign of one of the weaker Eleventh Dynasty pharaohs, within memory of the internal disruptions of the First Intermediate Period[44].

This chronology and interpretation was immediately accepted by H. Greßmann[45] who understood one text as referring directly to

[40] Mainly the position taken by W. F. Albright (esp. From the Stone Age to Christianity, 1957^3, 164; The Role of the Canaanites in the History of Civilization, in Albright Festschrift, 333; for further literature see below); and followed especially by G. E. Wright, Biblical Archaeology, 1957, 47; J. Bright, History of Israel, 47; and R. de Vaux, Les patriarches hébreux et les découvertes modernes, RB 53 (1946), 341 and Les patriarches hébreux et l'histoire, RB 72 (1965), 12. The interpretation of M. Noth (most recently: Thebes, Archaeology and Old Testament Study, ed. by D. Winton Thomas, 1967, 23—29), while in many respects resembling the interpretation put forward by Albright, distinguishes itself in several important points of detail. On this, see further below.

[41] K. Sethe, Ächtung. For Sethe's description of the finds, see 6—18.

[42] Ibid. 15.

[43] Ibid. 18.

[44] Ibid. 21.

[45] Wichtige Zeitschriften-Aufsätze, ZAW 44 (1926), 280—283.

Amenemes I, the founder of the Twelfth Dynasty, thus giving the texts a date immediately before Amenemes' rise to power. A. Mallon[46] and R. Dussaud[47] also fully accepted Sethe's interpretation. Dussaud supported the chronology by comparing the proper names of the Asiatic princes who are referred to as *ʿꜣmw* with the "Amorite" founders of the First Babylonian Dynasty. Because he used the old chronology for the Mesopotamian kings, which placed the First Dynasty of Babylon around 2000 B. C., the resulting synchronism appeared quite remarkable[48]. A. Alt accepted Sethe's chronology without discussion[49]. Noticing, however, that among those Asiatic place names that were identifiable, coastal cities were given without the names of their princes, he suggested that this area had contact with Eygpt through trade only (thus it would be quite possible that the names of the princes would not be known to the Egyptians) and consequently these cities were not to be considered as having been a threat of invasion to Egypt, in contrast to the cities whose princes were named in the texts. These appeared to present a direct threat to Egypt's borders. In this manner, Alt saw in the texts a division of Palestine into two distinct areas[50].

Albright, also accepting Sethe's dating of the texts in general[51], excluded the possibility of their having been written during the reign of *Mentuḥotpe*, because that reign, according to Albright, was a period of strong Egyptian government, and thus not a period in which we could expect the Egyptians to feel threatened[52]. He therefore placed the Sethe texts in the brief period of Egyptian weakness shortly after the death of *Mentuḥotpe*; i. e., almost exactly 2000 B. C.[53]. General support was found for this dating in the similar names which had been found at Mari which were at first dated by Albright at about 2000 B. C. as well[54]. The major thrust of

46 Jérusalem et les Documents Égyptiens, JPOS 8 (1928), 1—6.

47 Nouveaux Renseignements sur la Palestine et la Syrie vers 2000 avant notre ère, Syria 8 (1927), 216—231.

48 Ibid. 216f. 231.

49 Amurru in den Ächtungstexten der 11. Dynastie, ZAW 46 (1928), 77—78, and Die asiatischen Gefahrzonen in den Ächtungstexten der 11. Dynastie, ZÄS 63 (1928), 39—45.

50 Ibid., esp. 40f. Alt makes no comment on the similar lack of princes' names in the Libyan texts.

51 W. F. Albright, JPOS 8 (1928), 216—233; The Vocalization of the Egyptian Syllabic Orthography, AOS 5, 1934, 7; and JPOS 15 (1935), 193—234.

52 But see A. Alt, Herren und Herrensitze Palästinas im Anfang des zweiten Jahrtausends v. Chr., ZDPV 64 (1941), 26n1.

53 Albright, JPOS 8 (1928), 225f.

54 JPOS 15 (1935), 197f.

Albright's interpretation of these materials was to connect the Execration Texts with Palestinian archaeological finds, starting from the observation of Alt, that on the basis of the Execration Texts, Palestine seemed to be divided into two distinct zones, the northern coastal region on one hand, and the area of the hill country and the South on the other. The distinction which Albright saw, however, was not based on a difference of degree of danger to Egypt, but rather on a difference of the political structure of the Palestinian sites. Because the coastal cities such as Byblos, Ullaza, Yarimuta, and *Dm'tyw*[55] are listed in the Execration Texts without the names of any princes, or as in the case of ʿArqatum[56], listed with the name of but one prince, while the cities of southern Palestine, represented by Ashkelon and Jerusalem are given as many as two or three different times, each time with the name of a different prince, Albright concluded that the "Canaanite coastal towns" must have had the political structure of a city, under the rule of one prince, while the places of southern Palestine were still being ruled by a tribal form of government based on several rulers[57]. This division of Palestine into two different political and social types of occupation was used by Albright as strong supporting evidence for what he describes as a "well-defined period of Amorite invasion and settlement in Palestine, probably falling in the last third of the Third Millenium"[58]. In 1935 he spoke of the Sethe texts as giving evidence for "a radical change in the character of the population" which he, connecting it with the decline of the Palestinian material culture towards the end of the Third Millenium, explains by what he calls an "influx of barbarous tribes". For this reason, he places the entrance of the Hebrew patriarchs into Palestine at this time[59].

This interpretation of the Execration Texts as giving evidence for a type of tribal rule in Palestine had first been suggested by Sethe, who described it as a type of collegial rule[60]. This was, however, immediately and strongly objected to by Alt[61].

In 1940, a group of similar texts was published by G. Posener[62]. These new texts Posener conclusively dated to a period no earlier

[55] This site has not been identified. Albright groups it with the coastal cities for no other reason apparently than that no prince's name for this town is listed! Cf. JPOS 8 (1928), 250.

[56] Sethe e22.

[57] JPOS 8 (1928), 250f.

[58] Ibid.

[59] JPOS 15 (1935), 217ff.

[60] Ächtung 43f.

[61] ZÄS 63 (1927), 43.

[62] Princes et pays; preliminary reports: Nouvelles listes de proscription (Ächtungstexte) datant du Moyen Empire, Chronique d'Égypte 14 (1939), 39—46; and

than the Twelfth Dynasty. This introduced considerable change into the discussion of the chronology and interpretation of the Sethe texts. Alt immediately gave up his "Gefahrzonen Hypothese", which had been totally dependent on a dating of the Sethe texts in the 11th Dynasty and on the assumed weakness of the Egyptian government at the time of the writing of the texts. He suggested a new date for the Sethe texts during the reign of Amenemes I[63]. On the other hand, the new texts affirmed to some extent his objection to the theory of Sethe and Albright, that the earlier texts had given evidence for a type of collegial rule, since four different times in the texts published by Posener[64] a location is mentioned in two different ways, either as "Northern" and "Southern", or as "Upper" and "Lower", each time with a different prince. The cities which appeared with multiple princes in the Sethe texts had to be understood on this basis and not by assuming a special tribal or nomadic character for the cities[65].

Nevertheless, at first Alt saw a development between the period of the Sethe texts and that of the Posener texts, a gradual extension of Egyptian power into the region of Galilee, assuming that the sites which were in the Posener texts, but not in those published by Sethe, were to be understood as regions newly added to the Egyptian sphere of power[66]. On the basis of this political development he finds justification for understanding the Sethe texts as originating in a quite different historical situation than that from which the Posener texts came[67]. In 1954 Alt suggested that this difference between the Posener and Sethe texts is not so much to be understood as a broader extension of Egyptian power, as it was a sign of a new threat to an already existing sphere of influence. This new interpretation is made possible by his dating of the texts towards the end of

Nouveaux textes hiératiques de proscription. Mélanges Syriens offerts a R. Dussaud, I 1939, 313—317.

63 ZDPV 64 (1941), 25f.; again lowered in: Die Herkunft der Hyksos in neuer Sicht, KS III, 91—93 (originally published in 1954).

64 E 23/24; E 33/34; E 39/40; and E 52/53.

65 ZDPV 64 (1941), 37.

66 Ibid. 34—37; but see L. H. Vincent, Les pays bibliques et l'Égypte à la fin de la XIIe Dynastie Égyptienne, Vivre et Penser, RB 51 (1942), 206.

67 In this he approaches Albright's interpretation: "Vielmehr scheint in der Zeit zwischen Sethes und Poseners Text tatsächlich fast überall in Palästina ein Wechsel der Herrschaftsverhältnisse eingetreten zu sein, so daß in Poseners Text nur noch ein paar Ausnahmefälle den früheren Zustand zeigen, der zur Zeit von Sethes Text erst an wenigen Orten überwunden war." ZDPV 64 (1941), 37; cf. also Alt, Die älteste Schilderung Palästinas im Lichte neuer Funde, PJ 37 (1941), 34ff., where he, however, places the Sethe texts within the nineteenth century (35).

the Twelfth Dynasty and his seeing them as perhaps closely bound up with the rise of the Hyksos[68].

The adjustment of Albright's interpretation, presented primarily in two articles published in 1941[69], took an entirely different direction. The strength of his interpretation rests on his dating of the respective groups of texts. Asserting that the palaeography of the Sethe texts can only give us a basis for dating these texts to some unspecified period after the 21st century[70], he assigns the highest possible date to the Sethe texts, sometime before the end of the twentieth century, as well as the highest conceivable date to the Posener texts, perhaps early in the nineteenth century[71]. He emphasizes that neither of the groups of texts can be dated after the middle of the nineteenth century, since both lists mention "only the people or tribes of Byblos, without giving any names of princes"[72], (he assumes that since the princes are not mentioned they must not have existed) and because "we have an unbroken sequence of princes of Byblos" for the following century[73]. In spite of the obvious triviality of this argument[74], and in the face of Posener's demonstration that the Brussels texts could not possibly antedate the end of the reign of Sesostris III, Albright bases his entire argument for the early dating of these texts on the hypothesis that the inscriptions presuppose that no Byblian princes existed at the time[75]. He gives as a probable date of the Posener texts the early part of the reign of Amenemes III (1839—1791)[76]. Although Albright argues for a twentieth century date for the Sethe texts on the basis of the palaeographically and ortho-

[68] Alt, Die Herkunft der Hyksos, 94.

[69] New Egyptian Data on Palestine in the Patriarchal Age, BASOR 81 (1941), 16—20, and The Land of Damascus between 1850 and 1750 B. C., BASOR 83 (1941), 30—36. Albright had not yet seen Posener's Princes et Pays at the time of his writing the article in BASOR 81.

[70] BASOR 81 (1941), 16 n. 2.

[71] Ibid.

[72] Ibid. 18 n. 9.

[73] Ibid. Albright refers here to his dating of the reign of Entin, the king of Byblos, to sometime between 1770 and 1760 B. C.; New Light on the History of Western Asia in the 2nd Millenium B. C., BASOR 77 (1940), 27f. But see below Chapter 8.

[74] Albright had argued prior to 1940 that this same evidence (that no princes are mentioned for Byblos) showed that Byblos did not have a tribal structure: JPOS 8 (1928), 250.

[75] Albright, BASOR 83 (1941), 32.

[76] Ibid., also, The Archaeology of Palestine, 1949, 83; JAOS 74 (1954), 223 n. 2; The Chronology of MB I (Early Bronze-Middle Bronze), BASOR 168 (1962), 39; Remarks on the Chronology of Early Bronze IV-Middle Bronze IIA in Phoenicia and Syria-Palestine, BASOR 184 (1966), 27ff., and Yahweh and the Gods of Canaan, 1968, Jordan Lectures for 1965, 47f., esp. 232, where he reiterates the close relationship between the chronology of the Execration Texts and that of the Byblos kings.

graphically earlier characteristics of these texts, settling upon a probable date within the reign of Amenemes II (c. 1938—1907)[77], his main reason for dating the Sethe texts nearly a century before the Posener texts comes from his historical interpretation[78].

As Albright had earlier seen a political difference within the Sethe texts between the coastal sites which were understood to have a city culture, and the sites to the south, which were assumed to have a tribal and nomadic structure, which political difference represented what Albright understood to be the archaeological picture of the Middle Bronze I Period, so, subsequent to the publication of the Posener texts, this same interpretation is maintained, but now applies not to a distinction within the Sethe texts, but to a comparison of the Sethe texts as a whole, where most places occur with more than one prince and are therefore understood to be tribal settlements (Byblos and the other coastal sites are now included among the places with tribal structures because they do not have a prince!), and the Posener texts which most often mention only one prince by name for each region, giving evidence, according to Albright, for a growing urbanization during the period separating the two sets of texts[79]. The confirmation of both his chronology and his interpretation is drawn from Palestinian archaeology. When Albright first developed this interpretation, he dated the end of the MB I Period and the beginning of MB IIA at about 1900 B. C.[80]. He thus was able to understand the Sethe texts as reflecting the culture characteristic of Tell Beit Mirsim Stratum H (MBI), a settlement which he interpreted as tribal and "semi-nomadic"[81]. He understood the Posener texts to correspond closely with the increasing number of settlements and eventually the establishment of major cities during MB IIA, especially such cities that are found in the texts as Shechem, Apiqum, Hazor, Beth Shemesh[82], Shamuniya[83], Achsaph, and Pella, where

[77] BASOR 83 (1941), 32—34. Albright understands the recently discovered Mirgissa texts, which he tries to date between the Berlin and the Brussels texts, as supporting his chronology; see Yahweh and the Gods of Canaan, 47f. n. 3.

[78] BASOR 83 (1941), 33.

[79] Ibid.; BASOR 81 (1941), 19. It should be mentioned that there is no significant difference between the two sets of texts in their way of listing Byblos.

[80] W. F. Albright, A Third Revision of the Early Chronology of Western Asia, BASOR 88 (1942), 32.

[81] Ibid.; Archaeology of Palestine 82.

[82] The extent to which Albright forces his interpretation can be seen in his identification of *Bwt šmšw* with the Northern Galilee region rather than with the southern Beth Shemesh which, according to Albright, was only an "insignificant village" during MB IIA: BASOR 81 (1941), 19.

[83] Where MB pottery was found, ibid.

occupations contemporary to Tell Beit Mirsim G—F (MB IIA) were found[84]. The arbitrariness of this interpretation is seen in 1966, when on the basis of a further lowering of his dating of the Byblos royal tombs to c. 1800 B. C., he lowers the end of Middle Bronze I to the very end of the nineteenth century[85]. His dating of the Execration Texts remains unchanged however. Rather, both the earlier texts and the later texts are now seen to represent different stages of the Middle Bronze I culture! The Sethe texts are now seen to give us written evidence for the "nomadic" culture of EB IV (TBM Stratum J), and the Posener texts represent the culture characteristic not of Tell Beit Mirsim G—F, but of Stratum H, now understood as a settled culture[86]!

Albright's correlation of the names from the Execration Texts with those found at Mari has undergone a similar metamorphosis. As before 1940 the correspondence of the names from the Sethe texts, with the Mesopotamian names (then dated to c. 2000 B. C.) was seen as major support for an Eleventh Dynasty dating of the Sethe texts so, after the discovery of the Posener texts, the names from the Mari texts (now dated to the very end of the eighteenth century) are imagined to be "closer" to the names of the Posener texts and therefore can be used to support a dating of the Sethe texts to a considerably earlier period than the Posener texts[87]! In no way, however, has it been allowed to affect the dating of the Posener texts which has been tied first to the dating of the Byblos kings and second to the chronology of Middle Bronze I.

There has been a tendency in recent literature to date the Brussels texts even later than Posener recommended, as late as the Thirteenth Dynasty[88], connecting these texts more immediately with the Mari names[89] and the archaeology of the Middle Bronze II Period[90]. It must be stressed, however, that these opinions, like those of

---

84 Ibid., also BASOR 88 (1942), 28—36.

85 BASOR 184 (1966), 26—35.

86 Ibid., esp. 33.

87 BASOR 81 (1941), 18 n. 9.

88 J. van Seters, The Hyksos, 1966, 21. 78—81; and B. Mazar, The Middle Bronze Age in Palestine, IEJ 18 (1968), 74f.

89 So Mazar ibid. 81 and van Seters ibid. 77f.

90 Mazar, indeed, dating the Sethe texts to the reigns of Amenemes III and IV, sees them as adequately representing the culture of MB IIA and, dating the Posener texts to the third quarter of the eighteenth century, sees them as accurately descriptive of MB IIB. (Ibid. 74ff.). Unfortunately, he gives no reasons for his low dating of Posener, and misrepresents the general scholarly opinion (74 n. 22). J. van Seters, dating both sets of texts between 1790 and 1750 B. C., sees them within the context of early MB II (ibid. 80).

Albright, are strongly affected by an attempt to date the texts on the basis of a very tenuous interpretation of Palestinian archaeology and history[91], and on an understanding of the Execration Texts which is based much more on the peculiarities of the archaeological finds in Palestine than it is on these texts. When neither the chronology of Palestinian archaeology nor that of the Egyptian texts is clear, such historical reconstruction cannot be accepted as serious history. But, nevertheless, this is the way the historians have proceeded, and it is now necessary to ask how much of the historical interpretation of the Execration Texts is justified, particularly that which finds evidence for a gradual sedentarization, a movement away from an original tribal structure towards a city life, and how much of this interpretation is supported when we examine the dating and the content of these texts independently of what we know and don't know about Palestinian archaeology. The same must also be done in dating the royal tombs of Byblos. It obviously follows that the chronology for the end of the MB I Period and the beginning of MB IIA must also be established as much as possible independently of the Execration Texts[92]. Only then can we have a sound basis for historical interpretation.

D. THE DATING OF THE EXECRATION TEXTS

The uncertainty about the historical milieu of the Execration Texts has resulted more from attempts to extend already well-defined chronological limits in such a way that the texts could be used to support one specific archaeological interpretation of Palestine; it is not because there is any lack of clarity in the original attempts to date the texts. While no single criterion for dating the texts is absolutely certain or totally adequate, each aspect useful for the purposes of dating so confirms the others as to render a convincing chronology.

The most obvious means of dating the Execration Texts comes from the names of the Egyptians who are cursed in the texts. Many of these names are derived from the royal names of the Twelfth Dynasty. From the Posener texts we find abbreviations of the names *śḥtp-ib-rʿ* (Amenemes I), *nb-kȝw-rʿ* (Amenemes II), *ḫʿ-ḫpr-rʿ* (Sesostris II), and the name *ḫʿ-kȝw śnb* which is based on the name *ḫʿ-kȝw-rʿ*

---

[91] So Mazar, quite explicitly: "It seems to us that various historical and archaeological factors require that the early collection of Execration Texts be dated to the end of the Twelfth Dynasty . . ." (Ibid.).

[92] Cf. below, Chapter 8.

(Sesostris III)[93]. At least the last named, *ḫ'-kꜣw śnb* was born after Sesostris III came to power (1876—1839)[94]. Since it is reasonable to suppose that at the time of the writing of the Execration Texts this person was an adult[95], we derive an approximate date of c. 1850 B. C. as the earliest possible date for the Posener texts. The absence of names built on the names of the later pharaohs does not allow us, however, to suggest a date *ante quem* for our texts as Alt has suggested[96], since not only is the quantity of names very limited, but also since, because we find people named after the first king of this dynasty even later than the time of Sesostris III, we can probably expect these names to appear at almost any subsequent time during the Twelfth Dynasty and into the Thirteenth Dynasty.

Albright has shown that almost all of the names from the Egyptian section of the Sethe texts are also "taken from royal names and prenomina of the Twelfth Dynasty: "Amenemmes, Ameni, Seḥetepibrē', Sesostris, Sesostris the Younger, Wosret. Other Egyptians in the same list are called Sesostris son of Ameni, and Ameni son of Sesostris"[97]. Since it is to be assumed that the persons mentioned have reached adulthood, the earliest possible date for the Sethe texts must be considerably later than the beginning of the reign of Amenemes II (1928—1897), that is, hardly earlier than the beginning of the nineteenth century[98].

The use of palaeographical criteria has been plagued by uncertainty in the dating of many of the manuscripts that can be used for comparison. Nevertheless, some general conclusions seem valid. Since we are dealing with magical or ritual texts which normally have a tendency towards conservatism both in their orthography and in their palaeography, the relatively old forms are not so important for determining the date of the texts as the very latest forms which occur[99].

93 Posener, Princes et Pays, 32, followed by Alt, ZDPV 64 (1941), 24; PJB 37 (1941), 35; Die Herkunft der Hyksos, 91—93; M. Noth, ZDPV 65 (1942), 13; Vincent RB 51 (1942), 191; Albright, JAOS 74 (1954), 223 n. 2 and BASOR 184 (1966), 28 n.

94 Posener ibid.

95 If not already an old man as suggested by Alt, Die Herkunft der Hyksos, 92.

96 Ibid. 93.

97 BASOR 184 (1966), 28 n.; see also Sethe, Ächtung, 63—69.

98 Thus making Albright's suggested dating for these texts of 1925—1900 B. C. very unlikely. It must be stressed that these are the earliest possible dates. The Sethe texts give us only a very few Egyptian names and no conclusions can be safely drawn on the basis of the lack of later pharaonic names as, e. g., Alt (PJB 37, 1941, 35) attempts to do.

99 This principle is clearly stated by W. F. Edgerton, Egyptian Phonetic Writing, from its Invention to the Close of the Nineteenth Dynasty, JAOS 60 (1940), 492 n. 44.

Sethe observed that the palaeography of the Berlin texts called for a date within the Twelfth Dynasty[100]. In spite of Albright's observation that there is a lack of datable documents in cursive hieratic between the reigns of Menṯuḥotpe III (c. 2060 B. C.) and Sesostris III (1876—1839 B. C.)[101], a comparison of the Execration Texts with those datable texts that we do have suggests a much more definite date than that allowed by Albright[102].

Both the form of the script and the manner of writing in horizontal lines separate the Sethe texts from the earlier Eleventh Dynasty manuscripts, such as the correspondence of Hekanacht. The manner of writing in horizontal lines in contrast to the vertical writing of the Eleventh Dynasty is similar to that found in the Papyrus Prisse[103]. Sethe relates the palaeography to that of Kahun and Sinuhe B[104] (both c. 1800 B. C.)[105]. The Russian scholar Meščersky places the palaeography of the Sethe texts close to Kahun and Bulaq 18[106]. On the basis of the table given by Meščersky, however, the Sethe texts seem to be significantly earlier than Bulaq 18, and are rather to be compared with Prisse, but especially Kahun. The palaeography for the Sethe texts therefore suggests a date (although by no means firm) towards the end of the nineteenth century. Further, the

---

[100] Sethe, Ächtung, 15.

[101] BASOR 83 (1941), 33.

[102] While the palaeographical dating of Sethe is by itself inadequate, it is nevertheless valid, since the date derived also corresponds with other factors which are independent of the palaeography.

[103] Date uncertain; from the latter part of the Twelfth Dynasty to the Thirteenth; cf. Posener, Princes et Pays, 33f.

[104] Sethe, Ächtung, 15.

[105] Meščersky defends Borchardt's dating of Sinuhe B against Sethe (N. Meščersky, Zur paläographischen Datierung der altägyptischen Ächtungstexte, Comptes Rendus de l'Academie des Sciences de l'URSS, 13B, 1929, 254) giving a date towards the end of the Twelfth and the beginning of the Thirteenth Dynasty. L. Borchardt, Ein Rechnungsbuch des königlichen Hofes aus dem Ende des mittleren Reiches, ZÄS 28 (1890), 102; also A. H. Gardiner, Notes on the Story of Sinuhe, 2f.; and J. J. Clère, Sinouhé en Syrie, Mélanges Syriens offerts à René Dussaud, 1939, 829. J. A. Wilson dates Sinuhe B to the late Twelfth Dynasty, c. 1800 B. C. (ANET 18b). Kahun is to be dated to the end of the reign of Amenemes III (so van Seters, the Hyksos, 104 n. 28).

[106] Meščersky ibid. 256. Bulaq 18 is to be dated not at the end of the Thirteenth Dynasty with Meščerskij but more probably with Albright during the reign of Sebekḥotpe III (BASOR 83, 1941, 32) 1744—1741 B. C. (J. von Beckerath, Untersuchungen zur Politischen Geschichte der Zweiten Zwischenzeit in Ägypten. Ägyptologische Forschungen 23, 1964, 222), not 1770—1760 B. C. as Albright suggested in 1941, basing himeslf on a very high dating of Hammurapi: c. 1800 B. C.

Sethe texts appear to be palaeographically earlier than the Posener texts[107].

Posener has been able to show that the Brussels texts are earlier than Bulaq 18 (ca. 1744—1741) and Sinuhe R (early Thirteenth Dynasty), as well as that the Brussels texts are definitely later than the Kahun Papyri (the majority of the Kahun Papyri are from the reign of Sesostris III, 1876—1839 B. C. and Amenemes III, 1839 to 1791)[108]. There is some evidence to suggest that the Posener texts are also later than Sinuhe B[109]. The general conclusion on the basis of the palaeography seems to demand the latest possible Twelfth Dynasty date for the Brussels texts (c. 1800 B. C.). This opinion is even further strengthened by orthographic considerations.

Albright has argued for a relatively early date for the Sethe texts, in contrast to the date of the Posener texts, because the Sethe texts employ three reed leaves to transcribe an initial *y* (a characteristic of the Pyramid Texts), while the Posener texts use only two leaves, what is characteristic of later texts[110]. Granted that the Sethe texts do use this early form[111], such occurrence can easily be explained as an archaizing tendency much to be expected in this type of inscription. It should be observed that neither the Sethe nor the Posener texts are altogether consistent in their rendering of the *y*. We find in f 21 of the Sethe texts, for example, that the three reeds in *ʾIj-sipj* are not used to represent an initial *y* but rather אי[112], and that, on the other hand, in the Posener texts, the spelling of *Jʿnḳi* has one variant written with three reeds[113]!

Montet points out several orthographic innovations in the Sethe texts, especially with the spelling of the word *rsw.t*, which follows not the orthography of early Twelfth Dynasty texts, which would be expected if Albright's chronology were correct, but that of manu-

---

107 Posener, Chronique d'Égypte 14 (1939), 46; Mélanges Syriens 313f.; Princes et pays 35; W. F. Albright, BASOR 83 (1941), 32; Vincent, RB 51 (1942), 191; Alt, Herkunft der Hyksos, 91f., and R. Dussaud, Nouveaux textes égyptiens d'exécration contre les peuples syriens, Syria 21 (1940), 170.

108 Princes et pays 31. The Mathematical Papyri from Moscow offer a palaeographical transition between the Execration Texts and Bulaq 18. Cf. Posener, Princes et pays, 29, and Struve, Mathematical Papyri in Moskow, 1930, 8f.

109 Posener, Princes et pays, 31.

110 BASOR 81 (1941), 16 n. 2.

111 Cf. e1; *ʾIj-ʿnḳ* with Posener E 36: *Jʿnḳi*.

112 Cf. Posener E 12; *ʾIsipi* (one reed). In Sethe e2 we find the name *ʾIb-ij-mʿmʿw*, using a single reed to designate א and the triple reed to designate not the initial *y* but rather the vowel *i*. The three reeds often occur — particularly in proper names — in the Middle Kingdom as well, and not only in Old Kingdom texts. Cf. Sethe, Ächtung, 45.

113 Posener, Princes et pays, 83.

scripts such as Prisse, which Montet dates as late as the Thirteenth Dynasty[114].

The orthography of the Posener texts is placed by Albright himself closest to several manuscripts from about the time of Sebek-ḥotpe III (1744—1741)[115].

A significant orthographic peculiarity, which helps to determine what the chronology of our texts is, comes from the spelling of the name Byblos. In the Sethe texts we find the rendering *kbn*, a form derived from the end of the Eleventh Dynasty but also found in many Twelfth Dynasty texts[116]. The name appears four times in the Sethe texts, however, with an originally triconsonantal sign, *kꜣp*, given a biconsonantal value: *kp* or *kb*, a peculiar development which is quite rare until the very end of the Twelfth Dynasty[117]. These four texts also add the sign for the letter *y*, rendering Byblos by *kpny*, a spelling which elsewhere first occurs in the inscription of *Ib-šemu-abi*, a contemporary of Amenemes IV (1791—1781)[118]. This reading is also found in the Posener texts along with *kbny* (the form regularly found in early inscriptions, but with the suffix *y*), *kbn*, as well as the sign *kꜣp* which Posener sees as indicating the new pronunciation *kpny*[119]. The orthographic peculiarities of our texts thus indicate a date towards the very end of the Twelfth Dynasty or at the beginning of the Thirteenth Dynasty for both our groups of texts.

The closeness of the chronology of our texts that appears on palaeographic and orthographic grounds is confirmed by an examination of the Nubian sections of both sets of inscriptions. In the list of the princes, the first four regions out of the six listed in the Sethe texts are identical with the first four of five proscribed places in the Posener group. The sixth locality in the Sethe lists (which is not given with the name of any prince) is identical to the

114 P. Montet, Notes et documents pour servir a l'histoire des relations entre l'ancienne Égypte et la Syrie, Kêmi 1 (1928), 21.

115 Albright, JAOS 74 (1954), 224f.; The 18th Century Princes of Byblos and the Chronology of Middle Bronze, BASOR 176 (1964), 43; van Seters (The Hyksos 78) argues convincingly that the earlier character of Sethe's orthography in respect to these late texts is insufficient reason to give a date of 150 to 200 years earlier for the Sethe texts. Rather, it suggests a much later date for the Posener texts than Albright's 1850—1825 B. C.

116 Montet, Kêmi 1 (1928), 20.

117 In Papyrus Kahun, 28.5 and Sinuhe R 53; so, Edgerton, JAOS 60 (1940), 492. See also Sethe, Ächtung, 55f., who points out that the spelling in his texts is exactly the same as that in Sinuhe R. See, however, the Eleventh Dynasty text: Hekananakhte XX B 11/12.

118 Montet, Kêmi 1 (1928), 20; R. Dussaud, Syria 21 (1940), 171; Vincent, RB 51 (1942), 202; and Posener, Princes et Pays, 33.

119 Posener, Princes et Pays, 94.

fifth place given in the Posener list. The only place name from the Sethe list which is not also found in the Posener texts, *Mḏꜣ*, is perhaps not to be understood as an entirely new location, since the land called *ꜣwšḳ* in Sethe a6 and Posener A5 is in the territory with which *Mḏꜣ* people are associated[120]; thus Sethe's a5 and a6 may perhaps together be the counterpart of Posener's A5. In the proscription of Nubian cities the lists in both groups of texts follow the same order and list the same places, except that the Posener texts add eight localities between b4 and b5 of the Sethe texts[121].

Besides the close similarities in the order and structure of these lists, parallels are also noticeable in the names of the princes who are proscribed. Since a5 does not occur in the Posener texts, and since no prince is mentioned in Sethe's a6, in only one out of four possible cases can the personal names not be related, and clearly have nothing to do with each other; i. e., in a4 and A4. It is quite possible that in a3 with the prince *Bʿkwꜣjt* who bears the surname *ṯꜣj* and the prince *ʾIṯꜣw* in A3 we are dealing with the very same person[122]. In a2 the name of the prince *Stḳtnkẖ* (if de Walle's emendation to *St[ꜣ]kẖ*[123] is correct) might well be the same as the father's name of the proscribed prince in Posener's A2: *Stjkẖi*[124]. In a1 of the Sethe texts the name of the prince of *kꜣš*, *ꜣwꜣw* is to be identified with the name of the father of the prince of *kꜣš* in the Posener texts, which is normally written *ꜣwꜣꜣ*, but which has the variant spelling *ꜣwꜣw*[125].

If the above is correct, the Sethe texts are l e s s t h a n a g e n e r a t i o n o l d e r than those published by Posener. Such a possibility is in accordance with the palaeographic data and is confirmed by the orthography of our texts.

A recent discovery of similarly inscribed bowls and figurines from Mirgissa helps to complete our picture[126]. The palaeography of

120 Cf. Sethe, Ächtung, 37.

121 Vincent, RB 51 (1942), 191; Posener, Princes et pays, 54—62.

122 M. Noth, ZDPV 65 (1942), 13 n. 2; Posener, Princes et pays, 51. Certainty is lacking, however, since the parental names are not given in the Posener texts.

123 B. van de Walle, Remarques paléographiques sur les textes de proscription de Berlin, in Posener, Princes et Pays, 99—109, here 101.

124 Cf. esp. Posener, Princes et pays, 50; also Noth, ZDPV 65 (1942), 13 n. 2, Vincent RB 51 (1942), 191 n., and Dussaud, Syria 21 (1940), 170.

125 Posener, Princes et pays, 49. Albright's objection (JAOS 74, 1954, 34), in itself unconvincing, completely ignores the variant reading!

126 See A. Vila, Un dépot de textes envoûtement au Moyen Empire, Journal des Savants (1963), 135—160; J. Vercoutter, La Nubie au sud d'Abousimbel, Journal des Savants (1963), 129—134; Fouilles à Mirgissa, Revue d'Égyptologie 15 (1963), 69—75; Deux mois de fouilles à Mirgissa en Nubie Soudanaise, Bulletin de la Société d'Égyptologie 37/38 (1963), 28f.; Textes Exécratoires de Mirgissa, CRAI (1963), 97—102; Collections égyptiennes et soudanaises de l'Institut de Papyro-

these new texts is that of the Twelfth Dynasty[127]. On the basis of archaeological similarities such as the type of ware, as well as the order, composition and formulation of the texts, Posener is led to date these new texts to the same period as the Sethe finds[128]. Some minor indications, such as the use of vertical writing on some bowls, may suggest that these bowls are slightly earlier than the Sethe texts; however, this may just as well be a local or archaizing peculiarity of the Mirgissa texts[129].

Very little time can separate the Mirgissa texts from Sethe's inscriptions, since, according to Posener, the Nubian section of the Mirgissa inscriptions may mention some of the princes found in the Sethe texts:

> Dans la section nubienne, deux roitelets portent les mêmes noms à Mirgissa et à Berlin; il s'agit, sans discussion possible, des mêmes personnes puisque leurs parents sont identiques et que l'un des princes possède exactement le même surnom dans les deux cas. Pour un autre pays africain, le dynaste est différent dans les deux séries de textes, mais le nom de la mère est identique et celui du père, incomplet à Berlin, a la même longueur et se termine par le même signe de part et d'autre: il est raisonnable de penser qu'on a affaire à des frères qui se sont succédé sur le trône[130].

Similarly in the Asiatic section of the Mirgissa texts the prince of *'Iinq* in Mirgissa e2 is called *'Ibiiimmw* which is apparently the same name as that given to the prince of this place in the Sethe texts: *'Ib-ij-m'm'w* (Sethe e2)! It appears, then, that the Sethe and the Mirgissa texts are to be dated within the same generation, though not exactly contemporary. If the Mirgissa texts are earlier than Sethe, the three sets of texts must still be dated within less than two generations of each other.

---

logie et d'Égyptologie de Lille, 1964; Excavations at Mirgissa I, Kush 12 (1964), 61. Some of the texts are given in translation by G. Posener, Syria 43 (1966), 277—287. See further, J. van Seter's remarks: The Hyksos 79 n. A complete study of these texts has not yet been published. That the Mirgissa inscriptions are written on both bowls and figurines shows clearly that the distinction that the Sethe texts are written on bowls and the Posener texts are written on figurines is without any chronological significance.

127 Posener, Syria 43 (1966), 279.

128 Ibid. 279—283.

129 Albright's attempt to date these texts half-way between the Sethe and Posener texts, at the beginning of the nineteenth century (BASOR 184, 1966, 28 n.; Yahweh and the Gods of Canaan, 47f. n. 3) is completely arbitrary and without foundation. That figurines similar to the Posener figurines are also found at Mirgissa merely confirms the close contemporaneity of all our texts. See above note 126.

130 Syria 43 (1966), 285.

When all of the above material is taken into consideration, the earliest conceivable date for any of the Execration Texts seems to be about 1850 B. C. and the latest date about 1760 B. C., though both these dates are extreme. The more probable dates would seem to be c. 1810—1770 B. C., that is, from the latter part of the reign of Amenemes III to the beginning of the Thirteenth Dynasty[131]. On the basis of the chronology alone it becomes extremely difficult to identify the Early West Semites of the Execration Texts with either the *ʿꜣmw* of the First Intermediate Period of Egypt or the proposed immigrating nomads of the Middle Bronze I Period of Palestine. Such an identification would demand that we bridge a chronological gap of about two centuries.

E. THE EXECRATION TEXTS AND THE POLITICAL ORGANIZATION OF PALESTINE AT THE END OF THE TWELFTH DYNASTY

An examination of the content of the Execration Texts offers little confirmation to those attempts which find a process of sedentarization in Palestine at this time which developed into the Middle Bronze II culture, on the basis of a comparison of the levels of culture presupposed by the earlier and later sets of texts. Whether the Execration Texts reflect the rising power of the Palestinian city-states[132], or the Egyptian interest to protect their trade routes in the North[133], is by no means clear. That, however, there is no fundamental political or sociological distinction between the two sets of texts that can be ascertained[134], and that in both texts we are dealing with a settled culture centered around major population centers[135] is without doubt.

Nomadism (whether full nomadism, semi-nomadism in the sense of ass nomadism, or seasonal nomadism)[136] is an economic and socio-

[131] This excludes on one hand the very high dating of W. F. Albright (c. 1925—1825 B. C.) and the very low dating of B. Mazar on the other (Posener texts = MB IIB); it corresponds closely with the dates given by Helck (Die Beziehungen Ägyptens zu Vorderasien im 3. und 2. Jahrtausend v. Chr., Ägyptologische Abhandlungen 5, 1962, 49 and 53) and Ward (Egypt and the East Mediterranean in the Early Second Millenium B. C., Orientalia 30, 1961, 141). The chronology of J. van Seters (1790-1750: The Hyksos 78f.) appears a little too low, and does not seem to take the palaeographical evidence sufficiently into consideration.

[132] J. van Seters, The Hyksos, 80. [133] Helck, Beziehungen, 63f. [134] Ibid. 62.

[135] Van Seters, The Hyksos, 80. Whether they are fortified cities, however, is not clear.

[136] Shepherds who are closely connected and dependent on a sedentary culture and directly related to specific villages and towns cannot be distinguished archaeologically from villagers and should not be understood as nomads.

logically descriptive term, and describes a culture which is to be contrasted with a settled farming culture. It is not to be equated with tribal living which is a political structure that has existed among settled populations as well. The occurrence of tribal groups does not necessarily point to a nomadic culture nor a nomadic past. It is significant that when we examine the Execration Texts we find as much evidence for tribal structures in the Posener texts as we do in the Sethe texts. We also have adequate evidence from both sets of texts that we are dealing with a sedentary culture centered in town life.

That we are dealing with permanent settlements even in the Sethe texts and not merely with temporary camping sites is first of all obvious from the names of these settlements, some of which belong to the major cities of Palestine of later periods, such as Jerusalem, Ashkelon and Byblos. Nor is this exceptional, for of the nineteen Palestinian place names found in the Sethe texts, fifteen of them reappear in the Posener lists a generation later[137]. We have no reason to believe that the four places which do not appear in the Posener texts no longer exist, just as we have no reason for saying that the sites which are mentioned for the first time in Posener are newly founded. The texts reflect, after all, Egyptian concerns about Palestine rather than an objective and complete description of Palestine itself. While three of the four places that are found in Sethe alone are as yet unidentified, the fourth site *mut-i-r* still is in existence at the time of Rameses II *(mú-ta-r)*[138], and therefore in all likelihood existed at the time of the writing of the Posener texts[139]. Some observations make it clear that the sites mentioned in the Posener texts, but not found in the texts of Sethe, are not newly founded. The place name in Posener E1, *Ḥꜣim* occurs in the Sinai inscriptions from the time of Amenemes III (1839—1791) where "20 Asiatics from *Ḥꜣmi*" are mentioned[140]. More important is the place name from Posener E6, *Skmimi* which is surely to be identified with the *ŚKMM* mentioned in the Sebek-khu stele. An Egyptian campaign against this place was undertaken during the reign of Sesostris III (1876—1839). If the chronology for the Execration Texts which we have given is at all correct, then these settlements must have existed at the time of the Sethe inscriptions. Furthermore, the

137 See the comparative lists in Helck, Beziehungen, 62. Helck leaves out Byblos.

138 and is probably to be identified with the present day Mutariye, 17 km. East of El-Batrun. Helck, Beziehungen, 52.

139 A. van den Born and J. Simons, Syrisch-palästinische Ortsnamen in ägyptischen Texten in Bibellexikon List I, xiv—xv. Here *Ušu* is listed as if occurring in the Sethe texts but not in the Posener texts. This name does not occur in Sethe. In Posener a land *ꜣwsj* appears (E 59), but this is probably to be identified with the *Rws* of the Thutmosis III list.

140 Gardiner-Peet no. 110.

new texts from Mirgissa which, as we have seen, are to be dated only a few years from the Sethe texts and could be later than the Sethe texts, mention only five sites for Palestine and Syria in contrast to Sethe's nineteen different locations[141]. Obviously, no conclusions regarding the limitations of Palestinian settlement can be drawn from the Execration Texts.

Whether the peculiarity of the Sethe and the Mirgissa texts of listing some places several times, each time with a different prince, is to be explained along with Helck[142] as referring to several generations of rulers, with Alt[143] as evidence of territorial divisions of the sort that occur in the Posener texts between "Upper" and "Lower" or "North" and "South", with Sethe[144] as proof of a type of collegial or tribal rule, or in some other manner is a moot question. However, a close comparison of our texts does not allow the conclusion suggested by Albright, on the basis of the number of princes given for any particular site, that we have between the Sethe and the Posener texts a transition from a tribal organization to a city-state organization of society, and consequently evidence for a process of sedentarization[145]. That more caution must be used in discussing this material, so that we not confuse the peculiarities of rather unique Egyptian texts with Palestinian politics, can be seen, for example, in the Sethe texts: e23 to e25. While four of the manuscripts (2, 17, 18 and 22) mention the same site three times and give three different names for their princes, seven manuscripts (1, 7, 8, 11, 16, 59 and 60) mention only two princes[146]. The same site is given in the Posener texts (E2) with only one prince named.

Albright's description of the differences between the different bodies of texts is not quite as convincing as it first appears. In only four cases where we have the name of a town, with some indication as to the number of princes, does the pattern of multiple listings in Sethe in contrast to only a single listing in Posener follow[147]! A fifth

---

141 Posener, Syria 43 (1966), 285—287.

142 Helck, Beziehungen, 67.

143 Alt, ZDPV 64 (1941), 37. Alt's position seems to me to be more likely.

144 Sethe, Ächtung, 43f.

145 Albright, JPOS 8 (1928), 253; 15 (1935), 220f.; BASOR 81 (1941), 18 n. 9; Archaeology of Palestine, 83; JAOS 74 (1954), 34; and BASOR 184 (1966), 28f. It should be again stressed here that the same argument which Albright used in 1928 (JPOS 8, 252ff.) to show that Byblos did not have a tribal structure is used in 1966 (BASOR 184, 28f.) and 1968 (Yahweh and the Gods of Canaan, 232i) to show that it did not have a prince and must have had a tribal structure.

146 Sethe, Ächtung, 53.

147 So: *ʾIꜣḥbw* in e11—12, f 8 *ʾIꜣḥbwm* in E 14
ʾIsinw in e13—15, f10 *ʾIsinw* in E 3

case is perhaps *'Ij-sipi* for which the Sethe texts give the plural sign under the word *ḥḳꜣ* ("prince"), however the site is only listed once and no names of princes are given[148]. The Posener texts also list this place only once with the name of one prince[149]. *Ḳhrmw*, listed with three princes in the Sethe texts[150], occurs in the Posener texts in the form of a southern and a northern *ḳhrmw*, each with its own prince[151]. *Šwtw*, also with three princes in the Sethe texts[152], appears in Posener as Upper and Lower *Šwtw*, with a distinct prince for each division. However, the Mirgissa texts, which may perhaps be our earliest texts, attribute only one prince to *Šwtw*[153]! While both Mirgissa and Sethe list Byblos under the general listings "All the *ʿꜣmw* of..."[154], the Posener texts refer to the "tribes of Byblos" (*wḥjt* with the plural sign)[155]. In E 50 and E 51 of the Posener texts, we have two princes listed as rulers of the site *Kwšw* (which does not occur in the Sethe texts). These rulers, moreover, do not bear the title of "prince" *(ḥḳꜣ)* but rather *wr n wḥjt*, "The sheikh of *Kwšw*". Also very instructive is the case of the toponym *'Ijʿnḳ*, which in the Mirgissa texts is listed three times with the names of three different princes[156], and again a fourth time with the phrase "all the princes of *'Iiinq*"[157]. In Sethe this place name also appears three times with the names of three different rulers[158], but in Posener it is listed with the name of a single prince[159]. In Posener E 64, however, we find: "All the princes of *Jʿnḳi*"! This clearly shows us that E 36 does not list all the princes which the Egyptians considered to be in *Jʿnḳi*, and consequently proves that when only one prince is given for a given place in the Posener texts this does not mean that there was only one prince for that site or that the Egyptians thought there was only one. Even more conclusive are the references to *ʿꜣḳtm* for which the Sethe texts give us the name of only one

'Isḳꜣnw in e23—25, f15	*'Isḳꜣi* in E 2
ꜣwšꜣmm in e27—28, f18	*ꜣwšꜣmm* in E 45

148 Cf. Sethe, e31 and f21.

149 *'Isipi*, E 12.

150 e8—10, f7.

151 E 39 and E 40. The same division is found with two other places found in the Posener texts which do not occur in Sethe: *Mrḏḥkj* in E 23—24 and *'Ipwm* in E 33—34.

152 e4—6, f5.

153 Posener, Syria 43 (1966), 286: e4.

154 Ibid. f2 and Sethe, Ächtung, f2.

155 E 63.

156 Syria 43 (1966), e1—3.

157 Ibid. e6.

158 Sethe, Ächtung, e1—3, f4.

159 E 36.

prince[160], as does E 54 of the Posener texts. But Posener E 61 reads: "the tribes (*wḥjt* with plural designation) of *ʿɜḳti*".

The incomplete character of the Egyptian Execration Texts is perhaps best exemplified by comparing E 37 with E 62, both from the Posener inscriptions and both dealing with the land *Mkj* which appears neither in the Mirgissa nor in the Sethe texts. On one hand E 37 reads, "the prince (*ḥḳɜ*) of *Mkj* . . .", and on the other hand E 61 has "The sheikhs (*wrw* with plural designation) of *Mkj*"! What one "learns" about the political structure of Palestine from one text is entirely contradicted by the other. Clearly, we cannot learn on the basis of the Posener texts whether the proscribed sites in Palestine have a tribal and "nomadic" or a royal city-state political structure because the Egyptian scribes did not attempt to make such distinctions. It is all the more illegitimate to argue on the basis of a comparison of the Sethe and the Posener texts that a process of gradual sedentarization occurred between the time of the earlier and the later set of inscriptions.

It seems safe to conclude that the Execration Texts cannot be legitimately used as evidence for an immediate migration of semi-nomadic West Semites into Palestine in the early Second Millenium.

160 Sethe, Ächtung, 22e, f12.

Chapter 6

Egypt and the Amorite Question

A. THE INCURSION OF THE AMORITES INTO THE EASTERN DELTA

With the publication of the texts[1] and translations[2] of the Instructions to Merikarê and the Prophecy of Neferty, the suggestion Gardiner first made in his publication of the Admonitions of Ipuwer[3] that the First Intermediate Period witnessed major historical incursions of Asiatics into the Eastern Delta became widely accepted[4]. These three texts have continued to be the main sources around which this interpretation has been constructed; numerous other references in early Egyptian texts to Asiatics, especially in the Sethe Execration Texts[5], the Tale of Sinuhe[6], and the now famous painting from tomb 3 at Beni-Hasan[7], have been seen as fully supporting this thesis.

H. Frankfort, in an article published in 1926, brought together, in support of this interpretation, archaeological evidence for many Syrian related button seals which first appear in Egypt, according to Frankfort, during the Sixth Dynasty about the time of Pepi II, as well as the Inscription of Uni which mentions five expeditions against the land of the Asiatics during the reign of Pepi I[8]. On the

[1] W. Golénischeff, Les Papyrus Hiératiques no. 1115, 1116A, et 1116B de l'Ermitage Impérial à St. Pétersbourg, 1913.

[2] A. H. Gardiner, New Literary Works from Ancient Egypt, JEA 1 (1914), 20—36, and 100—106.

[3] A. H. Gardiner, The Admonitions of an Egyptian Sage, 1909, 111.

[4] Gardiner, JEA 1 (1914), 106. Here Gardiner speaks of the "period between the Middle and New Kingdoms", what seems from the context to be an obvious error for "the period between the Old and Middle Kingdoms". Erman, indeed, objected to Gardiner's interpretation rather strenuously at first in his comments on the Admonitions (Die Mahnworte eines ägyptischen Propheten, SBPAW 42, 1919, 809—815), but later he speaks of this interpretation as being historically possible (Die Literatur der Ägypter, 1923, 131).

[5] K. Sethe, Die Ächtung feindlicher Fürsten, Völker u. Dinge auf Altägyptischen Tongefässscherben des Mittleren Reiches, APAW 1926); but see my discussion of these texts in ch. 5 above.

[6] A. H. Gardiner, Notes on the Story of Sinuhe, 1916.

[7] P. E. Newberry, Beni Hasan I, 1893, plates xxx, xxxi, and xxxviii.

[8] H. Frankfort, Egypt and Syria in the First Intermediate Period, JEA 12 (1926), 80—99.

basis of the button seals, he concludes that the value of the Admonitions of Ipuwer (which was thought to refer to the time of Pepi II)[9] as an "historical document" was established[10]. He concluded from this evidence that "we are dealing with a major disruption of the entire Near East by the Amorites" and a "Syrian influx" into Egypt[11]. In the Inscription of Uni, he sees how already "under Pepi I's reign, the first waves come breaking on the eastern border (of Egypt), with anything but decreasing force"[12]. After such strong statements, it can hardly be surprising that Scharff would conclude from the Instructions to Merikarê that Egypt saw in the Ninth Dynasty an Asiatic occupation of the Delta; he suggests that this had already been begun during the reign of Pepi I[13]. Recently, this interpretation has been continued in the new edition of the Cambridge Ancient History where it has been related to materials from Mesopotamia and Palestine and placed into the context of widespread Amorite movements which were understood to involve the entire Near East during the period c. 2160—1780 B. C.[14]. Posener, who discusses the Egyptian material, bases his interpretation largely upon the Admonitions of Ipuwer and the Instructions to Merikarê, using other early Egyptian records to support his interpretation[15]. From the Admonitions, he sees evidence for a breakdown in trade between Palestine and Syria, and a weakening of the defenses along the Egyptian frontier, caused by internal disorder which resulted in a movement of Asiatics "in force into the Eastern Delta"[16]. He speaks of these Asiatics as „invaders", and on the basis of the Instructions, concludes that they are nomads who had come to Egypt from Palestine[17]. From the Prophecy of Neferty, he concludes that there must have been a repetition of this invasion during the Eleventh Dynasty, though he sees in the Prophecy also

---

[9] Erman, SBPAW 42 (1919), 813.

[10] Frankfort, JEA 12 (1926), 96.

[11] Ibid. 94f.

[12] Ibid. 88.

[13] A. Scharff, Über einige fremdartige Darstellungen auf Siegelbildern aus dem späten Alten Reich und der ersten Zwischenzeit, ZÄS 67 (1931), 101f. Interestingly, Scharff, who sees a very close relationship ("in engstem Zusammenhang") between the invasion of the "Asiatics" and the button seals spoken of by Frankfort, dates the introduction of these seals into Egypt to the reign of Pepi I (in contrast to Frankfort's dating them to the reign of Pepi II), apparently under the influence of the date for the Uni inscription.

[14] Posener, Bottéro and Kenyon, Syria and Palestine, c. 2160—1780, CAH², fascicle 29, vol. 1, ch. 21, 1965.

[15] Ibid. 3—8.

[16] Ibid. 3.

[17] Ibid. 4f.

a reflection of the invasion of the First Intermediate Period[18]. He points out the similarities of these movements to the Amorite movements in Mesopotamia; however, he does not feel that the evidence is adequate to show that we are dealing with the same people[19].

Kathleen Kenyon, on the other hand, writing in this same chapter of the Cambridge Ancient History on the archaeological material from Palestine for this period, does assert this identification, and sees a widespread movement of West Semitic nomads coming out of the Syrian desert into the settled regions around the Fertile Crescent, beginning in the region of Akkad about the time of Sargon, but not reaching the Syrian coast until after the time of Pepi II. In Egypt, this period of nomadic disruption is seen to extend from the time of Pepi II to the time of Sesostris I, and to some extent down to the time of Sesostris III. Its greatest effect is, however, on Palestine, where "From at least the twenty-fourth to the twentieth centuries B. C., Syria and Palestine were overrun by nomads, amongst whom the Amorites predominated, with a culminating period of complete nomadic control in the two centuries c. 2181—1991 B. C."[20].

This picture of Egyptian history has been defended by many Palestinian archaeologists and Biblical historians because it is seen to reflect and support what they understand about the transitional EB IV/MB I Period in Palestine. Kathleen Kenyon sums up this view of the First Intermediate Period very succinctly in her Archaeology of the Holy Land: "In 2294 B. C. (new dating following the Cambridge Ancient History: 2185) the Old Empire of Egypt fell before the attacks of Asiatic invaders, and the period known as the First Intermediate began. Such a period ranks with the Dark Age of Europe . . ."[21] and: "Palestine . . . received a great invasion of nomadic groups in the last centuries of the Second (Third!) Millenium, which completely blotted out the preceding urban civilization of the Early Bronze Age. E g y p t s u f f e r e d t h e s a m e f a t e. The Sixth Dynasty of Egypt came to an end . . . and Egypt was invaded by barbarians, some at least of them Asiatics. Peaceful conditions were not restored until Egypt was once more reunited under the Twelfth Dynasty . . ."[22].

---

[18] Ibid. 7f.

[19] Ibid. 6.

[20] Ibid. 58—61; quotation from 61. This same picture is presented very briefly in K. Kenyon, Amorites and Canaanites, 1966, 8.

[21] 1960, 135.

[22] Ibid. 159 (emphasis added). For similar statements cf. G. E. Wright, Biblical Archaeology, 1957, 45—49; J. Bright, History of Israel, 1959, 36. 44f. (The only significant difference in Bright's interpretation is that he would place the patriarchs in the Twelfth Dynasty; his understanding of the First Intermediate Period is substantially the same). See also, E. Anati, Palestine before the

There are three important theses around which this interpretation has developed: 1) That the Asiatics mentioned in the Egyptian texts of the First Intermediate Period, especially those who are called *ʿ3mw*, are at least in some general sense to be identified with the *Amurrū* of the Mesopotamian texts and the Amorites of the Old Testament. 2) That these people have come down into Egypt from Asia, most immediately from Palestine; and 3) That they form a new group of nomadic peoples in Egypt, who played a significant role in the breakup of the Old Kingdom.

B. THE *ʿ3MW* AND THE *AMURRŪ*

No objection can be made on onomastic grounds to the assumption that there is an ethnic similarity between the "Asiatics" found in Egypt and the Early West Semites mentioned in the Execration Texts or in the Thirteenth Dynasty Egyptian list of slaves from Palestine. The few names that we have from the Egyptian groups are either Egyptian in character, or West Semitic (e. g., *ibš3*, the *ʿ3mw* prince portrayed in the tomb painting at Beni-Hasan)[23].

That the term *ʿ3m* itself, however, can be etymologically related to the term *amurrū* and the Hebrew אמרי is not without its difficulties. It does seem phonetically possible, however, if unlikely: *ʿ3mw*〉 ערמו[24], by metathesis to עמרו〉 אמרו/*Amurrū*[25].

In considering this possible derivation, it should not be forgotten that the term *amurrū* is not West Semitic; nor did it originate as the *amurrū*'s description of themselves. It is the Akkadian word for "west" or "western" which was used for some of the Early West Semites in Mesopotamia[26]. This derivation of the term *ʿ3mw* presupposes that the term, once taken over by the (or some of the) West Semites, was brought from Mesopotamia to Egypt. It assumes not a general ethnic relationship, but a direct historical continuity between the two regions.

Other possible West Semitic derivations that have been suggested are *ʿ3m*〉 ערם〉 ערב, "Arab" or "Bedouin", which has been supported

Hebrews, 1963, 362—373; Y. Yadin, The Art of Warfare in Biblical Lands, 1963, 57; R. de Vaux, Les patriarches hébreux et l'histoire, RB 72 (1965), 11f.; J. Holt, The Patriarchs of Israel, 1964, 175f.; and J. C. L. Gibson, Light from Mari on the Patriarchs, JSS 7 (1962), 47.

23 ANET 29.

24 In the Execration Texts *3* is regularly used for Semitic ר or ל.

25 I am indebted to Professor W. Röllig of Tübingen for part of the here suggested etymology.

26 Cf. above, ch. 2—4.

by G. Posener[27], or a relationship to the Hebrew word עם "people" which Sethe sees as most probable[28]. Posener rightfully objects to this, however, because it ignores the *ꜣ* in *ʿꜣm*[29].

Much more probable seems to be the derivation which was long ago suggested by W. M. Müller, which is thoroughly unobjectionable and fits the textual and historical context admirably, that the word *ʿꜣm* is not Semitic at all but Egyptian, derived from the identically written word *ʿꜣm* "boomerang" or "throwing stick". Thus *ʿꜣmw* = "boomerang throwers"[30]. This etymology is supported by the orthography; for the abbreviated forms of the word *ʿꜣmw* generally include the boomerang sign. In later texts, this boomerang sign is extended to designate barbarians of various sorts: boomerang + *m* = *ʿꜣmw*, boomerang + *ś* = *nḥś* "negro", and boomerang + *nw* = *tḥnw* "Libyans"[31].

Boomerangs or throwing sticks are also found to be among the weapons used by some of the *ʿꜣmw* in early pictures of them, such as the group portrayed in tomb no. 3 at Beni-Hasan[32].

In further support of this Egyptian derivation, and in partial objection to the proposed derivation from the Akkadian *amurrū*, it is perhaps significant that the earliest witnesses of the term *ʿꜣmw* are, as we shall see, used in reference to groups which have a certain or probable location in or near Egypt, and that only in the Twelfth Dynasty is the term used for the peoples of Palestine and Syria, thus suggesting that the meaning "Asiatics" used in any literal sense may be derivative, and that an originally sociological and perhaps (from the Egyptian point of view) ethnic designation, referring to certain groups living in the eastern highlands and desert regions, was gradually extended to include Semites of all sorts[33].

---

27 G. Posener, Princes et Pays d'Asie et de Nubie, 1940, 42.

28 Ächtung 27.

29 Princes et Pays, 42; see also W. Max Mueller, Asien und Europa nach Altägyptischen Denkmälern, 1893, 123.

30 Mueller ibid. 121—125, here 123. See also, B. Gunn and A. H. Gardiner, New Renderings of Egyptian Texts, JEA 5 (1918), 37.

31 Mueller ibid. 125.

32 Newberry, Beni Hasan I, pl. xxx.

33 A thorough historical and philological study of the four related terms: *Iwn.tyw*, which is generally used for peoples of the desert east of Heliopolis but also for groups as far south as Nubia; *Mnṯw*, generally used for the people of Sinai; *sṯ.tyw*, used most often for the peoples of Palestine and Syria; and *ḥrj.w šʿ* used for some peoples in the Eastern Desert and along the Red Sea, would certainly help towards an understanding of the *ʿꜣmw*. The major difficulty is that already by the time of the Twelfth Dynasty, the four terms are frequently used interchangeably. Some clarification of these terms can be found in W. Helck, Die Beziehungen Ägyptens zu Vorderasien im 3. und 2. Jahrtausend v. Chr., AgAbh 5, 1962, 14—18.

C. THE "ASIATICS" OF THE EASTERN DESERT

While the most decisive text for the thesis that the *ʿꜣmw* of the First Intermediate Period had come from the region of Palestine and Syria has been the Instructions to Merikarê[34], the most influential single record, in the general discussion about the "Amorites" in Egypt and their relation to the biblical patriarchs has certainly been the Beni-Hasan tomb painting[35]. It is an influence which began with the earliest egyptologist's description of the painting[36]. It has been commonly asserted that the *ʿꜣmw n šw* pictured in tomb 3 at Beni-Hasan had come from Palestine or Transjordan, first of all, because of the identification of *šw* with the biblical name בני שת which is normally identified with the Moabites, but just as much because the *ʿꜣmw* have been identified with the *amurrū* and the "Amorites" of the Palestinian EB IV/MB I Period[37], and also because of the general effort to relate this painting as closely as possible to the biblical traditions. This interpretation was further aided by the general vagueness that exists about archaeological chronologies, which has allowed the mixing together of several different kinds of data on the assumption of a supposed contemporaneity. Once these correlations were generally accepted, the interpretation of the Beni-Hasan tomb painting expanded in direct proportion to the successive interpretations of the *amurrū* and of Palestinian archaeology[38].

[34] For a discussion of this, see below, section E.

[35] A wall painting in tomb 3 discovered at Beni-Hasan describing a group of 37 *ʿꜣmw n šw* presenting themselves at the border of Egypt in the sixth year of the reign of Sesostris II (c. 1890 B. C.). For the original publication of the picture and the accompanying text, see C. R. Lepsius, Denkmäler aus Ägypten und Äthiopien, 1849, II, 133. Translations can be found in ANET 29 and in AER I 281d. Cf. Newberry, Beni Hasan I, plates xxx, xxxi, and xxxviii. For the text see 69; also K. Sethe, Historisch-biographischen Urkunden des Mittleren Reiches I, Urkunden VII, 1935, 36f.

[36] As noted by Breasted in AER I 281.

[37] Based on references to *ʿꜣmw* in the Execration Texts.

[38] It is particularly interesting to note the variety of interpretations given this in more recent literature: In 1946, W. F. Albright (From the Stone Age to Christianity 121), comparing the people portrayed in the picture with the "Amorite nomads" of the EB IV/MB I Period, described the picture as portraying "a nomadic chieftain named Absha with his clansmen and their families". Again in 1949 (The Archaeology of Palestine 207) he refers to the picture as showing a "small clan of semi-nomadic tribesmen from Palestine in the early Patriarchal Age". He thinks of them as travelling metal workers, "something like the tinkers of later times". (208). In 1953, however, he altered his interpretation somewhat by saying that the "Asiatics" portrayed at Beni-Hasan probably represent a group similar to "the early Hebrew tribes of the Negev, south of Palestine proper", who were periodically "forced to abandon their country both during the dry season and during long arid periods". (Archaeology and the Religion of Israel, 1953, 98). He connects this with the patriarchal narra-

The thesis that these people came from southern Transjordan, based on the similarity between the supposedly archaic biblical name

---

tives by saying that it is this state of society which is reflected in Genesis, which describes the patriarchs moving back and forth between the Negev and the hill country of Central Palestine in what must have become regular seasonal movements (ibid.). Albright's interpretation of Beni-Hasan at this time corresponds with his view of the patriarchs as semi-nomads. By 1961, however, Albright had changed his interpretation of the type of life led by the patriarchs and, accordingly, he altered his interpretation of the Beni-Hasan painting (Abram the Hebrew. A New Archaeological Interpretation, BASOR 163, 1961, 40). He now speaks of them as a small band of "Asiatics" led by a desert chieftain, who had come into Egypt from the land of *šwt* (which he places in Transjordan) to trade (ibid.). Although he had stated in 1961 that these people "can hardly be considered as a typical caravan" (ibid. 42), in 1963 he uses this painting as evidence of "very active trade" between Palestine and Egypt. He describes the scene in the tomb painting as a "visit to Upper Egypt by a little caravan of travelling Semitic smiths and musicians". (The Biblical Period from Abraham to Ezra, 1963, 4). Most recently (Yahweh and the Gods of Canaan, 1968, 234), he gives added support to his identification of the land of *šwt* as being in Transjordan.

Over the past twenty years, we find the students of Albright, particularly G. E. Wright and H. M. Orlinsky, presenting in their work similar interpretations of the tomb painting. Orlinsky, in 1956, supported the connection of the patriarchal stories with the Beni-Hasan painting, particularly emphasizing the objects which were carried by the people; they are, he claims, all characteristic of semi-nomadic groups (Ancient Israel, 1956, 23f.). G. E. Wright, in his Biblical Archaeology, contents himself with merely pointing out that there is a parallel between the Beni-Hasan group and the biblical patriarchs "approximately contemporary with Abram and shows how he and his family must have looked" (46). He describes them as semi-nomads, emphasizing their physical characteristics, their clothing, and the tools and weapons they carry. He also connects them with the *amurrū* of the Mesopotamian texts (ibid. 47).

Among other scholars writing on this topic, I only point out here three whose opinions seem to comprise most of the significant variations of interpretation. B. Vawter's interpretation (A Path Through Genesis, 1965, 123) is eclectic, using Wright's language (Cf. Biblical Archaeology 46): "If one would know what Abraham and his caravan looked like, he can gain an idea from the rather well known illustration on page 124." He adopts Albright's interpretation, however, seeing both Abraham and the Beni-Hasan people as caravaneers (ibid.). R. de Vaux, in his interpretation, affirms the general certainty about the relevancy of the parallel; he also betrays the general confusion about what the material means: "Dans une tombe de Beni Hassan, une scène célèbre peint en couleurs vives une caravane de Bédouins (sic!). Sinuhe est accueilli par l'un de ces clans, fixé au sol, adonné à l'élevage et à la culture." (Les patriarches hébreux et les découvertes modernes, RB 53, 1946, 342).

While many of the commentaries seem to be confusing and contradictory, N. Glueck interprets the painting with simplicity, clearly and unequivocally. It is, for him, positive evidence for travel through the Negev: "They had to cross the Negev to get there." (Rivers in the Desert, 1950, 104).

for the Moabites, בני שת and the land *šw*[39], is extremely weak; for not only is the reading of the place name in the Beni-Hasan painting uncertain[40], but the biblical term is hardly more specific than a translation "sons of the desert" would suggest. A region called *šwtw* is mentioned in the Execration Texts[41], and Dussaud, in his discussion of the Sethe Texts, attempts to locate this region in Syria[42]. A similar name occurs in the Amarna letter 185 (line 37) in the form *šûtû*, and perhaps also in letter 197 (line 29) in the form *šaddu*. Vincent locates *šûtû* in Northern Galilee, commenting:

> On en peut déduire que *šûtû* est une désignation régionale, plutôt qu'un nom de localité. Dans cette perspective, et bien que ni Sethe, ni Dussaud n'en aient fait état, le rapprochement de *šwtw* avec *šûtû* qui revient si fréquemment dans les lettres d'el-Amarna, pour désigner les tribus nomades du désert syrien, parait s'imposer[43].

It seems possible that *šwtw* of the Execration Texts, *šûtû* of the Amarna tablets, as well as בני שת, and *šw* or *šwt* of the Beni-Hasan painting, have all the same vague general derivation, but are otherwise unrelated desert regions. In Egyptian the word *šw* is usually translated "dry" or "desert"[44]. The term *ḫ3śwt, ḫ3śt*, seems to have the primary meaning "hill country" or "highland" (i. e., the Eastern Desert of Egypt), and only by extension "foreign country"[45]. At least, it is clear that the appearance of the name is not by itself adequate to justify so specific an identification of the place *šw* with Transjordan.

Indeed, an examination of the tomb painting in its context makes such an assertion completely untenable. The text clearly points out[46] that the reason for the entry of the *ʿ3mw* on this occasion was

---

39 See especially Albright, BASOR 163 (1961), 40f.; Yahweh and the Gods 233f. and Helck, Beziehungen, 46.

40 So Wilson in ANET 229 n. Wilson renders the name tentatively as "shut". Newberry, however, reads *šw* (Beni-Hasan I 69).

41 Sethe e4, e5, and e6; Posener E 52, and E 53.

42 R. Dussaud, Nouveaux renseignements sur la Palestine et la Syrie vers 2000 avant notre ère, Syria 8 (1927), 220f.

43 Les pays bibliques et l'Égypte à la Fin de la XIIe Dynastie Égyptienne, Vivre et Penser II (RB), 1942/43, 200.

44 Breasted, AER I, 281d; Albright, Yahweh and the Gods, 234; A. H. Gardiner, Egyptian Grammar, 1927, 572.

45 Gardiner ibid. 477 no. 25. *śt* is the determinative for "desert"; see also: H. Gauthier, Dictionnaire des Noms Géographiques Contenus dans les Textes Hiéroglyphiques V, 1928, 130f.: "Chout (Beni Hassan = ... die Wüste)."

46 *rḥt n ʿ3mw n s3 ḥ3q-Ḫnmḥtp ḥr mśdmt ʿ3mw n šw (šwt or šw ḫ3śt) rḥt iri xxxvii*: "The list of Amu brought to the son of the *ha*-prince, Chnemhotep, on account of the *mśdm.t*: Amu of Shu, number of them: 37." (Newberry, Beni Hasan I, 69 = Urk. VII 30f.).

to bring *mśdm.t* "galena" (i. e., lead sulphide), an Egyptian eye cosmetic, into Egypt[47]. Galena can be mined in the mountains bordering on the Red Sea, both in Egypt and in southern Sinai. What galena there was in Egypt was worked exclusively for eye paint. Other galena was also imported from western Asia, Punt, and Coptos[48]. On the other hand, deposits are notably poor in Palestine, Syria, and Arabia, and these regions had to import lead. Consequently, black eye paint does not seem to have become common there until after 1400 B. C.[49]!

That these people are travelling metal workers as suggested by Albright[50] and Orlinsky[51] cannot be altogether excluded, since the processing of lead sulphide is a necessary aspect in the production of eye paint. Yet, since this suggestion is based on what seems to be a fanciful identification of the strange object prominently portrayed on the back of the second donkey, and the similar object carried by another donkey, as bellows, it is hardly justified. If the objects were bellows, they would have just two handles on one end of the sack[52].

Since these people are twice specifically described in the accompanying text as bringing eyepaint into Egypt, any interpretation which describes them as semi-nomads who periodically entered Egypt to feed their flocks (though this may be a valid description of other *ʿȝmw*) has no direct justification. While it may be difficult to determine whether they are engaged in the processing, transporting, or

---

47 Since stibium or stibnite is used for black eye paint only in relatively late times, here *mśdmt* must refer to the natural ore "galena", i. e., lead sulphide. Evidence for this is from eye paints taken from tombs. R. H. Forbes, Studies in Ancient Technology, III 18. J. R. Harris, Lexicographical Studies in Ancient Egyptian Minerals, Deutsche Akademie der Wissenschaften zu Berlin, Institut für Orientforschung Nr. 54, 1961, 174f. The material was ground into a powder, then mixed with water or a solution of some water-soluble gum into a paste ready for application (Forbes ibid. 19).

48 Ibid. 18. Black eye paint was extremely valuable in Egypt since it was a much-sought-for medical remedy against eye diseases (ibid.) and was also used to stop bleeding (Singer et alii, A History of Technology, 1965, I 293), as well as for cosmetic purposes. The black cosmetic was painted on the upper lids. A green paint, *wȝdw* "malachite" (a copper compound), was used on the lower lids up until the time of the Nineteenth Dynasty (Forbes loc. cit., but see Harris, Lexikographical Studies, 175).

49 Forbes ibid. Harris' reference to Syria (loc. cit. 175) is the Chnemhotep inscription from Beni-Hasan!

50 From the Stone Age to Christianity 121; Archaeology of Palestine 208.

51 Ancient Israel 24.

52 As pointed out by Professor K. Galling in a lecture in Tübingen in February, 1970.

the selling of the product, we are quite clearly told that they are involved in the very important Egyptian galena industry. We can then hardly look to Palestine or Transjordan for their place of origin.

Furthermore, it needs to be stressed that the painting is from the tomb of the high Egyptian official, *Ḫnmḥtp*, the *mr st ibtt m Mnʿt (Ḫwfw)*: Chnemhotep, "the Administrator of the Eastern Desert in the town of Menat-Chufu"[53]. The text relates that these *ʿ3mw* entered Egypt and presented themselves to the official in charge of the border at or near Beni-Hasan. If they had come from Palestine, they would not have entered Egypt here in the south, but by way of the Eastern Delta[54]. The most obvious place to look for the homeland of the Beni-Hasan *ʿ3mw* is the very Eastern Desert which Chnemhotep administered, in the mountains along the Red Sea where galena was to be found.

This location is decidedly supported by reference to other Egyptian pictures and texts from the Old and Middle Kingdoms. A survey of these texts will easily show this, and perhaps lead us into a clearer understanding of the role the *ʿ3mw* and other "Asiatic" groups played in the period between the Sixth and Twelfth Dynasties.

From the inscriptions in the tomb of Chnemhotep's grandfather, Chnemhotep I, (tomb 14 at Beni-Hasan)[55] we learn that Chnemhotep I had also been the Administrator of the Eastern Desert, and had originally been given the post as a reward for an expedition which he had undertaken during the reign of Amenemes I. The text reads: "I went down with his majesty to [. . .] in twenty ships of cedar [which] he [led], coming to [. . .]. He expelled them from the two regions (Egypt). Nubians [. . .], Asiatics *(sṯ. tyw!)* fell; he seized the lowland, the highlands . . ."[56]. In spite of the lack of clearly locatable place names in the text, it seems reasonable to conclude that we are dealing with but one expedition, (the reference to both Nubians and *sṯ. tyw* notwithstanding) near the shores of either the Nile or the Red Sea[57]. From the tomb paintings accompanying this inscription[58] we

---

53 Newberry, Beni Hasan I, 41. The title of one of his sons was "Superintendent of the Frontier", and that of one of his officers "Superintendent of the desert land" (ibid.).

54 That these *ʿ3mw* could not have entered Egypt by way of the Eastern Delta was first pointed out to me by Professor Galling.

55 Newberry, Beni Hasan I, esp. 81, and pl. xliv; see also K. Sethe, Urkunden VII, 12, ll. 5—6; and AER I, 465.

56 Ibid.; see also: T. Säve-Söderbergh, Ägypten und Nubien, 1941, 64; G. Posener, Littérature et politique dans l'Égypte de la XIIe Dynastie, 1965, 54 n. 1; W. A. Ward, The Nomarch Knumḥotep at Pelusium, JEA 55 (1969), 215f.

57 Against Breasted, who understands that the "Asiatics" were in the North and the Nubians in the South: AER I, 224. Ward (JEA 55, 1969, 215) reads the first line:

have a picture of *sṯ. tyw* allies or mercenaries of this battle. The *sṯ. tyw* remarkably resemble the *ʿꜣmw* we have already seen portrayed in tomb 3. They have the same hair and chin beard; the weapons they carry are bows, slings, and "epsilon" axes; and their short skirts have the same striped and chevron designs. Related as this battle is to the establishment of Chnemhotep I as Administrator of the Eastern Desert, and the painting from tomb 3 to Chnemhotep II's function in that office, it is hard to avoid the conclusion that we are dealing with at least closely related groups who lived somewhere in the Eastern Desert or highlands. Tomb 2 at Beni-Hasan, from the time of Sesostris I, also shows warriors of the same type[59]. An inscribed stele found in the Wadi Hamammat, just northeast of Luxor (Thebes) well south of Beni-Hasan, confirms this interpretation, speaking as it does of "smiting the Nubian, opening the land of the *ʿꜣmw* . . .". This "land of the *ʿꜣmw*" is the Eastern "Highlands": "I came to this highland in safety with my army by the power of Min, lord of the highlands"[60].

Other early texts which refer to *ʿꜣmw* in Egypt adequately confirm the contention that they are to be seen as occupants of the Eastern Desert. From even further to the south we have the *Iḳer* Inscription from the wadi el-Hudi (some twenty miles southeast of Aswân) which mentions an Egyptian conquest of the *ʿꜣmw*[61]. Closer to the region around Beni-Hasan we find two inscriptions (from the eleventh and thirteenth years of the reign of Sesostris I) from the alabaster quarries at Hatnub, which are in the hills just south of Beni-Hasan and Tell el-Amarna[62]. The first text refers to *ʿꜣmw* and Nubians as allies of the Egyptians, along with other groups of the

"I went down with his majesty to Imet (in) twenty ships of ʿš-wood. Then he came to Senu and expelled him (from) the Double-Banks-of-Horus." He identifies Senu with Pelusium at the mouth of the eastern branch of the Nile. Imet he identifies with the modern Tell Nabêsha, about 20 km north of Fâqus, which would be on the way to Pelusium. Ward compares this campaign with the construction of the line of fortresses: "The Wall of the Ruler", constructed along the frontier of the Eastern Delta. Unfortunately, Ward does not treat the second part of the inscription with the reference to Nubians.

58 Newberry, Beni Hasan I, pl. xlvii.

59 Ibid. pl. xvi, row 5, and vol. IV, pl. xxiii, 3.

60 From the 2nd year of Amenemes III, Lepsius, Denkmäler II, 138a; AER I, 707; J. Couyat and P. Montet, Les Inscriptions Hiéroglyphiques et Hiératiques du Ouâdi Hammâmât, 1912, 48.

61 A. Fakhry, The Inscriptions of the Amethyst Quarries at Wadi el Hudi, 1952, 46, fig. 39, and pl. XIXB; see also G. Posener, CAH^2 I, ch. 21, 5 n. 7.

62 W. Schenkel, Frühmittelägyptische Studien, BOS 13, 1962, 84—95, here 92—94; for texts, see R. Anthes, Die Felsinschriften von Hatnub, 1964, Graffiti 16,6 and 25,14; see also 37 and 47.

region, such as the *Mḏ3w*. The second text mentions among the friends of the Egyptians the *Mḏ3w*, the *ʿ3mw*, and, significantly, the *ḥ3śtjw* (the same name as that used for the group portrayed in Beni-Hasan tomb 14)[63]. The *ʿ3mw* prisoner pictured in the mortuary temple of Mentuḥotep III of the Eleventh Dynasty may also have come from the Eastern Desert, though the text is too damaged to tell[64]. Another important text which finds *ʿ3mw* in the Eastern Desert is that which mentions the military expedition undertaken in the reign of the Eleventh Dynasty pharaoh Mentuḥotep II (2060—2010 B. C.) against the *ʿ3mw* of the land of *Ḏ3ty*. The inscription was found at Abisko about ten kilometres south of Aswân. The best translation is that by Säve-Söderbergh which reads[65]:

> Befehl (oder Expedition), den *Ṭhm3w* ausgeführt hat im Jahre des . . . (?) Ich begann zu kämpfen in der Zeit des *Nb-ḥpt-Rʿ* als Soldat, als er stromauf fuhr nach *Bn* (Buhen ?). Mein Sohn stieg mit mir zum König hinab, nachdem er (der König) das ganze Land ergriffen hatte. Er gedachte, die Asiaten von *Ḏ3tj* zu töten. Ich (?) näherte mich Theben auf dem Rückmarsch (?). Der Nubier aber kehrte um. Da warf ich *Ḏ3tj* nieder. Er setzte Segel zur Stromauffahrt.

A second inscription from Abisko mentions the *ḥrj.w šʿ* people along with the land *Mʿ3*; a third mentions another campaign to Thebes[66]. The land of *Ḏ3tj* is apparently near Thebes, not far from the Wadi Hammamat. Again we find the expedition undertaken against both Nubians and *ʿ3mw*[67]. The second and third expeditions are possibly to the same general region. At least the term *ḥrj.w šʿ* is often used to refer to the "sanddwellers of the Eastern Desert", and other texts connect them closely with the *ʿ3mw*. The inscription of Uni from the reign of the Sixth Dynasty pharaoh Pepi I describes a campaign against the *ʿ3m-ḥryw-šʿ*[68] (the *ʿ3mw* and the *Ḥryw-šʿ* are either to be identified here, or the *ʿ3mw* are part of the *Ḥryw-šʿ*). The

---

[63] Posener (CAH² I, ch. 21, 4) seems to think that these "bedawin" are employed by the Egyptians as mercenaries, but the texts (particularly 25,14) give the impression that we are dealing here not with imported troops, but rather with local allies.

[64] J. J. Clère and J. Vandier, Textes de la Première Période Intermédiaire et de la XIème Dynastie, BiÄg 10, 1948, 37 no. 28, line x and 4. Ward's seeing this as evidence for an Egyptian "push northwards" is entirely arbitrary; see W. A. Ward, Egypt and the East Mediterranean in the Early Second Millenium B. C., Orientalia 30 (1961), 23f.

[65] T. Säve-Söderbergh, Ägypten und Nubien, 58.

[66] Ibid. 58—60; see also G. Roeder, Les Temples Immergés de la Nubie, Dehod bis Bab Kalabsche, 1911, I 104f. and II p. 107, no. 1.

[67] *Ḏ3tj* certainly has nothing to do with Sinai as suggested by Posener (CAH² I, ch. 21, 6).

[68] Sethe, Urkunden I, 101—110; AER I 311—315; ANET 228.

Egyptian army for the expedition was conscripted from Upper Egypt, from Elephantine in the south to Aphroditopolis in the north; the battle takes place in the "land of *Ḥryw-šʿ*", which, on the basis of other inscriptions, as we shall see, seems to be in the general region east of Heliopolis (and even further south), and in the desert region just east of the Delta. This location fits our present text perfectly. Five separate expeditions were undertaken and, in one of these, Uni proceeded by ship and got behind the enemy, to the north of the *Ḥryw-šʿ*. In this manner he was enabled to put down the rebellion. The place where he landed was called the "land of the gazelle nose"[69], which Helck has identified with Mons Cassius, just east of the Delta[70].

The land of the *ʿꜣmw* and of the *Ḥryw-šʿ* occur in another Sixth Dynasty text, in the inscription of *ppj-nḫt*, from the reign of Pepi II[71]. The Egyptians were building a ship in the "land of the *ʿꜣmw*" *(ḫꜣś.t ʿꜣmw)* for a voyage to Punt, when the *ʿꜣmw*, belonging to the *Ḥr(y)w-šʿ*, murdered Ka-Aper. This "land of the *ʿꜣmw*" is apparently in the south[72], since Pepi-Nakht was from Aswân, and there held office. Moreover, at least in Old Kingdom times, voyages to Punt left from the land of the *Ḥryw-šʿ* on the Red Sea[73]. Indeed, this trade with Punt may well explain the military expedition against the *Ḥryw-šʿ* mentioned in an Eleventh Dynasty inscription from the Wadi Hammamat[74].

Several other early texts refer to *ʿꜣmw* and other "Asiatic" groups who might be related to the *ʿꜣmw* in Egypt, but without completely clear indication as to their whereabouts. The Eleventh Dynasty pharaoh Mentuḥotep I had a relief in his temple in Upper Egypt at Gebelein, in which the king is shown killing a Nubian, a Libyan, an Egyptian, and an "Asiatic" *(sṯ. tyw)*. The references to the three non-Egyptians seem to refer to the immediate neighbors of Upper Egypt, those to the south, to the west, and to the east[75]. The text above the relief reads: "Binding the chiefs of the two lands,

---

69 Or: "Antelope-Nose", as in ANET.

70 Helck, Beziehungen, 18. It is certainly not Mount Carmel as Y. Aharoni (Mount Carmel as Border, in: Galling Festschrift 2) and others have suggested. Mount Carmel may well look much like an antelope's or gazelle's nose, but such a location does great violence to our texts.

71 Sethe, Urkunden I, 134; AER I 360.

72 Certainly not Syria as suggested by Helck (Beziehungen 21); also contra P. Montet, Notes et Documents pour servir a l'Histoire des Relations entre l'ancienne Égypte et la Syrie, Kêmi 13 (1954), 65f.

73 W. C. Hayes, Career of the Great Steward Ḥenenu under Nebḥepetrêʿ Mentuḥotep, JEA 35 (1949), 48.

74 From the reign of Mentuḥotep II; translation and text: ibid. 46 and plate.

75 Ward, Orientalia 30 (1961), 23; AER I 423 H.

capturing the south and the northland, the highlands and the two regions, the Nine Bows and the two lands", apparently referring not to foreign conquests, but to the conquest of Egypt itself; the three groups are the non-Egyptian elements found in Egypt. In spite of its more general character, this text fits well with those we have already seen.

There are several Middle Kingdom references to individual *ʿȝmw*, both male and female, from graves at Abydos[76], and perhaps from a stele in the Louvre[77] which seems to refer not to slaves but to private individuals[78].

From a magical text from the Middle Kingdom, Papyrus Berlin 3027, we have the interesting lines: "Laufe aus, du Asiatin *(ʿȝm.t)*, die aus der Wüste kommt, du Nubierin, die aus der Fremde kommt"[79]. The *ʿȝmw* is seen as an immigrant from the desert which borders on Egypt and it is, I think, in this light that we must see the reference to the "Asiatics" in the Satire on the Trades[80] from the reign of Amenemes I or Sesostris I (c. 1980 B. C.)[81]. The danger to the messenger's life is that he must go out into the desert: "Der Eilbote geht in der Wüste *(sṯt)*" where he has to face the dangers of lions and *ʿȝmw*. The danger is not to be found in foreign countries, as is implied in the ANET translation, so much as it is in the desert which he must enter when leaving the Nile valley. Such danger has been well represented by most of the texts that we have seen which refer to the *ʿȝmw* living in the desert. It may perhaps be suggested that it is just such disorganized danger from the *ʿȝmw* of the Eastern Desert which threatened many in Egypt during the time of political disunity during the First Intermediate Period, rather than any foreign invasion from Palestine. There is, at least, in the texts that we have seen so far, little basis from which one could argue that the *ʿȝmw* in Egypt had come from any place other than the desert and highlands east of the Nile.

We do have two early Twelfth Dynasty texts that speak of *ʿȝmw* in relation to Palestine, though they speak of *ʿȝmw* in, and not from, Palestine. The first, relatively late inscription, is from the

[76] H. O. Lange and H. Schäfer, Grab- und Denksteine des Mittleren Reichs im Museum von Kairo I, 1902, Kairo 20227k, 20231h, and 20392e.

[77] C. 170 (E. Gayet, Musée du Louvre, Stèles de la XIIe Dynastie, 1886, pl. xxviii).

[78] See, for further examples, Helck, Beziehungen, 79—84.

[79] For text and translation, see A. Erman, Zaubersprüche für Mutter und Kind, 1901, 14.

[80] For text and translation: H. Brunner, Die Lehre des Cheti Sohnes des Duauf, ÄgF 13 (1944); ANET 432—434.

[81] So Brunner ibid. 21. The translation in ANET is deceptive, and Brunner's rendering seems to be much more dependable.

reign of Sesostris III, the stele of *Ḫw-śbk*[82], which speaks of a military expedition to the land of *śkmm*, which is most likely biblical Shechem. The purpose of the expedition is not given, except that it is to overthrow the *Mnṯyw-sṯt*. The word *Mnṯw* is usually used to refer to the people of Sinai; here, however, it apparently refers to the people of the regions further north, since *Rṯnw* (usually considered to refer to southern Palestine, but may perhaps include part of Sinai) is defeated in the battle along with *śkmm*. The people that the Egyptians fight against are also called *ʿꜣmw*, and it seems that the terms *ʿꜣmw* and *mnṯyw-sṯt* are used synonymously. Whether we have here an extension of the use of the term *ʿꜣmw* to the Palestinian regions, or evidence that the *ʿꜣmw* were also thought to live in Palestine as well as in the Eastern Desert, or that these terms were used in such a fluid sense and with such little precision that the words *Mnṯw*, *sṯ.tyw*, *ʿꜣmw*, and *ḥryw-šʿ* can often be understood as synonymous, is not entirely clear, though the latter seems to be the more probable. We have already seen the word *ʿꜣmw* used in close relationship with the terms *śṯ.t* and *ḥryw-šʿ*, and here in the *Ḫw-śbk* inscription it is used with *mnṯw-sṯ.t*. This coalescence of meaning might also occur in the other early texts referring to *ʿꜣmw* in Palestine, though there does seem to be some significant differentiation.

The Tale of Sinuhe[83] has a manuscript tradition which goes back to the end of the Twelfth Dynasty; the original is probably to be dated to the end of the reign of Sesostris I. It, like the Teaching of Amenemes I[84], mentions the murder of Amenemes[85]. Sinuhe bears the title: "Der Erbfürst und Graf, der Verwalter der Bezirke des Königs in den Ländern der *sṯ.tyw*", and the following story relates his adventures there. When Amenemes I is assassinated, Sinuhe, in fear, escapes to Palestine. Just before leaving Egypt, he reaches the

[82] AER I 680f.; Helck, Beziehungen, 47.

[83] Maspero, Mémoires II, 1—23, pl. I and II; F. L. Griffith, Fragments of Old Egyptian Stories, PSBA 14 (1892), 453f.; A. H. Gardiner, Sinuhe, and AER I 490—497; see also J. J. Clère, Sinouhé en Syrie, Mélanges Syriens offerts à R. Dussaud, 1939, 829—840; also, G. Posener, Littérature et Politique, 87—115; for a good recent translation, see K. Galling, Textbuch zur Geschichte Israels, 1968², 1—12. The text used below is taken mostly from Galling.

[84] For text and translation see most recently, W. Helck, Der Text der Lehre Amenemhets I für seinen Sohn, 1969. Perhaps noteworthy for our discussion is the brief reference to Amenemes' conquest of the forces of the Eastern Desert: "Ich bändigte die Löwen und fing Krokodile, ich bezwang die Leute von Wawat und fing die Madjoi. Ich liess die Asiaten den Hundegang tun." Here the Semitic element is referred to as *sṯ.tyw*.

[85] The text of Sinuhe is most likely to be dated towards the end of the reign of Sesostris I as it relates the death of Sinuhe (line 310), in the context of the story, many years after the death of Amenemes I.

"Mauern des Herrschers" which had been constructed "um die *sṯ.tyw* abzuhalten und um die *ḥryw-š*ʿ zu vernichten" (lines B 16f.), apparently the same wall as is mentioned in the Prophecy of Neferty, built by Amenemes I against the *ʿ3mw*. In the story of Sinuhe, the *sṯ.tyw* seem to be the people living just east of the Delta. Beyond the Egyptian fortifications, Sinuhe arrives at the "Insel des *Km-wr*" (B 20), which is apparently just on the edge of Sinai near the salt lakes[86], where he is forced to stop because of thirst. He is saved by men of *sṯ.tyw*, whose sheikh he had known in Egypt. The rest of the geography is extremely vague, and it may be doubted whether it has any historical validity[87]. He went "in the direction of Byblos"[88], though nothing in the text implies that he ever arrived there[89]. He turned aside in the direction of Kedem ("the East"), where he spends a year and a half. He is then taken up by the prince of Upper Retenu, from whom he receives the land of Iaa, and is married to the prince's daughter. There he becomes the commander of the army against the *sṯ.tyw*. He fights a duel against one of the Retenu leaders who is jealous of him. The prince, his father-in-law, is called "son of *ʿ3mw*", and the people of Retenu are called *ʿ3mw* (ll. 142ff.).

While little precision is possible when discussing a story of this type, it seems that the term *ʿ3mw*, and conceivably also *Mnṯw*, is used for the farmers and shepherds of Upper Retenu (southern Palestine?). The term *sṯ.tyw*, on the other hand, refers to the shepherds living to the east of the Delta, and also to the enemies of Retenu. Only the *sṯ.tyw* along the Egyptian frontier are spoken of as ever having entered Egypt.

Evidence of *ʿ3mw* in Sinai comes from a stele of the sea captain or "transport officer" Akhtoy, in his tomb at Thebes, from the reign of the Eleventh Dynasty pharaoh Nebḥepetre. The text reads: "I punished the *ʿ3mw* in their countries". The region to which the expedition went is called *Bi3w*, a name which also occurs on the monuments of Sinai. Moreover, since turquoise and various metals are mentioned in the text, Sinai seems most probable[90]. Such contact with Egypt from this region, however, is not limited to the Middle Kingdom, but is found in the very earliest periods.

---

86 Gardiner, Sinuhe, 166.

87 See on this G. Posener, Littérature et Politique, 92—94.

88 *r Kpny*: Translation, as Gardiner suggests in Sinuhe, 21. Edel, in: Galling, Textbuch, translates: "ich reiste ab nach Byblos und kehrte um nach *Ḳdm*".

89 Byblos is the major port in Syria with which the Egyptians traded by sea.

90 Cf. A. H. Gardiner, The Tomb of a Much Travelled Theban Official, JEA 4 (1917), 34—38 and pl. IX (tomb 65, stele no. 2); Ward, Orientalia 30 (1961), 24.

D. SINAI AND THE DELTA IN OLD AND MIDDLE KINGDOM RECORDS

Already in the Badarian period Egypt had trade relations with Sinai, from which it obtained small quantities of turquoise[91]. From at least a very early period, Semitic elements apparently had a very strong influence on the eastern border of the Delta; since the god of the Wadi Tumilat, Sopdu, is portrayed as a Semitic nomad with a full beard during the Old Kingdom[92].

In the Narmer Palette we see the First Dynasty pharaoh celebrating his conquest of Upper and Lower Egypt[93]. On the front of the slate the pharaoh is pictured in the traditional stance of striking the fallen enemy, who appears to be an "Asiatic"[94]. By the fallen enemy's head there is a sign showing that he is from the Harpoon nome of the Eastern Delta. The pictograph above could be read: "The pharaoh Horus captures the 'Asiatic' in the marshland". In the lower field on the same side we see two other fallen or fleeing enemies. Next to them are two signs which Yadin has probably correctly identified as a fortified city and a corral. His identification of these structures as belonging to Transjordan, and his conclusion that this lower register must celebrate a conquest of "the area which lies near the highway between Transjordan, Syria, and Mesopotamia", however, stretches the evidence unduly[95]. The identification of the kite-shaped figure as a corral seems fairly clear on the basis of a comparison with a number of rock drawings published by G. L. Harding with several Safaitic inscriptions which had been found at Rijm el-Hawih just north of the Bagdad road[96]. These drawings have been compared by Yadin with a number of rock enclosures, some as much as 400 meters long, seen in the area to the east and northeast of Amman[97]. O. Eissfeldt has seen in this type of structure an illustration of the "sheepfolds" in the Song of Deborah (Judges 5 16)[98].

---

[91] W. A. Ward, Egypt and the East Mediterranean from Predynastic Times to the End of the Old Kingdom, JESHO 6 (1963), 3.

[92] Helck, Beziehungen, 6.

[93] ANEP nos. 296f.

[94] See also W. M. Flinders Petrie, Ceremonial Slate Palettes, British School of Egyptian Archaeology, 66A, 1953, Pl. C, 12, for similar foreigners on protodynastic monuments.

[95] Y. Yadin, The Earliest Record of Egypt's Military Penetration into Asia, IEJ 5 (1955), 1—16.

[96] G. L. Harding, The Cairn of Hani', ADAJ 2 (1953), Pl. VI, no. 73 shows a drawing of a corral; fig. 8, no. 71 reverse, shows a drawing just like the kite figure on the Narmer Palette.

[97] See A. S. Kirkbride, Desert Kites, JPOS 20 (1946), 1—5, and Yadin, IEJ 5 (1955), figures 2—6.

[98] O. Eissfeldt, Gabelhürden im Ostjordanland, FF 25 (1949), 9f.

While these identifications seem, in general, most reasonable, it should be recognized that the drawings found in Northern Transjordan are to be dated to the Safaitic period, just before the end of the fourth century A. D., and that the stone enclosures near Amman have not been dated at all. It is quite possible that we are dealing with structures used up into the Safaitic period, but having a much longer history, coextensive with a particular way of life. Nevertheless, Yadin's theory that the Narmer Palette gives evidence of an Egyptian campaign to Transjordan is still unacceptable, since these structures cannot be geographically limited to Northern Transjordan. S. Yeivin has reported that similar structures have been found in the Arabah much nearer to Egypt[99]. The Narmer Palette may indicate that these corrals were used in the desert regions to the east of the Delta. Ward has argued convincingly that the upper and lower fields of the palette must be read together[100]; thus what we have portrayed in the lower fields must relate to the subjugation of "Asiatic" groups in the Delta, or perhaps in the desert regions immediately to the east[101].

The foreigners shown in the central field of the reverse side of the Narmer Palette resemble those found on the "Schlachtfeld-palette" in the Ashmolean museum[102]. The remains of a hieroglyph identifies them as *Iwn.tyw*, a word which may be derived from *Iwnw* "Heliopolis", (or perhaps the land *wn.t* somewhere in the region of the Eastern Delta) and refers to the occupants of the desert region east of Heliopolis[103].

This name occurs in two other inscriptions of the First Dynasty during the reigns of the pharaohs Dwn and his son *ʿnḏ-ib* where "smiting of the *Iwn.tyw*" is mentioned in the texts, referring to groups living along the Wadi Tumilat. The texts are probably connected with Egyptian efforts to control the land of *wn.t*[104].

From the Third Dynasty we find a series of reliefs from the Wadi Mugharah in Sinai, which present the pharaoh in the traditional pose of smiting the "Asiatic"[105]. From the reign of the Fourth Dynasty king Snofru, the same scene is shown of the pharaoh clubbing an "Asiatic"; no reference to it is given in the accompanying text,

---

99 S. Yeivin, Early Contacts between Canaan and Egypt, IEJ 10 (1960), 201.

100 Ward, JESHO 6 (1963), 11f.

101 See also W. B. Emery, Archaic Egypt, 1961, 43.

102 S. Schott, Hieroglyphen, 1950, Pl. II, no. 4.

103 Ibid. 23 n. 3; Helck, Beziehungen, 13.

104 See W. Helck, Geschichte des alten Ägypten, Handbuch der Orientalistik, I, 3 1968, 33.

105 Gardiner, Peet, and Černy, The Inscriptions of Sinai, 1952², vol. I, Pl. I, 1, 2, 4.; Helck, Beziehungen, 14.

however[106]. In a stele from the reign of Cheops, with a similar scene, the text mentions "smiting the *Iwn.tyw*"[107]. A similar stele from the reign of Sahurê of the Fifth Dynasty mentions "smiting the *mntw n śwt*"[108], as does that of his fellow dynast Neuserrêʿ[109]. Though the name has changed, the portrayal of the "Asiatic" is basically the same as that in the earlier periods. The stele from the reign of the Fifth Dynasty king Dhedkarê-Asosi, however, speaks of "smiting the chief of the foreign country" (or "desert" *ḫꜣśt*), and the foreigner portrayed is beardless and does not resemble those of the other monuments in the least[110]. On a stele from the reign of Pepi I of the Sixth Dynasty, an "Asiatic" similar to those on the early steles is shown[111]. Finally, among the monuments from the Wadi Mugharah, one stele from the Eighteenth Dynasty, from the second year of the reign of Amenemes III, uses the head of an "Asiatic" for a hieroglyph which resembles most closely the "Asiatics" from the early Old Kingdom monuments[112]. Because of the strong similarity in the pictography from the Third to the Twelfth Dynasties, from monuments of one specific locality, which are all basically related to one artistic tradition, it appears reasonable to suspect that the Egyptians did not see any major shift in population in Sinai during this period. Posener's suggestion that there is a definite modification between the twenty-first and the twentieth-nineteenth centuries seems difficult to prove, and is not clearly supported by the evidence that he gathers[113]. It seems, in fact, important to stress rather his opinion that no firm conclusions about a change of population can be drawn on the basis of our present knowledge. Some continuity seems also to be indicated, as Posener is aware, between the portrayals of "Asiatics" from the early period and those from the Twelfth Dynasty. Most of the Twelfth Dynasty remains which Posener refers to are drawn from the Beni-Hasan tombs of that period, which form a very unique tradition. The "Asiatics" in some Twelfth Dynasty pictures from Serâbît el-Khadîm in Sinai[114] are pictured quite differently from the Beni-Hasan "Asiatics" of tombs 2, 3, and 14. The portrayal of the "Asiatics" from Serâbît el-Khadîm, especially the drawing with the multi-colored skirt shown on pl. 85 of Gardiner's The Inscriptions of Sinai, resembles

---

106 Gardiner ibid. vol. I Pl. II, and vol. II 56.

107 Ibid. vol. I Pl. II and III, and vol. II 57f. and Pl. I.

108 Ibid. vol. I Pl. V, and vol. II 58.

109 Ibid. vol. I Pl. VI, and vol. II 59.

110 Ibid. vol. II 61f., and Pl. VIII.

111 Ibid. vol. II Pl. VIII, 16.

112 Ibid. vol. I Pl. XI, 24A.

113 CAH² ch. 21, 7 and 22.

114 Gardiner, The Inscriptions of Sinai, vol. I Pl. 37, 39, 44 and 85.

in several characteristics the foreign warriors pictured in Beni-Hasan tombs XV and XVII which are dated to the Eleventh Dynasty, i. e., contemporary with Posener's suggested early type[115].

The Sinai relief from Serâbît el-Khadîm shown on plate 51[116], dated to the Twelfth Dynasty, which Posener sees as belonging to his later tradition, shows a bearded Asiatic who resembles those on the early Old Kingdom monuments from the Wadi Mugharah mentioned above, although it is possibly closest to the "Asiatics" shown on the pectoral from Dahshûr[117]. Both of these, however, hardly resemble either the Beni-Hasan paintings or the drawings from the other Sêrâbit monuments. A significant change in population, nevertheless, does not seem suggested. What we are probably dealing with, as Posener also suggests[118], are differences in artistic traditions. Note the traditional "smiting theme" among the Wadi Mugharah reliefs and the "donkey theme" among the Serâbît el-Khadîm reliefs, as well as the marked traditions in the two types of Beni-Hasan paintings. In the case of the Wadi Mugharah tradition, the portraiture of the "Asiatic", though not the smiting scene, is continued down into the Twelfth Dynasty.

E. THE INCURSION OF THE *ʿȜMW* INTO EGYPT DURING THE FIRST INTERMEDIATE PERIOD

Having reviewed very briefly in this chapter a number of texts and pictures from the Old and Middle Kingdoms relevant to *ʿȝmw* contacts with Egypt, we have seen that these contacts have been both friendly and hostile, and that they have been generally limited to the area of the Eastern Desert to the South and along the border of the Eastern Delta. Because of this, it seems doubtful that the generally used and convenient translation "Asiatic" for this and other related terms is precise, and indeed it has in the past been seriously misleading, particularly in reference to texts which antedate the middle of the Twelfth Dynasty.

---

115 Tomb no. 15 belonging to Baqt III (Newberry, Beni Hasan II, Pl. V, row 7). In tomb 17 these warriors appear to be allies of the Egyptians (ibid. Pl. XV, row 6). Khety, the owner of this tomb was, like Chnemhotep I and II, the "Administrator of the Eastern Desert" (Cf. ibid. vol. II 53). In spite of the absence of beards and the slightly different construction of their skirts, I am inclined to see these Eleventh Dynasty people as at least generally related to the *ʿȝmw/sṯ.tyw* of tombs 2, 3, and 14.

116 Gardiner, The Inscriptions of Sinai, no. 163.

117 E. Vernier, Bijoux et Orfèvreries, 1927, II Pl. II.

118 Posener, CAH², chapt. 21, 7.

The general picture which we have seen so far of Egyptian-*ʿɜmw* relationships appears to be borne out by an examination of the three major texts which have served as the basis of the theory that there was an Amorite invasion from Palestine during the First Intermediate Period: The Admonitions of Ipuwer, the Instructions to Merikarê, and the Prophecy of Neferty. In fact, as we shall see, no such invasion took place. What disturbances were caused by the *ʿɜmw* during the Herakleopolitan Period were of the same type, though perhaps more severe because of the concurrent Egyptian weakness, as those they had caused in the Old Kingdom, as well as those they continued to cause during the Twelfth Dynasty and later.

Certainly the Admonitions give no support to the invasion hypothesis; the usual terms *mnṯyw*, *ḥryw-šʿ*, and *ʿɜmw* are not even used in the text[119]. The text does present, however, a graphic description of the Egyptian upper class' view of social upheavals[120]. The complaints so eloquently expressed by Ipuwer are overwhelmingly complaints against the Egyptian officials, fellow Egyptians, and a situation which allows the poor and the lower classes to rise to positions of power. Until the very end of the text, reference to foreigners is very

---

119 J. van Seters, A Date for the "Admonitions" in the Second Intermediate Period, JEA 50 (1964), 15f.

120 For translation, see R. O. Faulkner, Notes on "The Admonitions of an Egyptian Sage", JEA 50 (1964), 24—36, and The Admonitions of an Egyptian Sage, JEA 51 (1965), 53—62. The traditional dating of this text places it in the First Intermediate Period (A. H. Gardiner, The Admonitions, 1—5). This dating has been challenged by J. van Seters (JEA 50, 1964, 13—23; The Hyksos, 1966, 103—120) who offers as an alternative a dating in the late Thirteenth Dynasty. The orthography, language, and terminology resemble the Twelfth Dynasty literary texts. However, that the breakdown of trade with Byblos and that the lack of cedar wood for coffins is related to a shift in burial customs that occurred in the Second Intermediate Period (The Hyksos 108f.) is hardly likely since, in such a case, the lack of cedar wood would not be a source of complaint. Moreover, the archaeological evidence from Byblos suggests a break in the close contact with Egypt after Pepi II, that is, during the First Intermediate Period.
Possible aspects of the social, administrative, and political developments may well reflect Egypt of the Twelfth and Thirteenth Dynasties (ibid. 110ff.). Van Seters' arguments, however, fail to be totally convincing, and, indeed, the First Intermediate Period cannot be completely excluded from consideration, simply because of the limitations of our knowledge about this period. His argument rests upon the philological and historical comparisons which he has made between the late Middle Kingdom on one hand, and the Old Kingdom on the other. Nor should the Eleventh and Twelfth Dynasties be excluded from possible consideration for the setting of this text, for they too were not without their periods of disruption, however brief. The reference to the "Residence" on the other hand, may restrict one to a choice between a dating at the end of the Sixth or at the end of the Thirteenth Dynasty. (Van Seters, JEA 50, 1964, 19f.).

superficial, referring to the people from the Egyptian desert whose actions are execrated, not because they are causing disruptions, but because they, like other of the poor, have obtained some wealth: "the tribes of the desert *(ḫꜣśtyw)* have become Egyptians everywhere" (1 : 9) and "desert dwellers *(ḫꜣśtyw)* are skilled in the crafts of the Delta" (4 : 8). Only in the very last lines (14 : 10ff.) of the Admonitions are foreigners mentioned in a significant way, but it is specifically to say that the trouble with Egypt is not the foreigners: "Is it Nubians *(nḥsyw)*? Then we will guard ourselves. Warriors are made many in order to ward off foreigners *(pḏtyw)*[121]. Is it Libyans? Then we will turn away. The Medjay *(Mḏꜣyw)*[122] are pleased with Egypt." The real difficulty is that Egyptian troops have "turned into foreigners and have taken to ravaging". (15 : 1) He ends by warning that the *Sṯ.tyw* and the desert peoples are aware of and disturbed by the disruptions in Egypt; apparently this is a warning that the *Sṯ.tyw* may be inclined to take advantage of the settled regions if law and order are not reestablished.

The Admonitions give as a picture of pillaging, disruption, and social change, of a situation in which the Egyptian soldiers, though organized for the purpose of protecting Egypt, can no longer themselves be controlled. There may be a reference here to a possible threat from the *sṯ.tyw*, but there is not the slightest reference throughout the Admonitions to anything which can be understood as an invasion from the north. The only reference conducive to such an interpretation (3 : 1b): "Barbarians from abroad have come to Egypt" is preceded by: "the desert is throughout the land; the nomes are laid waste", (3 : 1a) an apparent reference to non-Egyptian desert people coming into the fertile regions. The "barbarians from abroad" are from the desert lands along the Egyptian frontier. This same situation may be reflected in the poorly legible line: 15 : 3 "[. . .] without giving Egypt over to (?) the sand".

The Instructions to Merikarê is the one major relevant text that can be clearly dated to the First Intermediate Period. It is composed in the form of last minute instructions to the pharaoh's son and successor, similar to the Teachings of Amenemes I, which suggests a dating in the early years of the reign of Merikarê[123]. The Instructions relate the accomplishments of his father *wꜣḥꜣ r*ʿ (Achthoes II). The manuscript tradition stems from the New Kingdom period (Amenophis III)[124]; the language and content, however, place it with the very

---

[121] Perhaps to be read with J. van Seters (Hyksos 106): "Fighting police will hold off the bowmen *(pḏtyw)*".

[122] Egyptian allies, or perhaps mercenaries.

[123] See, however, P. Seibert, Die Charakteristik, ÄgAb 17, 1967, 88.

earliest Middle Kingdom texts[125]. The Instructions give advice on the various difficult problems which face Merikarê, and mention several times events from the life of Achthoes to illustrate possible solutions[126]. Lines 70ff. speak about the peaceful relations which exist with the South, and Merikarê is strongly advised to do nothing which would upset those relations. From lines 82 to 110, he speaks about the difficulties of the "Northland", i. e., the Delta region, which has been very troublesome to him. He has succeeded in pacifying the West, which now supplies Upper Egypt with wood from Syria (ll. 82f.). The situation is quite different, however, in the East, which is "rich in bowmen" *(pḏti)*. He mentions the steps which he has taken to bring the situation under control, first changing the administrative structure of the region, and then establishing a frontier line all the way from Hebenu (modern Minieh just north of Beni-Hasan) to the "ways of Horus" (perhaps modern Qantarah). He settled the frontier with "picked men of the entire land" to protect it. This enabled the people of the Eastern Delta to control the "bowmen" (ll. 95ff.), who now no longer offer a serious threat to Egypt: "He is only an *ʿꜣm*", who cannot threaten the fortified cities. Merikarê then receives further instruction in the methods of controlling these people. Mention is made of a garrison of 10 000 troops at *Djed-sat* (Memphis), who have been encouraged to stay there by the grant of tax-free status. This section ends with a warning (ll. 107ff.) that if the South should ever be threatened, the "bowmen" in the North will surely take advantage of the situation.

The text clearly speaks of a considerable threat from the *pḏtyw* and the *ʿꜣmw* of the "Northland". The line of fortifications which were set up along the frontier, stretching from Minieh to Qantarah, suggests that the base for these enemy groups lies in the desert regions to the east of Egypt, and between Sinai and the Delta. Apparently, as long as this frontier can be enforced, Egypt and the Delta are relatively safe. While there is no doubt that the threat is serious, one can only conclude from the passages referred to above, that the conflict is seen as basically a border problem, and that the fighting described is that of border raids and skirmishes. There is hardly a wholesale invasion from foreign lands.

The crucial text in understanding this aspect of the Instructions is a brief insertion into the narration which, in attempting to explain

[124] A. Scharff, Der historische Abschnitt der Lehre für König Merikarê, SBAW 8, 1936, 6f.; A. Volten, Zwei Altägyptische politische Schriften, AnÄg 4, 1945, 82; P. Seibert, Die Charakteristik, 87.

[125] C. 2100 B. C., according to Scharff: ibid. 53.

[126] For translations see Gardiner, JEA 1 (1914), 22ff.; Scharff, Merikarê, 18—21; ANET 414—418.

why the conflict with these people exists, describes the *ʿȝmw* and his homeland. Early commentators have generally read this description much as it is given in ANET:

Lo the wretched Asiatic — it goes ill with the place where he is, afflicted with water, difficult from many trees, the ways thereof painful because of the mountains. He does not dwell in a single place, (but) his legs are made to go astray. He has been fighting (ever) since the time of Horus, (but) he does not conquer, nor yet can he be conquered. He does not announce a day in fighting, like a thief who . . . for a gang.

The nearest region which has a lot of water, many trees, and mountains is Palestine; and it is hardly surprising therefore that so many have thought of these people as external invaders from this northern region. One must, nevertheless, wonder that the Egyptians could see an abundance of water and large forests as afflictions!

Posener corrects one line of the text (l. 93) to read: "He does not settle in one single place, for (lack of) food makes his legs take flight"[127]. The difficulties in the text, however, are not thereby diminished, though the amendment is undoubtedly correct. They rather become more apparent, since the abundance of water and forest lands seems to be a weak means of explaining why this "wretched *ʿȝmw*" has come because of lack of food, to threaten the frontiers of Egypt — and the purpose of the passage seems to be just such an explanation. Moreover, the line: "he has been fighting since the time of Horus", does not give the impression that these groups are newcomers on the scene in Egypt.

In fact, the text does not seem to be talking about Palestine at all, but refers rather to the desert regions and the hills bordering on Egypt. "Bad is the country where he lives"[128], *qsn n bw*, seems to refer to the region where the *ʿȝmw* are living at the time that they are threatening the frontier, and not some foreign land from which they were originally to have come. Secondly, in the phrase that is translated in ANET, "afflicted with water", the term *štȝ* has the basic meaning "hidden", with the sense of "difficult" or "impossible", and the phrase should be translated: "difficult of water"[129], with the sense "with little water". Similarly, the phrase "difficult from many trees" is rendered with the word *štȝ*, which, with the preposition *m*, has here the meaning "impossible" or more specifically "infertile

---

127 CAH², chapt. 21, 5; Trois Passages de l'Enseignement à Mérikarê, Rev d'Eg 7 (1950), 177f.

128 As translated by Posener, CAH², ch. 21, 5.

129 As convincingly argued by E. Drioton, Le Désert du Sinai couvert par une Forêt Impénétrable, Rev d'Eg 12 (1960), 90f.; So Posener: "Inconvenient in respect to water" (CAH², ch. 21, 5).

as to the number of trees"[130]. The entire passage should then read:

The wretched Asiatic, bad is the country where he lives, with little water, infertile in its number of trees, its roads are bad on account of the mountains. He does not settle in one single place, for (lack of) food makes his legs take flight. Since the time of Horus he has been at war; he does not conquer, nor yet can he be conquered[131].

We are then to look for a desert and mountainous region, which can best be found in the highlands along the eastern border of Egypt. This location fits well the implication that the region serves as the base for the *ʿȝmw* incursions against the Egyptian settlements, the impression that the situation is seen as permanent ("Since the time of Horus he has been at war"), and the fact that the protective frontier, which served to control these people, was set up over against this very region[132].

The Prophecy of Neferty[133], which was probably written during the reign of Amenemes I, tells about the disorders which occurred at the very end of the Eleventh Dynasty and which were put down

---

130 Drioton ibid.: "L'expression peut avoir deux sens. Ou bien l'auteur a voulu dire par là que beaucoup d'espèces d'arbres ne pouvaient pas pousser dans le pays désertique des Aamou. On en citerait en effet des dizaines. Ou bien il a entendu signifier que cette région était inapte à posséder de nombreux arbres. Quiconque évoquera la maigre végétation du désert, se maintenant péniblement ou fond des ouadys, et le rareté des arbres de taille normale qui arrivent à se développer dans ces conditions précaires, jugera certainement que le second sens est plus plausible." (ibid. 91). See further, Seibert, die Charakteristik, 92 n. 4 and 93 n. 6.

131 Following Posener (CAH² 5) with the above suggested corrections. Similarly, Seibert (Die Charakteristik, 90) suggests the translation: "[Gesagt wird zwar dies (jetzt) wieder vom Barbaren:] 'Der [schwächliche] Asiat, fürwahr', geplagt ist er wegen des Ortes, an dem er ist: Dürftig an Wasser, verborgen trotz der Menge der Wege dahin' (und) schlimm durch Berge. 'Er kann nicht wohnen' an einem Platz: Nahrung(smangel) treibt weiter seine Füße. Er ist am Kämpfen seit der Zeit des Horus: Er siegt nicht; (doch) er kann auch nicht besiegt werden, (denn) er kündigt nicht den Kampftag an: wie ein Räuber, den die Kraft von Vereinigten bannt."

132 See the remarks of Seibert (ibid. 93 n. 97): "die in der Lehre wenige Zeilen vor dem hier behandelten Text erwähnte Grenzsicherung 'von *Ḥbnw* bis zum Horusweg' zeigt ganz klar, daß das hier beschriebene Aufenthaltsgebiet des 'Asiaten' weder speziell der Sinai (gegen E. Drioton) noch speziell Südpalästina (gegen W. Helck) ist, sondern diese beiden Gebiete zusammen und vor allem vermehrt um die nördliche Ostwüste 'Ägyptens'."

133 For text and translation, see W. Golénischeff, Le papyrus No. 1 de St. Pétersbourg, ZÄS 14 (1876), 107ff.; Gardiner, JEA 1 (1914), 100—106; ANET 444—446; and W. Helck, Die Prophezeiung des *Nfr.tj*, Kleine ägyptische Texte, 1970: with brief commentary; see also the comments in Posener, CAH², ch. 21, 7f., and Littérature et Politique, 52—55.

by Amenemes. While not specifically about the First Intermediate Period, this text has often been used for a picture of the *ʿꜣmw*, since it tells about the time when the "*ʿꜣmw* approach in their might". (l. 18) In many ways it resembles both the Instructions and the Admonitions. It is written in the form of a prophecy and tells of a great famine when all the rivers are to go dry, even the Nile. At this time the *ʿꜣmw* will attack the people at the harvest and steal their cattle and generally "pervade the land" (l. 32). There will be general disorder, universal difficulties, social upheaval, and internecine strife: "I show you the land upside down" (l. 54). In the midst of these difficulties Amenemes will be born; all will rejoice; rebellion will cease; "the *ʿꜣmw* will fall by his sword, the Libyans shall fall before his flame, and the rebels before his wrath . . ." (ll. 63f.). In order that the peace might be permanent, "there shall be built the 'Wall of the Prince', and the *ʿꜣmw* will not be permitted to come down into Egypt that they might beg for water in the customary manner, in order to let their beasts drink".

If this text can be used for historical purposes at all, the *ʿꜣmw* here are seen to be much like those of our other texts, the sheep and goatherds of the Eastern Desert ("Foes have arisen in the East and *ʿꜣmw* have come down into Egypt" ll. 32f.)[134], who, though normally entering Egypt peacefully to water their cattle, in time of famine have broken forcibly into the settled regions to keep from starving. The Egyptians, because of internal disorder caused by the famine, are unable to prevent this, until the time when Amenemes was able to unite Egypt, and then, with the construction of a fortification wall, hold back the *ʿꜣmw* and restore order.

The *ʿꜣmw* incursions into Egypt during the First Intermediate Period and the Eleventh Dynasty are a direct concommitant of the weakness and disorder caused by a lack of political power and a lack of internal cohesion within Egypt itself, and were not a part of any widespread nomadic movement. The *ʿꜣmw* were people who lived along the eastern border of Egypt in peaceful as well as hostile relationship to the Egyptians. Their threat to the Egyptian borders seems to have been relatively constant throughout the periods in which they are met, becoming dangerous in times of famine or disorder when Egypt's ability to contain this threat was diminished.

[134] Note the parallelism of structure! The foes are the *ʿꜣmw*.

Chapter 7

EB IV / MB I: A Period of Amorite Semi-Nomadic Invasions?[1]

A. THE INFLUENCE OF THE AMORITE HYPOTHESIS ON ARCHAEOLOGICAL INTERPRETATION

The EB IV/MB I Period in Palestine and Syria is certainly among the least understood and most discussed periods in Near Eastern Archaeology. The limitedness of the stratified remains, in spite of the large body of ceramic material that has been found in hundreds of tombs, has made an analysis of the character of the settlements, particularly in Palestine, extremely difficult to pursue, and has left the relative chronology almost totally dependent on the highly dubious principles of ceramic typology, studied (by necessity!) for the most part, independent of the safeguards which the archaeologist has for other periods from a more precisely defined stratigraphy[2].

---

1 I am presently working on a brief monograph dealing with the distribution of settlements in Palestine and Syria during the EB IV/MB I Period in connection with the map: Die Übergangszeit FB IV/MB I in Palästina und Syrien, which I am preparing for the Tübinger Atlas des Vorderen Orients. In this monograph I hope to discuss the problems pertaining to the EB IV/MB I pottery. The following discussion is limited to a treatment of the historical questions related to this period in Palestine, particularly as they are connected with its identification as the "Patriarchal Period".

2 These remarks are by no means to be taken as derogatory of the work that has been done on the development of the ceramic forms of this period. It is merely to point out the limitations of the material. The most promising typological study of this period at present is that done by W. G. Dever, The Pottery of Palestine in the EB IV/MB I Period, c. 2150—1850 B. C., (Harvard Dissertation, 1966); cf. also his Vestigial Features in MB I: An Illustration of Some Principles of Ceramic Typology, BASOR 200 (1970), 19—30; and, The Peoples of Palestine in the Middle Bronze I Period, HThR 64 (1971), 197—217. E. D. Oren, in his article: A Middle Bronze Age I Warrior Tomb at Beth-Shan, ZDPV 87 (1971), 109—139, tries to carry the typological analysis beyond that of ceramic forms in arguing that the two major types of shafthole axes ("fenestrated" or "eye" axe, and "duckbill") can be used as dependable chronological criteria in classifying unstratified tomb deposits as MB I. (Oren's EB IV) and MB IIA (Oren's MB I) respectively. He tries to use these axes as criteria for his chronology on the basis of a detailed analysis of the deposits in which they have been found. However, it

Moreover, much of the material that is now available for the interpretation of EB IV/ MB I has been published only during the last decade, with the result that it has only recently become possible to get an overall view of the period; it is also only in the last few years that the archaeological remains for the whole of Palestine and Syria have been intensively studied.

The interpretation of the archaeological remains has several serious historical ramifications, particularly regarding the very touchy question of prehistoric migrations of peoples, and the extent to which

is on the basis of the existence of one or other axe type in specific deposits that he often establishes his "correction" of the dating and classification of many of the deposits that have so far been published (Cf. his remarks on Ugarit, Hama H!, Baghuz, and even tomb 92 at Beth Shan itself; cf., esp. 109—111 and 116f.). He attempts to give chronological clarity by introducing into the discussion two wall paintings from tombs in Egypt which portray axes carried by warriors (from Beni-Hasan; cf. Oren, 133. 136) on the grounds that the bearers of these axes are supposedly Asiatics (See, however, above, chapter 6!). In fact, the first is neither an "eye" nor a "duckbill" axe, and the second — certainly dated to 1890 B. C. — is an early form of the "duckbill" type. This would argue against his relatively late dating of MB IIA, and supports Kenyon's high dating. The main problem of this article, however, is its artificial introduction of chronological and typological precision into the classification of materials that do not allow such precise treatment.

His examination of the deposits parallel to Beth Shan T. 92, as well as his examination of the tomb itself (117—128), is quite unconvincing. His arguments are based on the presupposition that "homogenous" deposits can be asserted to exist because some of the material deposits (scarabs, spears, axes, and tomb types) followed a pattern of development similar to that of the pottery, and that the major divisions traditionally assigned to the pottery groups are in themselves real and total cultural complexes. However, can Ḫama H really be divided, as Oren would have it, so that early H = EB IV/MB I, and late H be assigned to MB II? (Ḫama H is, rather, a good example, as are most sites except of course TBM, of the limitations of our classification.) And does this same division really fall so neatly between Ugarit Moyen 1 and Ugarit Moyen 2? What about the pottery that is similar to MB IIA Palestinian pottery from U. M. 1? — and the "duckbill" axes from the same phase? What finally is Oren's oft-mentioned "evidence from homogenous and well-placed deposits elsewhere in Syria and Palestine" on the basis of which he is able to "correct" the deposits from Byblos, Ugarit, Beth Shan, Megiddo, Yabrud, Ḫama, and Baghuz? Only Tell et-Tin and Ras el-ʿAin are "homogenous and well-placed deposits" containing "duckbill" axes where we might without doubt classify the entire assemblage as belonging to MB IIA. But no one has ever doubted that the "duckbill" axe existed during the MB IIA period. That it is limited to this period, and not also found in MB IIB, is Oren's contention. Lebe'a, Kafer Djarra, and Sin el-Fil, Oren places in MB I—II (i. e., MB IIA—B); that is to say, there are in these tomb groups objects which can be placed in the MB IIA period and objects which, had they been found at TBM, would be dated to the MB IIB period!

such movements can be discerned on the basis of archaeological evidence. Does a significant difference in the pottery repertoire, combined with radical changes in living conditions, imply a change in the population? an immigration of a new nomadic people? An answer to this question, with regard to the shift between the Ghassulian Period and Early Bronze I, had been attempted on the basis of cranial material which at first appeared to allow of a sharp distinction between the Ghassulians and their successors.[3] No such direct anthropological evidence can be applied to the EB IV/MB I period. Rather, what has been found in the excavations has been linked with what was thought to be textual evidence for a widespread movement of semi-nomadic Amorites. We have already seen the inadequacy of this interpretation insofar as it is dependent on the written records. This chapter will attempt to examine the extent to which the interpretation of archaeological finds has been affected by this erroneous view of contemporary history. When taken by itself, does the archaeological evidence really reflect the arrival of new groups into Palestine coming from north of Palestine and ultimately from South Mesopotamia? Is the evidence really conclusive, that at this time Palestine is occupied and controlled by various semi-nomadic groups who were responsible for the destruction of the Early Bronze Age settlements? Finally, can the culture of EB IV/MB I really be described as nomadic? Only if all three of these questions are answered positively can support for the historicity of the patriarchs be claimed from the archaeological remains. Otherwise, the entire "Amorite Hypothesis" is without historical basis.

It has to be admitted that the general opinion of scholars who have written on this period is strongly inclined (though not with complete unanimity) to accept this interpretation. It is my opinion, however, that not only has this understanding been affected by faulty historical presuppositions, but it has also been misled by a premature evaluation of the archaeological materials, an evaluation based on excavations carried out at isolated sites, specifically, Tell Beit Mirsim and Jericho.

The pottery from this period was first recognized as belonging to an independent period during the excavations at Jericho in 1908 and 1909, when Sellin and Watzinger uncovered a level of mud brick houses with a unique type of pottery, having thin walls and

[3] R. de Vaux, Palestine During the Neolithic and Chalcolithic Periods, CAH², fascicle 47, 1966, 34 and 38; P. Lapp, Bab edh-Dhra Tomb A 76 and Early Bronze I in Palestine, BASOR 189 (1968), 13 and 20; Palestine in the Early Bronze Age, Glueck Festschrift, 104. This distinction now appears misguided; cf., Miroschedji, L'Époque Pré-Urbaine en Palestine, CRB 13 (1971), 105f.

incised and combed decoration[4]. Because of similarities seen with the pottery from Troy VI (then dated to the 14—12th centuries) the excavators gave the period the name "Spätkanaanitisch" dating it to the late pre-Israelite period, connecting it in Palestine with pottery found at Tell el-Mutesellim[5]. Petrie, in his excavations at Tell Ajjul in 1930 and 1931, found some evidence of this period on the edge of the tell, but primarily from a large number of graves. He dated this material to the Fifth and Sixth Dynasties and termed it the "Copper Age", because of the copper weapons found with the tombs[6].

The interpretation now current finds its beginnings in the publications of W. F. Albright on the excavations at Tell Beit Mirsim[7]. Three levels were distinguished: J, I, and H, with a gap in the occupation between J and I. The extent of the settlement was very slight, and the pottery of the later two periods was relatively homogeneous. On the basis of similarities of the pottery in I-H with what was known as the "caliciform ware" of Syria, Albright concluded that the origin of the pottery culture should be sought in Syria, and ultimately in North Mesopotamia[8]. Following the terminology that was being developed by archaeologists in the Aegean, he called the period, represented by TBM J, EB IIIB (or EB IV), and, on the basis of similarities with Egyptian pottery of the late Sixth Dynasty and early First Intermediate Period, he dated the level to the 23—21st centuries. The caliciform period (TBM I-H) he called MB I, and dated it from 2100 to 1900 B. C. In an article in 1935[9], he related TBM H to the Sethe Execration Texts (which he then dated c. 2000 B. C.)[10] and the Mari Texts (also dated c. 2000 "or a little later")[11]. He interpreted the decline in Palestinian culture that is evident in this period to a widespread nomadic immigration from the desert. These people he called "Amorites". He suggested that it was at this time that the patriarchs entered Palestine from North Mesopotamia[12]. In general, he understood the archaeological evidence to show that towards the end of the Third Millenium

---

4 Schicht f: E. Sellin and C. Watzinger, Jericho: Die Ergebnisse der Ausgrabungen 1913, 14f. 46f. and 108—112.

5 Ibid. 110—112.

6 W. M. Flinders Petrie, Ancient Gaza, 1931—1932, I 2. 9—12; II 2.

7 The Excavation of Tell Beit Mirsim, I: The Pottery of the First Three Campaigns, AASOR 12 (1932), 8—14; IA: The Bronze Age Pottery of the Fourth Campaign, AASOR 13 (1933), 62—67; and II: The Bronze Age, AASOR 17 (1938), 12—16.

8 Albright, AASOR 13, 66f.; cf. also Palestine in the Earliest Historical Period, JPOS 15 (1935), 220.

9 Ibid. 193—234.

10 Ibid. 197.

11 Ibid. 198.

(c. 2000 B. C.), there was a break in the continuity of the occupation in Palestine, and a gradual depopulation of the land; after about 2000 B. C., the population increased. This is attributed to nomadic penetration of Palestine, specifically by the Amorites[13].

This interpretation of Albright was strongly affirmed by G. E. Wright in the first comprehensive study of the period, in which Wright brought together parallel materials from other excavations in Palestine, particularly Bethel, Ajjul, Jericho, Megiddo, Tell ed-Duweir, and the sherds found by N. Glueck in his explorations of Northern Transjordan[14]. This interpretation has generally been supported in subsequent publications[15], particularly since so many of the major sites that had been excavated showed only slight occupation levels in contrast to the large number of tombs found. Typical is Tell ed-Duweir[16]. In her report on this site, Miss Tufnell identified the occupation during this period as belonging to the destroyers of the EB settlement. They are spoken of as "invaders" whose settlements are understood as "early attempts to adjust themselves to a settled way of life". Stressing the need to recognize several different subdivisions (whether chronological or cultural) within the entire period, she chose the term "caliciform", to represent the settlement at Duweir, TBM H, and the related finds at Ḫama[17].

Although regional and chronological differentiation must certainly be made, the pottery of the period does show a certain

---

[12] Ibid. 217—219.

[13] See further on the early position of Albright: From the Stone Age to Christianity, 1940, [3]1957, 163f. In his Archaeology of Palestine, 1949, Albright extends this nomadic period to the end of the 20th century, B. C., subsequent to the lowering of the dating for the Sethe Texts to the end of the 20th century (82). He also reemphasizes the dependence of the pottery culture on Syria (80), but states: "It is not necessary to suppose that this ceramic movement was connected with any shift of peoples; it seems rather to have been a cultural drift associated with the diffusion of the Syro-Mesopotamian Culture of the Period immediately preceding the Third Dynasty of Ur." (! emphasis added.) This statement is extremely significant for the history of the interpretation of MB I, since Albright later rejects the Amorite Hypothesis, particularly the nomadic character of the occupation contemporary with TBM H (see further, below).

[14] G. E. Wright, The Chronology of Palestinian pottery in Middle Bronze I, BASOR 71 (1938), 27—34; cf. also: The pottery of Palestine from the Earliest Times to the end of the Early Bronze Age, 1937, 78—81. This early position is also followed by J. Bright, History of Israel, 1959, 47f.

[15] See the brief discussion and bibliography in W. G. Dever, The "Middle Bronze I" Period in Syria and Palestine, Glueck Festschrift, 134f., as well as his dissertation, The Pottery of Palestine in the EB IV/MB I Period.

[16] Cf. O. Tufnell, Lachish IV, The Bronze Age, 1958, 41—45. 62. and 171—175.

[17] Ibid. 41f.

uniformity and homogeneity which justifies a single designation for the entire period. This homogeneity was stressed in the next general survey made of the pottery by Ruth Amiram in 1960[18], in which she established a relative chronology in three periods. Her family A (which consists largely of what Tufnell referred to as "caliciform") has close affinities with Syria and Mesopotamia, particularly Ḫama J 8—6, Akkadian graves at Ur, and Gawra VI (Akkad dynasty)[19]. Family C, which she considered to be the latest pottery, has close affinities with MB II pottery[20].

It is primarily because of what she understood as a line of continuity in the development of certain pottery forms ultimately ending in MB II, in contrast to what she interpreted as a very sharp break betweeen the ceramic traditions of this period and the Early Bronze pottery, that she has maintained the traditional terminology (MB I) for the period as a whole[21]. In 1962, Albright argued that Amiram's schema of pottery development should be turned about: that A, rather than being the earliest of the series, is the latest and that the development of the pottery groups should follow the order, B, C, A[22]. He pointed out rightly that Amiram's B and C groups, while showing no particular influence from Mesopotamia, do show a clear development from the EB III forms, and should therefore be dated early[23]. However, his reason for dating Amiram's group A later than B—C cannot be accepted. Not only does he neglect the close similarity of Group C to the MB II period which was stressed by Amiram[24], but his primary defense of this late dating is his hypothesis that Group A is related not only to the Syrian and Mesopotamian ware of Hama J and the Akkad Period, but also to the combing decoration found in

---

[18] The Pottery of the Middle Bronze Age I in Palestine, IEJ 10 (1960), 204—225.

[19] Ibid. 217—219.

[20] Particularly in the more frequent use of the potter's wheel (Ibid. 212).

[21] Ibid. 204f., see also her The Pottery of the Middle Bronze Age I, (Hebrew) Qadmoniot 2 (1969), 45—49, and especially, Ancient Pottery of the Holy Land, 1970, 78—89; for the similarities with the pottery from the Dynasty of Akkad, see R. J. and L. Braidwood, Excavations in the Plain of Antioch, I, The Earlier Assemblages, Phases A—J, 1960, 522f.

[22] The Chronology of Middle Bronze I (Early Bronze-Middle Bronze), BASOR 168 (1962), 36—42.

[23] Ibid. 38f. He dates B and C to the 22nd and 21st centuries. See also, Albright, Some Remarks on the Archaeological Chronology of Palestine before about 1500 B. C., in: Chronologies in Old World Archaeology, ed. by R. W. Ehrich, 1965, 53f., where, however, he dates these to the 21st and 20th centuries.

[24] IEJ 10 (1960), 204f., a similarity also to be found in Group A (cf. O. Tufnell, Lachish IV, Plate 66, no. 399).

Second Intermediate Period levels in Egypt[25]! This involves the elaborate hypothesis that, through what Albright calls "cultural diffusion", type A pottery spread from the Akkad Empire (his chronology: 24th—22nd centuries) westward under the influence of trade (2300-early 22nd century) to Syria, where it can be dated (in Ḫama J) from about 2300 to about 2000 B. C. The pottery then entered Palestine in the late 21st century and was used there until the end of the 19th century. From the South of Palestine, many of the decorative motifs were adopted by the potters of Egypt at the beginning of the Second Intermediate Period[26]. He dates type A pottery in Palestine from just before 2000 to about 1800 B. C., coextensive with the Twelfth Dynasty in Egypt, which late dating he defends by a correction of the chronology of the Royal Tombs of Byblos[27]. A completely new historical picture of the EB IV/MB I period is reconstructed around this thesis. Combining once again his archaeological hypothesis with the Execration Texts, he concludes that only the earlier part of the period (EB IV) is to be understood as nomadic, as is reflected in the Sethe Texts[28]. The later period (MB I) is now seen as sedentary (related to the Posener Texts), indeed closely tied to a thriving Amorite Caravan trade[29]. The patriarchs, now understood, not as wandering semi-nomads, but as caravaneers[30], are thought to have played a leading role in the furtherance of this trade[31].

Albright's new interpretation of the history of MB I has not been generally accepted by other archaeologists, though his correction of Amiram's thesis has been almost universally adopted[32]. J. van Seters,

25 Albright, Abram the Hebrew. A New Archaeological Interpretation, BASOR 163 (1961), 39; BASOR 168 (1962), 37f.; Chronologies in Old World Archaeology, 52—54.

26 BASOR 168 (1962), 38.

27 Albright's chronology will be discussed below in ch. 8, section B.

28 Albright, Remarks on the Chronology of Early Bronze IV—Middle Bronze II A in Phoenicia and Syria-Palestine, BASOR 184 (1966), 32f.

29 Ibid. 33; cf. also Chronologies in Old World Archaeology 54.

30 BASOR 163 (1961), 36—54.

31 This whole question will be taken up again in ch. 8.

32 So M. Tadmor (Contacts Between the Amuq and Syria-Palestine, IEJ 14, 1964, 253—269): "As has been repeatedly stressed, no occupational levels corresponding to the tomb-groups have as yet been excavated and the impression is that the major EB sites of Palestine still lay waste .... A very important point in the occurrence of the 'A' group in Palestine is the fact that the bearers of this pottery at some time abandoned their nomadic way of life and became sedentary." (266f.) However, Tadmor stresses the continuity that the 'A' group has with MB II: "This age of great upheavals — of destruction and changes — may have been more integrated in the archaeological sequence than has hitherto been suspected." (Ibid. 268f.) See also, B. Mazar, The Middle Bronze Age in Palestine, IEJ 18 (1968),

however, strongly objects to Albright's chronology, as well as his designation of MB I as "Amorite". He correctly sets aside Albright's terminus ad quem for this period, which was based on the ill-founded hypothesis that the incised decoration of the type A ceramic is related to similar decoration in 18th century Egypt, by pointing out that such decorative motifs are also extremely common in both Syria and Palestine in the MB II B—C period (contemporary with the Second Intermediate Period of Egypt). He also points out that Albright's understanding of a time lag of several centuries for the cultural diffusion of the MB I pottery is hard to correlate with Albright's thesis that the pottery was spread by means of trade[33]. His own interpretation, however, that MB I is an interlude of semi-nomadic groups[34], and that MB IIA is the result of an immigration from Syria by the Amorites[35], is hardly more acceptable, neglecting, among other things, the serious methodological issue stressed by Albright: that the transference of ceramic traditions from one region to another does not necessarily imply a migration of peoples[36].

Over the last 20 years, Kathleen Kenyon has developed the most dominant alternative interpretation to Albright's, though it shows strong affinities, particularly in its insistence on the Amorite and nomadic character of the period, with Albright's early interpretation. Based almost exclusively on her excavations at Jericho, her interpretation shows little significant change since the early 1950's[37].

68, n. 6, who, however, connects the beginning of MB IIA with the rise of the Twelfth Dynasty. De Vaux sees two waves of immigrants at this time. The first are the destroyers of the EB civilization; the second are the Amorites found in the Execration Texts (Bulletin: Archéologie palestinienne, RB 74, 1967, 474).

[33] J. van Seters, The Hyksos, 1966, 16f.

[34] Ibid. 10f.

[35] Ibid. 82.

[36] Albright, Archaeology of Palestine, 80.

[37] K. Kenyon, Some notes on the History of Jericho in the Second Millenium B. C., PEQ (1951), 101—138, esp. 106—113; British School of Archaeology in Jerusalem Excavations at Jericho, 1952: Interim Report, PEQ (1952), 4—6; Excavations at Jericho, 1952, PEQ (1952), 62—82, esp. 65—68. 74. 80; Excavations at Jericho, 1953, PEQ (1953), 81—96, esp. 90—93; Excavations at Jericho, 1954, PEQ (1954), 45—63, esp. 56—58; Tombs of the Intermediate Early Bronze-Middle Bronze Age at Tell Ajjul, ADAJ 3 (1956), 41—55; Digging up Jericho, 1957, ch. 8: "Nomadic Invaders," 186—209; Archaeology in the Holy Land, 1960, 135—161; Jericho I, 1960, 180—262; Jericho II, 1964, 33—166. 551—565; Syria and Palestine, c. 2160—1780 B. C., CAH², fascicle 29, 1965, 38—61; Palestine in the Middle Bronze Age, CAH², fascicle 48, 1966, 3—13; Amorites and Canaanites, 1966; Jericho, in: Archaeology and Old Testament Study, ed. by D. W. Thomas, 1967, 267—269. She is followed in her interpretation, among others, by J. Mellaart, The Chalcolithic and Early Bronze Ages in the Near East and Anatolia,

When Kenyon uncovered the latest EB wall at Jericho, she found a layer of intensely burnt debris giving evidence for a violent destruction of the EB city. Resting directly on top of this wall was a mud-brick building of the EB-MB (EB IV/MB I) Period. From this evidence, she was able to conclude that "the violent destruction of this wall and the ensuing cessation of the Early Bronze Age culture can undoubtedly be attributed to the newcomers"[38]. Further, it was discovered that the ditch of this latest EB town had silted up to a depth of 2.50 meters before any EB—MB structures appeared[39], from which Kenyon concluded that the EB—MB destroyers of the EB city initially used Jericho as a camping site and only after a considerable period of time began to build houses[40]. "The newcomers therefore were essentially nomads. They destroyed existing towns, but did not create their own"[41]. The building structures of the EB-MB Period were all very slight, and, spread over the mound, were, as far as is known, without any town wall.

Kenyon found added support for her interpretation in the large number of tombs at Jericho[42]. Among the 346 tombs excavated from this period, she distinguished seven different groups. Most of the pottery from the tombs was quite distinct from that found on the tell. One type of tomb (Dagger Type) contained mostly single burials with only a dagger, or a pin and a few beads, as grave offerings[43]. The Pottery Type tombs, also containing mostly single burials, usually had a lamp placed in a niche in the wall, and a skeleton that was partially or completely disarticulated[44]. This practice of disarticulated burial was explained by the hypothesis that the group consisted of nomadic pastoralists, following a seasonal pattern of migration, returning periodically to an ancestral burial ground. This coincided with her interpretation of the Dagger Type group who appeared to be warriors. The differences in burial customs was explained as due to a type of tribal organization, each tribe having its own customs.

1966, 91—95; J. B. Hennessy, The Foreign Relations of Palestine during the Early Bronze Age, 1967, 88—90, and J. N. Schofield, Megiddo, Archaeology and Old Testament Studies, 313f.

38 PEQ (1954), 56; see also PEQ (1952), 5. 68.

39 PEQ (1954), 56; Archaeology in the Holy Land 137.

40 PEQ (1954), 56—58. The obvious contradiction in this interpretation will be discussed in Section B.

41 Archaeology in the Holy Land 137.

42 The tombs are published in Jericho I—II.

43 Kenyon concludes from this that it reflects a group with "austere habits, possessing little in the way of worldly goods, amongst whom a warrior element was very important." (Amorites and Canaanites 15).

44 Ibid. 15—18.

It is primarily the distinction between the Dagger Type and Pottery Type tombs that the argument for tribal differences is based. The differences between these and the other groups could possibly be explained as evolutionary[45]. We have already discussed Kenyon's identification of these nomadic pastoralists with the Amorites of Mesopotamia and the *ʿȝmw* of the First Intermediate Period of Egypt[46]. On the basis of changes in burial practices, as well as what she sees as a complete break in the material culture both before and after this period, Kenyon calls the period: "Intermediate Early Bronze-Middle Bronze" (EB-MB), to designate a period totally unrelated to either the Early Bronze or the Middle Bronze periods[47]. She summarizes this extraordinary period as follows: "From at least the 24th to the 20th centuries B. C., Syria and Palestine were overrun by nomads, amongst whom the Amorites predominated, with a culmimating period of complete nomadic control in the two centuries c. 2181—1991 B.C."[48].

With the publication of a tomb group excavated at Dhahr Mirzbaneh, the late P. Lapp attempted a new interpretation of the Palestinian material[49]. After a critical review of the positions taken by Kenyon, Albright, and de Vaux[50], Lapp presents a new thesis which sees the prior EB settlement of Palestine, not as predominantly urban, but as dominated by urban centers in the midst of a generally non-urban population. The destruction of the cities was caused by non-urban invaders, which was followed by "a natural return to non-urban life"[51]. The indigenous element Lapp identifies as Semitic. The invaders are identified as non-Semitic on the basis of the names from Ur III which are neither Semitic nor Sumerian, variant Egyptian artistic traditions in the portrayal of "Asiatics", and the non-Semitic place names in Syria. These non-Semitic people he connects with Kenyon's Dagger Type tombs. The disarticulated

45 Digging up Jericho 143.

46 See above ch. 5 and 6.

47 PEQ (1951), 106n.

48 CAH² fascicle 29, 61.

49 The Dhahr Mirzbanêh Tombs, ASOR publication of the Jerusalem School: Archaeology, vol. 4, 1966, 86—116; See further his articles The Cemetery at Bab edh-Dhra, Archaeology 19 (1966), 104—111; Bab edh-Dhrâ Tomb A76 and Early Bronze I in Palestine, BASOR 189 (1968), 12—41; Palestine in the Early Bronze Age, Glueck Festschrift, 101—131, esp. 114—124; his interpretation is generally supported by M. Kochavi, The Settlement of the Negev in the Middle Bronze I Age (dissertation Jerusalem, 1967); The Middle Bronze Age I (The Intermediate Bronze Age) in Eretz-Israel, Qadmoniot 2 (1969), 38—44.

50 Dhahr Mirzbaneh 86—93. De Vaux in his review of Lapp's book (RB 74, 1967, 473f.) continues to hold his "Amorite" explanation of the period.

51 Dhahr Mirzbaneh 96.

burials are considered chronologically later, belonging to the second half of this period[52]. The metal-bearing non-Semitic invaders are linked with the destruction of Ras Shamra and Byblos[53], and the "porteurs de torques" are related to Cyprus, the Aegean, and the Beaker culture of the West Mediterranean. The ultimate origin of these people he traces to the region of Fergana in Soviet Central Asia where he says: "For the first time an assemblage of material published in some detail provides good parallels to material from IB Palestine"[54]. The pottery from Taš-Kurgan in the region of Fergana is at first sight remarkably similar to the Palestinian pottery, particularly that found in the South of Palestine. Lapp explained the easy assimilation of these newcomers by suggesting that the indigenous non-urban people of EB Palestine also had origins of a similar nature[55]. This also is used to explain the strong links between the pottery of EB III and EB IV in contrast to what he sees as a radical break between MB I and MB IIA[56].

However, this introduces serious contradictions in his interpretation of the period, rendering it totally unacceptable. Not only is there no real evidence for a non-Semitic portion of the population of Palestine during the EB IV/MB I Period[57], but Lapp's identification of these groups ethnically with the indigenous groups of EB I, as well as his argument that the pottery of EB III and EB IV are closely related, completely destroys the basis for his seeing two groups in the first place, or, indeed, any evidence for newcomers in Palestine! Furthermore, his identification of the MB I pottery with that of

---

52 Ibid. 97—100.

53 Ibid. 100f.

54 Ibid. 111f.

55 Only suggested in Dhahr Mirzbanêh 114f.; but more fully argued in BASOR 189 (1968), 26—31, and Glueck Festschrift, 114—123. G. E. Wright, however, suggests (The Archaeology of Palestine from the Neolithic through the Middle Bronze Age, JAOS 91, 1971, 285f.) that Lapp's "earlier" shaft tomb groups should perhaps be dated to the period between the 24th and 22nd centuries (i. e., EB IV)!

56 It is, indeed, because of this continuity (between EB III—EB IV) that Lapp suggests "EB IV A—B" (BASOR 31n) instead of the terminology he had suggested earlier; "Intermediate Bronze I—II" (Dhahr Mirzbanêh 115f.). In the Glueck Festschrift, he decided to use the terminology introduced by Dever ("EB IV/MB I") to avoid confusion.

57 That there were non-Semitic elements in the Near East goes without question, but the names from Ur III have nothing to do with Palestine (cf. above, ch. 4); The non-Semitic Syrian place names — in contrast to the Semitic place names of Palestine — give evidence that perhaps an earlier indigenous population in Syria was non-Semitic. That the Egyptian artistic traditions do not give evidence of a difference in the population has been argued above in ch. 6; this material is also not related to Palestine!

Taš-Kurgan is first of all very questionable, and secondly, even if the ceramics were related, does not really support the thesis that the Palestinian pottery is to be derived from Russia. Complete continuity with EB wares can be shown of the pottery in Palestine[58]. That is, the pottery can be shown to be indigenous to Palestine! Lapp would, however, take the Taš-Kurgan pottery out of its 1st century A. D. context, and relate it to Palestine of two thousand years earlier. If this could be done, then the Taš-Kurgan material must be seen as derived from Palestine. However, that it cannot be so disoriented, is strongly suggested by the report of Kozenkova which accompanies the publication of the tomb groups[59]. First of all the burial traditions appear to be radically different from Palestinian burials. The body (sometimes disarticulated) is placed in a shallow cist or on the surface, and is covered by a rounded mound of loose stones, in sharp contrast to the shaft tombs of both EB IV/MB I as well as the EB I tombs with which Lapp wishes to relate this group. The EB IV/MB I cairn burials, known from the Negev and Transjordan, are quite different[60]. All but one piece of the pottery found at Taš-Kurgan was made on a fast wheel, in contrast to all but the very latest EB IV/MB I pottery. The pottery is covered with a reddish-brown porous slip. The firing is medium. On the surface were found sherds of similar pots which were well-fired and covered with a white slip[61]. The description of the pottery, independent of the form, is entirely different form the Palestinian wares. Moreover, the late dating of these graves is fully supported by the metal objects found, some of which are iron, which cannot simply be explained on the basis of locally available ores, but implies a completely different level of technology[62]. Furthermore, the late dating of the finds at Taš-Kurgan is supported by the related pottery found in excavations throughout the Fergana plain, which are dated from the 1st or 2nd century B. C. to the 6th century A. D.[63]. Finally, these burials are identified as a

---

[58] Lapp, Glueck Festschrift. See further below, Section B.

[59] W. I. Kozenkova, Pogrebalnyje pamjatniki Fergany perwych wekow naschej ery, Sovetskaja Archeologija 1 (1966), 211—226. (I am indebted to Mr. Sitarz of the Biblical Archaeological Institute in Tübingen for providing me with a translation of this article.)

[60] Compare Kochavi, The Excavations at Tel Yeruḥam (Hebrew), BIES 27 (1963), 289, and Qadmoniot 2 (1969), 40, with Kozenkova, Sovetskaja Archeologija, 213. Lapp (Dhahr Mirzbaneh 112) refers to cairn burials of EB IV at Bab edh-Dhrâ, but these are not published.

[61] Kozenkova 217—219.

[62] Contra Lapp, Dhahr Mirzbanêh, 112. Lapp forgets here that according to his thesis these people are supposed to represent the copper metal-working traditions of the EB IV/MB I Period.

[63] Kozenkova 219—223.

late development of burial traditions of the early Iron Age in Northwest Fergana[64]. The only similarity with Palestine: the general form of the pottery, must apparently be accepted as simply coincidental.

Lapp, however, is correct in dismissing the "Amorite Hypothesis", and insisting that the origin of this culture has to be sought in the end of the EB III Period. As a result of Lapp's excavations at Bab-edh-Dhrâ, but also supported as we shall see by other recent excavations, the suggestion put forward earlier by Wright[65] that the EB IV/MB I pottery forms are survivals from and adaptations of the EB traditions, is shown to be completely justified[66].

William Dever, while fully accepting the EB III origins of the pottery forms, nevertheless, supporting the position of Kathleen Kenyon, presents an historical interpretation which understands the people who established this period as nomadic Amorite invaders from the North[67]. By emphasizing the geographical differences in the pottery found in Palestine[68], Dever has attempted to divide the pottery into six families: (1) The Northern Family (Amiram's B), (2) The Jezreel Family (Amiram's C), (3) The J. Family: Transjordan, Jericho, (4) The Southern Family (Amiram's A, including Negev and Sinai), (5) The Coastal Family (Azor, Ma'âbarot, etc.), (6) The Central Hills (area of Jerusalem).

On the basis of the degree of dependency of the pottery forms on the EB culture, he concludes that the J. Family is the earliest, and that in this region the EB traditions coalesced with Syrian influences, forming a distinctive hybrid culture. The Southern Family he under-

[64] Based on the construction of the cairns, the orientation of the body, and the placement of the pottery in the cist (Ibid.). For a further critique of Lapp's hypothesis, see W. G. Dever, HThR 64 (1971), 220—223.

[65] The Archaeology of Palestine, Albright Festschrift, 87**f.** Wright here suggests that the "new people" of this period lived along the desert fringes of the EB culture, and that the Syrian influence is "imported"; that is, he apparently rejects the Syrian origin of the people.

[66] Similarly, the recent article by E. D. Oren, A Middle Bronze Age I Warrior Tomb at Beth-Shan, ZDPV 87 (1971), 109—139, supports this relationship, and uses the terminology EB IVA and EB IVB to designate this period (see 109n).

[67] Cf. The Pottery of Palestine in the EB IV/MB I Period; also: Ethnic Movements in East Central Europe and the Near East, ca. 3300—1800 B. C., Yearbook of the American Philosophical Society for 1967 (1968), 500—503; The Middle Bronze I Period in Syria and Palestine, Glueck Festschrift, 132—163; BASOR 200 (1970), 19—30; and especially HThR 64 (1971), 197—226.

[68] Since Dever's dissertation, where he establishes these differences by pottery typology, is as yet unpublished, and since the interpretation given in the microfilm copy of his dissertation is radically different from the analysis given in his article in the HThR 64 (1971), 198—210, a detailed evaluation is here impossible.

stands as related, but, because of the absence of direct Syrian influences, to be regarded as later. He believes that most of the pottery in Palestine follows the EB tradition; the most common forms are clearly locally made and thoroughly indigenous.

Since the MB I pottery in Northern Transjordan and Jericho are thought to show strong Syrian influence, he concludes that the survivors of the EB culture could not have developed the MB I forms. He therefore sees the necessity of postulating the presence of newcomers from Syria in Transjordan at the end of EB IV. The Syrian influence in the Northern and Jezreel families he dismisses as peripheral, and apparently as late, assuming that Amiram's family B (and C?) is relatively late[69]. Dever then concludes that the route of the newcomers avoided the main routes of contact between Syria and Palestine, and came down through the Hauran into Transjordan, and then across into Palestine by Jericho. These newcomers are supposedly semi-nomads, organized into small groups without a definite ceramic tradition of their own (thus accounting for their borrowing from the Syrian tradition and being assimilated into the EB culture). They lived on the fringes of Syria (The "Syrian" influence in Transjordan is purely transitory) and migrated southward. This migration took more than a century. The pottery in the North is earlier; that in the South is later.

Stressing the so-called "nomadic" characteristics of the Palestinian MB I, particularly the practice of disarticulated burials familiar to us from Kenyon's study, Dever attempts to identify these newcomers with the Amorites of the Ur III Period, particularly the *MAR.TU* people mentioned in the texts from Drehem. He also cites the Sumerian literary texts describing the *MAR.TU*, "Knowing neither cereals nor house, feeding themselves on wild truffles and undressed meat, possessing no fixed abode in all the course of their life nor a tomb after their death"[70], as describing a distinctive

---

[69] In the Glueck Festschrift (completed in 1968), he arranges Amiram's chronology in the following manner: "C-early A—B-Late A" (139). The summary presented here is taken from Dever's article in the HThR. In his 1966 dissertation he suggested four families in which the Jezreel Family was the earliest. Largely on the basis of what Dever understood as Syrian influence, which he then by no means considered peripheral, he saw an immigration of semi-nomads from Syria into the Jezreel valley, down the Jordan to Jericho, from Jericho into the Central Hills and finally into the Negev. Those areas which had stronger Syrian influence were considered earlier, and those with less as later. This scheme has apparently been given up, and Dever seems now to follow the suggestion earlier made by G. E. Wright (Albright Festschrift 87f.) that the "Amorite" nomadic groups came from the fringes of the Syrian desert, and that the Syrian influence is secondary.

[70] CAH^2 fascicle 29, 34f. (emphasis added). See, Dever, HThR 64 (1971), 218.

trait that is unquestionably related to the disarticulated secondary burials of the tombs in Palestine.

Not only does this ignore Lapp's observation that no tombs similar to those in Palestine have ever been found in Southern Mesopotamia, but it is difficult to relate a people who are described as having no burial practices, with those we know primarily from quite elaborate tombs! Moreover, as was already pointed out in Chapter 4, the *MAR.TU* mentioned in the texts from Drehem are hardly to be thought of as semi-nomadic, and certainly not to be equated with the *MAR.TU* people described in this literary text.

Finally, it should be recognized that Dever's analysis of the geographic displacement of EB IV/MB I Palestinian pottery is only formally related to his historical assertion that the spread of ceramic influences from Syria is to be explained by a semi-nomadic infiltration from the North. Indeed, that there are "newcomers" to Palestine at all is a totally unnecessary hypothesis. For, as Dever rightly points out, the MB I forms are a hybrid; the Syrian influence on the Palestinian pottery does not imply that the pottery culture was brought from Syria. However, if the pottery was not brought from Syria, there is no need of an hypothesis for anyone to bring it. What the archaeological evidence shows, particularly the development of the EB IV/MB I pottery culture out of the EB traditions, and the coalescence with certain elements from the Syrian ceramic repertoire, is a diffusion of Syrian pottery motifs towards the end of the EB IV Period into Palestine. The necessity of Dever's conclusion, that the "newcomers" did not have their own pottery culture, only emphasizes the obvious implication that there is simply no archaeological evidence for an immigration. In fact, the indigenous character of the Palestinian pottery tradition positively excludes it. Furthermore, that the geographical differentiation of the pottery forms in Palestine, though showing a variation in the degree of Syrian influence (which in my opinion is far greater in Amiram's family A and at Megiddo than elsewhere)[71], is to be interpreted chronologically, that the farther the pottery is removed from Syrian influence the later it must be, can hardly be taken for granted. A priori, it can generally be assumed that those regions which have easiest access to Syria, by whatever route, will betray in their culture stronger Syrian influences than more distant regions.

Significant changes in pottery cultures do demand a cause, but even where they are combined with radical changes in the living

---

[71] Which is also to be expected, given the normal pattern of cultural diffusion in this region! I fail to understand how the pottery of Northern Transjordan can be understood as obviously earlier than much of the pottery elsewhere.

conditions, these developments need not imply a change in the population. While much necessarily depends on a careful analysis of the pottery types, there seems to be adequate evidence already available which seems sufficient to exclude the theory of Kenyon and Dever that the EB IV/MB I culture in Palestine reflects either an immigration or an invasion of semi-nomadic peoples. There was a very definite change in the culture of Palestine towards the end of the EB III Peroid, but it was a change that needs to be explained on the basis of events within Palestine itself. In Troy, Anatolia, and in Syria, the nomadic invasion theory, used to explain the end of the EB culture in these regions, has long been given up[72]. This explanation is also inapplicable to Palestine.

B. THE EVIDENCE FOR AN INVASION FROM THE NORTH

Essential to Kenyon's interpretation of this period, as well as to her terminology: "Intermediate EB—MB", is the belief that the Early Bronze Age came to a sudden and violent end, and that the destruction of this culture was caused by the invading Amorites, i. e., that there was a complete and radical break between the cultures. This she claims occurred in both Syria and Palestine[73]. Her claim that the people of the Intermediate Period destroyed the Early Bronze culture is based primarily on her understanding of the remains at Byblos and Jericho. Byblos was destroyed by a fire which left a deposit of ash almost a half meter thick above the main temple. The burnt layer contained objects with the name of Pepy II (2278—2185 B. C.). Kenyon concludes from this that Byblos was destroyed towards the end of the reign of Pepy II, at the same time that the Asiatics broke up the settled government of Egypt[74]. However, Dunand reports a radical shift in the architectural tradition at Byblos (the advent of the "logis monocellulaires") just before the destruction, which is

[72] M. J. Mellink, The Pratt Ivories in the Metropolitan Museum of Art-Kerma-Chronology and the Transition from Early Bronze to Middle Bronze, AJA 73 (1969), 285—287; M. van Loon, New Evidence from Inland Syria for the Chronology of the Middle Bronze Age, AJA 73 (1969), 276.

[73] E. g., K. Kenyon, Archaeology and Old Testament Study, 267f.; Amorites and Canaanites 46f.; CAH² fascicle 29, p. 38. Her argument, if taken literally, is certainly open to the criticism made by G. E. Mendenhall of historians in general (Review of M. Weippert, Die Landnahme, Bb 50 (1969), 434): "Large social organizations tend to be ephemeral, and therefore historians, not understanding the process which leads to the formation and disintegration of such large social organizations, have constantly engaged in mass genocide."

[74] See, however, my discussion of the Egyptian texts in ch. 6.

also continued after the destruction, along with a gradual but profound shift in the pottery repertoire[75], which, if true, would not permit the explanation that the destruction was caused by an invasion of Amorites, to whom Dunand attributes (and Kenyon here agrees) the new structures. Kenyon's dismissal of Dunand's stratigraphical interpretation appears forced[76], since Kenyon's simpler explanation that the destruction took place before the advent of the new structures would hardly have been missed by Dunand if the evidence had allowed it.

Kenyon's interpretation of the destruction of EB Jericho by the people who occupied Jericho during the Intermediate Period is equally forced. As we have already mentioned above, the final EB wall at Jericho was found buried in a thick layer of ashes and burned debris, giving clear evidence of a major destruction, at least of this part of the site. Immediately above this wall were found houses of the EB-MB period. Kenyon interprets this:

> ... the EB-MB houses are built directly over the top of the stump of the last Early Bronze Age wall, and are in part terraced into the levels contemporary with it. The violent destruction of this wall and the ensuing cessation of the Early Bronze Age culture can undoubtedly be attributed to the newcomers. Therefore, on the evidence of the upper end of the trench, (i. e. the houses overlying the EB wall) it appeared that immediately after destroying the Early Bronze Age city they built their own houses on top[77].

Not only does the pottery evidence contradict this interpretation (EB-MB pottery here is relatively late, comparable to TBM H!)[78], but Kenyon's very carefully drawn section[79] gives evidence that the EB-MB structures did not immediately follow the destruction of the EB wall! Above the EB debris surrounding the wall there are shown pockets of silt to the East and West of the wall. The eastern pocket also covers part of the stumps of the EB wall. The EB-MB level overlies this silt deposit. It seems quite clear that this area of Jericho was abandoned at the end of the EB III Period, and only after a considerable period of time was it reoccupied by people using EB-MB pottery. That is to say, the people living in the EB-MB settlement did not destroy the EB city.

[75] M. Dunand, Byblos au Temps du Bronze Ancien et de la Conquête Amorite, RB 59 (1952), 82—90, here 86.

[76] Cf. Amorites and Canaanites 47.

[77] PEQ (1954), 56 (emphasis added); see also PEQ (1952), 5. 68.

[78] Cf. PEQ (1952), 5. 74. As early as 1938, Wright was able to point out that "there is an ever increasing mass of material which is clearly transitional between such deposits as Tomb A (the latest EB deposit found at Jericho), and the TBM I—H culture." (The Pottery of Palestine 78).

[79] PEQ (1954), 57.

There is also considerable evidence from the rest of Palestine which makes it impossible to attribute the destruction of the EB culture to an invasion; in fact, in many sites we have evidence only that the EB settlements were abandoned. It is, furthermore, well known, though not sufficiently stressed, that the large fortified sites of the EB Age were not all abandoned at the same time; indeed, if an invasion theory is to be maintained, it must be thought of in terms of 400 to 500 years duration before the MB I Period proper begins. Already at the end of the EB II Period, many major cities in Palestine were either destroyed or abandoned, and apparently not reoccupied until the EB IV/MB I or MB II Periods. Megiddo[80], Arad[81], Tell el-Far'ah, Ras el'Ain[82], and others, were already abandoned before the appearance of EB III proper (c. 2600 B. C.). Ras Shamra[83], Beth Shan, Beth Yerah, Tell esh-Shuneh, Jericho, and Ai were all abandoned during or at the end of EB III[84]. Some of these, however, were, after a short gap, resettled[85]. Still other sites were at this time newly settled; e. g., Ader[86], Tell Beit Mirsim[87], Bethel[88], Aro'êr, and Iskander[89]. Corresponding approximately with the amalgamation of the EB traditions with the Syrian "caliciform" tradition, many sites, such as Jericho and Tell Beit Mirsim were reoccupied, and still countless others newly settled, such as Tell ed-Duweir and Jebel Q̰a'aqir[90].

---

80 Cf. Wright, Albright Festschrift, 86; J. N. Schofield, Archaeology and Old Testament Studies, 313f.; I have elsewhere shown (The Dating of the Megiddo Temples in Strata XV—XIV, ZDPV 86, 1970, 44 and note 32) that the EB round altar 4017 does not continue in use beyond the EB Period.

81 Aharoni, Negeb, Archaeology and Old Testament Study, 387.

82 de Vaux, Tirzah ibid. 374.

83 C. F. Schaeffer, Stratigraphie Comparée, 1948, 36.

84 Wright, Albright Festschrift, 86.

85 So Ugarit was partially reoccupied in Ugarit ancien 3 and was continuously, though only partially, occupied through Ugarit moyen 1. (Schaeffer, Stratigraphie, 39.)

86 Ray L. Cleveland, Soundings at Khirbet Ader, AASOR 34—35 (1960), 79—97, esp. 88ff. There was a very thin EB level, and, apparently, no signs of destruction.

87 Which was abandoned after a short period (after Stratum J), then reoccupied (Strata I—H).

88 J. L. Kelso, Excavations at Bethel, BA 19 (1956), 37; The Excavations of Bethel (1934—1960), AASOR 39 (1968), 22.

89 Cf. E. Olávarri, Sondages à 'Arô'er sur l'Arnon, RB 72 (1965), 77—94, and Fouilles à 'Arô'er sur l'Arnon, RB 76 (1969), 230—259, for these and other contemporary sites.

90 At the latter site, at least three distinct stratigraphic levels have recently been uncovered, two of which belong to the MB I period. (I have this information through personal correspondence with Dr. J. Landgraf in Jerusalem.)

When this evidence is taken together with the evidence for continuous occupation at many of the major sites in inland Syria[91], the concept of a nomadic invasion to account for the destruction of the EB culture seems highly inadequate. Finally, the hypothesis that there was a complete break between the EB culture and the EB IV/MB I Period does not seem tenable over against the already mentioned position, now held by most American and Israeli archaeologists, that the EB IV/MB I pottery forms clearly show a dependence on their EB predecessors, though such a break might be thought to exist on the evidence of Jericho alone because of a gap in occupation at that site.

Although the burial practices appear to be new, disarticulated burials[92] and burials in caves[93] also occurred in Early Bronze Palestine. In fact, shaft tombs, similar to those of the EB IV/MB I Period, with a limited number of disarticulated burials, have a tradition that goes back at least 800 years[94]. The basic structure of Palestinian fortifications in the MB II Period, going back as it does to the EB style of fortifications[95], argues against any complete break in the historical tradition.

However, most of the evidence comes from the pottery, and here the continuity is quite certain. The following examples should be sufficient to show this: (1) Early Bronze lamps, although rare, are clearly fore-runners of the EB IV/MB I tradition. The saucer-lamps, and particularly those with four indentations evenly spaced around the rim, are obvious predecessors of the typical EB IV/MB I four spouted lamp. Moreover, some four spouted lamps have been found in EB contexts[96], and at least one lamp has been found with EB red-burnishing[97]. (2) The EB IV/MB I envelope ledge handle is the final stage of a ceramic motif which ultimately goes back to the Neolithic period[98]. (3) The EB IV/MB I lug handles go back to the

[91] Cf. R. J. and L. S. Braidwood, Excavations in the Plain of Antioch; E. Fugmann, Ḫama, Fouilles et Recherches 1931—1938, II, 1, 1958; A. Davico et alii, Missione Archeologica Italiana in Siria, 1964, 1965, 1966; and M. van Loon, AJA (1969), 276f.

[92] Cf. K. Kenyon, Amorites and Canaanites, 12, fig. 4.

[93] W. G. Dever, The Pottery of Palestine in the EB IV/MB I Period, 183.

[94] See, for example, the tombs discussed by P. Lapp in BASOR 189 (1968), 14—26 and figs. 1—16; see however, G. E. Wright, JAOS 91 (1971), 285f.

[95] P. J. Parr, The Origin of the Rampart Fortifications of Middle Bronze Age Palestine and Syria, ZDPV 84 (1968), 18—45.

[96] E. g., Tomb A at Jericho (EB IIIA) and TBM J; cf. W. F. Albright, BASOR 168 (1962), 38.

[97] From Bab-edh-Dhrâ; cf. Lapp, Glueck Festschrift, 115.

[98] G. E. Wright, The Pottery of Palestine, Appendix; N. Glueck, Explorations in Eastern Palestine III, AASOR XVIII—XIX (1939), 251—256; O. Tufnell, Lachish

Late Chalcolithic period and perhaps earlier[99]. (4) The large jars of EB IV/MB I, the lug-handled jugs, the small "hole-mouth" jars, the ovoid storage jars with flat base and flaring neck, and the jars with spouts, all go back to the EB tradition, and some to as early as the Chalcolithic period[100]. (5) Pattern combing lasted throughout the EB Period and is found in TBM J, Megiddo Stratum XV, and Hama J4, after which it is replaced by band combing[101].

There is also some evidence of continuity, though, admittedly limited, between EB IV/MB I and MB IIA[102]. The radical changes in the pottery repertoire at the beginning of MB IIA might possibly be explained by the adoption of new techniques in pottery making, particularly the use of the fast wheel, as well as the stronger influences of the more technologically advanced pottery traditions of Syria. This might perhaps be understood in the context of the rapid rise of trade during the Twelfth Dynasty which enabled the culturally more advanced settlements of the North, particularly those in Syria and Lebanon, to reassert their dominance over the relatively improverished South. However that may be, there are a number of characteristics which preclude any complete break between the cultures[103]. (1) Several sherds found by Glueck in the Negev have been classified by Albright as transitional between MB I and MB IIA[104]. (2) Band combing connects EB IV/MB I with MB II[105].

IV, 148—155; Albright, BASOR 168 (1962), 38; Chronologies in Old World Archaeology, 53f.; and R. Amiram, Ancient Pottery of Palestine, 35—40.

99 Dever, BASOR 200 (1970), 22.

100 G. E. Wright, BASOR 71 (1938), 29 and 32; P. J. Parr, A Cave at Arqub el Dhahr, ADAJ 3 (1956), 61—73 (see forms 124, 201, 202, 204 and 205); Dever, BASOR 200 (1970), 20—22.

101 M. W. Prausnitz, Abydos and Combed Ware, PEQ (1954), 96; Albright, BASOR 168 (1962), 40; J. van Seters, The Hyksos, 14f.

102 Similarly, G. E. Wright, JAOS 91 (1971), 287bf.; contra Kenyon, CAH², fascicle 48, 3—8, and Dever, HThR 64 (1971), 224f.

103 The scarcity of excavated MB IIA deposits in Palestine make it extremely difficult to evaluate this transition; moreover, the traditionally inflated chronology of the EB IV/MB I Period (400 to 500 years for EB IV/MB I over against 250 to 350 years for the entire Middle Bronze Period (see below, Chapter 8), as well as the general confusion in Middle Bronze Age typological studies, (cf. Thompson, ZDPV 86, 1970, 38—49, and U. Müller, Kritische Bemerkungen zu den Straten XIII bis IX in Megiddo, Ibid. 50—86) have made the use of Syrian parallels extremely tenuous.

104 W. F. Albright, BASOR 163 (1961), 40 n. 17: "One piece struck me in particular; it is a large piece from the wall of a vessel found with exclusively MB I sherds. Color and decoration are identical with MB I, but a primitive wheel had been used in turning the body of the vase, and the paste is typical MB II!" (ibid. 40n).

(3) The cooking pot is common to both EB IV/MB I and MB IIA, and transmits EB features[106]. (4) The four spouted lamp has been found in MB IIA contexts[107], and the single spouted lamp has often been found in unequivocal EB IV/MB I contexts[108]. (5) The MB II duckbill axe is a direct development out of the earlier fenestrated form which has been found in both EB IV/MB I and MB II contexts[109]. (6) If the double temples 5269/5192 in Megiddo

That most of the pottery which Glueck has found in the Negev is quite different from MB IIA pottery is insufficient reason to dismiss Albright's quite concrete observation; for just such continuity is only to be expected. There never was a time when the EB IV/MB I culture no longer existed and MB IIA had not yet begun. Nor is every EB IV/MB I corpus of pottery earlier than every MB IIA corpus.

105 Cf. Albright, AASOR 12, pl. 7; AASOR 13, pl. 21; E. Grant, Beth Shemesh, 1929, 131; C. W. McEwan, The Syrian Expedition of the Oriental Institute of the University of Chicago, AJA 41 (1937), 10; G. E. Wright, BASOR 71 (1938), 32; Braidwood, Excavations in the Plain of Antioch, 464; M. Tadmor, IEJ 14 (1964), 268; J. van Seters, The Hyksos, 16; G. E. Wright, JAOS 91 (1971), 287. One clear example of the closeness of these two periods regarding this particular motif of band combing is the jar found in an MB II A tomb near Dalhamiya (coord: 2066. 2300). Cf. the Israeli General Archives of the Israel Department of Antiquities.

106 G. E. Wright, BASOR 71 (1938), 32; JAOS 91 (1971), 287; M. Tadmor, IEJ 14 (1964), 268. The inverted-rim bowl (a hallmark of the MB II pottery repertoire) might also be mentioned as a point of ceramic continuity between EB IV/MB I and MB II. Cf. Dever, Glueck Festschrift, fig. 4, nos. 1, 2, and 3; also idem, Archaeology 25 (1972) 233. Also note the ring-base ware found in the unequivocal EB IV/MBI levels in Parr, ADAJ 4/5 (1960) 133.

107 R. Amiram, IEJ 10 (1960), 205f. and Fig. I. To dismiss these as misattributed to MB II levels, while always possible, requires some justification other than typological. I see no reason to doubt the excavation reports here. Mention should also be made of the miniature four-spouted lamp from the MB II Nahariya temple displayed in case 70. 5 of the Israel Museum, Jerusalem.

108 P. Guy and R. M. Engberg, Megiddo Tombs, 1938, Pl. 10:27, 12:10 and 11; O. Tufnell, Lachish IV, 171; R. Amiram, IEJ 10 (1960) 212; and W. G. Dever, BASOR 200 (1970), 29 n. 29. Also at Tell Ḥalif in an MB I burial: cf. RB 74 (1967), 77f.

109 Contra Oren, ZDPV 87 (1971), 137. Cf. Thompson, ZDPV 86 (1970), 46—49. Subsequent to the publication of my article in ZDPV, R. Gophna published a fenestrated axe found at Maʿabarot (A Middle Bronze Age I Tomb with Fenestrated Axe at Maʿabarot, IEJ 19, 1969, 174—177), which shows beyond doubt that this axe was used in the EB IV/MB I Period as well. While it is now clear that fenestrated axes were first developed contemporary to some of what we understand as EB IV/MB I culture in Palestine, it is also clear that the "duckbill" axe is a direct development from this type. The evidence from Byblos shows that this development was a gradual one (Note the intermediate types; it was not suddenly decided that the cutting "fenestrated" axe would be changed into the piercing "duckbill" form); the evidence from Megiddo (and the evidence for the dating

Stratum XV are to be dated to the EB IV/MB I Period[110], then we have extremely strong evidence for architectural continuity between this and the succeeding MB II Period, since the similar temple 4040 must be dated to MB II[111]. (7) Tumulus burials, commonly met in EB IV/MB I contexts, have also been found with MB II A pottery; e. g., the tomb reported in the Israel Archaeological survey: coord. 15661. 22314 (Courtesy of Israel Department of Antiquities). It is because of this continuity with both the preceding and succeeding periods that the terminology EB IV/MB I seems to me to be not only traditional, but adequate, implying a transitional though depressed stage between the more thriving Early Bronze and Middle Bronze cultures.

C. THE SO-CALLED NOMADIC CHARACTER OF EB IV/MB I

The description of the EB IV/MB I Period as a period in which Palestine was occupied by semi-nomadic groups is either the result of a careless use of language or one of the most serious misinterpretations in the history of Palestinian archaeology. It is in either case, totally indefensible, based on a concentration on what has not been found and a disregard for what has been. It is largely the association made between the shaft tomb people and the Amorites that has led scholars to think of the population of EB IV/MB I Palestine as semi-nomadic, and to interpret the archaeological evidence in this light[112].

The description of this period as giving evidence of only limited settlements in contrast to a large number of tombs is in general accurate, but to draw the conclusion that this is proof that the EB IV/MB I Period is semi-nomadic, and that most of the stratified

of temple 4040 can not be ignored here) shows that this shift did not occur throughout Palestine at a time contemporaneous with the major shifts in ceramic forms. Rather, we have here clear evidence of true continuity in at least one important aspect of the material culture. Merely that the fenestrated axe has been found in EB IV/MB I contexts — and there is no one who would dispute that — offers us a firm basis (namely, the development of the shaft-hole axe) for rejecting the claim that there is a total break in the continuity between EB IV/MB I and MB IIA in Palestine.

110 They could conceivably belong to the early MB IIA Period at Megiddo; Cf. Thompson, ZDPV 86 (1970), 38—46; Dever, HThR 64 (1971), 206 n. 21.

111 Thompson ibid. Kempinsky's report of Dunayevsky's excavation (to appear shortly in ZDPV) does not offer sufficient grounds for changing my datings of these temples. Unfortunately, Kempinsky does not take into consideration the literature on Megiddo published during the last five years.

112 See the remarks of P. Lapp, Dhahr Mirzbanêh, 115.

occupations should be understood as "camping sites" is a distortion. A significant proportion of the tombs owe their initial discovery to accidental finds in the process of modern construction, followed by a search for other tombs in the area, as well as to the thriving industry of illegal tomb robbing carried out with the purpose of finding whole pieces of pottery for sale in the antiquities market. When intensive tomb robbing in a given area comes to the attention of the authorities, archaeologists often attempt to clear as many tombs as possible in the area in an effort to save as much scientific evidence as possible; this, however, can add to the statistical distortion[113]. Excavation of the lower levels in the major tells is very difficult and extremely expensive. Consequently only limited areas are uncovered at this depth; in contrast, the excavation of tombs is relatively simple. At Jericho, spurred by the remarkable finds in the MB II tombs, the excavators made elaborate efforts to find and clear as many tombs as possible. Similar efforts were not made to find EB IV/MB I levels on the tell. Moreover, since most EB IV/MB I burials were single interments, the relationship of a large number of tombs in contrast to a thin level of settlement is perhaps not so great a disproportion as is often assumed[114].

The problem of the difference in pottery that is at times observable between some of the tomb groups at a given site, and also between the pottery of the tombs and the tell, has not yet found a satisfactory clarification. Some of the pottery is possibly made for funerary purposes only[115]. The proposal that the differences are to be explained by supposing several different tribal groups used the cemetery for their burials, would be more convincing if major differences did not exist in the pottery, and if these differences could not be explained as developmental changes in the pottery forms. Kenyon herself points out that of the eleven different tomb types that she has distinguished, all but two can be explained on the basis of evolutionary change; and all of the pottery can be so explained, even that found on the tell.

During the MB II Period there is also a great variety of burial practices, but there is hardly sufficient reason to attribute these

---

[113] The discovery of a major EB IV/MB I cemetery at Jebel Qaʿaqîr is a good example of this; particularly since, through continued digging, carried out under the direction of William Dever, the initial impression of a large cemetery connected with only a very slight occupation, has subsequently been corrected. Three levels of occupation have been discovered, two of which belong to MB I. There is also a cave settlement at El-Ful with stratified levels of EB IV/MB I uncovered in 1971.

[114] In his dissertation, Dever remarks: "The lack of evidence of town-life can be explained as simply due to the accidents of excavation; after all, the few sites that have been extensively excavated at deep levels have produced some evidence of occupation" (375).

[115] Kenyon, ADAJ 3 (1956), 42.

differences to different ethnic groups, and even less to the existence of nomadic tribes[116]. Similarly, it does not seem necessary to posit distinct nomadic immigrations to explain the problems at Jericho. As we have already seen, Jericho (Tell eṣ-Ṣultan) was abandoned at the beginning of the EB IV/MB I Period. The pottery from the tell (resembling TBM H) appears to be typologically later than the tomb pottery which shows a much closer relationship to EB pottery. The two distinct kinds of tombs are the dagger type tombs and the pottery type tombs. The dagger type tombs, however, had no pottery. These tombs could then conceivably be connected with the settlement on the tell, who must have buried their dead somewhere. This does not leave us with the necessity of assuming that all of the other tombs must belong to nomadic tribes, since there is another large EB IV/MB I site which is unexcavated in the immediate vicinity of the tomb area at ʿAin eṣ-Ṣultan, which may well have been occupied during the gap on the tell[117].

Similarly, at Dhahr Mirzbanêh, an important tomb group from the EB IV/MB I Period was excavated and no signs of permanent occupation were found by the excavators. However, recently, a large line of stones and walls have been noticed up on the Mirzbanêh ridge that might possibly be associated with the burials[118].

Apart from the question of the tombs and pottery analysis, archaeological exploration and excavation in Syria, Palestine, Transjordan, and the Negev, over the last fifty years, have brought to light a massive amount of evidence that these regions were extensively settled during the EB IV/MB I Period[119]. That major settlements existed in Syria at this time is universally recognized. In Palestine proper, over thirty excavated sites, including most of the major sites, have contained as many as three distinct strata datable to this period, and many more settlements have been recognized on the basis of surface explorations. While hundreds of sites have been recognized in Transjordan and the Negev, very few have been excavated. Nevertheless, those in Transjordan that have been excavated have contained several layers of occupation, and Kochavi's excavation at Yeruḥam in the Negev clearly shows that the settlements there were not

[116] J. van Seters, The Hyksos, 45.

[117] This site is mentioned in the survey of the Jordan Valley reported by J. Mellaart (List of Sites Examined, ADAJ 6—7, 1962, 156, site no. 84).

[118] The Department of Antiquities found EB IV/MB I and MB II pottery here in addition to walls (coord. 181. 154).

[119] This evidence will be systematically treated in the work now in progress mentioned in note 1. The pattern and extent of the EB IV/MB I settlements in Palestine, which I hope to show in this study, prove beyond question that we are dealing with permanent agricultural settlements.

nomadic[120]. It should be stressed that at Yeruḥam, the earlier level is much larger than the later more ephemeral occupation, making it extremely difficult to assume a theory of a gradual sedentarization of nomads in this area[121]. That more sites have been identified in the fringe areas than the more amenable fertile regions has several reasons. Thanks to the energy of Nelson Glueck these regions have been more systematically surveyed. Furthermore, most EB IV/MB I sites seem to be shallow and are easily obliterated either by later occupations, or, when not on a tell, by the intensive farming that has been carried out in Palestine over the centuries and particularly in modern times.

That these settlements are not "campsites" seems clear from the finds that have been recorded. Stone foundations and mud brick walls have been found at Khirbet Ader[122]. At Jericho houses from this period were found all over the tell, and in some areas three levels of superimposed buildings were uncovered[123]. Fortifications have been found at Khirbet Iskander[124] and Tell Beit Mirsim[125]. Similar finds have been observed elsewhere. Temples found at Megiddo can perhaps be dated to this period[126], and the recent publication of the Beitin excavation shows, though not a temple or similar monumental structure, a considerable village belonging to this period[127]. An even larger settlement can be expected from the excavations at Tell el-Ḥesi.

The use of grinding stones, sickle blades, and extensive terracing shows that agriculture was more than ephemeral.

That the people of Jericho did not only live in houses, but had a tradition of living in houses, is indicated by finds both on the tell and in the pottery tombs containing disarticulated skeletons. In these tombs a four-spouted lamp was typically placed in a niche carved into the wall, even when it was obvious (from the fact that there were holes in the base of the lamp) that the lamp was not being used for the burial[128]. Such a practice possibly reflects the placing of lamps on shelves or niches in the houses of the living!

---

120 M. Kochavi, BIES 27 (1963), 284—292.

121 On the settled character of the Negev in general see Aharoni, Negeb, Archaeology and Old Testament Study, 387f.

122 Ray L. Cleveland, Soundings at Khirbet Ader, AASOR 34—35 (1960), 79—97.

123 Kenyon loc. cit., PEQ 1951—1954.

124 P. Parr, Excavations at Khirbet Iskander, ADAJ 4—5 (1960), 128—133.

125 W. F. Albright, Debir, Archaeology and Old Testament Study, 211.

126 Thompson, ZDPV 86 (1970), 38—46.

127 Cf. J. Kelso, The excavation of Bethel, 22f. In evaluating the EB IV/MB I evidence at Beitin, the corrective remarks of Dever (Archaeological Methods and Results: A Review of Two Recent Publications, Orientalia 40, 1971, 464—466) are very important.

128 Cf. Kenyon, Jericho I—II, passim.

Much more convincing evidence that the people who settled Jericho did not have a nomadic tradition comes from one of the buildings overlying the silt deposit in the EB ditch. Underneath a wall separating two rooms a foundation cist was uncovered in which a bag was found, containing the disarticulated bones of an infant[129]. Such a foundation sacrifice can only be understood within the context of a building tradition!

A tradition of building is also suggested by the construction of plaster floors at Megiddo[130].

The construction of the tombs themselves, rather than reflecting the tradition of nomads, who generally have extremely simple burials with small tumuli, betrays a rather sophisticated architectural tradition, with deep shafts (as much as 4 meters deep) and carefully dug burial chambers cut into the rock. This burial practice itself seems sufficient to exclude the attribution of these burials to nomads. Kenyon is forced to see these tombs as the products of professional tomb diggers[131].

The pottery also makes it extremely difficult to see these people as nomadic wanderers[132]. The well-made, large thin-walled jars, the well-levigated paste, the generally even firing (implying the development of a good kiln), the widespread use of a fairly fast wheel for shaping the neck and rims of vessels, all reflect a relatively advanced technology. This is also indicated in the copper industry and the construction of the carnelian beads found in several tombs, some of which appear to have been lathe turned[133].

The most consistently mentioned single characteristic of the EB IV/MB I Period that is thought to give evidence that the people buried in the shaft tombs were nomads is the frequent practice of "disarticulated" or secondary burials[134]. The practice of secondary burial, however, is not suggestive of a nomadic way of life. We have already mentioned that secondary burials were practiced at Early Bronze Jericho. Disarticulated burials, moreover, are widely known both inside and outside of Palestine in all periods of ancient history from the Neolithic period. This practice, to the extent that it is known to archaeologists, is most often connected with settled cultures.

---

[129] K. Kenyon, PEQ (1954), 58 and Plate XIII.

[130] Pavement 4009; for chronology, cf. Thompson, ZDPV 86 (1970), 46.

[131] Kenyon, Amorites and Canaanites, 17; Jericho I 217—219. See further on this below.

[132] This is also the opinion of P. Lapp, Dhahr Mirzbanêh, 112, and Y. Aharoni, Archaeology and Old Testament Study, 388.

[133] For this last, cf. Kenyon, ADAJ 3 (1956), 46.

[134] This is stressed both by W. G. Dever, HThR 64 (1971), 208f.; and by K. Kenyon, Amorites and Canaanites, 15—18.

This material has recently been conveniently gathered together by E. M. Meyers[135].

Secondary burials during the Neolithic period are best known (connected with one of the first town settlements in Palestine) from the plastered skulls found at Jericho. At Çatal Hüyük, the largest Neolithic site known in the Near East, secondary burials were the ordinary form of burial. A great deal of evidence for disarticulated interments has been found in the coastal region of Palestine from the clearly non-nomadic Chalcolithic house urn burials. Secondary burial was also practiced at Jericho and Gezer during EB I, and Bab edh-Dhrâ gives evidence of it throughout the entire Early Bronze Age[136]. Many sites have secondary burials during the MB I Period. During MB II they are found at Ras el-ʿAin, Munḥata in the Jordan Valley, and elsewhere. During the Late Bronze Age such tombs are found at Ras Shamra, Tell Faraʿ, and Baḥan, and they are found also in the Iron Age and later. Biblical references to this practice are, for example, I Sam 31 11-13, II Sam 21 13 and I Chr 10 12. On the basis of II Sam 22 10 ff., the process of decomposition took approximately 8 months[137]. This alone, aside from any of the archaeological evidence, makes it an extremely unlikely practice of wandering groups of nomads. It also helps to explain the riddle from one of the Jericho tombs, on the basis of which Kenyon constructs her hypothesis that the EB IV/MB I people of these tombs were nomadic!

In tomb J 21 a brown band of small gypsum crystals was formed from moisture in the walls of the tombs. "The drop of the gypsum band towards the doorway . . . can be explained only by the assumption that the door was open to the air, and indeed the sun, while the crust of the brown band was forming"[138]. The formation of the band must have taken several weeks after the tomb was completed. A careful analysis of the sediment on the tomb floor showed that the tomb must have remained open at least two weeks and perhaps longer after the tomb had dried out. Only after this was the skeleton brought in completely disarticulated, and the tomb sealed.

In her book, Amorites and Canaanites, Kenyon argues that the disarticulated interments are not explainable simply by the length

---

135 E. M. Meyers, Secondary Burials in Palestine, BA 33 (1970), 2—29. Cf. also his doctoral dissertation: Jewish Ossuaries and Secondary Burials in their Ancient Near Eastern Setting (Harvard, 1969). The following information is taken from Meyers' article in BA; the reader is referred to these works for fuller discussion and bibliography.

136 But it is not found here during the EB IV Period!

137 Meyers, BA 33 (1970), 11.

138 Jericho I 218; for entire discussion see 217—219.

of time the tombs took to dig, since this tomb J 21 was clearly completed long before it was used. She, therefore, suggests that the tombs were prepared by professional gravediggers, and first used when the nomadic pastoralists, following a seasonal pattern of migration, returned to their ancestral burial grounds[139].

Aside from the fact that the hypothesis that a professional gravedigging class existed in order to fulfill the needs of groups of semi-nomadic pastoralists is simply fantastic[140], the time necessary for disarticulation itself is sufficient explanation of the length of time tomb J 21 was open. An explanation for the existence of disarticulated burials during this period, as at any other, is rather to be found, with Meyers, in the religious attitudes these people had towards the dead[141].

The difficulty of finding West Semitic nomadic tribes in a land where the indigenous population is West Semitic, and where textual evidence does not exist, is extremely great; for nomads generally do not leave much evidence of an archaeological nature.

---

139 Amorites and Canaanites 17.

140 Though the tombs were indeed quite probably done by, if not professional, experienced tomb-diggers.

141 BA 33 (1970), 3.

Chapter 8

Abraham as a Caravaneer

A. THE THESIS OF C. H. GORDON AND W. F. ALBRIGHT

In 1958, in his article "Abraham and the Merchants of Ura", C. H. Gordon argued that Abraham is to be understood historically, not as a shepherd or semi-nomad, but as a merchant; more explicitly, a travelling "merchant-prince"[1]. Gordon's thesis relates the patriarchal narratives to several thirteenth century tablets from Ugarit which refer to Hittite merchants from the city of Ura (somewhere in North Mesopotamia)[2]. One of these tablets (PRU IV, 103) restricts the ability of the merchants to buy real estate in Ugarit. Gordon sees a connection between this and the story of Abraham's purchase of the cave at Machpelah from the Hittite Ephron, which he believes follows Hittite law[3]. Asserting that the verb סחר in Gen 34 10 and 42 34 "to wander about" really means "to trade" (cf. Gen 23 16 סֹחֵר!)[4], and pointing out that Abraham was rich in gold and silver (Gen 13 2 and 24 35), he comes to the conclusion that Ura must be Ur of the Chaldees, Abraham's birthplace[5], and that Abraham was not a wandering shepherd, but "a tamkârum ("merchant") from Ur of the Chaldees in the Hittite realm. Like many others from Ur, (!?) he embarked on a career in Canaan. But unlike the others, he succeeded in purchasing land and laying the foundation for his descendants' settlement there"[6]. He suggests that Abraham engaged in the profitable trade of "importing silver into Egypt and gold into the Hittite realm"[7], and concludes that Abraham, coming as an immigrant from Ur under Hittite sponsorship, "need not be a unique phenomenon in cultural history, but rather is part of a movement for which we have authentic documentation"[8].

---

[1] JNES 17 (1958), 28—31. See further: C. H. Gordon, The World of the Old Testament, 1958, 132; Before the Bible: The Common Background of Greek and Hebrew Civilizations, 1962[1], 25—36; 1965[2], 35f.; and Abraham of Ur, Driver Festschrift, 77—84.

[2] Gordon, JNES 17 (1958), 28; cf. PRU IV 103—5. 190. 203. 256.

[3] This has recently been shown to be false by H. Petschow (Die neubabylonische Zwiegesprächsurkunde und Gen 23, JCS 19, 1965, 103—120) and G. M. Tucker (The Legal Background of Genesis 23, JBL 85, 1966, 77—84). See further, below, ch. 10, L.

[4] This will be discussed below in C.

[5] This is surely wrong; see below ch 11A.

[6] Before the Bible 34f. (parentheses added).

[7] Driver Festschrift 78.

[8] Ibid. 82.

The thesis, as presented by Albright, although equally unconvincing, is much more sophisticated[9]. While Albright takes over much of Gordon's interpretation of the biblical passages involved, particularly the meaning of the verb סחר, he sees the context of Abraham's trading activities at a much earlier time, during the EB IV/MB I Period. Beginning with a reexamination of Nelson Glueck's survey of the Negev[10], and a readjustment of the chronology of the EB IV/MB I Period which he bases on a new date for the kings of Byblos, Albright comes to the conclusion that the EB IV/MB I Period was not a period in which Palestine was overrun by seminomads, but rather Palestine had a settled culture and was the center of a thriving caravan trade which is reflected in the Execration Texts and the patriarchal traditions of the Bible. With the lowering of MB I chronology to 2000—1800 B. C., Albright is able to connect his new interpretation of the MB I culture with the revival of trade brought about by the Twelfth Dynasty of Egypt (1991—1786), as well as the trading

---

[9] Albright's new interpretation of the patriarchs was developed over a period of eight years in the following articles: Abram the Hebrew. A New Archaeological Interpretation, BASOR 163 (1961), 36—54; Some Remarks on the Meaning of the Verb SḤR in Genesis, BASOR 164 (1961), 28; The Chronology of MB I (Early Bronze-Middle Bronze), BASOR 168 (1962), 36—42; The Biblical Period from Abraham to Ezra, 1963, 1—9; The 18th century Princes of Byblos and the Chronology of Middle Bronze, BASOR 176 (1964), 38—46; A Question About Origins, Interpretation 18 (1964), 191—198; Some Remarks on the Archaeological Chronology of Palestine before about 1500 B. C., in: Chronologies in Old World Archaeology, ed. by. R. W. Ehrich, 1965, 47—60; Further Light on the History of Middle Bronze Byblos, BASOR 179 (1965), 38—43; Remarks on the Chronology of Early Bronze IV-Middle Bronze IIA in Phoenicia and Syria-Palestine, BASOR 184 (1966), 26—35; Debir, in: Archaeology and Old Testament Study, ed. by D. W. Thomas, 1967, 207—220; Yahweh and the Gods of Canaan, 1968, 47—95. 232—234.

[10] For Glueck's survey see: N. Glueck, Exploration in Western Palestine, BASOR 131 (1953), 6—15; Further Explorations in the Negev, BASOR 137 (1955), 10—22; The Age of Abraham in the Negev, BA 18 (1955), 2—9; The Third Season of Exploration in the Negeb, BASOR 138 (1955), 7—29; The Fourth Season of Exploration in the Negeb, BASOR 142 (1956), 17—35; The Fifth Season of Exploration in the Negeb, BASOR 145 (1957), 11—25; The Sixth Season of Archaeological Exploration in the Negeb, BASOR 149 (1958), 8—17; The Seventh Season of Archaeological Exploration on the Negeb, BASOR 152 (1958), 18—38; Rivers in the Desert, 1959; An Aerial Reconnaissance of the Negev, BASOR 155 (1959), 2—13; The Negev, BA 22 (1959), 82—97; Archaeological Exploration of the Negeb in 1959, BASOR 159 (1960), 3—14; Further Explorations in the Negev, BASOR 179 (1965), 6—29; Some Edomite Pottery from Tell El-Kheleifeh, BASOR 188 (1967), 8—38.

activity known in Mesopotamia from texts from the early part of the Second Millenium, including the Ur economic texts and the Cappadocian tablets. That Abraham took part in this new caravan activity is concluded not simply on the basis of the verb סחר, but by the entire Genesis tradition: He came out of Ur which was a major trading center and went to Harran, (the name Harran means "Caravan City"); He went on to Damascus (sic!)[11] where he adopted a merchant to "obtain credit in order to buy donkeys, equipment and supplies for caravaneering or related activities"[12]. From Damascus he went further south visiting the major trading centers of Palestine mentioned in Genesis, which, according to Albright, were occupied during the EB IV/MB I Period. In Gen 20 we are told that he settled for a time in the Negev between Kadesh and Shur, where, Albright further argues, Abraham could only have survived if he had been engaged in the caravan trade between Palestine and Egypt. It was exactly during this time, as shown by Glueck, that the Negev was settled by a network of caravan stations.

In Gen 14, Albright finds the final justification for his interpretation. He sees this tradition as centering on the ancient north-south trade routes, connecting Transjordan with Egypt. The battle narrated in Gen 14 is a battle over control of the trade routes. Finally, in this chapter of Genesis, Abraham is referred to explicitly as a Hebrew, whom Albright identifies with the Ḫapiru. He then goes on to argue that the word Ḫapiru means "caravaneer". Moreover, they can be identified with the "*Banū-yamina*"[13], who, he claims, were engaged in the caravan trade of North Mesopotamia in the early Second Millenium.

While Albright indiscriminately mingles archaeological, biblical, and historical materials, the cumulative weight of the material that he gathers is every bit as impressive as the nomadic-Amorite hypothesis. The thesis of Gordon and Albright has already been sufficiently reviewed by others, and I am in basic agreement with the criticisms of Saggs[14], Ginsberg[15], Emerton[16], and especially Weippert[17].

---

[11] Yahweh and the Gods 58.

[12] Ibid., see also BASOR 163 (1961), 47. For a criticism of this, see my discussion in ch. 10c.

[13] On the "*Banū-yamina*" at Mari, see above ch. 3.

[14] Ur of the Chaldees, Iraq 22 (1960), 200—209.

[15] Review of C. H. Gordon, Before the Bible, in Commentary (October, 1963), 333—336.

[16] Some false clues in the study of Genesis XIV, VT 21 (1971), 24—27.

[17] Abraham der Hebräer? Bemerkungen zu W. F. Albright's Deutung der Väter Israels, Bb 52 (1971), 407—432.

The arguments in support of the historicity of Abraham, dealt with in this and the following chapter, have not gained wide adherence[18]. The recent article of M. Weippert discusses most of the important elements of this hypothesis with clarity and accuracy. There is, therefore, no need to repeat his arguments here. This and the following chapter are offered in the spirit of complementary notes to Weippert's article. Since, in my opinion, the central weight of Albright's argument lies in the question of the chronology of EB IV/MB I, and since this has not received adequate treatment elsewhere, a more thorough treatment of this aspect of the problem is called for. In Chapter 9, I will give my reasons for believing that Weippert's interpretation, "daß Gen 14 eher einem Flickenteppich als einer guten historischen Tradition gleicht und eine sekundäre literarische Kompilation darstellt", has the most promise of solving the riddle of Gen 14[19]. My reasons for being somewhat more sceptical than Weippert in seeing the historical background of the patriarchal narratives in the prehistory of Israel, and for reaffirming the well-known statement of Wellhausen, that there is "über die Patriarchen ... kein historisches Wissen zu gewinnen"[20], will be given in Chapters 11 and 12A.

B. SOME CHRONOLOGICAL NOTES ON EB IV/MB I

We cannot here undertake a complete survey of the chronology of the EB IV/MB I Period. While there are two basic opinions: that followed by Kenyon and others, which assigns this period generally to the time of the First Intermediate Period of Egypt, and that of Albright, which sees the entire later part of the EB IV/MB I Period (that corresponding with the TBM I-H) to be dated after the beginning of the Twelfth Dynasty[21], there is a great deal of disagreement about the date for the end of the period among those who accept the former chronology, varying from as early as 2000 B. C. to as late as 1850[22].

---

[18] See, however, J. Kelso, Archaeology and Our Old Testament Contemporaries, 1966, 16—21.

[19] Bb 52 (1971), 424.

[20] J. Wellhausen, Prolegomena zur Geschichte Israels, 1905, 316.

[21] J. van Seters, The Hyksos, 1966, 10.

[22] E. g., B. Mazar dates the end of the period to c. 2000 B. C. (The Middle Bronze Age in Palestine, IEJ 18, 1968, 65—97). Kenyon offers a date somewhere within the range of 2300 to 1900 B. C. (Amorites and Canaanites, 1966, 35); Cf. her remarks on p. 33: "From contacts with Egypt we can only say that EB III overlapped the time of the IVth Dynasty of Egypt (2600—2500) and that the MB Age (MB IIA) begins during the time of the 12th Dynasty (1991—1786)." G. E. Wright dates the

The wide range of disagreement is caused by the lack of any objects found among EB IV/MB I remains that can clearly be dated later than 2000 B. C. The evaluation of the material dated before 2000 B. C., however, cannot be used for a terminus ad quem of the period until the relative chronology of the pottery is established and the relationship between the pottery of Palestine and the more clearly dated deposits of Syria is better understood than at present.

There is, however, sufficient evidence to show that Albright's chronology and his attempt to relate the remains of MB I to the influence of the Twelfth Egyptian Dynasty in Palestine are completely without foundation.

We already discussed in Chapter 7 Albright's contention that the end of MB I in Palestine corresponds with the introduction of the combing motif on some of the early Second Intermediate ware in Egypt. Albright's argument that the Byblos kings (whose tombs contain MB IIA pottery) must be dated later than the Posener Execration Texts can also be set aside as irrelevant on the basis of our discussion in Chapter 5, sections D and E. Albright, however, tries to establish an absolute chronology for these tombs, and consequently, an absolute date for the beginning of MB IIA, on the basis of the inscriptions found in the tombs. His argument briefly is that the first four royal tombs postdate the end of the 19th century. The pottery in the tombs marks the beginning of MB IIA; therefore, the end of the EB IV/MB I Period in Palestine must be lowered to c. 1800 B. C. In my opinion, however, this chronology must be rejected for the following reasons: (1) the Byblos kings cannot all be dated in the 18th century; rather, their dates must be considerably raised. (2) The pottery of the Byblos tombs is not the earliest pottery of MB IIA, and the end of the MB IIA Period cannot be dated later than the middle of the 18th century. (3) MB I cannot postdate the beginning of the 19th century, and probably comes to an end much earlier.

(1) Essential to Albright's lowering of the chronology of the Byblos kings to the 18th century and his claim that MB IIA is to be dated to this later period, is his identification of the Byblos prince buried in tomb IV, *'ntn*, who was a contemporary of Neferḥotep I (1738—1727), with *Yantin-ḫammu*, Prince of Byblos, a contemporary

MB I period to the 22nd to 20th centuries: (The Significance of Ai in the Third Millenium B. C., Galling Festschrift, 311). R. Amiram dates the end of MB I somewhere between 2000 and 1950 B. C. Ancient Pottery of the Holy Land, 1970, 12; and W. Dever, who earlier gave a date of 1850 B. C. for the end of MB I(The Pottery of Palestine in the EB IV/MB I Period, c. 2150—1850 B. C., unpublished Harvard dissertation, 1966) now dates the end of the period c. 1950: The Peoples of Palestine in the Middle Bronze Period, HThR 64 (1971), 197—226.

of Zimri-Lim of Mari (according to Albright's dating 1728—1697)[23]. Recent discoveries, however, make this identification impossible to maintain. W. Röllig has been able to show that Zimri-Lim ruled in Mari from either the eleventh or the seventeenth year of Hammurapi at the earliest, until the thirty-second year; i. e., 1716/1710—1695 B. C.[24]. The father of *ʾntn* was *Rꜣn* (certainly not *Ykn,* nor to be identified with *Yakin-ilum,* vassal of *Sḥtp-ib-Rʿ* II)[25]. A cylinder seal from Byblos mentions Si-Ḥatḥor, the eldest son of Nefer-ḥotep (who ruled for a brief period c. 1725) together with the prince of Byblos *Ḥasrûrum,* the son of *Rûm*[26]. Though this does not suggest any final solution to the chonology of the Byblos kings, it seems, nevertheless, clear that the Byblos prince *ʾntn* cannot be identified with *Yantin-ḫammu* if the low chronology for Mesopotamia is to be followed. The skeleton of the chronology for Byblos is as follows, showing that *ʾntn* could not have lived as late as the reign of Zimri-Lim:

(1)	*Abi-šemu*	(Tomb I)	reign of Amenemes III (1839—1791)
(2) his son:	*Yapi-šemu-abi*	(Tomb II)	reign of Amenemes IV (1791—1781)
(3)	*Rꜣn*		
(4) his son:	*ʾntn*	(Tomb IV)	reign of Neferḥotep I (1738—1727)
(5) (his son?)	*Ilimi-yapi*		
(6)	*Rûm*		
(7) his son:	*Ḥasrûrum*		reign of Si-Ḥatḥor (ca. 1725)
(8)	*Yantin-ḫammu*		reign of Zimri-Lim (1716/1710—1695)

In addition we know of an *Abi-šemu* (tomb VIII?) and his son *Yapaʿ-šemu-abi* (tomb XI), as well as the already mentioned *Ykn,* contemporary of *Sḥtp-ib-Rʿ* II (c. 1763) and *ʿkꜣi.* On the basis of the

[23] For Albright's arguments, see esp. BASOR 176 (1964), 38—46; BASOR 179 (1965), 38—43; and BASOR 184 (1966), 26—35; This identification had been earlier proposed in New Light on the History of Western Asia in the Second Millenium, B. C., BASOR 77 (1940), 27; New Egyptian Data on Palestine in the Patriarchal Age, BASOR 81 (1941), 18; and An Indirect Synchronism Between Egypt and Mesopotamia cir. 1730 B. C., BASOR 99 (1945), 9—18.

[24] W. Röllig, Zur Datierung Zimri-Lims, XVe RAI 42 (1967), 97—102.

[25] So Albright, BASOR 99 (1945), 10.

[26] For text cf. P. Montet, Notes et Documents pour servir a l'Histoire des Relations entre l'ancienne Égypte et la Syrie, Kêmi 13 (1954), 65f.; See also Albright, BASOR 184 (1966), 29.

finds in tomb XI, it appears that *Yapaʿ-šemu-abi*, as well as his father *Abi-šemu* (tomb VIII?), must be placed prior to *Abi-šemu* of tomb I[27]; that is, sometime during the 19th century. Finally we have one other king of Byblos, a contemporary of Bûr-Sin (1978 to 1970). I see no compelling reason to assume that there was a break in the continuity of the rule of Byblos[28].

(2) That the beginning of MB IIA cannot be set as early as 1800 B. C. follows from our discussion of the Byblos kings, but there are also other indications. The pottery from the royal tombs of Byblos does not give us a terminus a quo for MB IIA in Palestine and Syria, but only a date within that period. In a recent article on the pottery of tombs I—III, O. Tufnell argues that the pottery at Byblos must be dated towards the end of MB IIA[29]. Forms 44 and 45 (dipper juglets with ring bases) are found in Level II at Kültepe dated between 1980 and 1880/1850 B. C. There is no evidence that these forms survived much later than the finds at Byblos[30]. This is confirmed by the comparisons Albright makes between the carinated bowls with flaring rims and high ring bases from Byblos and similar finds in TBM G-F and Megiddo[31]. At Megiddo these bowls first appear in strata XIIIA/XII, that is, in the second Middle Bronze level found at Megiddo[32]. Furthermore, TBM G-F can hardly be considered to span the entire MB IIA Period, since TBM E ("Hyksos") corresponds to Megiddo XII/XI. At Megiddo there are at least five building phases from MB IIA above XII/XI, namely: XIIIA/XII, XIIIB/XIIIA and three phases from XIV[33].

(3) That EB IV/MB I cannot be dated as late as Albright would like seems certain because of the evidence that MB IIA must be placed in the 19th century. Unfortunately, our clearest evidence comes from literary texts that do not have an archaeological context in Palestine itself, and their value for Palestinian chronology is

---

[27] Mazar, IEJ 18 (1968), 74 n.

[28] On the other hand, I assume that we do not have all of the names of the Byblos kings at present. Cf., for instance, G. T. Martin, A Ruler of Byblos of the Second Intermediate Period, Berytus 18 (1969), 81—83.

[29] O. Tufnell, The Pottery from Royal Tombs I—III at Byblos, Berytus 18 (1969), 5—33: "Except for the sophisticated burnished jugs and dippers which have been described, the rest of the pottery is clearly local and undistinguished, turned out by potters who were still working in a style and technique long since obsolete in Palestine" (16).

[30] Ibid. 13f.

[31] BASOR 168 (1962), 41.

[32] Cf. U. Müller, Kritische Bemerkungen zu den Straten XIII bis IX in Megiddo, ZDPV 86 (1970), 78—86.

[33] T. Thompson, The Dating of the Megiddo Temples in Strata XV—XIV, ZDPV 86 (1970), 46.

largely based on what has not been found in Palestine. The earliest Mesopotamian reference to Hazor is in a letter sent by Šamši-Adad, king of Assyria (c. 1734—1724). There are also several references to Hazor during the reign of Zimri-Lim. Malamat concludes that these must refer to the MB IIB settlement at Hazor, since the settlement in MB IIA was not a proper city[34]. If Malamat is correct, the end of MB IIA cannot be set as late as proposed by Albright. In the Khu-sebek stele found at Abydos, dated to the reign of Sesostris III (1878—1843), the conquest of Skmm (i. e., Shechem) is mentioned. Shechem, however, was not occupied during MB I[35]. Therefore, the large MB IIA settlement must antedate this conquest. That MB IIA is to be set back even further is suggested by the portrayal of a "duck-bill" axehead (a type which has been found only in MB II contexts)[36] in tomb 3 at Beni Hasan, which has been clearly dated to 1890 B. C.

This chronology is confirmed by datable objects found in MB II archaeological contexts. Besides the inscriptions from the tombs at Byblos a number of objects datable to Twelfth Dynasty pharaohs have been found in MB II levels. Among them are a sphinx of Amenemes III (1842—1797) found in Ugarit Moyen 2 (= MB IIB)[37], a basalt statue found at Megiddo of Thut-ḥotpe, the nomarch of the Hare Nome, who lived during the reign of Sesostris III (1878—1843)[38], an inscription bearing the name of the wife of Sesostris II (1897—1877) and a scarab of this same pharaoh from Ugarit Moyen 2[39], and a sphinx of Amenemes II (1929—1895) from Qatna[40]. From Ugarit Moyen 1 (= MB I and MB IIA) comes a head with the cartouche of the Pharaoh Sesostris I (1971—1928), and many scarabs bearing the name of the same pharaoh have been found all over Palestine, from Tell Beit Mirsim, Megiddo, Gezer, Beisan, Lachish, and Ajjul[41].

While some of these objects have certainly been found out of context, and some of the scarabs of Sesostris I may perhaps be later forgeries, the cumulative evidence, and especially the finds related to

---

34 A. Malamat, Northern Canaan and the Mari Texts, Glueck Festschrift, 164—171.

35 Cf. Dever, The Middle Bronze I Period in Syria and Palestine, Glueck Festschrift, 144 and esp. 159 note 64!

36 E. D. Oren, A Middle Bronze Age I Warrior Tomb at Beth Shan, ZDPV 87 (1971), passim.

37 Schaeffer, Stratigraphie comparée, 22.

38 Dever, Glueck Festschrift, 142.

39 Schaeffer, Stratigraphie comparée, 22.

40 Van Seters, The Hyksos, 73.

41 Schaeffer, Stratigraphie comparée, 25f. For other scarab finds cf. A. Rowe, Topography and History of Beth-Shan, 1930, 9ff., and his Catalogue of Egyptian Scarabs, 1936. Gezer has no certain MB I occupation level.

Ugarit Moyen 2, can hardly be dismissed, especially when the only similar find in an MB I context, a silver goblet clearly to be attributed to the Ur III Period found recently at ʿAin Samia in deposits belonging to the very end of the EB IV/MB I Period[42], confirms a chronology which places the end of MB I and the beginning of MB II sometime during the 20th century B. C.

M. W. Prausnitz has shown that EB IV (TBM J) is to be dated to the end of the Sixth Dynasty[43]. Ruth Amiram has shown that her family A is closely related to the Mesopotamian pottery of the Akkad Dynasty (2242—2098) and to Ur III (2044—1936), and that it is comparable to the pottery found in ʿAmuq I—J and Ḫama J[44]. The remarkably consistent Carbon 14 readings from Ḫama J confirm this chronology:

K-530 from J6 2310 ± 140 = before 2170
K-531 from J5 2230 ± 120 = before 2110
K-533 from J4/5 2210 ± 120 = before 2090[45]

That is, Ḫama J 1—8 existed during the dynasties of Akkad and Ur III[46]. This seems to be a likely date for the EB IV/MB I Period in Palestine as well.

C. ABRAHAM THE CARAVANEER AND EB IV/MB I

The low chronology attributed to EB IV/MB I by Albright is the central key to his thesis. Once this is seen as untenable, the rise

---

[42] Dever, HThR 64 (1971), 216. B. Shantar and Y. Labadi, Tomb 204 at ʿAin Samiya, IEJ 21 (1971), 73—77; Z. Yeivin, A Silver Cup from 204a at ʿAin Samiya, IEJ 21 (1971), 78—81; Y. Yadin, A Note on the Scenes Depicted on the ʿAin Samia Cup, IEJ 21 (1971), 82—85.

[43] Abydos and Combed Ware, PEQ (1954), 91—96.

[44] The Pottery of the Middle Bronze Age I in Palestine, IEJ 10 (1960), 204—225. This judgment has been confirmed by M. Tadmor, Contacts between the ʿAmuq and Syria-Palestine, IEJ 14 (1964), 253—269.

[45] E. Fugmann, Hama, Fouilles et Recherches 1931—1938, II 1, 1958, 281f.

[46] If the new half-life value is followed with a doubling of the tolerance figure, according to the suggestions of Braidwood (Further Remarks on Radioactive Carbon Age Determination and the Chronology of the Late Prehistoric and Protohistoric Near East, in: Moortgat Festschrift, 57—67; A Note on the Present Status of Radioactive Carbon Age Determination, Sumer 23, 1967, 39—43), we arrive at the following dates:

K-530 from J6 2438 ± 280 = before 2158
K-531 from J5 2355 ± 240 = before 2115
K-533 from J5/4 2335 ± 240 = before 2095

of the caravan trade under the Twelfth Dynasty pharaohs can no longer be associated with the settlements of MB I either in Palestine or the Negev.

Commercial activity was carried out from Ur from the time of Šulgi (2026—1979) until the city was destroyed by the Elamites in 1936[47]. There is little evidence of Egyptian trade into Asia during this period, though trade with Byblos by ship was probably continued during the Intermediate Period and the Eleventh Dynasty. There is no evidence, however, of any overland trade[48]. During the 19th century there is a revival of trade throughout the Near East, in Ur under the Larsa Dynasty[49] and throughout South Mesopotamia[50], in the Assyrian colonies in Cappadocia[51], and in Egypt along the Red Sea[52], and, increasingly from the time of Sesostris III (1876—1839) in Sinai[53], Palestine[54], and the entire Eastern Mediterranean[55].

The Egyptian campaign against Shechem and the contacts that existed between Palestine and the Sinai mines during the time of Sesostris III suggest that trade was carried out overland. Contacts between Palestine and Egypt increased during the Second Intermediate (= Middle Bronze II B—C), and especially during the New Kingdom (= Late Bronze Age). The absence of any known system of caravan stations through the Negev and Sinai during these later periods only emphasizes the obvious fact that these deserts offered no insurmountable obstacles to the caravan trade between Egypt and Palestine. Nor are they uninhabitable wastelands, but appear to have been occupied by semi-nomadic tribes, and at times by settled peoples, throughout the history of the ancient Near East[56]. There is no reason whatever to insist that the Twelfth Dynasty trade with Palestine

---

47 Albright, BASOR 163 (1961), 44. My dates are taken from van der Meer, The Chronology of Ancient Western Asia and Egypt, 1963.

48 W. A. Ward, Egypt and the East Mediterranean in the Early Second Millenium B. C., Orientalia 30 (1961), 22—45. 129—155; Egypt and the East Mediterranean from Predynastic times to the end of the Old Kingdom, JESHO 6 (1963), 1—57; Relations between Egypt and Mesopotamia from Prehistoric Times to the End of the Middle Kingdom, JESHO 7 (1964), 1—45. 121—135; and W. A. Ward and O. Tufnell, Relations between Byblos, Egypt, and Mesopotamia at the End of the Third Millenium, B. C., Syria 43 (1966), 165—241.

49 Albright, BASOR 163 (1961), 44.

50 W. Leemans, Foreign Trade in the Old Babylonian Period, 1960.

51 M. T. Larsen, Old Assyrian Caravan Procedures, 1967.

52 W. C. Hayes, The Middle Kingdom in Egypt, CAH^2, fascicle 3, 1964, 23 f.

53 Ward, Orientalia (1961), 38.

54 Ibid. 39—42.

55 Ibid. 27.

56 See Glueck, BASOR 152 (1958), 18.

required caravan stations in the middle of the desert[57]. The fact is: caravan trade was carried out across Sinai and the Negev when, as far as we know, no caravan stations existed; and this includes the time of the Twelfth Dynasty. Moreover, the EB IV/MB I settlements of the Negev can hardly be explained by the trade with Egypt no matter how active that trade may have been. There were hundreds of settlements in the Negev at this time, and they could not all have been caravan stations. Within one 5 km. square area southwest of Avdat over 27 MB I sites were found[58]. Moreover, that some of these settlements — indeed some of the largest — were found in areas where the richest water supplies are to be found, such as Ein el Qudeirat, is only to be expected. Desert settlements also need water. The fact that these same springs were used by the caravans of later periods, is not evidence that the line of access between these water sources across the Negev were caravan routes during the EB IV/MB I Period[59]. Nothing has been found in the remains of these settlements that gives any indication that they were connected with trade. There are no foreign objects, and all the evidence for cultural relationships shows a close dependence on Southern Palestine. In fact, throughout Palestine there is very little evidence of international trade at this time. The archaeological evidence we have excludes the possibility of any important trade through Palestine and the Negev during the EB IV/MB I Period[60], in contrast to any other known historical period. Any period other than EB IV/MB I would have been well chosen to support a hypothesis of widespread caravan activity.

Albright's thesis that the patriarchal wanderings are related to the major caravan stations of the EB IV/MB I Period in Palestine is also not supported by the archaeological knowledge we have of the cities mentioned in Genesis. Some of them, such as Sodom and Gomorrah are mythological[61], others such as Qadesh-Barnea and Hebron have not been adequately located. Only Bethel, Beth

---

57 Albright (Yahweh and the Gods of Canaan 62 n. 42) himself, mentions that under Amenemes II and in the Sixth Dynasty, caravans traversed the much more forbidding Nubian desert by carrying water and food with them!

58 Y. Aharoni et alii, The Ancient Desert Agriculture of the Negev V., An Israelite Agricultural Settlement at Ramat Matred, IEJ 10 (1960), 25.

59 At Ein el Qudeirat and other Negev sites there are also remains of palaeolithic settlements. (M. Dothan, The Fortress of Kadesh Barnea, IEJ 15, 1965, 134—151). Are we to conclude that there was a thriving caravan trade during the Palaeolithic period?

60 Cf. P. Lapp, The Dhahr Mirzbanêh Tombs, 1966, 91f., and Palestine in the Early Bronze Age, Glueck Festschrift, 123.

61 See below ch. 9 A, and D. Irvin, Mytharion. The Comparison of Tales from the Old Testament and the Ancient Near East, AOAT, 1974, 32f. (seen in typescript).

Shemesh, and possibly Dothan[62] existed at this period. Hazezon Tamar was built by Solomon (I Kings 9 18)[63]. Beersheba did not exist before the Iron Age[64]. Succoth, which is identified with Tell Deir ʿAlla by Glueck[65], was not occupied before the Late Bronze Age. Jerusalem (Salem?) has not yet shown (though the excavations so far have been very limited) any settlement from this period[66]. The excavations at et-Tell have shown a gap in the occupation of Ai from 2500 B. C. until the Iron Age[67]. Finally, Shechem, as we have already seen, does not seem to have been occupied before the MB IIA Period[68]. The only period in which all of the known sites mentioned in the patriarchal stories were occupied is the Iron Age!

That the patriarchs are to be understood as caravaneers from the biblical tradition is based entirely on Gordon's translation of the verb סחר in Gen 34 10 34 21 and 42 34 as "to trade"[69]. E. A. Speiser, in his article The Verb SHR in Genesis and Early Hebrew Movements[70], objects strongly to this interpretation, pointing out that the meaning of the verbal noun "trader" has never been in doubt. Postbiblical Hebrew and Jewish Aramaic developed a secondary verb *sḥr* meaning "to trade"[71]. Speiser, however, shows that the nominal form *sōḥēr* must necessarily be understood as derived from the verb, "to circle about", and that the verb could not have been formed from the noun[72]. The use of the verb in Ps 38 10 obviously is based on the meaning to "circle" and cannot mean "trade"[73]. In Gen 34 10 the form of the verb is סחרוה, with the pronoun referring back to הארץ; in 34 21 the syntax is יסחרו אתה, the direct object אתה referring back

62 Cf. J. P. Free, The Fifth Season at Dothan, BASOR 152 (1958), 10—18.

63 Y. Aharoni, Tamar and the Road to Elath, IEJ 13 (1963), 30—42.

64 J. Perrot, Les VIe et VIIe campagnes des fouilles à Beerseba, CRAI (1959), 133 to 140; H. Haag, Erwägungen über Beersheba, Sacra Pagina, I 1959, 335—345.

65 Transjordan, Archaeology and Old Testament Study 431; cf. also The River Jordan, 1946, 147; and Three Israelite Towns in the Jordan Valley: Zarethan, Succoth, Zaphon, BASOR 90 (1943), 14—17. Franken's reasons for rejecting this identification are primarily that it did not exist before the Late Bronze Age! (Cf. H. J. Franken, Excavations at Tell Deir ʿAlla, I 1969, 4—8).

66 See my article, Jerusalem, in: H. Haag, Biblisches Wörterbuch, 1971.

67 J. A. Callaway, The 1964 ʿAi (et Tell) Excavations, BASOR 178 (1965), 39f.

68 W. G. Dever, Glueck Festschrift, 142—144.

69 Gordon, JNES 17 (1958), 29; followed by Albright, BASOR 163 (1961), 44, and BASOR 164 (1961), 28.

70 BASOR 164 (1961), 23—28.

71 Ibid. 24.

72 Ibid. 24f.

73 Ibid. 25. The only other occurrence is in Jer 14 18. The context here, though obscure, does not allow the translation "to trade" or the like.

again to "the land"[74]; in Gen 42 34 the syntax in which the verb is used is: ואת־הארץ תסחרו. That is to say, in every case the verb סחר is found with "the land" as its direct object. This clearly excludes the meaning of "to trade", and demands the translation "to wander about"[75]. It is this sense which is also demanded by the context[76].

D. ABRAHAM AND THE ḪAPIRU CARAVANS

M. Weippert has already adequately refuted Albright's claim that the Ḫapiru of the early Second Millenium were caravaneers[77]. Only one point of Albright's interpretation needs to be taken up here. By identifying the *Banū-yamina* of the Mari Texts[78] with the Ḫapiru of North Mesopotamia, and by identifying these both with two "lost" tribes of Judah[79], Albright attempts to make a connection between the Hebrew Abraham of Gen 14 and the caravan trade of North Mesopotamia[80].

Albright bases his argument on an article by A. Finet[81] which identifies the tribal group, the *Benê-Sim'âl*, with the Ḫapiru. Finet observes that the general area of activity of the "Sim'âlites" is largely limited to an area centering on the triangle of the Ḫabur, which is the same general area where, according to the Mari letters, the Ḫapiru are known as mercenaries for the kings of Ilanṣurâ, Ašlakka, and Niḫriya. Otherwise, they live as "nomads". He concludes that, since the "Sim'âlites" are known as mercenaries working for the king of Mari, the term "Ḫapiru" must be synonymous at Mari with "Sim'âlite"[82]. This conclusion is partially based on the generally accepted view offered by J. R. Kupper[83], and here referred to by Finet[84]: "le terme Ḫapiru ne serait qu'un adjectif designant un genre de vie et non un gentilice", which conclusion is in turn based on the clear evidence that the names of the Ḫapiru are not all of the same linguistic type. That no historian today is justified in claiming ethnic unity for the many groups of Ḫapiru is one thing; it is quite another

[74] In contrast to the preceding clause וישבו בארץ!

[75] Speiser ibid. 25f.

[76] See further the, in my opinion, unconvincing remarks of B. Landsberger, Akkadisch-Hebräische Wortgleichungen, VTS 16 (1967), 188—190.

[77] Biblica 52 (1971), 407—432.

[78] See above ch. 3.

[79] W. F. Albright, Yahweh and the Gods of Canaan, 69—88.

[80] The following is taken from my review of Albright's book in CBQ 32 (1970), 251f.

[81] Iawi-Ilâ, Roi de Talḫayûm, Syria 41 (1964), 117—142.

[82] Ibid. 140—142.

[83] Les nomades en Mésopotamie au temps des rois de Mari, 1957, 257.

[84] Syria 41 (1964), 141.

to claim that they were not understood to be a distinct group by their contemporaries in any given area — as distinct as the *Rabbû* were from the Ḫaneans or from the people of Mari themselves[85]. It is again clear, from the evidence which Finet brings forward, that these people did not all have the same social function; e. g., some served as mercenaries, others as shepherds, but all are known as Ḫapiru. It hardly seems correct to assert that the term Ḫapiru comes from their activities as mercenaries. It is an even more serious mistake to assume that since some Ḫapiru were used as mercenaries, all mercenaries must be Ḫapiru. Would Finet make Ḫapiru out of Ḫaneans also?

In spite of the fact that it is clearly obvious that the *DUMU.MEŠ.iamina* and the *DUMU.MEŠ.sim'al* are not actually related, and in spite of the fact that the northern group is used as mercenaries to control the movements of the southern group[86], Albright not only accepts the thesis of Finet, but extends the argument further to include the *DUMU.MEŠ.iamina* among the Ḫapiru: "The southern 'Apiru *(Banū-yamīna)* were chiefly found in Upper Mesopotamia, south of the hill country, while the northern 'Apiru *(Banū-Sim'al)* were to be found in the more mountainous region to the north"[87]. In extending the argument in this manner, however, Albright ignores what little foundation there was to Finet's argument. For Albright, the mercenary activity of these people is not of any decisive importance (the *DUMU.MEŠ.iamina* were not involved in that sort of work anyway), and the Ḫapiru's main activity becomes the task of running donkey caravans (hiring themselves out as soldiers and raising sheep and goats during the slack season) in the "early patriarchal period". Needless to say, there is no textual evidence for this anywhere.

Albright tries to bring support to his theory by claiming that two of the tribes of the "*Banū-yamina*" can be identified with the names of two "extinct clans of Judah"[88]. "Er and Onan died without leaving any offspring and so may safely be identified with extinct clans of the tribe of Judah"[89]. The very fact that no children are attributed to Er and Onan shows rather that there were no tribes to become extinct. Childless people in folktales are not the eponymous ancestors of whole tribes, whether extinct or not. Albright identifies the name Onan with the name of the tribe *Awnânum* and the name

---

[85] For a more thorough treatment of this question, see Weippert's article in Bb 52 (1971), 412—418.

[86] See above ch. 3.

[87] Albright, Yahweh and the Gods of Canaan, 88.

[88] Ibid. 69.

[89] Ibid.

Er with the name of the tribe *Yaḫrurum*[90]. These identifications are based on no more than a single letter in each case and cannot be taken seriously. On the basis of a newly discovered genealogy of the king ʿAmmiṣaduqa (among these names are, according to Albright, "the eponymous (sic!) founders of the tribes of *Awnânum* and *Yaḫrurum*"), Albright concludes that it is apparently thereby proven "that the ancestral Hebrews founded the First Dynasty of Babylon . . ."[91]!

The only other evidence which Albright brings forward to connect the Ḫapiru with caravans of the early Second Millenium are a literary text from Sumer which reads:

> From the watch-towers the watch has fled, On the caravan road the *SA.GAZ* lie in wait[92].

the letters from Mari mentioning the danger of Ḫapiru raids against the caravans[93], and a passage from the Lipit-Ishtar code which uses the word *SA.GAZ* in a verbal form[94]:

> If a man has rented a ship and has sent it on a trading expedition under contract, but bad luck has attended that trading expedition, where the crew that mans the ship gives itself to *SA.GAZ* activity, the man who has rented the ship must pay compensation for the ship[95].

In other words, the only contact the Ḫapiru have with trade are as disrupters of peaceful trade and as pirates! The claim that these passages give evidence that the Ḫapiru themselves were caravaneers is hardly "analysing all the material now available as objectively as possible"[96].

---

[90] Ibid. 69f.
[91] Ibid. 70f.
[92] Ibid. 67.
[93] Ibid. 94.
[94] Which may or may not refer to the Ḫabiru.
[95] Albright, Yahweh and the Gods, 68.
[96] Ibid. 64.

Chapter 9

The Problem of Historicity and Genesis 14

In recent literature the consideration of Gen 14 as historical has generally been given up, and few authors would argue seriously with the remarks of Roland de Vaux that Gen 14 "appears as an erratic block and is more a hindrance than a help to the historian"[1]. Gen 14 is quite different from the rest of the narratives about the patriarchs in Genesis, at the same time presenting the reader with an historiographical character, which appears particularly amenable to the tools of the historian, and a context that is obviously unhistorical. The formal historiographical form of Gen 14 has been admirably treated by H. Cancik[2].

As Cancik points out, however, to designate the form of a tradition as historiographical does not imply that it is history in the modern sense, nor is it to grant it historicity[3]. Historiography is an "Übergattung"[4]. A similar historiographical character is found in many different traditions[5], some of which, however, must be understood — in the context of the question of historicity — as saga or legend, and as basically unhistorical[6]. These traditions are developed through an eclectic gathering of historical and legendary bits of information available to the storyteller, and offered as incidents in the life of a hero of the past, or as amplifications of some great event of the past. The legend of the birth of Sargon is one example of this form of literature[7], which attaches a fictitious story, constructed from

---

1 R. de Vaux, The Hebrew Patriarchs and History, ThD 12 (1964), 240.

2 Grundzüge der hethitischen und frühisraelitischen Geschichtsschreibung (Tübingen Dissertation, 1970), 183f. That Gen 14 is an early example of Israelite historiography, as Cancik suggests (333f. n. 43), is hardly likely; however, see also J. A. Emerton, The Riddle of Genesis XIV, VT 21 (1971), 435—437.

3 Ibid. 18f.

4 Ibid. 19.

5 Cf. Jos. 10 1-15 13 21 Num 31. See also the Prism of Assurbanipal (G. Cornfeld, Adam to Daniel, 1961, 444) and the Zakir Stela (ANET 501f.).

6 E. g., the Arab tradition of the tribes of Ishmael and their battle with Nebuchadnezzar II, placed in the time of Adnân, is obviously unhistorical, since the birth of Adnân can not be placed earlier than 130 B. C. Cf. J. I. M'Lennan, Studies in Ancient History, The Second Series, 1896, 154.

7 ANET 119.

basic folktale motifs, to a great historical figure of the past[8]. Similarly, Gen 19 brings together the mythical tradition of the destruction of Sodom and Gomorrah with the ancestral hero Lot, placing the story into the historiographical context of the lives of the patriarchs[9]. Perhaps much closer to Gen 14, however, are some of the Serbo-croatian oral traditions collected by Milman Parry[10]. Some of these tales recount historical events, particularly battles. However, they gather together indiscriminately different historical figures and heroes who do not historically belong together, and who often had nothing historically to do with the events recounted. Sometimes centuries are spanned in this manner, and the tales are always generously sprinkled with legendary and fictitious incidents. For instance, the tale of the Greek War begins:

> All the seven kings gathered in Paris, that French city, and they summoned Sultan Aziz and divided his lands. They gave Batun to the King of Moscow, and with Batun thirty and two cities. Tuna the level they gave to the Bulgarian king; Egypt, to the Queen of England; Bosnia the level to King-Emperor Joseph. Spuž and Žabljak, Bar and Tivar, and the city of Podgorica they gave to the Montenegrin prince; Niš and Vidin to the Serbian king; Thessaly to the Greek king. Thus they apportioned all the lands. Then they assembled and maligned the sultan and intrigued with the Greek king. Thus Europe instructed the Greek king: "Declare war upon the sultan!" And the Greek king wrote an ultimatum and sent it to Sultan Hamid. "Sultan Hamid, may the sun shed its warmth upon you! The time has come for us to fight. Either deliver to me the city of Salonika and the city of Manastir, or prepare to meet me at Stambol, which is my ancestral land"[11].

The story than relates the origin of the First Balkan war which began in October, 1912.

The treaty of Paris took place in 1856, but the division of land mentioned in the above lines took place at the Treaty of San Stefano and Berlin in 1878. Sultan Aziz, however, who ruled from 1861—1876, took part in neither of these treaties. Similarly, Sultan Hamid was deposed in 1909 before the beginning of the war. Tuna (perhaps referring to the southern half of Dobrija) was given to Bulgaria in 1918 by the Treaty of Bucharest. England took Egypt in 1881 and

---

[8] See D. Irvin, Mytharion. The Comparison of Tales from the Old Testament and the Ancient Near East, AOAT, 1974, 138 (seen in typescript).

[9] Cf. the similar story in Judges 19. For examples of how similar stories can exist outside of a historiographical setting; cf. Irvin, ibid. 97—205; see also her methodological remarks on 234—236.

[10] Serbocroation Heroic Songs, ed. and trans. by A. B. Lord, 1954, Cf. also A. B. Lord, The Singer of Tales, 1960; and Homer and Other Epic Poetry, in: A Companion to Homer, ed. by Wace and Stubbings, 1963, 179—211, esp. 188ff.

[11] M. Parry, Serbocroation Heroic Songs, 119.

Austria annexed Bosnia in 1908. Bar and Tivar are two names for the same city[12]!

The story ends:

> All Europe has mobilized, and they have entered Crete; they have enterd Crete, and all the seven kings are in Crete. When this telegram arrived, the sultan turned back and retreated before the Greeks. He gave back Thessaly. The army returned. They had shed much blood[13].

Historically, Crete was evacuated by the Turkish soldiers in 1898, following a revolt in 1897. It was not ceded to Greece until 1913[14].

In one version of the "Song of Baghdad"[15], the hero who captures Baghdad is Ibrahim who is presented as the son of Suleyman. Historically, Baghdad was captured twice, in 1533 by Suleyman, and again in 1638 by Sultan Marad IV (whose brother happened to be Sultan Ibrahim I!)[16]. The tale relates the capture of both Baghdad and Kandija, though the cities are in totally different regions and the capture of Kandija belongs to a different campaign[17].

Mustajbey is mentioned though he never took part in a campaign in Persia. Moreover, his presence (he was sanjakbey of Bihac from 1642—1676), as also the presence of his contemporary Mujo Hrnjica, is anachronistic, whichever battle of Baghdad is referred to[18]. This same Mujo Hrnjica plays a role in the tale "Mujo and Captain Dojčič" as well[19]. Captain Dojčič, however, was Ban of Jajce in Bosnia in the fifteenth century[20]! Also significant for our purposes is the song of the "Battle of Temišvar", in which the enemy king Rákóczy is attacked in the city of Rakoče. In fact, no such city exists; the name is constructed from that of the king[21].

These examples should be sufficient to show the type of "history" involved in popular lore, and something of the manner in which these tales are formed. Needless to say, any attempt to extract an "historical core" from such traditions is essentially misdirected. It cannot be on the basis of the Sargon birth story that Sargon of Akkad is to be seen as an historical figure, nor is it on the basis of Milman Parry's folksinger, that we can understand Sultan Ibrahim as a real historical figure of the past; so too, it cannot be on the basis of Gen 14 that we can lay claim to the historicity of Abraham.

---

[12] Ibid. 371.

[13] Ibid. 121.

[14] Ibid. 371.

[15] Ibid. 268—276, No. 26.

[16] Ibid. 330.

[17] Ibid. 417.

[18] Ibid. 336.

[19] Ibid. 144—153, No. 13.

[20] Ibid. 378.

[21] Ibid. 278 and 421 n. 7.

Most recent efforts to understand Genesis 14 presuppose some such form for the tradition and, because of this, offer much more hope in solving the enigma of this chapter than many earlier efforts[22].

Gen 14, itself, offers certain indications that this approach is correct. We need only mention here the Postdeuteronomic character of the tradition[23], the symbolism of the number 318 (318 = אליעזר: א = 1, ל = 30, י = 10, ע = 70, ז = 7, ר = 200)[24], the eponymous nature of Abraham's confederates[25], the connection with the mythical cities of Sodom and Gomorrah[26], and the addition of the Melchisedech-Abraham incident. This new effort at the interpretation of Gen 14 is not simply opposed to those older efforts which tried to find the historical background of the story by identifying the Mesopotamian kings mentioned in Gen 14, since the results of this earlier investigation, though meager and ambiguous, lend themselves to just such an interpretation[27]. Albright[28], Böhl[29], and Cornelius[30] have together offered the various possibilities of identification:

---

[22] N. A. van Uchelen, Abraham de Hebreer, 1964, esp. 5—13 and 91—105; M. C. Astour, Political and Cosmic Symbolism in Genesis 14 and in its Babylonian Sources, in: Biblical Motifs, ed. by. A. Altmann, 1966, 65—112; R. de Vaux, Les Hurrites de l'histoire et les Horites de la Bible, RB 74 (1967), 498 and 503; S. Gevirtz, Abram's 318, IEJ 19 (1969), 110—113; M. Weippert, Die Landnahme der israelitischen Stämme in der neueren wissenschaftlichen Diskussion, 1967, 94ff.; Abraham der Hebräer? Bemerkungen zu W. F. Albrights Deutung der Väter Israels, Bb 52 (1971), 422—424; J. A. Emerton, Some False Clues in the Study of Genesis XIV, VT 21 (1971), 24—47; VT 21 (1971), 403—439.

[23] Cf. Astour, Biblical Motifs, 69ff. Astour's argument must now be read in the context of Weippert's judicious critique: "Nun sollte man mit dem Etikett 'deuteronomistisch' vorsichtig sein; wenn man die Bezeichnung aber als 'nachdeuteronomisch und vom Buch oder einem Teil (Schicht) des Buches Deuteronomium abhängig' interpretiert, kann man m. E. der These Astours zustimmen." Bb 52, 1971, 423; see, however, Emerton, VT 21 (1971), 404—406.

[24] The objection of S. Gevirtz notwithstanding (IEJ 19, 1969, 110); the nature of this narrative does not limit the material to any single symbolic nuance.

[25] Gen 14 13; Eshcol is near Hebron (Num 13 23) and Aner is in Manasseh (I Chr 6 70).

[26] Gen 19 Dtn 29 23 Ez 16 56; cf. D. Irvin, Mytharion, 32f.

[27] For the early attempts at identification see especially F. M. th. de Liagre Böhl, Het Tijdperk der Aartsvaders, 1925; Das Zeitalter Abrahams AO (1930); (with major revisions, = Opera Minora, 1953, 43—49. 476—479); Abraham, Encyclopedia Britannica I (1947), 59f.; Amraphel, RGG³ I, 332f.; Babel und Bibel II. Die Patriarchenzeit, JEOL 17 (1963), 132f.; W. F. Albright, esp.: A Third Revision of the Early Chronology of Western Asia, BASOR 88 (1942), 33—36; for a review of the early literature, see H. H. Rowley, Recent Discovery and the Patriarchal Age, BJRL 32 (1949/1950), 58f.

[28] Abram the Hebrew. A New Archaeological Interpretation, BASOR 163 (1961), 49f.; Yahweh and the Gods of Canaan, 1968, 60.

(1) Amraphel, king of Shinar: While Shinar is identified as Babylonia or Babel by Cornelius and Albright, Böhl suggests Sanḫara in North Syria. Cornelius identifies Amraphel with Hammurapi of Babylon (1726—1686 B. C.). Böhl, however, suggests that the name rather reflects something like Amar-pi-el, and Albright suggests Emudpal. No kings bearing these names, however, are known.

(2) Arioch, king of Ellasar: Cornelius suggests that the name is Hurrian and that Ellasar is the kingdom of Alziya in the Hurrian region. Both Albright and Böhl identify this name with Arriyuk, who appears in the Mari correspondence as the son of Zimri-Lim[31]. The identification of Ellasar is, however, uncertain.

(3) Kedarlaomer king of Elam: Elam of course is well known, and all seem to agree that Kedarlaomer is a good Elamite name. Böhl and Cornelius both suggest that it might refer to the Elamite royal name *Kuter-Naḫḫunte* (assuming the identification of the divine names *Laḳ/gamar/Naḫḫunte*), although there is some difficulty in determining whether it is Kuter-Naḫḫunte I (ca. 1670 B. C.), or perhaps the very last Kassite king of the same name (ca. 1160 B. C.). Albright, with more caution, suggests simply that it is an Elamite name: *Kudur-X*.

(4) *Tidʿal*, King of Goyim: All are agreed that this is to be equated with Tudḫaliya, king of the Hittites (Ug. *TDḠL*). But it is not clear which Tudḫaliya might be referred to, whether Tudḫaliya I (ca. 1675), or any of the other Tudḫaliyas, including Tudḫaliya V (12th century).

Some of the suggested names may well be the original of one or other of the names in Genesis, but they need not all be contemporary, and their identification may (even if they are correct) be irrelevant to an attempt at discovering the historical background of the tradition in Genesis.

If the results of the attempt to identify the kings in Gen 14 must end finally in disappointment, those attempts which have tried to identify and date the "event" related in the Abraham story cannot be taken seriously.

---

29 RGG³ I, 332f.; JEOL 17 (1963), 132f.

30 Genesis XIV, ZAW 31 (1960), 1—7.

31 M. Noth (Arioch-Ariwwuk, VT 1, 1951, 136—140) raises three important questions concerning this identification: (1) Is the name of the son of Zimri-Lim in the Mari Texts really to be read Ariwwuk? (2) Can the name Ariwwuk really be identified with the Biblical form Arioch? and (3) Since the son of Zimri-Lim was never a king, can we assume that he is to be identified with the biblical king, Arioch?

Nelson Glueck long claimed that the historicity of Gen 14 has been fully substantiated by his explorations in Transjordan[32]. He claims that the "trade routes" and the entire civilization of MB I came to a sudden and catastrophic end throughout most of Transjordan. This widespread destruction of the country is attributed to the armies of the kings led by Chedorlaomer as recounted in Gen 14:

> They subdued and destroyed one after another all the fortified sites which lay in their path from Ashteroth and Ham at the northern end to El-Paran at the southern end of the territory which later on became known as Edom. . . . When the Edomites and others came across these sites, they could hardly have recognized them as ancient places of dwelling of civilized settlers who made pottery distinctively characteristic of their period. The Old Testament record of the existence of this Middle Bronze Age I civilization as reflected particularly in Gen 14 must be attributed to the phenomenon of historical memory[33].

Aside from the fact that Gen 14 does not mention the conquest of Transjordan by Chedorlaomer and his forces (rather, they were defeated by Abraham's army), the pottery which Glueck collected on the mounds of Transjordan gives no evidence at all for the destruction of any of the MB I sites, let alone the abandonment of all of the sites at any single time. Nor does it give any evidence of a caravan route through Transjordan at this time[34]. We have already discussed the general inadequacy of the present knowledge of relative pottery chronology during this period. Even if all the pottery were the same at these sites, and a sound chronology for this period were available, no serious archaeologist could suggest that the sites were abandoned within a period of less than fifty years. Pottery forms do not develop so rapidly that greater precision is possible. Furthermore, the summary of Glueck's own findings[35], that only in the region south of the *wādi ez-zerḳa* are the sites abandoned at the end of MB I, and that in North Gilead and the Jordan Valley the sites

---

[32] For the reports of Glueck's surveys in Transjordan, see his Explorations in Eastern Palestine I, AASOR 14 (1934) 1—114; II, AASOR 15 (1935); III, AASOR 18—19 (1939); and IV, AASOR 25—28 (1955); for preliminary reports, see the bibliography under Glueck.

[33] N. Glueck, Transjordan, in: Archaeology and Old Testament Study, ed. by. D. W. Thomas, 1967, 445. Similar remarks are found throughout Glueck's writings; cf. esp. The Other Side of the Jordan, 1940, 15f. 114f.; The Age of Abraham in the Negev, BA 18 (1955), 7f.; The Seventh Season of Archaeological Exploration in the Negeb, BASOR 152 (1958), 20. He has been followed in this by M. Burrows, What Mean these Stones?, 1941, 279; G. E. Wright, The Achievement of N. Glueck, BAR I, 1961, 12—14; W. F. Albright, BASOR 163 (1961), 36f.; and Y. Aharoni, The Land of the Bible, 1967, 126—128.

[34] For a discussion of the caravan trade during MB I, see above ch. 8.

[35] Given in AASOR 25—28, 423.

continued through MB II A, does not seem to suggest the sudden and catastrophic end that Glueck would read into Gen 14.

Glueck's argument then reduces itself simply to the claim that since Southern Transjordan was abandoned during the Middle Bronze II and Late Bronze Periods, Gen 14, if it is historical, must be connected with the settlements of MB I. But this is hardly an argument for the historicity of Gen 14; it assumes the historicity of the tradition from the outset.

Even so much cannot be accepted without question. Although Glueck has certainly shown that Transjordan did support a settled population during MB I, that the population of Transjordan during the Middle and Late Bronze Periods was nomadic is doubtful; that Transjordan was totally without a settled population is unquestionably false. Glueck's cursory and superficial examination of the sites of Transjordan cannot be expected to yield a dependable history of their occupation[36]. That this picture is in fact not dependable has been recently decidedly proven by the systematic survey of Northern Transjordan by S. Mittmann carried out from 1963 to 1966. In his publication of this survey Mittmann writes:

> Neben den früheisenzeitlichen Siedlungen steht eine relativ große Anzahl von Niederlassungen der FB-sowie der MB II- und SB-Periode (MB II- und SB-Siedlungen: Nr. 147, 168, 185, 193, 196, 204, 210, 213, 228). Ein ähnliches Bild zeigen, wie wir sogleich sehen werden, die östlich benachbarten Bereiche der *ǧeraš-* und *mefraq-*Region. Dieses Ergebnis stellt die gewichtigste der Glueckschen Thesen zur Siedlungsgeschichte Transjordaniens in Frage, seine Behauptung nämlich, daß in der mittleren Bronzezeit II ein weitgreifender Verfall der seßhaften Kultur eingetreten sei, dem erst in der frühen Eisenzeit ein neuer Aufschwung folgte. Glueck hat diese These speziell

[36] E. g., in the months of April, May, and June of 1933, Glueck visited "whenever time permitted" 115 sites! Between July 9—15 over 30 sites were visited! Of course, some sites were more intensively investigated, such as Tell el-Medeyneh and ʿArʿir where he found LB and MB IIA sherds respectively! (Further Explorations in Eastern Palestine, BASOR 51, 1933, 9—18). It is hard to agree with Albright's earlier evaluation of Glueck's evidence: "I am inclined to think that the situation brought to light by Glueck's exploration is due to the fact that occupation became concentrated in fortified towns and castles during the Hyksos period, instead of being distributed through unwalled settlements. Sherds belonging to the 17—15th centuries would be buried in the accumulating debris inside the walls and would seldom appear on either surface or slopes of a site." (Note to Glueck, Three Israelite Towns in the Jordan Valley, BASOR 90, 1943, 18). The establishment of more concentrated settlements during MB II in Palestine does not occur at the expense of the small village settlements. It seems unlikely that this would then have been the case in Transjordan. The MB II period of Palestine has the densest population of the entire Bronze Age in the countryside as well. (This question will be treated in detail in a monograph which I am now preparing on the Bronze Age sites of Palestine.)

im Hinblick auf den Südrand des nördlichen Ostjordanlandes wiederholt: "Nowhere in the entire Jerash region were sites found where history of occupation could bridge the gap between the end of MB I and the beginning of Iron Age I. MB II and LB, so far as surface finds are concerned are wholly absent." Wie wenig das zutrifft, mag eine statistische Gegenüberstellung verdeutlichen. Im Bergland zwischen *ǧeraš* und *mefraq* haben Glueck und ich jeweils etwa gleichviel Siedlungs-Stätten (27 und 26) aufgenommen. Dabei ist jedoch zu berücksichtigen, daß Glueck sich vornehmlich die Plätze mit der am meisten versprechenden Siedlungsgeschichte ausgesucht hat. Das zeigt sich schon am unterschiedlichen Anteil der nacheisenzeitlichen Niederlassungen in Gluecks und meiner Liste (11 gegenüber 20). Dementsprechend überwiegen bei Glueck die eisen- und voreisenzeitlichen Siedlungen, und zwar in folgendem Verhältnis zu den von mir entdeckten: N-C 6: 0; FB 3 (5) ?: 3; MB I 1: 0; E 6: 4. Während Glueck nun bei den 16 Plätzen, auf die sich diese Siedlungen verteilen, nur zwei mit angeblich unsicherer mittel (II)- und spätbronzezeitlicher Keramik aufweisen kann, befinden sich schon bei den nur sechs von mir untersuchten vier mit vollkommen eindeutiger MB II- bzw. SB-Keramik (Nr. 290, 296, 311, 316). Daß dieses Ergebnis nicht zufallsbedingt ist, bestätigt der Befund im Becken von *ǧeraš* und im *wādī sūf*, wo sechs eisenzeitlichen vier mittel- bzw. spätbronzezeitliche Siedlungen (Nr. 240, 246, 252, 282) gegenüberstehen. Ich bin überzeugt, daß eine sorgfältige Nachprüfung auf den Glueckschen *ḫereb* jene These von der mittel- und spätbronzezeitlichen Siedlungslücke vollends umstoßen würde[37].

Nor can the thesis of W. F. Albright that the "Cities of the Plain" mentioned in Genesis were MB I settlements now buried by the southern end of the Dead Sea be taken seriously[38]. Not only would

---

[37] S. Mittman, Beiträge zur Siedlungs- und Territorialgeschichte des Nördlichen Ostjordanlandes, ADPV, 1970, 221 n. 32. For other Middle and Late Bronze finds in Transjordan, including a temple and tombs with Mycenaean pottery at Amman, as well as a plastered glacis fortification at Tell Safut, cf. G. Lankester Harding, Excavations in Jordan, 1951—1952, ADAJ 2 (1953), 82—88; Four Tomb Groups from Jordan, PEFA 6 (1953); A. Dajani, A Hyksos Tomb at Kalandia, ADAJ 2 (1953), 75—77; F. Ma'Ayah, Recent Archaeological Discoveries in Jordan, ADAJ 4—5 (1960), 114—116; Recent Discoveries in Jordan, ADAJ 6—7 (1962), 110; W. A. Ward, Cylinders and Scarabs from a Late Bronze Temple at Amman, ADAJ 8—9 (1964), 47—55; G. R. H. Wright, The Bronze Age Temple at Amman, ZAW 78 (1966), 351—357; J. B. Hennessy, Excavation of a Late Bronze Age Temple at Amman, PEQ 98 (1966), 155—162; Supplementary Note, ZAW 78 (1966), 357—359; D. Gilead, Burial Customs and the Dolmen Problem, PEQ 100 (1968), 18. There are also a considerable number of sites from the Middle and Late Bronze Periods mentioned by Glueck himself: Cf., e. g.: The Archaeological Exploration of El-Hammeh on the Yarmûk, BASOR 49 (1933), 23; BASOR 51 (1933), 9—18; The Earliest History of Jerash, BASOR 75 (1939), 22—30; BASOR 90 (1943), 22; Some Ancient Towns in the Plains of Moab, BASOR 91 (1943), 7—26; see also the volumes of AASOR, passim.

[38] W. F. Albright, The Jordan Valley in the Bronze Age, AASOR 6 (1926), 56—62; Archaeology of Palestine and the Bible, 1932, 133—135; followed by J. P. Harland, Sodom and Gomorrah: Part I. The Location of the Cities of the Plain, BA 5 (1942), 17—32; Part II, The Destruction of the Cities of the Plain, BA 6 (1943),

the existence of MB I sites at the southern end of the Dead Sea not be proof that they were the Cities of the Plain, nor, if the sites were identifiable and datable to this early period, would it be evidence that the stories about them were historical, but nothing was found by Albright at the southern end of the Dead Sea, except two sites (possibly to be identified with the Byzantine-Arabic Zoar) that were not occupied in either Israelite or earlier periods[39]! What was found from the early period was a large Early Bronze Age Settlement at Bab edh-Dhrâ', not at the southern end of the Dead Sea, but a considerable distance away overlooking the Lisân. The excavations of Paul Lapp have shown that the settlement at Bab edh-Dhrâ' no longer existed after EB IV[40]!

The answer to the question of historicity for Gen 14, as well as the other patriarchal traditions, has not and obviously cannot be solved on the basis of archaeological and historical study. It is hoped that the foregoing chapters have shown that the claim that the archaeology and history of the early Second Millenium can serve as the historical mileu of the patriarchal narratives remains not only unproven, but is a methodological distortion of both history and the Bible. The study of the archaeology and the history of the early Second Millenium has nothing to offer directly to the interpretation of the traditions about Abraham, Isaac, and Jacob, though it has much to offer to an understanding of the culture of the ancient Near East, of which the Bible and the patriarchal narratives form a part.

41—52; and surprisingly, Lapp, Bab ehh-Dhrâ' Tomb A76 and Early Bronze I in Palestine, BASOR 189 (1968), 114. See however, D. Irvin, Mytharion, 32f.

39 AASOR 6, 57.

40 The Cemetery at Bab edh-Dhrâ, Archaeology 19 (1966), 104—111; BASOR 189 (1968), 12—14. See also S. Saller, Bab edh-Dhrâ, Studii Biblici Franciscani Liber Annuus XV (1964—1965), 137—219; and the Chronique Archéologique, in RB 73 (1966), 556—561 and RB 75 (1968), 86—93. Recently, G. E. Wright has suggested (The Archaeology of Palestine from the Neolithic through the Middle Bronze Age, JAOS 91, 1971, 285f.) that some of the previously dated EB I—II burials might properly be related to the burials of MB I. Nevertheless, he redates these finds to the "period between the 24th and 22nd centuries", which suggests that he places them in the EB IV period, just before the beginning of MB I.

Chapter 10

Nuzi[1] and the Patriarchal Narratives

A. THE DISCOVERY OF THE TEXTS AND THEIR DATING

As early as 1894 cuneiform tablets from the region of modern Kirkuk in Northern Mesopotamia had found their way to the British Museum and elsewhere[2]. Since 1896 these and similar tablets (both from Kirkuk and from Yorghan Tepe, 12 km southwest of Kirkuk) have been published in various places[3]. In 1925, Miss Gertrude Bell,

1 On the orthography of the name "Nuzi", see E. A. Speiser, Nuzi or Nuzu, JAOS 75 (1955), 52—55.

2 C. J. Gadd, Tablets from Kirkuk, RA 23 (1926), 49.

3 T. G. Pinches, Cuneiform Texts in the British Museum, II 1896, pl. 21 (one tablet: copy); also Some Early Babylonian Contracts or Legal Documents, JRAS (1897), 589ff. (transliteration and translation of the text published in 1896); B. Meißner, Thontafeln aus Vyran Sehir, OLZ 6 (1902), 245f. (one tablet: copy, transliteration, and translation, from Vyran Sehir, near Kirkuk); A. Ungnad, VAS I, 1907, 106 to 111 (five tablets); V. Scheil, Lettre Assyrienne de Kerkouk, Recueil de Travaux 31 (1909), 56—58 (one tablet: transliteration and translation); also Tablettes de Kerkouk, RA 15 (1918), 65ff. (two texts: copies, transliterations, and translations); L. Speleers, Recueil des Inscriptions de l'Asie antérieure, 1925, nos. 309f. (two tablets); G. Contenau, Textes Cuneiformes de Louvre, 1926, pls. 1—46 (46 texts: copies); C. J. Gadd, RA 23 (1926), 49—161 (82 tablets: copies, transliterations and translations); P. Koschaker, Neue Keilschriftliche Rechtsurkunden aus der El-Amarna-Zeit, ASAWL 39, 1928, 166f. 171. and 174ff. (transliterations and translations of TCL IX, nos. 46—48, p. 171 and 174—176); G. Contenau, Tablettes de Kerkouk du Musée du Louvre, RA 28 (1931), 27—39 (eight tablets: copies, transliterations and translations); H. F. Lutz, A Legal Document from Nuzi, UCP IX, 11 (1931), 405—412, and pl. 12 (one tablet: copy, transliteration and translation); F. M. Th. de Liagre-Böhl, Mededeelingen uit de Leidsche verzameling van spijkerschrift-inscripties II: Oorkonden mit de periode van 2000—1200 v.Chr., MKAW, deel 78, Serie B, nr. 2 (1934), 2; C. H. Gordon, Nuzi Tablets Relating to Women, AnOr 12 (1935), nos. XXXVI—XLIV (nine tablets from the Louvre: transliterations and translations); E. M. Cassin, L'Adoption à Nuzi, 1938 (171 texts from the Louvre: transliterations and translations); P. Koschaker, Drei Rechtsurkunden aus Arrapḫa, ZA 48 (1944), 161ff.; G. Contenau, Les tablettes de Kerkouk et les origines de la civilisation assyrienne, Babyloniaca 9 (1926), 69—151. 157—212; E. Ebeling, Ein Brief aus Nuzi im Besitz des Athener archäologischen Museums, Orientalia 22 (1953), 355—358 (one tablet: copy, transliteration, and translation); N. B. Jankowska, Legal Documents from Arrapha in the Collections of the USSR, 1961 (100 tablets: copies and transliterations); and E.

Director of the Department of Antiquities in Iraq, noticing the large number of tablets appearing on the market in Baghdad, recommended to E. Chiera (the Annual Professor of the American Schools of Oriental Research) that an excavation be undertaken. Chiera accordingly began the excavation on a site a few hundred yards from Yorghan Tepe. He uncovered there a private residence of about twenty rooms, finding about 1000 tablets written in cuneiform script from the middle of the Second Millenium. Examination of the tablets showed that they formed the archives of a single family. The excavations were interrupted for about two years, but were continued in 1927, when two houses a few hundred yards from the first were excavated. Here again, more than 1000 tablets were found[4]. From 1928 to 1931 the excavators concentrated on the tell of Yorghan Tepe itself, uncovering the palace and bringing the total number of cuneiform tablets found to more than 4000. A deep pit was sunk to bedrock, showing that the site had been occupied in fifteen levels from the second aeneolithic period (second half of the Fourth Millenium, B. C.). On the basis of some 200 Akkadian tablets found, it was learned that the earlier city of levels 5 to 12 had been named Ga-sur. In level 13, according to the excavators, Hurrian names begin to appear on the tablets. Levels 14 and 15 belong to the palace of the Hurrian city of Nuzi, from which most of the tablets were found. This palace proved to be contemporary to the private houses that had been uncovered earlier[5].

Cassin, Tablettes Inédites de Nuzi, RA 56 (1962), 57—80 (nine tablets: copies, transliterations, and translations); A. Shaffer, Kitru/kiterru: New Documentation for a Nuzi Legal Term. Studies presented to A. Leo Oppenheim (1964), 181ff.; E. R. Lacheman, Les tablettes de Kerkouk au Musée d'Art et d'Histoire de Genève, Genava 15 (1967), 5ff.

[4] That 1000 tablets were found in the "House of Tehiptilla" may well be an exaggeration. E. R. Lacheman, the final editor of the tablets, is aware of only somewhat less than 600 tablets (cf. Lacheman, HSS XVI, p. v., n. 2).

[5] For the preliminary reports on the discovery and excavation, see E. Chiera, Report of the Professor in Charge of the School in Baghdad, BASOR 20 (1925), 19—25; D. G. Lyon, The Joint Expedition of Harvard University and the Baghdad School at Yargon Tepa near Kirkuk, BASOR 30 (1928), 1—6; E. Chiera, Report of the Director of the School in Baghdad, BASOR 32 (1928), 15—17; R. H. Pfeiffer, Yorghan Teppe, BASOR 34 (1929), 2—7; R. F. S. Starr, Notes from the Excavation at Nuzi, BASOR 38 (1930), 3—8; Kirkuk Expedition, Fogg Art Museum Notes, vol. II, 5 (1930), 182—197; Report from Our Expedition in Iraq, BASOR 41 (1931), 24—27; R. H. Pfeiffer, The Excavations at Nuzi, BASOR 42 (1931), 1—7; Nuzi and the Hurrians, Annual Report of the Smithsonian Institution I (1935), 535—558; for the final excavation report see R. F. S. Starr, Nuzi I—II, 1939, and appendices; for the study and publication of the seals found on

Publication of copies of the cuneiform tablets proceeded very rapidly, and the first volume appeared as early as 1927. Today, there are 13 volumes of copies or transliterations of the tablets from the Nuzi levels available, and there is one volume of the tablets from the earlier levels[6]. The publication of translations has been very sporadic; yet, when the tablets discovered independent of the excavations are considered, we now have more than 600 Nuzi and Kirkuk contracts in translation, most of which are easily accessible[7].

Most of the tablets are family contracts dealing with sales, rentals, marriage settlements, adoptions, and the like. They cover a

---

the tablets, see E. Porada, Seal Impressions of Nuzi, AASOR 24 (1947), and for the pottery see S. M. Cecchini, La Ceramica di Nuzi, 1965.

6 Six volumes are published in the JEN series: E. Chiera, Inheritance Texts, JEN I, 1927; Declarations in Court, JEN II, 1930; Exchange and Security Documents, JEN III, 1931; Proceedings in Court, JEN IV, 1934; Mixed Texts, JEN V, 1934; E. R. Lacheman, Miscellaneous Texts, JEN VI, 1939; Eight volumes of texts are published in the Harvard Semitic Series; E. Chiera, Texts of Varied Contents, HSS V, 1929; T. J. Meek, Old Akkadian, Sumerian, and Cappadocian Texts from Nuzi, HSS IX, 1935; R. H. Pfeiffer, Archives of Shilwateshub, Son of the King, HSS X, 1942; R. H. Pfeiffer and E. R. Lacheman, Miscellaneous Texts from Nuzi, Part I HSS XIII, 1942; E. R. Lacheman, Miscellaneous Texts from Nuzi, Part II, HSS XIV, 1950; The Administrative Archives, HSS XV, 1955; Economic and Social Documents, HSS XVI, 1958; Family Law Documents, HSS XIX, 1962; 112 tablets were also published by E. R. Lacheman in the form of copies in his articles: Nuziana I—II, RA 36 (1939), 81—95 and 113—219. Some of these were republished in subsequent volumes of HSS.

7 Besides those listed in note 3 above, translations are available in the following publications: E. Chiera and E. A. Speiser, Selected "Kirkuk" Documents, JAOS 47 (1927), 36—60; E. A. Speiser, New Kirkuk Documents Relating to Family Laws, AASOR X (1930), 1—73; P. Koschaker, Neue Keilschriftliche Rechtsurkunden, 168—176; E. A. Speiser, New Kirkuk Documents Relating to Security Transactions, Part I: JAOS 52 (1932), 350—367, and Part II: JAOS 53 (1933), 24—46; T. J. Meek, Some Gleanings from the Last Excavations at Nuzi, AASOR 13 (1933), 1—11; A. Saarisalo, New Kirkuk Documents Relating to Slaves, Studia Orientalia V 3, 1934; E. R. Lacheman, New Nuzi Texts and a New Method of Copying Cuneiform Tablets, JAOS 55 (1935), 429—431; E. A. Speiser, Notes to Recently Published Nuzi Texts, JAOS 55 (1935), 432—443; C. H. Gordon, Nuzi Tablets Relating to Women, AnOr 12 (1935), 163—184; Fifteen Nuzi Tablets Relating to Women, Le Muséon 48 (1935), 113—132; E. A. Speiser, 100 New Selected Nuzi Texts, AASOR 16 (1936), 1ff.; E. M. Cassin, La Caution à Nuzi, RA 34 (1937), 159—162. 167ff.; E. M. Cassin, L'Adoption à Nuzi, 1938; H. Lewy, The *Aḫḫûtu* Documents from Nuzi, Orientalia 9 (1940), 369—373; J. B. Pritchard, ANET 119f.; E. M. Cassin, RA 56 (1962), 57—80; H. Donner, Adoption oder Legitimation?, Oriens Antiquus 8 (1969), 117f. A collection of about 800 similar tablets have recently been excavated from the site of Tell al-Fikhar, about 45 km. southwest of Kirkuk (cf. F. El-Wailly, Tell al-Fikhar, Sumer 23, 1967, e—f.).

period of four or five full generations[8], and can be dated from the time of Šauššatar, king of Mitanni to the reign of Tušratta; i. e., from c. 1480 to c. 1355 B. C.[9].

The tablets were written in Akkadian by people whose mother tongue was Hurrian[10].

B. NUZI FAMILY CUSTOMS AND THE HISTORICITY OF THE PATRIARCHAL NARRATIVES

The cuneiform tablets that have been excavated give evidence of family customs among the Hurrians living at Nuzi which were immediately thought to be remarkably similar to biblical customs, particularly those in Genesis, many of which, it was felt, could not be explained by later biblical practice. The similarity was thought to be so strong, and the agreement among scholars was so clearly unanimous, that it quickly became common opinion that the patriarchs must have lived according to Nuzi or Hurrian law.

These parallels were seen to support the attempts to establish a "patriarchal period" in the Second Millenium, because they added to the arguments based on external historical and archaeological sources a means for relating the question of historicity to the history of the transmission of the biblical narratives. But because of this attempt to establish a direct relationship between Genesis and the Nuzi customs, the comparison created an argument which avoided

---

8 C. J. Gadd, RA 23 (1926), 61; W. F. Albright, Some Important Recent Discoveries: Alphabetic Origins and the Idrimi Statue, BASOR 118 (1950), 17; and C. H. Gordon, Adventures in the Nearest East, 1957, 105.

9 Following E. Cassin, L'influence Babylonienne à Nuzi, JESHO 5 (1962), 114; see also Albright, BASOR 118 (1950), 17; Also: E. A. Speiser, A Letter of Šauššatar and the Date of the Kirkuk Tablets, JAOS 49 (1929), 269—275; G. Furlani, Review of R. Pfeiffer, HSS X, JRAS (1935), 747; E. Forrer, Assyrien, RLA I, 249ff., esp. 252b; B. Landsberger, Assyrische Königsliste und "Dunkles Zeitalter", JCS 8 (1954), 54; A. Goetze, Hethiter, Churriter, und Assyrer, 1936, 119n; The Predecessors of Šuppiluliumaš of Hatti, JAOS 72 (1952), 68f.; H. Lewy, The Nuzian Feudal System, Orientalia 11 (1942), 318—329; and A. Pohl, Review of E. Chiera, JEN IV and V, Orientalia 5 (1936), 141.

10 I. J. Gelb, P. M. Purves, and G. MacRae, Nuzi Personal Names, 1943; E. Chiera and E. A. Speiser, A New Factor in the History of the Ancient East, AASOR 6 (1926), 75—92; L. Oppenheim, Zur Landessprache von Arrapha Nuzi, AfO 11 (1936), 56ff.; C. H. Gordon, The Dialect of the Nuzi Tablets, Orientalia 7 (1938), 32—63 and 215—232; F. Imperati, I Hurriti, 1964; R. de Vaux, Les Hurrites de l'Histoire et les Horites de la Bible, RB 74 (1967), 481—503 (also see de Vaux's review of C. Epstein, Palestinian Bichrome Ware, in RB 74, 1967, 268—271); and especially: G. Wilhelm, Untersuchungen zum Ḫurro-Akkadischen von Nuzi, AOAT 9 (1970).

the weakness of any of the other arguments for historicity, and was offered as a self-sufficient proof that the biblical narratives must be early. The uniqueness of the Nuzi-type customs allowed the commentators to argue more completely that the historical background of the traditions had to be placed prior to the Israelite Conquest. This argument has proven even more convincing to many because it has not been based on an historical analogy, but is drawn out of the biblical narratives themselves, elements of which could now be identified as uniquely early and as separated from the later developments which the traditions underwent.

Most of the parallels that have been claimed, and the arguments for relating them to the dating of the patriarchs, have been developed by E. A. Speiser and C. Gordon[11]. On the basis of their comparison of the family relationships and customs implied in the Genesis stories with the family legal contracts found at Nuzi Speiser and Gordon have sought to discover and to reestablish the common historical tradition which they believe must have lain behind the now diverging narratives, with their many variant and even conflicting details. The historical character of this original tradition is assumed on the basis of the clearly historical, rather than literary nature, of the Nuzi parallels, and the verifiability of this Tradition is directly related to the early age at which the background of the tradition must be placed.

That Speiser chooses to date the patriarchal traditions at the beginning of the Second Millenium, and that Gordon prefers the "Amarna Age" is of some, though only peripheral, significance. Speiser sees the Nuzi parallels as a means of supporting the early Second Millenium dating of the patriarchs, and for establishing the Mari period firmly as the original historical background of the narratives. In doing this, of course, he might appear to be open to the criticism of de Vaux that if the type of customs which have been found at Nuzi are not limited to the time that Nuzi was occupied, the Nuzi tablets cannot be used to date the patriarchs[12]. Speiser, however, not only dates the Nuzi tablets relatively early (c. 1500 B. C.), but sees the contracts of Nuzi as representative of general Hurrian practice. His dating of this general Hurrian influence in North Mesopotamia is placed vaguely from the early part of the Second Millenium. At least it is clear that the Hurrians were in North Mesopotamia at the time that the Mari texts

[11] Complete bibliographical information would be far too cumbersome to include here. The reader is referred to the footnotes in the following sections of this chapter as well as to the bibliography at the end of the book.

[12] R. de Vaux, Method in the Study of Early Hebrew History. The Bible in Modern Scholarship, ed. by J. P. Hyatt, 1966, 26f. De Vaux's remarks are here not directed specifically against Speiser, but are general in nature.

were written. Speiser's date for the patriarchs is not based so much on the Nuzi tablets as it is on the date of the supposed "Amorite" movement which we have already discussed. Nuzi is seen to support this chronology, since the contracts, according to Speiser, identify the patriarchal customs as specifically and uniquely Hurrian.

In contrast, Gordon uses the Nuzi parallels to the patriarchal narratives as a constitutive part of his argument for the dating of the patriarchs to the Amarna Period. Indeed, his argument does not require that the customs be exclusively dated to this period, only that they be practiced during this period. Nevertheless, that Nuzi is to be dated to the fifteenth and early fourteenth centuries, and that comparable parallels have not been recognized elsewhere at any other period, have been major factors in the growing preference for this later dating of the patriarchs which avoids so many of the inconsistencies of the earlier chronology. On the other hand, the Amarna Period dating is almost totally dependent on the reality of the Nuzi parallels for its adherence, for no other substantial argument has been raised which would require a date for the narratives of Genesis prior to the Conquest. In this respect, the validity of the Nuzi parallels is more important for a fourteenth century date of the patriarchs than for a date at any earlier period.

As we have already pointed out, however, the importance of the Nuzi parallels is of far greater significance for the question of historicity than for establishing a very specific patriarchal period; for if the presentation of these parallels is as valid and as unique as has been claimed, the thesis that the stories do go back to a period prior to that of the Conquest must undoubtedly be accepted, and that at least a position similar to that of Martin Noth, that the patriarchal narratives do have at least an historical core, must be seen not only as historically possible but as likely[13].

The need for a critical review of the Nuzi parallels to the patriarchal narratives has long been recognized[14]. What follows is, as far as I know, the first attempt to place the stories from Genesis and the proposed Nuzi parallel customs into their historical-legal context[15].

---

[13] M. Noth, Die Ursprünge des alten Israel im Lichte neuer Quellen, 1961, 22f. This is of course aside from the question of the relationships with Mari; on this last see above ch. 2 through 5.

[14] A. Alt, Erwägungen über die Landnahme der Israeliten in Palästina, PJ 35 (1939), 63 n. 1 (= KS I 175n): "Manches an diesen Vergleichungen bedarf noch der Nachprüfung."

[15] A few articles have examined single parallels: M. Greenberg, Another Look at Rachel's Theft of the Teraphim, JBL 81 (1962), 239—248; J. van Seters, The

The Nuzi parallels to Genesis are said to exist, according to Speiser, not specifically between Nuzi and the narratives we now find in Genesis, but rather between the customs of Nuzi and a proposed original tradition (T) about the patriarchs which had once served as the historical "Grundlage" for the Genesis narratives[16]. The positing of this hypothetical "Tradition" or "Grundlage" makes it insufficient merely to point out that the Nuzi contracts are not similar to the biblical customs as they are now described in the text of Genesis. Speiser's interpretation does not claim that the Nuzi customs and those of Genesis itself are identical; it only claims that the Nuzi customs and those that are implied in the original "Tradition" are. Subsequent redaction — so it is argued — no longer understood the customs that were portrayed in the earliest forms of the narratives. The narratives we now find in Genesis are later quasi-legendary versions of what once was an original history, no longer understanding the social structure which once underlay the events related.

It is important to realize in the following investigation that the Genesis narratives only indirectly reflect actual practices of individuals in history. Because Genesis is composed of stories, these stories can be expected at times to follow not the actual customs of people but the exigencies of the narrative form which has its own traditions and context. So, for example, we cannot assume on the basis of Gen 38 alone, that the ancestors of the tribe of Judah, or anyone at all, actually used burning as a punishment for adultery. So too, the assumption that patriarchal authority is actually exemplified by Lot's willingness to sacrifice his daughters to save his guests is not adequately justified. This story is perhaps more influenced by the literary necessities of the ancestral hero offering hospitality to strangers, which hospitality is to result in his being saved[17]. The literary form of the

---

Problem of Childlessness in Near Eastern Law and the Patriarchs of Israel, JBL 87 (1968), 401—408; Jacob's Marriages and Ancient Near East Customs. A Reexamination, HThR 62 (1969), 377—395; H. Donner, Oriens Antiquus 8 (1969), 87—119; D. Freedman, JANESC 2 (1970), 77—85.

[16] E. A. Speiser, Genesis, Anchor Bible Commentary, 1964, xxvii—lii; cf. also my remarks above, pp. 6—8. Speiser's position is indirectly supported, for example, by G. Cornfeld (Pictorial Biblical Encyclopedia, 1964, 562): "(it is) possible that the Biblical authors did not fully understand the motivating social factors in the lives of the patriarchs".

[17] For an example of the quite different ways that the same legal custom might appear in laws and stories, cf. Th. and D. Thompson, Some Legal Problems in the Book of Ruth, VT 18 (1968), 79—99. For an extensive discussion of the influence which literary motifs have on the Genesis narratives, see the dissertation of D. Irvin, Mytharion. The Comparison of Tales from the Old Testament and the Ancient Near East, AOAT, 1974, Chapters 4—6.

story is not bound to the limitations of actual legal practices, and in several cases in our Genesis stories where the motivation of the patriarchs' actions has been explained by reference to Nuzi customs, traditional literary practices appear to offer a more adequate explanation[18].

C. GEN 15 2-4

Gen 15 2-4, particularly v. 2, because of the enigmatic בן־משק, is untranslatable. The various translations that have been offered affect so strongly the question of whether and how this passage is related to Nuzi — and indeed in some cases they are inseparable from the attempt to explain the passage on the basis of one or other proposed parallel — that it is essential to examine the basis of these translations before proceeding to the question of whether the narrative does seem to assume a background like that offered by the Nuzi tablets[19]. In my opinion, none of the translations is totally convincing, though the suggestions of Gordon and Snijders both seem possible, that of Snijders being the most complete. For the present, at least, it seems that interpretation (and consequently a consideration of the Nuzi "parallels") must be the arbiter of translation.

The passage is particularly complex since v. 2 seems to be paralleled by v. 3, and v. 4 by v. 5, suggesting the possibility of two sources: E and J[20]. Moreover the phrase הוא דמשק could well be a later gloss explaining the no longer (?) understood בן־משק[21].

Snijders suggests a way in which v. 2-5 can be understood as a unity[22], by interpreting בן־משק with an understanding of the word משק as used in Is 33 4: from the root שקק "rushing", "assault"; thus בן־משק would be "the attacker", or "he who overcomes" (cf. בן־עַן "a miserable man"). Eliezer is seen as a usurper of Abraham's position and name — an unwanted successor[23]. This, according to

[18] It is because of the neglect of this aspect of his material that A. van Selm's, Marriage and Family Life in Ugaritic Literature, 1954, is practically unusable for the history of culture in the ancient Near East. This is also a serious drawback in many textbooks on biblical legal customs.

[19] Only those possibilities are here discussed which relate to the question of the Nuzi parallel. M. Weippert (Abraham der Hebräer? Bemerkungen zu W. F. Albright's Deutung der Väter Israels, Bb 52, 1971, 421f. n. 1) has conveniently gathered together most of the relevant literature related to the translation of this passage, which does not need to be repeated here.

[20] G. von Rad, Das erste Buch Mose, 1964[7], 153f.

[21] Cf. critical apparatus in BHS, Genesis, by O. Eissfeldt.

[22] L. A. Snijders, Genesis XV. The covenant with Abram, OTS 12 (1958), 269—271.

[23] Ibid. 270.

Snijders, is emphasized by parallelism in v. 3: בן־ביתי יורש אתי which uses the verb ירש, which has the basic meaning "subdue" or "take possession", not necessarily used in the context of legal inheritance[24].

The key to an understanding of this pejorative stress in Abraham's words is the interpretive parenthetical remark or "gloss" הוא דמשק, "that is, Damascus", a pun on בן־משק. Thus Abraham complains to Yahweh that, since he is childless, the usurper of his property will be Eliezer; a servant born in his house is to be his successor, namely Damascus[25]. The significance of Yahweh's answer is that not Damascus, but Abraham's own children will be the heirs of Abraham. This anti-Damascus tendency could reflect the historical antagonism between Israel and the Aramaeans of Damascus[26], a motif which fits well with other Stammessagen in the Patriarchal narratives. This interpretation does not need an understanding of legal inheritance or adoption for its sense, and thus can be understood independent of the Nuzi customs.

Gordon, on the other hand, understands דמשק as a gloss giving the Aramaic equivalent or translation of בן־משק[27]. To דמשק Gordon gives the meaning "servant" on the basis of a comparison of the cuneiform transliteration and translation of the name Damascus; *Dimašq* = *ša imēri/e-šu. ša imēri šu* is translatable as "he of his donkey" or "servant"[28]. The ד is the Aramaic relative pronoun, with the same meaning as the Akkadian *ša*. משק as well as בן־משק, he relates to Hebrew, משקה, "cupbearer", "household servant" (from שקה). Thus דמשק is a clear rendering of *ša imēri šu*, and a translation of בן־משק[29].

Following Gordon, then, one could translate "and the servant (i. e., aramaic דמשק) of my house is Eliezer", parallel to v. 3b. The difficulty of this interpretation is that v. 2 must be understood as saying the same as v. 3, i. e., that the servant will be Abraham's heir, but, by itself — and if בן־משק is to be understood as "servant" the text seems to demand that v. 2 and 3 are variants — it does not say that; only that Abraham's servant is Eliezer, an inconsequential statement following v. 2a.

---

[24] ירש in Is 54 3 has more the sense of "to succeed" than to "inherit". Snijders (ibid.) notes that the closeness of the words שקק and ירש can be seen by comparing Is 33 4 with Deut 28 42 where both verbs are used to describe the activity of locusts.

[25] Snijders ibid.

[26] O. Kaiser, Traditionsgeschichtliche Untersuchung von Genesis 15, ZAW 70 (1958), 116.

[27] C. H. Gordon, Damascus in Assyrian Sources, IEJ 2 (1952), 174f.

[28] C. H. Gordon, Review of J. B. Pritchard, ANET, JBL 70 (1951), 161.

[29] Gordon, IEJ 2 (1952), 174f.

Speiser's translation of v. 2b: "the successor to my house is Dammesek Eliezer" is impossible, and conflicts with the little justification that he gives for it. First, his interpretation of the clause on the basis of 3b, is obviously a circular argument. Second, Speiser states that דמשק is a gloss on בן־משק, and is "etymologized" in Aramaic as *di masqya*.

He argues that בן־משק, then, must be understood as analogous to this Aramaic phrase. The juxtaposition of the two terms is supposed to signify hereditary succession[30]! The "explanation" is little more than obfuscation. His final interpretation that "a servant by the name of Eliezer, apparently a Damascene by birth, was the only prospective heir to Abraham's estate", is in no way a conclusion from his discussion, but is a harmonization of v. 2 and 3 of his translation. דמשק cannot be understood as the adjective "Damascene"[31], as the meaningless hybrid translation of Speiser "Dammesek" itself implies. That בן־משק means "successor", must presuppose an interpretation similar to Snijders, and is neither obviously implied in the word בן־משק, nor consistent with the interpretation of Damascus as adjectival. Speiser seems to translate the text so that it will fit what he proposes as a parallel from Nuzi. This parallel we will examine shortly.

M. F. Unger, following unpublished suggestions of W. F. Albright, argues that משק is itself the place name Damascus, an older form of the name דמשק. Thus the gloss הוא דמשק is to explain the antiquated משק[32].

Albright had suggested an emendation involving haplography and transposition so that ובן־משק ביתי would read ובן־ביתי [בן־] משק "and the son of my house is the son of Meśeq" which Unger simplifies: ובן־משק [בן־] ביתי "and the son of Meśeq is the son of my house"[33]. הוא דמשק אליעזר is then understood as an explanatory gloss[34]. He gives as a translation of the passage: "And the 'son of my house' is the son of Meśeq, which is Damascus . . . (sic!) and behold, the 'son of my house' shall be my heir". Unger then maintains that the phrase "son of my house" refers specifically to the heir presumptive and can be simply rendered "my heir"[35].

There are three major difficulties in this interpretation. First, the equation משק = Damascus is without justification and is merely

---

30 Speiser, Genesis, 110—112.

31 G. von Rad, Das erste Buch Mose, 154f.

32 M. F. Unger, Some Comments on the Text of Genesis 15 2. 3, JBL 72 (1953), 49f.; O. Kaiser, ZAW 70 (1958), 116; G. von Rad, Das erste Buch Mose, 154n; recently, Albright himself: Abram the Hebrew. A New Archaeological Interpretation, BASOR 163 (1961), 47, and Yahweh and the Gods of Canaan, 1968, 57f.

33 Unger, JBL 72 (1953), 50.

34 Ibid.

35 Ibid.; see also Albright, BASOR 163 (1961), 47.

asserted; second, the phrase הוא דמשק could well be a gloss meaning "which is Damascus", but the phrase הוא דמשק אליעזר understood as a gloss makes no sense (as perhaps is already felt by Unger when he left אליעזר out of his translation!); third, if Unger and Albright's translation for v. 2 were accepted, v. 3b must read — if "son of my house" has the meaning not "servant", but "heir": "and behold, my heir shall be my heir", which is a hardly acceptable redundancy.

This is not overly critical, as becomes clear when we observe that when Albright sees Eliezer as a citizen of Damascus he does not see him as a member of Abraham's household; rather בן־ביתי is understood as a terminus technicus for "heir". In this way, Albright's interpretation of Gen 15 2 departs radically from both Speiser's and Gordon's interpretations. Moreover, when he explains the passage as implying that Abraham has adopted Eliezer of Damascus, which is to be understood on the basis of the Nuzi customs, he refers to a completely different practice than the adoption of a servant, the custom which Speiser and Gordon consider; rather, he is relating the Genesis text to those contracts which are commonly referred to as "sale-adoptions".

This divergence from the interpretation of Speiser and Gordon coincides with Albright's recent attempts to prove that Abraham is a caravaneer[36]. In fact, it appears that Albright's translation of the passage and the parallel which he claims with Nuzi are both designed to support this picture of the patriarch as a leader of a caravan who "in order to purchase donkeys and buy supplies"[37] adopted a rich citizen of Damascus in lieu of the necessary collatoral[38]. Thus Eliezer is not seen as Abraham's servant, but rather as a "rich Damascene merchant"[39]. The proposed parallel to Nuzi is that the requirement of adoption for the transference of property suggests to Albright that the property must be inalienable, and according to him, the Nuzi *ṭuppi mārūti* ("tablet of sonship") contracts offer many examples "in which a man of means was adopted as heir by another man who needed credit, but who had property collateral"[40].

---

[36] This change in interpretation is not well understood by Albright himself. In BASOR 163 (1961), 47 he states: "Soon after the discovery of the Nuzi tablets from the 15th century B. C. it was recognized that Abraham had adopted Eliezer in much the same way that the capitalists of Nuzi had themselves adopted by persons who borrowed from them." In 1932, however, (The Archaeology of Palestine and the Bible 138 and 209 n. 25) Albright's interpretation was substantially that of Speiser and Gordon!

[37] BASOR 163 (1961), 47.

[38] Yahweh and the Gods 58 n. 31.

[39] W. F. Albright, New Horizens in Biblical Research, Whidden Lectures no. 6, 1966, 9.

[40] Ibid.

An examination of the referred-to practice at Nuzi shows that such an interpretation is not justified, and, moreover, in respect to the so-called "sale-adoption" contracts and the social structure that they presuppose, Nuzi society is extremely unlike the society reflected in the Old Testament and in the patriarchal narratives.

In order to understand better these "sale-adoption" contracts, it seems useful to understand them in the context of the different types of "adoption" contracts which were used not only at Nuzi but throughout the Near East[41].

The term "adoption", which we use here, is a terminus technicus derived from Roman legal usage that is not entirely the same as the practices under discussion in the Near Eastern legal structure. This quite obvious fact alone should make one hesitate to speak of the Nuzi *ṭuppi mārūti* documents as sales disguised as adoptions, or as means of circumventing established social norms[42], since these descriptions assume that the Near Eastern legal concept of family, and hence "adoption", differs little from the Roman or modern. Moreover, the establishment of two classes of adoption, one real and one nominal[43], obscures the extent to which the Nuzi "sale-

---

[41] Cf. A. L. Oppenheim, On an Operational Device in Mesopotamian Bureaucracy, JNES 18 (1959), 121.

[42] E. A. Speiser, New Kirkuk Documents Relating to Family Laws, AASOR X (1930), 1—73, esp. 13f.: "the object of the Nuzi nominal adoptions is to provide a legally unimpeachable by-path for transferred ownership of property, the sale of which in a direct way was not sanctioned by the law of the country, etc." Koschaker, Rechtsurkunden, 54—64, gives a more complete discussion. Koschaker's concept of "Nachgeformte Rechtsgeschäfte" seems to have more the meaning "extended legal concept" than Speiser's "borrowed". See esp. 88—90.
The often stated explanation of Nuzi property practice as, e. g., found in Gordon, The World of the Old Testament, 1958, 114: "Inasmuch as land could not be sold legally (at Nuzi) sale of land was often masked as adoption," is misleading, since rights to property were bound up with family, and the manner of the transference of property was by means of a legal extension of the family; such an extension of the family was a basic legal conception widely practiced for various reasons throughout the Near East: namely, adoption.
One of the most recent treatments of this practice tends to make it even more obscure and peculiar — effectively isolating the Nuzi contracts from the res. of Near Eastern law: "A curious legal fiction at Nuzi was nominal 'filial adoption' of a purchaser of land by its seller, presumably to satisfy some obsolescent religious taboo or legal restriction against transfer of land outside the family." (C. J. M. Weir, Nuzi, in: Archaeology and Old Testament Study, ed. by D. W. Thomas, 1967, 73).

[43] E. A. Speiser, AASOR 10, 7—18; C. H. Gordon, Adventures in the Nearest East, 1957, 110f.; M. David, Die Adoption im altbabylonischen Recht, LRS 23 (1927), 112; J. Holt, The Patriarchs of Israel, 1964, 119f.

adoption", and, subsequently other Nuzi legal practices, share a generally consistent Near Eastern legal consciousness about the obligations involved in family relationships and landed property. In agreement with general Near Eastern practice the contracts dealing with immovable property at Nuzi involve two fundamental aspects of the structure of the society: the implied rights and duties of familial relationships, and the order of the normal inheritance of property. The purpose of the various types of "adoption" contracts at Nuzi is not to "circumvent" an objectionable law or custom; these practices are rather the ordinary means (generally common to the Near East) of maintaining the basic structural order and the responsibilities involved in family relationships and the transference of property, and at the same time allowing considerable freedom to extend these structures beyond the ordinary limits given by custom. The tablets of Nuzi show that the people there had a well integrated legal structure, very similar and fully comparable to what we know of other Mesopotamian societies.

Although the term "adoption" is a terminus technicus referring to a practice in Roman law for the transferral of parental authority over a dependent person with its legal consequences[44], it nevertheless seems justified to use this same term for the earlier Near Eastern practices. While it seems important to emphasize that, in the Near Eastern context, the practices involved are much more varied, and that the term is often used in both an extended as well as a more limited way, with the result that we must be careful not to impose the implications of Roman law on these earlier arrangements, some of the contracts at Nuzi, as well as contracts from several cuneiform sources, are similar to adoption proper and can be spoken of as full adoption. These full-adoption contracts normally have three characteristics: 1) A statement of the intention to adopt, involving the person who possesses the patria potestas and the person to whom this is to be transferred; 2) A statement about the rights of inheritance, in case of the existence of present or future children of the adopter. The inheritance portion is not related to a specific piece of land or goods, but to a share in the total family property; and 3) A mutual penalty clause, in case the contract is broken. For example, a standard full adoption text reads[45]:

> Ubār-Šamaš, Sohn des Sin-idinnam, haben von Sin-idinnam, seinem Vater und Bititum, seiner Mutter, Ningir-abi und Taram-Ulmaš zur Kindschaft angenommen.

---

[44] Following H. Donner, Oriens Antiquus 8 (1969), 88—90. Donner's entire discussion is particularly helpful for judging the extent of the relationship implied in the Nuzi adoption contracts.

[45] These characteristics are discussed by Donner ibid., 94f.

Selbst wenn Ningir-abi und Tarām-Ulmaš Kinder bekommen sollten, so ist Ubār-Šamaš ihr ältester Erbsohn. Sobald Ningir-abi, sein Vater, oder Taram-Ulmaš, seine Mutter, zu Ubār-Šamaš, ihrem Sohne, "Nicht bist du unser Sohn" sagen, gehen sie des Hauses und Hausgerätes verlustig. Sobald Ubār-Šamaš zu Ningir-abi seinem Vater, oder Tarām-Ulmaš, seiner Mutter — "nicht (bist du) meine Mutter", bzw. "Nicht (bist du) mein Vater", sagt, werden sie ihn marken, in dem sie ihm ein Sklavenmal machen, und werden ihn alsdann für Geld dahingeben. Bei Šamaš, Aja, Marduk und Ḫammurapi schworen sie[46].

The basic concept involved in these Near Eastern contracts is the extension of familial relationships by legal means; the clearest type is the extension of the relation of sonship in the form as seen above of full adoption. But other familial relationships, as we shall see further on, may also be similarly extended beyond the customary blood ties. The extension of sonship characteristic of full adoption can also be limited in various ways to achieve purposes of a different nature. Since the concept of family is closely related to landed property, a wide variety of limited adoptions is possible. In each case, however, the adoption involves the extension of one's family or property, or both, to some defined extent, whether the purpose of the contract is to gain a son or daughter when childless, or whether it is to determine that one's property be given to a grandchild or a wife, to reward a servant, to ensure care in one's old age, or for other similar reasons.

If this general view is sound, then the practice referred to as "sale-adoption" at Nuzi is best understood as one form of adoption limited to one aspect of the filial relationship: namely, the rights to a specific piece of property. These sale-adoption contracts have three characteristic clauses and are similar to the Old Babylonian sale contracts[47]:

1) The *zittu* clause:
   After the statement of intention to adopt, a statement that a clearly specified portion of property — not an unlimited share of the inheritance — has been handed over to the person adopted.
2) The *qištu* clause:
   That a specific sum of money is handed over to the adopter (this clause is not absolutely necessary)[48]; and

---

[46] From the reign of Hammurapi, J. Kohler, P. Koschaker, and A. Ungnad, Hammurabi's Gesetz, III 1909—1923, 9f., text 19. The Nuzi form will be discussed below.

[47] For examples of the Old Babylonian sale contracts, cf. J. Kohler, Ham. Ges., IV 33—41, texts 921—950; V 15—20, texts 1133—1150; and VI 51—83, texts 1552—1632.

[48] Cf. E. Cassin, L'adoption, texts nos. 42 and 98, pp. 96f. and 147f., which do not have this clause. H. Lewy's objections to seeing these as outright sales may well

3) Penalty clause:
Usually, but not always, a substantial sum of money[49].

Typical of this type of contract is HSS V 64:

> Tablet of adoption of Šukriya and of Šurukaya; Akkuya son of Katiri they adopted. 6 *awihari* of land in ⟨the district of⟩ Katiri to Akkuya they have given. And Akkuya to Šurukaya and to Šukriya 20 minas of copper, (and) 2 imer of grain has given. Whoever breaks the contract shall pay one mina of gold and one mina of silver.[50]

That this type of contractual arrangement, rather than an outright sale, was used for the transferral of property rights is easily understood on the basis of the feudal structure and state control of most of the property that is referred to in the Nuzi tablets[51]. Evidence for this feudal structure is found in the often recurring *ilqū* clause which refers to the feudal duties to the king attached to the land, a practice which goes back to Old Babylonian times (cf. Code of Hammurapi, Nos. 35—41), connected with land granted by the king to his vassals, which land was inalienable[52]. Because of this feudal structure certain crown properties were in a real sense inalienable, entailed in a form, in all likelihood, after the manner which we know from the recurring clause in the feudal grants made by the kings of Ugarit: "No man shall take these fields from the hand of PN or from the hands of his sons forever"[53]. Feudatory lands are also mentioned in the Mari tablets[54], and both at Mari and at Ugarit we

---

be correct (Review of Cassin, L'Adoption à Nuzi, JAOS 59, 1939, 119). What we have is the transferral of some of the familial rights to property by means of adoption.

49 Two other clauses which often appear are the statement that, if there are claims on the property, they will be removed, and the *ilqū* clause. These will be discussed below.

50 Speiser, AASOR X, 40, no. 10. For others, see ibid., texts 9—16 (nos. 17 and 18, which Speiser classifies as "sale adoptions" are not. No. 17 *ṭuppi zitti*, is a mutual division of property and no. 18, *ṭuppi tamgurti* seems to be a contract through which two men enter into a partnership. The sale-adoption contracts are conveniently available in E. Cassin, L'Adoption, 51—254.

51 On the feudal structure at Nuzi see especially H. Lewy, The Nuzian Feudal System, Orientalia N. S. 11 (1942), 1—40, 209—250. 297—347; but also E. Cuq, Études sur le droit babylonien, 1929, 419; P. Koschaker, Rechtsurkunden, 54; Gordon, Adventures, 1957, 110; Holt, The Patriarchs, 119f., and Donner, Oriens Antiquus 8 (1969), 97f.

52 Cf. Nos. 28—31, and also P. Koschaker, Rechtsurkunden, 59f.; H. Lewy, JAOS 59 (1939), 119, and R. H. Pfeiffer, On Babylonian-Assyrian Feudalism, AJSL 39 (1922), 66f.

53 A. F. Rainey, Family Relationships in Ugarit, Orientalia 34 (1965), 13.

54 ARM VIII, no. 12, cf. Malamat, Mari and the Bible, JAOS 82 (1962), 148.

find examples of the sale-adoption contracts[55]. These feudatory lands, with which the sale-adoption contracts dealt, coexisted with other land which was held absolutely[56] and which could apparently be sold outright[57].

Although this inalienable character of the feudal lands at Nuzi — so similar to that in Babylon, Mari, and Ugarit — has often been related to the biblical prohibition against the sale of land outside the family[58], the two structures in fact are quite different. On one hand we have a feudal structure, based on land grants from the king. On the other hand we have a tribal structure of society based on family ownership of land. In the first case land is indeed inalienable and cannot be sold outright. In the second case we have protective laws which "for social and religious reasons, disapproved of and tried to control land alienation"[59] (Lev 25 23-34 Num 36 2-12). But land in Israel was ultimately salable! Not only does Abraham buy land in Gen 23, and Omri, the hill of Samaria, in I Kings 16 23, but even those passages that find the sale of land reprehensible imply that it could be and was sold: I Kings 21 and Is 5 8[60].

In Israel there existed a tradition which created a moral necessity to maintain property within the family, and the customs of the *go'el* and of the levirate were developed to promote this aim. Both of these customs, in fact, imply that property could be alienated; for they are in Israel specifically designed to prevent the property from going out of the family[61].

To return now to the question of Albright's claim that Gen 15 is paralleled by the *ṭuppi mārūti* documents of Nuzi, a number of observations can be made.

---

55 For Mari, cf. ARM VIII 11. 13 and 14. In no. 11 no payment is made (Malamat, ibid.); for Ugarit, see A. F. Rainey, Orientalia 34 (1965), 16, and J. Pirenne and M. Stracmans, Le testament à l'époque de l'Ancien Empire Égyptien, RIDA 1 (1954), 80f. (RS no. 16, 200). 56 CH no. 39.

57 For the Old Babylonian period, see above note 47; one text at Nuzi (JEN V, 552) mentions the outright sale of 100 imer of land for 1 shekel of gold. (Cf. H. Lewy, JAOS, 1939, against E. Cassin, L'adoption, 22).

58 Especially Gordon, who claims that the biblical prohibition cannot be divorced from the picture we have of Hurrian society! (Review of A. van Selms, Marriage and Family Life in Ugaritic Literature, Orientalia 24, 1955, 329; World of OT, 114). See also C. J. M. Weir, Arch and OT, 73; Malamat (JAOS, 1962, 140) sees the practice at Mari as similar to that in Israel.

59 Quotation from Weir, Arch and OT, 73.

60 See on this question further K. H. Henrey, Land Tenure in the Old Testament, PEQ 86 (1954), 7 and 11.

61 For the practice of the *Go'el*, Jer 32 6-25, esp. v. 15 is particularly instructive; for the relationship of the *ge'ulah* and the levirate to property laws and inheritance see my: Some Legal Problems in the Book of Ruth, VT 18 (1968), 79—99.

1) The social structure of Nuzi, as it relates to the sale-adoption contracts, is substantially different from that of Israel.
2) The social structure which seems to lie behind the sale-adoption is not unique to Nuzi. Further, Albright's understanding of the *ṭuppi mārūti* contracts is seriously distorted.
3) The transferral of land in the sale-adoptions is immediate[62].
4) In these contracts a specifically defined tract of land is the object of the exchange. The purchaser is not the heir to a share of the adopter's total property.
5) Albright's understanding of this type of contract, as providing collatoral for the purpose of a loan in time of need, does not fit the *ṭuppi mārūti* contracts at all. It does, however fit the *ṭuppi ditennūti* contracts, which have nothing to do with either adoption or inheritance, but are simple rentals of land for specified periods of time[63].

In no way then do these contracts give us a social structure analogous to that implied by Gen 15 1-4. If a *ṭuppi mārūti* contract had been undertaken by Abraham and Eliezer, not only would Eliezer not be Abraham's heir, but he would already be in possession of the land[64]. Finally, even if there were not these objections to Albright's interpretation, the difficulty would still remain — whatever the social background supposed — that if Eliezer were Abraham's creditor and this were the ground of Abraham's complaint, Yahweh's promise of personal descendents would hardly put Abraham's mind at rest in regards to Eliezer, for Albright's hypothetical debt would still remain.

The parallel between Gen 15 2-4 and Nuzi, suggested by Speiser and Gordon, on the other hand, rests on different grounds, since these writers refer, not to the sale-adoption contracts, but to other adoption contracts. While the sale adoption seems explainable on the basis of the feudal structure at Nuzi, those adoptions which have as their basis the extension of familial relationships do not necessarily imply this type of social structure. Those that involve inheritance — and as we shall see not all do — imply a specific order of inheritance within the family, with the eldest son usually given a greater share. A person adopted as son can also be given the normal inheritance share of a son. However, since these adoptions are basically contractual arrangements, a considerable degree of freedom

---

62 Koschaker's analysis here is particularly clear (Rechtsurkunden 55f.): "(Die Eviktionsklausel) ist bei einer adoptio in hereditatem undenkbar", and "Der Adoptierte (sofort bekam) Besitz und Eigentum des Grundstücks."

63 So, for example, Pfeiffer and Speiser, AASOR XVI, nos. 65 and 66, 113—115.

64 What land does Abraham own?

was exercised in the specification and at times limitation of the adopted person's portion of the inheritance.

The vast majority of the *ṭuppi mārūti* contracts at Nuzi are contracts which are limited to the extension of property rights — i. e., the "sale-adoptions". A few, however, as we have already mentioned, resemble full adoptions[65], and it is in these contracts that most scholars, following primarily Speiser and Gordon, find the social structure in which Gen 15 2-4 is to be understood[66].

The claimed Nuzi parallel to this passage is often seen to be among the clearest examples of how archaeological finds have given clarity and understanding to an otherwise difficult text[67]. The Nuzi tablets are particularly important here, since, according to these scholars, the custom which this passage presupposes cannot be explained on the basis of Mosaic law[68].

The basic understanding of the parallel has been most fully developed by C. Gordon[69]. According to this thesis, both at Nuzi and in the patriarchal traditions, it was important, for religious, social, and practical reasons, for a man to have an heir; the continuity of a man's estate within his family was essential. According to Nuzi custom, a man could in the case of childlessness adopt a free-born child or even a slave, who would then take care of him during his

65 So H. Donner, Oriens Antiquus 8 (1969), 97f.

66 Presupposing, of course, a translation of the biblical text similar to Gordon's or Speiser's, in that Eliezer, as a "servant of Abraham's house" is adopted as heir.

67 Holt, The Patriarchs, 119, and Speiser, Genesis, 112: "Our Dammesek Eliezer — whoever he may have been and whatever the first word might mean — was juridically in the position of an *ewuru*. Here, then, is another instance of Hurrian customs which the patriarchs followed, but which the tradition and its later expounders were bound to find perplexing."

68 R. de Vaux, Les patriarches hébreux et les découvertes modernes, RB 56 (1949), 25f.; M. H. Prévost, Remarques sur l'adoption dans la Bible, RIDA 14 (1967), 68f.

69 Biblical Customs and the Nuzi Tablets, BA 3 (1940), 2; Adventures, 1957, 107—111 and 118; The World of the OT, 114 and 117f.; perhaps dependent on Albright, The Archaeology of Palestine and the Bible, 138 and 209 n. 25; and followed without substantial difference by R. T. O'Callaghan, Historical Parallels to Patriarchal Social Customs, CBQ (1944), 402; H. H. Rowley, Recent Discoveries and the Patriarchal Age, BJRL 32 (1949/50), 73f.; R. de Vaux, RB 56 (1949), 25., Les Institutions de L'Ancien Testament I—II, 1958, 85f.; Schofield, Some Archaeological Sites and the Old Testament: Nuzu, ET 66 (1955), 318; J. Bright, History of Israel, 1959, 71; G. von Rad, das erste Buch Mose, 155; J. Holt, The Patriarchs, 119—121; E. A. Speiser, Genesis, 110—114; C. J. M. Weir, Arch and OT Study, 73f., and M. Prévost, RIDA (1967), 168—171; It has not been accepted (apparently for reasons of translation) by O. Eissfeldt, OLZ 49 (1954), 108, and H. Donner, Oriens Antiquus 8 (1969), 109, followed by M. Weippert, Bb 52 (1971), 420f.

old age and take care of the burial and mourning rites when he was dead[70]. In return for this the adopted would inherit the man's property.

The immediate objection to be raised to this parallel is that if the obligations of such a contract were fulfilled by Eliezer, it seems he would of necessity be Abraham's heir. Could his rights be set aside as implied by Gen 15 4? Rowley and de Vaux explicitly ask this question, and answer it: "Here again we find illustration in the Nuzu texts, where it is provided that if the adopter should subsequently beget a son, the adopted son must yield to him the place of chief heir"[71]. "D'autres contrats font l'hypothèse d'un enfant engendré par l'adoptant après l'adoption d'un étranger: dans ce cas, le fils adoptif perd le droit à l'héritage principal, et cette règle juridique donne tout son sens à la réponse que Dieu fait à Abraham: non, mais l'héritier sera le fils issu de tes entrailles"[72].

So it is claimed that Eliezer was adopted by Abraham, under the condition that he would serve him (thus his continued condition of household servant) and carry out the necessary funeral rites. In turn he was Abraham's heir. However, as a result of Yahweh's promise to Abraham (Gen 15 4), Isaac is born, and Eliezer's rights are superseded.

This interpretation is based on the Nuzi *ṭuppi Mārūti* texts HSS V, 7, 60 and 67[73] and JEN 59[74], where we find adoptions of free born persons. HSS IX 22 is also referred to by Gordon[75] which (according

---

[70] Gordon speaks of these contracts as a kind of social security or annuity provision. (Adventures, 1957, 107). Bright goes so far as to speak of "slave adoption as practiced at Nuzi. Childless couples would adopt a son who would serve them as long as they lived and inherit on their death." (History 71).

[71] Rowley, BJRL (1949/50), 74.

[72] De Vaux, RB 56 (1949), 26; So also Gordon, The World of the Old Testament, 117f.: "if a real son should be born, the real son would be the heir. (Gen 15 4)." So Speiser (Genesis 112) speaks of Eliezer as an *ewuru* or indirect heir "whom the law recognized when normal inheritors were lacking." J. Holt, alone, (The Patriarchs 121) sees a discrepancy here: "We cannot say what the terms of the servant's adoption were, since we are not told any more than that he had been made an heir. If the adoption was according to the standard pattern, however, we might wonder what the ultimate fortune of the man was.... If still alive at the time of Abraham's death, he should have received his share ...."

[73] For translations: Chiera and Speiser, AASOR X, nos. 1. 2 and 4, p. 30—35 and also Cassin, L'adoption, 285—289. 292f.

[74] JAOS 47 (1927), 40.

[75] BA 3 (1940), 2, and O'Callahan CBQ 6 (1944), 402; translation and transliteration: Cassin, L'adoption, 280—282; some discrepancies of interpretation seem to be caused by the fact that most of our commentators are, apparently, not aware of this text!

to Gordon) is an adoption of a slave for the same purpose — an observation which is thought to strengthen the parallel between Nuzi and Genesis. This text we will discuss in some detail later.

In order to judge with clarity the accuracy of this apparently obvious parallel it is useful to compare the form of these Nuzi contracts with the ordinary Near Eastern full adoption contracts that have been discussed above[76].

There are five relatively standard clauses in these Nuzi contracts:

I. Statement of the adoption.
II. Right to Property clause.
III. Protective clause in case sons are born.
IV. Service clause.
V. Mutual penalty clause in case contract is broken.

Clause I is comparable to the handing over of the patria potestas in the normal Near Eastern full adoption (cf. p. 208 above). HSS V 7, 57 and 67 all mention explicitly that the natural father has given his son for adoption, and, in this respect are identical to the normal full adoption. In HSS V 59 Shennima adopts his brother Arzizza. HSS V 60. 65 and Gadd 9, are also ambiguous in this clause stating only that PN adopts PN_2. It is impossible to tell whether the person adopted is a child. In the other three tablets, however, it is clear that we are dealing with a contract between two independent adults. In JEN 59 Hanadu adopts his "companion" *(awêl TAB-šu-ma ana mārūti ītepuš)* Ḫutiya (ll. 3f.) and the document is given directly to the adopted son: ll. 24ff.: *(ṭuppu ša šīmtiya ana Ḫutiama attadin)*. In Gadd 51 Wullu is the adopted son and he is given the daughter of his adopted father as his wife *(ù mārtišu SALnuhuia ana aššatūti ana mWullu iddin)*. In HSS V 66 the extension of the clause is even further broadened to include a woman, the wife of Šilwatešup son of the king, who is *ana mārūti ītepuš* "adopted into sonship".

Similar extensions of the adoption contracts are also found outside of Nuzi, although, particularly in Babylonian law, small children are usually the objects of adoption. Several contracts mention simply that a certain person is adopted without any clear sign that it is a child. As in the Nuzi texts, it appears that the contract is made between the adopter and the adopted. Such clauses are found in contracts from the Old Babylonian period from Tell Sifr and Mari

[76] It will also be useful to include in our discussion here the related contracts HSS V, 57 (Ch. Sp., AASOR X, no. 6, p. 37f.) HSS V, 66 (ibid., no. 5, p. 36f.); Gadd 9 (RA 23, 1926, 94f.), and Gadd 51 (ibid. 126f.); the flexibility of these contractual arrangements will also become clearer if we include in our discussion HSS V 59 (AASOR X, no. 3, p. 33f.) and HSS V 65 (ibid. p. 38) which have been written for more limited purposes.

and also from Ugarit[77]. One Old Assyrian text from Kültepe is perhaps equally ambiguous, except that it adds the clause: "Subbianika wird eint[reten] und sie werden das Haus gemein[sam] bewohnen", possibly suggesting that the adopted son Subbianika is an adult[78]. Several Old Babylonian contracts extend the full adoption involving inheritance to women[79]. One text from Nippur[80] mentions that the adopted son immediately takes over his adopted father's property, clearly implying that we are dealing here with an adult. Another Old Babylonian text deals with the adoption of a man "mit seiner Einwilligung", explicitly mentioning the independent responsibility of the one adopted[81]. So also a text from the Middle Assyrian period[82]. A text from Alalakh is of this same type, except for the unusual first clause: "Before Niqmepa the King: Ilimilimma has made Tulpuri his father". It is clear here that not only is Ilimilimma an independent person, but he is apparently of greater consequence than the man who adopts him[83].

The Nuzi tablets seem to share with other cuneiform contracts this characteristic, that the full adoption contracts can deal with both free-born children and adults[84]. The second clause, dealing with the handing over or declaring the adopted son's right to the property, is found in nearly all of the Nuzi tablets, and, though there are variants, the following is typical: *minummê eqlētūia, ḫitātuia, manaḫātuia [kal]ummanuia ištēn mimia [ana] Zigi addin.* "A[ll] my lands, my [build]ings, [an]d my earnings, my domestics, one (part) of all my property, to Zigi I have given"[85]. In the three cases which do not

[77] For text from Tell Sifr, J. Kohler, Ham Ges III, text 20, p. 10 — also see undated texts: ibid. no. 22, p. 10 and no. 23, p. 11; For Mari text, see J. J. Finkelstein, Additional Mesopotamian Legal Documents, ANETS 545; Ugaritic text RS 15. 92; see Donner, Oriens Antiquus 8 (1969), 101.

[78] G. Eisser and J. Lewy, Die altassyrischen Rechtsurkunden vom Kültepe, MVÄG 33/35, I—II 1930/1935, text 7, p. 8.

[79] So, for example, M. Schorr, Urkunden des altbabylonischen Zivil und Prozeßrechts, VAB V, 1, 1913, text no. 14, p. 29f., and I. Mendelsohn, The Family in the Ancient Near East, BA 11 (1948), 38 (Mendelsohn is clearly wrong in seeing this as merely a financial arrangement.)

[80] Dated to eighth year of Šamšuiluna; cf. Schorr, Zivil und Prozeßrecht, text 21, p. 40f.

[81] J. Kohler, Ham. Ges. VI, text 1425, p. 3f.

[82] M. David, Adoption, 101.

[83] It is clear from the rest of the text that the contract here is mutual, but apparently instigated by Ilimilimma (note the one-sided penalty clause). D. J. Wiseman, The Alalakh Tablets, Occasional Publication of the British Institute of Archaeology at Ankara, no. 2, 1953, 39, text 16.

[84] The question of the adoption of a slave will be taken up later, particularly with reference to HSS IX 22.

[85] HSS V 60 ll. 5ff.; AASOR X, 30.

include this clause, it seems implied[86]. HSS V 7 is particularly interesting and brings out very clearly the truly adoptive character of these contracts: *māria šelluni ana mārūti ana Akapšenni mār Zigi nadnu ina eqlētia ù ina bītātia lā šummuḫ lā izzuzzū.* "My son Shelluni into sonship to Akapshenni son of Zigi has been given; of my lands and of my buildings he shall have no part or share"[87]. This resembles the neobabylonian tablet which records the disinheritance of a first-born son on the grounds that he has been adopted by another[88]. Gadd 51 and HSS V 7 also imply that the right of inheritance has been given since they both contain a protective clause (III) which guarantees them their inheritance.

In the frequency which clause II occurs in the texts, the records of Nuzi are unusual, for it is rare in other cuneiform texts. However, this does not show that the Nuzi contracts are written for different purposes, for we not only find some examples of this clause in other texts[89], but the full adoption contracts from our cuneiform sources

---

[86] HSS V 67, ll. 12ff., states that if Paltešup does not bear the feudal duties, he has to give up the lands. This implies, of course, that the adoption has given him the right to the lands with this condition. Similarly Gadd 51, ll. 22ff., states that in the case that Wullu marries again he must vacate the lands.

[87] AASOR X 34f.

[88] British Museum 84. 2—11. J. Kohler and F. E. Peiser, Aus dem babylonischen Rechtsleben, Bde 1—4, 1890—1898, II, 16f. These texts stress the reality of the adoption and its close connection with inheritance; it is doubtful, however, that such disinheritance is the effect of every such adoption as Kohler and Peiser suggest (ibid. 15).

[89] So, for example: "Dem Nachlaß der Sallurtum, soviel da ist, wird Šāt-Ninurta erben." (Old Babylonian: J. Kohler, Ham Ges. IV, text 780, p. 2f.); another formulation is found in the Old Babylonian contract translated by Mendelsohn: "Immertum . . . Lamassum, daughter of Inib-šarri, has adopted as her child (and) appointed her as heiress" (I. Mendelsohn, BA 11, 1948, 38) Alalakh 16 has the formulation: "When Tulpuri dies whatever is his inheritance, all he possesses and the *tilu* of Tulpuri shall belong to Ilimilimma" (Wiseman, Alalakh Tablets, 39). As at Nuzi, some texts only indirectly imply this clause. So, a text from Nippur in the reign of Šamšuiluna mentions that the adopted immediately enters upon his inheritance (Schorr, Zivil und Prozeßrechts, text 21, p. 40f.); see also the similar contract in J. Kohler, Ham Ges VI, p. 3f., text 1425. The same type of contract is found from Sippar from the reign of Apil-Sîn (Schorr, 29f., text 14) but this text also has clause II: "Ḫunābātiya, die Tochter des Ellil-malik, ist die Erbin ihrer Hinterlassenschaft." It seems to me that this clause is also implied in the one Mari adoption contract that we possess, in the phrase: "He shall rejoice in their joys and commiserate in their miseries." (Finkelstein, ANETS, 545), a formula that occurs very often in the Old Babylonian adoption texts. In the adoption contract from Ugarit (RS 15. 92) clause II is implied, in my opinion, by the statement that the wife of the adopter, upon the death of her husband, need

are almost universal in possessing clause III (see above, p. 215) which, as we have just mentioned in reference to Gadd 51 and HSS V 7, presupposes that the right to inheritance exists. In other words, the existence of clause III makes clause II of our contracts superfluous.

Clause III, the protective clause which guarantees the adopted son's right to the inheritance, is widely attested outside of Nuzi. It is on the basis of this clause more than any other that the nature of our contract is made clear[90]. Moreover, it seems that this clause is used exclusively in full adoption contracts, though it is not a sine qua non for a full adoption.

This clause is particularly important in reference to the claimed parallels with Gen 15 2-4, whereby this clause is understood as a limitation upon clause II, in the case that a natural son is born subsequent to the adoption. Indeed, the interpretation is often so formulated[91] to give the impression that clause III gives the conditions in which the effects of clause II might be cancelled. This is, of course, necessary if the parallel with Gen 15 2-4 is to succeed completely, for it is Isaac that is the eventual heir of Abraham.

In its most typical form (judging on the basis of the Near Eastern texts in general), the clause occurs in only four of the texts which we are here considering (HSS V 7. 60. 67 and Gadd 51). However, the purpose of the clause is on one hand to allow for the possibility of sons born subsequently, who might have a claim on the adopter's inheritance, and on the other to protect[92] the right of the one adopted to his share in the inheritance. The variety of the ways which these needs are met brings out clearly that in this type of contract we are not dealing with a custom or law which is reflected in our texts; rather we are dealing with negotiable aspects of a contract. The usual purpose of an adoption contract is to supply a childless man with a son and heir, and this purpose is reflected in the typical forms of clause III. However, the same type of agreement might be undertaken where this is not the primary purpose, or where the adopter is not childless. In such cases clause III is not needed.

The absence of this clause in JEN 59 is puzzling as there is no apparent reason why it should be omitted. It deals with the adoption of a friend, and, moreover, there seems to be no other heir at the

---

not leave the house. By implication, the house would then belong to the adopted son. For text, cf. H. Donner, Oriens Antiquus 8 (1969), 101.

90 Cf. M. David, Adoption, 1f.; E. Szlechter, Des droits successoraux dérivés de l'adoption en droit babylonien, RIDA 14 (1967), 92 and 106.

91 See above, p. 213 and n. 67 and 68.

92 The protective character of clause III is paralleled by no. 191 of the Hammurapi Code.

time of the contract[93]. Are we to assume that he is an old man and not married, or that his wife is beyond childbearing? that, nevertheless, he needs a son in his old age, and, that it is for this reason, as well as that he wants to leave his goods to his friend, that the adoption agreement is drawn up? The unusual phrase: *umma Ḫanaduma ṭuppu ša šimtiya ana Ḫutiyama attadin:* "Ḫanadu said: "The document which is my will I have given to Ḫutiya."[94], may well point to such an interpretation.

The reason for the absence of the Protective Clause in our other texts is clearer. A brief survey of these texts will help to draw out the significance of this clause's function.

In HSS V 57, a specific plot of land (*2 imēr eqlāti ina Zamite*: "Two imers of land in Zamite") is given to the adopted son. This is unusual in that the exact inheritance is specified. This is made understandable by the following lines which mention sons of the adopter. Thus the specification is itself all that is necessary to fulfill the purpose of clause III. Similarly in HSS V 65 the possibility that the adopted son might be the exclusive heir does not exist, for other heirs are mentioned in the contract. The adopted son is made "joint heir"[95]. Akuya and his daughter shall receive equal portions. Furthermore, this contract is made in connection with the adoption of yet another man who will be the second son *(šanâ māra)*.

In Tablet HSS V 66, a woman is the adopted "son" and the property is given to her with the provision that, if a third party, *Šušiya*, performs the duties belonging to a son[96] for the woman who is adopted, he will inherit the property after her. Furthermore, a number of valuable goods are given outright to a woman or girl by the name of Ummiya. That the adopter Akapurḫi is an *arad* Šilwitešup[97] and that the woman adopted is Našmunnaya the wife of Šilwitešup suggests the possibility that both Ummiya and Šušiya are actually the children of Akapurḫi whom he has given into the care of Našmunnaya. Thus the tablet might be a contract by which an old or sick man assures the care of his children (paid for by the usufruct of his property) and the ultimate inheritance of his property

---

93 Cf. ll. 6ff., "All of the fields and buildings, my inherited portion, which my father Kuššiya gave (to me), these I myself have now given to Ḫutiya".

94 JAOS 47 (1927), 40.

95 However, the final clause: "(As for) Tulpunnaya, him as second son he shall adopt with regard to land and building(s)." (emphasis added) implies that in this respect Akuya seems to be guaranteed the right to the primary inheritance. The possibility of natural sons does not seem to be foreseen.

96 Cf. the discussion of clause IV below.

97 On the meaning of *arad*, see below, p. 226—228.

by his son[98]. If this interpretation is correct, there is no need of clause III since the adopted "son" is the means by which the inheritance passes to the physical son. Gadd 9 also deals with a woman, but here in the position of adopter. Since inheritance by women in cuneiform contracts seems to extend the possibility of inheritance beyond the normal line of inheritance[99], it might well be that the purpose of this adoption contract is not so much to see the property continued within the family by way of sons (thus the normal threat that real sons offer to the adopted son), but rather to supply the wife (not necessarily her husband!) with a son who will perform for her the duties of a son. HSS V 59 also deals with special circumstances. It is a contract in which a man adopts his brother. However, the property mentioned in the contract may well not be all the adopter Šennima owns; it is specified as all that he, an adopted son, had received from Šurihil (text given in HSS V 67); this would then be the "portion" of the inheritance which is guaranteed to the adopted Arzizza.

In HSS V 7, 60 and 67, clause III states that if a son is born subsequent to the adoption, he will receive a double portion of the inheritance and the adopted son will be the second heir. Gadd 51 shows the flexibility of this clause as it is here specified that the adopted son will share equally with the natural heir. However, apparently Wullu's position in the family is still secondary since the gods of the adopter would go to the natural heir[100]. HSS V 67 has the added protective clause (ll. 30ff.) that a second adopted son shall not be brought into the family.

In all our cases it is clear that the adopted sons do share in the inheritance even in the case that a natural heir is born. The greater variety of examples of this clause in the adoption contracts of our comparative materials brings this out even more clearly, and moreover shows that the contractual arrangement need not always give the advantage to the natural heir. Very similar to the Nuzi clauses is the Middle Assyrian contract mentioned above

---

98 This text calls to mind the ubiquitous cuneiform (including Nuzi) clauses which specify that the inheritance first go to the wife, and then to those children who treat her properly. Thus, in the above text, if Šušiya does not fulfill his obligations, Našmunnaya can give the property "to whomever she pleases". In Egyptian contracts the wife at times is appointed as heir, and then has the freedom to leave the property to the child who treats her best: P. W. Pestman, Marriage and Matrimonial Property in Ancient Egypt, Papyrologica Lugdonu-Batava, vol. IX, 1961, 124.

99 Cf. the recurring phenomenon that women (albeit, mostly priestesses) leave their property to other women. Cf. Kohler, Ham. Ges., and Schorr, Urkunden, passim.

100 See below H.

where the natural heir is to receive a double share while the adopted Gimillu is to receive a share equal to that of the younger sons[101]. In two Old Babylonian tablets the adopter already has a son and the adopted takes the position of a second son[102]. In another, two brothers are adopted and the eldest gets the special share with the remainder divided "für alle Zeit"[103]. In another text the adopter has 5 other heirs. The adoptive son is "gleich einem Erben. Für alle Zeit"[104]. Three other Old Babylonian texts state that in the case that the adopter should have natural children, the adopted son remains an heir. Nothing is said of the preferential portion[105]. Several texts, however, from the Old Babylonian period, in the South as well as at Mari, and one text from the neo-Assyrian period (656 B. C.), state that in the case that the adopter has children subsequent to the adoption, the adopted son will remain as the primary heir[106]!

Clearly, what we are dealing with in this clause is n o t a provision declaring that the inheritance rights of the adopted son will be set aside in the advent of a natural son. In no single case is this said. Rather, it is a prior contractual agreement specifying the rights of the adopted in the case that he must share it with others. What is negotiated is the position of first-born and not the right to inheritance.

Clause IV, which specifies the obligations of the adopted son, is frequently found in the Nuzi contracts, but only rarely in other Near Eastern contracts. It is extremely important for our discussion since it is the clause that is most seriously misinterpreted. It directly impinges on the parallel to Genesis, since it is largely on the basis of this clause, that most who accept the parallel with Gen 15 2-4, see the Nuzi adoption contract as a contract for service.

---

101 M. David, Adoption, 101.

102 J. Kohler, Ham. Ges. IV, text 783 (time of Šamšuiluma) p. 3f., and Schorr, Zivil- und Prozeßrecht, text 10, p. 23f.

103 J. Kohler, ibid. text 782, p. 3.

104 Ibid. III, text 20, p. 10.

105 Ibid. III, text 22, p. 10; IV, text 779, p. 2; and M. Schorr, Altbabylonische Rechtsurkunden aus der Zeit der ersten babylonischen Dynastie, IIIte Heft. SKAWW 165, 2, 1910, text: VAT 694, p. 22f.

106 Kohler, Ham. Ges. III, text 17, p. 9, dated to the 14th year of Hammurapi; Schorr, Zivil- und Prozeßurk., texts 8 and 9, p. 21—23, Mendelsohn, Slavery in the ancient Near East, 1949, 21f. — a text from Sippar; In the Mari text (Finkelstein, ANETS, 545) it is stated: "regardless of how many sons they shall have acquired — Yehetti-el is primary heir, and he shall take a double share of the estate of Hillalum, his father. His younger brothers shall divide in equal shares." The Assyrian text (AO 2221) can be found in J. Kohler and A. Ungnad, Assyrische Rechtsurkunden, 1913, 36, text 41: "Selbst wenn 7 Erben des Sinḳi-Ištar und der Ra'imtu noch zur Welt kommen sollten, so ist Aššur-ṣabātsu-iḳbi (doch) sein ältester Erbsohn." See also 451.

In the Nuzi texts we are discussing, there appear to be two quite distinct types of this clause[107]. One type (A), found in HSS V 7, 57, and 67 simply states, for example: "As long as Šurihil is alive, Šennima shall serve him"[108]. All these texts deal with people who are given into adoption by their parents; i. e., they deal with children. Text HSS V 60, a tablet in which the adopted son is himself the contrahent, also has this clause, but it is followed by: "with garments he shall provide him"; that is, the service to be provided is not only physical service but also material remuneration. This clause is made clearer with the examination of the three texts of type B: Gadd 9 and 51 and JEN 59. All these tablets apparently deal with adopted sons who are adults. JEN 59 is the most complete: "As long as Ḫanadu lives Ḫutiya shall serve him, and every year Ḫutiya shall deliver to Ḫanadu one garment as his clothing, five imers of barley and two imers of wheat as his sustenance. When Ḫanadu dies Ḫutiya shall weep for him and bury him". Gadd 51 gives the clause with brevity: "Wullu will give him food and clothing, and when Našwa is dead, Wullu will give him burial"[109]. The clause in Gadd 9 is particularly useful as it gives us a hint as to the proper interpretation of this clause (both types A and B): "So long as Kašummenni is alive, Pinteššenni shall revere (her) as his mother. When Kašummenni is dead he shall mourn her . . . and bury (her) . . .".

What we are dealing with in clause IV are the obligations which belong to the adopted as a son. Moreover, the difference between types A and B seem best explained by the observation that type A deals with adopted sons who are apparently minors — who at least do not yet share the inheritance with the father, while type B deals with independent persons, who have already entered into the inheritance which they receive from their adopted father, and as a result of this have the filial obligation to support their father, which includes also

---

[107] HSS V 59 and HSS V 65 are missing this clause. However, HSS V 59 deals with the adoption of a brother *ana mārūti*, whose purpose in an adoption contract would be more concerned with the inheritance than with the familial relationship. HSS V 65 also lacks clauses III and V, and seems to be largely designed for testamentary purposes.

HSS V 66 has this clause, but it has been tailored to the specifications of this contract, which is to give the inheritance ultimately to Šušiya; thus Šušiya is placed in a position of son to the woman, Našmunnaya, who has been adopted.

[108] HSS V 67.

[109] The vagueness in this last contract — in contrast to JEN 59 — must make one doubt that we are dealing with anything like an annuity, as Gordon (see above, n. 66) suggests. The detailed character, on the other hand, of JEN 59 precludes the suggestion of Bright's (see above ibid.) that we are dealing with some sort of slave-adoption contract.

the responsibilities of burial and mourning. What we have here specified are the minimum required duties that the adopted will have as a son[110].

This interpretation is born out by records outside of Nuzi, that the obligation of service for the lifetime of the father, and on his death the obligation to bury and mourn him, as well as the obligation to support the father materially once the inheritance portion is received, are the normal obligations of a son. Because of this, Nuzi clause IV has nothing to do with servitude, nor is it in any way "mercenary".

Although the explicit connection between the obligation to care for the burial of one's parents and inheritance appears to be peculiar to the Nuzi adoption contracts among cuneiform literature, the Egyptian records relate this obligation with the right to inheritance quite emphatically[111].

In Egypt it is specifically the obligation of the eldest son to care for his parents and to arrange for a fitting burial[112], though it is also shared by the other children, perhaps in proportion to their share in the inheritance[113]. The need of a son for the care of one's burial was of social as well as financial significance.

Although the cuneiform sources generally do not lay emphasis on the burial obligation of the son, both types of clause IV nevertheless do occur. Type A is found, for instance, at Alalakh in the following formulation: "So long as he (Tulpuri, the adopter) lives, he (Ilimilimma, the adopted) shall be responsible for him"[114]. The first part of the

---

[110] Gadd 51, ll. 22ff. imply that he already has possession of his adopted father's property. This seems also to be the case in JEN 59. Gadd 9 is too badly damaged.

[111] "'Let the possessions be given to him who buries', says the law of pharaoh . . ."; J. J. Janssen and P. W. Pestman, Burial and Inheritance in the Community of the Necropolis Workmen at Thebes, JESHO 11 (1968), 140 and 168, which refers to the man Minurpu who died without traceable relatives. "A woman buries him at the instance of her husband who says, 'bury him and act as an heir towards him'". In Egypt the right of inheritance is at times decided on the basis of who has buried the deceased (ibid. 140). In the papyrus Bulaq 10, 10 (20th Dyn.) it is stated "Die Sachen werden wegen des Begräbnisses gegeben . . ." (E. Seidl, Vom Erbrecht der alten Ägypter, ZDMG 107, 1957, 273) The connection between burial and inheritance is perhaps strongest reflected in a number of deeds from Demotic papyri in which a man sells his whole property to a woman (perhaps his wife) because she has been the person who has cared for him in life and who will bury him. Cf. W. Spiegelberg, Ägyptische Verpfründungsverträge, SHAW 6, 1923, 3—12; and Pestman, Marriage, 122f.

[112] R. Tanner, Untersuchungen zur ehe- und erbrechtlichen Stellung der Frau im pharaonischen Ägypten, Klio, BAG 49 (1967), 29.

[113] M. El-Amir, The Unpublished Demotic Papyri in the Turin Museum, AcOr 25 (1960), 206.

[114] Wiseman, Alalakh Tablets, text 16, p. 39.

penalty clause of this same contract emphasizes the filial character of this obligation: "If Ilimilimma shall continually be responsible for his father, but then insults his father and frees (himself), then he is deprived (?) from whatever is his"[115]. The filial character of type A is also perhaps to be discovered in the context in which it is placed in the Middle Assyrian text VAT 8947: "Azukiya ist sein Vater und ... seine Mutter. Solange sie leben, wird er sie ehren und sie versorgen"[116].

The cuneiform materials also show that type B is not to be considered less personal, and that the explicitness of the obligations is not evidence of a disguised, purely commercial transaction, but is a result of the property having already been given to the adopted son[117].

Clause IV is found in the cuneiform adoption contracts either as an independent clause[118] or is implied in the penalty clause[119]. The penalty clauses are especially instructive as they clearly state the cost of not fulfilling these obligations: "Derjenige Erbsohn der den Unterhalt nicht zahlt, geht seiner Erbsohnschaft verlustig"[120]. Other Old Babylonian contracts show that these same obligations and these same penalties, for failure to fulfill the obligations, also applied to physical sons. So, one text, which is concerned with the father's division of his property between his two sons, reads: "W. und N. werden ihrem Vater, A., monatlich 60 ka Gerste und 1/3 ka Öl und Kleider abliefern. Wer Verpflegung, Öl, und Kleidung (als) Verpflegung ihm nicht leisten wird, dessen Erbeinstellung wird er (der Vater) nicht machen, etc."[121]. In one Old Babylonian text we find the actual

115 Ibid.

116 M. David, Adoption, 101.

117 Cf. the remarks of J. Klima, Untersuchungen zum Altbabylonischen Erbrecht, MArOr 8 (1940), 76f.

118 So the Old Babylonian text 1425: J. Kohler, Ham. Ges. VI, 3f.: "Jährlich wird Sin-išmeanni $1^1/_5$ (?) Kur Gerste, 6 minen Wolle, 6 ka Öl dem Aḫum, seinem Vater, und der Muḫadditum, seiner Mutter geben." (N. B.: That the payment is given not simply to the father, but also to the mother, emphasizes its character as a filial obligation); see also Schorr, Zivil- und Prozeßrechts, 37, text 19 (from the reign of Hammurapi) and text 14, p. 29f. (from reign of Apil-Sin).

119 E. g., "Derjenige Erbsohn der den Unterhalt nicht zahlt, geht seiner Erbsohnschaft verlustig." Schorr ibid. text 21 (from reign of Šamšu-iluna), p. 40f., also: Kohler, Ham. Ges. III, 8f., text 14. Schorr, text 21, is particularly important, as it is a typical example which makes clear the normal situations where the adopted son takes over the land immediately, and shows that this is the basis for the annual payments.

120 Schorr 21, Kohler Ham. Ges. III, text 15, has: "Desgleichen darf sie Sîn-šadûni, gibt er ihr Kleidung, Salböl und Pflege nicht, enterben."

121 Klima, Erbrecht, 74: Old Babylonian text from Nippur; cf. also J. Kohler, Ham. Ges. III, 62, text 1047.

disinheritance of a son for failure to provide support and make his annual payments to his father[122].

Clause V deals with the penalties to be applied if one or other party of the contract does not live up to the agreement. In most of the cuneiform contracts the penalties are directly proportionate to the contract being broken. If the adopting father rejects the adopted son, the penalty is the loss of his property; i. e., the inheritance which the adopted would normally receive. If the son, on the other hand, did not live up to his obligations and rejects the adopted father, he can be sold into slavery: "they shall have him shaved, and shall sell him for money"[123]. In some cases the penalty to the son is milder, and involves only disinheritance[124]. In rare instances, the penalties involve money only, usually a significant sum[125]. In Nuzi, the penalty clause is always in money, usually given as one mina of silver and one mina of gold[126].

The most significant characteristic of the penalty clauses of these contracts is that they are mutual, showing that both parties have stipulated in the contract certain minimal requirements which the other must undertake, indirectly reflecting the free and responsible character of the adopted even after the contract is entered into.

On the basis of our analysis of the Nuzi contracts and comparable contracts from the Near East, the following conclusions can be made. Most important of all, there is no question but that the Nuzi contracts are quite typical of Near Eastern, especially cuneiform, adoptions of free-born children and are to be understood within the context of Near Eastern legal custom. In this Near Eastern context, the parallel to Gen 15 is unacceptable, first of all because, according to the suggested translation, Eliezer is Abraham's household servant. Clauses I and V of the Nuzi contracts, however, are incompatible with this status. Moreover, clauses I and IV show that the adopted person has the status of a son, similar to that of a physical son. Secondly, Gen 15 4 implies that Abraham's servant would not be

---

122 J. Kohler ibid. text 1056, p. 65f.

123 From text from Mari ARM VIII, 1, ANETS, 545; similarly, the Old Babylonian text from the time of Hammurapi: Kohler, Ham. Ges. III, text 19, p. 9f. These examples are typical. See Mendelsohn, BA 11 (1948), 38 and R. Haase, Einführung in das Studium Keilschriftlicher Rechtsquellen, 1965, 76—78.

124 Wiseman, Alalakh Tablets, text 16, p. 39. HC no. 168f. See also No. 191 which regulates the limitations of the adoptive parent.

125 E. Szlechter, RIDA 14 (1967), 99—101, and H. Donner, Oriens Antiquus 8 (1969), 101.

126 JEN 59 has a penalty clause of 2 minas of silver and 2 minas of gold, and HSS V 57 has a penalty clause of 6 oxen. HSS V 66 has no penalty clause. This may, however, be explained by the special character of this contract.

his heir, if Abraham were to have children. Clauses II and III (as well as V) of the Nuzi tablets, on the other hand, guarantee the right to an inheritance portion by the adopted.

The critical difference between Gen 15 and these Nuzi contracts is that Abraham's "heir" is a servant, a slave of Abraham's household, a dependent of Abraham, and as such could not enter into a mutually binding contract with Abraham. Similarly, that Eliezer's "right" to the inheritance could be as easily set aside as is implied in Gen 15 4 shows that he was not the free and responsible person required by this type of contractual arrangement. Gen 15 2-4 specifically refers to a servant, and the vulnerability of his inheritance requires that we are dealing with either a slave or a similarly dependent person. These Nuzi texts, on the other hand, do not deal with the adoption of servants[127].

It is true that Gordon refers to HSS IX, 22 as the adoption of a slave[128], but both the form and text of the contract show that we are dealing not with a servant but an independent, fully responsible person. The text reads:

> Tablette d'adoption par laquelle Tupkiya, fils de Šurkitilla, a adopté comme fils Pai-Tešup, *arad ša šilwa-tešup mār šarri*. Ainsi (a parlé) Tupkiya: "J'ai adopté comme fils Pai-tešup et mes champs et mes maisons et tout ce qui forme ma richesse je remets comme part (d'héritage) à Pai-Tešup. Tant que Tupkiya vivra Pai-Tešup [logement et nourriture] lui donnera (et) quand (Tipkiya) mourra Pai-tešup le pleurera et l'enterrera. Un autre fils en plus de Pai-Tešup, il n'adoptera pas. (Pai-Tešup) les champs et les maisons ne vendra pas. Les charges de Tupkiya, Tupkiya supportera, Pai-Tešup ne supportera pas". Ainsi (a parlé) Tupkiya: "Tout l'argent de mes filles, quand elles siégeront à la porte, Pai-Tešup fera payer et recevra". Quiconque parmi eux transgressera (l'accord), paiera 1 mine d'argent (et) 1 mine d'or[129].

That we are not dealing with the adoption of a slave, but of a free and independent adult, is clear in several points of the contract.

(1) The contract is made between Tupkiya and Pai-Tešup. If Pai-Tešup were Šilwatešup's slave, Šilwatešup would take part and give Pai-Tešup into adoption[130]!
(2) Clause V, containing the mutual penalty clause, also stresses the independence and responsibility of Pai-Tešup.
(3) The conjunction of clauses II and IV may imply that Pai-Tešup takes over title to the property immediately[131], in return for which

127 For the adoption of slaves outside of Nuzi see below.

128 C. H. Gordon, Biblical Customs and the Nuzu Tablets, BA 3 (1940), 2.

129 E. Cassin, L'adoption, 280—282.

130 That Pai-Tešup be Tupkiya's slave is necessary if the parallel with Eliezer is to be supported. This, however, is not the case in clause I of the contract.

131 This may also be implied by the abbreviated character of the protection clause (Clause III). Has Tupkiya daughters but no son?

he has the obligation to care for Tupkiya; this is hardly the condition of a servant.
(4) Moreover, the statement, "Tout l'argent de mes filles, quant elles siégeront à la porte, Pai-Tešup fera payer et recevra", shows clearly that Pai-Tešup is put in the position of a son, not that of a servant.

On formal grounds alone then we must conclude that this contract is not basically different from those discussed above, and deals with the adoption of a free-born person and not a slave.

That Pai-Tešup is the *arad Šilwatešup*, who is the "son of the king", should perhaps be stressed, for *arad* here does not have the meaning "servant" or "slave"[132], but rather should be translated "official", a term which designates not status, but profession[133]. This position of *arad* to Šilwatešup son of the king is also held by Akapurḫi who we find in HSS V 66 as the adopter of Šilwatešup's wife, a contract which would have little meaning if Akapurḫi were Šilwatešup's slave. Similarly, in Gadd 9 Kašummenni, an *amat ēkallim* "a palace official", also acts as the adopter in a contract which shows her not only to be a landholder, but the owner of slaves. In this tablet, Pai-tešup, undoubtedly the same man as is adopted in HSS IX 22, acts as witness to the contract, a function that is hardly congruent with the status of a slave[134]. Similar to the adoption of Pai-Tešup is the badly damaged tablet HSS XIII 69 in which a *warad ēkalli*, like Pai-Tešup, is apparently taken into a real adop-

---

[132] As it does in Nuzi text no. 7 (Chiera, Speiser, JAOS 47, 1927, 44): *Ṣilikupi* [awêl]*ḫāpiru ana ardūti . . . ušēribšu*: "Zilikupi, a Ḫapiru, into servitude . . . has entered", parallel to text 8 (ibid): [sal il] *Sînpālti* [sal]*Ḫāpiru . . . ana amtūti ušēribšu.* "Sin-palti, a Ḫapiru woman . . . has entered into servitude."

[133] CAD A, part 1, esp. 248: "*ardu*"; cf. also 211.

[134] Also to be considered are the texts 30—32 and 42—44, transliterated and translated in AASOR XVI. In text 32 the girl Kisaya, an *amat* of the woman Tulpunnaya, a major official of the palace, is identified as "daughter of Ariya" and has apparently the status of a free-born person. In text 30 she is adopted *ana mārtūti u kallūti* by Tulpunnaya and in 31 wins a court decision against Tulpunnaya, enabling her to marry the man of her choice. Texts 42—44 speak of another *amat* Tulpunnaya, called Hanate, in which Hanate adopts another girl *ana mārtūti u kallūti* and gives her away in marriage. In text 42 the agreement states that Hanate shall treat her adopted daughter: "as a daughter of Arrapḫa; she shall not give her into slavery." Surely, the implication is that Hanate herself does not have the status of a slave. The term *amat* as attributed to Hanate as well as to Kisaya should perhaps best be translated as "employee" or perhaps as "civil servant", for Tulpunnaya is a major official in charge of the palace archives. The six tablets referred to in this note are all from these archives (room C 120).

tion. The text reads: "*Ṭuppi mārūti ša* *ᵐ[Gel]ia mār [Milki]tešup [xxx] warad ēkalli ana mārūti ītepuš* (?), which I translate: "Tablet of sonship in which [Gel]ia son of [Milki]tešup [xxx], the palace official, into sonship has taken." (The rest of the tablet is badly destroyed. The translation is uncertain, since it requires the form *ītepušu*.)

Many cuneiform contracts do treat of the adoption of slaves, but the contracts have their own form quite distinct from the form of adoption that we have been considering and that occurs at Nuzi. The contracts deal with the adopter's own slaves and is entirely one-sided. There are five basic clauses to the typical form: (1) PN is said to be son. (2) Declaration of emancipation. (3) So long as the adopter lives, the adopted will serve him. (4) Upon the death of the adopter, no one shall have any claims on the adopted, and (5) A one-sided penalty clause: usually the return to the status of a slave[135]. First, it is to be noticed that the contract is, as is to be expected, one-sided, and apparently can be broken by the adopter; second, the slave is freed, a necessary prerequisite for his entry into the position of a son of the family; third, no inheritance is mentioned and it is unlikely that any right to inheritance is implied[136]. Except for the clause of adoption, these contracts resemble simple manumissions[137]. There are also a few rare texts which connect inheritance with the adoption of a slave. The interpretation of these texts is, however, very uncertain[138].

---

135 For examples see J. Kohler, Ham. Ges. III, texts 25—31, p. 11—13; IV, text 785, p. 4; V, texts 1089 and 1090, p. 4; M. Schorr, Altbabylonische Rechtsurkunden aus der Zeit der ersten babylonischen Dynastie, 3. Heft, SKAWW 165, 2, 1910, text VAT 750, p. 15; from the neo-Babylonian Period cf. Kohler and F. E. Peiser, Aus dem babylonischen Rechtsleben, IV 15, and from the Greek period cf. C. B. Welles, Manumission and Adoption, RIDA 3 (1949), 508—515. See also the discussion of E. Szlechter, RIDA 14 (1967), 80f.

136 Cf. CH no. 190 and H. Donner, Oriens Antiquus 8 (1969), 92f.

137 For examples cf. Kohler, Ham. Ges. IV, 4, text 786; and VI, 5, text 1427. Contra Welles, RIDA 3 (1949), 517.

138 ARM VIII, 1 (contra M. Noth, Die Ursprünge des alten Israel im Lichte neuer Quellen. Arbeitsgemeinschaft für Forschung des Landes Nordrhein-Westfalen Geisteswissenschaften, Heft 94, 1961, 19f.), is certainly not an adoption of a slave, but belongs with the full adoption texts.
Among the arabs, inheritance rights were not an aspect of adoption. In the pre-Islamic period, however, the adopted son shared in the inheritance with naturally born members, even slaves could be adopted and share in the inheritance. Muhammed, before preaching Islam, adopted his slave Zayd ibn Ḥaritha, who then was known as Zayd ibn Muhammed, and was Muhammed's heir. (R. Levy, An Introduction to the Sociology of Islam, I—II 1931/1933, I 210.).

One 5th century neo-Babylonian text, dated to the reign of Artaxerxes I, refers to the manumission and adoption of a male slave. This manumission is moreover connected with the cultivation of a specific piece of land, which is to be the adopted son's inheritance[139]. Also in a text from the 9th year of Cyrus (c. 340), we have a similar text, which however is very badly damaged. The final clause reads: "... 1 ... Gewand ... wird Ḫibta (the adopter) für ... in seinen Besitz geben." Whether this refers to property that is given to the adopted son is a moot question, but it seems possible if not likely[140]. In both these texts — if they are at all relevant — the inheritance deals with a specified piece of property and is not the unspecified share of the father's possessions that is normally given to sons.

We must also mention here an Egyptian contract from the Ramesside period, whose interpretation is still much debated[141]. It is generally referred to as the "Extraordinary Adoption" text and deals with two different legal acts. The first gives the adoption of a woman by her husband, because they had no children. The second part is dated 18 years later and deals with the adoption by the wife of three children who were originally slaves. They, along with a brother-in-law, also adopted as a son, are to divide the full inheritance. It may well be that we have here the adoption of slaves with the right to inheritance; however, the statement "We purchased the female slave Diniḥetiri and she gave birth to these three children, etc." may well suggest that the three children are the children of a concubine, in which case, the purpose of the contract is more exactly one of legitimation than adoption proper[142].

In conclusion it can be said that the interpretation of Gen 15 2-4 which attempts to see Eliezer as a servant whom Abraham has adopted or will adopt can only with the greatest difficulty be supported by the known legal practices of the ancient Near East, and can in no way be related to the *ṭuppi marūti* adoption contracts of Nuzi.

Any interpretation of Gen 15 2-4 which seeks its explanation on the basis of adoption has the additional difficulty that the practice

---

139 M. San Nicolo and A. Ungnad, Neubabylonische Rechts- und Verwaltungsurkunden, I 1935, no. 10, p. 15f.; C. B. Welles, RIDA 3 (1949), 519.

140 Kohler and Peiser, Babyl. Rechtsleben, IV 13.

141 For text see A. H. Gardiner, Adoption Extraordinary, JEA 26 (1940), 23f. For interpretation, ibid. 25—27; J. J. Rabinowitz, Semitic Elements in the Egyptian Adoption Papyrus Published by Gardiner, JNES 17 (1958), 46; A Théodoridès, Le Papyrus des Adoptions, RIDA³ 12 (1965), 79—142 (against Gardiner and Rabinowitz); and above all the excellent remarks of S. Allam, Zur Stellung der Frau im alten Ägypten in der Zeit des Neuen Reiches, 16—10. Jh. v. u. Z., BiOr 26 (1969), 157f.

142 Cf. below the discussion of similar contracts in G.

of full adoption of a free-born person, let alone the adoption of a slave, is not clearly found in any text of the Old Testament[143]. For the present, it seems, that if Snijders' translation and interpretation is not to be accepted, we must see this passage along with Pedersen[144] as "very extraordinary" and "without analogy". In any case, it is clear that the solution has not been found among the Nuzi tablets or "Hurrian customs".

D. GEN 11 29[145]

Another type of extended adoption at Nuzi is that found in those contracts titled *ṭuppi mārtūti ù kallatūti*, "Tablet of daughtership and daughter-in-law-ship". The relationship established by this agreement was widely known throughout the Near East[146]. We find this

143 See above all the very thorough article of H. Donner, Oriens Antiquus 8 (1969), 104—110. See on the other hand, F. Nötscher, Biblische Altertumskunde, 1940, 90; E. Neufeld, Ancient Hebrew Marriage Laws, 1944, 265f., and Z. W. Falk, Hebrew Law in Biblical Times, 1964, 118 and 162f. II Sam 7 14 Ps 2 7 and perhaps the enigmatic Ps 80 16-18 do seem to use an adoption formula, but to argue from these texts to the existence of a practice of full adoption among the Israelites is to give too much weight to poetic religious texts. Gen 48 12 50 23 and Ruth 4 16f. have to be interpreted with Job 3 12 and do not imply adoption. These imply no more than legitimation (Donner ibid. 107f.). Concerning Gen 48 5f., see Donner ibid. 108f. I Chr 2 34f. does not deal with the adoption of a slave, but rather with the transmission of the inheritance to the grandchildren through the daughter. Ex 21 7-11 is adoption only in an extended sense, and will be discussed below. Ex 2 10, the adoption of Moses, and Est 2 7, the adoption of Esther, are not full adoptions, but deal with the adoption of a foundling and an orphan, and thus do not imply a right to inheritance; they are therefore no help to an understanding of Gen 15 2-4. Prov 17 2: "A wise slave may give orders to a disappointing son and share the inheritance with the brothers." does give the possibility of a slave inheriting, but this shows us more the extent to which a man has control over the division of his estate, even where there are sons. A man can also include others than his sons into the patrimony, particularly for purposes of reward — a practice that was widespread in the Near East (see further on this below, in section K of this chapter). It seems to me unlikely that we can understand this passage with Neufeld (Anc Heb Mar Laws 261f.) as an application of the legal principle defined in Num 27 8-11.

144 Israel, Its Life and Culture, I—II 1926, 511.

145 Since my purpose is limited to the examination of the extent to which the Nuzi contracts can be compared to the social customs presupposed by the Genesis narratives, I have limited my discussion of the nature and function of these contracts to a minimum; the result is a simplification, but I hope no serious distortion.

146 Contra I. Mendelsohn, The Conditional Sale into Slavery of Free Born Daughters in Nuzi and the Law of Ex 21 7-11, JAOS 55 (1935), 190; Slavery in the Ancient

practice reflected in the texts and laws of the Old Babylonian period[147], in the Middle Assyrian Law code[148], in a text dated to the Cassite period (c. 1342)[149], as well as in the Ugaritic tablets[150] and in the Old Testament[151]. The contracts of this type from Nuzi are quite numerous and show a wider variety of intention than those found elsewhere. Nevertheless, there seems to be no reason to see the development of this legal form at Nuzi as significantly different from its development elsewhere in the ancient Near East[152]. This type of contract is particularly close to the adoption of daughters, but without the right to inheritance[153]. However, the emphasis on the terḫatu, as well as on the conditions under which the girl can be given in marriage by the adopter, mark this as a type of adoption that can have quite limited purposes. There are wide variations of intention in these contracts ranging from the establishment of a relationship fully comparable to that of a real daughter[154] to a relationship that is close to but not entirely equal to slavery[155].

Near East, BA 9 (1946), 76—78. See rather, M. Burrows, The Basis of Israelite Marriage, AOS 15, 1938, 23; The Ancient Oriental Background of Hebrew Levirate Marriage, BASOR 77 (1940), 14. R. Yaron, On Divorce in Old Testament Times, RIDA 4 (1967), 123; and especially A. van Praag, Droit Matrimonial Assyro-Babylonien, AHB 12 (1945), 79 and 84, and Neufeld, Anc. Heb. Mar. Laws, 68—76.

147 Cf. J. Kohler, Ham. Ges. VI, texts 1418 and 1419; Code of Hammurapi no. 155f. Cf. van Praag, Droit Matrimonial, 79; Yaron, RIDA 4 (1957), 123; M. Burrows, The Basis of Israelite Marriage, 23. Also, Kohler, Ham. Ges. III, text 3, may well presuppose that Šamaš-tutum is the adoptive father of Iltāni [compare with text 2]: so Schorr, Zivil und Prozessrecht, 11 n.

148 Esp. nos. 30 and 33 (see also no. 29). For discussion see Burrows, BASOR 77 (1940), 14, and J. Lewy, TC 100, LC 242 und das Eherecht des altassyrischen Rechtsbuches KAV Nr. 1, ZA 36 (1925), 147.

149 Kohler, Ham. Ges. III, text 23; Mendelsohn, Slavery, 22; David, Adoption, 1.

150 See A. F. Rainey, Orientalia 34 (1965), 17.

151 Esp. Ex 21 7-11.

152 Some of the Nuzi tablets which either are this type of contract or include or imply such a contract are: Gadd 35 (Gadd, RA 23, 1926); HSS V 11, 17, 79, and 80 (Chiera and Speiser, AASOR X, no. 25, no. 26, ll. 25ff., no. 30, and no. 31, ll. 10ff.); Pfeiffer and Speiser, AASOR XVI, nos. 23, 30—33, and 42—44, TCL IX 7 (Koschaker, Rechtsurkunden, 171); Chiera-Speiser, JAOS 47 (1927), nos. 4 and 5; C. H. Gordon, AnOr 12 (1935), 177 and 180; JEN VI 638 (H. Lewy, Orientalia 10, 1941, 216); JEN V 441 (M. Burrows, BASOR, 1940); JEN 26, 50, 429, 431, 432, 433, and HSS IX 119 and 145 in E. Cassin, L'adoption à Nuzi, 299—308 and 312—314.

153 As e. g., Texts 1422 and 1424 in J. Kohler, Ham. Ges. VI, 2f.

154 This seems true of the Cassite text dated to the 21st year of Kurigalzu: "[Ina-Uruk-rîšat] die Tochter des [. . .]-muššallim, hatte keine Tochter; deshalb adoptierte sie die Eṭirtum die Tochter des Ninurta-mušallim.

Because of the very wide range of use of these contracts it is impossible to give a single text or even a number of texts as typical. Almost every clause has several variants: (1) There is the statement of intention: adoption either as *ana mārtūti*, or *ana kallatūti*, or both[156]. (2) A settlement about the brideprice and sometimes the dowry[157]. The payment of the brideprice can be completed at the time the girl is married[158]. (3) A statement that the adopter has the right to give the girl in marriage (the type of bridegroom can be specified; e. g., the eldest son, or even a slave)[159]. (4) The penalty clause (usually, but not always, mutual, and with great variety)[160]. Some tablets also include clauses that determine the status of the girl and of her children[161]; others include specifically filial obligations contracted by the girl, similar to those of the full adoption contracts[162].

The basic legal principle which seems to underlie all these contracts is the possibility of receiving, upon payment of the *terḫatu*, the right to give a girl in marriage.

---

7 Sekel Gold gab sie. Sei es, daß sie sie einem Manne geben will, sei es, daß sie sie zur Hierodulenschaft bestimmt, (jedenfalls) darf sie sie nicht zu ihrer Magd machen. Macht sie sie zu ihrer Magd, so soll sie in ihr Vaterhaus fortgehen. Solange Ina-Uruk-rīšat lebt, soll Eṭirtum ihr Ehrfurcht erweisen. Stirbt Ina-Uruk-rīšat so soll Eṭirtum als ihre Tochter ihr Wasser spenden. Sagt Ina-Uruk-rīšat '(du bist) nicht meine Tochter' so geht sie des Silbers, das sie besitzt (?) verlustig. Sagt Eṭirtum '(du bist) nicht meine Mutter', so wird sie zur Magd gemacht." (as translated by J. Kohler: Ham. Ges. III, 11.)

155 This is particularly true of some of the contracts from Nuzi; esp. Cassin, L'adoption, JEN, 432 and 433, pp. 302—306.

156 The difference of terminology does not seem to be significant. Cf. Gadd 35: *ana mārtūti*, HSS V 79 (AASOR X 25): *ṭuppi kallūti*, and JEN 26 (Cassin 299): *ṭuppi mārtūti ù kallatūti*.

157 E. g., HSS V 11 (AASOR X no. 31, ll. 10ff.) and HSS V 80 (AASOR X no. 26).

158 HSS V 80, ibid., and Gordon, AnOr (1935), 177.

159 Compare HSS V 79 (AASOR X no. 25) with AASOR XVI no. 23. The often recurring clause which states that the adopter may give the girl in marriage as often as he pleases may perhaps only signify: (1) That the contract is not limited by any single marriage, and (2) The extent of the patria potestas that the adopter has over the girl. There is one text in which a girl, adopted under such unlimited conditions, does nevertheless protest successfully the choice of her husband (AASOR XVI 30—33).

160 HSS V 79 has one mina of silver and one mina of gold. AASOR XVI no. 23 has 2 minas of gold; AASOR XVI 42 has a one-sided penalty of 2 slave-girls. JEN 433 (Cassin, L'adoption, 304—306) has no penalty clause.

161 Most texts explicitly protect the adopted girl from being made a slave or from being married to a slave. On the other hand, see above note 159.

162 See above the discussion of clause IV of the full-adoption contracts on p. 215.

E. A. Speiser, in an article published in 1963[163] as well as in his commentary on Genesis[164], maintains that the Nuzi *ṭuppi mārtūti ù kallatūti* contract lies behind and explains Gen 11 29, which, according to him, speaks of Nahor having married his niece Milcah. In 1964 Speiser wrote: "Juridically, cases of this kind (Gen 11 29) involve adoption (here of an orphaned niece) followed by marriage. The pertinent document in Nuzi would be called *ṭuppi mārtūti ù kallatūti* ... since the husband was also the adoptive father and thereby father-in-law[165]." That is, the husband, before himself marrying the girl, had adopted her and made her his daughter and daughter-in-law. Earlier he had written, "This (Gen 11 29) agrees closely with a practice which Hurrian law recognizes by a *ṭuppi mārtūti ù kallūti* ... whereby a man adopts a girl as his daughter for the declared purpose of either marrying her himself or giving her in marriage to his son ... Since the latter (Haran) was Nahor's brother, the marriage would come simultaneously, in accordance with Hurrian law, under the classification of brotherhood[166]." (!)

It is unfortunate that Speiser does not refer to any specific texts from Nuzi on which he bases his interpretation, for there is a great deal of confusion here, not only in his understanding of the Genesis text, but also in his understanding of this Nuzi or, rather, Near Eastern type contract. First, Gen 11 29 can have nothing to do with the *aḫḫūti* ("brothership") contracts, for the significant characteristic of the *aḫḫūti* contracts is not that they are drawn up between brothers; rather they deal with the transference of a legal relationship of brothership. It need hardly be argued that neither Nahor (her uncle) nor Haran (her father) is Milcah's brother. Second, and much more important, Gen 11 29 speaks of Milcah as the wife of Nahor, but the purpose of the *ṭuppi martūti ù kallatūti* contracts is generally not to marry the girl oneself[167]; the authority obtained over her is rather the right to give her in marriage. Here, Speiser has simply misunderstood these contracts.

Third, if there is anything obscure about this passage it is that Nahor marries his niece by blood, a curiosity which is neither altered nor explained by the Nuzi contracts.

Furthermore, it may be doubted that the Genesis text requires such a bizarre interpretation since a marriage between an uncle and

---

163 The Wife-Sister Motif in the Patriarchal Narratives, in: Biblical and Other Studies, ed. by A. Altmann, 15—28 (= OBS 77ff.).

164 Genesis 78f.

165 Genesis 78.

166 OBS, WS, 77f.

167 Though it is possible; cf. JAOS 47 (1927), text no. 5, p. 42: "Or, if he so desires, Takku himself may take her as wife."

his niece is not forbidden in the Old Testament[168] and is found in other Near Eastern sources as well[169].

E. GEN 12 10-20 20 1-18 and 26 6-11

The parallels from Nuzi which Speiser claims for these passages raise some significant, if peculiar, methodological issues, since Speiser's reconstruction of the Genesis tradition presupposes that this tradition has lost all awareness of the "real" social forms that had been the basis of the "events" behind these stories, to such an extent that the present form of the stories reflects a context, motivation, and use completely different from the original. What now are completely evolved tales of a deception for purposes of safety and personal gain[170] were originally diplomatic visits of Abraham and Isaac to neighboring capitals, where the exceptionally high status of the patriarchs was carefully noted by the tradition which was particularly interested in the purity of line and the prestige of the fathers of Israel. However, since this status was marked by a purely local Hurrian custom, whereby a man not only married a woman but also adopted her as his sister, it is hardly surprising that the tradition garbled the original events and transposed some elements, to emerge with stories that on the surface presuppose an unbridgeable distinction between being a wife and being a sister, for in the later social milieu in which the tradition developed, it was an unbridgeable distinction.

The methodological issue here is very serious, since it is not on the basis of the similarities of the Nuzi texts and the Genesis accounts that Speiser develops his interpretation. On the contrary, he clearly recognizes their differences and lack of similarity. What the Bible has

---

168 Neufeld, Anc Heb Mar Laws, 201f.; S. Krauss, Die Ehe zwischen Onkel und Nichte, in: Festschrift K. Kohler, 1913, 165—175.

169 E. g., at Alalakh, Text no. 92 (D. J. Wiseman, The Alalakh Tablets; see also I. Mendelsohn, BASOR 156, 1959, 38, and Marriage in Alalakh, 356f.), as well as from Egypt in a text from the reign of Ramses III (A. H. Gardiner, The Goddess Nekhbet at the Jubilee Festvial of Rameses III, ZÄS 48, 1911, 50f.) and in the genealogical trees (Pestman, Marriage, 4 and 83—86).
Finally, it is not entirely clear that Milcah's father, Haran, is the same Haran as Abraham's brother; for in v. 27 Haran is the father of Lot and in v. 29 Milcah's father is the father of Milcah and Iscah. There are also two Nahors in the Genealogy. At any rate, there are serious source difficulties in the text here which Speiser ignores. Certainly, Milcah-bat-Haran is not a "serial-name" as Speiser claims, (Genesis 79) for that would bring the succeeding clause "the father of Milcah" into apposition with Milcah, making her her own father!

170 Gen 12 13 aα.

presented as a lie, was, in fact, according to Speiser, historically the truth[171].

Speiser's "interpretation" of Gen 12. 20 and 26 is not based on the Genesis texts (how far he departs from them will be discussed below), but is rather the construction of a historical hypothesis based on historical records. His interest is in what happened to the biblical patriarchs, and, while he refers to the traditions about the patriarchs, they are not for him dependable criteria. The Nuzi tablets, on the other hand, offer to him a much sounder basis for understanding the "real" events of the patriarchs' lives: "Of the two interpretations, one based on original and contemporary records of a society that is closely involved, and the other in much later literary narratives, the first is obviously to be preferred[172]." But this first interpretation, it is important to stress, is not of Genesis, even though that the Nuzi customs are related to the patriarchs at all can only be suggested on the assumption that the patriarchs did live according to what Speiser speaks of as Hurrian law. This question about the relevance of the Nuzi tablets to an understanding of the patriarchal way of life, depends to a great extent on the uniqueness of this particular parallel, because, as we shall see, the contracts which Speiser refers to here, the *aḫātūti* contracts, are the basis for claiming not only that the biblical tradition no longer understands this custom but that the custom is so unique to Nuzi that its existence in the patriarchal stories shows that they are based on "Hurrian" law! It should be then fair to ask on what basis the patriarchs are said to live according to this Hurrian law, for this type of contract is certainly rare — even at Nuzi. Some credence could be given, of course, to Speiser's historical reconstruction by the accummlative weight of other parallels between Genesis and the Nuzi contracts, but in that case a necessary connection between Nuzi or the Hurrians and the patriarchs is not obvious. Speiser's historical alternative to the Genesis traditions of Chapters 12. 20 and 26 should then offer an adequate explanation of these narratives which the stories would not have independent of the proposed historical basis. Briefly, it must first be shown that the Nuzi contracts do give an adequate interpretive base for the history of the patriarchs. Secondly, a significant relationship must be shown between this historical view and the patriarchs we know, that is between the Nuzi *Aḫātūti* contracts and Gen 12. 20 and 26.

These are then serious questions that must be asked about Speiser's biblical interpretation. Equally serious questions must be

---

171 Speiser, OBS, Wife-Sister, 80f., and Genesis XL.

172 Speiser, Genesis, XL.

asked about his interpretation of the Nuzi *aḫātūti* contracts. (1) It is hoped that the following brief examination will show that while the specific legal concept of *aḫātūti* seems peculiar to Nuzi, there may be some doubt whether the contracts that are involved reflect any significantly unique custom or social structure. (2) That the people of Nuzi had a special legal arrangement according to which by separate contracts a woman became both wife and sister to her husband; i. e., that we can speak of a "wife-sister" custom at Nuzi, must be seriously doubted, and perhaps completely discarded.

In his interpretation of the *aḫātūti* contracts, Speiser has come to expand an interpretation first suggested by Koschaker[173], who is followed by Korošec[174], that the Nuzi adoption "for sistership" reflects a vestigial fratriarchy[175].

This thesis of Koschaker has enabled Speiser to speak of fratriarchy as a "normal feature of the (Hurrian) upper classes"[176]. The claim for fratriarchal authority among the Hurrians and at Nuzi primarily rests upon Koschaker's understanding of the Hittite treaty of Šuppiluliumaš, according to which a marriage agreement would make a girl also her husband's sister. Consequently, as a brother, he would have fratriarchal authority over the woman's female siblings[177].

This, however, offers an extremely weak basis for Speiser's subsequent interpretations. Not only can this concept of fratriarchy not be reconciled with some of the Nuzi practices, but the *aḫātūti* contracts themselves are directly antipathetic to fratriarchy.

First, that a man, married in a "sistership" contract, does not attain authority over his wife's female siblings is clearly shown in HSS V 80 (AASOR X 26), in which contract the husband adopts his sister-in-law *ana mārtūti* and promises to pay for her! Furthermore, JEN 78, ll. 23f.[178]. "Ich selbst zur Schwesterschaft dem Ḫutarrapḫi gebe (mich)", causes one to doubt that the authority involved in these contracts is fratriarchal.

173 P. Koschaker, Fratriarchat, Hausgemeinschaft, und Mutterrecht in Keilschriftrechten, ZA 41 (1933), 1—89.

174 V. Korošec, Ehe in Nuzi, RLA II, 296—299.

175 Cf. Burrows, Basis of Israelite Marriage, 23 n. Burrows' objection, that AASOR XVI no. 23 speaks of a woman who gives her brother into adoption, is not to the point, for Koschaker speaks of a vestigial fratriarchy in a patriarchal structure (ZA 41, 1933, 14f.!). Speiser's expansion on Koschaker's interpretation is quite another matter. A. Skaist's article (The Authority of the Brother at Arrapha and Nuzi, JAOS 89, 1969, 10—17) unfortunately does not carry us much beyond Koschaker. It is, on the other hand, a very clear explication of the interpretations of Koschaker and Speiser.

176 OBS, WS, 73.

177 Koschaker, ZA 41 (1933), 1—13. 33, and Speiser, OBS, WS, 73.

178 Cassin, L'adoption, 311f., and Koschaker, Rechtsurkunden, 173f.

Koschaker contrasts "Brudergewalt", the authority of the brother, to patriarchal authority; i. e., for Koschaker, the authority of the girl's father[179]. But this is a misrepresentation of the difference between fratriarchy and patriarchy. What Koschaker describes is in both cases patriarchal authority. Fratriarchal authority is that which the wife's family maintains — particularly her brother — over her, but more importantly over her children. This authority is to be contrasted to the authority of the husband's family — usually his father — over the bride, which authority in the Near East is generally consequent on the payment of the bride price. That the *aḫātūti* contracts from Nuzi are concerned with the transference of just these rights is sufficient to describe the custom as oriented to a patriarchal type society. That brothers have important positions, and, upon the death of their father, authority and responsibility for their sisters before they are married, is a normal characteristic of the patriarchal family.

If the *aḫātūti* contracts are not to be understood as a remnant of fratriarchy, it becomes important to determine more exactly what type of contract the *ṭuppi aḫātūti* was. Speiser speaks of it as a special and unique arrangement of upper class Hurrians, whereby a man not only married a woman, but also adopted her as his sister[180]. Thus the woman was legally both his wife and his sister. This not only gave greater authority to the husband, but also was a mark of superior status to the wife, accordingly protected by what Speiser calls a "special socioreligious solicitude"[181]. This fraternal authority possessed by the husband is identical to that of a real brother, and, according to Speiser, whenever a woman was given in marriage by a real or an adoptive brother, she was subsequently considered both the wife and sister of her husband, whether or not an *aḫātūti* contract was used[182]. The status of "wife-sister" was such that the terms for "wife" and "sister" "could be interchanged in official use under the right circumstances"[183]. This type of relationship is thought to be effected by two separate contracts, one establishing the couple as brother and sister, and the other as husband and wife[184]. Each contract required a separate payment.

---

179 ZA 41 (1933), 31—34.

180 Speiser, OBS, WS, 70—76; Genesis XL and 92; Speiser, Nuzi, IDB, 574; Speiser, The Biblical Idea of History in its Common Near Eastern Setting, IEJ 7 (1957), 210ff. (= OBS 204f.).

181 Speiser, OBS, WS, 75.

182 Speiser, Genesis, 92.

183 Speiser IDB, 574.

184 Speiser, OBS, WS, 92 and Genesis XL.

There are numerous serious objections of detail that can be made to this thesis: e. g., Speiser speaks of "brother-husbands" in HSS V 26 and Gadd 31[185]. However, in HSS V 26 this term clearly does not apply, since Akawatil, the legal brother *(ana aḫatūti)*, is not himself the husband, but will be the recipient of half the brideprice from the husband. Nor is such a term readily applicable to Gadd 31. Šeqai is the brother of Ḫalase and supplies her dowry (ll. 1 and 14f.). Šalab-urḫe, on the other hand, is apparently the husband (ll. 21ff.).

The contracts themselves do not support Speiser's interpretation, which he rests almost solely on three tablets dealing with the same couple: HSS V 25, 69, and 80[186]. Speiser believes that HSS V 69 is a separate contract in which Akkulenni gives his sister Beltakkadummi as sister *(ana aḫāti)* to Hurazzi; that is, Akkulenni has ceded his fraternal rights to Hurazzi. For this right, 40 shekels of silver were paid: "The juridical basis of the transaction is thus a form of adoption. The adoptive brother may then marry the girl himself, as is the case in HSS V 80, or he may give her in marriage to another in return for the customary brideprice[187]." HSS V 80 is seen as an independent contract according to which Akkulenni gives his sister Beltakadummi into marriage *(ana aššūti)*. For this an additional payment is made. HSS V 25 records Beltakkadummi's consent to the arrangement. There are obvious objections to Speiser's understanding of these three texts. First, if the transferal of brothership rights, as effected in HSS V 69, gives Akkulenni the right to give Beltakkadummi in marriage and to receive the brideprice for her, how then is the payment in HSS V 80, which Speiser insists is independent, to be explained? Moreover, if HSS V 80 were the earlier contract, and HSS V 69 were made for the purpose of contracting special privileges of "brotherhood", then Speiser's thesis, that a brother, who gives his sister in marriage (HSS V 80), thereby transfers his fratriarchal rights, must obviously be rejected. Moreover, if the man is already married to the woman, independent of the special "brotherhood" rights, what the special rights are needs to be explained, for it can no longer simply be the right to receive her *terḫatu*.

Both H. Lewy and H. Donner have attempted to explain these three tablets in ways which would exclude anything like a "wife-sister" relationship. Lewy sees the *ana aḫātūti* contracts as reflecting a special form of concubinage[188]. HSS V 69 is the earliest of the

[185] Speiser, OBS, WS, 70.

[186] Chiera and Speiser, AASOR X nos. 26—28. Speiser's treatment is very cursory; however, see OBS, WS, 68f.

[187] Ibid. 69.

[188] H. Lewy, Gleanings from a New Volume of Nuzi Texts, Orientalia 10 (1941), 209—217.

tablets, and contracts a sort of tentative marriage. Later, however, Hurazzi decides to marry Beltakkadummi. To facilitate this, Akkulenni repurchases Beltakkadummi by giving his other sister Kapulanza to Hurazzi *ana mārtūti* (HSS V 80, ll. 25ff.), with the result that Hurazzi is able to take Beltakkadummi *ana aššūti* in HSS V 80[189]. The basis of this form of concubinage is that, according to Lewy, a brother in Nuzi "had ipso facto the right to live in concubinage with his sister".

Lewy's reconstruction cannot, however, be accepted. In HSS V 80 Kapulanza is not given in exchange for Beltakkadummi; rather the adoption of Kapulanza *ana mārtūti* appears unexceptionable, and Hurazzi undertakes to hand over the brideprice (perhaps minus the dowry) to Akkulenni[190]. Any separation between the two contracts creates the necessity of explaining what then appears to be a double payment.

In favor of Lewy's interpretation on the other hand is JEN 636[191], which involves the dissolution of an *aḫātūti* contract and the settlement concerning the children. There is no indication, however, if it existed here, that concubinage is characteristic of *aḫātūti* arrangements, let alone brother and sister relationships. The explicit reference to marriage to someone other than the adoptive brother in JEN 78 and HSS XIX 68[192] inclines one to the contrary opinion. However, examples of *ṭuppi aḫātūti* contracts are so rare, that it is particularly difficult to define its purpose, except as it is stated in a specific contract. JEN 78 is the only text that is itself an *aḫātūti* contract and offers some adequate grounds for understanding its purpose. If it had been drawn up for the purpose of establishing a concubinage, that aspect of the relationship is entirely missing from the contract.

H. Donner understands the *aḫātūti* contract as a disguised form of sale of a sister into slavery[193]. In this way he understands HSS V 69, which he sees as the earliest of the contracts involving Beltakkadummi. Donner understands HSS V 80 as establishing a full marriage. A slave, however, could not enter a full marriage. It is for this reason that this contract is seen to cancel and to replace HSS V 69. The contracts are understood consecutively rather than —as Speiser would have it — as complimentary.

---

[189] Ibid. 213.

[190] "When Kapulanza with her husband has lain, straightway 20 shekels of *ḫašaḫušenni* money Hurazzi to Akkulenni shall pay." AASOR X, no. 26.

[191] Lewy, Orientalia 10 (1941), 209f.

[192] (Untranslated).

[193] Oriens Antiquus 8 (1969), 110; cf. Koschaker, Rechtsurkunden, 90f.

While Donner accurately points out the weakness of Speiser's interpretation on the grounds that we do not know the order in which the contracts were written, in placing HSS V 69 as the earlier contract later superseded by HSS V 80, he fails to offer a reason for the payment of the *terḫatu* in HSS V 80. If Beltakkadummi were the slave of Hurazzi, Hurazzi would not have to pay the brideprice. Moreover, his claim that the *aḫātūti* contracts are disguised sales into slavery is without adequate justification.

One major difficulty in ascertaining the significance of the *aḫātūti* contracts is the enigmatic character of HSS V 69:

> Tablet of sistership of Akkulenni son of Akiya, whereby his sister [f]Beltakkadummi as sister to Hurazzi son of Ennaya he has sold (i. e., "given" *ittadin*). And Hurazzi 40 shekels of silver to Akkulenni has given. If there is a claim against [f]Beltakkadummi, Akkulenni shall clear her and to Hurazzi restore her. Whoever breaks the agreement shall furnish one mina of silver and one mina of gold[194].

JEN 78 is perhaps more complete: Beginning in the same manner, it adds the clause that Ḫutarrapḫi may give the girl Ḫinzuri to whomever he pleases: *[ana aššūt]i ašar ḫadû inandin.* The brideprice is split, 20 shekels going to the real brother, and the other 20 is to be used for the dowry. At the end of the contract, immediately before the penalty clause, is a declaration from the girl that she has given herself into sistership: *ana iqtabi mania a[n]a aḫātūti Ḫutarrapḫi ittadin.*

The absence of the first clause in HSS V 69 may well be understood by the fact that the bridegroom — namely Ḫurazzi himself — had already been determined. The declaration of the woman is found in the declaration of Beltakkadummi in HSS V 25, ll. 11ff. Both of these suggestions of course assume the possibility that HSS V 25 and 69 belong together. Since HSS V 25 is a declaration asserting that Beltakkadummi has been given *ana aššūti* ("into wifeship"), the relating of this text to HSS V 69 assumes that this *aḫātūti* contract (HSS V 69) is in fact a marriage contract.

This interpretation seems moreover to be justified, as far as can be judged, by the few texts that can be brought into relationship with those we have already considered.

Aside from the declaration clause, JEN 78 resembles the *mārtūti* contracts, and we may well be correct in seeing a close resemblance[195]. That is, the *aḫātūti* contract regulates the transference of the right to give a girl in marriage and to receive the *terḫatu*[196]. The closeness of these types of contracts is suggested for instance by HSS V 79

194 AASOR X 60f.

195 M. Burrows, Basis of Isr. Marr., 23, and Koschaker, Rechtsurkunden, 90f.

196 See above section D.

(AASOR X 25) in which a man gives his sister *ana kallatūti* (into "daughter-in-law-ship"). The brideprice is here referred to as *ḫaša-ḫušenni*, a term also used in HSS V 80 and JEN 475[197], in which another brother gives his sister *ana aššūti*. This same term is used in the *martūti* contract JEN 751[198].

At least one text seems to identify the *martūti* and the *aḫātūti* concepts. It is a *mārtūti* contract in which the girl is given by her father (*ana aḫātia*, "as sister"). Unfortunately, the last part of the text is too badly damaged to read: HSS XIII 15:

ṭuppi mārtū[ti]ša ᵐApazi mar Malia u mārāzu ᶠAsuli ana aḫātia Bekušše iddinaššu ù Bekuššḫi ana [aššū]ti ana 1 amēli iddin[a] . . .

Which I translate: "Tablet of daughtership belonging to Apazi son of Malia. Thus, his daughter ᶠAsuli as sister to Bekušše gave and Bekušše as a wife (or "into wifeship") to a man gave . . .".

It is significant that the man to whom she is given into sistership — as in JEN 78 — is not to be her husband. Rather what appears to be involved, as we have seen with other *ana mārtūti* contracts is the right to give the girl in marriage. It is also noteworthy that the man who gives the girl "into sistership" is not the brother but the father of the girl[199]. We have already seen that in HSS V 79 a man gives his sister as daughter-in-law. That these contracts are closely related in content as well as in terminology is clear from JEN 475[200]. Here we have a *ṭuppi riksi* whereby a man gives his sister *ana aššūti*, however, ll. 12—19 (*šumma Ḫanaya imât u ana šanîm mārišu Itḫipšarru inandinši adî Kulimmadu bāltalu u ištu bīt Itḫipšarru lā uṣṣi arkaṣṣa ša Kulimmadu ša Itḫipšarruma* . . . "If Ḫanaya dies Itḫipšarru shall give her to a second son. While Kulimmadu is alive she shall not leave the house of Itḫipšarru. The estate that is Kulimmadu's belongs to Itḫipšarru.") show that the contract is identical to an *ana mārtūti* contract. This is confirmed by the fact that the contractor is not the husband Ḫanaya but his father

[197] Chiera-Speiser, JAOS 47 (1927), no. 6, p. 43.

[198] Ibid. text no. 5, p. 42. Speiser's attempt to translate this as "brothership money" AASOR X 60) is certainly false, as is clear from this text. See also AASOR XVI 55, l. 33f.; CAD Ḫ, 136f., von Soden, AHW, 333a.

[199] Skaist (JAOS 89, 1969, 15) does not seem to be aware of this text when he argues that the Nuzi *aḫātūti* contracts are limited to brothers. The whole weight of his interpretation unfortunately depends on this distinction. Similarly Freedman's distinction (Journal of the Ancient Near Eastern Society of Columbia University 2, 1970, 77—85) between the *aḫātūti* and *mārtūti* documents, on the basis of the relative age of the person receiving her, is largely imaginary (cf. HSS V 80, ll. 25ff.!). This article, otherwise, offers nothing new to the discussion.

[200] Chiera-Speiser, JAOS 47 (1927), no. 6, p. 43f.

Itḫipšarru. It is similar to HSS V 69 in that who the husband is to be has already been determined. It is itself a marriage contract. It differs from HSS V 69 primarily in that this contract is concerned with bringing the girl under the patriarchal authority of Itḫipšarru, and thus considers the possibilities of marriage in the case that one son dies. In HSS V 69 on the other hand the bridegroom appears to have his own independent household[201].

Similar to the *ana mārtūti* contracts, the *aḫātūti* arrangement seems only indirectly concerned with marriage, i. e., the adopter receives the right to give the girl in marriage and to receive the *terḫatu*.

Happily two tablets (HSS V 26[202] and AASOR XVI 54) which are written in the form of declarations mention some of the obligations of the adopter, and indirectly inform us about the social significance of the *aḫātūti* contracts. AASOR XVI 54 is a declaration of the woman Kunyašu that her former husband and the person who had given her in marriage were both dead and that now her brother has taken *(ītepušmi)*[203] her *ana aḫātūti*, "into sistership"! When he gives her into marriage he will receive 10 shekels of silver. The tablet does not reflect the assertion of fratriarchal rights as Speiser suggests[204]. The fact that the declaration is made by Kunyašu and that the penalty clause is mutual suggest that there are mutual obligations undertaken here and not merely the one-sided assertion of a right. That this was so is supported by HSS V 26 which is also the declaration of a woman:

> (To) Akawatil son of Elli upon the street my strength I offered, and as sister (or "into sistership") I have been adopted. And Akawatil shall manage my possessions; what is in my stores is in his stores; since he has adopted me as sister he shall be of assistance unto me. And Akawatil shall receive from my (future) husband 20 shekels of the money (paid) for me, and he shall have the usufruct thereof; and twenty shekels of silver my brother Elhinnamar shall use[205].

Thus, like the *mārtūti* contracts, the *aḫātūti* contract approaches that of a real though mitigated adoption, with its concommitant responsibilities: The natural relationship between the woman and Akawatil is not clear; however, the reference to Elhinnamar (a minor ?) and the splitting of the *terḫatu* between him and the adopter may

[201] This seems to be confirmed by the *ana mārtūti* contract in HSS V 80, ll. 25ff.

[202] AASOR X no. 29, and Cassin, L'adoption, 314f.

[203] Speiser's "Seized" (AASOR XVI 104) is too strong.

[204] Ibid.

[205] AASOR X 62. This may well resemble the text from Ugarit described by A. F. Rainey (Orientalia 1965, 20) — "a brotherhood adoption, in which some woman adopted a man as her brother. He came to her house to live bringing at least 1000 shekels, 10 slaves, expensive household goods and lots of livestock."

well suggest that Akawatil and Elhinnamar are not related. Gadd 31[206] also records an adoption of a woman *ana aḫātūti*. The contract then describes the dowry that the adopter Šeqai gives to the woman whom he has adopted. The responsibility of the brother (i. e., the person giving her in marriage) to supply the dowry is also reflected in HSS V 79, ll. 26ff.[207]: "Thus (declares) Šuwarninu: 'I am sister to Šartešup'. 5 shekels of silver, each year, he shall pay."[208]

In only one respect do these contracts significantly differ from the *mārtūti* contracts and that is in the recurrence of the declaration of the woman, usually towards the end of the contract (so in JEN 78, AASOR XVI 55, Gadd 31 and HSS V 79) but at times, as in HSS V 25, in a separate tablet, signifying her consent or even her concurrent responsibility. This may well be related to the right to the children which the payment of the *terḫatu* effects. HSS V 53[209] is a court record in which the fact that the wife is dead significantly affects the outcome of the hearing in which her brother Kinni tried to lay claim to the child of her marriage. AASOR XVI 55, ll. 38ff. is a particularly interesting addition to a marriage contract between the woman Haluya and the man Zilikkušu. In this passage Haluya gives — apparently without payment — a daughter (which she bore to Zilikkušu apparently prior to the marriage agreement) *ana mārtūti* to her husband Zilikkušu. Apparently a woman (whose father was dead?) had some rights over her children, and thus some concern with arrangements involving the *terḫatu* and the dowry[210].

In considering the three tablets which Speiser stresses in his interpretation of the *aḫātūti* contract, the following reconstruction seems to make the most sense: HSS V 25 is a declaration on the part of the three principals, confirming the contract made in HSS V 69. Akkulenni declares that he has given his sister as wife to Hurazzi and has received 40 shekels of silver (the same sum that is mentioned in HSS V 69). The form of the HSS V 69 contract *ana aḫātūti*, may well be determined by the fact that Akkulenni is Beltakkadummi's brother. Like the *ṭuppi mārtūti* form the *aḫātūti* contracts may be

206 RA 23 (1926), 109f.

207 Chiera-Speiser, AASOR X no. 25, p. 57f.

208 Compare HSS V 80, ll. 11ff. where half the *terḫatu* is given as dowry and AASOR XVI 55, ll. 33ff. where the 5 shekels per year is not an annuity but a time payment: "And Zilikkušu fifty shekels of silver, as afore-mentioned, *ḫašaḫušennu* for Haluya and for Šehalitu, in installments of five shekels year by year to Šukritešup shall pay until he has [paid it] off (?)!"

209 AASOR X 35, p. 69f.

210 Skaist, (JAOS 89, 1969, 16) comparing these texts with Roman law, makes a similar suggestion.

used per accidens for a marriage agreement, for they have the same purpose as the marriage contract, namely, the transference of patriarchal authority.

Beltakkadummi's declaration is to give consent to this arrangement. This seems in this case particularly important, since the terms of the agreement in HSS V 25 and 69 give the entire 40 shekels of the *terḫatu* to her brother Akkulennni, although in HSS V 80 it had been agreed that this payment would be split between Akkulenni and Beltakkadummi. This discrepancy between HSS V 25 and HSS V 80 may be explained by Hurazzi's declaration at the end of HSS V 25: *aššum Kap[luanza] ina arki Akkulenni la ašassi ša ina berišunu ibalkatu.* "Concerning Kapluanza, against Akkulenni I shall raise no claims", which can only mean that the agreement between Akkulenni and Hurazzi concerning Kapluanza in HSS V 80, ll. 25ff. has been cancelled, and Hurazzi is stating that he will not raise any future claims on the basis of the contract in HSS V 80. If this is accurate, the contract recorded in HSS V 25 and HSS V 69 has been formed to replace the earlier agreement in HSS V 80. HSS V 80 then, the earliest of the contracts, is an agreement that has been made between Akkulenni and Hurazzi but not fulfilled[211].

Finally, Speiser's claim that the *aḫātūti* contracts confer a special status on the woman that has "socioreligious" ramifications is based on what he sees as a type of "Ceremonial Payment" that is found in these contracts whose classical form can be seen in HSS V 79. That is, one ox, one ass, and ten sheep[212]. This payment is seen to reflect the "seriousness" and the "demonstrable solemnity of the occasion" and is directly related to the type of contract involved.

Speiser's evidence for this, however, is particularly disappointing. HSS V 79 is not an *Aḫātūti* contract but a contract *ana kallūti!* The brother-sister relationship is natural and lies between the girl and her guardian, not the girl and her husband. Moreover, the payment includes 10 shekels of silver. The only other two tablets that Speiser considers along with this "classical form" of payment are HSS V 43 and 52. In both cases they are fines and have nothing to do with the *aḫātūti* documents. HSS V 69, which is an *aḫātūti* contract, has a payment simply of 40 shekels in silver. JEN 78, also an *aḫātūti* contract, is also different as Speiser recognizes[213]. It mentions a payment of 40 shekels of silver, twenty of which is silver and the

[211] It may be important that the payment to be given to Akkulenni in HSS V 80 of 20 shekels of silver — or its equivalent — is not recorded as having been given but is rather contracted to be given: *inandin.*

[212] AASOR X no. 25. Speiser's most complete discussion of this is to be found in: Nuzi Marginalia, Orientalia 25 (1956), 9—15.

[213] Ibid. 12.

rest is given in kind: 1 ox, [× × ×] sheep, 1 imer of corn, 2 minas of copper and 9 minas of wool. HSS V 80 which is a *ṭuppi riksi ana aššūti* mentions that the payment is to be given in the form of one ox and 10 shekels of silver, and JEN 179 mentions the payment of 2 oxen, 1 ass and 10 sheep. This, however, is the payment for the purchase of a girl. That many payments at Nuzi are given in kind — which may indeed be a more original type of payment — is known to everyone, but that this type of payment is particularly related to the *aḫātūti* documents, and that this is a ceremonial kind of payment, is false.

It is difficult to see that the *aḫātūti* contracts significantly affect the general social structure at Nuzi. Like the *mārtūti* documents they seem little more than a means of facilitating the transferral of parental rights from the family of the bride to that of the groom, and on this basis are related to the attempt to supply a structure of responsibility and care for the female members of the family. It is certainly not a unique custom by which a woman through separate contracts achieves the status of both sister and wife to her husband.

Speiser's attempt to relate this custom to the patriarchal stories is somewhat fanciful and need only be treated briefly. 1) As we saw in section D, Speiser tried to identify Milcah's marriage with (her uncle?) Nahor with the *mārtūti* contracts. Since Haran and Nahor were brothers, he also believes that the marriage could be classified under "brotherhood" contracts[214]! This however would not reflect even *his* interpretation of the *aḫātūti* contracts. What Speiser does not seem to understand about Gen 11 28 is that the relationships there, according to the narrative, are biological and the Nuzi relationships dealt with here are only legally contracted. 2) Similarly, Speiser tries to claim that Sarah must have been adopted by Terah and thus she qualified "as Abraham's sister in the broader sense of the term"[215]. This somehow makes her eligible for "sistership status" on the basis of the *aḫātūti* contracts "with all its attendant safeguards and privileges". In saying this Speiser not only ignores Gen 20 12 but he is also relating Abraham and Sarah to the *mārtūti* and the *aḫātūti* contracts at the same time!

We have already seen that the *aḫātūti* contracts did not confer special status, let alone make husbands into brothers. Even so, the most important objection to Speiser's interpretation is that he does violence to the biblical stories. The story element found in each of our passages in which the patriarch calls his wife, his sister, is

[214] Speiser, OBS, WS, 78.

[215] Ibid.

basically integrated into the stories as a motif of intended deception[216]. Each of the three stories in Genesis implies that if Sarah/Rebecca were in fact Abraham's/Isaac's sister, she could not be his wife, and each of the stories builds independently from that basis. If Speiser's understanding of Nuzi social practice were correct, then Nuzi or "Hurrian" society would be the one society which could not presuppose such a dichotomy.

The literary character of Gen 12 is particularly clear. The basic motif is that of "Despoiling the Egyptians"[217], which motif affects the treatment of every detail of the story. The story begins with the plot: Out of fear for his own safety, because of Sarah's beauty, Abraham plans to say that Sarah is his sister for two purposes: 1) that למען ייטב־לי בעבורך "it will go well for me for your sake" and 2) that his life will be safe. When they enter Egypt, the Egyptians do notice that Sarah is very beautiful[218]. The plan succeeds, and Pharaoh takes Sarah into his harem לאברם היטיב בעבורה "For Abram he made it go well for her sake". Thus Abraham became very rich. The story ends with Yahweh intervening, enabling Abraham to regain Sarah. If one were to assume that this literary superstructure was the result of misunderstanding what really happened, then where is there any indication that anything happened. What is the basis for connecting Gen 12 with Nuzi?

If the "events" did not happen as they are related in Genesis, far better "parallels" could be found to them than the *aḫātūti* contracts from Nuzi. The legendary material of the Near East is rich with examples of gods and heroes marying their "sisters", "sister", being used, as are other familial terms, in a very broad sense. Isis was the wife and "sister" of Osiris as Anat was of Baal. Kronos married his "sisters" Rhea and Dione[219], and the titans freely married

---

[216] This is even the case in Gen 20, where, although it was not a complete lie — Sarah was Abraham's half-sister — it served the function of deceiving the king. That Deuteronomy forbids the marriage of half-brothers and sisters (Deut 27 22; see also Lev 18 11f.) is seen by Gordon (The World of the Old Testament, 1958, 122f.) to favor the historicity of the "incident". This not only neglects II Sam 13 13 (and Ex 6 20 where Amram marries his father's sister), but also neglects to consider the literary tendency of the E tradition to see Abraham as a prophet and as an ideal hero who could neither lie nor sin. Similarly, sexual relationships between Sarah and Abimelech are explicitly denied. Even the innocence of Abimelech is stressed.

[217] G. W. Coats, Despoiling the Egyptians, VT 18 (1968), 450—457, esp. 453; see also C. A. Keller, Die Gefährdung der Ahnfrau, ZAW 66 (1954), 181—191.

[218] Cf. Iliad 24:765f.

[219] M. H. Pope, El in the Ugaritic Texts, 1955, 36.

their "sisters"[220]. One late Babylonian text lists successive gods who married their "mothers" and "sisters" such as Amakandu who married earth his "mother" and sea his "sister"[221]. Finally, there is the Demotic tale of Seton Chaemwese in which the girl Ahwere marries her older brother[222]. There are also several historical cases of men marrying their sisters; this was particularly true in Egypt from very early times[223], and has been thought to occur in Hatti[224] as well as possibly in Elam[225]. As interesting as actual marriages between brothers and sisters is the extremely common custom since the 18th Dynasty in Egypt of referring to one's wife as "sister" — a term of endearment[226]. This same use of the term "sister", as a term of endearment, is reflected in the Old Testament in the Canticle of Canticles:

---

220 Tethys married Okeanos; Theia married Hyperion, Phoebe married Kaios and Rheia married Kronos (W. G. Lambert and P. Walcot, A New Babylonian Theogony and Hesiod, Kadmos IV (1965), 72.

221 Ibid. 65f. Albright, Yahweh and the Gods, 81f.

222 E. Brunner-Traut, Altägyptische Märchen. Die Märchen der Weltliteratur, 1965², 175f.

223 We have no evidence from the Old Kingdom, but perhaps a majority of Eighteenth Dynasty pharaohs were married to their sisters or half sisters: Tao II, Ahmose, Amenhotep I, Thutmosis I, II, III, Amenhotep II and Thutmosis IV as well as Ramses II and Merneptah of the 19th dynasty (R. Middleton, Brother-Sister and Father-Daughter Marriage in Ancient Egypt, ASR 27, 1962, 60f.). The marriage of commoners with their sisters is not as certain. However, there seems to be two relatively clear and three doubtful cases from the Middle Kingdom (J. Černý, Consanguineous Marriages in Pharaonic Egypt, JEA 40, 1954, 23—29, esp. 29; R. Tanner, Klio BAG 49, 1967, 25). From the New Kingdom during the 22nd Dynasty, we have one certain case of a Libyan mercenary chieftain who married his sister (During reign of Sheshonk III, 823—772 B. C.); Černý 23f.; Middleton 605 and Tanner 25. In later periods, it becomes extremely common (cf. H. I. Bell, Brother and Sister Marriage in Graeco-Roman Egypt, RIDA 2, 1949, 83—92, and Pausanius, Att. VIII, 1).

224 H. Otten, Geschwisterehe, RLA III, 1964, 231; Das Königspaar Arnuwanda-Ašmunikal (scheint) jedoch als Kinder eines Königs Tutḫaliya auszuweisen. — which is forbidden in no. 29 of the Hittite laws; however, this is very doubtful.

225 F. W. König, Geschwisterehe in Elam, RLA III, 224—231. Koschaker's (ZA 33, 1941) and König's (Mutterrecht und Thronfolge im alten Elam, 1926, 529—552) treatments of this question are now too old to be dependable.

226 Černý, JEA 40 (1954), 24f.; G. Möller, Zwei ägyptische Eheverträge aus vorsaitischer Zeit, APAW 3, 1918, 14; S. Wenig, Die Frau im alten Ägypten, 1967, 22. Similarly, in the story of the Shipwrecked Sailor the snake refers to its wife as "little daughter". In one of the Aramaic papyri a slave girl who is manumitted is referred to as the "sister" of the son of the manumitter (R. Yaron, Introduction to the Law of the Aramaic Papyri, 1961, 45).

5 1aα "I am come into my garden, my sister, my spouse." and 5 2bα "Open to me, my sister, my love."

None of these examples, however, inclines one to suspect that they might reflect the "real history" of Gen 12. 20 or 26.

F. GEN 24

The *aḫātūti* contracts have also been related to the story of Rebekah's marriage in Gen 24, which, it is claimed, because of the "dominant" role played by Rebekah's brother Laban, reflects the type of fratriarchy which was thought to be found in the Nuzi tablets[227]. Speiser has argued that the story in Chapter 24 of Genesis is so remarkably similar to a Nuzi *aḫātūti* contract, that it could not have been invented, but must reflect the Nuzi type of marriage agreement[228]. Of the five constitutive elements of a "sistership" contract, only the last, the penalty clause — which in any case does not have a place in a story like Rebekah's — is missing from Genesis. "What we have ... is virtually a restatement, in suitable literary form, of such a 'sistership' document"[229]. These five clauses he gives as follows:

a. The principal in the case
b. Nature of the transmission
c. Details of Payment
d. Girl's declaration of concurrence
e. Penalty clause

When due allowance is made for the literary form of Gen 24, Speiser identifies, on the basis of these similarities, the marriage of Rebekah as a Nuzi sistership contract.

Before investigating the clauses in detail, it should be noticed that the most characteristic clause of the Nuzi *Aḫātūti* contracts — that which confers the right to give the girl in marriage to another[230] — is left out of Speiser's schema. The only *aḫātūti* contract that this schema resembles is HSS V 69 (in conjunction with HSS V 25, ll. 11f.).

---

227 C. H. Gordon, אלהים in its Reputed Meaning of Rulers, Judges, JBL 54 (1935), 226 and note 20; World of the OT, 124f.; R. de Vaux, Les Institutions, 37; J. Holt, Patriarchs of Israel, 111—114; E. Speiser, OBS, WS, 79f.; Genesis 93f. 182—185; and Weir, Arch and OT Study, 77.

228 Speiser, Genesis, 184f. Holt (Patriarchs 113) says that this is part of the "shared culture with the Hurrians we know from Nuzi, where fratriarchy . . . is amply attested".

229 Speiser ibid.

230 See above p. 240.

a. The principals of the "contract" in Genesis are, according to Speiser, Abraham's servant and Laban: "The transaction is thus necessarily of the 'sistership' type, since it is the girl's brother who acts on the request"[231]. But this is not correct for several different reasons: 1) As we have seen in Section E, that a brother is the principal in a Nuzi contract does not by that fact make it a "sistership" type of agreement. Brothers have also given their sisters *ana mārtūti* and *aššūti*, as well as *ana amtūti* ("into slavery")! 2) Conversely, not all *ana aḫātūti* agreements involve the brother of the girl[232]. 3) The servant represents not Isaac, but Isaac's father Abraham. In no *aḫātūti* contract does a man adopt a girl to be married to his son — though this does occur in the *ana mārtūti* and the *ana aššūti* contracts which are known throughout the Near East. 4) Finally, it must be questioned whether Laban really is a principal in this "contract", and whether he is so obviously a "fratriarch". In Gen 24 15. 24. 47 and 25 19 Rebekah is referred to as the daughter of Bethuel. The only place in the story of Gen 24 that Laban acts independently is in vv. 29-31, where he takes care of the servant's camels! v. 50: "Laban and Bethuel spoke in reply", does betray some uncertainty in our text (cf. Gen 29 5)[233], and the following references may well suggest that Bethuel does not belong here[234]. Nevertheless, vv. 53. 55 and 57f. do not present Laban as the principal but rather "her brother and her mother". This does not reflect a special type of structure of society. An Old Babylonian contract, dated to the 14th year of Ammiditana, reflects the same kind of arrangement of a mother and a brother exercising patriarchal authority — here in a contract *ana mārtūti ù kallatūti*:

> 1 (Frau) Narubtum, Tochter des Iltāni, die Iltāni, ihre Mutter, und Adad-šarrum, ihr Bruder, in das Haus des Šamaš-liwwir, Sohnes des Rīš-Šamaš, als Schwiegertochter und Tochter hineingingen, als ihre *terḫatu* hat 5 Sekel Silber Šamaš-liwwir der Iltāni, ihrer Mutter, und dem Adad-šarrum ihrem Bruder, dargewogen[235].

Nor is it correct to argue that, because Laban has an important role to play in the marriage of his sister, this reflects a fratiarchal society. A large number of Near Eastern texts show that the brother, particularly the eldest son of the father, holds a very important position in regard to his sisters[236]. This is characteristic of patriarchal

---

231 Genesis 185.

232 Cf. HSS XIII 15 where it is the girl's father who gives her *ana aḫātūti*.

233 Von Rad, Das erste Buch Mose, 210.

234 However, the reference in v. 28 to "her mother's house" is no evidence for "matriarchy" (cf. v. 67).

235 J. Kohler, Ham. Ges. VI, text 1419.

236 E. g., one OB text (Kohler Ham. Ges. III, 6, text 8) where a brother and a sister give their sister away in marriage. See also the OB marriage contract BM 78296,

authority, and specifically does not reflect what we know about fratriarchy. What is spoken of as fratriarchy in the Old Testament and the ancient Near East are all natural concommitants of a patriarchal society[237].

Fratriarchy is not simply the recognition of the importance of the brother of a girl who was still a member of her father's household. Rather, it is an essential feature of the organization of matrilineal kinship, and directly antipathetic to patriarchy. It refers to the "power and influence of the mother's brother" (not the daughter's brother, i. e., the son!):

> In (the matrilineal) organization he was the head, or at least the administrator of the family. It was he who held the potestas. Nor was he ousted from that position when the husband came to reside with his wife, nay even when the husband was the acknowledged master of the house or tent . . . even when the father-right is dominant, the mother's brother . . . has undoubted rights and privileges in regard to her and her children, which we are justified in regarding as survivals of a much more extensive jurisdiction. A third characteristic of mother-right is succession to property or to dignities from the mother to her children or through her from her brother to her children[238].

Fratriarchy has nothing to do with the son sharing in the authority over his father's family. Fratriarchal authority is the authority which a brother has over his sister after she is married, and particularly the authority which he has over his sister's children. If Laban were Rebekah's maternal uncle, and if there were other male members of Rebekah's family who were either brothers, father, or paternal uncles to Rebekah, only then could we possibly say that we have some evidence of residual fratriarchy. However, in both the story of Genesis, whether Bethuel is alive or dead, as well as in the Nuzi tablets, we have aspects of patriarchal authority alone.

b. Nature of the Transaction: Speiser derives the nature of the transaction in Gen 24 on the basis of (a), The Principals in the case,

in which the brother is made responsible for the word of the bride (J. J. Finkelstein, ANETS, 544, text no. 8). In two old Assyrian texts it is implied that the brothers of the wife have significant rights that must be considered (G. Eisser and J. Lewy, Die Altassyrischen Rechtsurkunden vom Kültepe, text 1 and 3, p. 1—3). In the Neobabylonian records, mention should be made of one text, dated to the eighth year of the reign of Cyrus, where the brother gives his sister in marriage (Kohler and Peiser, Babylonisches Rechtsleben, II 7f.). In only one of the marriage contracts of the Aramaic Papyri does the father give away the bride (R. Yaron, Aramaic Papyri, 44). See further on this point, especially as regards the OB Period: Cuq, Droit Babylonien, 23.

237 C. H. Gordon: "All the fratriarchal elements in the OT seem to be developments within patriarchy." (Fratriarchy in the Old testament, JBL 54, 1935, 231).

238 Emphasis added; from: Hartland, Matrilineal Kinship, and the Question of its Priority, MAAA 17 (1917) — in reference to the Sioux American Indian tribes.

which we have seen is not correct; nor is it the case at Nuzi. There, the nature of the transaction is stated explicitly: NN gives his sister *ana mārtūti*, *ana aššūti*, or *ana aḫātūti*. If clause (b) is to be found in Gen 24, it is in vv. 48 and 51, where the purpose and intention of the persons involved is made explicit. The explicit intention of Abraham's servant is: לקחת את־בת־אחי אדני לבנו "to take the daughter of my master's brother for his son", and that of Laban and Bethuel is expressed: הנה־רבקה ליפנך קח ולך ותהי אשה לבן־אדניך "Here, Rebekah is before you, take her and go, and she will be the wife of the son of your master". The intention of the agreement is on one hand that Abraham's son receive (obviously, for purposes of marriage) the daughter of Bethuel. That she is also the sister of Laban has nothing to do with the nature of the contract. On the other hand, it is the expressed intention of Laban and Bethuel to give Rebekah as a wife (the akkadian would have to be *ana aššūti!*) to the son of Abraham and to this end the agreement is made through the servant with Abraham. In no way does this reflect the *ana aḫātūti* contracts of Nuzi.

c. Details of payment: "The emissary gives presents to the girl, but does not neglect the gifts for her brother and mother which must cover the customary bride payment"[239]. In the Ancient Near East, gifts were often given at a marriage, but these were not necessarily related to the *terḫatu* or "bride price"[240]. v. 53 emphasizes the gifts which were given to Rebekah, which surely cannot be equated with the *terḫatu*. The other gifts are given to Rebekah's brother and mother. These also cannot be identified with the *terḫatu* if the text is to be related to the Nuzi *aḫātūti* contracts, since then, Rebekah's mother would have no claim to such a payment.

It might also be mentioned in passing, that, according to Speiser, the payment in the *aḫātūti* contracts is supposed to be made in the ceremonial form of 1 ox, 1 ass, and 10 sheep.

d) Girl's declaration of Concurrence: While, as we have seen above in section E, the declaration of the girl is characteristic of the *aḫātūti* contracts, it is in itself only significant in contrast to the more common *ṭuppi mārtūti* agreements. That a woman would have some say about her marriage is not at all uncommon in the Near

---

239 Speiser, Genesis, 185.

240 So Gadd 31 mentions a gift to the value of 15 shekels which the bride gives to her husband. In Egyptian marriages jewelry was commonly given to the bride by the husband, which gifts would be returned to the husband if the couple were divorced. Cf. E. Lüddeckens, Ägyptische Eheverträge, ÄgAb, I (1960), passim; and Pestman, Marriage, 13. See further Mendelsohn, Marriage in Alalakh, 353f., and Falk, Hebrew Law, 151.

East[241]. This is implied in Egyptian marriages not only by the fact that the woman could unilaterally divorce her husband, but also by the fact that some Egyptian marriages are contracted not by the man but by the woman herself[242], as well as by the expression *iri ḥy* "to take a husband"[243]. Paragraph 156 of the Code of Hammurapi uses the phrase that occurs often in the Old Babylonian contracts: "that the man of her choice may marry her", which implies something more than complete passivity on the part of the woman. In one text from Sippar, a marriage contract is recorded in the normal manner, except that the bride herself receives and acknowledges the brideprice[244]. This consultation of the bride might also be reflected in Judges 14 7f.

However, a much more serious objection to seeing the consultation of Rebekah as reflecting the declaration clause of the woman in the Nuzi *aḫātūti* contracts is the simple observation that, in our story at least, Rebekah is not consulted as to whether she will marry Isaac! Rebekah is not asked whether she consents to the marriage; that has already been decided the day before[245]. Rather her consent (אלך: "I will go") is to leaving her family without delay, without remaining even ten days (vv. 54d-58)!

The only point at which the suggested interpretation of Speiser and others can be affirmed is that clause (e) the Penalty Clause finds no echo in Genesis. Since Gen 24 is a story, it may well be questionable whether it can be legitimately compared with any legal contract; that it cannot be compared with the *aḫātūti* contracts of Nuzi, is, however, clear.

G. GEN 16 21 1-21 and 29 31—30 24

The Nuzi text HSS V 67 was published in 1929 and translated in 1930[246]:

---

[241] J. Neubauer, Beiträge zur Geschichte des biblisch-talmudischen Eheschließungsrechts, MVÄG 24, 1920, 22 and 34; S. Allam, BiOr 26 (1969), 155—159; M. Burrows, Basis of Israelite Marriage, 24f.

[242] E. g., Pap. Berlin 3078 (493/492 B. C.): "(Es) hat gesagt (die) Frau *'Is-ḫb* . . . Gemacht hast du (mich zur) Ehefrau etc. . . ." (Lüddecken, Eheverträge, 18f.; as also the Pap. Libbey (387 B. C.): ibid. 23.

[243] Pestman, Marriage, 11 and n. 3.

[244] Schorr, Zivil- und Prozessrecht, text 2, p. 7f. Texts 1. 2 and 3, from Nippur, also state that the bride has the right to divorce the husband, which would imply her consent to the marriage. Contrast p. 8f.

[245] The division of the action here is particularly marked. See D. Irvin, Mytharion, 34f.

[246] AASOR X no. 2, p. 31f.

Tablet of adoption belonging to [Zigi] son of Akkuya; his son Šenni[ma] as son to Šu[rihil he has given.] And Šu[rihil], as far as Šennima is concerned, all these lands, his earnings, whatever their description, one (portion) of it all to Šennima he has given. If Šurihil has a son (of his own,) firstborn (he shall be;) a double share he shall take. Šennima shall then be second and according to his allotment his inheritance share he shall take. As long as Šurihil is alive, Šennima shall serve him. When Šurihil [dies,] Šennima shall become h[eir.] Further, Gilimninu as wife to Šennima has been given. If Gilimninu bears (children,) Šennima shall not take another wife; and if Gilimninu does not bear, Gilimninu a woman of the Lullu as wife for Šennima shall take. As for (the concubine's) offspring, Gilimninu shall [not] send (them) away. Any sons that out of the womb of Gilimninu [to Še]nnima may be bor[n, all the] lands, buildings, [whatever their description,] to (these) sons are given. [In case] she does not bear [a s]on, then the daughter of Gilim[ninu of] the lands and buildings one portion shall take. As for Šurihil, another son in addition to Šennima he shall not adopt.

Whoever among them breaks [the contract] shall furnish one mina of silver and one mina of gold.

Moreover, Yalampa as handmaid to Gilimninu has been given, and Šatimninu for supervision has been assigned. As long as she is alive, she (Yalampa) shall se[rve her;] and Šatimninu [. . .] shall not annul.

If Gilimninu bears (children) and Šennima takes another wife, her "bundle" she shall pick up and she shall leave.

As early as 1933 Speiser pointed out the similarity that this contract had with Gen 16. 21 and 29f.[247]. and his interpretation has been generally followed with some amplification[248]. The main grounds for the similarity that has been claimed between this text, which Speiser speaks of as a contract that "might have been written for Abraham and Sarah"[249], and the biblical stories are: 1) That the husband cannot take a second wife unless his wife fails to bear him children[250].

---

[247] E. A. Speiser, AASOR 13 (1933), 44.

[248] E. g., R. Pfeiffer, Annual Report of the Smithsonian Institution I (1935), 554; Gordon, Parallèles Nouziens aux lois et coutumes de l'ancien Testament, RB 44 (1935), 35; BA 3 (1940), 3; M. Burrows, The Ancient Oriental Background of Hebrew Levirate Marriage, BASOR 77 (1940), 2f.; R. O'Callaghan, CBQ 6 (1944), 398; R. de Vaux, RB 56 (1949), 26—28; H. H. Rowley, BJRL (1949/1950), 74f.; J. Bright, Hist. of Israel, 71; C. H. Gordon, Adventures, 118f.; The World of the OT 115. 118 and 123; R. de Vaux, Les Institutions, 46; S. Kardiman, Adoption as a Remedy for Infertility in the Period of the Patriarchs, JSS 3 (1958), 123—126; E. A. Speiser, Nuzi, IDB, 574; J. Gray, Archaeology and the Old Testament World, 1962, 37; Speiser, Genesis, 119—121. 157 and 230; J. Holt, The Pat. of Israel, 102ff.; Weir, Arch and OT Study, 75; F. C. Fensham, The Son of a Handmaid in Northwest Semitic, VT 19 (1969), 312—321.

[249] AASOR XIII 44; see also Genesis 120.

[250] Ibid. Except for Speiser, most commentators ignore this first provison, which ommission has led, as we shall see, to considerable distortion in the understanding of the social purpose of this practice.

2) If the wife fails to bear children she has the obligation to provide the husband with a concubine. This is the primary basis for the comparison with Genesis[251]. Rowley points out that a foreign slave is specified in HSS V 67, making the observation that Hagar, an Egyptian, was also a foreign slave[252]. 3a) That the wife could not expel the children of the concubine (some say without justification: the concubine and her children) from the home[253]. This has led most authors to support a type of dispensation theory to explain Gen 21. On the basis of the Nuzi tablets the concubine could not be sent away. Abraham, however, did send Hagar away. Therefore, "it was necessary for God to give Abraham a special dispensation to allow this"[254]. or 3b) That the wife has the authority over and legal rights to the offspring of the concubine[255]. It is important to note that clauses 3a and 3b are mutually exclusive. 3a is based on v. 22 of HSS V 67 as it is transliterated and translated in AASOR X: "As for (the concubine's) offspring, Gilimninu shall [not] send (them) away". *(ù še-ir-ri Gi-li-im-ni-nu l[a] ú-ma-ar)*. In his Genesis commentary[256], though, Speiser transliterates this line *u šerri Gilimninu-ma uwâr*[257], which he translates: "Gilimninu herself shall have authority over the offspring". If 3b is the correct reading then 3a can have nothing to do with Nuzi. Speiser, nevertheless, argues that the inclusion of 3a is supported by CH no. 146 and Deut 21 14[258].

Until recently almost no one offered any objection to this proposed parallel[259]. In a brief article in 1968, however, J. van Seters objects

251 See above note 243. Almost all commentators stress this obligation strongly.

252 Rowley, BJRL (1949/1950), 74f.

253 Instead of this clause, Speiser said in AASOR, 1933, that the bride was obligated to treat the concubine humanely. This is not mentioned in his later references to the parallel and is implicitly denied in his Genesis 121. I see no basis for it in the Nuzi contracts. It is possibly partially derived from Gen 16.

254 As quoted from Gordon, Adventures, 119; or, BA 3 (1940), 3: "Doubtless Sarah was not acting within her rights, for a divine dispensation is required to permit the unwilling Abraham to comply."

255 Speiser, IDB, 574; Genesis 121.

256 Ibid.

257 On the basis of the Chiera copy, either *la* or *ma* is possible, since the text is damaged at this point, enabling only the final wedge to be read, which, however, could form part of either syllable.

258 Genesis 121.

259 J. Hempel (Zusammenfassung und Einzelforschung in der Archäologie, ZAW 70, 1958, 168) suggested that Gen 16 could just as well be explained by CH 146. But this is said only in passing. CH 146 is normally excluded from consideration because Old Babylonian law supposedly restricts the custom of taking a concubine to specific temple personell (cf. de Vaux, RB 56, 1949, 26—28, and J. van Seters, JBL 87, 1968, 403f.).

to the Nuzi parallel and indicates three specific points where he sees the Nuzi text to be different from Genesis: 1) That the children of the slave-girl do not become the children of Gilimninu: "The fact that the slave-girl's children could not inherit equally with Kilim-ninu's children clearly indicates that they have no relationship to her"[260]. 2) The slave-girl in the Nuzi text is not the personal maid of Gilimninu, as is clearly shown in ll. 35ff. 3) That HSS V 67 is an adoption contract, in which the groom is adopted by his father-in-law, gives a special context to the Nuzi contract — which does not exist in the Genesis stories — and explains the terms concerning the inheritance.

Van Seters rather proposes a text like that from 7th century Nimrud as far closer to the customs presupposed by Genesis[261].

Unfortunately van Seters' arguments are not well tested and fail to convince. It could well be argued that van Seters' first objection does more to support than to injure the Nuzi parallel since Ishmael is also clearly not Sarah's child. Nevertheless, van Seters has pointed out an inconsistency that exists, however, not between Nuzi and Genesis, but between the different stories of Genesis. Second, that the slave girl is not the personal maid of Gilimninu is a discrepancy, and van Seters does well to point it out, but it is not clear that it makes any significant difference in judging our parallel, since, in HSS V 67, it is Gilimninu who supplies the maid. It should not go unnoticed, moreover, that the Nimrud text favored by van Seters also does not satisfy these first two objections. Van Seters' third objection on the basis of the context of the proposed parallel is perhaps the most significant point he makes. However, his own neglect of the context not only of this tablet but also of the Old Babylonian laws, leads him to commit similar errors in his alternative proposal. The question, as we shall see, cannot be simply put whether certain First Millenium texts are closer to the Genesis stories than the Nuzi or Old Babylonian texts. Moreover, we are not dealing with earlier and later forms of a custom in a process of development. Rather, we are dealing with individual situations within a social context of polygamy. HSS V 67 does not reflect a law or custom which determines the type of clauses that are there specified. It is rather an individual agreement, that reflects more the relative influence and intention of Zigi and Šurihil than the practice of a people. To a certain extent because of this I will later argue that the Old Babylonian laws and contracts, the Nuzi contracts, as well as the Nimrud text, all help to some extent in understanding the stories in

---

260 Ibid. 405. J. van Seters here follows Speiser's AASOR reading of clause 3a.

261 Ibid. 407. A discussion of this text will be reserved for later.

Gen 16. 21 and 29f., but that none of them can be considered in a strict sense as parallel to the biblical tales, nor be offered as the background in which these tales are to be understood.

A reevaluation of this parallel is perhaps best begun by reference to our biblical texts, for they do not readily present themselves as reflecting the coherent and consistent custom that is presupposed by those who favor the Nuzi parallel. There is nevertheless a relative consistency in the various biblical traditions, and certain common presuppositions become clear particularly when we stress the myriad differences from the Nuzi contract that they betray.

(1) Fundamental to the contractual arrangement of HSS V 67 is that the concubine is given to the husband by his wife to prevent him from taking a second wife — perhaps more accurately: as a concession to what is thought to be his right to progeny in a society that normally accepted polygamy. It is a clause in the marriage contract which protects or defines the future status of the wife. Gen 16 and 21, however, do not seem to presuppose such an agreement[262]. On the contrary, there is much — albeit drawn from originally independent traditions — that argues against the existence of such an agreement: Nahor, Abraham's brother, according to Gen 22 20-24, had eight children by his first wife; nevertheless, he took a concubine who bore Nahor four further children. Either Nahor did not live according to what Speiser calls Hurrian law, or the clause: "If Gilimninu bears (children), Šennima shall not take another wife" does not represent binding law or custom, but only individual agreement.

(2) That the wife, in the case of sterility, is obliged to give her handmaid to her husband might perhaps be seen to resemble the troubles of Sarah and Rachel, but that this is the custom reflected in the biblical stories is contradicted by the example of Leah who gives her handmaid to Jacob not because of sterility — she had already had four children by him — but in order to give him more children. The motivation of the women in the Genesis stories is moreover not that of the Nuzi tablet. The concubine is not given as a concession to the husband's right to progeny, or even to prevent the husband from taking further wives. The wives are rather trying to overcome — if only vicariously — the shame[263] of their own lack of fertility, and, in the case of Leah, to win the love of her husband.

(3) As in HSS V 67, but contrary to the opinion of the commentators[264], the children that are borne by the maids are not attributed

---

[262] Jacob's agreement with Laban not to take further wives is made after he already has 11 sons — and has nothing to do with the question of the handmaids.

[263] See I Sam 1 6 and Gen 30 1-3.

[264] Particularly Weir, Arch and OT Study, 75.

to the wives. In Gen 30 20 Leah says: "I have borne him six (not eight) sons; it is not until the birth of Joseph by Rachel herself that Rachel's disgrace is removed (Gen 30 23), and the children of Rachel are the children she herself bore: Joseph and Benjamin. In Gen 21 10f., Sarah could hardly be more explicit that she did not consider Ishmael her son[265].

Gen 16 6 indeed shows that Sarah has authority over Hagar, but Gen 21 14 (and this is not to be harmonized with Gen 16) shows that the authority to send Hagar and the boy away belongs to Abraham.

There is no doubt that the children were already recognized as the biological children of Abraham and Jacob. As H. Donner has clearly shown[266], we are not dealing with adoption in Gen 16. 21 and 29f., but rather with a type of legitimation[267]. The question is about inheritance — whether the sons borne by the handmaids will be recognized as the direct descendents of the patriarchs. Jacob's children were, but Abraham's were not. On the other hand, whether this has any significance at all for the history of real law in the Near East must remain extremely doubtful, for the inheritance of the sons of Jacob and the disinheritance of the sons of Abraham are both for the same reason. But that reason is literary: The 12 tribes of Israel are heirs to the promise of Abraham; namely, the Davidic empire. Such dominating literary motivations of our stories make any history of law based on these stories extremely tenuous, and perhaps ultimately impossible.

(4) According to HSS V 67, if Gilimninu were herself to bear children after the birth of children by the handmaid "all the lands, buildings, [whatever their description] to (these) sons are given", that is, they are to be the heirs to the exclusion of the slave's children. In Gen 29f., however, not only are the children of the handmaids accepted among the heirs of Jacob, but Rachel's children are counted as the youngest. Moreover, if such a contract as HSS V 67 lay behind the story of Gen 21, as suggested by Speiser, the fear of Sarah that Ishmael might also be Abraham's heir (v. 10) would be groundless.

(5) A very minor, probably insignificant, difference between this contract and the Genesis stories is that Hagar, Bilhah and Zilpah are all, like Yalampa, the maids of their mistresses, in contrast to the

---

265 Gen 30 3 "upon the knees" does not signify adoption as claimed by Neufeld, Anc Heb Mar Laws, 125f., and E. A. Speiser, Genesis, 230. See H. Donner, Oriens Antiquus 8 (1969), 106f.

266 Ibid. 104—109.

267 Falk's speculation (Testate Succession in Jewish Law, JJS 12, 1961, 72) that Hebrew society did not have the concept of legitimacy, because they were not aware of the ovum, is not to be taken seriously.

foreign slave-girl of HSS V 67. That Hagar is an Egyptian is not an important parallel to the Nuzi contract, since the maids of Rachel and Leah are not foreigners.

(6) Rachel and Leah do not send the children of their maids away; nor does Sarah in Gen 16; in Gen 21, however, Abraham does. On the basis of one reading of the Nuzi contract it must be admitted that Gilmninu could not have sent her competitor's children away. This is so obviously a discrepancy between the stories of Genesis and Nuzi, that only a belief that there were other parallels between the patriarchal stories and the Nuzi tablets, or a belief that the patriarchs did live according to Hurrian type law, could enable one to ignore it. The idea that the speech of Elohim represents a "divine dispensation" can only be countered with the all too obvious argument that we have no other example of an ancient Near Eastern contractual arrangement being countermanded by a divinity. The sending away of Ishmael has much more in common with Judges 11 1-3 than with Nuzi. Both Jephthah and Ishmael are sent away for the same reason: to keep them from possible future inheritance, and, in the case of Jephthah there is no question, and certainly no need, of divine intervention[268].

(7) Finally, Gen 21, is farthest from the Nuzi contracts, and from the consideration of any possible legal parallels, in that Abraham, in sending Hagar and the boy away, abandons them to wander in the desert. This makes no sense whatever in any legal context, but is a typical example of the literary motif: Cruelly treated or abandoned child, a motif that is quite common in Near Eastern literature[269]. Indeed, the story of the rescue (of Hagar and Ishmael) follows a pattern that is paralleled in at least 13 other extra-biblical ancient Near Eastern legends[270].

Similar inadequacies in the prevailing interpretation become apparent through an examination of the Nuzi contracts themselves. A serious distortion of the significance of HSS V 67 has been created by the almost exclusive dependence on and isolated use of it in the discussion of what is supposedly Nuzi custom. We have already seen that one of the central clauses of HSS V 67 has been rendered in two radically different ways; l. 22: "As for the offspring, Gilimninu shall not send them away", and "Gilimninu herself shall have authortity over the offspring", and that the choice of the translation significantly

---

268 On Judg 11 1ff. see M. David, Adoptie in het oude Israel, MKNAW 18 (1955), 90—93, esp. 91; also with care J. Feigin, Some Cases of Adoption in Israel, JBL 50 (1931), 186ff.

269 Cf. the "Plot-Motif Table" under S: Unnatural Cruelty, in D. Irvin's Mytharion.

270 Cf. "Traditional Epiphany Episode Table", ibid.

affects the supposed parallel with Genesis. Unfortunately, texts from Nuzi that are similar to HSS V 67 do not have either of these proposed clauses, and a judgement on the basis of comparative witness is not possible. These other texts do help us however in understanding the other clauses of the contract and render a decidedly different picture than has been customary. To my knowledge only Mendelsohn[271], who is aware of other Nuzi contracts similar to HSS V 67, has given an adequate presentation of the significance of these contracts: "The stipulation restricting the husband from marrying a second wife was probably inserted in all marriage contracts of well-to-do brides where the girl's father was in a position to impose such a pledge on his future son-in-law. The reason underlying it was, of course, to safeguard the status of the woman in the household and to spare her the humiliation of sharing the husband with a rival wife[272]." This judgement is borne out by several contracts from Nuzi, and indeed fits HSS V 67 admirably. We are not dealing with codified law or even necessarily custom, but rather with individual legally acceptable efforts of the bride's family — made possible by the contractual nature of marriage in the Near East — to deal with the undesirable effects of polygamy. The differences in the strictness of these several clauses may well be explained by the relative influence and the variable intentions of the principals in the contract. HSS V 67 is an agreement between Šurihil and Šennima according to which Šennima agrees not to take another wife if Gilimninu (probably the daughter of Šurihil) bears him children. The concession is made on the other side, however, that if Gilimninu does not bear children, she will supply Šennima with a slave girl for a concubine. In any case, the sons of Gilimninu will be the heirs to all of the property. Even a daughter will receive a share of the inheritance. A similar clause is found in HSS V 80[273]: "If Beltakkadummi bears a son, Hurazzi another wife shall not take. If Beltakkadummi a son does not bear, Hurazzi may take another wife *(aššata šanīta ileqqe)*." However, no mention is made of a slave girl or of a concubine; nor that it is the wife's obligation to supply her husband with a second wife; it is agreed that Beltakkadummi shall be Hurazzi's only wife, unless she proves to be childless.

AASOR XVI 55 also limits the husband to one wife: "And Zilikkušu another wife in addition to Haluya shall not take." (ll. 29f.) In this contract, no mitigation of the requirement is made, apparently because Haluya has already borne a daughter to

[271] Marriage in Alalakh 355—357.

[272] Ibid. 355.

[273] AASOR X no. 26, p. 59f.

Zilikkušu. It may well be supposed that if Haluya bore no other children, this daughter, Kanzuššalli, is intended as the heir.

HSS IX 24[274] stipulates that the husband Zigi is not allowed to take a second wife; nor is he allowed to take a concubine. No concessions are given, and his wife's eldest child is to be his heir. The strictness of this contract may perhaps be explained by the status of the bride, who is Šuwarhepa, the sister of Šilwatešup, son of the king[275].

Equally strict is Gadd 51, according to which Wullu is forbidden to take a second wife, and no concession is made in case there are no children. However, the girl's father is in a particularly strong position since he has adopted Wullu as his heir, and the punishment for breaking this aspect of the contract is the loss of the inheritance.

Gadd 12 is particularly noteworthy because in this contract the husband is not forbidden to take a second wife, nor is he forbidden to take a concubine. Nevertheless, the status of his first wife is assured by the stipulation that only her children will be the husband's heirs.

JEN 666 and 671 are also important to an understanding of this clause, since they make it clear that the son of a concubine — provided that he had not been especially recognized as heir — had no claims whatever to his father's property. The two tablets form the record of a litigation in which Mušteia son of the woman Zilikiaše claimed a right to the inheritance of his father Tarmiia. His suit was objected to by Tarmiia's brother on the grounds that Zilikiaše was not the wife, but only the concubine *(ḫarimtu)* of Tarmiia. Since the opposing litigant was the brother of Tarmiia, it may well be supposed that Tarmiia had no other sons than Mušteiia. Nevertheless, Mušteiia was not recognized as heir.

An examination of other ancient Near Eastern contracts and even some codified laws shows us that the concerns met with in the Nuzi records are also reflected elsewhere, and that there is no indication that these few contracts from Nuzi display a special type of social value or legal principle. These other records, along with the Nuzi tablets, form the general legal background in which, but not according to which, the Genesis stories become understandable. We will also see that the possibility of establishing a chronological development on the basis of the variations of the form of these clauses as attempted by van Seters, so that we might suggest at least a relative chronology for our biblical stories, may well have to be excluded;

---

274 Gordon, AnOr 12 (1935), 171f.

275 Mendelsohn (Marriage at Alalakh 355) limits this restriction to the lifetime of Šuwarhepa. This may well in fact be true, but it is not in the contract.

for the variations, in the terms of the contract or the legal code, is determined more by immediate concern that by custom: a concern for the position of the wife; for the protection of the concubine; for the questions of inheritance; or for the right of the husband to progeny. Any specific contract or legal codification may address itself to but one or more of these concerns, but when we have several records from a single period, we find, as at Nuzi, that a "typical" custom characteristic of this period cannot be described. Van Seters' attempt, then, to see the Genesis stories as reflecting more the practice of the First Millenium than that of the early Second Millenium rests on the very weak basis that there are fewer clear discrepancies between the biblical stories and the very difficult to understand Nimrud contract than between the biblical stories and the clear and detailed Nuzi contract, but this fact alone does not make the Nimrud text more amenable as a parallel.

From as early as the laws of Ur-Nammu (c. 2100 B. C.) we find attempts to deal with some of the difficulties that arise directly out of the practice of polygamy, in this case the possible confict between the wife and the concubine. No. 23, unfortunately, is not complete: "If a man's slave-woman, comparing herself to her mistress, struck her . . . (rest of text missing)". But No. 22 tells us the punishment alloted for a somewhat lesser offense: "If a man's slave woman, comparing herself to her mistress, speaks insolently to her, her mouth shall be scoured with 1 quart of salt[276]."

No. 25 of the Lipit Ištar Code (early 19th century B. C.)[277] addresses itself to the problem of inheritance in the case that a man has sons both by a wife and by a concubine whose children have been granted their freedom. The decision is that the children of the concubine, in that case, will not divide the estate with the children of the wife, similar to what is specifically contracted in Gadd 12. An almost identical law is found in the Sumerian Laws No. 14 (c. 1800 B. C.)[278]. No. 18, however, considers the possibility that the wife is childless but that the husband had children by a harlot off the streets. The children of the harlot w o u l d in this case be his heirs (all the more so, we might suppose, if she were a concubine)[279]. The rights of the wife are also considered, in that, as long as the wife lives, the harlot is not allowed to live in the house, though she is to be supported[280].

---

[276] J. J. Finkelstein, The Laws of Ur-Nammu, ANETS 525.

[277] S. N. Kramer, Lipit-Ishtar, ANET 160; Falk, Hebrew Law, 163.

[278] H. Gressmann AOT^2, 411.

[279] Contrast, for instance, the court decision in JEN 666 and 671 where the son of the concubine is not recognized as heir.

[280] Gressman, AOT^2, 411.

From the Old Assyrian period, we have three marriage contracts which have clauses similar to those we have seen in the Nuzi tablets. Two are much alike: I 490[281] and ICK 3[282]. These are marriage contracts of Assyrian merchants. The first one states that, besides his wife in Aššur, the husband cannot take another. The second contract allows that in the city the husband may take a *qadištum*. In the country, however, he is limited to his wife Ḫatala. Both contracts state that if — within a certain period (the one three years, the other two) — the wife remains childless, the husband will take a concubine. One states that the husband will purchase the concubine himself. The other that the maidservant will be supplied by the wife and then, after the child is born, immediately sold by the wife. A third contract[283] is a marriage contract that states simply that the husband will not take a second wife; and if he does, he must pay one mina of silver. No concession is contracted in the case that the wife is childless, and, as we have seen in the Nuzi texts, it need not be supposed that any is intended. In these three contracts we find almost as much variety as in the Nuzi material.

From the Old Babylonian period there is considerably more variety, as well as a much clearer picture of what is involved in these contracts. Especially helpful are Nos. 144—147 of the Code of Hammurapi[284]. It is true that these laws have been excluded by some from comparison with the Nuzi tablets and the stories in Genesis, because apparently Old Babylonian society "restricted this expediency of using a slave girl in order to have children to priestesses who must remain childless by law"[285]. In Nuzi and the Old Testament, however, the practice is not so restricted. However, this interpretation, particularly of Nos. 144f. is somewhat distorted. Moreover, that Nos. 144—147 refer to the problems of hierodules does not mean that they do not reflect more general practice. That the class of people explicitly referred to are hierodules does not create any (for our purposes) significant legal implications. Further, that the practice extends to a group much broader than is specifically referred to in this law is clear both from other paragraphs of the code as well as from private contracts[286].

---

281 J. Lewy, On some Institutions of the Old Assyrian Empire, HUCA 27 (1956), 6—8.

282 Ibid. 9f.; also see H. Hirsch, Eine Kleinigkeit zur Heiratsurkunde ICK 1, 3, Orientalia 35 (1966), 279, and J. J. Finkelstein, ANETS, 543.

283 TC 67: Eisser and Lewy, Urkunden aus Kültepe, 1f.

284 T. J. Meek, Hammurapi Code, ANET 171f.

285 J. van Seters, JBL (1968), 404.

286 For a discussion of these passages in the CH see A. Jeremias, Das alte Testament im Lichte des alten Orients, 1906, 355—357; B. Meissner, Assyriologische Studien,

Paragraphs 144 and 145 of the Code of Hammurapi deal not so much with the use of a concubine for bearing children — that this can be done is taken for granted — but rather with the problem of whether, when a man's wife is a "hierodule" and therefore childless, he can take a second wife, a "lay priestess" who can give him children. No. 145 states that he can unless his first wife the "hierodule" had provided him with children (namely, by means of a slave girl). The text here does not restrict itself to marriages with hierodules, but rather refers to the context in which the law is most applicable[287]. It should also be noticed that it is the wife who supplies the slave-girl, and, apparently on the basis of No. 146, has authority over her.

No. 146 takes up the question of the slave girl who, having borne children, claims equality with her mistress. Similar to one of the proposed readings of HSS V 67, l. 22, the mistress is forbidden to sell her[288]; as punishment, however, the concubine can be reduced to slavery. A similar situation might be reflected in Abraham's answer in Gen 16 6: "Look, she is your maid. Do whatever you like to her[289]." That the concubine remains under the authority of the mistress is clear from No. 147: "If she did not bear children, her mistress may sell her."

Paragraphs 170 and 171 can be compared very favorably with Gen 21 and 29f. When a man has had children by both his first wife and by a concubine, if the father has acknowledged[290] the children of the concubine as sons, then they share in the inheritance equally with the sons of his wife (Gen 29f.). If, however, he has not so acknowledged them, then the children of the concubine do not share in the estate. Nevertheless, they have specific rights and are to be given their freedom (Gen 21). The Nuzi contracts which prevent the husband from giving the children of a concubine an equal position in the family do not necessarily presuppose an entirely different under-

MVÄG 10, 4 (1905), 44—55; Cuq. Droit Babylonien, 49; L. Epstein, Marriage Laws in the Bible and the Talmud, HSS 12, 1942, 35; I. Mendelsohn, BA 11 (1948), 28; Slavery 50. 56—58; J. Miles, RIDA 1 (1954), 123; E. Szlechter, RIDA 14 (1967), 82.

287 Mendelsohn (Slavery 50) goes so far as to say that the Babylonian family was monogamous on the basis of nos. 145 and 148. Without question these laws reflect a tendency towards monogamy.

288 No. 119 shows that a slave-girl who has borne children to her master, if sold because of debt, can be redeemed like other members of the family. This agrees well with this clause in no. 146.

289 The Genesis passage, however, does not speak of a reduction to slavery, but rather implies a condition of slavery.

290 Not adoption but legitimation, see above p. 257.

standing of law; for they are individual enactments designed particularly to prevent just some such action on the part of the husband. They are agreements made at the time of the marriage to give preferential treatment to the children of the bride. Moreover, the correspondence that we see between these paragraphs of the Hammurapi Code and the biblical texts does not support the conclusion that the biblical stories presuppose the Old Babylonian legal structure or the Old Babylonian concept of marriage; it only shows that the widely different destinies of the sons of Jacob and Ishmael need not be considered contradictory and may well have a common legal basis[291].

Some of the Old Babylonian contracts also reflect this practice of using the maid-servant of the wife as a concubine for the husband, and at the same time maintaining the servant's subordinate position to the wife. This is particularly clear in a text from Sippar, dated to the 12th year of the reign of Hammurapi, according to which a girl is bought as a servant to the wife and as a concubine to the husband: "Dem Bunene-abī ist sie Ehefrau, der Belessunu Sklavin[292]."

In two contracts the concubine is given in the wife's dowry[293]. The second example is particularly interesting, since, besides the expected clause dealing with the ensured subordination of the concubine[294] (the punishment in this case is that she can be sold into slavery), is the clause "Die Kinder, soviel sie geboren haben und gebären werden, sind ihre (beider) Kinder"[295], thus apparently establishing in the marriage contract that the children of the concubine will share equal rank with those of the wife[296].

One text, particularly, resembles some of the Nuzi contracts in that it attempts to guarantee the right to the inheritance for the future children of the wife: "Kikkinu, der Sohn des Abaja, hat bei seinen Lebzeiten die Rechtsverhältnisse der Bitti-Dagan, seiner

---

[291] However, see bove p. 257.

[292] Schorr, Zivil- und Prozessrecht, text 77, p. 121; J. Kohler, Ham. Ges. III, text 424, p. 116.

[293] J. Kohler, ibid. text 9, p. 6, and texts 2 and 3, p. 4f. (= Schorr, Zivil und Prozessrecht, 10—12).

[294] For a good example of this type of clause in a contract, cf. text 1420 in J. Kohler, Ham. Ges. VI, 2: "Am Tage da Ištar-ummī (the concubine) das Herz der Ḳadimātum (the wife) kränkt, wird Ḳadimātum die Ištar-ummī für Geld (weg)-geben."

[295] Schorr, Zivil- und Prozessrecht, text 5.

[296] Schorr suggests (ibid. 11 note), probably correctly, that Šamaš-tutum is the natural father of Tarâm-sagila and the adoptive father of Iltāni (Notice the similarity of the punishment clause to the similar clauses of adoption contracts). This may also explain the relatively favorable treatment contracted for Iltāni's children.

Ehefrau, festgesetzt ... Die Kinder, die Bitti-Dagan dem Kikkinu, ihrem Ehemanne, gebären wird, werden [gesetzlichen] Anteil am Hause des Kikkinu haben[297]."

But these concerns are by no means limited to the Old Babylonian contracts and Nuzi; they are found in the contracts of quite distant places in both the Second and the First Millenium. Three contracts from Alalakh help to bring out the extent of the possibilities open to those contracting a marriage settlement and are particularly instructive, since the society of Alalakh so closely resembles that of Nuzi. The family structure was apparently polygamous, and a man could have as many wives as he could afford, unless this was specifically limited by the marriage contract[298]. These three texts, like the Nuzi contracts we have seen, are just such contracted limitations on the husband's freedom. Text 91[299] is a declaration that provides that, if the woman Išara has children, they will be of the Mariannu class. If, however, she has no sons, a second wife, Aria-abon, and her sons will be of this rank. The husband is not allowed to take a third wife unless both fail to bear sons. Text 92 resembles the Nuzi contracts very closely, except that, in the case of childlessness, the second wife is not to be a slave-girl, but the daughter of the husband's brother: "If Naidu does not give birth to a son (then) the daughter of his brother Iwaššura shall be given; if ... (another wife) to Iriḫalpa gives birth to a son first and after that Naidu gives birth to a son, the son of Naidu alone shall be the first born[300]." The third text (text 93) allows the husband to have but one wife as in HSS IX 24 and Gadd 51; however, if his wife does not give him a child after seven years, he can take another wife[301].

A tablet from Ugarit offers an example of a case in which a concubine is raised to the position of her mistress (who was previously divorced). The position of her son is also altered accordingly: "My wife is free from her slave status; she is mistress of the house with her son[302]." Paragraph 41 of the Middle Assyrian laws[303], which are in

---

[297] J. Kohler, Ham. Ges. III, text 5, p. 5.

[298] Mendelsohn, Marriage in Alalakh, 354f.

[299] Wiseman, Alalakh Tablets, 54.

[300] I. Mendelsohn, On the preferential Status of the Eldest Son, BASOR 156 (1959), 38.

[301] Wiseman, Alalakh Tablets, 55. Text 94 seems to have a similar clause: ... *Mu 7. KAM ... DAM-tam ša-na-am*: "... seven years ... a second wife ..." (Mendelsohn, Marriage in Alalakh, 355).

[302] A. F. Rainey, Orientalia (1965), 19. On the texts from Ugarit, see also, O. Eissfeldt, The Alphabetical Cuneiform Texts from Ras Shamra published in: Le Palais Royal d'Ugarit, II 1957, JCS 5 (1960), 44.

[303] Meek, Middle Assyrian Laws, ANET 183. The tablets are dated to the 12th century (Tiglathpileser I), but the laws may be as early as the 15th century.

other respects remarkably close to the Nuzi contracts, seems irreconcilable with JEN 666 and 671, which seem to resemble more closely CH 170 and 171. According to this law, like No. 18 of the Sumerian laws, the sons of a concubine, in the event that their father has no other sons, receive a share in the estate[304].

There is also one Egyptian text which has two parts dated to the first and eighteenth year of Ramses XIth[305]. It is unfortunately not clear who the father is of the children mentioned in the second part of the text. If they are not children of Nebnûfer, then we have an extraordinarily clear case of the full adoption of slaves. If they are, however, the children of Nebnûfer by a concubine, then we have a very detailed example from Egypt, of a man who, in spite of a childless marriage, was able to have children through a concubine who ultimately became his heirs. General minor details allow it to be compared with the biblical stories rather closely. First of all, in this Egyptian text, as in Genesis, we are not dealing with contracts or laws which have as their purpose the protection of the rights of the wife, but rather a concern, shared by the wife, for sons who might receive the inheritance from their father: "We purchased the female slave Dinihetiri, and she gave birth to these three children . . .[306]." Secondly, the wife has considerable influence (as in Gen 21) — perhaps for different reasons — in the determination of who should receive the inheritance, and thirdly, the children are referred to up to the time of the second part of this contract as slaves: "They are indeed no longer with him as servants, but are with him as brothers and children, being freedmen of the land." Similarly in Gen 21 10 Sarah refers to the status of Hagar as that of a slave. One might suppose that in this case, as in the Code of Hammurapi, and at Nuzi (JEN 666 and 671), as elsewhere, but in contrast to, for instance, the Middle Assyrian Laws, the son of a concubine would normally have to be specifically recognized as an heir before he could share in the estate of his father. To some extent van Seters is correct, that this Egyptian text is a "more useful parallel to the biblical stories" than the Nuzi texts[307], since, because of its detail, its meaning is less ambiguous. On the other hand, it is far less useful, since the most essential detail, whether we are dealing with a concubine at all, is open to question. It can not be said, however, that it is "closer" as van Seters does[308]

---

304 See also Neufeld, Anc. Heb. Mar. Laws, 127.

305 A. H. Gardiner, JEA 26 (1940), 23—29; B. Welles, RIDA 3 (1949), 515; J. J. Rabinowitz, JNES 17 (1958), 146; A. Théodoridès, RIDA[3] 12 (1965), 79—142; J. van Seters, JBL 87 (1968), 405f.

306 Text in Gardiner, JEA 26 (1940), 23f.

307 van Seters, JBL 87 (1968), 406.

308 Ibid. and 407.

(in the sense that the Genesis stories should be grouped with this and later texts over against the Nuzi and Old Babylonian material), simply because there is no single element nor combination of elements which these later texts show, that is not found also in earlier material. It, on the other hand, becomes clear, on the basis of this later material, that we are not dealing in Genesis with customs which existed in any single limited area for a short period of time, which then were no longer understood in the First Millenium when the stories of Genesis were written.

The Neo-Assyrian Text referred to by van Seters[309] is in fact not remarkably close to our Genesis stories. Moreover, it is unfortunately extremely ambiguous, and van Seters' adjusted translation neither solves all of the important problems nor is it in itself convincing. The text begins by declaring that if Ṣubietu is childless, her husband shall take a handmaid (not—as in Genesis — that the wife is to give the handmaid; nor are we led to suppose that the husband, as in Gen 29f., could take a handmaid though his wife had borne him children). Then line 45 begins a series of four *šumma* clauses followed by the apodosis *iddan(an)*. In Parker's translation[310] this makes little sense: "If she curses, strikes, if she is furious (and) treats her (the handmaid) improperly, (47) if Ṣubietu (with) Milkiramu is at enmity (lit: is furious) and (. . .) if Milki-ramu (with her) is at enmity (even then) if he divorces her, he is to give. The witnesses, etc.". Van Seters tries to clarify the text by seeing the last two protases (ll. 47f.) as a divorce clause, and reading the *šumma* as a strong negative command — on the strength of a non — existent meaning of Hebrew אם: "She (the wife) shall not curse, strike, nor be furious and treat her (the handmaid) improperly, etc.". Aside from the fact that this moves the Nimrud text significantly further from the Genesis stories (Sarah in Gen 16 does mistreat Hagar), it may well be unnecessary. Both van Seters and Parker in understanding the subject of the *šumma* clause in line 45 to be the wife — rather than the concubine — introduce a change of subjects from the previous line, which is not indicated in the text. Further, l. 47: *šum-ma(sal) Ṣu-bi-*[*e-tu*] *(m) Mil-ki-ra-mu*, suggests a possible change in subject, since it gives explicitly the wife's name, which change cannot be expressed in van Seters' and Parker's translations. If, however, the subject of ll. 45 and 46 is the servant and the object of l. 46 is the wife, then not only do these minor difficulties disappear, but the clauses themselves make better sense, if it is the mistress and not the handmaid who is

[309] Ibid. 407; for a different translation see B. Parker, The Nimrud Tablets, 1952 — Business Documents, Iraq 16 (1954), 37—39.

[310] Ibid. 39.

in danger of being treated "improperly". In the comparative material, we have seen that this type of clause normally protects the wife from the caprice of the concubine. Though I hardly mean to imply that the text thereby becomes lucid, I do think that the lack of an apodosis is no longer so strongly felt; or perhaps the apodosis may be the *iddan(an)* of line 50. Thus (after Parker):

She (the handmaid) shall bring into being (even) her grandsons[311]. If she curses, strikes, if she is furious (and) treats her (the wife) improperly, (also) if Ṣubietu (with) Milki-ramu is at enmity . . . (considerable break in the text) and if Milki-ramu (with his wife) is at enmity (and) if he divorces her, he is to give (probably, her *terḫatu*). The witnesses, etc.

That is, the husband has the obligation to protect the status of his wife, rendering the text fully consonant with our comparative material.

Among the later contracts there is yet to be mentioned one from the Neo-babylonian period, which prevents the husband from taking a second wife by imposing a considerable fine. No concession is made to the possibility of the first wife being childless[312]. Also to be mentioned are the two contracts from the Aramaic Papyri[313] which forbid the husbands to marry a second wife. These also resemble to some extent the Graeco-Egyptian marriage contracts from the second and first centuries B. C. which forbid the husbands to take a second wife, a concubine, or a boy[314].

In a polygamous society, it is not at all surprising to find attempts, especially on the part of the wife's family at the time of marriage, to limit the husband's freedom to take other wives. It is also only to be expected that the husband's concern for an heir — and at times the wife's as well — will mitigate this tendency when the wife proves to be childless. The practice of concubinage, by protecting the status of the first wife, readily lends itself to a satisfactory solution. This solution, however, particularly because of the inferior status of the slave, produces its own problems, as we have seen. The Nuzi tablets prove to be helpful in understanding the way that these conflicting relationships were resolved in the Near East, and the understanding of Near Eastern marriage that we derive from them is confirmed by other Near Eastern records and laws. It should not be

---

311 That is, she is to remain in the family as a permanent member. Compare CH no. 146.

312 J. Kohler and Peiser, Babylonischen Rechtsleben, I 7; J. Kohler, Das Recht als das Lebenselement der Völker, 1892, 17.

313 C 15: 31ff. and K 7: 36f.; R. Yaron, Aramaic Papyri, 60 and n. 4.

314 Papyrus Giessen 2 (173 B. C.); Papyrus Genève 21 (2nd century B. C.) and Papyrus Tebtunis 104 (92 B. C.) see further: R. Yaron, Aramaic Papyri, 106.

assumed, however, that this is what is behind the stories in Genesis, particularly Chapters 16 and 21. For in Genesis, as perhaps in the Egyptian "Extraordinary Adoption" text, there is nothing given to imply that the husband's right to take a second wife has been restricted. The restriction on Jacob imposed by Laban in Gen 31 50, however, is certainly to be related to the attempts of the bride's father to restrict the husband's freedom to marry again, but here, obviously, it is in no way related to childlessness or to the taking of a concubine. It is, however, related to the marriage contract which is only here completed between Jacob and Laban. What also reflects the Near Eastern Material as a whole is the use to which concubines were put in Genesis, their position in the family as a result of their bearing children, and the consequent ambiguous position of the son of the concubine in his father's household.

H. GEN 29 9-30 AND 30 25—31 54

It is among the most widely accepted conclusions of those who have discussed the Nuzi parallels to the patriarchal traditions, that the Jacob-Laban story has been adequately illustrated by the Nuzi texts; in particular, it is thought that one text, Gadd 51, has firmly established this parallel. That Jacob is forbidden to take another wife in Gen 31 50 is only one relatively minor detail[315] among a series of extensive parallels that have been claimed between the text Gadd 51 and the Laban-Jacob stories in Gen 29—31[316]. However, since this is the one aspect of the proposed parallel that is acceptable, it is important to point out that it is only so in a very limited and a very vague sense. The clause in Gadd 51 forbidding the remarriage of Wullu, and that in Gen 31 50 forbidding Jacob to take another wife, are both limitations on the polygamous rights of the husband imposed by the

---

315 This is doubtless paralleld by the Nuzi tablets, but the parallel must be understood in the wider context of general Near Eastern practice of the Second and First Millenium B. C., as discussed above in section G. Gen 31 50 was compared to Gadd 51 as early as 1926 by S. Smith (Gadd, RA 23, 1926, 127 n.) who has been followed by C. H. Gordon, The story of Jacob and Laban in the Light of the Nuzi Tablets, BASOR 66 (1937), 25; BA 3 (1940), 5; O'Callaghan, CBQ 6 (1944), 339; Rowley, BJRL (1949/1950), 75f.; Bright, Hist. of Israel, 71; and Weir, Arch and OT Study, 75.

316 Several of these parallels have been recently challenged in an article by J. van Seters: HThR 62 (1969), 377—395. Van Seter's arguments are not substantially different from that given here below. His discussion of the *errēbu* marriage is particularly to be recommended (ibid. 377—388).

bride's father in the marriage contract[317]. But here the similarity ends. Gadd 51 reads:

> Tablet of adoption, whereby Našwa, son of Aršenni, has adopted Wullu, son of Buhišenni. So long as Našwa is alive, Wullu will give him food and clothing, and when Našwa is dead, Wullu will give him burial. If there be a son of Našwa, he shall divide (the estate) equally with Wullu, and the gods of Našwa the son of Našwa shall take. But if there be no son of Našwa then Wullu shall take also the gods of Našwa. Also he has given his daughter Nuhuia to Wullu to wife; if Wullu shall take another wife he shall vacate the lands and houses of Našwa. Whoever infringes (the agreement) shall pay in full one mina of silver and one of gold[318].

The reason for the prohibition here is clear: Našwa, who has adopted Wullu, wants to ensure that his own property be ultimately given to the children of his daughter, and the punishment for non-compliance is disinheritance. It is also to be noticed that no concession is made for possible childlessness. It has already been seen that similar prohibitions are given in various ways at Nuzi and in other Near Eastern marriage contracts, reflecting a variety of motivations[319]. Similar prohibitions, therefore, cannot be assumed to be based on similar causes. In fact, in Gen 31 50 Jacob already has children, both by Laban's daughters and by concubines, and we must assume that they are all intended to share equally in the inheritance of Jacob. Secondly, we will try to show below that Jacob is not the adopted son of Laban, and thirdly, that, in returning to Canaan Jacob cannot be affected by a penalty of disinheritance; rather, Elohim is the guarantor of Jacob's compliance. Gadd 51 and Gen 31 50 are related in the sense that they can both be placed within a broad spectrum of texts, from the laws of Ur-Nammu to the Graeco-Egyptian papyri, which have similar clauses. One other unessential similarity is claimed to support the parallel between the Nuzi tablets and Gen 29—31, and this should be discussed first.

Gen 29 24. 29 states that Laban gave to his daughters Leah and Rachel, the maids Zilpah and Bilhah. Most commentators do not attribute these passages to J with the main body of Chapter 29, but see them rather as later additions of P[320]. Speiser, however, remarks:

---

[317] That the marriage agreement between Jacob and Laban does not appear to be completed until the end of Chapter 31 seems probable. See further below.

[318] Gadd, RA 23 (1926), 127.

[319] See above section G. Interestingly, HSS V 67, which has often been used to support the parallel between Gen 29—31 and Gadd 51, is not absolute in its prohibition as is Gadd 51, but allows the possibility of children through a maid; moreover, the punishment for taking a second wife, is not disinheritance as in Gadd 51, but divorce from Gilimninu at the husband's cost. It is also not entirely clear that Gilimninu is Šurihil's daughter.

[320] O. Eissfeldt, Hexateuch-Synopse, 1922, 1962², 55f.

"It is precisely these two verses that are most likely to constitute direct transcripts from some old and authentic document[321]." He bases this claim on the Nuzi tablet HSS V 67[322]. Speiser then argues that the statement that Yalampa has been given as handmaid to Gilimninu is just as abrupt and marginal as the references in Genesis 29, and that therefore the verses in Genesis should be considered as part of J[323]. He goes on to say that this practice of giving the bride a handmaid at the wedding "was the norm in the upper stratum of Hurrian society"[324].

The reason that these verses are attributed to P, is not so much their abruptness, as that they break the discernible continuity between v. 23 and 25, and between 28 and 30! This is not the case with HSS V 67 where the statement about Yalampa is placed as an additional clause at the end of the contract. The attribution to P moreover does not imply that verses 24 and 29 are inauthentic, in the sense that they are not appropriate to their context, only that they are later additions to that context. As Speiser correctly points out, such a gift is very much in place in a marriage agreement. However, it cannot be said that such a gift was a "norm" at Nuzi, nor that it was unique to Hurrian society. Gadd 51 and almost all of the Nuzi marriage contracts do not have such a clause. But the practice of the father giving his daughter a maid at her wedding is abundantly witnessed to elsewhere, from the Old Babylonian Period to the time of Cyrus, as well as in the Old Testament[325].

The main point at issue in the discussion of the proposed parallel between Gadd 51 and Gen 29—31 does not depend on such incidental similarities. They are only supportive to the main thesis that the relationship between Jacob and Laban is identical to that between Wullu and Našwa. Several different arguments have been emphasized. Along with the transliteration and translation of the text in 1926,

---

[321] Genesis 226f.

[322] See translation above in section G, p. 253.

[323] Genesis 227.

[324] Ibid. In 1962 (IDB, 574) Speiser said that this is "occasionally" found in the Nuzi marriage contracts. For this parallel, see the earlier remarks of Gordon, BASOR 66 (1937), 25 and BA 3 (1940), 6.

[325] Schorr, Zivil- und Prozessrecht, text 209, p. 291—293; J. Kohler, Ham. Ges. III, 6, text 9; at Ugarit: C. H. Gordon, Adventures in the Nearest East, 98; Ugaritic Literature, Scripta Pontificii Instituti Biblici 98, 1949, 70; in Twentieth Dynasty Egypt: J. Černy, and T. E. Peet, A Marriage Settlement of the Twentieth Dynasty, JEA 13 (1927), 30—33; at the end of the 4th century in neo-Babylonian records: Kohler and Peiser, Babylonischen Rechtsleben, Cyrus 111, 143, 312, and Camb. 215, p. 7f., 11f. and 13; in the Old Testament, see I Sam 25 42 and Gen 24 61.

Gadd added the interpretive note of Sydney Smith which pointed out a parallel between Gadd 51, ll. 10—17: "If there be a son of Našwa, he shall divide (the estate) equally with Wullu, and the gods of Našwa the son of Našwa shall take. But if there be no son of Našwa then Wullu shall take also the gods of Našwa!" and the theft of Laban's gods by Rachel mentioned in Gen 31. He adds that "Jacob's possession of these (gods) would mark him as the legitimate heir of the family"[326]. This interpretation was expanded in an article by Smith in 1932[327], where he concluded that the value of these images was not so much that they were gods, but that they gave a legal claim to property[328]. Moreover, he concluded that, since similar use was not made of such gods in tablets from purely Babylonian cities, this must reflect a distinctively Hurrian law.

Speiser, accepting Smith's basic interpretation, drew the parallel out more clearly. According to him, on the basis of Gadd 51, a son-in-law was considered the heir of his father-in-law's property on condition that he possessed the household gods. Rachel's theft, then, made Jacob the heir to Laban's property[329]. Possession of the gods was a prerequisite to the inheritance of the property[330]. Gordon sees the gods of Našwa and of Laban as the equivalent of the title to the chief inheritance portion and to the leadership of the family[331].

In 1957 A. E. Draffkorn published a study of the entire issue, and was able to show that the use of the term *ilāni*, "gods", in some of the Nuzi tablets paralleled some of the atypical uses of the term "Elohim" in the Old Testament, particularly Ex 21 6 and 22 7-10[332]. She further discusses other tablets from Nuzi where the use of the *ilāni* is apparently similar to that of Gadd 51, particularly Gadd 5 and HSS XIV 108, where the eldest sons are given the household gods[333]. Her understanding of the purpose of the gods is basically

[326] S. Smith, as cited by Gadd, RA 23 (1926), 127 n.

[327] What were the Teraphim?, JTS 33 (1932), 33—36.

[328] Smith also gives this interpretation to Michah's teraphim in Jud 18 14ff. (ibid. 34). But here, surely such an interpretation cannot apply! Micah made his own teraphim; he did not inherit them.

[329] Speiser, Mesopotamian Origins, 1930, 162 n,; also see Speiser, AASOR 13 (1933), 44.

[330] Speiser, IEJ 7 (1957), 213. Speiser and Smith were followed in this interpretation by W. F. Albright, The Archaeology of Palestine and the Bible, 138f. L. Woolley, Abraham, 1935, 164. R. O'Callaghan, CBQ 6 (1944), 39; H. H. Rowley, BJRL (1949/1950), 76; J. N. Schofield, ET 66 (1955), 318; H. M. Orlinsky, Ancient Israel, 1956, 19; J. Bright, Hist. of Israel, 71.

[331] BASOR 66 (1937), 26; see also: Gordon, RB 44 (1935), 35f.; BA 3 (1940), 5—7; JNES 13 (1954), 56; Adventures in the Nearest East, 119f.

[332] Following Gordon, JBL 54 (1935), 139—144; A. E. Draffkorn, Ilani/Elohim, JBL 76 (1957), 216—224.

[333] Ibid. 220f.

that of Speiser and Gordon. However, her view of Gen 31 is startlingly different: "A daughter's right to a share in her father's estate would have to be safeguarded, according to Hurrian law as reflected in Nuzi, by possession of the house gods. Thus Rachel had every reason to make sure that she would not be deprived of her rights; her removal of the house gods would have been a case of self-protection[334]." Draffkorn's interpretation of Gen 31, however, has been ignored, and the effect of her article was to bolster, with added documentation, the interpretations of Speiser and Gordon, which remained essentially unaltered[335].

Their argument, however, is by no means self-sufficient and depends on the recognition that Jacob is in some way the heir of Laban. That Jacob was Laban's heir, and that both the Genesis story and Gadd 51 were examples of what is called an *errebu* marriage was argued independently by Gordon and M. Burrows[336]. The *errebu* marriage was a type of marriage in patriarchal societies which provided a man, who did not have a son, with a male heir through the adoption of the son-in-law[337]. Gadd 51 is seen as normative for the understanding of this practice: "Laban, who has no sons of his own, adopts Jacob and makes him heir[338]."

---

[334] Ibid. 220. Draffkorn shifts the emphasis of Gen 31 to the possible inheritance of Rachel on the strength of HSS V 67, 28ff., which says that a daughter of Gilimninu should receive a single share if Gilimninu has no other children (n. 17). Draffkorn's argument is weak, however, since the inheritance by a daughter is not dependent on the general absence of sons to the husband Šennima, but only on the absence of sons to Gilimninu. This is to ensure that Gilimninu, the daughter (?) of Zigi, maintains her place in the inheritance of Zigi. From the Old Testament side, this interpretation is excluded for two reasons: (1) Laban has sons, and the inheritance of the daughter in HSS V 67 requires that the daughter be the only child, and (2) Rachel is the younger daughter.

[335] C. H. Gordon, The World of the OT, 114f.; Speiser, IDB, 574; OBS, WS, 76, n. 40; Genesis 250; and also Weir, Arch. and OT Study, 74f.; H. H. Rowley, Worship in Ancient Israel, 1967, 20.

[336] Gordon, BASOR 66 (1937), 25—27, and M. Burrows, The Complaint of Laban's Daughters, JAOS 57 (1937), 259—276.

[337] Burrows ibid. 261—263, as in Ezr 2 61 and Neh 7 63.

[338] Gordon, BA 3 (1940), 5f. See also Burrows, BASOR 77 (1940), 3: "Laban's action . . . in taking Jacob into his own household and giving him his daughters in marriage, corresponds to the Babylonian custom of *errēbu* marriage, by which a man who had no son gave his daughter as wife to a young man who instead of taking her into his own home and family 'entered' *(erābu)* her father's family, receiving only in part the ordinary powers of a husband over her. Either this practice or one closely related to it appears in two of the Nuzu tablets (Gadd 51 and HSS V 67), recording the adoption of young men who at the same time received their adoptive fathers' daughters in marriage."

That Laban has no sons at the time he adopts Jacob is argued from the fact that they are not mentioned until later (Gen 31 1), when Laban's manner had changed towards Jacob (31 2)[339].

That Jacob is Laban's adopted son and not simply his son-in-law is seen to be further confirmed by Gen 31 43; "The daughters are mine', Laban replied to Jacob, 'and the children are mine; so too is the flock. Everything you see belongs to me'." That is, Laban is understood as exercising patriarchal authority over Jacob's wives and family[340].

The similarity of the phrase אכול כסף in Gen 31 15: "Not only did he sell us, but he has 'eaten up the money', he got for us", to the recurrent phrase at Nuzi: *akalu kaspa* "to eat the money"[341], has led scholars to understand correctly that both refer to the girl's *terḫatu*[342]. Laban had used up the *terḫatu,* instead of holding it for the daughters, and thus has "sold" them. This is obviously understood as reprehensible in the biblical context[343]. That this is in direct conflict with the Nuzi tablets cited, where the guardian is given full rights over the *terḫatu,* to "eat it", is not seen as very significant, since, on the basis of other texts from Nuzi, it becomes clear that there too the money from the *terḫatu* sometimes formed part of the dowry[344].

What is not seen, however, is that the complaint of Laban's daughters in Gen 31 15, as understood by Burrows and Speiser (and, I think, correctly), proves that Jacob's marriage was not an *errēbu* marriage, what Koschaker has correctly described as essentially "eine muntfreie Ehe". That is, the *errebu* marriage is a marriage in which a brideprice is not paid[345]. Moreover, in this most important characteristic, Jacob's marriage differs from both Gadd 51 and

339 Gordon, BA 3 (1940), 6; see also Holt, The Pat. of Israel, 100.

340 Gordon ibid.

341 Gadd 35: "Give my daughter Ašte to wife either to your son or in the gate; the silver for her I declare I have consumed." AASOR X 31: "and forty shekels of silver for her from her husband she (a third party) shall receive and consume." and Contenau, Textes Cuneiformes du Louvre, no 2: "The woman who adopts the girl in question shall choose a husband for her and consume her money." (Burrows, JAOS 57, 1937, 269).

342 Burrows ibid.; Gordon, RB 44 (1935), 36; The Status of Woman Reflected in the Nuzi Tablets, ZA 43 (1935), 157f.; O'Callaghan, CBQ 6 (1944), 403.

343 J. Neubauer, Beiträge zur Geschichte des biblisch-talmudischen Eheschließungsrechts, 205; Z. W. Falk, Hebrew Law in Biblical Times, 145. 150; see also J. Miles, Some Remarks on the Origins of Testacy, with some References to the Old-Babylonian Laws, RIDA 1 (1954), 123.

344 Burrows, JAOS 57 (1937) 271ff.; Speiser, AASOR X 22—24; O'Callaghan, CBQ 6 (1944), 403.

345 P. Koschaker, Quellenkritische Untersuchungen zu den altassyrischen Gesetzen, MVÄG 26 (1921), 60f.; ZA 33 (1941), 84f. See further below.

HSS V 67, for in neither of these texts is a *terḫatu* paid, nor, as we shall see, can the payment of a brideprice be assumed. Furthermore, the use of the verb "to eat" meaning "to take into possession", as used at Nuzi is not peculiar to these tablets. Text 8, l. 23 from Alalakh[346] reads: *i-za-ak-kar be-li-mi-im-ma ša na-da-nim li-di-nam-ma lu-ku-ul*, "Let my lord give (me) whatever is to be given and I will accept (lit. "eat") it." Nor are the Nuzi tablets the closest to the meaning of the phrase as used in Gen 31 15, in the sense of to "consume" with the pejorative connotation "to use up" unfairly. Much closer is the expression found in a relatively modern Arabic story told by Granqvist:

Zarîfe Aḥmad was a widow when Smaʿīn married her. After [her first husband] Mūsa died, she was angry with [her mother-in-law] Ṣabḥa and went back to her father's house. Then [her brother-in-law] Smaʿīn was betrothed to her but said, I have no money. [Then they said] Acknowledge that the garden belongs to us! And they wrote the document in the name of Aḥmad [the bride's father]. When on the wedding day, she should leave her father's house, she refused and said: I will not go until you bring the document and transfer the land to me. My father ate up my first brideprice, and now this is for me. Bring the document and inscribe it in my name! The document was brought to her and she went. She has the document in her possession and she plants and uses the ground[347].

The question of whether the *errēbu* form of marriage as practiced in the Near East is a remnant of matriarchal society need not be discussed here[348], for the contracts from Nuzi, in particular Gadd 51, and perhaps HSS V 67, are, like the customs implied in I Chr. 2 34f. and perhaps Ezr 2 61, means by which a man without sons can nevertheless have male descendants through his daughter. The adoption of the son-in-law offers the possibility for the bride's father to obtain grandsons in the direct line of inheritance. This is very clear in I Chr 2 34f. and also in Gadd 51, since, happily, we possess the sequel to this contract: Gadd 5.

Tablet of disposition whereby Našwa [son of Aršenni] disposed (their) lots to Hašib-tilla, to Buitae, to Akawatil and to Mukri-Tešup, the sons of Wullu. Našwa

[346] Wiseman, Alalakh Tablets.

[347] Granqvist, Marriage, 128.

[348] Nor do we need to go into the diffcult problems of the possible relationship between this practice and the Middle Assyrian laws nos. 26. 27. 28. 31. 33. 34. 37 and 39 which refer to married women who remain in the houses of their father. See however: J. Lewy, ZA 36 (1925), 147 and 152f.; von Praag, Droit Matrimoniale, 181 to 183. On no. 25 of the Laws of Eshnunna, see R. Yaron, The Rejected Bridegroom, Orientalia 34 (1965), 23—29. For the *errēbu* in general see, e. g., Koschaker, MVÄG (1921), 56—61; ZA 41 (1933), 84f.; Neufeld, Anc. Hebr. Mar. Laws, 56—62; The Hittite Laws, 1951, 124; Mendelsohn, BA 11 (1948), 25; de Vaux, Les Institutions, 52; Falk, Hebrew Law, 124f.; Driver-Miles, Assyrian Laws, 134ff.; J. van Seters, HThR 62 (1969), 377—388.

(spoke) thus: Formerly I had adopted Wullu; all my lands and houses and all (that was) mine I gave to Wullu. Now all my lands, my houses, the whole of my servants everything of mine, and ... I give to Hašib-tilla, to Buitae, to Akawatil, and to Mukri-Tešup. Of the lands, of the houses and of everything that is mine Hašib-tilla [is] the eldest and his share [is] double. Buitae, Akawatil, and Mukri-Tešup after Hašib-tilla [shall-share] according to their strength (?) My gods dwelling ... and let me obtain burial ... jointly (?) to Hašib-tilla ... the impost and ... [according to] his strength bears. The four men ... one house of seven ells? ... and of five ells? ... they shall [vacate?] the houses of Aršenni and jointly (?) to Akabšušše. they shall give them. This one house and one imer of land to Akabšušše is given ... Kalwašimma (?) to [Hašib-tilla?] the eldest son, is given. If the land [and]. the houses, there is (anyone) to bring an action ... the four men, sons of Wullu, shall go into court together (?) and clear ... and together they shall divide. This tablet was written behind the [pit?] of the palace.

Našwa (says) thus: These four men, sons of Wullu, are my sustainers (?) and other there is none; and all that was willed before is cancelled (?) and this tablet is the (authentic) one, and other there is none[349].

Here, Našwa wills his property, that he had previously given to Wullu in the adoption contract Gadd 51, to his grandchildren, the sons of Wullu; Wullu's eldest son Hašib-tilla receiving a double share. The patria potestas here is still maintained by Našwa.

This understanding is confirmed by an Old Babylonian contract of the *ana ittišu* type which reads: (ll. 32ff.)

Die Urkunde seiner Erbeinstellung hat er ihm geschrieben, seine Tochter hat er in seinen Schoss gegeben, das Haus und dessen Hausrat hat er ihm übergeben; dieser Ausreisser (sic?) hat in das Haus seines Vaters alles, was er erworben hat, ihm hineingebracht. Wenn er gegen seinen (Adoptiv) vater Abscheu fasst, alles dessen, was er ihm eingebracht hat, wird er verlustig geben, ausserdem 2 Minen Silber, die terḫatu seiner Ehefrau, wird er darwägen[350].

Here, as in Gadd 51, the property of the father-in-law is placed in the hands of the adopted son; however, in both cases the father-in-law maintains the potestas.

The same intention as that of the *errēbu* type contract is shown by an adoption at Ugarit in which a man adopted his grandson, the son of his daughter, as his heir[351]. What we here speak of as an *errēbu*

349 Gadd, RA 23 (1926), 91.

350 R. Haase, Einführung in das Studium keilschriftlicher Rechtsquellen, 65 (emphasis added).

351 A. F. Rainey, Orientalia (1965), 15. The same type of motivation is also reflected in one Egyptian ostracon: (B. M. Ostracon 5624. 0,4) "On the day of induction which the workman Ḥai, my father, underwent, the majordomo of Ne, Thutmosis, apportioned the places which were in the necropolis to the work people [of] pharaoh. And he [Tuthmosis] gave the tomb of Amun(mose) to Ḥai my father, as a charge, it being that Ḥel, my mother, was his own daughter, and he had no male

marriage, however, is not to be understood in every case in which a man enters the house of his father-in-law, particularly when the husband is a foreigner, as Moses in Ex 2 19 or Hadad in I Kings 11 20[352]. The *errēbu* marriage is not a special form of agreement whose major result is that the husband lives with the father-in-law; that is but one highly noticeable, but, legally insignificant, result. The *errēbu* marriage is the normal result of the combination of a full adoption of a younger man and a marriage with the adoptive father's daughter. Gadd 51 and HSS V 67 are basically adoption contracts which follow the same form as HSS V 7 and HSS V 60[353].

That an *errēbu* marriage is made without the payment of the *terḫatu* is a direct result of the adoption by the father-in-law. The position that the adoptive son has to the inheritance is determined by the agreement reached in the Guarantee Clause (Clause II) of the adoption contract. In most cases of the Nuzi adoption clauses at least one share is guaranteed (so HSS V 7, 60 and 67) in the case that the father-in-law, himself, has a son. In Gadd 51 the guaranteed share is equal in any case. This is not affected by the possession, or lack of possession, of the household gods. According to Gadd 5, Gadd 51 and HSS XIV 108, the household gods are normally given to the primary heir, but they do not themselves cause the recognition of who the eldest son is. That is done in one of two ways: either on the basis of who was born first, or in the case of adopted sons, by clause II in the contract of adoption.

Aside from the question of whether Jacob is an heir of Laban at all, that Rachel's theft of the gods of Laban has nothing to do with Jacob being recognized as the heir of Laban[354] was clearly shown by M. Greenberg in 1962[355]. In one point, however, Greenberg's inter-

child, and his places were becoming forsaken." A. M. Blackman, Oracles in Ancient Egypt, JEA 12 (1926), 177.

352 The marriage of Sinuhe seems at first to follow the *errēbu* pattern very closely ("He set me at the head of his children. He married me to his eldest daughter.") ANET 19. However, since Sinuhe goes back to Egypt without his family, it might be suggested that we are not dealing here with adoption in any strict sense, but with poetic language, and that Sinuhe is to be compared more with I Reg 11 20 and Ex 2 19.

353 For an explanation of the adoption contracts, see above section C.

354 If the proposed interpretation of the Jacob story on the basis of Gadd 51 were aceptable, one would have to conclude that Jacob's inheritance portion would still be equal to that of Laban's sons, since the primary heir, according to Gadd 51, would receive no more — except for the gods — than would the other hiers. The difficulty of Laban's sons is not so much that they are only mentioned in the latter part of the story and, therefore, might not have existed when Jacob first married, but that only J refers to them.

355 M. Greenberg, JBL 81 (1962), 239—248.

pretation must be criticized. The bequeathal of the household gods does not determine who is to be the paterfamilias[356]. Rather, the household gods are given to that son. In this respect, the possession of the gods does not have legal significance in its own right, and is to be compared with the possession of a family heirloom; it is secondary to the inheritance. Clearly, Rachel has stolen the gods because, as gods, they are valuable to her[357].

The passage from Josephus offered by Greenberg[358], while it in no way presents us with a complete explanation of Rachel's motives, is nevertheless emphatically enlightening, as it shows that household gods could be important to people even though they were unrelated to inheritance rights: The quotation is taken from the Antiquities 18, 9, 5 which relates the adventures of the brothers Asineus and Avileus. Here, we have the story of a woman, the wife of a Parthian, who has been taken captive in battle:

> When, after the death of her husband, she had been taken captive, she took along the ancestral images of the gods belonging to her husband and to herself — for it is the custom among all the people in that country to have objects of worship in their house and to take them along when going abroad. She too therefore secretly carried them off in observance of her national custom in these matters.

Nor should the strong literary character of the narration about Rachel's theft be ignored. When Jacob is accused of stealing Laban's gods, he answers — not knowing that his most loved wife Rachel had stolen them — "Whoever you find has your gods shall not live!" (v. 32). That is, he unwittingly condemns the one who is closest to him, a motif that is similar to the story about Jephthah's daughter, and also resembles the story in II Sam 12 where David declares that a ruthless thief deserves the death penalty, little knowing that he himself is the thief under discussion[359].

Finally, there are several other aspects of the Jacob story which make it impossible to understand his marriage with Rachel and Leah as *errēbu* marriages. More than one passage makes it quite clear that Jacob was neither Laban's adopted son nor his heir.

---

356 Ibid. 242—244.

357 Moreover, as Greenberg notes (ibid. 245f. and 246 n. 22) Jacob is leaving Laban's household, while Laban is still alive, thus removing any possible motivation of the sort suggested by Smith and Speiser. The complaint of Laban's daughters, again, emphasizes — against Draffkorn — that Rachel has nothing to expect from Laban.

358 Ibid. 246.

359 For other related motifs see D. Daube, Error and Accident in the Bible, RIDA 2 (1949), 190—192.

In Gen 31 39 Jacob argues: "That which was torn by beasts I did not bring to you; I bore the loss; you demanded it from me whether they were stolen during the day or at night[360]."

This clearly shows that Jacob was working for Laban as a shepherd, and, from his own point of view, Jacob was scrupulously honest with Laban. The relationship is not that of a son and heir, but of an employee. In fact the whole structure of the story in Gen 29 to 31 is built around Jacob and Laban's conflicting interests. Jacob works for Laban, but for his own gain. Jacob becomes rich, not through the expanding value of his share in his inheritance from Laban, but at Laban's expense.

The claim of Laban in 31 43: "The daughters are my daughters and the sons are my sons and the flocks are my flocks, and whatever you see is mine[361]," has to be interpreted as an answer to Jacob's argument in verses 38ff. where Jacob obviously does not agree with Laban. Especially verse 41: "I served you fourteen years for your two daughters, and six years for your cattle, and you have changed my wages ten times." Jacob claims that he more than earned all that he has, and, except for the help of Yahweh, Laban would have cheated him and have sent him away empty-handed (v. 42). To this Laban retorts (v. 43) that everything is really his, in the sense that everything that Jacob has is from Laban — which is true, but ineffectual. And so Laban finally agrees to the full settlement that Jacob demands which had been put off for so long. Only here is the conflict fully resolved, the marriage agreement completed (v. 50), and Laban and Jacob are quits with each other. This (for Jacob) happy ending of the story is the culmination of the agreement between Jacob and Laban in Chapter 30 25-34, when, six years earlier Jacob had asked: "Send me away that I may go to my own place, and into my own country. Give me my wives and my children for whom I have served you, and let me go (v. 25f.).". Laban, seeing possible advantage to himself in keeping Jacob, does not want to do this — though he does not deny Jacob's rights to them — and asks Jacob to stay and work for wages. It is this agreement which enables Jacob to ruin Laban and become rich at Laban's expense.

What separates Jacob's marriages most from the type of *errēbu* marriage we have discussed above, however, is the marriage agreement itself in Chapter 29. The affectionate meeting in verse 14: "Surely you are my bone and my flesh." is not a kind of adoption. Jacob is, after all, Laban's nephew. Moreover, Jacob has declared no intention

[360] Cf. CH no. 266 and Ex 22 13; also J. J. Finkelstein, An Old Babylonian Herding Contract and Genesis 31 38f., JAOS 88 (1968), 30—36.

[361] Cf. Gordon's interpretation in BASOR 66 (1937), 26.

of staying with Laban permanently, and he certainly does not stay there during the first month in the legal position of a son, since, after a month, Laban brings up the question of Jacob's wages (v. 15): "Because you are my brother (אחי) should you serve me for nothing?"

Jacob wishes to marry Rachel and offers to work for Laban seven years in lieu of the brideprice. That this is equivalent to the *terḫatu*, and therefore, Jacob's marriage cannot be considered to be an *errēbu* marriage, is made particularly clear from the fact that it is not until after Jacob fulfills the seven years labor, i. e., until after he pays the full *terḫatu*, that he receives his bride.

This practice of working out the brideprice is quite widespread and the term of seven years is not unusual[362].

Two such stories among the Arabs are found in Granqvist, and are remarkably close to the story of Jacob:

> Ḥasan Abu Šawriye came [to Arṭas]. He said to my uncle: wilt thou not allow me to serve for one of your daughters? He said: I take thee into my service. Thus fate had willed it and he served. He said: I will have Ḫaḍra. He served eight years for her. After that he took her ...

and:

> ʿAbd-il-Nebi was herdsman for the sheep and goats of Aḥmad Jēdallah. Then he said to him: 'Oh my father's brother Aḥmad wilt thou not give me one of thy daughters? I will serve for her brideprice.' He replied: There are three girls. Thou art the wolf of them, whichever thou wishest, only name her [to me]! He said, I will have Nijme. I will be herdsman and serve for her brideprice. [Aḥmad replied:] Go and bring thy father's brother so that we may sign the agreement before men of authority, good men. Then he went, brought his father's brother from Ḥalḥūl and they drew up the agreement. Whoever-breaks it shall give compensation to his partner in the agreement. And he served [his years] and when the time was finished he took her.
>
> He was an orphan and sought service, because his mother had married again and he therefore left her and his home village. In that way he came to Aḥmad Jēdallah a man of Arṭas who lived on his land in Bet Skārye and was at that time the father of three girls but had no son. He remained a long time with his father-in-law and is said to be now in Bet Jāla[363].

J. GEN 25 29-34

The often proposed parallel between the Nuzi tablets and Esau's sale of his birthright to Jacob for some food, appears to be much more

---

[362] See the many examples of this given by J. G. Frazer, Folk-Lore in the Old Testament, 3 vols., 1919, II 342—371. Three, five, six, and seven years labor are usually demanded. See also E. Westermarck, The History of Human Marriage, 1901, 394.

[363] Granqvist, Marriage, 108f.

the result of an enthusiasm for possible points of contact between Genesis and Nuzi than of real similarities.

The story was first related to HSS V 99:

Tablet of agreement whereby Manniya son of Tultukka and Ilanu son of Tayuki between themselves made an agreement. Thus (says) Manniya: "As for all the accumulations of Tayuki, I will take a double portion and Ilanu a single portion shall receive. And after Tayuki, whatever we may accumulate, I and Ilanu shall evenly divide. And from this day on, the one shall not raise complaints against the other. Whichever breaks the contract one mina of silver and one mina of gold he shall furnish[364].

Speiser speaks of this tablet as a "disposition of the birthright: one of the parties acquires the rights of the firstborn, while the other, whose claims to the privilege would have been actually justified by reason of birth, is satisfied to accept a minor share in his father's estate". He sees this as a precedent for the agreement made between Esau and Jacob[365]. There are several difficulties with the comparison however. As Gordon pointed out[366], the Nuzi text does not deal with brothers. Even more than that, the text does not deal with a sale at all (Ilanu receives no money in return!), and there is no reason to assume that the proportion of Tayuki's property which is to be received by Manniya, should be designated as the "right of the firstborn". The agreement is not with Tayuki but between Manniya and Ilanu and concerns the inheritance that Ilanu is expected to or has received from his father. What is being transferred is not a right to inheritance, but goods that have been inherited. Much more important is that the main point of the agreement is that a partnership is being established between the two men: "and after Tayuki, whatever we may accumulate, I and Ilanu shall evenly divide". The division of Tayuki's goods merely established the basis for this agreement.

The text most often cited as a parallel to the Jacob-Esau story is JEN 204. This text does deal with real brothers, who moreover enter into an *aḫḫūti* ("Brothership") agreement. The following text of this tablet is as translated by Cassin:

Tablette d'adoption en fraternité par laquelle Tupkitilla, fils de Ḫilbiššuḫ, a adopté Ḳurpazaḫ, fils de Ḫilbiššuḫ, son frère. Dans (ce) jour il partage: le verger sur la route de la ville de Lumti, (mesurant) 45 coudées en longueur au nord, 42 coudées au sud, 33 coudées à l'ouest, 33 coudées à l'est, à l'est du verger de Akkulenni à coté du champ fertile (?) de Ḫilbiššuḫ Tupkitilla à Ḳurpazaḫ comme sa part (d'héritage) a livré. D'autre part, Ḳurpazaḫ 3 moutons comme sa part (d'héritage) à Tupkitilla a

---

364 AASOR X no. 18, p. 48f.

365 AASOR 13 (1933), 44. He is followed, with reservations, by Gordon, BA 3 (1940), 3—5, and Rowley, BJRL (1949/1950), 75.

366 BA 3 (1940), ibid.

remis. Si le verger est l'objet d'une revendication, alors Tupkitilla après (l') avoir libéré, à Ḳurpazaḫ (le) remettra. Quiconque transgressera ce qu'il a dit, 1 mine d'argent (et) 1 mine d'or paiera etc. . . . Ces hommes le verger ont arpenté et les moutons ont livré etc. . . .[367].

Gordon describes this as a contract in which a man sells his inheritance rights to a grove to his brother for three sheep. This sale of a birthright is described as a disguised adoption into brotherhood. The apparent disproportion between the value of three sheep and the man's patrimony leads Gordon to conclude that Tupkitilla could only have been driven to such a bargain through severe hunger. "But just as Kurpazaḫ exploited Tupkitilla's hunger so did Jacob take advantage of the famished Esau[368]."

Elsewhere Gordon speaks of JEN 204 as a tablet in which Tupkitilla "sells his future inheritance rights"[369]. In his discussion of this parallel in 1957[370], he stresses the interpretation that Tupkitilla was driven into this agreement by dire necessity, "specifically to avert starvation". Thus he nearly completely identifies the sale of Esau's birthright and the Nuzi contract. That this is the case is clear when in The World of the Old Testament, he stresses the uniqueness of this parallel: "Jacob purchased from Esau the 'birthright' which means the title to the position of first born. This is no longer a peculiar incident without parallel. In the Nuzu tablets, inheritance prospects are negotiable (though only from brother to brother) much as stocks and bonds are today. One Nuzu tablet records how a man in need of food sold his inheritance portion to his own brother in exchange for livestock, even as the hungry Esau had sold his to Jacob for a 'mess of potage'[371]."

Aside from the issue of whether this parallel is unique, the two major points of similarity that are said to exist between JEN 204 and Gen 25 is that a man has sold his birthright to his brother, and that this was done in an obviously disproportionate bargain under

---

367 Cassin, L'adoption, 231.

368 Gordon, BA 3 (1940), 5.

369 JNES 13 (1954), 56 (emphasis added).

370 Adventures 119.

371 Gordon, World of the OT, 125f. See also similar interpretations by R. O'Callaghan, CBQ 6 (1944), 401; Rowley, BJRL 32 (1949/1950), 75; and Weir, Arch and OT Study, 76f. J. Holt (The Patriarchs of Israel 124f.) refers to AASOR XVI 58 as another parallel. This, however, is a simple sale adoption (see above section C). The phrase "as his inheritance share" does not refer to what Eḫeltešup might have once received from his father, but is Utḫaptae's (the receiver's) "inheritance share", i. e., it is simply the property being sold.

the duress of hunger. However, the only real similarity between JEN 204 and Gen 25 is that they are agreements between brothers. There is no indication in JEN 204 that we are dealing here with the sale of a birthright, that is, the transference of the rights of the first-born; for we cannot tell whether Tupkitilla or Kurpazaḫ is the elder. Second, it is quite clear that we are not dealing with the sale of an inheritance share or the right to some future inheritance. This is based on two observations: (1) The very last line of the above quoted tablet: "Ces hommes le verger ont arpenté et les moutons ont livré" shows that the sale is immediate and that the property had already been inherited by the sons; (2) much more important, the clear description of a specific field shows that we have to do not with an inheritance portion of the father's property, but rather only with the sale of a specific piece of land that happens to have been inherited.

In fact, the tablet closely resembles the type of contract known as "sale-adoption" discussed above in section C[372]. We have already discussed the similarities that the Nuzi sale adoption contracts had to other Near Eastern and biblical sales of land and inherited property. That these sales were contracted not only in the *ana marūti* but also in the *ana aḫḫūti* form is clear from the Mari text ARM VIII 11[373].

Several outright sales of land mention that the property being sold is the inheritance of the man making the sale[374].

JEN 204, however, differs from these somewhat in that it deals with an agreement between two brothers; that is, the agreement is made within the family. This perhaps can be compared profitably with no. 38 of the Laws of Eshnunna: "If one of several brothers wants to sell his share (in a property common to them) and his brother wants to buy it, he shall pay . . .[375]." In the Old Babylonian contracts, we find several examples of this kind of arrangement. One text from Nippur records an agreement by which a son buys the inheritance

---

372 Cassin (L'adoption 320f.) also identifies this text as a sale-adoption.

373 See Malamat, JNES (1962), 148.

374 See the Middle Assyrian contracts in: Koschaker, Rechtsurkunden, KAJ 149, p. 149f.; KAJ 153, p. 150f. and KAJ 164, p. 164, but especially the sale of a man's house recorded in a British Museum Papyrus from 4th century (B. C.) Egypt (A. F. Shore, The Sale of the House of Senkhonsis Daughter of Phibis, JEA 54, 1968, 194—198). In spite of the fact that the sale of inherited property in Egypt was strongly discouraged (see E. A. E. Jelinková, Sale of Inherited Property in the First Century B. C., P. Brit. Mus. 10075, Ex Salt Coll. No. 418, JEA 43 1957, 50f.) this sale was made in order to defray the costs of the burial of his wife. See further the discussion in section C above.

375 As translated by A. Goetze, The Laws of Eshnunna, ANET 163. This may possibly be compared with the Old Testament concept of the *ge'ulāh*.

share (a specific piece of his father's property) belonging to his paternal uncle for six shekels of silver[376].

Much more interesting for our purposes is a contract from the time of Hammurapi[377], in which two brothers, who have together inherited one slave, carry out the division of the inheritance by one brother selling the other his half-share in the slave. The Nuzi text seems to have a similar purpose. Indeed, it seems difficult to maintain that we are dealing with a sale at all. The overwhelmingly typical form of the sale-adoption is the contract *ana marūti*[378]. JEN 204, however, has the title: *ṭuppi aḫḫūti* ("Tablet of brothership") which is normally the form used for partnership agreements. Tupkitilla and Ḳurpazaḫ are also real brothers. The form of the clauses in the sale-adoption contract is also quite standardized. The property that is being sold is typically referred to with the phrase *kīma zitti-šu*, "as his share of the inheritance", and the money or the goods given in return for it are typically described by the phrase *kīma qīštišu* "as his gift". Lines 14ff. of JEN 204, however, read: *Tupkitilla ana Ḳurbazaḫ kīma zittišu iddin (din) u Ḳurbazaḫ 3 immerē (meš) kīma zittišu ana Tupkitilla ilqe*: "Tupkitilla has given to Ḳurpazaḫ (the field) as his share of the inheritance and Ḳurpazaḫ has delivered three sheep as his share of the inheritance to Tupkitilla."

This can be compared to the text JEN 87 which deals with a similar agreement between Ḳurpazaḫ and another brother[379], and also JEN 221, which deals again with brothers *ana aḫḫūti*. In these texts both parts of the exchange are also referred to as "part of the inheritance".

This is certain in JEN 221. In JEN 87 the property is referred to as *kīma zittišu* as in JEN 204 and most sale adoption contracts. The clause dealing with what is given in exchange is however damaged at this point. Cassin reconstructs the text on the basis of the standard sale-adoption forms *ki-i [-ma qišti]* etc. ... "as a gift". Since, however, the text resembles JEN 204 and 221 in all other respects, particularly as an *aḫḫūti* contract between brothers, it might perhaps be argued that the text should be reconstructed: *ki-i -[ma zitti-šu]* etc. with the implication that what we have in each of our tablets is a contract between brothers dealing with the division of their inheritance and not a sale[380].

---

376 Schorr, Zivil- und Prozessrecht, text 192, p. 266—268. Several examples of such arrangements within the family can also be found in Egypt; cf. Jelinková, JEA 43 (1957), 45 and 50f.; Pestman, Marriage, 83 and 137—139.

377 Schorr, Zivil- und Prozessrecht, text 80, p. 121.

378 See Cassin, L'adoption, 51—254.

379 Cassin, L'adoption, 232f.

380 Cassin (L'adoption, p. 231 n. 17) suggests: "Il faut penser qu'il s'agit d'une adoption en fraternité, les deux frères partageront donc leurs biens en parties égales."

I see no reason to suppose that the bargain made by Tupkitilla is to his disadvantage, and there is certainly no reason to assume that he was driven to such an agreement by starvation. Sheep, it is true, are food, but there is no further similarity between this and Esau's porridge. The garden that is exchanged is quite small, and three sheep, though they cannot be compared with the large sums of money paid in some of our tablets, nevertheless, have a significant value. The value of three sheep at Nuzi is three shekels of silver[381], which need not be considered necessarily as an unfair exchange for a piece of land. A field bought in HSS IX 116 costs 6 shekels of silver[382]. In the Old Babylonian period (when the value of a shekel was slightly different) a garden was sold for 5½ shekels. Another garden (the size of 5 *sar* is given) with date palms was sold for the full price of 1½ shekels of silver. 1½ *sar* of land with a house on it was sold complete for 3½ shekels of silver[383]!

K. GEN 27 1-45

A number of interpreters have claimed that Gen 27, the story of Isaac's last blessing, is closely paralleled by several Nuzi tablets[384]. However, the tablets that have been most commonly put forward as reflecting practices that might be related to Genesis do not seem to imply what has been claimed for them. It cannot be doubted that there is a real basis for comparison between the Nuzi inheritance practices, particularly the father's discriminating power over the inheritance, and the rules governing inheritance reflected in several places in the Old Testament. However, the claim that the patriarchal stories and the contracts of Nuzi reflect a common practice that is so different from other Near Eastern societies that we are justified in suggesting that they are related cannot be upheld. What is common to Nuzi and Genesis is characteristic of Nuzi as well as the rest of the Near East, and of Genesis as well as the rest of the Old Testament.

HSS IX 34 l. 9: *u inanna anāku altīb*: "Now that I have grown old" is compared by Speiser with the biblical phrase הנה־נא זקנתי in

[381] Cf. for example, HSS V 79 where the value of 10 sheep is given at 10 shekels of silver.

[382] Cassin, L'adoption, 240.

[383] J. Kohler, Ham. Ges. VI, texts 1602. 1624 and 1578 (p. 61. 70. and 79). Slaves were variously priced from as low as five or six shekels of silver to as high as a mina (60 shekels) of silver.

[384] Gordon, BA 3 (1940), 8; JNES 13 (1954), 56; World of the OT 127; E. A. Speiser, I Know not the Day of my Death, JBL 74 (1955), 252—256 (= OBS 89—96); IEJ 7 (1957), 213; IDB 574; Genesis 208. 210—213; and Weir, Arch. and OT Study, 76.

Gen 27 2, which he translates (I believe, correctly): "See now, I have grown (so) old (that)" לא ידעתי יום מותי: "I do not know the day of my death"[385]. On the basis of this comparison, Speiser concludes, that the statement "I have now grown old" was at Nuzi "a recognized formula accompanying a solemn final declaration; and such declarations had special standing precisely because they expressed a man's last wish. The phraseology, in short, had definite sociojuridical implications"[386].

If this were a formulaic statement with the well-established legal significance that Speiser suggests, one would expect that other testaments (e. g., HSS XIX 17) would also have this statement. The statement, is, on the other hand, just what one might expect to hear from a man who was old and dying, no matter what the purpose or general context of the statement. It is important to recognize that the context of this phrase at Nuzi is quite different from the deathbed blessing in Genesis. HSS IX 34 is not a personal testament, and, while the fact that the man is dying may well be the cause of the tablet, it does not have much bearing on its content. By this tablet Hannaya appoints five men — not as "executors"[387] but as apprentices[388] — to carry out his administrative work! These appointments are apparently effective, not as a result of the man's death — of which we know nothing — but of his present incapacity.

Nor is the phrase in Gen 27 2 entirely identical to the Akkadian phrase in HSS IX 34. The Akkadian *u innana anāku altīb* "now I have grown old" does not obviously imply that Hanaya is dying, only that he considers himself too old to carry on his work. The rest of the text is not a "final disposition"[389] but an administrative transfer of authority. Similarly, by itself, the biblical phrase, "Behold I have now grown old", is not a terminus technicus as Speiser says, but means no more than what it says. That Isaac is dying is clear only from the following phrase: "I do not know the day of my death." A similar event is related in Gen 48, and the entire sentence in Gen 27 might be compared with the simple and direct הנה אנכי מת in 48 21 "Behold, I am dying", which is obviously no terminus technicus[390].

Lest too much be made of a coincidence in phraseology between the Nuzi text and Genesis, we should also consider a similar phrase in

385 Speiser, OBS, 89; Genesis 205.

386 Speiser, OBS, 91.

387 See Speiser ibid.

388 Ibid. note 7. 389 Ibid. 91.

390 Compare also the similar phrase in Gen 24 1: אברהם זקן בא בימים "And Abraham was old and advanced in days", and I Reg 1 1: והמלך דוד זקן בא בימים "And King David was old and advanced in days."

the "Testimony of Naunakhte", an Egyptian text from the 20th dynasty, which is far closer to the biblical context. Here too the phrase "But behold, I have grown old", is so appropriate in its primary meaning to the context of a testament, that one is not justified considering it a terminus technicus. Young people do not ordinarily write testaments, and old age — not necessarily dying — is certainly an understandable motivation. The Egyptian text reads:

As for me, I am a free woman of the country of (the) Pharaoh; I have raised these eight servants of yours; I have given them an allowance of everything, as one is wont to do for those who are in their position. But behold, I have grown old, and behold, they do not take care of me anymore. As regards the one of them who has laid his hand on my hand: I will give my possessions to him, (but) as regards the one who has not given to me. I will not give to him of my possessions[391].

Speiser refers to HSS V 48 also as illustrating the legal background of Gen 27. Speiser's 1926 translation of the entire tablet reads:

[Thus] (says) Paitilla son of Giliya: "Ehlipapu son of Nupanani, Haištešup son of Puhišenni, Šatikintar son of Turikintar, Uthaptae son of Zigi, Turari son of Emuya, Nihriya son of Akaptukki, Akaptukki son of Kakki; these 8 judges sent me to Šurihil son of Ellaya (and) thus they (instructed me), 'Take with you 5 men and say to Šurihil, Thus (say) the judges: (Long) life to you now. There has been a claim against you. If I may trouble you, declare to us your son so that we might verily know'. Ehlitešup (and) Šarteshup sons of Tehiptilla, Arihhaya son of Šurukkaya, Akipšarru son of Ahuya, Artae son of Ennamilki, these 5 men I took with me (and) I spoke to Šurihil. Šurihil in my presence and in the presence of these witnesses declared as follows, 'Šennima son of Zigi is my (adopted) son as regards my fields and my buildings, and all that I have; there is no other son'."

The judges pronounced judgment in accordance with the declaration of Palteya and with the statements of these men. Šennima prevailed in the lawsuit, the judges ⟨assigning⟩ the fields and buildings of Šurihil to Šennima, son of Zigi.

Seals of 7 judges and signature of scribe.

The declaration of Tuppaya daughter of Arzizza, wife of Šurihil; she spoke as follows: "Yes, my husband Šurihil [adop]ted Šennima son of Zigi with regard to his land and his buildings[392].

In 1954 Speiser corrected the reading of the extremely difficult phrase in l. 15: *šumma aktatamatkimi* to *šumma atta tamāt kīmi*, and retranslated this part of the text to read "Thus (say) the judges: You are now alive and claims are being raised against you. Since you may die, then point out your son to us so that we may know.", which gives a much better reading[393]. Speiser understands the text to state that Šurihil is asked to "declare formally who his heir was to be", and he concludes that this text gives us "unusually vivid confirmation of the repeatedly established fact that at Nuzi, and

[391] Pestman, Marriage, 163.

[392] AASOR X no. 33, p. 67.

[393] OBS 94.

by extension also in Hurrian society in general, sonship could legally be determined by fiat, i. e., adoption, as much as by birth"[394].

It is unfortunately not very clear what Speiser is trying to stress in his argument. Is it that the principle of adoption implies the father's at least partial control over the inheritance? That is true, of course, but why choose this particular text which only refers indirectly to an adoption when we have so many good adoption contracts? Moreover, if this is his point, how is it particularly related to Hurrian society? Adoption, with a right to the inheritance, is, as we have seen, known elsewhere in the Near East. But what has adoption to do with Gen 27, for neither Jacob nor Esau is an adopted son?

Or does Speiser try to stress that sonship can be declared "by fiat", and to imply that since we have a declaration here from a dying man, we have what approximates the creation of an heir by a verbal "deathbed" testament?

That this is his intention seems confirmed by his reference to the adoption contract HSS V 7, particularly the lines: "If a son of my own is born to me, he shall be the oldest, receiving two inheritance shares. Indeed, should the wife of Akabšenni bear ten sons, they shall (all) be major (heirs), Šelluni (becoming) a secondary heir"[395]. with the conclusion that "The primacy of the birthright is here a matter of the father's discretion and not of chronological priority. To be sure, in the present instance the distinction involves actual offspring as against an adopted relative. Elsewhere, however, a similar distinction is made between sons of the same father but of different mothers, an understandable procedure in a polygamous society. In any case, in matters of birthright, the father's decree could reverse the natural order"[396].

Speiser's argument, however, does not show this. The adoption contracts, including HSS V 7, all take for granted the real son's right to the inheritance. What is negotiated by contract is the adopted son's place in the inheritance, and, in those few cases in which the adopted son is guaranteed the place of primary heir (in no tablet known to me from Nuzi), the adoption is contracted before the birth of biological sons, so that we cannot say — even in the case of adoption — that the father has the right to arbitrarily displace his eldest son.

In those cases where the children are from different wives, elder children of a secondary wife may well have only a secondary right

[394] Ibid.

[395] So ibid. 95. Line 15 might also be read: "Šelluni (shall be) a secondary heir."

[396] Ibid. (emphasis added).

to the inheritance — or perhaps no right at all, as we have seen above in section G, but this is based, not so much on the powers of discretion held by the father, as by the status of the wife as established in the marriage contract, and the question of whether the children by the secondary wife have been made legitimate.

HSS V 48 does not resemble a last testament nor any special decretal power possessed by Šurihil. The tablet is concerned only with asking Šurihil to declare who had already been made his heir. There has been a claim made against him (l. 14), and it cannot be settled without the assurance from Šurihil that he had adopted Šennima. The declaration made by Šurihil is not a decree that makes Šennima the heir, but merely one that confirms Šennima's status. What makes Šennima Šurihil's heir is that Šurihil had previously adopted him. So ll. 42ff.: "The declaration of Tuppaya daughter of Arzizza, wife of Šurihil; she spoke as follows: 'Yes, my husband Šurihil adopted Šennima son of Zigi with regard to his land and his buildings'." We have this adoption contract in HSS V 67[397]. In HSS V 59 we learn that Šennima later gives this property to his brother Arzizza[398].

The text that has been related to Gen 27 which deserves the most serious attention is AASOR XVI 56[399]. Speiser and Gordon claim that this text gives conclusive proof that a death-bed statement could be legally binding, that an oral will made to a son by a dying father had legal validity[400].

> Tarmiya son of Huya with Šukriya and with Kulahupi, with (these) two of his brothers, sons of Huya, on account of the slave-girl [Zululi-Ištar] in a lawsuit before the judges of Nuzi appeared, and thus Tarmiya before the judges spoke: "My father Huya was ill and on (his) couch he lay. And my hand my father seized and thus to me he spoke, 'The other sons of mine are older (and) wives they have taken. But you have not taken a wife. So Zululi-Ištar as your wife to you herewith I am giving'." And the judges witnesses of Tarmiya requested. [And Tarmiya] his witness [before the judges] produced: . . . son of Huršaya, . . . son of Ekkiya, . . . son of Itruša, (and) . . . son of Hamanna, [these] witnesses of [Tarmiya] were examined before the judges. And the judges to Šukriya and to Kulahupi spoke: "Go and (against) the witnesses of Tarmiya take the oath of the gods. From the gods Šukriya and Kulahupi shrank, and in the lawsuit Tarmiya prevailed [and] the judges assigned the slave-girl Zululi-Ištar to Tarmiya[401].

This Nuzi tablet is about a young man who claims that his father had promised him the slave girl Zululi-Ištar as his bride, but

397 AASOR X 2.

398 AASOR X 3.

399 See on this, Speiser, OBS, 91f., and Gordon, BA 3 (1940), 8; JNES 13 (1954), 56, and World of the OT 127.

400 Ibid.

401 AASOR XVI no. 56, p. 107.

now that his father has died, his brothers object to it. When he is able to establish witnesses, his plea is upheld. Several observations need to be made about this text in reference to Speiser's and Gordon's claims. (1) This is not a deathbed testament, but rather a claim, that the father who is now dead wished to give his son a wife over and beyond his normal inheritance share. (2) Nor is the claim upheld because the promise had been made orally when the man was dying, but rather because, although oral, it was upheld by witnesses. (3) The Nuzi tablet does not deal with a change in the relative position of the sons to each other; nor does it declare the younger son the primary heir, or even concern the basic inheritance shares of the brothers. What is at stake is a specific slave girl. The text deals with the young man's bride whom the father, because of his death, failed to give the son while he was alive. This is not a case of inheritance. The promise which the father made to the son itself established the son's right to the girl. It is not a right which he acquired upon the death of the father.

An interesting parallel to this Nuzi text is the CH no. 166 where this right is stated as law:

> If a seignior, upon acquiring wives for the the sons that he got, did not acquire a wife for his youngest son, when the brothers divide after the father had gone to (his) fate, to their youngest brother who did not acquire a wife, to him in addition to his share they shall assign money (enough) for the marriage-price from the goods of the paternal estate and thus enable him to acquire a wife[402].

That these tablets fail to show what they have been claimed to prove does not mean, however, that the general law governing inheritance in Israel, Num 27 8-11, is to be so understood that a man had no discretionary rights over his property. This is manifestly not true. In I Kings 1 1-39, David bypasses his son Adonijah (with cause, cf. v. 5 f.) and chooses the younger brother Solomon over him (see also, I Kings 2 1-9). Also Hosah in I Chr 10 26 made Simri the chief of his clan though he was not the eldest. The law of Numbers gives us the general principle that governs the law of inheritance. This guarantees the succession of the property in the case that the head of the family dies intestate. In turn, there were rules, like Deut 21 16, which protected the sons from some of the more obvious injustices. The rule in Deut 21 16 is often presented as contradicting the story in Gen 27[403]. I do not see that this is true, since Deuteronomy deals with the respective inheritance rights of two sons born of different, nevertheless equal, wives (such as, e. g., Leah and Rachel). It forbids discrimination against an eldest son based merely on the grounds of

[402] ANET 173.
[403] So Speiser, IDB, 574.

preference for another wife. This does not imply that an eldest son could not be disinherited, nor that a younger son could not be raised to a higher position. In a similar way, CH nos. 168f. require that a man have grave cause before he can disinherit a son, and then only after a second offense (cf. I Kings 2 15 I Chr 5 1). That the father could also give a part of the inheritance to those who otherwise would not receive a share, if he were to die without some form of testament, is shown above all by Job 42 15 and by Prov 17 2. In fact, these texts imply the possibility of testament to ensure someone the succession to property or valuables who would otherwise not inherit in the normal course of succession. This interpretation seems to be supported by many different records from the ancient Near East. The purpose of the testament is very clearly stated in the legal Code of Hermopolis West, which though dated to the reign of Philadelphus, probably goes back in the original to a much earlier date. The text states: "If a man dies leaving lands, gardens, temple offices (?) and slaves; if he had children and he did not assign shares to them while alive, it is his eldest son who takes possession of the property of his father"[404].

In most cases where our evidence is sufficient, it seems that the right of testation and especially the possibility of disinheriting a son was severely restricted, and hedged with difficulties. Nevertheless we have several examples of testaments according to which property is left to people who otherwise could not inherit[405]. We have several such texts from the Old Babylonian period, though most seem to be contracts which create someone other than a member of the family as heir[406]. At least in one text[407] the father leaves the property to his four sons and his daughter. Another text concerns a litigation in which an oral testimony is upheld in court[408]. The CH no. 165 also allows the father to give gifts over and above the inheritance shares to a favorite son[409], and quite often records of gifts have been found which are, in fact, testaments[410].

Examples of testaments are rarer in other bodies of documents. Nevertheless, one text from Egypt should be mentioned, dated to the reign of Ramses II, in which the woman Urnero is recognized as

404 G. Mattha, A Preliminary Report on the Legal Code of Hermopolis West, BIdEg 23 (1941), 308.

405 A testament from Nuzi is HSS XIX, 17.

406 So Kohler, Ham. Ges. IV, no. 1043, 1046 and 1048; VI, 1741—1743.

407 Ibid. IV 1044.

408 ANETS 543.

409 For the general rules in the OB period, cf. Schorr, Zivil- und Prozessrecht, 359 to 361; Cúq, Droit Babylonien, 54f. 62—64.

410 Schorr ibid.

the "eldest" and appointed trustee and administrator of the estate[411]. As might be expected, it appears that it is most often a man's wife to whom he wishes to leave his property by special testament. We have contracts of this sort from Egypt[412], from the Old Babylonian Period[413], as well as from Ugarit[414]. It is particularly interesting that in these texts, the wife is made the heir, and the property is to descend ultimately to the sons. This is, however, not merely a delay in the son's inheritance, for the wife is almost invariably given the power to disinherit any son who does not treat her properly, and she is often allowed to give the inheritance to the son of her choice. This, of course, implies the possibility that the inheritance may be given to a younger son. Similarly, we learn from one Old Babylonian text, that a man, who has remarried, requires of the sons that they care for their stepmother under the threat of disinheritance[415]. Another text records the actual disinheritance of a son (apparently not adopted) for failing to meet his annual payments to his father from the family property[416]. Records of other acts of disinheritance are relatively common[417], and the basic possibility of disinheritance was already established in the Sumerian Laws no. 4:

---

411 Gardiner, The Inscription of Meš, UGAA 4, 1905. On inheritance in Egypt in general see, J. J. Janssen and P. W. Pestman, Burial and Inheritance in the Community of the Necropolis Workmen at Thebes, JESHO 11 (1968), 165—168.

412 J. Pirenne and M. Stracmans, Le testament à l'époque de l'Ancien Empire Egyptien, RIDA 1 (1954), 49; A. J. Gardiner, JEA 26 (1940), 23f.: "All profit that I have made with her, I will bequeath it to Nenūfer, my wife, and if [any of] my own brothers and sisters arise to confront her at my death tomorrow or thereafter and say 'Let my brother's share be given (to me)'" etc. (the apodosis has been left off.); S. Wenig, Die Frau im alten Ägypten, 12f.; see however, especially the "Testimony of Naunakhte" (Pestman, Marriage, 1961, 163) where a woman, who was apparently the heir of her husband, (Théodoridès, RIDA 13, 1966, 48 and esp. 68f.) gives the inheritance to five of her eight children. Three are totally and one partially disinherited.
There are also some contracts in which men leave property to women who are apparently not their wives: Pap. Louvre 2439 (330—329 B. C.), Pap. Louvre 2429b (292/1 B. C.), Pap. Rylands XI (285/4 B. C.), and Pap. Marseille (235/4 B. C.). Cf. Spiegelberg, Ägyptische Verpfründungsverträge, 3—12.

413 Esp. Schorr, Zivil- u. Prozessrecht, texts 183, 202 and 204; see also, however, texts 13 and 210, where the heir is the daughter.

414 F. Thureau-Dangin, Trois Contrats de Ras-Shamra, Syria 18 (1937), 245—255, and ANETS 546, text no. 17.

415 Schorr, Zivil- u. Prozessrecht, text 6, p. 13f.

416 J. Kohler, Ham. Ges. IV, text 1056.

417 Cf. e. g., ibid. III, texts 737—739, and Rainey, Orientalia (1965), 19 and 21. Acts of disinheritance at Nuzi are HSS XIX 17 and 27. Moreover, HSS V 21 (AASOR X 8) refers to a previous disinheritance of a son and his reinstatement to his position as firstborn.

If (a son) has said to his father and to his mother: "You are not my father; you are not my mother", he forfeits (his heir's rights to) house, field, orchard, slaves and (any other) property, and they may sell him (into slavery) for money at full value[418].

The possibility of a younger son being appointed the primary heir by the father, without the disinheritance of the elder, is clear from the Egyptian Legal Code of Hermapolis West:

If a man dies, leaving his property in the hands of the younger son, and if the elder son brings complaint against his younger brother on account of the property; and if the younger son says "the property, for which he has brought action against me, is mine, my father is he who gave it to me, he is made to swear saying it is my father who gave me this property, saying take it for thyself". If he swears, his elder brother is not given the property. If he does not swear, the property is given to his elder brother, and a title is written for him to the property of his father[419].

While it seems clear that the inheritance of a younger son is legally possible, this is not to say that the story of the deathbed blessing in Gen 27 is to be explained on legal grounds. For in this story Isaac has the intention of giving Esau the blessing. Through trickery, however, Jacob gets it. If this were a real situation, then we would expect that Isaac, in discovering the deception, would reverse his decision[420]. In fact, Jacob's offense, in a legal sense, would be quite serious. We, however, have here a story, and the power of Isaac's word has determined Jacob's and his brother's future. Gen 27 does not mention property, and so we are not dealing here with the inheritance of property, but rather the determination of destiny. Destiny once determined is irreversible. The reason that Jacob is able to usurp Esau's place and become Isaac's primary heir is not explained by Near Eastern law, let alone the legal contracts from Nuzi. It is rather found in the literary motif: The Success of the Unpromising; more explicitly, the Youngest son receives the Birthright, and is paralleled in Ugaritic literature[421].

In this context, the story of Jacob and Esau, as well as that of Keret gives added support to the traditional structure of inheritance, as, for example, found in Numbers, and could not exist in a society in which the inheritance of the younger was common; for it is the very extraordinary character of this event which enables it to function as a literary motif effectively. The Jacob-Esau story is therefore a confirmation of Num 21 and cannot be dated as necessarily early merely on the basis of the supposed disagreement of these texts.

418 ANETS 526.

419 G. Mattha, BId'Eg 23 (1941), 308.

420 Such reversals are always possible, cf. HSS V 21 (AASOR X 8)!

421 In the Keret Legend, UH 128, col III, l. 16; cf. also A. van Selms, Marriage and Family Life, 41; C. H. Gordon, Review of Cassuto, The Goddess Anath, JAOS 72 (1952), 180f.; The World of the OT 96.

L. CONCLUSION TO CHAPTER 10

In considering the different laws and contracts which might possibly help us to understand the stories in Genesis, we have been able to make more explicit several methodological difficulties involved in a discussion of the legal background of the narratives. (1) The difference in the basic form of our texts (stories in Genesis, and laws, records, and contracts in our Near Eastern legal corpus) presents us with the difficulty of not being certain whether our materials, even when similar, are truly comparable; for it cannot be taken for granted that the Genesis stories reflect, even indirectly, the customs and practices of any people. There is sufficient evidence in some cases that they do not. (2) Those Genesis stories which do seem to presuppose the assumptions of every day life, nevertheless do so in such a general way, that any attempt to place them chronologically or geographically seems hopeless. (3) Equally troublesome is the wide variability of our Near Eastern contracts. While given groups of texts may show common presuppositions and concerns, in the most typical contracts our material is far too limited to allow the type of distinctions necessary for a chronology based on form. (4) Consequently, it is impossible to determine whether the biblical practices that can be defined can be dated to any specific period in Near Eastern history[422].

Nevertheless, some important negative conclusions can be made about patriarchal customs, particularly, that they do not seem to be in conflict with later biblical practice. Moreover, there is no apparent reason to suppose that they are not Palestinian in origin. There are many a priori reasons to believe that practices dealing with marriage, adoption, and particularly inheritance, are not easily imported[423].

Positively, it can be said that many of the customs in Genesis, that cannot be directly related to known literary motifs, fit very well into the general context of ancient Near Eastern family law, and a comparison of these stories with this legal material is quite helpful in understanding the intention of these narratives.

The Nuzi tablets offer us one of the richest sources for Near Eastern legal contracts related to family customs. A comparison with Old Babylonian and other legal materials shows that the basic presuppositions, system of values, and purpose, as well as all of the customs that we have examined, are shared with other Near Eastern

---

422 In spite of the recent attempts of J. van Seters: JBL 87 (1968), 401—408, and HThR 62 (1969), 377—395.

423 Cf. P. Koschaker, Keilschriftrecht, ZDMG 89 (1935), 32; M. David, Hammurabi and the Law in Exodus, OTS 7 (1950), 154; Th. and D. Thompson, VT 18 (1968), 83.

societies. Since there do not seem to be major elements in these contracts which can be identified specifically as Hurrian, it seems more correct to speak of these practices, and what laws they might presuppose, as "Nuzian". The Hurrians at Nuzi have obviously shared the basically Sumero-Akkadian legal practices of the region in which they settled.

The value that the Nuzi texts have for the study of Genesis is extremely limited. Our survey has shown the practices at Nuzi to be relatively different from those presupposed by Genesis. Certainly no historical connection can be drawn between Genesis and Nuzi. Nevertheless, the Nuzi texts are indirectly very valuable for an understanding of Genesis, and indeed the entire Old Testament treatment of family laws, since they are a large body of texts from a single site, dated to a limited period, and thus may well serve as a good basis for the understanding of Near Eastern contracts in general[424].

The attempt to date Genesis on the basis of the type of customs the stories reflect does not seem to be a promising pursuit, for we are totally without chronological criteria. In 1953 M. Lehmann attempted to date the story of the purchase of the cave at Machpelah to the Late Bronze Age and to draw what he thought might show an authentic historical relationship by comparing the biblical story with the Hittite Law Code nos. 46—48 and 169. He saw elements of the conversation between Ephron and Abraham as perhaps best explained by the type of feudal structure reflected in the Hittite laws. He felt that his hypothesis was supported by verse 17 which mentioned the trees that were on the plot that Abraham purchased[425].

This coincidence, however, is only superficial, since, aside from the fact that trees are an important element in any land purchase, Gen 23 17 does not mention the exact number of trees on the plot of land; only that all the trees belonged to Abraham. Moreover, if Lehmann were correct in relating Gen 23 to the feudal structure reflected in the Hittite law, he would not thereby identify the background of the story as Hittite, nor would he be able to determine

---

[424] As far as I am aware, this work is yet to be done. Only a relatively small number of texts are easily available even in transliteration. The very important volume of family contracts, HSS XIX, published in 1962, is still only available in cuneiform copy.

[425] M. R. Lehmann, Abraham's Purchase of Machpelah and Hittite Law, BASOR 129 (1953), 15—18. His interpretation was generally accepted and widely followed: Gordon, JBR 21 (1953), 242; The World of the OT 124; J. Bright, History of Israel, 72; G. E. Wright, Biblical Archaeology, 51; H. Haag, Homer, Ugarit und das Alte Testament, 1962, 25.

the period in which the story originated, since the elements that Gen 23 is said to have in common with the Hittite laws are neither ethnically nor chronologically limited to a single place and time. Feudal structures related to the purchase of land cannot be defined as peculiarly Hittite.

In 1965 H. Petschow argued that Gen 23 had remarkably strong similarities to several Neobabylonian sale contracts. He decisively proved thereby that the story need not be dated to the Second Millenium. He also judiciously pointed out that the contracts need not necessarily be dated to the Neobabylonian period[426]. In 1966 G. M. Tucker discussed similar neobabylonian contracts and argued convincingly that the story in Genesis "has many general characteristics in common with Near Eastern legal forms from many periods"[427].

That the story is in any way historically related to Babylonian laws is seriously to be doubted, but that the story probably reflects in some measure — perhaps in caricature — the way the storyteller understood how people bought and sold land comes from the story itself, and the general authenticity of this picture is confirmed to some extent by the parallels suggested by Petschow and Tucker.

Similar to the contracts dealing with family laws, these dealing with land sales aid biblical interpretation, in that they enable the student to see more clearly the meaning and general context of the different elements of a story. They supply him with the necessary details that help him to discern nuances of interpretation that would otherwise lie hidden. They do not help him, however, to determine a date for these stories, nor to relate them to any specific geographic region. Even less do they help him to confirm the historicity of the patriarchal narratives.

In chapters 1 through 9 of this book we have discussed the major current arguments that are used to support the thesis that the patriarchs of Israel are historical and that they can be dated to the Second Millenium B. C. There does not seem to be any single argument that supports this thesis either historically or exegetically. If the patriarchs are historical, they are not reflected in any records of the Second Millenium that we possess. Indeed, aside from the still enigmatic Gen 14, I have tried to show that what we know about the history of Palestine in the Second Millenium seems to argue definitely against any such historicity.

Not only is there no evidence to support a dating of the patriarchal narratives prior to the existence of Israel, there are some indications

---

[426] H. Petschow, Die neubabylonische Zwiegesprächsurkunde und Gen. 23, JCS 19 (1965), 103—120.

[427] G. M. Tucker, The Legal Background of Genesis 23, JBL 85 (1966), 77—84.

to suggest that these stories may well have to be dated to a much later period.

In the earlier chapters of this book I spent considerable time discussing the proposed arguments for the historicity of Abraham's wandering from Ur of the Chaldees to Canaan, and, ultimately to Egypt. In the following chapter, I will try to discuss something of the intention of Gen 11 26 ff. and I hope to be able to show to the reader's satisfaction that not only is the claim of historicity for the patriarchal stories a serious distortion of history, but that it is also a misunderstanding of the formation and intention of the biblical tradition.

Chapter 11

Genesis 11 10—12 9 and the Wanderings of Abraham

A. The Patriarchs and the Aramaeans

The patriarchs, and especially Abraham, are the means by which the biblical tradition has expressed Israel's political, sociological and geographical ties with the world surrounding it. This is effected in the tradition through the personification of peoples, tribes, and territories, and their relation to each other by means of genealogies and Stammessage. This structure lends itself readily to the development of tales about the ancestral heroes which expand and fill out the genealogies, and which in turn, when originally self subsistent, are ordered by the genealogies. Understandably, the stories often are aetiological in intent and are used to explain the historiographical relationship between the eponymous ancestor or hero and the tribe, village, or region bearing his name.

Examples of such names are found throughout the Bible, especially in Joshua and Judges. A large number of the geographical and tribal names known to Israel take on personalities in the stories and genealogies dealing with the prehistory of Israel: ארם, כנען, אשר, מצרים, etc. The Aramaeans of the Syrian desert are gathered together in the form of a genealogy of Abraham's kinsman Nahor, including place names from this region: Uz, Buz, Hazo, Chesed, Tebah, and Maacah[1]. The Arabs, including such well known places as Midian, Sheba and Dedan are introduced as the descendants of Abraham[2]. Similarly the twelve tribes of Israel are personified by eponymous ancestors as sons of Jacob[3], and above all, the name Israel itself is similarly used, appearing also in the forms בני ישראל (cf. בני קדם, בני שכם, בני שמשי, בני עמון, and בני אדם) and בית ישראל (cf. בית יוסף, בית יהודה, בית אפרים, and בית בנימן)[4].

It is uncertain whether the names Jacob and Isaac are originally eponymous, or whether they are names of folk heroes which have been used eponymously. Jacob is found, particularly in the prophetic writings, as a name for the people Israel. In Mic 1 5 it is the northern kingdom of Israel: in Neh 2 3, the southern kingdom of Judah. The

[1] Cf. Job 1 1 32 2. 6 Jer 25 20. 23 II Sam 10 6. 8 I Chr 19 6f.

[2] R. A. Bowman, Genealogy, IDB II 363.

[3] M. Noth, Die Welt des alten Testaments, 1962⁴, 48ff.

[4] F. Delitzsch, Wo lag das Paradies ?, 1881, 98.

name appears in the form בני יעקב in I Kings 19 3 and Mal 3 6, and in the form בית יעקב in Gen 46 27 Ex 19 3 Is 2 5f. 8 17 Am 3 13 9 8 and Mic 2 7. In Gen 37 2a we find the beginning of a genealogy of Jacob which has been lost (or suppressed in favor of the genealogy of Israel)[5]. Similarly, the name Isaac appears as a synonym for Israel in Am 7 9 and in the form בית ישחק in Am 7 16[6].

Names like Lot, Esau, Laban, and probably Abraham[7], are originally not names of eponymous ancestors but are rather names of folk heroes, who perform the function in the tradition of Urväter, giving expression to the political and social ties that Israel has with its neighbors, above all the Aramaeans of the north and northeast, and related tribes to the south and southeast[8].

Although these traditions cannot confidently be used for the reconstruction of history, or to answer questions about the origin of Israel, they do reflect Israel's view of the world after its formation as a people. According to the tradition of Genesis the Israelites understood themselves to be living in the land of the Canaanites, Amorites and Philistines, but as related to the Aramaeans and the desert tribes of the South: through Esau with the tribes of Edom; through Lot with the Moabites and Ammonites; through the sons of Keturah with the Arabs, and through Ishmael with the Ishmaelites[9].

The relationship with the Aramaeans is expressed in several traditions, and three different geographical regions are referred to.

---

[5] In the Genesis text, this follows Chapter 36, the genealogy of Esau (Edom) and of Seir the Horite.

[6] For further discussion of the eponymous character of Israel's ancestors, see: E. Meyer, Der Stamm Jakob und die Entstehung der israelitischen Stämme, ZAW 6 (1886), 1—16; K. Albrecht, Das Geschlecht der hebräischen Hauptwörter, ZAW 16 (1896), 41—121 (passim); Th. Nöldeke, Names, EncBb III, 3264—3331; Robertson Smith Kinship and Marriage in Early Arabia, ZDMG 40 (1886), 158f.; E. von Mülinen, Das Nomaden Abschied, ZDMG 4 (1925), 150—161; H. Gunkel, Genesis, 1966^{7}, LXXVIf.; H. Gressmann, Sage und Geschichte in den Patriarchenerzählungen, ZAW 30 (1910), 1—34; M. Noth, Das Amt des Richters Israels, in: Festschrift A. Bertholet, 404ff.; K. Schunck, Benjamin, BZAW 86, 1963, 4; H. Haag, Patriarchen, Bibellexikon, 1326; and especially recently, M. D. Johnson, The Purpose of the Biblical Chronologies, 1969, passim.

[7] See, however, above ch. 2. Isaac and Jacob, as mentioned earlier, might also possibly be seen as folk heroes rather than as eponymous ancestors.

[8] E. Meyer, Die Israeliten und ihre Nachbarstämme, 1906, 230—234; O. Eissfeldt, Stammessage und Novelle in den Geschichten von Jakob und von seinen Söhnen, Festschrift H. Gunkel, I 56—77.

[9] On these last two groups see R. Dussaud, La Pénétration des Arabes en Syrie avant l'Islam, Institute Francais d'Archéologie de Beyrouth, Bibliothèque Archéologique et Historique 59, 1955, 174—179; S. Moscati, The Semites in Ancient History, 1959, 72.

(1) The Aramaeans of Transjordan: The genealogy of Nahor, the brother of Abraham, connects the patriarch with the Aramaeans of Transjordan through a list of 12 sons, comparable to the 12 sons of Jacob and Ishmael[10]. Although the identification of the names is not in every case certain, it seems nevertheless clear that the sons of Nahor are a list of tribes and regions in the Syrian and North Arabian deserts. The name Nahor itself, however, appears secondary, serving as a link with the Abraham traditions[11]. The groups referred to are the Aramaeans settled to the east and northeast of Palestine. עוץ, in Job 1 1-3, lies in the region of the בני קדם, which is the desert area east of Palestine. Such a location is also demanded by Gen 32 20 and suits Lam 4 21 and Jer 25 20 well (cf. also Josephus, Ant. I, 145)[12]. The place name בוז is closely related to עוץ and in Jer 25 23 is listed alongside Dedan and Tema in NW Arabia. In I Chr 5 14, בוז is listed as one of the ancestors of the tribe of Gilead. The name is also probably to be identified with the land of *Ba-a-zu* which appears as one of the regions conquered by Asarhaddon during a campaign in Arabia[13]. The land of חזו is also mentioned in Asarhaddon's campaign in the form *Ha-zu-u*, and lay in the highlands just north of *Ba-a-zu*[14]. There may be some doubt that קמואל (the head of the tribe of Ephraim in Num 34 24) is either a tribal or geographical name, but

---

[10] Cf. F. Delitzsch, Neuer Commentar über die Genesis, 1887⁵, 239; E. Meyer. Die Israeliten, 241—243; J. Skinner, Genesis, 1917, 232; G. von Rad, Das erste Buch Mose, 1964⁷, 210; E. A. Speiser, Genesis, 1964, 167; O. Eissfeldt, Stammessage und Menschheitserzählung in der Genesis, Sitzungsberichte der Sächsischen Akademie der Wissenschaft zu Leipzig, 110, 4 (1965), 9.

[11] Eissfeldt's attempt to contrast Gen 22 20-24 to Gen 29 15—30 24, showing the development of a Stammessage into a story about individuals (Stammessage 9), seems unquestionably correct. However, this process is already begun in Gen 22 20-24 with the introduction of the North Arabian tribes into the Israelite patriarchal traditions as the sons of Nahor. Furthermore, unless Nahor can be shown to really belong to this region, it is doubtful that the tradition is correctly to be understood as referring to either a tribal or a geographical unity. I am much more inclined to identify Nahor with the Aramaean city-state Til Naḫiri in North Mesopotamia and to see the names listed in Gen 22 20-24 as a willful collection of place names from the Transjordanian region, patterned after the traditional twelve-tribe confederation.

[12] Further, see E. Meyer, Die Israeliten, 239; Th. Nöldeke, ZDMG 40 (1886), 183f.; P. Dhorme, Le Pays de Job, RB 8 (1911), 104f.; J. Skinner, Genesis, 332; R. Dussaud, La Pénétration, 173; R. Smend, Die Erzählung des Hexateuch auf ihre Quellen untersucht, 1912, 49; E. A. Speiser, Genesis, 166.

[13] Cf. E. Meyer, Die Israeliten, 239; J. Skinner, Genesis, 332f.; P. Dhorme, RB 8 (1911), 104.

[14] E. Meyer, Die Israeliten, 240; P. Dhorme, RB 8 (1911), 104; J. Skinner, Genesis, 333.

rather appears (like Isaac?) to be one of the patriarchs of the Aramaeans.[15] His son Aram is, of course, the eponym of the Aramaeans. The name כשד apparently refers to the Aramaean tribal group mentioned in II Kings 24 12 and Job 1 17 (next to the Sabaeans); i. e., כשד must lie in the neighborhood of עוץ and בוז. This tribe is probably not to be connected with the Chaldaeans of Gen 11 29. 31[16]. The character of the name Bethuel is not clear, and its insertion here may well be dependent on the Laban/Jacob tradition (cf. Gen 28 5 29 5). טבח is unknown; possibly the Aramaean city of בטח in II Sam 8 8. The identification of the last named son of Nahor: מעכה is the most certain. It was a small Aramaean state just to the south of Mount Hermon (Deut 3 14 II Sam 10 6 20 14f. Jos 13 11. 13)[17].

The Israelites are also closely connected to the Aramaeans of Transjordan through the Jacob tradition in Gen 29—31. In Gen 29 1 (E) Jacob comes to the land of the בני קדם (contrast Gen 29 4: J) which is the steppeland on the fringe of the Syro-Arabian desert east of Palestine (Gen 49 26 Deut 33 15 Num 23 7)[18]. Similarly, in the Stammessage in Genesis, Jacob's argument and covenant with Laban, establishing the border between Israel and the Aramaeans takes place in the mountains of Gilead in Transjordan. Only later is the tradition transplanted to Ḫarran in North Mesopotamia[19].

While the traditions portray a close relationship between the Israelites and the Aramaeans of Transjordan, seeing the brother of

---

[15] E. Meyer, Die Israeliten, 239; B. Mazar, The Aramaean Empire and its Relations with Israel, BA 25 (1962), 99.

[16] See especially H. Winckler, Altorientalische Forschungen, 1900, II 250—252, who is followed by E. Meyer, Die Israeliten, 240; J. Skinner, Genesis, 333; R. Smend, Erzählung, 49.

[17] E. Meyer, Die Israeliten, 241; M. Streck, Über die älteste Geschichte der Aramäer, mit besonderer Berücksichtigung der Verhältnisse in Babylonien und Assyrien, Klio 6 (1906), 200; M. Noth, Die Nachbarn der israelitischen Stämme im Ostjordanlande, Beiträge zur Geschichte des Ostjordanlandes III, ZDPV 68 (1951), 29; E. A. Speiser, Genesis, 167.

[18] E. Meyer, ZAW 5 (1885), 46; Die Israeliten 242—249; R. Smend, Erzählung, 49; R. Dussaud, La Pénétration, 175—178; J. Skinner, Genesis, 334; H. Gunkel, Jakob, RGG², 14—17. The name is also found in Egyptian texts (cf. e. g., A. Gardiner, The Kadesh Inscriptions of Ramesses II, 1960, 7 and 58 n. 14: *Ḳd-y*). Unfortunately, the identification of the place name from the Egyptian texts usually follows the traditional interpretation of the Sinuhe text, placing Qedem somewhere in North Syria to the East of Byblos. But, as we have already seen, such a location is not required by this text (See above ch. 6).

[19] E. Meyer, Die Israeliten, 244. 280; J. Skinner, Genesis, 334; H. Gunkel, RGG², 14; Jakob, PrJ 176 (1919), 352f.; M. Noth, Das Land Gilead als Siedlungsgebiet israelitischer Sippen, PJ 37 (1941), 61—65; O. Garcia-Treto, Genesis 31 44 and Gilead, ZAW 79 (1967), 13—17; A. van den Born, Jakob, Bibellexikon, 801.

Abraham as the ancestor of the Aramaeans and presenting Jacob's father-in-law as Laban the Aramaean, they also, in doing this, distinguish the patriarchs from the Aramaeans. As Stammessage, the traditions are not historical but aetiological, and attempt to describe and explain the divisions as well as the relationships that exist. The story of Jacob and Laban explains the boundary that separates the Aramaeans from the Israelite tribes. Therefore, to see Jacob himself as an Aramaean is to misinterpret the tradition[20]. That Laban names the stone in Aramaic: יגר שהדותא and Jacob calls it in Hebrew גלעד, emphasizes this intention of the storyteller. Jacob is also the brother of Esau (albeit in an originally independent tradition); and this expresses a distinction which the tribe of Judah understood between themselves and the Edomites. They were descendents of Jacob and not of Esau. The divisions continue down into the present; the unity existed in the "Urzeit", before Israel was a people! It seems, therefore, highly unlikely that the patriarchal tradition of Jacob can be seriously used for evidence of an historical memory connecting the people of Israel originally with the Aramaeans. That they would naturally understand themselves to have been more closely attached to the tribal elements in their cultural milieu (the Aramaeans, Moabites, Ammonites, Edomites, and Ishmaelites) is readily explainable on sociological grounds. On the other hand, Deut 26 5: "My father was a wandering Aramaean who went down to Egypt ..." is a completely different kind of tradition and may perhaps be understood to have an historical intention, but it is not related to any of the patriarchal traditions that connect the patriarchs with the Aramaeans. If it is early, it should be understood independently of the traditions discussed here.

Chronologically, these traditions should be placed sometime after the establishment of Israel in Palestine. In the Amarna period the Aramaeans were still nomadic tribes in the Syrian desert, and sometime before the end of the 11th century they began settling in the areas bordering on the desert in the northern part of Transjordan[21]. Similarly, the Moabites and Ammonites became settled no sooner than the twelfth century, B. C.[22], and the Edomites first entered Southern Transjordan as a settled people at the very end of the Bronze Age. The Arabs can hardly be dated before the beginning of the ninth century[23].

---

[20] Contra A. Parrot, Abraham et son temps, 1962, 50.

[21] S. Schiffer, Die Aramäer, 1911, VII; M. Noth, ZDPV 68 (1951), 19; B. Mazar, BA 25 (1962), 101f. This chronology, it must be emphasized, is largely based on uncritically examined biblical texts, and may in fact be much lower.

[22] M. Noth, Die Welt des Alten Testaments, 73.

[23] S. Moscati, The Semites in Ancient History, 72.

(2) The Chaldaeans of South Mesopotamia: Both J (Gen 11 28f. 15 7) and P (Gen 11 31) have traditions which place Abraham's homeland in אור כשדים, usually identified with Ur of South Mesopotamia[24]. There have been many attempts to cast doubt on this identification — particularly since the LXX does not have Ur in its text, but rather gives χώρα: "the land of the Chaldees" — and to seek a location somewhere in North Mesopotamia[25]. The objection to the identification, however, does not seem to be based on the lack of unanimity between the Hebrew and Greek texts[26], but rather on the fact that the Chaldaeans are not to be found in Southern Mesopotamia before the beginning of the First Millenium B. C.! The reading כשדים/χαλδαιοι = *māt Kaldi* (originally **Kašdu*) is certain, and both the Hebrew "Ur of the Chaldees" (= *Ūr ša māt Kaldi*), or the Greek "the land of the Chaldaeans", can only refer to the region of Southern Mesopotamia occupied by the Chaldaean Aramaeans from the beginning of the First Millenium to the end of the sixth century B. C.[27]. That such a reference could not be made before the First Millenium does not affect the identification whatever, but rather is clear evidence that this part of the tradition at least must be later than the arrival of the Chaldaeans in Southern Mesopotamia; that is, it must be dated sometime between the tenth and the sixth centuries B. C. It is among this branch of the Aramaeans that traditions in both J and P place the birthplace of Abraham. That these traditions may have an historiographical intent (i. e., that the tradition may well presuppose

---

24 H. Winckler, Ur-Kasdim als Heimat Abrahams, Altorientalische Forschungen, I 1893, 98; H. C. Rawlinson, On the Inscriptions of Assyria and Babylonia, JRAS 12 (1850), 481f.; J. Skinner, Genesis, 236f.

25 So, for example, E. König, Die Genesis, 1925³, 442f.; F. Delitzsch, Genesis, 239—242; H. Gunkel, Die Genesis, 158; W. F. Albright, Historical and Mythical Elements in the Joseph Story, JBL 37 (1918), 133—135 (Albright subsequently — A Question about Origins, Interpretation 18, 1964, 194 — reasserts the identification with Southern Ur). See also most recently C. H. Gordon, Abraham and the Merchants of Ura, JNES 17 (1958), 28—31; Abraham of Ur, Driver Festschrift, 79—83. Gordon's thesis has been decisively set aside by H. W. F. Saggs, Ur of the Chaldees, Iraq 22 (1960), 200—209, esp. 208.

26 In fact, all the alternative hypotheses have sought some other city by the name of Ur, or have identified Ur Chasdim with Arpakshad. Gordon points to as many as seven different Urs in the North Mesopotamian region before deciding on the identification with Ura (cf. Driver Festschrift 83; also D. J. Wiseman, The Alalakh Tablets, 1953, 48 and 157).

27 See further on the Chaldaeans: S. Schiffer, Die Aramäer, 1—6; S. Moscati, Semites in Ancient History, 68f.; S. Ahmed, Southern Mesopotamia in the Time of Ashurbanipal, 1968, passim; and, esp. M. Dietrich, Die Aramäer Südbabyloniens in der Sargonidenzeit, AOAT 7, 1970.

that Abraham did in fact come from there) is certainly possible. The tradition is, however, without question, unhistorical.

(3) The Aramaeans of North Mesopotamia: The ancestors of Abraham given in the genealogy of Shem in Gen 11 10-26 consist of a collection of appellatives and names of cities and regions that can probably be located and identified with the Aramaean city-states in the region of Ḫarran in North Mesopotamia. The probability of identifying most of these names with areas of North Mesopotamia makes it extremely difficult to attribute an historical character to this tradition, as is so often done[28]. It rather shows that Gen 11 10 ff. is to be understood in a way that other genealogies are understood, and not as a history of the family of Abraham.

The city of חרן is not in the genealogy itself and is probably not to be identified with הרן the brother of Abraham[29]. In a tradition from P (Gen 12 4b-5) it appears as the homeland of Abraham. Historically, it is a well-known city on the upper Baliḫ, which first appears in the Cappadocian and Mari texts, but again in the Assyrian records of the 13th century, and most commonly in Neo-Assyrian times. In the eighth and seventh centuries the city name appears commonly as a component of personal names in the Neo-Assyrian texts[30]. Excavation of the site shows that the city was occupied in the following periods: Early Dynastic II—III (Mid-Third Millenium); Sargonid or Ur III (late Third Millenium); and the Late Assyrian period (probably destroyed in 610 B. C.)[31].

In the genealogy itself, the patriarch שם is obviously the eponym of the Semites. The identification of ארפכשד (cf. also 10 22. 23) on the other hand, is much debated, and several suggestions, none of them completely convincing, have been offered. F. Hommel has suggested that the first three letters be identified with Babylonian *arpū*, a synonym of *ṭiḫū* "boundary wall" and that כשד be understood as

---

28 See above ch. 2.

29 Common opinion, see U. Cassuto, A Commentary on the Book of Genesis, II 1964, 268.

30 K. L. Tallqvist, Assyrian Personal Names, 1918, 56f.; J. J. Stamm, Die akkadische Namengebung, MVÄG 44, 1939, 84f.

31 K. Prag, The 1959 Deep Sounding at Ḫarran in Turkey, Levant 2 (1970), 63—94; Further on Ḫarran, see H. Winckler, KAT³, 29f.; F. Delitzsch, Die Genesis, 245; H. Gunkel, Die Genesis, 158; J. Skinner, Genesis, 236; S. R. Driver, The Book of Genesis, 1904, 141; F. M. Th. de Liagre Böhl, Het Tijdperk der Aartsvaders, 1925; Das Zeitalter Abrahams, AO 29 (1930), 52 n. 43; W. F. Albright, New Light on the History of Western Asia in the Second Millenium, B. C., BASOR 78 (1940), 29f.; S. Lloyd, Harran, Anatolian Studies 1 (1951), 77—112; A. Parrot, Abraham et son Temps, 34; H. Schunk, Benjamin, 10 n. 46.

referring to the Chaldaeans: so ארפכשד = "the border of Chasdim"[32]. Delitzsch and Jensen have attempted the unlikely identification with the Babylonian royal title: "König des Vierufer Landes", arriving at a hypothetical Babylonian original **Arba-kišādu*. Far more serious, and the only suggested identification that seems likely to be correct, is the identification with 'Αρραπαχιτις which Ptolemy (VI, I, 2) described as an Assyrian province bordering on Armenia[33]. Albright has suggested that Ptolemy has placed 'Αρραπαχιτις too far north[34], and that it should probably be identified with the territory and city of Arrapḫa (probably modern Kirkuk), which is well known from both Egyptian and cuneiform sources of the Second and First Millenia[35]. He suggests a solution to the problem of the ending שד by comparing it with Assyrian references to the place name *Tirqan šadi* (= "Eastern Tirqan"). Thus ארפכשד = *Arrapḫa šadi*. If such a reading is acceptable, it fits well with the other locatable sites in this genealogy, as well as its use in Gen 10 22, following Elam and Asshur.

The identification of שלח is not entirely certain. Knobel has suggested the city of *Ṣ/Salaḫ* in Northeast Mesopotamia, referred to in Assyrian texts[36].

עבר is the eponymous ancestor of the עברים. While there is considerable disagreement among the commentators about what geographical region is referred to here[37], it is not at all necessary that any geographical location is presupposed, since the use of the eponym

---

[32] F. Hommel, The True Meaning of Arpakshad, ET 13 (1901—1902), 285; A. H. Sayce, Ur of the Chaldees, ET 13 (1901—1902), 65f. In a like manner, Gordon would see the first three letters as equivalent to Hurrian *arip* + *chasdim* (Arpachshad, IDB I 231). Similar, although improbable, is Hommel's earlier suggestion that the name should be identified with Ur of the Chaldees, taking the פ as the Egyptian (sic!) article *pa*. A later refinement of this thesis is the suggestion of a hypothetical city: Urfa Chasdim (see J. Skinner, Genesis, 205).

[33] J. Skinner, Genesis, 205.

[34] Near the sources of the Upper Zab, between Lakes Van and Urumia.

[35] W. F. Albright, A Babylonian Geographical Treatise on Sargon of Akkad's Empire, JAOS 45 (1925), 193—245; see also W. M. Müller, Asien und Europa nach altägyptischen Denkmälern, 1893, 278f.; A. van den Born, Arpaksad, Bibellexikon, 109f.

[36] A. Knobel, Die Genesis, 1852[11], 122; the name may well be connected with the root *šiliḫtu*, "canal" (cf. W. F. Albright, Contributions to Biblical Archaeology and Philology, JBL 43, 1924, 389).

[37] E. Meyer (ZAW, 1886, 11) and H. Weinheimer (Hebräer und Israeliten, ZAW 29, 1909, 276), following Wellhausen and others, prefers to see the phrase עבר הירדן "the other side of the Jordan" as the source of this term (cf. Driver, Genesis, 138); while Delitzsch (Die Genesis 238), König (Die Genesis 439f.), Schiffer (Die Aramäer 80—85), and Kraeling (Aram and Israel, 1918, 31) would prefer עבר הנהר of Jos 24 2f. 14f.; that is, Mesopotamia.

in this context refers to the Hebrews and not necessarily to the place from which they came. If the origin of the Hebrews is also intended here, it must refer to עבר הנהר, given the location of the other names in the genealogy.

In Gen 10 25 the name פלג is used as an appelative: "For in his days the earth was divided" (נפלגה)[38]. Here, however, the name may well have a geographical significance. Of the three suggested identifications: *'el-Falǧ* in NE Arabia at the head of the Persian Gulf, *'el-Aflāǧ* in central Arabia, and *Phalga* on the Euphrates above the mouth of the Ḫabur, only the last seems plausible. It is known from Hellenistic times (it appears at Dura Europos as Paliga)[39].

A satisfactory identification of רעו has not been found. The only possible identification available at present seems to be with the city *rêʿû* mentioned in the Ugaritic texts[40].

The other names of the list are more certain. שרוג is to be identified with the well known city of the seventh century, *Sarūgi*, approximately 60 km. west of Ḫarran[41]. נחור, the father of Terah, is to be identified with the city *Til Naḫiri*, located south of Ḫarran near the Baliḫ, which belonged to the district of Ḫarran in the seventh century[42]. This same city appears in the Mari texts and at Kültepe as Naḫur[43]. תרח, the father of Abraham, is to be identified

---

38 Cf. A. Malamat, King Lists of the Old Babylonian Period and Biblical Genealogies, JAOS 88 (1968), 166.

39 Albright seems to suggest (Archaeology of Palestine and the Bible, 1949, 139) that it is known in the Assyrian records, but no references are given; cf. also, U. Cassuto, Genesis, II 218.

40 P. Nougayrol, PRU III, MRS VI, 235.

41 See C. H. W. Johns, An Assyrian Doomsday Book, 1901, 29f. 33. 43. 48; for comment, cf. Delitzsch, Genesis, 239; J. Skinner, Genesis, 232; Driver, Genesis, 139; H. Gunkel, Genesis, 156; W. F. Albright, Contributions to Biblical Archaeology and Philology, JBL 43 (1924), 385; From the Stone Age to Christianity, 1957³, 180; J. Lewy, Les Textes paléo-assyriens et l'Ancien Testament, RHR 110 (1934), 46; Malamat, JAOS 88 (1968), 166.

42 C. H. W. Johns, Assyrian Deeds and Documents, nos. 420, 3 and 421, 5; Doomsday Book no. 21, 2.

43 ARM XV 130; Lewy, RHR 110 (1934), 46 n. 2. For fuller discussion, see E. Schrader, Die Keilinschriften und das Alte Testament, 1903³, 477; Driver, Genesis, 140; Skinner, Genesis, 232—234; A. Lods, Israel, Des Origines au milieu du VIIIᵉ siècle, 1949, 188f.; W. F. Albright, JBL 43 (1924), 386; BASOR 78 (1940), 28f.; From the Stone Age to Christianity, 179; J. Bright, History of Israel, 1959, 69f.; E. A. Speiser, The Biblical Idea of History in its Common Near Eastern Setting, IEJ 7 (1957), 201; H. Klengel, Benjaminiten und Hanäer zur Zeit der Könige von Mari (Berlin Dissertation, 1958), 61; J. Lewy, Orientalia 21 (1952), 84; A. Goetze, JCS 7 (1953), 67; A. Parrot, Abraham et son Temps, 33f.; Speiser, Genesis, 79f.; A. Malamat, JAOS 88 (1968), 166.

with the Aramaean city-state *til-ša-turâḫi*, located north of Ḫarran on the Baliḫ, found in the Assyrian texts from the middle of the ninth century and later[44]. The sons of Terah are Abram, Nahor, and Haran, and here the genealogy is brought to an end. These last three names are probably not, strictly speaking, eponymous. Abram is the patriarch of the Ishmaelites, Edomites and Israelites; Nahor (not to be confused with the father of Terah the eponym of Til-Naḫiri) is the patriarch of the Aramaean tribes of northern Transjordan; Haran (possibly derived from the place name בית הרן in Moab: Num 32 36) is, in the genealogy here, probably to be understood as the patriarch of Moab and Ammon (displaced by Lot under the influence of the traditions in 11 27 and 12 5)[45].

The genealogy of Gen 11 10-26 is a later expansion of the ספר תולדת אדם from Gen 5 1a. 3 ff. Its motivation is basically mythological and historiographical. In the form of a genealogical introduction to the P patriarchal traditions, it attempts to ground Israel's past in the Urzeit of Gen 1—11 and to describe the transition from this original time to the immediate past of Israel. The genealogy of Shem places the origin of man in North Mesopotamia. If the general picture of the occupation of the sites in Gen 11 10 ff. in North Mesopotamia is representative, this biblical tradition seems to connect the origin of the Israelites and the related tribes of the South and East with the Aramaean citystates which were established sometime during the eleventh and tenth centuries[46]. The identification of this tradition with the Aramaeans is very uncertain, and is based largely on the lack of evidence for *Sarûgi* and *Til ša turâḫi* at any earlier period. The connection, however, in 10 26 with the patriarchs Nahor and Haran, who are more easily related to the Aramaean and West-Semitic tribes of Transjordan, makes this a likely interpretation.

The historiographical intention of this tradition is to place the origin of the Israelites and related groups in North Mesopotamia. That this runs directly contrary to the dominant biblical traditions which understand Israel to have entered Palestine from Transjordan and from Egypt, and encounters insurmountable difficulties as a true historical reconstruction, affects only the question of its historicity. The historiographical intention is affected far more by the demands of composition and formation of a consistent world-view in the larger task of relating the patriarchs to the traditions of Gen 1—11, than it is by any hypothetical historical memory. That it runs counter to

[44] F. Delitzsch, Prolegomena eines neuen Hebräisch-Aramäischen Wörterbuchs zum alten Testament, 1886, 80; E. Kraeling, Miscellen-Terach, ZAW 40 (1922), 153f.

[45] See further below.

[46] See S. Moscati, The Semites in Ancient History, esp. 66; 96; J. C. L. Gibson, Light from Mari on the Patriarchs, JSS 7 (1962), 53.

the tradition found also in P, which brings Abraham out of Ur of the Chaldees, however, is a much more serious descrepancy and presents a conflict which the P tradition takes great pains to overcome.

B. THE EDITORIAL CONSTRUCTION OF THE WANDERINGS OF ABRAHAM

The J tradition about the wandering of Abraham (Gen 12 1f. 4a. 6-9 13 1-4. 14-18) is largely unhistorical in character. By means of the theological leitmotif of the wandering obedient servant of Yahweh, it gives a structure to the many independent stories at J's disposal. It is an editorial device used to unite the many disparate Abraham and Lot traditions[47]. It has, however, a strong aetiological interest in connecting the patriarch with the establishment of sanctuaries at Shechem, Bethel, and Hebron. The resulting saga is infinitely expandable, and amenable to the further addition of any tale that comes to hand (so 15 7ff). However, the stories in 12 10-20 and especially 13 5-13 seem to be presupposed by the wandering motif (cf. 12 9 and 13 1b-3 13 14). Gen 13 18, together with 18 1a, seems to introduce the story in 18 1bff. Gen 19 30 abα, on the other hand, may be an expansion of the editorial structure — now independent of Abraham — to introduce the tale of Lot and his daughters.

Throughout, there is no noticeable interest in the homeland of Abraham. He is commanded to leave his own country and his own kindred and to go to a land which Yahweh will show him. Nothing more exact is stated, and, given the theological implications of these verses, it is unlikely that any specific region is presupposed. On the other hand, the unconnected J fragment (11 28-30) refers to Ur of the Chaldees as the land of Haran's birth, and the J insertion (15 7) states that the call of Abraham (12 1f.) took place in Ur of the Chaldees. This interpretation indeed is secondary in J, but already quite prominent by the time the tradition is restructured by P.

Not only does P have to deal with the tradition of J, which he treats with respect, but the traditions which stem from his own sources are sharply divergent. In the reconstruction of these traditions, P's intention is thoroughly historiographical: to create a history which will trace the patriarchs, by genealogical tradition, back to Adam, on the basis of the traditions that P has at hand.

Central to his reconstruction is the addition of the genealogy of Shem to the ספר תולדת אדם. This genealogy, as we have seen, places the ancestors of Abraham, Haran, and Nahor in North Mesopotamia

[47] See also Gressmann, ZAW 30 (1910), 9f.; Gunkel, PrJ 176 (1919), 339 and 351.

in the region of Ḫarran from which stem the tribes of Israel and Transjordan. J, however, places the homeland of Abraham in Ur, among the Aramaeans of South Mesopotamia, in 11 28-30, and has the homeland of Abraham unlocated in 12 1f. P has, in addition, two variant traditions of its own which radically conflict with each other. The one (12 4b) is that Abraham was 75 years old when he left Ḫarran. The other is completely different: a tradition not about Abraham but about Terah. It is found in 11 31abα. It is Terah, not Abraham, who leaves his homeland in Ur of the Chaldees to go (ללכת) to the land of Canaan. Possibly connected with this is the tradition in 11 32a (since this tradition is about Terah) that Terah lived 205 years.

The problem of Terah's age — Terah was 70 years old when Abram was born (11 26), and Abram was 75 years old when he left Harran (12 4b) — was never solved by P. The Samaritan Pentateuch attempts to harmonize the tradition by drawing the obvious conclusion that Terah was only 145 when he died[48]. P, however, was much more successful in resolving the other internal contradictions of his material; and, presupposing a full acceptance of the traditions that he used, his historiographical reconstruction is both ingenious and highly satisfactory. On one hand, he has the genealogical construction which understands Haran as the patriarch of the Ammonites and Moabites (11 26) over against the J fragment which knows Haran, the father of Iscah and Milcah, to have died in Ur of the Chaldees. On the other hand, he has his own tradition of the migration of Terah from Ur to Canaan which involves Abram and Lot (who is called the son of Haran): 11 31abα. The "seeming" conflict is deftly resolved by the editorial structure — which does not reject or alter but merely interprets the material — found in 11 27, patterned after the toledoth formula of 11 10: ואלה תולדת תרח: "These are the generations of Terah. Terah begat Abram, Nahor and Haran and Haran begat Lot" (which he knew from 11 26. 31a). Then, with the insertion of the J tradition (11 28-30), he is able to replace Haran of 11 26 with Lot of 11 31abα. The reader is left to himself to conclude that Haran had three children: Lot, Milcah and Iscah[49].

---

[48] Similarly, Archbishop Ussher, in his notes to the Authorized Version (following perhaps Acts 7 4) attempts to harmonize the tradition with the impossible interpolation: "And Terah lived 70 years, and [60 years afterwards] begat Abram, Nahor and Haran." Cf. Driver, Genesis, 142; Gunkel (Genesis 158) maintained that the Samaritan Pentateuch was the original. This, however, leaves the Masoritic and LXX traditions of 205 years unexplained. A reason for an emendation on the part of the Samaritan Pentateuch is much easier to understand.

[49] The New English Bible tries, but unsuccessfully, to find this in the text itself of verse 29: "She (Milcah) was Haran's daughter; and he was also the father of Milcah and Iscah" (sic!).

P is then faced with the difficulty of explaining the conflicting P traditions of Terah's journey from Ur to Canaan together with Abraham and Lot (11 31abα), and the variant tradition that Abraham left Ḫarran at the age of 75, (12 4b) as well as to interpret both of these in the light of the J tradition of Yahweh's call (12 1f. 4aα. 6-9) to Abraham, which originally does not seem to involve Lot. (Contrast 12 5 ויבאו ארצה כנען with J 12 6: ויעבר אברם בארץ!) These difficulties are overcome; first, by drawing the obvious conclusion that if Terah left Ur with Abraham and Lot, and if Abraham left Ḫarran, they must have stopped in Ḫarran: (11 31bβ) "But when they reached Ḫarran they settled there[50]."

Second, Terah is replaced in the leadership of the family by Abraham, by having Terah die in Ḫarran (so: 11 32b), and Lot is joined to Abram by means of 12 5: "He took his wife Sarai, his nephew Lot, all the property they had collected, and all the dependants they had acquired in Ḫarran, (cf. 13 5-13) and they started on their journey to Canaan." 12 4b-5, then, becomes P's historicization of Abraham's call. Gen 15 7, itself an interpretation of two variant J traditions which saw Yahweh to have called Abraham out of Ur of the Chaldees, now no longer so harshly conflicts with the P traditions, and can be passed over as a simplification of the more complex course of "real events" found in 11 10—12 9.

Recapitulation:

J Tradition

a. J "wandering" tradition: 12 1f. 4aα. 6-9 13 1-4. 14-18 18 1a 19 30abα.
b. J fragment: 11 28-30.
c. J interpretation: 15 7.

P Tradition

a. Genealogy: 11 10-26.
b. Abram/Ḫarran: 12 4b.
c. Teraḫ/Ur: 11 31abα. (32a).
d. Editorial bridge: 11 27. 31bβ. 32b 12 5.

Gen 11 27ff. is not an historical remnant of a tradition, nor even a half-legendary saga which brings Abraham out of Ur to Palestine by way of Ḫarran. It is a very late editorial development which on one hand attempts to explain in a literary manner the complex relationships which bind Israel to its neighbors. On the other hand, it is an attempt by historiographical interpretation to establish a link between the Urzeit and the later history of Israel. The wandering of Abraham

[50] Such editorial detours may cause trouble for an historian; they are, however, quite common in this literary genre (cf. Gen 12 9 and 13 1-3; also see below section C).

from Ur to Ḫarran and then through Palestine and into Egypt is more a development based on the necessity of binding together the widely scattered stories about Abraham and Lot, than an independent tradition in itself.

C. SOME NOTES ON THE STRUCTURE OF GENEALOGIES AND SAGAS IN ANTIQUITY

The verification of the above interpretation depends largely on its inner consistency and its ability to understand and explain the myriad conflicts of the final traditon. That some such method of interpretation must be used is suggested by the similar method of constructing the stories of ancestral heroes found in the literature of cultures closely related to Israel. That the collections of the traditions of other ancient cultures require a similar interpretation is generally accepted, and a few brief notes should here suffice to draw out the structural parallels to Genesis.

Eponymous ancestors are well known from Greek and Latin literature. The ancestral hero Aeolus has twelve children who are the eponymous ancestors of their settlements[51]. Individual eponymous ancestors are explained by means of tales: In Pindar, Opus is adopted by Lokrus and becomes the eponymous hero of the city with the same name in the territory of Lokris[52]. Similarly, an eponymous hero (or God?) is used to explain the very ancient and enigmatic name Lakedaimon used for Sparta and its territories[53].

Often, the development of these eponyms involve travel: "Aetôlus, son of Endymion, quitted Peloponnêsus in consequence of having slain Apis. The country on the North of the Corinthian Gulf . . . received from him the name of Aetolia . . .! He had two sons, Pleurôn and Kalydôn, and from them the two chief towns in Aetôlia were named[54]." A variant etymology explaining Aetôlia comes in the form of a genealogy. "Orestheus son of Deukaliôn first passed into Aetôlia and acquired the kingdom: he was father of Phytios who was father of Oeneus. Aetôlus was son of Oeneus[55]."

---

[51] Diodorus Siculus IV 67, 2—7.

[52] Pindar, Olymp. IX, 62; G. Grote, History of Greece, 1854⁴, I 193.

[53] Cf. Stephanus Byzantinus, De Urbibus, ed. by Guilielmi Xylandri Augusta, 1568, 180f.; Th. de Pinedo, Stephanus Byzantinus cum Annotationes IV, 1825, 731, paragraph 412b; Eustathii in Homerum, ed. by A. Polito, 1830, I 326; O. Szemerenyi, The Origin of the name Lakedaimon, Glotta 38 (1960), 14—17.

[54] Grote, History, 193f.

[55] Ibid. 208; compare Aram, son of Kemuel, son of Nahor in Gen 22 21 with Aram, son of Shem in Gen 10 22.

Like the biblical genealogies those of the Greeks are expanded with stories about the exploits of the eponymous heroes. These stories proceed according to the logic of the genealogy as continuously expanding narrative. Such is the story of Danaos and his brother Aegyptus. Aegyptus had fifty sons who wished to marry Danaos' fifty daughters. To prevent this Danaos sent his daughters on a ship with fifty oars bound for Argos. The sons followed and all but one were murdered. He became the king of Argos[56]. This has nothing to do with history or the memory of an Egyptian settlement in the Aegean.

In the Latin traditions, the wandering of Aeneas, like that of Abraham, was remarkably suited to the construction of genealogies; and Aeneas becomes an ancestor to the settlements in Thrace, Delos, Arcadia, the islands of Kythera and Zakynthus, areas of southern Italy, Sicily, Carthage, Misenum and Latium[57].

"The motive of most of these genealogies was to account for the origin of the various groups they referred to, and in each case, the local distribution of the sections of the group . . . the persons connected in the pedigrees were personified districts, nations, tribes, gentes, towns, mountains, springs, lakes, and rivers, connected as fathers and sons or daughters, or as brothers and sisters, etc., a narrative of the personal adventures of the more prominent of these persons completing the pedigree[58]."

Of course, the biblical genealogies are much more restrained, though their structural development is similar to what is found in the traditions of the classical world. Understandably, the early Arab genealogies are much closer to the biblical genealogies in their development. A good example of this comes from the Berber genealogy of North Africa. Etymologically, the name Berber comes from the Latin Barbarus; genealogically, however, it is derived, under Mohammedan influence, from the eponymous ancestor Berr who is a descendent of Noah. A variant genealogy has the eponym Berber who is "son of Temla, son of Mazîgh, son of Canaan, son of Ham, son of Noah"[59]. The pure Arabs trace their ancestry to Qaḥṭam, the Yoktan of Gen 10 25[60], a region in Arabia northeast of Ǧisān, known from the third century, A. D.[61]. The son of Qaḥṭam is Ya'rab the eponym of the Arabs. Ya'rab's grandson was Saba from whom the Sabaeans are understood to derive their name. The son of Saba, Himyar, established

[56] Ibid. 120; Apollodorus II, I. 4.

[57] J. F. M'Lennan, Studies in Ancient History, 1896, 2nd Series IX, 127. M'Lennan remarks that some Scots families also trace their lineage to Aeneas.

[58] Ibid. 117.

[59] Ibn Khaldous, I 167ff.; cf. M'Lennan ibid. 145—148.

[60] Ibid. 151; J. Henninger, Altarabische Genealogie, Anthropos 61 (1966), 861.

[61] J. Henninger ibid.

a dynasty which ruled the Sabaeans for 2020 years which explains the reason that the Sabaeans are also known as Himyarides[62].

As in the Bible, some of the tribal groups derive their names from wives and daughters of the ancestral and eponymous heroes. The tribe Adwân, one of the four Moaddique tribes derives its name from its ancestress Adwân, wife of Modha[63].

The Arabic genealogies are schematic constructions of traditions, and are not historical. They attempt to express relationships between groups by means of family ties, which relationships were, however, much more complicated in their origin[64]. The difficulties encountered in attempting to circumscribe the present complex reality by the simple familial structure, lends added impetus to the evolution of the traditions. Henninger describes one aspect of this process with clarity:

> Wenn Ismāʿil, der Sohn Ibrahīms, der Stammvater der Nordaraber war und mit seinen Söhnen in der Gegend von Mekka gewohnt hatte, dann mussten die Ahnen der Stämme, die später über einen grossen Teil Nordarabiens und seiner Randgebiete verbreitet waren, dort zu Hause gewesen sein. Daher das Thema der 'Zerstreuung der Nordaraber", das in mehreren Varianten, unter Verwendung von vielerlei historischem und pseudo-historischem Material, behandelt wurde ... Nunmehr aber konstituierte sich die Genealogie als eine umfassende Wissenschaft, die sämtliche Nordaraber auf ʿAdnān und über ihn hinaus auf Ismāʿil, alle Südaraber auf Qaḥṭan als Stammvater zurückführte ... Von vielen Parteien muss man sagen, dass sich dort weniger die historische Wirklichkeit als der Ehrgeiz und das Machtstreben der politisch-genealogischen Parteien spiegelt[65].

Recently, A. Malamat has published a brief study of a newly found Old Babylonian cuneiform text giving a complete genealogy of the Hammurapi Dynasty. In this study he points out several characteristics that I think should be compared with the biblical material[66]. This genealogy, going back to the Old Babylonian period, is constructed in the same manner as some of the biblical genealogies, connecting true historical persons to fictitious eponyms such as tribes, cities and geographical regions. A variant tradition is found in the upper portion of the Assyrian King List, which Malamat sees, with some justification, as deriving from a common genealogical tradition[67].

[62] M'Lennan, Studies in Ancient History, 151. [63] Ibid.

[64] W. Caskel, Ǧambaret an-Nasab, I—II 1966; J. Henninger, Anthropos 6 (1966), 854; see also M'Lennan, Studies in Ancient History, 160.

[65] J. Henninger, Anthropos 61 (1966), 858.

[66] A. Malamat, JAOS 88 (1968), 163—173; for text of the genealogy, cf. J. J. Finkelstein, The Genealogy of the Hammurapi Dynasty, JCS 20 (1966), 95—118; see also, W. Röllig, Zur Typologie und Entstehung der babylonischen und assyrischen Königslisten, AOAT 1 (1969), 265—277.

[67] Ibid. 96; Cf. B. Landsberger, Assyrische Königsliste und "Dunkles Zeitalter", JCS 8 (1954), 33ff. and 109ff.; for text see I. J. Gelb, JNES 12 (1954), 209ff.

By means of structural analysis, Malamat distinguishes four distinct types of genealogy, each of which is also represented in the biblical traditions. The first type describes the "genealogical stock" or background of the West Semitic peoples in a list of nine to eleven names composed of personal names, appellatives, tribal names and toponyms in the form of eponyms, which in some ways are comparable to the genealogy of Shem in Gen 11 10-26. The second type he calls the "determinative line" which is the tables of ancestors linking the "genealogical stock" with the historical West Semitic dynasties of Babylon and Assyria. These are basically composed of West Semitic tribes (e. g., *Amnānu* and *Yaḫruru*: nos. 12 and 13). This type is comparable to the various genealogies found in Joshua and Judges as well as to most of the genealogical "Stammessage" of Genesis, such as Gen 22 20-24, and the genealogies of Jacob, Ishmael, etc. The third type, the "Table of Ancestors" is composed of real and possibly fictitious tribal chieftains who preceded the establishment of the dynasties. They are not, however, to be understood as the historical ancestors of Sumuabum and Šamši-Adad[68]. This type of genealogy is comparable to the genealogy of David in Ruth 4 18-22. It is extremely difficult to evaluate historically, however, since the early names in the list are often linked with earlier "Stammessage" and other literary expansions. Characteristic of this type in biblical literature is the genealogy of Saul in I Sam 9 1. It is extremely difficult to distinguish in this material what may be real ancestors and historical predecessors from fictitious eponyms personifying tribal groups or villages.

The fourth type is the "Historical Line", listing the true rulers of the dynasty. In the biblical tradition this is comparable to the king lists of Judah and Israel. It is at this stage that the Old Babylonian king lists and the biblical traditions take on a firm historical character. It is here that the historian can first be confident that the traditions of Israel have a sound historical base, to be analyzed and evaluated in the manner of comparable ancient Near Eastern historical documents.

To assume such an historical basis for the patriarchal traditions of Genesis, however, is to distort their real significance and to lose sight of the rich literary sources of the Pentateuch. When we set ourselves the task of understanding the patriarchal narratives, we are not so much involved with the history of Israel as with the history of the development of Israel's literature.

---

[68] Aminu was not the father of Šamši-Adad. His father was Ila-kabkabu, though apparently Aminu did precede Šamši-Adad on the throne, and may well have been Šamši-Adad's brother as Malamat suggests (JAOS 88, 1968, 169).

Chapter 12

Summary and Conclusions

A. THE HISTORICAL BACKGROUND OF THE PATRIARCHAL NARRATIVES

We have seen in the foregoing chapter that the received tradition about Abraham's journey from Ur of the Chaldees to Canaan by way of Ḫarran is not an originally independent tradition about Abraham. Rather it is a historiographical reconstruction which is based on several originally independent and conflicting traditions. It not only must be understood as unhistorical, but any attempt to find movements analogous to Abraham's in the history of the Near East are essentially misdirected for the purposes of biblical interpretation. The intentions of the biblical traditions about the patriarchs are not comparable to those of the modern historian. They are rather sociological, political, and religious. Those attempts at interpretation of these traditions which willfully neglect the implications of their formation and structure can justly be dismissed as historicism.

Moreover, we have seen that the biblical chronologies are not grounded on historical memory, but are rather based on a very late theological schema that presupposes a very unhistorical worldview. Those efforts to use the biblical narratives for a reconstruction of the history of the Near East, in a manner comparable to the use of the archives of Mari and similar finds, can justly be dismissed as fundamentalist[1].

Though we have argued that the quest for the historical Abraham is a basically fruitless occupation both for the historian and the student of the Bible, the question about the historical background of the patriarchal narratives is a question to which historical criticism, with the help of ancient Near Eastern history and archaeology, can give very concrete answers.

There are generally three possible periods that have been suggested for the historical background of the patriarchal narratives. (1) The early Second Millenium, (2) The fifteenth and fourteenth centuries B. C. and (3) A period approximate to the time when the traditions became part of the literature of Israel; that is, sometime

[1] A very recent example of fundamentalistic historiography in the field of Near Eastern history is K. Prag's reconstruction of the history of Ḫarran: The 1951 Deep Sounding at Ḫarran in Turkey, Levant 2 (1970), 63—94.

around the end of the tenth or during the ninth century B. C. (the time of the J author).

(1) The Early Second Millenium B. C.

The central argument for dating the "patriarchal period" to the early Second Millenium is that the movement of the patriarch's family from Ur of the Chaldees to Ḫarran, and from there into Palestine, and finally into Egypt, is paralleled by a remarkable series of coincidences gleaned from history, the sheer mass and coherence of which seem to require a dating of the patriarchs to this period.

The very distinctive names of the patriarchs, especially Abraham and Jacob, belong to the type of West-Semitic names often referred to as "Amorite" or "Proto-Aramaean" which were thought to occur in the ancient Near Eastern extrabiblical sources only during the period between 2000 and 1600 B. C. The ethnic group identified by these names shows up as semi-nomadic groups in texts from South Mesopotamia in the region of Ur at the very end of the Third Millenium and at the beginning of the Second Millenium, where they gradually gain power and establish the First Dynasty of Babylon, of whose rulers Hammurapi is the most famous. Shortly after this, semi-nomadic groups bearing the same kind of names show up further to the North at Mari. From the eighteenth century texts of Mari, a tribe of "Benjaminites" was discovered living in the region of Harran. These West Semitic groups were then seen to move southwards into Palestine where we discover them in two groups of Execration Texts, dated by Albright to the twentieth and nineteenth centuries B.C. The Execration Texts were moreover thought to show that these Amorite groups were semi-nomadic tribes at the time of the earlier group of texts, and were in the process of gradually settling down in Palestine. This understanding of the Execration Texts corresponded to the interpretation of many archaeologists that Middle Bronze I was a period when Palestine was overrun by semi-nomadic tribal groups who had migrated to Palestine from the north.

These West-Semitic semi-nomadic groups were also thought to have moved down into Egypt in large numbers where they were called *ʿȝmw*, a title which has been identified by Kenyon and others with the "Amorites".

Given this understanding of the history of the early Second Millenium, it is easily understood how those who saw the patriarchs as leaders of tribal groups would also see them as taking part in this nomadic migration which moved from Ur in South Mesopotamia to Ḫarran, and from there to Palestine and finally down into Egypt. In this way, the patriarchal narratives have taken on major historical significance, representative of almost every well known historical movement of the early Second Millenium.

When this interpretation found support in the discovery of over 4000 cuneiform tablets from Nuzi which gave evidence of family customs that were remarkably similar to the customs portrayed in Genesis — so similar that major scholars could argue that the patriarchs lived according to Nuzi law — the final summary of Albright's seemed perfectly justified: "Abraham, Isaac, and Jacob no longer seem isolated figures, much less reflections of later Israelite history; they now appear as true children of their age, bearing the same names, moving about over the same territory, visiting the same towns, practicing the same customs as their contemporaries. In other words, the patriarchal narratives have a historical nucleus throughout[2]."

However, this argument which places the historical background of our narratives in the early Second Millenium has been developed almost entirely on the basis of a harmonization of historical hypotheses that have been drawn from several distinct bodies of material involving West Semitic onomastics, comparative Semitic philology, the history of Mesopotamia, of Palestine, and of Egypt, archaeology of the Middle Bronze Period, ancient Near Eastern law, and biblical interpretation. Historical reconstructions which would appear extremely hypothetical or even totally untenable on their own merits and within their own field of discipline, achieve, nevertheless, the appearance of plausibility when they are interpreted in the light of similar reconstructions of possibly related materials, which reconstructions themselves first appear plausible in the projection of the total synthesis. It is on the basis of such mutual affirmation and harmonization that this chain of evidence has been constructed, a chain which in the scholarly literature has proved far stronger than its very strongest link.

The patriarchal names: Abraham, Isaac, Jacob, Israel, and Ishmael, are indeed peculiarly West Semitic names, and can even be classified typologically as Early West Semitic, the origin of which type long precedes the class of "Phoenician" or "Canaanite" names in which the majority of biblical names can be placed, but the claim that such Early West Semitic names are found only, or even for the most part, in the period from 2000 to 1600 B. C. is simply not true, and is based on a myopic fascination for history's earliest witnesses and archaeology's latest discoveries, a faddish disregard for knowledge that is old. Names of exactly the same type as Abram are found from the time of eighteenth century Mari down through the Neo-Assyrian period, and names directly parallel or identical to the name

[2] W. F. Albright. Archaeology of Palestine. 236.

Abram are found from the second half of the Second Millenium until long after the Genesis traditions had been formed in the literature of Israel. Names similar to Abram appear not only in the first half of the Second Millenium but in nearly every period from which we possess names from West Semitic peoples. The name Abram also accords well with other biblical names, and is typologically associated with such names from the Bible as *Râm, Yehurâm, Malkirâm, Amrâm, Aḫirâm, Ḫirom,* etc., as well as such names as *Abšâlom, Ebpelet, Ebyasaf, Abyâdâ'*, etc.

In considering the name Jacob, we find that it is one of the most common West Semitic names used in the ancient Near East and it is found in the records of almost every century from the Old Babylonian Period in the early Second Millenium to early post-Christian times, as well as several times in the Bible itiself, in the forms *Ya'aḳobah* and *'aḳob.*

The patriarchal names are names of a quite common sort, and can be expected to appear wherever we find names form West Semitic peoples. The discovery of related names in the extrabiblical records, and even exact parallels, can help in no way in dating the patriarchs. The names are not related to any specific period. The large number of similar names found at Mari is in direct proportion to the large number of texts found there.

The failure of the reconstruction of history involved in this attempt to date the patriarchs to the early Second Millenium, when the individual aspects of the reconstruction are independently examined, is all too evident.

Early West Semites do appear in South Mesopotamia in the region of Ur at the beginning of the Second Millenium. However, the historical evidence shows that we are not dealing with one unified group of Amorites, but with many independent groups and individuals whose only common trait is the similar type of name they bear. They live not only in the region of Ur, but all over South Mesopotamia. Moreover, the texts show these people migrating into and settling down in Southern Mesopotamia, but there is no historical evidence whatever for a migration away from the South. The West Semites of North Mesopotamia came not from the South, but independently from the North Arabian desert. Moreover — here too — the texts give us the picture of immigrating settlers, and nowhere do we find evidence for a West Semitic migration from Mesopotamia to Palestine, indeed the philological evidence argues directly against any such migration.

The "tribes" of sheep and goatherds near Harran turn out after all not to be proto-Benjaminites, but merely one of the many West

Semitic groups of sheep and goatherds which happens to be referred to by the Mari administration as the "southern tribe" in contradistinction to another group called the "northern tribe" which is settled farther North. They are no more to be related to the Benjaminites than are the Biblical Temenites of northern Edom or the modern Yemenites.

Instead of giving evidence for the gradual sedentarization of Palestine in the twentieth and nineteenth centuries B. C., the Execration Texts show us that the Egyptian enemies in Palestine at the end of the nineteenth and the beginning of the eighteenth centuries were localized around major settlements. Whether we are dealing with indigenous West Semitic peoples in Palestine is not entirely certain; however, the Early West Semites are the earliest linguistic group known to be in Palestine, and the names of the rivers and mountains of Palestine, for example the Jordan and Mount Carmel, suggest that the West Semites had already been there from a very early period, further supporting the impression that we do not have any evidence of a migration into Palestine at the beginning of the Second Millenium.

The philological structure of the personal names found in the Execration Texts relates them not to the groups of North Mesopotamia, but rather to those of South Arabia.

Likewise, the *ʿ3mw* mentioned in many Egyptian texts of this period are West Semitic, though the name *ʿ3mw* is not related to the name *Amurrū*, but rather is an Egyptian word meaning "boomerang thrower", a typical Egyptian classification for a foreign group. It is important to note that the Egyptian texts give us our earliest references to the West Semites in the entire Near East, from as early as the beginning of the Old Kingdom, who are at times referred to as *ʿ3mw* from as early as the beginning of the Sixth Dynasty. These West Semitic groups in Egypt, however, do not seem to have come from Palestine, but appear to be indigenous to the eastern desert bordering on Middle Egypt, the desert region between Sinai and the Delta, perhaps the Eastern Delta, and the region across the Red Sea in southwestern Arabia. Nor is there any evidence for a West Semitic invasion of the Egyptian Delta at this early period, but only border skirmishes and disruptions caused by famine and the breakdown of internal security in Egypt. The famous mural painting from Beni-Hasan shows not a West Semitic caravan from Transjordan but rather a group of people who lived in the eastern desert of Egypt not far from Beni-Hasan itself.

Finally, the archaeological evidence from Palestine shows that the Middle Bronze I period, far from being a period in which semi-nomads overran the country, was a period of extensive, albeit poor, agricultural settlement, with many major settlements. The pottery culture grows out of an indigenous Early Bronze repertoire, incorporating into it modifying elements and techniques drawn from the increasingly richer culture of Syria. The material culture of this period is poor and degraded when compared with the Blütezeit of the Early Bronze and Middle Bronze sedentary cultures, but, aside from poverty, it has nothing in common with a nomadic economic culture. Moreover, the culture is thoroughly indigenous, significantly characterized (outside of a few of the major settlements in the north) by an almost total lack of imported ware.

The recent efforts of W. F. Albright to offer an alternative interpretation to the "Amorite hypothesis", finding the patriarchal stories reflected in the growing caravan trade during the period of the Twelfth Dynasty connected both with the Ḫapiru and hypothetical caravan stations of the EB IV/MB I Period has been shown to be completely groundless. His reconstruction hinges on his adjustment of the chronology of EB IV/MB I downwards to as late as 1800 B. C. The end of EB IV/MB I, however, cannot be placed later than ca. 1900 B. C. Moreover, there is no evidence of any caravan stations in Palestine or the Negev at all during the EB IV/MB I Period, and only a few of the places mentioned in Genesis were occupied at this time. The only connection the Ḫapiru are known to have with the caravans was antagonistic to peaceful trade.

Nor is Albright's and Glueck's effort to discover the destruction and subsequent abandonment of the EB IV/MB I sites of Transjordan in the biblical narrative of Genesis 14 any more successful. Not only was the settlement of Transjordan not abandoned any time during the Bronze Age, but there is no evidence that the EB IV/MB I sites were destroyed at any single time. The attempt to identify the kings mentioned in Genesis 14 with historical figures of the ancient Near East, rather than suggesting a historical basis for the tradition, lends itself to the interpretation of Genesis 14 as folklore.

Returning to the question of the historical background of the patriarchal narratives: it can be seen that the methods used by those who have sought the background in the early part of the Second Millenium are wholly inadequate for dealing with a period from which the historical materials are so limited and so chronologically and geographically scattered.

Because of the limitations of our primary data, particular care must be taken in the isolation of our material and in its independent evaluation. Before general conclusions can be drawn encompassing all available materials, we must be careful that the relationships we trace between distinct bodies of evidence are themselves concretely supported by our evidence.

Such conservative methodology may indeed make any unifying history of the early Second Millenium impossible for the present. On the other hand, it is only through such methodology that we will be able to see the historical significance — and also insignificance — of the little material that we do have, and that we will be able to establish a basis for the intrepretation of future discoveries.

This is not to say that comparative materials are not to be profitably used. On the contrary, such methodology offers the possibility of a sound foundation on the basis of which comparative materials become highly significant for interpretation; for it is only within the context of comparable data that any given discovery may be understood. Just as archaeological data cannot be understood outside of their archaeological context and apart from comparable archaeological materials, and Egyptian historical texts cannot be understood apart from comparable records, so the patriarchal narratives cannot be understood apart from comparable biblical narratives and apart from the body of ancient Near Eastern and East-Mediterranean narrative material. And so consistently — only when the initial interpretation drawn from such comparative study suggests a correlation with other distinct types of sources — can we be justified in making such a connection and in basing our interpretation on it.

(2) The Fifteenth and Fourteenth Centuries B. C.

The second suggested possibility for the historical background of the patriarchal narratives, in the "Amarna Period" of the fifteenth and fourteenth centuries, avoids many of the difficulties which the suggestion for the earlier period faces, if primarily only because it is much less specifically grounded in the events of the period.

It, however, takes more seriously the problems of the history of the transmission of the biblical traditions, recognizing fully that if the historical background of the traditions is to be placed prior to the Israelite conquest, the traditions themselves must be traced back to that early period, and this early phase of the traditions must be clearly and uniquely identifiable as pre-Israelite on internal grounds.

While the biblical chronology that is used, based as it is on the genealogical data of the Bible, offers but little more dependability than the chronology calculated according to years, the methodology used to relate the period at which they understand the Bible to place the "events" to the extrabiblical material of that period is worthy of a great deal more respect, proceeding as it does, not from arguments of analogy and probability, but from an attempt to identify elements of the patriarchal tradition itself as uniquely early.

This argument has been developed primarily by Speiser and Gordon (Speiser indeed continued to hold an early Second Millenium date for the patriarchal period. However, his interpretation of the relationship between the Nuzi tablets and the Genesis narratives has served as the basic argument for the dating of the patriarchs to the Amarna period). This argument rests primarily upon a comparison of the family relationships and customs implied in the Genesis stories with family legal contracts that have been excavated from Nuzi in North Mesopotamia — dated to the fifteenth century B. C. Speiser and Gordon have sought to discover and to reestablish from the biblical texts a common historical tradition which consequently must have lain behind the now diverging narratives with their many variant and even conflicting details. Since this resulting common denominator is seen by Speiser to reflect customs which can only be explained according to the customs of the fifteenth century Nuzi, which customs are unexplainable or contradicted by later practice, the necessity of assuming a common source for the biblical traditions seems unavoidable. The historical character of this tradition is assumed on the basis of the clearly historical, rather than literary nature of the Nuzi parallels, and the verifiability of this tradition is directly related to the early age at which the background of the tradition must be placed.

The chronology that the Bible gives for the patriarchs, calculated by generations, achieves a certain methodological importance and forms a necessary aspect of the argument for the historicity of the original Tradition; for the external evidence is understood to prove that the tradition, though not the stories as we now have them, does go back to the time at which the tradition itself claims that the "events" took place.

What we now possess, according to this thesis, are later quasi-legendary versions of the original history which no longer understand the original social structure which once underlay the events related. That the argument is patently circular — the primary basis for establishing this proposed original Tradition and for showing that it extends back into preconquest times, are the very parallels themselves which Nuzi is supposed to offer — does not make the process of rebuttal any less difficult, though it calls into question the validity of the method used to claim that the parallels existed in the first place. On what basis are the Nuzi contracts called parallels if not the Genesis narratives? An examination of the proposed Nuzi parallels reveals two things: (1) The significance and meaning of the Nuzi contracts in the context of Near Eastern law and social practice has in most cases been seriously distorted by the interpretation of Speiser and Gordon.

(2) Most of the claimed Nuzi parallels are quite different from the customs presupposed by the biblical narratives.

Only two or three minor parallels can be affirmed on the basis of the present form of our narratives. When we notice further that the customs which have been identified in Nuzi are not in fact customs at all but very specific legal contracts, formed to expedite the immediate wishes of concrete individuals, the suggestion that the patriarchs had lived according to Nuzian type law is an error of serious significance.

When the Nuzi tablets are examined in the context of Near Eastern law and contracts, it becomes apparent that most of the customs claimed for Nuzi appear to be harmonizations constructed as much on the basis of the biblical narratives as on the tablets discovered at Yorghan Tepe (the site of ancient Nuzi). This leads us to the perhaps justifiable assumption that in those cases where the hypothetical original Tradition lying behind the biblical narratives diverges from the patriarchal stories, we are dealing with nothing more than artificial constructions, the result of a harmonization of the Bible with those Nuzi customs that vaguely resemble but are really distinct from the biblical material.

Furthermore, it must be remembered, that however impressive the Nuzi parallels to the Genesis narratives appear, they only affect the question of the historical background of our narratives to the extent that they can be shown to be more than illustrative of biblical-type customs — to the extent that they in fact are the very same customs that the Bible presupposes.

In this respect, whether the biblical customs are in fact paralleled in the contracts of Nuzi, and, if so, to what extent they are paralleled, is completely subordinate to the question about the uniqueness of the parallels. It is on the basis of this second question that the claim for the historical background of the patriarchal narratives must be completely set aside; for the character of unparalleled uniqueness for the Nuzi contracts is grossly misapplied. Customs and contracts of this sort are found throughout the entire Near East, in Mesopotamian legal codes and contracts from the Old Babylonian Period to the Persian Period, in Alalakh, in Ugarit, in the Old Testament itself outside of Genesis, and in Egypt from the Middle Kingdom to the time of the Ptolemies. In most large collections of texts that contain family contracts or legal codes referring to family relationships, similar practices of marriage, adoption and inheritance are found.

Nuzi still maintains a position of pre-eminence in the field of comparative family law, if only because of the unusually large number of such contracts found there, but their importance for the Bible is basically illustrative. They offer us neither the historical background nor the constitutive legal structure for our stories, but only a background over against which some aspects of our stories can be better understood, and on the basis of which a more careful delineation of the specifically Israelite character of the patriarchal customs can be pursued.

The scarcity of the evidence for actual family practices in the Near East can easily lead to an over-confidence about similar traits in related cultures. The situation is similar to what we find in the field of comparative literature of the Near East, where one close parallel gives sufficient conviction so that we can speak of literary borrowing, but two or three such parallels from different sources and different regions show us rather the distinctiveness and uniqueness of each.

(3) The Historical Background of the Patriarchs in the Israelite Period

In considering the third suggested possibility for the historical context of the patriarchal narratives — the period approximating the collection of the stories into the J tradition, it should be pointed out that the hypotheses which placed the historical background in the early part of the Second Millenium or in the Late Bronze Age were forced to understand many aspects of the traditions as anachronistic, as later accretions to the stories over the centuries up to the time at which the stories reached their completed form. However, when we examine some of these supposed anachronisms we find that they tend to be characteristically those aspects of the traditions which specifically distinguish the narratives from the rest of Near Eastern folk-literature as Israelite and Palestinian, namely those aspects which give the patriarchal traditions their viable and distinctive character as the traditions about the ancestors of the historical Israel! In addition, those aspects of the stories are called "anachronistic" which are the very aspects that allow one to determine a chronological limit to our stories; in fact, that some aspects of the stories can be dated to the Israelite period is the very basis for calling them anachronistic.

Even such arbitrary judgement would be allowable if it were not for the difficulty that the removal or "bracketing" of these "anachronisms" would render the stories either totally without significance for Israel, or it would destroy them structurally.

When we examine the traditions with these questions in mind it becomes obvious that we are dealing only rarely with real anachronistic accretions, and in most cases we have identifiable criteria for discovering the historical context of our stories.

The tradition about Terah setting out with his family from Ur of the Chaldees for the land of Canaan, the genealogical tree of Abraham in Gen 11, the genealogy of Nahor the brother of Abraham, the tradition that Lot is the father of the Ammonites and the Moabites and his settlement to the east of Abraham the father of the Israelites, and the Jacob-Laban traditions, all bring the patriarchs inescapably in close relationship to the Aramaeans — those of Transjordan who were not there before the end of the Late Bronze Age in the twelfth century, the Aramaeans of North Mesopotamia who can probably be dated there post twelfth century, and certainly post-fourteenth century, and the Aramaeans of South Mesopotamia, the Chaldaeans, who were not there before the beginning of the tenth century. Similarly, the tradition which connects Esau with Edom can hardly antedate the beginning of the Iron Age, and the disinheritance of Ishmael is in its origin bound up with the conflicts between Israel and the Ishmaelites. The identification of Jacob with Israel and the inheritance of his twelve sons presupposes the existence of Israel as a political and geographical entity, and the promise to Abraham presupposes the existence of the political boundaries of the Davidic kingdom. The story of the conquest of Shechem presupposes the possession of Shechem by the Israelites for a considerable period of time. That Abram is given the name Abraham because he is the father of many peoples presupposes that the tradition already knows about the Israelites.

We also have other criteria: Abraham is closely associated with the Amorites who, according to the biblical traditions, were the successors of the Aramaean related Ammonites. The reference to the Philistines in the patriarchs's conflict over water rights can only arbitrarily be excluded from the story; and specifically because we do not have other evidence for the Philistines in this region, the reference appears to be original to our story.

Archaeological research is also of some help. On the basis of the extensive archaeological study of Palestine, we can now say with some confidence that only during the Iron Age are all the cities of Palestine that are mentioned in the patriarchal narratives and which can be located with some certainty known and occupied. The geographical picture we get from the Genesis stories is that of Iron Age Palestine. I refer especially to such sites as Bethel, Ai, and Beersheba[3].

Furthermore, no aspect of the patriarchal stories, as far as I am aware, can clearly and exclusively be dated to a period earlier

[3] For a more complete discussion of the historical background of these narratives, see, most recently: B. Mazar, The Historical Background of the Book of Genesis, JNES 28 (1969), 73—83, esp. 77ff.; G. Wallis, Die Tradition von den drei Ahnvätern, ZAW 81 (1969), 18—40.

than the Iron Age, nor has any concrete detail been shown to be in conflict with this late dating.

Only one tradition shows the least promise of being early, Gen 14, which may well be historiographical, if not historical, in form, but only that part of it which is independent of the patriarchs themselves; that is, we may have here an historiographical tradition about a single or several Mesopotamian campaigns in Palestine, which has been attached to the patriarchal traditions. The identification of any such campaign in history, however, has not only been unsuccessful, but there is clear evidence that the story, as we now have it, connected with Abraham and his 318 retainers, is very late and probably post-exilic.

For reasons of source criticism and the history of the development of the traditions (Redaktionsgeschichte), it is clear that many of our individual pericopes and groups of stories antedate the Yahwistic composition. Nevertheless, since some of the traditions — such as the El naming stories — seem to have been taken up by the Yahwistic writer with relatively little change, it seems possible to suggest — but here only as a suggestion — that the stories were taken up into the Yahwistic tradition directly from the contemporary Canaanite/Israelite milieu. To search beyond this source seems to carry us outside of the context in which the traditions had meaning and significance for Israel, that is, beyond their significance as patriarchal traditions. For it is at the point that they are taken up and become a part of the traditions belonging to the Israelite people that they achieve a constitutive existence as traditions about Israel's ancestors.

B. HISTORICAL AND CHRISTIAN FAITH

"Do not presume to say to yourselves, 'we have Abraham for our father'. I tell you that God can make children for Abraham out of these stones here." (Matt 3 9).

More than forty years ago, Kurt Galling referred to this New Testament passage as an example to show that the theological significance of Israel's piety lies not in the history or the historicity of the Old Testament phenomena, but in the traditions themselves, and in the understanding which these traditions bring[4].

Recently, however, many Old Testament scholars have been inclined to believe that not only is history central to the message of Israel, but that an acceptance of the historicity of Israel's early traditions, particularly those about the biblical patriarchs, is essential to Christian faith, even, that belief in the resurrection depends

[4] K. Galling, Die Erwählungstraditionen Israels, BZAW 48, 1928, 1f.

directly on the historical facticity of the promise to the patriarchs[5]. Roland de Vaux has asserted several times that the task of scientifically establishing the historical foundations of these biblical traditions is of the utmost importance, "for if the historical faith of Israel is not founded in history, such faith is erroneous, and therefore, our faith is also"[6]. De Vaux maintains that if faith is to survive, the close relationship between "religious history" and "objective history" must be maintained[7]. He claims that to reject the historicity of Israel's "religious history" would be to question, in an ultimate way, the ground of faith itself[8].

In a similar manner, George Ernest Wright believes that Christian faith depends ultimately on questions of historicity: "In biblical faith everything depends upon whether the central events actually occurred.[9]" God is seen as one who acts in the events of Israel's history. Indeed, it soon becomes clear, it is not ultimately in the Bible that this "biblical faith" is grounded, but in the events of history, and in the Bible only insofar as the Bible retells historical events. This neo-orthodoxy is by no means a "biblicism" or a "fundamentalism" as it is often accused of being. In fact, there is very little room for any theology of the word. It is rather a deistic and positivistic historicism, which searches in its construction of a "biblical history" — to be found neither in the Bible nor in history — for the "real revelation" which could be learned if only the events which lie behind the biblical stories could be discovered[10].

For those that are less agile than they, as indeed for those who do take history seriously, the neo-orthodox have set up an exceedingly

[5] B. Vawter, A Path Through Genesis, 1965², 8: "If God did not covenant with Israel, neither did the God of Abraham and Isaac and Jacob raise Jesus from the dead, for there is no fullfillment without a promise."

[6] English translation from: The Hebrew Patriarchs and History, ThD 12 (1964), 22; cf. Les patriarches hébreux et l'histoire, RB 72 (1965), 7: "si la foi historique d'Israel n'est pas fondée dans l'histoire, cette foi est erronée, et la notre aussi." See also, Method in the Study of Early Hebrew History, in: The Bible and Modern Scholarship, ed. by J. Ph. Hyatt, 1966, 16.

[7] Ibid.

[8] Ibid.

[9] God Who Acts, 1962, 126, and: "To assume that it makes no difference whether they are facts or not is simply to destroy the whole basis of the faith" (ibid. 127). See also J. C. L. Gibson, Light from Mari on the Patriarchs, JSS 7 (1962), 45, and R. de Vaux, Method, 16.

[10] Wright speaks of history as the "primary data of faith," (ibid. 127) and that "history is the chief medium of revelation" (ibid. 13). The "biblical word is not primarily a truth, but an event ... completely and entirely within history" and "The event brings into being ... etc." (emphasis added): History and Reality, The Old Testament and Christian Faith, ed. by B. W. Anderson, 1964, 186.

serious barrier to any acceptance of the biblical tradition as constitutive of faith; for not only has "archaeology" not proven a single event of the patriarchal traditions to be historical, it has not shown any of the traditions to be likely. On the basis of what we know of Palestinian history of the Second Millenium B. C., and of what we understand about the formation of the literary traditions of Genesis, it must be concluded that any such historicity as is commonly spoken of in both scholarly and popular works about the patriarchs of Genesis is hardly possible and totally improbable.

A serious evaluation of history — as well as of the literary forms used in the past — is essential for a clear elucidation of the theological significance of the Old Testament, for it is only in this way that we can understand the Old Testament as it was meant; but historical understanding, and, concomitantly, historical and archaeological research, is not the essential aspect of a Christian's commitment of faith. In respect to the commitment of faith, the question is not whether we take history seriously. The question of whether the Bible is a true source of faith will not be decided on the basis of the Bible's historical acceptability. Of far more importance is the question whether we are prepared to see literary forms which are foreign to us, and philosophical presuppositions which are antagonistic to historical positivism, as media of truth; for it is only then that we can take the Bible seriously[11].

If we seriously affirm a "biblical faith", then it must be from the Bible that we begin to understand what that faith ought to be. And if it is true that the Bible does not speak about an historical Abraham, then a recognition of this leads us one step further towards an understanding of biblical faith. To learn that what we have believed is not what we should have believed is not to lose our faith.

Salvation history is not an historical account of saving events open to the study of the historian. Salvation history did not happen; it is a literary form which has its own historical context. In fact,

---

[11] Similarly, W. Stählin, Auch darin hat die Bibel recht, 1964, 36: "Die Frage, ob die Bibel wirklich recht hat, entscheidet sich nicht an archäologischen Beweisen für die geschichtliche Zuverlässigkeit biblischer Berichte, sondern an der Frage, ob wir in der Lage und bereit sind, auch in Sage, Märchen, und Mythos als Denkformen, die der Bibel nicht fremd sind und die aus der Bibel nicht eliminiert werden können, die Stimme der Wahrheit zu vernehmen, die uns unbedingt angeht, weil darin die Grundstruktur unseres menschlichen Seins als Menschen und als Christen ihren Ausdruck gefunden hat. Und allein diese Freiheit, zu der ich damit aufrufe, gibt uns das gute Gewissen, die Bibel auch da ernst zu nehmen, wo alles rein historische Denken mit Notwendigkeit versagt, und ihr recht zu geben gerade darin, worin sie recht haben und recht behalten will."

we can say that the faith of Israel is not an historical faith, in the sense of a faith based on historical event; it is rather a faith within history. It is a faith that is structured by the experience of Israel's history, and as such has the freedom and openness to the future which is characteristic of reflection on historical experience. It is a faith, however, which has its justification, not in the evidence of past events, for the traditions of the past serve only as the occasion of the expression of faith, but in the assertion of a future promise. The promise itself arises out of an understanding of the present which is attributed to the past and recreates it as meaningful. The expression of this faith finds its condensation in an historical form which sees the past as promise. But this expression is not itself a writing of history, nor is it really about the past, but it is about the present hope. Out of the experience of the present, new possibilities of the past emerge, and these new possibilities are expressed typologically in terms of promise and fulfillment. Reflection on the present as fulfillment recreates the past as promise, which reflection itself becomes promise of a future hope. What is historical and therefore very much open to the historical-critical disciplines are the events and the historical situation in which Israel's past traditions achieve significance as promise, but prior to this new understanding, the traditions do not have significance for the understanding of faith.

Implicit in the writings of those theologians, who see revelation as the historical event itself, is that revelation is not in word or language, not in an existential experience of man reunderstanding his situation in history. Rather, for them there is little theology of the word; revelation is understood as a series of interventions in history by the divinity, which acts have been recorded and passed down through many generations. These acts of God are seen to culminate in the act of the resurrection. According to this view, the Old Testament has value according to its reportorial accuracy, and its theological significance is seen primarily as preparation. The acts of God recorded in the Old Law give confidence in the promise which is fulfilled in the New. It is not difficult to understand how questions of historicity must necessarily be of crucial significance in the authentication of such a faith; for, the argument goes: if these actions which have been reported did not happen, then there could not have been a real historical promise, and hence there could hardly be a fulfillment of what was not promised. The theological orientation is toward the past; for it is the events of the past which are seen as authentication of the present belief.

It is hardly accidental that this view of Christianity, while patterning itself on the biblical view of history, does not see the Bible itself as constitutive of faith. Such a theological structure creates serious difficulties for Christian faith, if only because it makes great demands on the credulity of Christians. Moreover, by presenting the faith of Israel as history, they demand for it a legitimation according to the norms of historical criticism. In maintaining that the history of Israel is the revelation to Israel, they have given to the historical disciplines the ultimate competence to decide what is and what is not revealed among the biblical traditions. The rejection of the historicity of large parts of the Old Testament, thought by them to be historical, is understood as a challenge to faith because it challenges their identification of revelation with event.

But the stories about the promise given to the patriarchs in Genesis are not historical, nor do they intend to be historical; they are rather historically determined expressions about Israel and Israel's relationship to its God, given in forms legitimate to their time, and their truth lies not in their facticity, nor in their historicity, but in their ability to express the reality that Israel experienced. To the extent that this experience can be communicated, it is a revelation of the faith that was Israel's. And it is through this communication in word that Israel's experience can become ours, and Israel's faith our faith; for it is through this revelation that we are enabled to see through to the reality and the truth of the human experience which transcends the historical forms in which this experience has been expressed.

Abbreviations

AAb	Alttestamentliche Abhandlungen
AAS	Les Annales Archéologiques de Syrie
AASOR	Annual of the American Schools of Oriental Research
AcOr	Acta Orientalia
AcOr Hung	Acta Orientalia Hungarica
ADAJ	Annual of the Department of Antiquities of Jordan
ADPV	Abhandlungen des Deutschen Palästina-Vereins
ÄgAb	Ägyptologische Abhandlungen
ÄgF	Ägyptologische Forschungen
Aegyptus	Rivista Italiana di Egittologia e di Papirologia
AER	Breasted, Ancient Egyptian Records
AfO	Archiv für Orientforschung
AHB	Archaeologish-Historische Bijdragen
AJA	American Journal of Archaeology
AJSL	American Journal of Semitic Languages and Literatures
Albright Festschrift	The Bible and the Ancient Near East, ed. by G. E. Wright, 1961.
Alt Festschrift	Geschichte und Altes Testament, Beiträge zur historischen Theologie 16, 1953.
AN	J. J. Stamm, Die Akkadische Namengebung
AnÄg	Analecta Ägyptiaca
ANEP	The Ancient Near East in Pictures, ed. by J. B. Pritchard
ANET	J. B. Pritchard, Ancient Near Eastern Texts related to the Old Testament
ANETS	Supplement to ANET
AnOr	Analecta Orientalia
AnSt	Anatolian Studies
AO	Der Alte Orient
AOAT	Alter Orient und Altes Testament
AOS	American Oriental Series
AOSG	Arbeiten aus dem Orientalischen Seminar der Universität Gießen
AOT	H. Gressmann, Altorientalische Texte zum Alten Testament
APAW	Abhandlungen der königlich-preußischen Akademie der Wissenschaften zu Berlin, philosophisch-historische Klasse
APN	K. Tallqvist, Assyrian Personal Names
APNM	H. B. Huffmon, Amorite Personal Names from Mari
ARM	Archives Royales de Mari
ArOr	Archiv Orientální
ASAWL	Abhandlungen der philologisch-historischen Klasse der Sächsischen Akademie der Wissenschaften zu Leipzig
ASOR	American Schools of Oriental Research

ASR	American Sociological Review
BA	The Biblical Archaeologist
BAR	The Biblical Archaeologist Reader
BASOR	Bulletin of the American Schools of Oriental Research
Bb	Biblica
BBB	Bonner Biblische Beiträge
BHS	Biblica Hebraica Stuttgartensia
BiÄg	Bibliotheca Ägyptiaca
Bibellexikon	H. Haag, Bibellexikon, 1968
BId'Eg	Bulletin de l'Institut d'Égypte
BIES	Bulletin of the Israel Exploration Society
BIFAO	Bulletin de l'Institut Français d'Archéologie Orientale du Caire
BiOr	Bibliotheca Orientalis
BJRL	Bulletin of the J. Rylands Library
BM	British Museum
BOS	Bonner Orientalische Studien
BWA(N)T	Beiträge zur Wissenschaft vom Alten (und Neuen) Testament
BZAW	Beihefte zur Zeitschrift für die Alttestamentliche Wissenschaft
CAD	Chicago Assyrian Dictionary
CAH	The Cambridge Ancient History
CBQ	The Catholic Biblical Quarterly
CH	The Code of Hammurapi
CHL	Commentationes Humanorum Litterarum
CRAI	Comptes rendus des séances (Académie des Inscriptions et belles-lettres)
DBS	Supplément au Dictionnaire de la Bible
Driver Festschrift	Hebrew and Semitic Studies, 1963
EB	Early Bronze
e. g.	for example
EncBb	Encyclopedia Biblica
esp.	especially
ET	The Expository Times
f. (ff.)	following
FB	Frühbronzezeit
FF	Forschungen und Fortschritte
Gadd	C. J. Gadd, RA 23 (1926), 49—161.
Glueck Festschrift	Near Eastern Archaeology in the Twentieth Century, ed. by J. A. Sanders, 1970
HAT	Handbuch des Alten Testaments
HDB	Hasting's Dictionary of the Bible
HSS	Harvard Semitic Series
HThR	Harvard Theological Review
HUCA	Hebrew Union College Annual
IB	Intermediate Bronze
ibid.	the same (as the last cited reference)
IDB	International Dictionary of the Bible
i. e.	that is

IEJ	Israel Exploration Journal
JAOS	Journal of the American Oriental Society
JBL	Journal of Biblical Literature
JBR	The Journal of Bible and Religion
JCS	Journal of Cuneiform Studies
JEA	Journal of Egyptian Archaeology
JEN	Joint Expedition with the Iraq Museum at Nuzi
JEOL	Jaarbericht van het Vooraziatisch-Egyptisch Genootschap Ex Oriente Lux
JESHO	Journal of the Economic and Social History of the Orient
JJS	The Journal of Jewish Studies
JNES	Journal of Near Eastern Studies
JPOS	Journal of the Palestine Oriental Society
JRAS	Journal of the Royal Asiatic Society
JSS	Journal of Semitic Studies
JTS	Journal of Theological Studies
KAI	H. Donner and W. Röllig, Kanaanäische und Aramäische Inschriften
KAJ	Keilschrifttexte aus Assur juristischen Inhalts
Kohler Festschrift	Studies in Jewish Literature, 1913
KS	Kleine Schriften
l. (ll.)	line(s)
LB	Late Bronze
LCL	Loeb Classical Library
loc. cit.	place cited
LRS	Leipziger rechtswissenschaftliche Studien
LXX	Septuagint
MAAA	Memoirs of the American Anthropological Association
MArOr	Monographien des Archiv Orientální
MB	Middle Bronze
MKAW (MKNAW)	Mededeelingen der Koninklijke (Nederlandse) Akademie van Wetenschappen
Moortgat Festschrift	Vorderasiatische Archäologie, ed. by K. Bittel, 1964
MRS	Mission de Ras Shamra
MVÄG	Mitteilungen der Vorderasiatisch-Ägyptischen Gesellschaft
NBN	K. Tallqvist, Neubabylonisches Namenbuch
no. (nos.)	number
NThT	Nederlands Theologisch Tidsskrift
OB	Old Babylonian
OBS	E. A. Speiser, Oriental and Biblical Studies
OIP	Oriental Institute Publications
OLZ	Orientalische Literaturzeitung
op. cit.	work cited
OTS	Oudtestamentische Studiën
p. (pp.)	page(s)
PEFA	Palestine Exploration Fund Annual
PEQ	Palestine Exploration Quarterly
PJ	Palästinajahrbuch

PN	A. T. Clay, Personal Names from Cuneiform Inscriptions of the Cassite Period
PrJ	Preußische Jahrbücher
PRU	Palais royal d'Ugarit
PSBA	Proceedings of the Society for Biblical Archaeology
QDAP	Quarterly of the Department of Antiquities of Palestine
RA	Revue d'Assyriologie et d'archéologie orientale
RAI	Rencontre Assyriologique Internationale
Revd'Eg	Revue d'Egyptologie
RB	Revue Biblique
RGG	Die Religion in Geschichte und Gegenwart
RHPR	Revue d'Histoire et de Philosophie religieuses
RIDA	Revue Internationale des Droits de l'Antiquité
RLA	Reallexikon der Assyriologie, ed. by E. Ebeling and B. Meissner, 1928ff.
RL'HR	Revue de l'Histoire des Religions
RS	Ras Shamra
RSO	Rivista degli Studi Orientali
SAOC	Studies in Ancient Oriental Civilization
SBAW	Sitzungsberichte der Bayerischen Akademie der Wissenschaften
SBPAW	Sitzungsberichte der Preußischen Akademie der Wissenschaften
SBS	Stuttgarter Bibelstudien
SBTh	Studies in Biblical Theology
SHAW	Sitzungsberichte der Heidelberger Akademie der Wissenschaften, Philosophisch-historische Klasse
SKAWW	Sitzungsberichte der kaiserlichen Akademie der Wissenschaften in Wien
Syria	Syria, Revue d'Art Oriental et d'Archéologie
TCL	Textes Cunéiformes, Musée du Louvre — Département des Antiquités Orientales
ThD	Theology Digest
ThQ	Theologische Quartalschrift
TLZ	Theologische Literaturzeitung
UCP	University of California Publications in Semitic Philology
UGAA	Untersuchungen zur Geschichte und Altertumskunde, ed. by K. Sethe
VAB	Vorderasiatische Bibliothek
VAS	Vorderasiatische Schriftdenkmäler der Staatlichen Museen zu Berlin
VAT	Tafelsignaturen der Vorderasiatischen Abteilung der Berliner Museen
VT	Vetus Testamentum
VTS	Supplements to Vetus Testamentum
WO	Die Welt des Orients
WZKM	Wiener Zeitschrift für die Kunde des Morgenlandes

WZL	Wissenschaftliche Zeitschrift der Karl-Marx-Universität zu Leipzig
YOS	Yale Oriental Series
ZA	Zeitschrift für Assyriologie und verwandte Gebiete
ZÄS	Zeitschrift für Ägyptische Sprache und Altertumskunde
ZAW	Zeitschrift für die Alttestamentliche Wissenschaft
ZDMG	Zeitschrift der Deutschen Morgenländischen Gesellschaft
ZDPV	Zeitschrift des Deutschen Palästina-Vereins

Bibliography

Abel, F. M., Exploration du Sud Est de la Vallée du Jourdain, RB 40 (1931), 214—226.

Ackroyd, P. R., The Teraphim, ET 62 (1950/1951), 378ff.

Aharoni, Y., The Land of Gerar, IEJ 6 (1956), 26—32.

—, The Negeb of Judah, IEJ 8 (1958), 26—38.

—, et alii, The Ancient Desert Agriculture of the Negev: Early Beginnings, IEJ 8 (1958), 231—268.

—, et alii, The Ancient Desert Agriculture of the Negev, V; An Israelite Agricultural Settlement at Ramat Matred, IEJ 10 (1960), 23—36, 97—111.

—, Kadesh Barnea and Mount Sinai, in: B. Rothenberg, God's Wilderness, 1961, 115—189.

—, The Expedition to the Judean Desert-1960-Expedition B, IEJ 11 (1961), 11—24.

—, Expedition B — The Cave of Horror, IEJ 12 (1962), 186—199.

—, Tamar and the Road to Elath, IEJ 13 (1963), 30—42.

—, The Negeb, in: Archaeology and Old Testament Study ed. by D. W. Thomas, 1967, 384—401.

—, The Lands of the Bible, 1967.

—, Mount Carmel as Border, in: Galling Festschrift, 1—7.

Ahmed, S. S., Southern Mesopotamia in the Time of Ashurbanipal, 1968.

Aistleitner, J., Studien zur Frage der Sprachverwandtschaft des Ugaritischen, AcOrHung 7 (1957), 251—307; 8 (1958), 51—98.

Albrecht, K., Das Geschlecht der hebräischen Hauptwörter, ZAW 16 (1896), 41—121.

Albright, W. F., Historical and Mythical Elements in the Joseph Story, JBL 37 (1918), 111—143.

—, Palestine in the Earliest Historical Period, JPOS 2 (1922), 110—138.

—, The Babylonian Antediluvian Kings, JAOS 43 (1923), 323—329.

—, Egypt and the Early History of the Negev, JPOS 4 (1924), 131—161.

—, Contributions to Biblical Archaeology and Philology, JBL 43 (1924), 363—393.

—, A Babylonian Geographical Treatise on Sargon of Akkad's Empire, JAOS 45 (1925), 193—245.

—, The Jordan Valley in the Bronze Age, AASOR 6 (1926), 13—74.

—, Review of F. Th. de Liagre Böhl, Genesis, in JPOS 6 (1926), 224—228.

—, Review of Th. Bauer, Die Ostkanaanäer, AfO 3 (1926), 124—126.

—, The Names of Israel and Judah, JBL 46 (1927), 151—185.

—, The Egyptian Empire in Asia in the 21st Century, B. C., JPOS 8 (1928), 223—256.

—, On the Map Found at Nuzi, BASOR 42 (1931), 7—10.

—, Review of E. A. Speiser, Mesopotamian Origins, JAOS 51 (1931), 60—66.

—, The Fourth Joint Campaign of Excavation at Tell Beit Mirsim, BASOR 47 (1932), 3—17.

—, The Archaeology of Palestine and the Bible, 1932.

—, The Excavation of Tell Beit Mirsim I: The Pottery of the First Three Campaigns, AASOR 12 (1932).

Albright, W. F., The Excavation of Tell Beit Mirsim IA: The Bronze Age Pottery of the Fourth Campaign, AASOR 13 (1933), 55—127.

—, Archaeological and Topographical Explorations in Palestine and Syria, BASOR 49 (1933), 23—31.

—, The Vocalization of the Egyptian Syllabic Orthography AOS 5, 1934.

—, The North-Canaanite Poems of Al'êyân Ba'al and the "Gracious Gods", JPOS 14 (1934), 101—140.

—, The Names Shaddai and Abram, JBL 54 (1935), 173—204.

—, Palestine in the Earliest Historical Period, JPOS 15 (1935), 193—234.

—, New Canaanite Historical and Mythological Data, BASOR 63 (1936), 23—32.

—, Western Asia in the 20th Century; the Archives of Mari, BASOR 67 (1937), 26—30.

—, The Northwest-Semitic Tongues before 1000 B. C., Atti del XIX Congresso Internazionale degli Orientalisti, 1938, 445—450.

—, Archaeology Confronts Biblical Criticism, American Scholar 7 (1938), 176—188.

—, The Present State of Syro-Palestinian Archaeology, Haverford Symposium on Archaeology and the Bible, 1938, 1—46.

—, Was the Patriarch Terah a Canaanite Moon-God?, BASOR 71 (1938), 35—40.

—, Review of The Two Sources of the Predeuteronomic Primeval History (JE) in Gen 1—11, JBL 57 (1938), 230f.

—, The Chronology of a South-Palestinian City, Tell El-'Ajjûl, AJSL 55 (1938), 337—359.

—, The Excavation of Tell Beit Mirsim II: The Bronze Age, AASOR 17 (1938).

—, A Hebrew Letter from the 12th Century B. C., BASOR 73 (1939), 9—13.

—, The Israelite Conquest of Canaan in the Light of Archaeology, BASOR 74 (1939), 11—23.

—, The Babylonian Matter in the Pre-deuteronomic Primeval History (JE) in Gen 1—11, JBL 58 (1939), 91—103.

—, From the Stone Age to Christianity, 1940, 1957³.

—, The Ancient Near East and the Religion of Israel, JBL 59 (1940), 85—112.

—, New Light on the History of W. Asia in the 2nd Millenium B. C., BASOR 77 (1940), 20—31; 78 (1940), 23—31.

—, Review of Z. Harris, Development of the Canaanite Dialects JAOS 60 (1940), 414—422.

—, New Egyptian Data on Palestine in the Patriarchal Age, BASOR 81 (1941), 16—20.

—, The Land of Damascus between 1850 and 1750 B. C., BASOR 83 (1941), 30—36.

—, A Teacher to a Man of Shechem about 1400 B. C., BASOR 86 (1942), 28—31.

—, A Case of Lèse-Majesté in Pre-Israelite Lachish, with Some Remarks on the Israelite Conquest, BASOR 87 (1942), 32—38.

—, A Third Revision of the Early Chronology of Western Asia, BASOR 88 (1942), 28—36.

—, Two Little Understood Amarna Letters from the Middle Jordan Valley, BASOR 89 (1943), 7—17.

—, An Archaic Hebrew Proverb in an Amarna Letter from Central Palestine, BASOR 89 (1943), 29—32.

—, Note to article of N. Glueck, Three Israelite Towns in the Jordan Valley, BASOR 90 (1943), 17—18.

—, EB Pottery from Bâb Ed-Drâ' in Moab, BASOR 95 (1944), 3—13.

—, The Old Testament and Canaanite Language and Literature, CBQ 7 (1945), 5—31.

Albright, W. F., An Indirect Synchronism Between Egypt and Mesopotamia, cir. 1730 B. C., BASOR 99 (1945), 9—18.

—, The Phoenician Inscriptions of the Tenth Century B. C. from Byblos, JAOS 67 (1947), 153—160.

—, The Early Alphabetic Inscriptions from Sinai and their Decipherment, BASOR 110 (1948), 6—22.

—, and Moran, W. L., A Re-interpretation of an Amarna Letter from Byblos (EA 82), JCS 2 (1948), 239—248.

—, The Archaeology of Palestine, 1949.

—, Some Important recent Discoveries: Alphabetic Origins and the Idrimi Statue, BASOR 118 (1950), 11—20.

—, The Origin of the Alphabet and the Ugaritic ABC Again, BASOR 119 (1950), 23f.

—, and Moran, W. L., Rib-Adda of Byblos and the Affairs of Tyre (BA 89), JCS 4 (1950), 163—168.

—, Review of J. Pritchard, ANET, JAOS 71 (1951), 259—264.

—, Archaeology and the Religion of Israel, 1953,

—, Northwest Semitic Names in a List of Egyptian Slaves from the 18th. Century, B. C., JAOS 74 (1954), 222—233.

—, Recent discoveries in Bible Lands, 1955.

—, Albrecht Alt, JBL 75 (1956), 169—173.

—, From the Stone Age to Christianity, 1957[3].

—, Archaeology and Religion, Cross Currents 9 (1959), 107—124.

—, Dunand's New Byblos Valume: A Lycian at the Byblian Court, BASOR 155 (1959), 31—34.

—, The Role of the Canaanites in the History of Civilization, in: Albright Festschrift, 328—362.

—, Abram the Hebrew, a New Archaeological Interpretation, BASOR 163 (1961), 36—54.

—, Some Remarks on the Meaning of the verb SHR in Genesis, BASOR 164 (1961), 28.

—, The Chronology of MB I (Early Bronze-Middle Bronze), BASOR 168 (1962), 36—42.

—, Jethro, Hobab, and Revel in Early Hebrew Tradition, CBQ 25 (1963), 1-11.

—, The Biblical Period from Abraham to Ezra, 1963.

—, History, Archaeology and Christian Humanism, 1964.

—, The Beth-Shemesh Tablet in Alphabetic Cuneiform, BASOR 173 (1964), 51—53.

—, The 18th. Century Princes of Byblos and the Chronology of Middle Bronze, BASOR 176 (1964), 38—46.

—, A Question About Origins, Interpretation 18 (1964), 191—198.

—, Some Remarks on the Archaeological Chronology of Palestine before about 1500 B.C., in: Chronologies in Old World Archaeology, ed. by R.W. Ehrich, 1965, 47—60.

—, Further Light on the History of Middle-Bronze Byblos, BASOR 179 (1965), 38—43.

—, New Horizons in Biblical Research, Whidden Lectures 6, 1966.

—, The Amarna Letters from Palestine, CAH fasc. 51, 1966[2], 1—20.

—, Remarks on the Chronology of Early Bronze IV—Middle Bronze IIA in Phoenicia and Syria-Palestine, BASOR 184 (1966), 26—35.

— Debir, in: Archaeology and Old Testament Study, ed. by D. W. Thomas, 1967, 207—220.

Albright, W. F., Yahweh and the Gods of Canaan, 1968.
—, The Proto-Sinaitic Inscriptions and Their Decipherment, Harvard Theological Studies 22, 1969[2].
Allam, S., Zur Stellung der Frau im alten Ägypten in der Zeit des Neuen Reiches, 16—10. Jh. v. u. Z., BiOr 26 (1969), 155—159.
Alt, A., Ein Reich von Lydda, ZDPV 47 (1924), 169—185.
—, Amurru in den Ächtungstexten der 11. Dynastie, ZAW 46 (1928), 77—78.
—, Die asiatischen Gefahrzonen in den Ächtungstexten der 11ten Dynastie, ZÄS 63 (1928), 39—45.
—, Der Gott der Väter, BWANT 12, 1929.
—, Erwägungen über die Landnahme der Israeliten in Palästina, PJ 35 (1939), 8—63 (= KS I, 126—175).
—, Herren und Herrensitze Palästinas im Anfang des zweiten Jahrtausends v. Chr., ZDPV 64 (1941), 21—39.
—, Die älteste Schilderung Palästinas im Lichte neuer Funde, PJ 37 (1941), 19—49.
—, Der Rhythmus der Geschichte Syriens und Palästinas im Altertum, Beiträge zur Arabistik, Semitistik, und Islamwissenschaft (1944), 284—306 (= KS III, 1—19).
—, Die Herkunft der Hyksos in neuer Sicht, KS III, 72—98.
Amir, M. El., The Unpublished Demotic Papyri in the Turin Museum, AcOr 25 (1960), 203—228.
Amiram, D. H. K., and Ben Arieh, Y., Sedentarization of Beduin in Israel, IEJ 13 (1963), 161—181.
Amiram, R., The Pottery of the Middle Bronze Age I in Palestine, IEJ 10 (1960), 204—225.
—, The Pottery of the Middle Bronze Age I, (Hebrew) Qadmoniot 2 (1969), 45—49.
—, Ancient Pottery of the Holy Land, 1970.
—, The Beginnings of Urbanization in Canaan, in: Glueck Festschrift, 1970, 83—100.
Anati, E., Palestine before the Hebrews, 1963.
Anderson, B. W., (ed), The Old Testament and Christian Faith, 1964.
—, The Living World of the Old Testament, 1967.
Anthes, R., Die Felseninschriften von Hatnub, 1964.
Apollodorus. The Library LCL edition by J. G. Frazer, I—II 1921.
Astour, M., Benê-iamina et Jéricho, Semitica (1959), 5—20.
—, The Origin of the terms "Canaan", "Phoenician" and "Purple", JNES 24 (1965), 346—350.
—, Political and Cosmic Symbolism in Genesis 14 and in its Babylonian Sources, in: Biblical Motifs, ed. by A. Altmann, 1966, 85—112.
Avigad, M., The Expedition to the Judaean Desert 1960-Expedition A, IEJ 11 (1961), 6—10.
—, Expedition A — Nahal David, IEJ 12 (1962), 169—183.
Avi Yonah, M., Our Living Bible, 1962.

Bacher, W., יְשֻׁרוּן, ZAW 5 (1885), 161—163.
Bar-Adon, P., The Expedition to the Judaean Desert — Expedition C, IEJ 11 (1961), 25—35.
Baramki, D. C., The Pottery from Khirbet El Mefjer, QDAP 10 (1940), 65—104.
Bardtke, H., Bibel, Spaten und Geschichte, 1969.
Bartlett, J. R., Sihon and Og, Kings of the Amorites, VT 20 (1970), 257—277.

Barton, G. A., The Religion of Israel, 1918.
—, The Present State of Old Testament Studies, in: Haverford Symposium on Archaeology and the Bible, ed. by E. Grant, 1938, 47—78.
Bauer, Th. Die Ostkanaanäer, 1926.
—, Eine Überprüfung der "Amoriter"-Frage, ZA 38 (1929), 145—170.
Bayd, R. M. Arpachshad, HDB I, 157.
Beckerath, J. von, Untersuchungen zur politischen Geschichte der Zweiten Zwischenzeit in Ägypten, ÄgF 23, 1964.
Beek, M. A., Das Problem des aramäischen Stammvaters (Deut. 26 5), OTS 8 (1950), 193—212.
Bell, B., The Dark Ages in Ancient History, I. The First Dark Age in Egypt., AJA 75 (1971), 1—26.
Bell, H. I., Brother and Sister Marriage in Graeco-Roman Egypt, RIDA 2 (1949), 83—92.
Ben-Arieh, Y., and Amiram, D. H. K., Sedentarization of Beduin in Israel, IEJ 13 (1963), 161—181.
Bernhardt, K. H., Die Umwelt des Alten Testaments, I 1967.
Bialoblocki, S., Materialien zum islamischen und jüdischen Eherecht, AOSG 1, 1928.
Bilgic, E., Die Ortsnamen der kappadokischen Urkunden im Rahmen der alten Sprachen Anatoliens, AfO 15 (1945/1951), 1—37.
Birot, M., Trois textes économiques de Mari (II), RA 47 (1953), 161—174.
—, Un recensement de Femmes au Royaume de Mari, Syria 35 (1958), 9—26.
—, Textes Économiques de Mari (III), RA 49 (1959), 15—31.
Blackman, A. M., Oracles in Ancient Egypt, JEA 12 (1926), 176—185.
Böhl, F., Kanaanäer und Hebräer, BWAT 9, 1911.
Böhl, F. M. Th. de Liagre, Het Tijdperk der Aartsvaders, 1925.
—, Volksetymologie en Woordspeling in de Genesis-Verhalen, MKAW Letterkunde 59 A, 1925, 49—79.
—, Die bei den Ausgrabungen von Sichem gefundenen Keilschrifttafeln, ZDPV 49 (1926), 321—327.
—, Das Zeitalter Abrahams, AO, 1930 (revised, Opera Minora, 1953, 26—49, 476—479).
—, Mededeelingen uit de Leidsche verzameling van spijkerschrift-inscripties II: Oorkonden uit de periode van 2000—1200 v. Chr., MKAW, deel 78, Serie B, Nr. 2 (1934).
—, Abraham, Encyclopedia Britanica 1 (1947), 59—60.
—, Amraphel, RGG^3 I, 332f.
—, Babel und Bibel II. Die Patriarchenzeit, JEOL 17 (1963), 125—140.
—, De Bijbel in het Licht der Opgravingen, Commentar op de Heilige Schrift, no date, 58—61.
Bonnet, H., Die Waffen der Völker des alten Orients, 1926.
Borchardt, L., Ein Rechnungsbuch des königlichen Hofes aus dem Ende des mittleren Reiches, ZÄS 28 (1890), 65—103.
Borée, W., Die alten Ortsnamen Palästinas, 1930.
Born, A. van den, and Simons, J., Syrisch-palästinische Ortsnamen in ägyptischen Texten, $Bibellexikon^2$ List I, XIV—XV.
—, Abraham, $Bibellexikon^2$, 13—15.
—, Arpaksad, $Bibellexikon^2$, 109f.
—, Jakob, $Bibellexikon^2$, 800—802.

Born, A. van den, Joseph, Bibellexikon², 880—882.
—, Kanaan, Bibellexikon², 914f.
Bottéro, J., and Finet, A., Répertoire Analytique des Tomes I à V, ARM 15, 1954.
Bowman, R. A., Genealogy, IDB II 362—365.
Boyer, G., Contribution à l'Histoire Juridique de la 1re Dynastie Babylonienne, 1928.
—, Sur quelques emplois de la fiction dans l'ancien droit oriental, RIDA 1 (1954), 73—100.
—, ARM VIII, TCL XXIX, Textes Juridiques et Administratifs, 1957.
Braidwood, L. S. and R. J., Excavations in the Plain of Antioch I, OIP 61, 1960.
Braidwood, R. J., Mounds in the Plain of Antioch, OIP 48, 1937.
—, Report on Two Sondages on the Coast of Syria, South of Tartous, Syria 21 (1940), 183—221.
—, and L. S., Excavations in the Plain of Antioch I, OIP 61, 1960.
—, Further Remarks on Radioactive Carbon Age Determination and the Chronology of the Late Prehistoric and Protohistoric Near East, in: Festschrift A. Moortgart, 57—67.
—, A Note on the Present Status of Radioactive Carbon Age Determination, Sumer 23 (1967), 39—43.
Branden, A. von den, Le Déchiffrement des Inscriptions Protosinaïtiques, Al-Mašriq (1958), 361—397.
Breasted, J. H., When did the Hittites enter Palestine, AJSL 21 (1904/1905), 153—158.
—, The Earliest Occurrence of the Name of Abram, AJSL 21 (1904/1905), 22—36.
—, Ancient Records of Egypt, I—V 1906.
—, The "Field of Abram" in the Geographical List of Sheshank I, JAOS 31 (1911), 290—295.
—, The Ras Shamra Statue of Sesostris-Onekh, Syria 16 (1935), 318—320.
Bright, J., Early Israel in Recent History Writing, SBTh 19, 1956.
—, History of Israel, 1959.
—, Modern Study of Old Testament Literature, in: The Bible and the Ancient Near East, Albright Festschrift, 13ff.
Brooks, B. A., The Babylonian Practice of Marking Slaves, JAOS 42 (1922), 80.
Brown, Driver, and Briggs, Hebrew and English Lexikon of the Old Testament, 1959.
Brunner, H., Die Lehre des Cheti Sohnes des Duauf, ÄgF 13, 1944.
Brunner-Traut, E., Altägyptische Märchen. Die Märchen der Weltliteratur, 1965².
Buccellati, G., The Amorites of the Ur III Period, 1966.
Budde, K., Ellä toledoth, ZAW 34 (1914), 241—253; 36 (1916), 1—7.
Buisson, Le Comte de Mesnil du, L'Ancienne Qatna ou les Ruines d'El-Mishrifé au N. E. de Homs (Émèse), Syria IX (1928), 6—24.
Buit, M. Du., Quelques Contacts Bibliques dans les Archives Royales de Mari, RB 66 (1959), 576—581.
Burke, M., Un nouveau nom d'Année du Règne de Zimri-lim, RA 52 (1958), 57—59.
Burney, C. F., Israel's Settlement in Canaan. The Biblical Tradition and its Historical Background, Schweich Lectures, 1921.
Burrows, E., Notes on Harrian, JRAS (1925), 277—284.
Burrows, M., The Complaint of Laban's Daughters, JAOS 57 (1937), 259—276.
—, The Basis of Israelite Marriage, AOS 15, 1938.
—, The Ancient Oriental Background of Hebrew Levirate Marriage, BASOR 77 (1940), 2—5.

Burrows, M., What Mean these Stones?, 1941.
Buttrick, G. A., International Dictionary of the Bible, I—IV 1962.
Byzantinus, Stephanus, De Urbibus, ed. by Guilielmi Xylandri Augusta, 1568.
Byzantinus, Stephanus, cum Annotationes IV. ed. by Th. de Pinedo, 1825.

Callaway, J. A., The 1964 ʿAi (et Tell) Excavations, BASOR 178 (1965), 13—40.
—, The Emerging Role of Biblical Archaeology, Review and Expositor 63 (1966), 200—209.
Campbell, A. F., Homer and Ugaritic Littératures, Ab-Nahrain vol. V for 1964—1965, (1966), 29—56.
Campbell, E. F., Jr., The Ancient Near East: Chronological Bibliography and Charts, in: Albright Festschrift, 214f.
—, Archaeological News from Jordan, BA 28 (1965), 17—32.
Cancik, H., Grundzüge der Hethitischen und Frühisraelitischen Geschichtsschreibung (Tübingen Dissertation, 1970).
Caquot, A., Remarques sur la Langue et le Panthéon des Amorites de Mari, Les Annales Archéologiques de Syrie I, 2 (1951), 206—225.
Cardascia, G., Les lois assyriennes, Littératures anciennes du Proche-Orient 2, 1969.
—, Adoption Matrimoniale et Lévirat dans le Droit d'Ugarit, RA 64 (1970), 119—126.
Caskel, W., Gambaret an-Nasab, I—II 1966.
Cassin, E. M. La Caution a Nuzi, RA 34 (1937), 154—168.
—, L'Adoption à Nuzi 1938.
—, L'influence Babylonienne à Nuzi, JESHO 5 (1962). 113—138.
—, Tablettes Inédites de Nuzi, RA 56 (1962), 57—80.
—, Nouvelles données sur les relations familiales à Nuzi, RA 57 (1963), 113—119.
Cassuto, U., The Documentary Hypothesis, 1961.
—, A Commentary on the Book of Genesis, II 1964.
Cazelles, H., Der Gott der Patriarchen, Bibel und Leben 2 (1961), 39—49.
—, Patriarches, DBS VIII col. 81—156.
—, Mari et L'Ancien Testament, RAI XVe (1967), 73—90.
Cecchini, S. M., La Ceramica di Nuzi, 1965.
Černy, J., Le Culte d'Amenophis Ier chez les Ouvriers de la Nécropole Thébaine, BIFAO 27 (1927), 159—197.
—, and Peet, T. E., A Marriage Settlement of the Twentieth Dynasty, JEA 13 (1927), 30—39.
—, The Will of Naunakhte and the Related Documents, JEA 31 (1945), 29—53.
— (ed.), Gardiner, A. H., and Peet, T. E., The Inscriptions of Sinai I—II, 1952/1955.
—, Consanguineous Marriages in Pharaonic Egypt, JEA 40 (1954), 23—29.
—, A Note on the Ancient Egyptian Family. Studi in onore di Aristide Calderini e R. Paribeni, II 1956, 51—55.
Cheyne, T. K., Arpachshad, ZAW 17 (1897), 190.
—, and Sutherland-Black, J. Encyclopedia Biblica, I—IV 1899—1903.
—, Abram, EncBb, 28.
—, Eber, EncBb, 1152f.
—, Haran, EncBb, 1961f.
—, Isaac, EncBb, 2174—2179.
—, Lot, EncBb, 2824f.
—, Moses, EncBb, 3203—3219.

Cheyne, T. K., Nahor, EncBb, 3258f.
—, Peleg, EncBb, 3644.
—, Shelah, EncBb, 4448.
—, Shem, EncBb, col. 4449.
—, Terah, EncBb, cols. 4973f.
Chiera, E., Report of the Professor in Charge of the School in Baghdad, BASOR 20 (1925), 19—25.
—, and Speiser, E. A., A New Factor in the History of the Ancient East, AASOR 6 (1926), 75—92.
—, and Speiser, E. A., Selected "Kirkuk" Documents, JAOS 47 (1927), 36—60.
—, Inheritance Texts JEN I, 1927.
—, Report of the Director of the School in Baghdad, BASOR 32 (1928), 15—17.
—, Excavations at Nuzi I — Texts of Varied Contents, HSS V, 1929.
—, Declarations in Court, JEN II, 1930.
—, Exchange and Security Documents, JEN III, 1931.
—, Proceedings in Court, JEN IV, 1934.
—, Mixed Texts, JEN V, 1934.
—, They Wrote on Clay, 1938.
Clark, G. H., The Bible as Truth, Bibliotheca Sacra 114 (1957), 157—170.
Clay, A. T., Personal Names from Cuneiform Inscriptions of the Cassite Period, YOS 1, 1912.
—, The Origin of Biblical Traditions, YOS 12, 1923.
Clements, R., Abraham and David, 1967.
Clère, J. J., Sinouhé en Syrie, in: Melanges Syriens offerts à René Dussaud 2 (1939), 829—840.
—, and Vandier, J., Textes de la Première Période Intermédiaire et de la XIeme Dynastie, BiÄg 10, 1948.
Cleveland, R. L., Soundings at Khirbet Ader, AASOR 34/35 (1960), 79—97.
Coats, G. W., Despoiling the Egyptians, VT 18 (1968), 450—457.
Cohen, S., Peleg, IDB III, 709.
Conder, R. E., Districts in Palestine, PEQ 17 (1885), 18—19.
Contenau, G., Babyloniaca, Textes Cuneiformes de Louvre, IX, 1926, 1—46.
—, Les Tablettes de Kerkouk, 1926.
—, Les tablettes de Kerkouk et les origines de la civilisation assyrienne, Babyloniaca IX (1926), 69—151. 157–212.
—, Textes et Monuments, Tablettes de Kerkouk du Musée du Louvre, RA 28 (1931), 27—39.
Couroyer, B., Les Nouveaux Textes Egyptiens de Proscription, Vivre et Penser I, RB 50 (1941), 261—264.
Cornelius, F., Chronologie: Eine Erwiderung, JCS 12 (1958), 101—104.
—, Genesis 14, ZAW 31 (1960), 1—7.
—, Moses urkundlich, ZAW 78 (1966), 75—78.
Cornfeld, G., From Adam to Daniel, 1961.
—, Pictorial Biblical Encyclopedia, 1964.
Couyat, J., and Montet, P., Les Inscriptions Hiéroglyphiques et Hiératiques du Ouâdi Hammâmât, 1912.
Cross, F. M. Jr., and Freedman. D. N., The Blessing of Moses, JBL 67 (1948), 191—210.

Cross, F. M. Jr., and Lambdin, T. O., An Ugaritic Abecedary and the Origins of the Proto-Canaanite Alphabet, BASOR 160 (1960), 21—26.
—, The Priestly Tabernacle, BAR, 1961, 201—228.
—, Yahweh and the God of the Patriarchs, HThR 55 (1962), 225—259.
Cuq, E., Études sur le Droit Babylonien, 1929.

Dahood, M., Hebrew Ugaritic Lexicography III, Bb 46 (1965), 311—332.
—, Hebrew-Ugaritic Lexicography IV, Bb 47 (1966), 403—419.
—, The Name Yišma''el in Genesis 16 11, Bb 49 (1968), 87—88.
Dajani, A., A Hyksos Tomb at Kalandia, ADAJ 2 (1953), 75—77.
—, Middle Bronze Age Pottery, ADAJ 4—5 (1960), 99—113.
—, Transportation in the Middle Bronze Periods, ADAJ 8—9 (1964), 56—67.
Dajani, R. W., Iron Age Tombs from Irbed, ADAJ 8—9 (1964), 99—101.
—, Jabal Nuzha Tomb at Amman, ADAJ 11 (1966), 48—52.
—, Four Iron Age Tombs from Irbed, ADAJ 11 (1966), 88—101.
Dalman, G., Arbeit und Sitte in Palästina, I—VII 1964.
Danell, G. A., Studies in the Name Israel in the Old Testament, 1946.
Daube, D., Studies in Biblical Law, 1947.
—, Error and Accident in the Bible, RIDA 2 (1949), 189—213.
—, and Yaron, R., Jacob's Reception by Laban, JSS 1 (1956), 60—62.
Davico, A., et alii., Missione Archeologica Italiana in Siria, I—III 1965—1967.
David, M., Die Adoption im altbabylonischen Recht, LRS 23 (1927).
—, The Codex Hammurabi and its Relation to the Provisions of Law in Exodus, OTS 7 (1950), 149—178.
—, Zabal (Gen. 30 20), VT 1 (1951), 59f.
—, Adoptie in het oude Israël, MKNAW 18 (1955), 85—104.
Delitzsch, Franz, Neuer Commentar über die Genesis, 1887[5].
Delitzsch, Friedrich, Wo lag das Paradies?, 1881.
—, Prolegomena eines neuen Hebräisch-Aramäischen Wörterbuchs zum alten Testament, 1886.
—, Assyrische Lesestücke, 1912[5].
Dever, W., The Pottery of Palestine in the EB IV/MB I Period ca. 2150—1850 B. C., Harvard diss., 1966.
—, Ethnic Movements in East Central Europe and the Near East ca. 2300—1800 B. C., Yearbook of the American Philosophical Society for 1967 (1968), 500—503.
—, The "Middle Bronze I" Period in Syria and Palestine, in: Glueck Festschrift, 132—163.
—, Vestigial Features in MB I: an Illustration of Some Prinicples of Ceramic Typology, BASOR 200 (1970), 19—30.
—, The People of Palestine in the Middle Bronze Period, HThR 64 (1971), 197—226.
—, Archaeological Methods and Results. A Review of Two Recent Publications, Orientalia 40 (1971), 459—471.
Dhorme, E., Un nouveau fragment de l'épopée de Gilgamès, RA 55 (1961), 153f.
Dhorme, P., Les Pays Bibliques au Temps d'El-Amarna, RB 6 (1909), 50—73.
—, Les Pays Bibliques et l'Assyrie, RB 7 (1910), 368—390.
—, Le Pays de Job, RB 8 (1911), 102—107.
—, Les Amorrhéens, RB 37 (1928), 63—79, 161—180.
—, Abraham dans le Cadre de l'Histoire, RB 37 (1928), 367—385. 503—518.

Dietrich, M., and Loretz, O., Zur ugaritischen Lexikographie (I), BiOr 23 (1966), 127—133.
—, Die Aramäer Südbabyloniens in der Sargonidenzeit, AOAT 7 (1970).
Dillmann, A., Die Genesis, 1892.
Donner, H., Zur Formgeschichte der Aḫiram-Inschrift, WZL 3 (1953—1954), 283—287.
—, and Röllig, W., Kanaanäische und aramäische Inschriften, I—III 1966—1969².
—, Adoption oder Legitimation? Erwägungen zur Adoption im Alten Testament auf dem Hintergrund der altorientalischen Rechte, Oriens Antiquus 8 (1969), 87—119.
Dossin, G., Les Archives Epistolaires du Palais de Mari, Syria 19 (1938), 105—126.
—, Signaux Lumineux au Pays de Mari, RA 35 (1938), 174—186.
—, NQMD et Niqme-ḫad, Syria 20 (1939), 169—176.
—, Les Archives Économiques du Palais de Mari, Syria 20 (1939), 97—113.
—, Benjaminites dans les Textes de Mari, Melanges Syriens offerts à R. Dussaud, II 1939, 981—996.
—, Correspondance de Samši-Addu et de ses Fils, ARM I, 1950.
—, Correspondance de Samši-Addu et de ses Fils, ARM IV, 1951.
—, Correspondance de Iašmaḫ-Addu, ARM V, 1952.
—, A Propos du Nom des Benjaminites dans les Archives de Mari, RA 52 (1958), 60—62.
—, Les Bédouins dans les Textes de Mari, Studi Semitici, 2 L'Antica Società Beduina, 1959, 35—51.
Dothan, M., The Fortress of Kadesh Barnea, IEJ 15 (1965), 134—151.
Draffkorn, A. E., Ilani/Elohim, JBL 76 (1957), 216—224.
Drioton, E., Le Désert du Sinai couvert par une Forêt Impénétrable, Revd'Eg 12 (1960), 90f.
Driver, G. R., and Miles, J. C., Ordeal by Oath at Nuzi, Iraq 7 (1940), 132—138.
Driver, S. R., Nahor, HDB III, 472f.
—, The Book of Genesis, 1904.
Dunand, M., Les Égyptiens à Beyrouth, Syria 9 (1928), 300—302.
—, Fouilles de Byblos Tome I, 1926—32, Tome II, 1933—1938, I—V 1937—1958.
—, Byblos au Temps du Bronze Ancien et de la Conquète Amorite, RB 59 (1952), 82—90.
—, Phénicie, DBS 7 (1966), 1141—1204.
Dunayevski, I., and Kempinski, A., Notes and News: Megiddo, IEJ 16 (1966), 142.
Dupont—Sommer, A., Les Araméens, L'Orient Ancien Illustré, 1949.
Dussaud, R., Les Inscriptions Phéniciennes du Tombeau d'Ahiram, Roi de Byblos, Syria 5 (1925), 135—157.
—, Nouveaux Renseignements sur la Palestine et la Syrie vers 2000 avant notre Ere, Syria 8 (1927), 216—231.
—, Review of E. Dhorme, La Religion des Hébreux Nomades, Syria 18 (1937), 395—398.
—, Nouveaux Textes Égyptiens d'Exécration contre les peuples Syriens, Syria 21 (1940), 170—182.
—, L'origine de l'alphabet et son évolution première d'après les découvertes de Byblos, Syria 25 (1946—1948), 36—52.
—, La Pénétration des Arabes en Syrie avant l'Islam, Institute Français d'Archéologie de Beyrouth, Bibliotheque archéologique et historique, 59, 1955.
—, Une Traduction Nouvelle de la Bible, Syria 35 (1958), 1—8.

Ebeling, E., Ein Brief aus Nuzi im Besitz des Athener archäologischen Museums, Orientalia 22 (1953), 355—358.

Eberharter, A., Das Ehe- und Familienrecht der Hebräer, AAb 5, 1914.

Edgerton, W. F., Notes on Egyptian Marriage, SAOC 1, 1931.

—, Egyptian Phonetic Writing, From its Invention to the Close of the Nineteenth Dynasty, JAOS 60 (1940), 473—506.

Edwards, I. E. S., The Early Dynastic Period in Egypt, CAH² fascicle 25, 1964.

Edzard, D. O., Die "Zweite Zwischenzeit" Babyloniens, 1957.

—, Altbabylonisch nawûm, ZA 53 (1959), 168—173.

—, Mari und Aramäer?, ZA 22 (1964), 142—149.

Eisser, G. and Lewy, J., Die Altassyrischen Rechtsurkunden vom Kûltepe, MVÄG 35/35, I—IV 1930/1935.

Eissfeldt, O., Hexateuch-Synopse, 1922, 1962².

—, Stammessage und Novelle in den Geschichten von Jakob und von seinen Söhnen, Eucharisterion, H. Gunkel zum 60. Geburtstag, 1923, I, 56—77.

—, Gabelhürden im Ostjordanland, FF 25 (1949), 9f.

—, Recht und Grenze archäologischer Betrachtung des Alten Testaments, OLZ 49 (1954), cols. 101—108.

—, Das Alte Testament im Lichte der safatenischen Inschriften, ZDMG 104 (1954), 88—118.

—, Der Beutel der Lebendigen, 1960.

—, The Alphabetical Cuneiform Texts from Ras Shamra published in Le Palais Royal d'Ugarit, II 1957, JCS 5 (1960), 1—49.

—, Achronische, anachronische und synchronische Elemente in der Genesis, JEOL 17 (1963), 148—164 (= KS IV, 153—169).

—, Stammessage und Menschheitserzählung in der Genesis, Sitzungsberichte der Sächsischen Akademie der Wissenschaft zu Leipzig, Phil.-hist. Kl. Bd 110, 4 (1965), 5—21.

—, Neue keilalphabetische Texte aus Ras Schamra-Ugarit, Sitzungsberichte der Deutschen Akademie der Wissenschaften zu Berlin, 1965.

—, Kleine Schriften, I—IV 1962—1968.

—, Liber Genesis, BHS, 1969.

Elgavish, Y., Shiqmona, in Chronique Archéologique, RB 75 (1968), 146f.

Elliger, K., Review of G. E. Wright, Biblische Archäologie, TLZ 84 (1959), col. 94—98.

Elrington, C. R., and Todd, J. H., The Whole Works of the Most Rev. James Ussher, 1847—1864.

Emerton, J. A., Beth-Shemesh, in: Archaeology and Old Testament Study, ed. by D. W. Thomas, 1967, 197—206.

—, Some False Clues in the Study of Genesis XIV, VT 21 (1971), 24—47.

—, The Riddle of Genesis XIV, VT 21 (1971), 403—439.

Emery, W. B., Archaic Egypt, 1961.

Emmet, C. W., Genealogy, HDB.

Engberg, R. M., and Shipton, G. M., Notes on the Chalcolithic and Early Bronze Age Pottery of Megiddo, 1934.

—, and Guy, P. Megiddo Tombs, 1938.

—, Tombs of the early second millenium on the Middle Euphrates, BASOR 87 (1942), 17—23.

Engnell, I., Methodological Aspects of Old Testament Study, VTS 7, (1959), 13—30.
Epstein, C., Palestinian Bichrome Ware, 1966.
Epstein, L., Marriage Laws in the Bible and the Talmud, HSS 12, 1942.
Erichsen, W., and Nims, C. F., A Further Category of Demotic Marriage Settlements, AcOr 23 (1958), 119—133.
Erman, A., Zaubersprüche für Mutter und Kind, 1901.
—, Die Mahnworte eines ägyptischen Propheten, SBPAW 42 (1919), 804—815.
—, Die Literatur der Ägypter, 1923.
—, and Grapow, H. (eds.), Wörterbuch der ägyptischen Sprache, I—VII 1955.
—, and Grapow, H., Wörterbuch der ägyptischen Sprache. Die Belegstellen, I—V 1955.
—, The Ancient Egyptians, 1966.
Evenari, M. et alii., The Ancient Desert Agriculture of the Negev, III; Early Beginnings, IEJ 8 (1958), 231—268.

Fabretti, Rossi, and Lanzone. Regio Museo di Torino I—II, 1882—1888.
Fabricus, W., et alii., Die Geschichte der Jakobtradition, Wissenschaftliche Zeitschrift der Martin Luther Universität Halle 13 (1964), 427—440.
Fakhry, A., The Inscriptions of the Amethyst Quarries ar Wadi el Hudi, 1952.
Falk, Z. W., Review of R. de Vaux, Les Institutions de L'Ancien Testament, JJS 9 (1958), 201—203.
—, Testate Succession in Jewish Law, JJS 12 (1961), 67—77.
—, Hebrew Law in Biblical Times, 1964.
Faulkner, R. O., Notes on "The Admonitions of an Egyptian Sage", JEA 50 (1964), 24—36.
—, The Admonitions of an Egyptian Sage, JEA 51 (1965), 53—62.
Feigin, S., Some Cases of Adoption in Israel, JBL 50 (1931), 186—200.
Fensham, F. C., The Son of a Handmaid in Northwest Semitic, VT 19 (1969), 312—321.
Fichtner, J., Die etymologische Ätiologie in den Namengebungen der geschichtlichen Bücher des Alten Testaments, VT 6 (1956), 372—396.
Finegan, J., Handbook of Biblical Chronology, 1964.
Finet, A., and Bottéro, J., Répertoire Analytique des Tomes I à V, ARM XV, 1954.
—, Iawi-Ilâ, Roi de Talḫayûm, Syria 41 (1964), 117—142.
Finkelstein, J. J., Subartu and Subarians in Old Babylonian Sources, JCS 9 (1955), 1—7.
—, The Bible, Archaeology, and History, Commentary 27 (1959), 341—349.
—, An Old Babylonian Herding Contract and Genesis 31: 38f., JAOS 88 (1968), 30—36.
—, The Laws of Ur-Nammu, ANETS, 523—525.
—, Sumerian Laws, ANETS, 525f.
—, Additional Mesopotamian Legal Documents, ANETS, 542—547.
Flanagan, M., Salvation History, 1964.
Flight, J. W., The Nomadic Idea and Ideal in the Old Testament, JBL 42 (1923), 158—224.
Fohrer, G., and Galling, K., Ezechiel, HAT, 1955.
Forbes, R. J., The Coming of the Camel, Studies in Ancient Technology, II 1955, 187—204.
—, Studies in Ancient Technology, 1954.

Forrer, E., Assyrien, RLA I.

—, Aramu, RLA I.

—, Eine Geschichte des Götterkönigtums aus dem Hatti-Reiche, Melanges F. Cumont, Annuaires de l'Institut de Philologie et d'Histoire Orientales et Slaves 4, 1936, 687—713.

Franken, H. J., Excavations at Tell Deir 'Alla I, 1969.

—, and Power, W. J. A., Glueck's Explorations in Eastern Palestine in the light of recent evidence, VT 21 (1971), 118—123.

Frankfort, H., Egypt and Syria in the First Intermediate Period, JEA 12 (1926), 80—99.

Frazer, J. G., Folk-Lore in the Old Testament, I—III 1919.

Free, J. P., The Third Season at Dothan, BASOR 139 (1955), 3—9.

—, Archaeology and Biblical Criticism, I: Is Rationalistic Biblical Criticism Dead?, Bibliotheca Sacra 113 (1956), 123—129.

—, Archaeology and Biblical Criticism, II: Archaeology and the Historical Accuracy of Scripture, Bibliotheca Sacra 113 (1956), 214—226.

—, Archaeology and Biblical Criticism, III: Archaeology and Liberalism, Bibliotheca Sacra 113 (1956), 322—338.

—, Archaeology and Biblical Criticism, IV: Archaeology and Higher Criticism, Bibliotheca Sacra 114 (1957), 23—29.

—, Archaeology and Biblical Criticism, V: Archaeology and Neo-Orthodoxy, Bibliotheca Sacra 114 (1957), 123—132.

—, Archaeology and Biblical Criticism, VI: Archaeology and Neo-Orthodoxy, Bibliotheca Sacra 114 (1957), 213—224.

—, The Fifth Season at Dothan, BASOR 152 (1958), 10—18.

Freedman, D. N., and Cross, F. M. Jr., The Blessing of Moses, JBL 67 (1948), 191—210.

—, The Chronology of Israel and the Ancient Near East, in: Albright Festschrift 203—228.

—, The Original Name of Jacob, IEJ 13 (1963), 125f.

—, A New Approach to the Nuzi Sistership Contract, Journal of the Ancient Near Eastern Society of Columbia University 2 (1970), 77—85.

Fugmann, E., Hama, Fouilles et Recherches 1931—1938 II, 1; L'Architecture des Périodes Pré-Hellénistiques, 1958.

Furlani, G., Review of R. Pfeiffer HSS vol. X, The Archives of Shilwateshub, JRAS (1935), 747.

Gadd, C. J., Tablets from Kirkuk, RA 23 (1926), 49—161.

—, History and Monuments of Ur, 1929.

—, Tablets from Chagar Bazar, Iraq 4 (1936), 178—185.

—, Tablets from Chagar Bazar and Tell Brak 1937—38, Iraq 7 (1940), 22—66.

Galling, K., Die Erwählungstraditionen Israels, BZAW 48, 1928.

—, Biblisches Reallexikon, HAT I, 1937.

—, Review of N. Glueck, AASOR 25—28, ZDPV 68 (1951), 284—286.

—, Archaeologisch-historische Ergebnisse einer Reise in Syrien und Libanon im Spätherbst 1952, ZDPV 69 (1953), 88—93.

—, and Fohrer, G., Ezechiel, HAT, 1955.

—, Kritische Bemerkungen zur Ausgrabung von eğ-ğib, BiOr 22 (1965), 242—245.

—, Textbuch zur Geschichte Israels, 1968².

Garcia-Treto, F. O., Genesis 31 44 and "Gilead", ZAW 79 (1967), 13—17.
Gardiner, H. A., The Inscription of Meš, UGAA 4, 1905.
—, The Admonitions of an Egyptian Sage, 1909.
—, The Goddess Nekhbet at the Jubilee Festival of Rameses III, ZÄS 48 (1911), 47—51.
—, New Literary Works from Ancient Egypt, JEA 1 (1914), 20—36. 100—106.
—, Notes on the Story of Sinuhe, 1916.
—, The Tomb of a Much Travelled Theban Official, JEA 4 (1917), 28—38.
—, and Gunn, B., New Renderings of Egyptian Texts, JEA 5 (1918), 36—56.
—, Egyptian Grammar, 1927,
—, Adoption Extraordinary, JEA 26 (1940), 23—29.
—, and Peet T. E., The Inscriptions of Sinai, I—II 1952–1955.
—, The Kadesh Inscriptions of Ramses II, 1960.
—, Once Again the Proto-Sinaitic Inscriptions, JEA 48 (1962), 45—48.
Gaster, T. H., A Canaanite Magical Text, Orientalia 11 (1942), 41—79.
—, Thespis, 1950.
Gauthier, H., Dictionnaire des Noms Géographiques Contenus dans les Textes Hiéroglyphiques V, 1928.
Gayet, E., Musée du Louvre Stèles de la XIIe Dynastie, 1886.
Gelb, I. J., Purves, P. M., and MacRae, G., Nuzi Personal Names, 1943.
—, The Early History of the West Semitic Peoples, JCS 15 (1961), 27—47.
—, An Old Babylonian List of Amorites, JAOS 88 (1968), 39—46.
Geus, C. H. J. de, De Amorieten in de Palestijnse Archeologie: een Recente Theorie Kritisch Bezien, NThT 23 (1968/1969), 1—24.
Gevirtz, S., Abram's 318, IEJ 19 (1969), 110—113.
Gibson, J. C. L., Observations on Some Important Ethnic Terms in the Pentateuch, JNES 20 (1961), 217—238.
—, Light from Mari on the Patriarchs, JSS 7 (1962), 44—62.
Gilead, D., Burial Customs and the Dolmen Problem, PEQ 100 (1968), 16—26.
Ginsberg, H. L., and Maisler, B., Semitized Hurrians in Syria and Palestine, JPOS 14 (1934), 243—267.
—, The Brooklyn Museum Aramaic Papyri, JAOS 74 (1954).
—, Review of C. H. Gordon, Before the Bible, Commentary (October, 1963), 333 to 336.
—, Aramaic Papyri from Elephantine, ANETS, 1969, 548f.
—, Abram's "Damascene" Steward, BASOR 200 (1970), 31f.
Glueck, N., The Archaeological Exploration of El-Hammeh on the Yarmûk, BASOR 49 (1933), 22f.
—, Further Explorations in Eastern Palestine, BASOR 51 (1933), 9—18.
—, Explorations in Eastern Palestine I, AASOR 14 (1934).
—, Explorations in Eastern Palestine and the Negeb, BASOR 55 (1934), 3—21.
—, Explorations in Eastern Palestine II, AASOR 15 (1935).
—, Explorations in Eastern Palestine III, BASOR 64 (1936), 9—10; 65 (1937), 8—29.
—, An Aerial Reconnaissance in Southern Transjordan, BASOR 66 (1937), 27f.; 67 (1937), 19—26.
—, Explorations in the Land of Ammon, BASOR 68 (1937), 13—21.
—, Explorations in Eastern Palestine III, AASOR 18—19 (1939).
—, The Earliest History of Jerash, BASOR 75 (1939), 22—30.
—, The Other Side of the Jordan, 1940.

Glueck, N., Further Explorations in Eastern Palestine, BASOR 86 (1942), 14—24.
—, Three Israelite Towns in the Jordan Valley: Zarethan, Succoth, Zaphon, BASOR 90 (1943), 2—23.
—, Some Ancient Towns in the Plains of Moab, BASOR 91 (1943), 7—26.
—, The River Jordan, 1946.
—, Explorations in Western Palestine, BASOR 131 (1953), 6—15.
—, Further Explorations in the Negeb, BASOR 137 (1955), 10—22.
—, The Age of Abraham in the Negev, BA 18 (1955), 2—9.
—, The Third Season of Explorations in the Negeb, BASOR 138 (1955), 7—29.
—, Explorations in Eastern Palestine IV, AASOR 25—28 (1955).
—, The Fourth Season of Exploration in the Negeb, BASOR 142 (1956), 17—35.
—, The Fifth Season of Exploration in the Negeb, BASOR 145 (1957), 11—25.
—, The Sixth Season of Archaeological Exploration in the Negeb, BASOR 149 (1958), 8—17.
—, The Seventh Season of Archaeological Exploration in the Negeb, BASOR 152 (1958), 18—38.
—, Rivers in the Desert, 1959.
—, An Aerial Reconnaissance of the Negev, BASOR 155 (1959), 2—13.
—, The Negev, BA 22 (1959), 82—97.
—, Archaeological Exploration of the Negeb in 1959, BASOR 159 (1960), 3—14.
—, Further Explorations in the Negev, BASOR 179 (1965), 6—29.
—, Some Edomite Pottery from Tell El-Kheleifeh, BASOR 188 (1967), 8—38.
—, Transjordan, in: Archaeology and OT Study, ed. by D. W. Thomas, 1967, 428—452.

Goetze, A., Kleinasien zur Hethiterzeit, 1924.
—, Hethiter, Churriter und Assyrer, 1936.
—, Review of Ugnad, Subartu, JAOS 57 (1937), 104—109.
—, Is Ugaritic a Canaanite Dialect?, Language 17 (1941), 127—138.
—, Mesopotamian Laws and the Historian, JAOS 69 (1949), 115—120.
—, The Predecessors of Suppiluliumas of Hatti, JAOS 72 (1952), 67—72.
—, The Laws of Eshnunna, ANET 161—163.
—, The Hittite Laws, ANET 188—197.
—, On the Chronology of the Second Millenium B. C., JCS 11 (1957), 63ff.
—, Remarks on Some Names Occuring in the Execration Texts, BASOR 151 (1958), 28—33.
—, Review of J. R. Kupper, Les nomades en Mésopotamie au temp des rois de Mari, JSS 4 (1959), 142—147.
—, Amurrite Names in Ur III and Early Isin Texts, JSS 4 (1959), 193—203.
—, and Levy, S., Fragment of the Gilgamesh Epic from Megiddo, Atiquot 2 (1959), 121—128.

Golénischeff, W., Le Papyrus No. 1 de St. Pétersbourg, ZÄS 14 (1876), 107—111.
—, Ermitage Impérial Inventoire de la Collection Egyptienne, 1891.
—, Les Papyrus Hiératiques nos 1115, 1116A et 1116B de l'Ermitage Impérial à St. Pétersbourg, 1913.

Good, E. M., Hosea and the Jacob Tradition, VT 16 (1966), 137—151.

Gophna, R., Ma'abarot, in Chronique Archéologique, RB 75 (1968), 268f.
—, A Middle Bronze Age I Tomb with Fenestrated Axe at Ma'abarot, IEJ 19 (1969), 174—177.

Gordon, C. H., Numerals in the Nuzi Tablets, RA 31 (1934), 53—60.
—, Points of the Compass in the Nuzi Tablets, RA 31 (1934), 101—108.
—, Nuzi Tablets Relating to Women, AnOr 12 (1935), 163—184.
—, Parallèles Nouziens aux lois et coutumes de l'Ancien Testament, RB 44 (1935), 34—41.
—, אלהים in its Reputed Meaning of Rulers, Judges, JBL 54 (1935), 139—144.
—, Fratriarchy in the Old Testament, JBL 54 (1935), 223—231.
—, Fifteen Nuzi Tablets Relating to Women, Le Muséon 48 (1935), 113—132.
—, A New Akkadian Parallel to Deuteronomy 25 11-12, JPOS 15 (1935), 29—34.
—, The Status of Woman Reflected in the Nuzi Tablets, ZA 43 (1935), 146—169.
—, An Akkadian Parallel to Deuteronomy 21 1ff., RA 33 (1936), 1—6.
—, Nuzi Tablets Relating to Theft, Orientalia 5 (1936), 305—330.
—, Evidence for the Horite Language from Nuzi, BASOR 64 (1936), 23ff.
—, A Marriage of the Gods in Canaanite Mythology, BASOR 65 (1937), 29—33.
—, The Story of Jacob and Laban in the Light of the Nuzi Tablets, BASOR 66 (1937), 25—27.
—, The Dialect of the Nuzi Tablets, Orientalia 7 (1938), 32—63. 215—232.
—, Biblical Customs and the Nuzi Tablets, BA 3 (1940), 1—12.
—, Ugaritic Literature, Scripta Pontificii Instituti Biblici 98, 1949.
—, The Ugaritic "ABC", Orientalia 19 (1950), 374—376.
—, Review of J. B. Pritchard, ANET, JBL 70 (1951), 159—163.
—, Damascus in Assyrian Sources, IEJ 2 (1952), 174f.
—, Review of Cassuto, The Goddess Anath, JAOS 72 (1952), 180—181.
—, Introduction to Old Testament Times, 1953.
—, The Patriarchal Age, JBR 21 (1953), 238—243.
—, The Patriarchal Narratives, JNES 13 (1954), 56—59.
—, Review of van Selms, Marriage and Family Life in Ugaritic Literature, JAOS 74 (1954), 267—268.
—, Homer and Bible, HUCA 26 (1955), 43—108.
—, Review of A. van Selms, Marriage and Family Life in Ugaritic Literature, Orientalia 24 (1955), 327—329.
—, Ugaritic Manual, AnOr 35 (1955).
—, Adventures in the Nearest East, 1957.
—, Abraham and the Merchants of Ura, JNES 17 (1958), 28—31.
—, The World of the Old Testament, 1958.
—, Before the Bible, 1962.
—, Arpachshad, IDB, I, 231.
—, Haran, IDB, II, 524.
—, Hebrew Origins in the Light of Recent Discovery, in: Biblical and Other Studies, ed. by A. Altmann, 1963, 3—14.
—, Abraham of Ur, in: Hebrew and Semitic Studies, G. R. Driver Festschrift, 1963, 77 to 84.
—, The Common Background of Greek and Hebrew Civilizations, 1965.
—, Ugarit and Minoan Crete, 1966.
—, Evidence for the Minoan Language, 1966.
—, Forgotten Scripts, 1968.

Graham, W., Culture and Conscience, 1936.
—, Higher Criticism Survives Archaeology, American Scholar 7 (1938), 409—427.

Granqvist, H., Marriage Conditions in a Palestinian Village, CHL 3, 8, 1931.
Grant, E., Beth Shemesh: Progress of the Haverford Archaeological Expedition, 1929.
—, Ain Shems Excavations, I—II 1931/1932.
—, and Wright, G. E., Ain Shems Excavations IV—V, 1938—1939.
Grapow, H., and Erman, A., Wörterbuch der ägyptischen Sprache, 7 vols., 1955.
—, and Erman, A., Wörterbuch der ägyptischen Sprache, Die Belegstellen, 5 vols., 1955.
Gray, G. B., Studies in Hebrew Proper Names, 1896.
Gray, J., Archaeology and the Old Testament World, 1962.
—, The Canaanites, 1964.
—, The Legacy of Canaan, VTS 5, 1965.
—, Hazor, VT 16 (1966), 26—52.
Greenberg, M., Hebrew segulla: Akkadian sikiltu, JAOS 71 (1951), 172—174.
—, Another Look at Rachel's Theft of the Teraphim, JBL 81 (1962), 239—248.
—, Response to R. de Vaux's "Method in the Study of Early Hebrew History", in: The Bible in Modern Scholarship ed. by J. Philip Hyatt, 1966, 37—43.
Greengus, S., The Old Babylonian Marriage Contract, JAOS 89 (1969), 505—532.
Gressmann, H., Sage und Geschichte in den Patriarchenerzählungen, ZAW 30 (1910), 1—34.
—, Ursprung und Entwicklung der Joseph-Sage, in: Eucharisterion, Festschrift für H. Gunkel, hrsg. von H. Schmidt, I 1923, 1—55.
—, Review of Th. Bauer, Die Ostkanaanäer, ZAW 44 (1926), 301f.
—, Wichtige Zeitschriften-Aufsätze, ZAW 44 (1926), 280—283.
—, Altorientalische Texte zum Alten Testament, 1926.
Griffith, F. L., Fragments of Old Egyptian Stories, PSBA 14 (1892), 451—472.
—, The Millingen Papyrus (teaching of Amenemhat), ZAS 34 (1896), 35—49.
—, Beni Hasan, III—IV 1896/1900.
—, Hieratic Papyri from Kahun and Gurob, I—II 1897/1898.
Grimme, H., Der Name Jerusalem, OLZ 16 (1913), 152—158.
Grintz, J. M., On the Original Home of the Semites, JNES 21 (1962), 186—206.
Gröndahl, F., Die Personennamen der Texte aus Ugarit, 1967.
Gross, W., Jakob, der Mann des Segens. Zu Traditionsgeschichte und Theologie der priesterschriftlichen Jakobsüberlieferungen, Biblica 49 (1968), 321—344.
Grosvenor, M. V., Journey into the Living World of the Bible, The National Geographic Magazine 132 (1967), 495—507.
Grote, G., History of Greece, I, 1854^4.
Gunkel, H., Jakob, PrJ 176 (1919), 339—362.
—, Genesis, 1966^7.
—, Jakob, RGG^2 III, 14—17.
Gunn, B., and Gardiner, A. H., New Renderings of Egyptian Texts, JEA 5 (1918), 36—56.
Gurney, O. R., The Hittites, 1952.
Gustavs, A., Die Personennamen in den Tontafeln von Tell-Ta-ʿannek, ZDPV 50 (1927), 1—18.
—, Die Personennamen in den Tontafeln von Tell-Ta-ʿannek II, ZDPV 51 (1928), 169—218.
Güterbock, H., Die historische Tradition und ihre literarische Gestaltung bei Babyloniern und Hethitern bis 1200, ZA 44 (1938), 45—145.

Güterbock, H., The Hittite Version of the Hurrian Kumarbi Myths: Oriental Forerunners of Hesiod, AJA 52 (1948), 123—134.

—, The Song of Ullikummi, Revised Text of the Hittite Version of a Hurrian Myth, JCS 5 (1951), 135—161; 6 (1952), 8—42.

Guthrie, H. H. Jr., Eber, IDB, II, 5.

Guy, P., and Engberg, R. M., Megiddo Tombs, 1938.

H. R. H., A Sphinx of Amenemhet IV, British Museum Quarterly 2 (1927/1928), 87f.

Haag, H., Erwägungen über Beersheba, Sacra Pagina, Miscellanea Biblica Congressus Internationalis Catholici de re Biblica, I 1959, 335—345.

—, Homer, Ugarit und das Alte Testament, 1962.

—, Die Archäologie im Dienste der Bibel, in: Seine Rede geschah zu mir, ed. by F. Leist, 1965, 144—172.

—, Der gegenwärtige Stand der Erforschung der Beziehungen zwischen Homer und dem Alten Testament, JEOL 19 (1967), 508—518.

—, Bibellexikon, 1968².

—, Patriarchen, Bibellexikon, cols. 1325—1328.

—, Review of H. Seebass, Der Erzvater Israel, ThQ 148 (1968), 107.

—, Biblisches Wörterbuch, 1971.

Haase, R., Einführung in das Studium keilschriftlicher Rechtsquellen, 1965.

Hachmann, R., Das Königsgrab V von Jebeil (Byblos), Istanbuler Mitteilungen 17 (1967), 93—114.

Hahn H., The Old Testament in Modern Research, 1966.

Hall, H. R., The Ancient History of the Near East, 1960.

Hansen, D. P., Some Remarks on the Chronology and Style of Objects from Byblos, AJA 73 (1969), 281—284.

Haran, M., The Religion of the Patriarchs, Annual of the Swedish Theological Institute 4 (1965), 30—55.

Harden, D., The Phoenicians, 1962.

Harding, G. L., The Cairn of Hani, ADAJ 2 (1952), 8—56.

—, Four Tomb Groups from Jordan, PEFA 6 (1953).

—, Excavations in Jordan, 1951—52, ADAJ 2 (1953), 82—88.

Harland, J. P., Sodom and Gomorrah: Part I, The Location of the Cities of the Plain, BA 5 (1942), 17—32.

—, Sodom and Gomorrah: Part II, The Destruction of the Cities of the Plain, BA 6 (1943), 41—52.

Harrelson, W., Shechem in Extra-Biblical References, BA 20 (1957), 2—10.

Harris, J. R., Lexicographical Studies in Ancient Egyptian Minerals, Deutsche Akademie der Wissenschaften zu Berlin, Institut für Orientforschung, N. 54, 1961.

Harris, R., The Archive of the Sin Temple in Khafajah (Tutub), JCS 9 (1955), 31—88. 91—120.

Harrison, R. K., History of Old Testament Times, 1961.

Hartland, E. S., Matrilineal Kinship, and the Question of its Priority, MAAA 17 (1917).

Harvey, P., Oxford Companion to Classical Literature, 1966.

Hastings. J., (ed.), Dictionary of the Bible, I—V 1898—1904.

Haupt, P., Midian und Sinai, ZDMG 63 (1909), 506—530.

—, Die "Eselstadt" Damaskus, ZDMG 69 (1915), 168—172.

Hawkes, J., and Woolley, L., Prehistory and the Beginnings of Civilization, History of Mankind, I 1963.
Hayes, W. C., Career of the Great Steward Henenu under Nebhepetre' Mentuhotpe, JEA 35 (1949), 43—49.
—, The Scepter of Egypt, I 1953.
—, The Middle Kingdom in Egypt, CAH fascicle 3, 1964².
—, From the Death of Ammenemes III to Seqenenre II, CAH fascicle 6, 1965².
Helck, W., Die Beziehungen Ägyptens zu Vorderasien im 3. und 2. Jahrtausend v. Chr., ÄgAb 5, 1962.
—, Geschichte des alten Ägypten, Handbuch der Orientalistik 1, 3, 1968.
—, Der Text der "Lehre Amenemhets für seinen Sohn", Kleine Ägyptische Texte, 1969.
—, Die Prophezeiung, Kleine Ägyptische Texte, 1970.
Hempel, J., Zusammenfassung und Einzelforschung in der Archäologie, ZAW 70 (1958), 165—173.
Hennessy, J. B., Excavation of a Late Bronze Age Temple at Amman, PEQ 98 (1966), 155—162.
—, Supplementary Note, ZAW 78 (1966), 357—359.
—, The Foreign Relations of Palestine during the Early Bronze Age, 1967.
Henninger, J., Altarabische Genealogie, Anthropos 61 (1966), 852—870.
—, Zum Erstgeborenrecht bei den Semiten, in: Festschrift W. Caskel, ed. by E. Gräf, 1968.
Henrey, K. H., Land Tenure in the Old Testament, PEQ 86 (1954), 5—15.
Hermann, A., Review of S. Schott, Altägyptische Liebeslieder, ZDMG 101 (1951), 361—366.
Herrmann, S., Israels Aufenthalt in Ägypten, 1970.
Hicks, L., Abraham, IDB, I, 15—21.
—, Isaac, IDB, II, 728—731.
—, Haran, IDB, II, 524.
—, Lot, IDB, III, 162f.
—, Lotan, IDB, III, 163.
—, Nahor, IDB, III, 497f.
—, Reu, IDB, IV, 53.
—, Serug, IDB, IV, 291.
—, Shem, IDB, IV, 321.
—, Terah, IDB, IV, 574.
Hillen, C., A Note on Two Shafthole Axes, BiOr 10 (1953), 211—215.
Hillers, D. R., An Alphabetic Cuneiform Tablet from Taanach, BASOR 173 (1964), 45—50.
Hirsch, H., Eine Kleinigkeit zur Heiratsurkunde, ICK 1, 3, Orientalia 35 (1966), 279—280.
Höfner, M., Altsüdarabische Grammatik, 1943.
Hoftijzer, J., Die Verheißungen an die drei Erzväter, 1956.
Holladay, J. S. Jr., The Day(s) the Moon Stood Still, JBL 87 (1968), 166—178.
Holladay, W. L., Chiasmus, the Key to Hosea 12 3-6, VT 16 (1966), 53—64.
Holt, J., The Patriarchs of Israel, 1964.
Hommel, F., The True Meaning of Arpakshad, ET 13 (1901/1902).
Horn, S. H., Scarabs from Shechem, JNES 21 (1962), 1—14.

Horn, S. H., Scarabs and Scarab Impressions from Shechem-II, JNES 25 (1966), 48—56.

Huffmon, H. B., Amorite Personal Names in the Mari Texts, 1965.

—, Prophecy in the Mari Letters, BA 31 (1968), 101—124.

Hughes, G. R., Saite Demotic Land Leases, SAOC 28, 1952.

Hulst, A. R., Geschiedenis von Israel tot aan de Ballingschap, Commentar op de Heilige Schrift, (no date) 66—72.

Hyatt, J. P., ed. The Bible and Modern Scholarship, 1966.

Hyslop, R. Maxwell, Western Asiatic Shaft-Hole Axes, Iraq 11 (1949), 90—130.

Imperati, F., I Hurriti, 1964.

Irvin, D. (with Thompson, Th.), Some Legal Problems in the Book of Ruth, VT 18 (1968), 79—99.

—, Mytharion. The Comparison of Tales from the Old Testament and the Ancient Near East, AOAT, 1974.

Isserlin, B. S. J., Place Name Provinces in the Semitic Speaking Ancient Near East, Proceedings of the Leeds Philosophical and Literary Society 8 (1956), 83—110.

Jack, J. W., The Date of the Exodus, 1925.

Jacob, G., Der Name Jacob, Litterae Orientales 54 (1933), 16—19.

Jacobsen, Th., The Reign of IbbI-suen, JCS 7 (1953), 36—47.

Jankowska, N. B., Legal Documents from Arrapha in the Collections of the USSR, 1961.

Janssen, J. J., and Pestman, P. W., Burial and Inheritance in the Community of the Necropolis Workmen at Thebes, JESHO 11 (1968), 137—170.

Jastrow, M., A Dictionary of the Targumim, The Talmud Babli and Yerushalmi, and the Midrashic Literature, I—II 1903.

Jean, C.-F., Métaphonie i‘am> i‘em dans les Lettres de Mari, RA 34 (1937), 169—171.

Jeffrey, A., Review of T. Ashkenazi, Tribus semi-nomades de la Palestine du Nord, JNES 5 (1946), 282f.

Jelínková, E. A. E., Sale of Inherited Property in the First Century B. C. (P. Brit. Mus. 10075, Ex Salt Coll. No. 418), JEA 43 (1957), 45—55; 45 (1959), 61—74.

Jensen, P., Vorstudien zur Entzifferung des Mitanni, ZA 6 (1891), 34—72.

—, Grundlagen für eine Entzifferung der (hatischen oder) cilicischen (?) Inschriften, ZDMG 48 (1894), 235—352. 429—485.

—, Nik(k)al-Šarratu-שׂרה in Harran, ZA 11 (1896), 293—301.

—, Hittiter und Armenier, 1898.

—, Kiš, ZA 15 (1900), 210—256.

Jepsen, A., Die Hebräer" und ihr Recht, AfO 15 (1945/1951), 55—68.

—, Zur Überlieferungsgeschichte der Vätergestalten, WZL 3 (1953/1954), 265—281.

—, Ama^h und Schiphcha^h, VT 8 (1958), 293—297.

—, Ama^h und Schiphcha^h — Nachtrag VT 8, 3, VT 8 (1958), 425.

Jeremias, A., Das Alte Testament im Lichte des Alten Orients, 1906.

Jirku, A., Die ägyptischen Listen palästinensischer und syrischer Ortsnamen, Klio 25 (1937).

Johns, C. H. W., An Assyrian Doomsday Book, 1901.

—, The Relations Between the Laws of Babylonia and the Laws of the Hebrew Peoples, 1917^2.

Johnson, M. D., Purpose of the Biblical Chronologies, 1969.

Johnston, C., Assyrian qanânu "to coil" and Xarâpu "to abound", JAOS 29 (1908), 224—226.

Kaiser, O., Traditionsgeschichtliche Untersuchung von Genesis 15, ZAW 70 (1958), 107—126.

Kantor, H. J., The Relative Chronology of Egypt and its Foreign Correlations before the Late Bronze Age, in: Chronologies in Old World Archaeology, ed. by B. W. Ehrich, 1964.

Kapelrud, A. S., Hvem var Abraham ?, NTT 64 (1963), 163—174.

—, The Ras Shamra Discoveries and the Old Testament, 1963.

—, The Role of the Cult in Old Israel, in: The Bible in Modern Scholarship, ed. by J. P. Hyatt, 1965, 44—56.

—, Israel, 1966.

Kardimon, S., Adoption as a Remedy for Infertility in the Period of the Patriarchs, JSS (1958), 123—126.

Karošec, V., Ehe in Nuzi, RLA II, 296—299.

Kaufman, Y., The Religion of Israel, 1961.

Keller, C. A., Die Gefährdung der Ahnfrau, ZAW 66 (1954), 181—191.

—, Über einige alttestamentliche Heiligtumslegenden I, ZAW 67 (1955), 141—168.

Kelso, J., The Second Campaign at Bethel, BASOR 137 (1955), 5—10.

—, Excavations at Bethel, BA 19 (1956), 36—43.

—, The Third Campaign at Bethel, BASOR 151 (1958), 3—8.

—, The Fourth Campaign at Bethel, BASOR 164 (1961), 5—19.

—, Condensed Report of the 1960 Beitin Expedition, ADAJ 6/7 (1962), 122f.

—, Archaeology and Our Old Testament Contemporaries, 1966.

—, The Excavation of Bethel (1934—60), AASOR 39 (1968).

Kempinski, A., and Dunayeveski, I., Notes and News: Megiddo, IEJ 16 (1966), 142.

Kennett, R. H., Ancient Hebrew Social Life and Custom as Indicated in Law, Narrative, and Metaphor, 1933.

Kenyon, F. G., The Bible and Modern Scholarship, 1949.

—, The Bible and Archaeology, 1949.

Kenyon, K., Some Notes on the History of Jericho in the Second Millenium B. C., PEQ (1951), 101—138.

—, British School of Archaeology in Jerusalem Excavations at Jericho 1952: Interim Report, PEQ (1952), 4—6.

—, Excavations at Jericho, 1952, PEQ (1952), 62—82.

—, Excavations at Jericho, 1953, PEQ (1953), 81—96.

—, Excavations at Jericho, 1954, PEQ (1954), 45—63.

—, A Crescentic Axehead from Jericho, and a Group of Weapons from Tell el Hesi, University of London Institute of Archaeology, Eleventh Annual Report (1955), 10—18.

—, Tombs of the Intermediate Early Bronze—Middle Bronze Age at Tell Ajjul, ADAJ 3 (1956), 41—55.

—, Digging up Jericho, 1957.

—, Some Notes on the Early and Middle Bronze Age Strata of Megiddo, Eretz Israel 5 (1958), 51—60.

—, Archaeology in the Holy Land, 1960.

—, Jericho, I—II 1960—1964.

—, Excavations in Jerusalem, 1965, PEQ 98 (1966), 73—88.

—, Palestine in the Middle Bronze Age, CAH fascicle 48, 1966².

—, Amorites and Canaanites, 1966.

Kenyon, K., Jericho, in: Archaeology and Old Testament Study, ed. by D. W. Thomas, 1967, 264—275.
—, The Middle and Late Bronze Age Strata at Megiddo, Levant 1 (1969), 25—60.
Kilian, R., Die vorpriesterlichen Abrahamsüberlieferungen, BBB 24, 1966.
—, Isaaks Opferung, SBS 44, 1970.
Kirk, G. E., Archaeological Explorations in the Southern Desert, PEQ 70 (1938), 211—235.
Kirkbride, A. S., Desert Kites, JPOS 20 (1946), 1—5.
Kirkbride, D., Appendix E: Scarabs, in: Jericho II, ed. by K. Kenyon, 1965, 580—655.
Klengel, H., Benjaminiten und Hanäer zur Zeit der Könige von Mari (Dissertation Berlin, 1958).
—, Zu einigen Problemen des altvorderasiatischen Nomadentums, ArOr 30 (1962), 585—596.
Klima, J., Untersuchungen zum altbabylonischen Erbrecht, MArOr 8 (1940).
Knaur Lexikon für ägyptische Kultur, 1960.
Knierim, R., Oberflächenuntersuchungen im Wadi el-Far'a II, ZDPV 85 (1969), 51—62.
Knobel, A., Die Genesis. Kurzgefaßtes exegetisches Handbuch zum AT, 1852[11].
Knudzton, J., Die El-Amarna Tafeln, I—II 1964.
Koch, K., Der Tod des Religionsstifters, Kerygma und Dogma 8 (1962), 100—123.
Kochavi, M., The Excavations at Tel Yeruham, (Hebrew) BIES 27 (1963), 284—292.
—, The Settlement of the Negev in the Middle Bronze I Age (Jerusalem dissertation, 1967).
—, Review of K. Kenyon, Jericho II, IEJ 18 (1968), 59—62.
—, The Middle Bronze Age I (The Intermediate Bronze Age) in Eretz-Israel, (Hebrew) Qadmoniot 2 (1969), 38—44.
Kohler, J., and Peiser, F. E., Aus dem babylonischen Rechtsleben, I—IV 1890—1898.
—, Das Recht als das Lebenselement der Völker, 1892.
—, Koschaker, P., and Ungnad, A., Hammurabi's Gesetz, III—VI 1909—1923.
—, and Ungnad, A., Assyrische Rechtsurkunden, 1913.
König, E., Die Genesis, 1925[3].
König, F. W., Mutterrecht und Thronfolge im alten Elam, 1926.
—, Geschwisterehe in Elam, RLA III, 224—231.
Kornemann, E., Die Stellung der Frau in der vorgriechischen Mittelmeerkultur, Orient und Antike 4, 1927.
Koschaker, P., Ungnad, A., and Kohler, J. Hammurabi's Gesetz, III—IV 1909 bis 1923.
—, Rechtsvergleichende Studien zur Gesetzgebung Hammurapis, 1917.
—, Quellenkritische Untersuchungen zu den altassyrischen Gesetzen, MVÄG 26 (1921).
—, Neue keilschriftliche Rechtsurkunden aus der El-Amarna-Zeit, ASAWL 39, 1928.
—, Keilschriftforschung, OLZ 35 (1932), 399—405.
—, Fratriarchat, Hausgemeinschaft und Mutterrecht in Keilschriftrechten, ZA 41 (1933), 1—89.
—, Keilschriftrecht, ZDMG 89 (1935), 32.
—, Drei Rechtsurkunden aus Arrapha, ZA 48 (1944), 161ff.
—, Eheschließung und Kauf nach alten Rechten, mit besonderer Berücksichtigung der älteren Keilschriftrechte, ArOr 18 (1950), 210—296.
Kozenkova, W. I., Pogrebalnyje pamjatniki Fergany perwych wekow naschej ery, Sovetskaja archeologija 1 (1968), 211—226.

Kraeling, E., Aram and Israel, 1918.
—, Miscellen. 1. Terach, ZAW 40 (1922), 153f.
—, The Significance and Origin of Genesis 6 1-4, JNES 6 (1947), 193—208.
—, and Avi-Yonah, M., Our Living Bible, 1962.
Kramer, S. N., The Verb in the Kirkuk Tablets, AASOR XI (1931), 63—119.
—, Lipit-Ishtar Lawcode, ANET, 159—161.
Krauss, S., Die Ehe zwischen Onkel und Nichte, in: Festschrift K. Kohler, 165—175.
Krückmann, O., Die neuen Inschriften von Hatra, AfO 16, 1 (1952), 141—148.
Kupper, J. R., Les Nomades en Mesopotamie au temps des rois de Mari, Bibliothèque de la Faculté de Philosophie et Lettres de l'Université de Liège fasc. 142, 1957.
—, ed. XVe Rencontre Assyriologique Internationale, Bibliothèque de la Faculté de Philosophie et Lettres de l'Université de Liège no. 182, 1967.
Kuschke, A., Beiträge zur Siedlungsgeschichte der Bikâ', ZDPV 70 (1954), 104—129.
—, Beiträge zur Siedlungsgeschichte der Bikâ' (Fortsetzung), ZDPV 71 (1955), 97—110.
—, Har(r)an, RGG^{3} III, 73f.
—, and Kutsch, E., ed., Archäologie und Altes Testament, Festschrift K. Galling, 1970.
Kutsch, E., and Kuschke, A., Archäologie und Altes Testament, Festschrift K. Galling, 1970.
Kyle, M. G., The "Field of Abram" in the Geographical List of Shoshenq I, JAOS 31 (1911), 86—91.

Labat, R., Le Rayonnement de la Langue et de l'Écriture Akkadiennes au deuxième millénaire avant notre Ère, Syria 39 (1962), 1—27.
Labuschagne, C. J., Teraphim: A New Proposal for its Etymology, VT 16 (1966), 115—117.
Lacheman, E. R., New Nuzi Texts and a New Method of Copying Cuneiform Tablets, JAOS 55 (1935), 429—431.
—, Miscellaneous Texts, JEN VI, 1939.
—, Nuziana, I—II RA 36 (1939), 81—95; 113—219.
—, Epigraphic Evidences of the Material Culture of the Nuzians, in: Nuzi, ed. by Starr, 1939, 528—544..
—, and Pfeiffer, R. H., Miscellaneous Texts from Nuzi, Part I, HSS XIII, 1942.
—, Miscellaneous Texts from Nuzi, Part II, HSS XIV, 1950.
—, The Administrative Archives, HSS XV, 1955.
—, Economic and Social Documents, HSS XVI, 1958.
—, Family Law Documents, HSS XIX, 1962.
—, Les tablettes de Kerkouk au Musée d'Art et d'Histoire de Genève, Genava 15 (1967), 5ff.
Lambdin, T. O., and Cross, F. M., Jr., An Ugaritic Abecedary and the Origins of the Proto-Canaanite Alphabet, BASOR 160 (1960), 21—26.
Lambert, W. G., The Domesticated Camel in the 2nd Millenium — evidence from Alalakh and Ugarit, BASOR 160 (1960), 42—43.
—, and Walcot, P., A New Babylonian Theogony and Hesiod, Kadmos 4 (1965), 64—72.
Landsberger, B., Über die Völker Vorderasiens im dritten Jahrtausend, ZA 35 (1924), 213—238.
—, Assyrische Königsliste und „Dunkles Zeitalter", JCS 8 (1954), 31—73. 106—133.
—, Akkadisch-Hebräische Wortgleichungen, VTS 16 (1967), 176—204.

Lange, H. O., and Schäfer, H., Grab- und Denksteine des Mittleren Reichs in Museum von Kairo, I 1902
Langhe, R. de, Les Textes de Ras Shamra-Ugarit et leurs Rapports avec le Milieu Biblique de L'Ancien Testament, Dissertationes Louvaniensis Series II, Tomus 35, 1 and 2, 1945.
Lanzone, Fabretti, and Rossi, Regio Museo di Torino, I—II 1882—1888.
Lapp, P., Palestine: Known but Mostly Unknown, BA 26 (1963), 121—134.
—, The Dhahr Mirzbanêh Tombs, ASOR publication of the Jerusalem School: Archaeology, IV 1966.
—, The Cemetery at Bab edh-Dhra, Archaeology 19 (1966), 104—111.
—, Bâb edh-Dhrâ' Tomb A 76 and Early Bronze I in Palestine, BASOR 189 (1968), 12—41.
—, Palestine in the Early Bronze Age, in: Glueck Festschrift, 101—131.
Larsen, M. T., Old Assyrian Caravan Procedures, 1967.
Lawrence, T. E., and Woolley, C. L., The Wilderness of Zin, PEFA (1914/1915).
Leemans, W., Foreign Trade in the Old Babylonian Period, 1960.
Lefèvre, A., Note d'exégèse sur les généalogies des Qehatites, Recherches de Science Religieuse 37 (1950), 287—292.
Legrain, L., Le Temps des Rois d'Ur, 1912.
Lehmann, M. R., Abraham's Purchase of Machpelah and Hittite Law, BASOR 129 (1953), 15—18.
Leibovitch, J., Deux Nouvelles Inscriptions Protosinaïtiques, Muséon 74 (1961), 461—466.
Lepsius, C. R., Denkmäler aus Ägypten und Äthiopien, I—VI 1849—1859.
Lesky, A., Review of C. H. Gordon, Homer and Bible, Gnomon 29 (1957), 321—325.
Levy, R., An Introduction to the Sociology of Islam, I—II 1931—1933, 210—212.
Levy, S. and Goetze, A., Fragment of the Gilgamesh Epic from Megiddo, Atiquot 2 (1959), 121—128.
Lewy, H., Review of E. Cassin, L'Adoption à Nuzi, JAOS 59 (1939), 118—120.
—, The aḫḫûtu Documents from Nuzi, Orientalia 9 (1940), 362—373.
—, Gleanings from a New Volume of Nuzi Texts, Orientalia 10 (1941), 201—222.
—, The Nuzian Feudal System, Orientalia N. S. 11 (1942), 1—40. 209—250. 297—347.
—, Assyro-Babylonian and Israelite Measures of Capacity and Rates of Seeding, JAOS 64 (1944), 65—73.
Lewy, J., TC 100, LC 242 und das Eherecht des altassyrischen Rechtsbuches KAV Nr. 1, ZA 36 (1925), 139—161.
—, Zur Amoriterfrage, ZA 38 (1929), 243—272.
—, Review of A. Gustav, Die Personennamen in den Tontafeln von Tell-Ta'annek, OLZ 32 (1929), 172—174.
—, and Eisser, G., Die altassyrischen Rechtsurkunden vom Kültepe, MVÄG 33/35, 1930 and 1935.
—, Les Textes paléo-assyriens et l'Ancien Testament, RHR 110 (1934), 29—65.
—, Habiru and Hebrews, HUCA 14 (1939), 587—623.
—, The Late Assyro-Babylonian Cult of the Moon at its Culmination at the Time of Nabonidus, HUCA 19 (1945/1946), 405—489.
—, On Some Institutions of the Old Assyrian Empire, HUCA 27 (1956), 1—79.
Lieberman, S. J., An Ur III Text from Drehem Recording Booty from the Land of Mardu, JCS 22 (1968/1969), 53—62.

Liebesny, H., The Oath of the King in the Legal Procedure of Nuzi, JAOS 61 (1941), 62ff.

—, Evidence in Nuzi Legal Procedure, JAOS 61 (1941), 130—142.

—, The Administration of Justice in Nuzi, JAOS 63 (1943), 128—144.

Linage, J. de, L'Acte d'Établissement et le Contrat de Mariage d'un Esclave sous Thoutmes III, BIFAO 38 (1939), 217—234.

Littmenn, E., Safaitic Inscriptions, 1943.

Liverani, M., and Matthiae, P., La Ceramica di Superficie in Missione Archeologica Italiana in Siria 1964, 1965, 23—33.

—, I Tell Pre-Classici in Missione Archeologica Italiana in Siria 1964, 1965, 107—133.

Lloyd, S., Harran, AnSt 1 (1951), 77—112.

Lods, A., Quelques remarques sur les poèmes mythologiques de Ras Chamra et leurs rapports avec l'Ancien Testament, RHPR 16 (1936), 101—130.

—, Israël des Origines au milieu du VIIIe siècle, 1949.

Long, B. O., The Problem of Etiological Narrative in the Old Testament, BZAW 108, 1968.

Loon, M. van, New Evidence from Inland Syria for the Chronology of the Middle Bronze Age, AJA 73 (1969), 276f.

Lord, A. B., The Singer of Tales, 1960.

—, Homer and Other Epic Poetry. A Companion to Homer, ed. by Wace and Stubbings, 1963, 179—211.

Loretz, O., and Dietrich, M., Zur ugaritischen Lexikographie (I), BiOr 23 (1966), 127—133.

—, Texte aus Chagar Bazar und Tell Brak, Teil 1, AOAT 3/1, 1969.

Los, F. J., The Table of Peoples in the Tenth Chapter of Genesis, The Mankind Quarterly 7 (1967), 144—152.

Loud, G., Megiddo, II 1948.

Luckenbill, D. D., Azariah of Judah, AJSL 41 (1925), 217—232.

—, Ancient Records of Assyria and Babylonia, I—II 1926—1927.

Lüddeckens, E., Ägyptische Eheverträge, ÄgAb 1, 1960.

Lutz, H. F., A Note Regarding the Garment Called لالان and its Etymology, JAOS 42 (1922), 207.

—, The Meaning of Babylonian bittu, JAOS 42 (1922), 206.

—, A Legal Document from Nuzi, UCP IX, 11 (1931), 405—412, and pl. 12.

Lyon, D. G., The Joint Expedition of Harvard University and the Baghdad School at Yargon Tepa near Kirkuk, BASOR 30 (1928), 1—6.

Ma'Ayah, F. S., Recent Archaeological Discoveries in Jordan, ADAJ 4/5 (1960), 114—116.

—, Recent Discoveries in Jordan, ADAJ 6/7 (1962), 104—113.

Mace, D. R., Hebrew Marriage, 1953.

Mackay, L. A., The Wrath of Homer, 1948.

MacRae, G., Gelb, I. J., and Purves, P. M., Nuzi Personal Names, 1943.

Maisler (Mazar), B., Untersuchungen zur alten Geschichte und Ethnographie Syriens und Palästinas, Arbeiten aus dem Orientalischen Seminar der Universität Gießen 2, 1, 1930.

—, and Ginsberg, H. L., Semitized Hurrians in Syria and Palestine, JPOS 14 (1934), 243—267.

Maisler (Mazar), B., Canaan and the Canaanites, BASOR 102 (1946), 7—12.
—, The Aramaean Empire and its Relations with Israel, BA 25 (1962), 98—120.
—, The Middle Bronze Age in Palestine, IEJ 18 (1968), 65—97.
—, The Historical Background of the Book of Genesis, JNES 28 (1969), 73—83.
Malamat, A., Hazor "The Head of all Those Kingdoms", JBL 79 (1960), 12—19.
—, Mari and the Bible, JAOS 82 (1962), 143—150.
—, Aspects of Tribal Societies in Mari and Israel, RAI 15 (1967), 129—138.
—, King Lists of the Old Babylonian Period and Biblical Genealogies, JAOS 88 (1968), 163—173.
—, Northern Canaan and the Mari Texts, in: Glueck Festschrift, 164—177.
Mallon, A., Les Hébreux en Égypte, Orientalia 3, 1921.
—, Jérusalem et les Documents Égyptiens, JPOS 8 (1928), 1—6.
—, Teleilât Ghassûl, I 1934.
Mallowan, M. E. L., The Excavations at Tall Chagar Bazar and an Archaeological Survey of the Habur Region, Second Campaign, 1936, Iraq 4 (1936) 92—177.
—, The Syrian City of Til-Barsip, Antiquity 11 (1937), 328—339.
—, Excavations at Brak and Chagar Bazar, Iraq 9 (1947), 1—259.
Maly, E. H., Genesis 12_{10-20}, 20_{1-18}, 26_{7-11} and the Pentateuchal Question, CBQ 18 (1956), 255—262.
—, Genesis, Jerome Biblical Commentary, ed. by Brown, Fitzmyer and Murphy, 1968, 7—46.
Marcus, R., The Hebrew Sibilant Śin and the Name Yiśra'el, JBL 60 (1941), 141—150.
Margoliouth, D. S., Ham, HDB II, 288f.
Mariette-Bey, A., Les Listes Géographiques des Pylônes de Karnak, 1875.
Martin, G. T., A Ruler of Byblos of the Second Intermediate Period, Berytus 18 (1969), 81—83.
Mattha, G., A Preliminary Report on the Legal Code of Hermopolis West, BId'Eg 23 (1941), 297—212.
Matthiae, P., and Liverani, M., La Ceramica di Superficie, Missione Archeologica Italiana in Siria 1964, 1965, 23—33.
—, Mission archéologique de l'Universite de Rome à Tell Mardikh, AAS 15 (1965), 83—100.
May, H. G., The Patriarchal Idea of God, JBL 60 (1941), 113—128.
—, Response to A. S. Kapelrud's "The Role of the Cult in Old Israel", in: The Bible in Modern Scholarship, ed. by J. Philip Hyatt, 1965, 65—73.
McEwan, C. W. The Syrian Expedition of the Oriental Institute of the University of Chicago, AJA 41 (1937), 8—13.
McNamara, M., De Populi Aramaeorum primordiis, Verbum Domini 35 (1957), 129 to 142.
Meek, T. J., Some Gleanings from the Last Excavations at Nuzi, AASOR 13 (1933), 1—11.
—, Old Akkadian, Sumerian, and Cappadocian Texts from Nuzi, HSS IX, 1935.
—, Hebrew Origins, 1950.
—, The Code of Hammurabi, ANET, 163—180.
—, The Middle Assyrian Laws, ANET, 180—188.
—, The Neo-Babylonian Laws, ANET, 197f.
—, Mesopotamian Legal Documents, ANET, 217—222.
Meer, P. van der, The Chronology of Ancient Western Asia and Egypt, 1963.

Meissner, B., Thontafeln aus Vyran Sehir, OLZ 6 (1902), 245f.
—, Assyriologische Studien, MVÄG 10, 4, 1905.
Mellaart, J., The Chalcolithic and Early Bronze Ages in the Near East and Anatolia, 1965.
Mellink, M. J., Anatolian Chronology, in: Chronologies in Old World Archaeology, ed. by R. W. Ehrich, 1965, 101—131.
—, The Pratt Ivories in the Metropolitan Museum of Art — Kerma — Chronology and the Transition from Early Bronze to Middle Bronze, AJA 73 (1969), 285—287.
Mendelsohn, I., The Conditional Sale into Slavery of Free Born Daughters in Nuzi and the Law of Ex 21 7-11, JAOS 55 (1935), 190—195.
—, Slavery in the Ancient Near East, BA 9 (1946), 74—88.
—, The Family in the Ancient Near East, BA 11 (1948), 24—40.
—, Slavery in the ancient Near East, 1949.
—, On the Preferential Status of the Eldest Son, BASOR 156 (1959), 38—40.
—, On Marriage in Alalakh, in: Essays on Jewish Life and Thought, ed. by J. L. Blau, 1959, 351—357.
Mendenhall, G. E., Mari, BA 11 (1948), 1—19.
—, The Hebrew Conquest of Palestine, BA 25 (1962), 66—87.
—, Response to R. de Vaux's "Method in the Study of Early Hebrew History", in: The Bible and Modern Scholarship, ed. by J. P. Hyatt, 1966, 30—36.
—, Review of M. Weippert, Die Landnahme der israelitischen Stämme in der neueren wissenschaftlichen Diskussion, Bb 50 (1969), 432—436.
Meščerskij, N., Zur paläographischen Datierung der altägyptischen Ächtungstexte, Comptes Rendus de l'Académie des Sciences de l'URSS, 13B (1929), 253ff.
Meyer, E., Der Krieg gegen Sichem und die zugehörigen Abschnitte, ZAW 5 (1885), 36—52.
—, Der Stamm Jakob und die Entstehung der israelitischen Stämme, ZAW 6 (1886), 1—16.
—, Miscellen: Bemerkungen zu Bd VI 5.1ff., ZAW 8 (1888), 42—47.
—, Forschungen zur Alten Geschichte, 1892.
—, Die Israeliten und ihre Nachbarstämme, 1906.
—, Geschichte des Altertums, I—III 1910^3, 1913, 1939.
Meyers, E. M., Jewish Ossuaries and Secondary Burials in their Ancient Near Eastern Setting (Harvard dissertation, 1969).
—, Secondary Burials in Palestine, BA 33 (1970), 2—29.
Mezger, F., Promised but not Engaged, JAOS 64 (1944), 28—31.
Middleton, R., Brother-Sister and Father-Daughter Marriage in Ancient Egypt, ASR 27 (1962), 603—611.
Miles, J., and Driver, G. R., Ordeal by Oath at Nuzi, Iraq 7 (1940), 132—138.
—, Some Remarks on the Origins of Testacy, with Some References to the Old-Babylonian Laws, RIDA 1 (1954).
Mittmann, S., Aroer, Minnith und Abel Keramim, ZDPV 85 (1969), 63—75.
—, Beiträge zur Siedlungs- und Territorialgeschichte des nördlichen Ostjordanlandes ADPV, 1970.
M'Lennan, J. F., Studies in Ancient History, The Second Series, 1896.
Möller, G., Zwei ägyptische Eheverträge aus vorsaitischer Zeit, APAW 3, 1918.
Montet, P., and Couyat, J., Les Inscriptions Hiéroglyphiques et Hiératiques du Ouâdi Hammâmât, 1912.

Montet, P., and Couyat, J., Un Egyptien, Roi de Byblos, sous la XIIe Dynastie, Syria 8 (1927), 85—92.
—, Notes et Documents pour servir à l'histoire des relations entre l'ancienne Egypte et la Syrie, Kêmi 1 (1928), 19—28.
—, Sur Quelques Objets Provenant de Byblos, Syria 10 (1929), 12—15.
—, Note sur les Inscriptions de Sanousrit-Ankh, Syria 15 (1934), 131—133.
—, Notes et Documents pour servir à l'Histoire des Relations entre l'ancienne Égypte et la Syrie, Kêmi 13 (1954), 65f.
—, Everyday Life in Egypt, 1958.
—, Notes et Documents pour servir à l'Histoire des relations entre l'Egypte et la Syrie, Kêmi 16 (1962), 76—96.
—, Notes et Documents pour servir à l'histoire des relations entre l'Egypte et la Syrie, Kêmi 17 (1964), 61—68.
—, Egypt and the Bible, 1968.
Montgomery, J. A., Mythological Epic Texts from Ras Shamra, JAOS 53 (1933), 97—123.
Moortgat, A., and Scharff, A., Ägypten und Vorderasien im Altertum, 1950.
Moran, W. L., and Albright, W. F., A Re-interpretation of an Amarna Letter from Byblos, JCS 2 (1948), 239—248.
—, Mari Notes on the Execration Texts, Orientalia 26 (1957), 339—345.
—, The Hebrew Language in its Northwest Semitic Background, in: Albright Festschrift, 54—72.
Moscati, S., Sulle origini degli Aramei, RSO 26 (1951), 16—22.
—, I Predecessori D'Israele, Studi orientali publicati a cura della scuola orientale, IV 1956.
—, Israel's Predecessor's: A Re-Examination of Certain Current Theories, JBR 24 (1956), 245—254.
—, The "Aramaean Ahlamu", JSS 4 (1959), 303—307.
—, The Semites in Ancient History, 1959.
—, Sulla Storia del Nome Canaan, Studia Biblica et Orientalia 3 (1959), 266—269.
Moskowitz, S., and Negbi, O., The "Foundation Deposits" or "Offering Deposits" of Byblos, BASOR 184 (1966), 21—26.
Mowinckel, S., The Babylonian Matter in the Predeuteronomic Primeval History (JE) in Gen 1—11, JBL 58 (1939), 87—91.
Mülinen, E. von, Des Nomaden Abschied, ZDMG 4 (1925), 150—161.
Müller, K. F., Das assyrische Ritual, MVÄG, 41/3, 1937.
Müller, U., Kritische Bemerkungen zu den Straten XIII bis IX in Megiddo, ZDPV 86 (1970), 50—86.
Müller, W. M., Asien und Europa nach altägyptischen Denkmälern, 1893.
—, Die Palästinaliste Thutmosis III, MVÄG 12, 1, 1907.
Müller, W. W., Die Wurzeln Mediae und Tertiae Y/W im Altsüdarabischen (Tübingen dissertation), 1962.

Negbi, O., and Moskowitz, S., The "Foundation Deposits" or "Offering Deposits" of Byblos, BASOR 184 (1966), 21—26.
Neubauer, J., Beiträge zur Geschichte des biblisch-talmudischen Eheschließungsrechts, MVÄG 24, 1920.
Neufeld, E., Ancient Hebrew Marriage Laws, 1944.

Neufeld, E., The Hittite Laws, 1951.
Newberry, P. E., Beni Hasan I—II, 1893/1894.
—, A Middle Kingdom Mayor of Byblos, JEA 14 (1928), 109.
Nicolo, M. San, and Ungnad, A., Neubabylonische Rechts- und Verwaltungsurkunden I, 1935, No. 10, pp. 15f.
Nielsen, E., Oral Tradition, 1954.
—, Shechem, 1955.
Nilsson, M. P., Homer and Mycenae, 1933.
Nims, C. F., and Erichsen, W., A Further Category of Demotic Marriage Settlements, AcOr 23 (1958), 119—133.
Nöldeke, Th., Zur Topographie und Geschichte des Damascenischen Gebietes und der Haurângegend, ZDMG 29 (1875), 419—444.
—, Robertson Smith's Kinship and Marriage in Early Arabia, ZDMG 40 (1886), 148—187.
—, Harran, ZA 11 (1896), 197—209.
—, Names, Enc. Bb III, 3264—3331.
Nötscher, F., Biblische Altertumskunde, 1940.
North, R., Flesh, Covering, and Response, Ex. 21 10, VT 5 (1955), 204—206.
—, Stratigraphia Geobiblica, 1970.
Noth, M., Gemeinsemitische Erscheinungen in der israelitischen Namengebung, ZDMG 81 (1927), 1—45.
—, Die israelitischen Personennamen im Rahmen der gemeinsemitischen Namengebung, BWANT, 1928.
—, Das System der zwölf Stämme Israels, 1930.
—, Zum Problem der Ostkanaanäer, ZA 39 (1930), 213—222.
—, Erwägungen zur Hebräerfrage, in: Festschrift O. Procksch, 1934.
—, Das Land Gilead als Siedlungsgebiet israelitischer Sippen, PJ 37 (1941), 50—101 (= Aufsätze I 347—390).
—, Die syrisch-palästinische Bevölkerung des zweiten Jahrtausends v. Chr. im Lichte neuer Quellen, ZDPV 65 (1942), 9—67.
—, Die Herrenschicht von Ugarit im 15/14. Jahrhundert v. Chr., ZDPV 65 (1942), 144—164.
—, Israelitische Stämme zwischen Ammon und Moab, ZAW 60 (1944), 11—57 (= Aufsätze I 391—433).
—, Überlieferungsgeschichte des Pentateuch, 1948.
—, Das Amt des "Richters Israels", in: Festschrift A. Bertholet, 1950, 404—417.
—, Die Nachbarn der israelitischen Stämme im Ostjordanlande, Beiträge zur Geschichte des Ostjordanlandes, III ZDPV 68 (1951), 1—50 (= Aufsätze I 434—475).
—, Arioch-Arriwuk, VT 1 (1951), 136—140.
—, Mari und Israel. Eine Personennamenstudie, in: Festschrift A. Alt, 127—152 (= Aufsätze II 213—233).
—, Jabes-Gilead, Ein Beitrag zur Methode alttestamentlichen Topographie, ZDPV 69 (1953), 28—41 (= Aufsätze I 476—488).
—, Geschichte Israels, 1954².
—, Das Deutsche Evangelische Institut für Altertumswissenschaft des Heiligen Landes, Lehrkursus 1956, ZDPV 73 (1957), 1—58.
—, Der Beitrag der Archäologie zur Geschichte Israels, VTS 7 (1960), 262—282 (= Aufsätze I 34—52).

Noth, M., Die Ursprünge des alten Israel im Lichte neuer Quellen, Arbeitsgemeinschaft für Forschung des Landes Nordrhein-Westfalen, Geisteswissenschaften Heft 94, 1961 (= Aufsätze II 245—272).
—, Eine siedlungsgeographische Liste in I Chr 2 und 4, ZDPV 55 (1962), 97—124.
—, Die Welt des Alten Testaments, Theologische Hilfsbücher 3, 1962[4].
—, Thebes, in: Archaeology and Old Testament Study, ed. by D. W. Thomas, 1967, 21—35.
—, Aufsätze zur biblischen Landes- und Altertumskunde, I–II 1971.
Nougayrol, J., Le Palais Royal d'Ugarit. III Textes Accadiens et Hourrites, MRS 6, 1955.
—, Documents du Ḫabur, Syria 37 (1960), 205—214.
—, L'influence Babylonienne à Ugarit d'après les Textes en Cunéiformes Classiques, Syria 39 (1962), 28—35.

O'Callaghan, R. T., Historical Parallels to Patriarchal Social Customs, CBQ 6 (1944), 391—405.
—, Aram Naharaim, AnOr 26, 1948.
Olávarri, E., Sondages à ʿArôʿer sur l'Arnon, RB 72 (1965), 77—94.
—, Fouilles à ʿArôʿer sur l'Arnon, RB 66 (1969), 230—259.
Olmstead, A. T., History of Palestine and Syria, 1931.
—, History, Ancient World, and the Bible, JNES 2 (1943), 1—34.
Oppenheim, L., Zur Landessprache von Arrapḫa Nuzi, AfO 11 (1936), 56ff.
—, On an Operational Device in Mesopotamian Bureaucracy, JNES 18 (1959), 121 to 128.
O'Rahilly, T. F., Early Irish History and Mythology, 1946.
Oren, E. D., A Middle Bronze Age I Warrior Tomb at Beth-Shan, ZDPV 87 (1971), 109—139.
Orlinsky, H. M., Ancient Israel, 1956.
—, Whither Biblical Research?, JBL 90 (1971), 1—14.
Otten, H., Geschwisterehe, RLA, III 1964, 231.

Page, D. L., History and the Homeric Iliad, 1959.
Palmer, L. R., Mycenaeans and Minoans, 1961.
Parker, B., The Nimrud Tablets, 1952 — Business Documents, Iraq 16 (1954), 29—58.
Parr, P. J., A Cave at Arqub el Dhahr, ADAJ 3 (1956), 61—73.
—, Khirbet Iskander, ADAJ 3 (1956), 81.
—, Excavations at Khirbet Iskander, ADAJ 4—5 (1960), 128—133.
—, The Origin of the Rampart Fortifications of Middle Bronze Age Palestine and Syria, ZDPV 84 (1968), 18—45.
Parrot, A., Les Tablettes de Mari et l'Ancien Testament, RHPR 30 (1950), 1—11.
—, Mission Archéologique de Mari. II Le Palais, 2, Peintures Murales, 1958.
—, Abraham et son Temps, 1962.
—, A propos de la "jarre Montet", Syria 44 (1967), 448f.
Parry, M., Serbocroation Heroic Songs, ed. and trans. by A. B. Lord, 1954.
Pedersen, J., Israel. Its Life and Culture, I–IV 1926—1940.
Peet, T. E., and Černy, J., A Marriage Settlement of the Twentieth Dynasty, JEA 13 (1927), 30—39.
—, and Gardiner, A. H., The Inscriptions of Sinai, I—II 1952/1955.
Peiser, F. E., and Kohler, J., Aus dem babylonischen Rechtsleben, I—IV 1890 to 1898.

Perrot, J., Les VIe et VIIe campagnes de fouilles à Beerseba, CRAI (1959), 133—140.

—, The Dawn of History in Southern Palestine. Archaelogical Discoveries in the Holy Land, compiled by the Archaeological Institute of America, 1967, 2—8.

Pestman, P. W., Marriage and Matrimonial Property in Ancient Egypt, Papyrologica Lugduno-Batava, IX 1961.

—, and Janssen, J. J. Burial and Inheritance in the Community of the Necropolis Workmen at Thebes, JESHO 11 (1968), 137—170.

Petrie, W. M. F., The Royal Tombs of the First Dynasty, Egyptian Exploration Fund Nos. 18 and 21, 1900 and 1901.

—, Ancient Gaza, I—II, 1931—1932.

—, Ceremonial Slate Palettes, British School of Egyptian Archaeology LXVI (A), 1953.

Petschow, H., Die neubabylonische Zwiegesprächsurkunde und Gen 23, JCS 19 (1965), 103—120.

Pfeiffer, R. H., On Babylonian-Assyrian Feudalism, AJSL 39 (1922), 66—68.

—, Yorghan Teppe, BASOR 34 (1929), 2—7.

—, Review of E. Chiera, ASOR Publications of the Baghdad School, Texts I, JAOS 49 (1929), 178—180.

—, A Non-Israelitic Source of the Book of Genesis, ZAW 48 (1930), 66—73.

—, Review of E. Chiera, ASOR Publications of the Baghdad School II, JAOS 51 (1931), 76—78.

—, The Excavations at Nuzi, BASOR 42 (1931), 1—7.

—, HSS IX, Excavations at Nuzi, II: The Archives of Shelwateshub, Son of the King, 1932.

—, Nuzi and the Hurrians, Annual Report of the Smithsonian Institution, I 1935, 535—558.

—, Archives of Shelwateshub, Son of the King, HSS X, 1942.

—, and Lacheman, E. R., HSS XIII, Miscellaneous Texts from Nuzi, Part I, 1942.

Pinches, I. A., Haran, HDB II, 301.

Pinches, T. G., Cuneiform Texts in the British Museum II, 1896.

—, Some Early Babylonian Contracts or Legal Documents, JRAS (1897), 489—613.

—, Ur of the Chaldees, HDB IV, 835—837.

—, The Old Testament in the Light of the Historical Records and Legends of Assyria and Babylonia, 1903.

—, A Cylinder-Seal Inscribed in Hieroglyphic and Cuneiform in the Collection of the Earl of Carnarvon, JEA 7 (1921), 196—199.

Pirenne, J., and Stracmans, M., Le testament à l'époque de l'Ancien Empire Egyptien, RIDA 1 (1954), 49—72.

Pohl, A., Review of E. Chiera, JEN IV and V, Orientalia 5 (1936), 140—141.

—, Review of Ungnad, Subartu, Orientalia 6 (1937), 387—389.

—, Review of Götze, Hethiter, Churriter und Assyrer, Orientalia 6 (1937), 387—389.

—, Review of Cross, Movable Property in the Nuzi Documents, Orientalia 8 (1939), 268f.

—, Miszellen, Bb 20 (1939), 200—201.

Pope, M. H., El in the Ugaritic Texts, 1955.

Porada, E., Seal Impressions of Nuzi, AASOR 24 (1947).

—, Appendix F: Cylinder Seals, in: Jericho II, ed. by K. Kenyon, 1965, 656—661.

—, Les cylindres de la jarre Montet, Syria 43 (1966), 243—258.

Porter, J. R., Son or Grandson, JTS 17 (1966), 54—66.

Posener, G., Une Liste de Noms propres étrangers sur deux Ostraca Hieratiques de Nouvel Empire, Syria 18 (1937), 183—197.

—, Nouvelles Listes de Proscription (Ächtungstexte) datant du Moyen Empire, Chronique d'Égypte 1 (1939), 39—46.

—, Nouveaux Textes Hiératiques de Proscription, Mélanges Syriens offerts a R. Dussand, I 1939, 313—317.

—, Princes et Pays d'Asie et de Nubie, 1940.

—, Trois Passages de l'Enseignement à Mérikarê, Revue d'Egyptologie 7 (1950), 176—180.

—, Littérature et Politique dans l'Égypte de la XIIe Dynastie, fascicule 307 de la Bibliotheque de l'École des Hautes Études, 1956.

—, Les Asiatiques en Égypte sous les XIIe et XIIIe Dynasties, Syria 34 (1957), 145 to 163.

—, Bottéro, J., and Kenyon, K., Syria and Palestine, c. 2160—1780, CAH[2] fasc. 29, 1965.

—, Les Textes d'envoûtement de Mirgissa, Syria 43 (1966), 277—287.

Power, W. J. A., and Franken, H. J. Glueck's Explorations in Eastern Palestine in the Light of Recent Evidence, VT 21 (1971), 118—123.

Praag, A. van, Droit Matrimonial Assyro-Babylonien, AHB 12 (1945).

Prag, K., The 1951 Deep Sounding at Harran in Turkey, Levant 2 (1970), 63—94.

Prausnitz, M. W., Abydos and Combed Ware, PEQ (1954), 91—96.

Prévost, M. H., Remarques sur l'Adoption dans la Bible, RIDA 14 (1967), 67—77.

Pritchard, J. B., ANET, 1946.

—, Gibeon's History in the Light of Excavation, VTS 7, 1959), 1—12.

—, Gibeon: Where the Sun Stood Still, 1962.

—, The Bronze Age Cemetery at Gibeon, 1963.

—, El-Jib Excavations 1962, ADAJ 8—9 (1964), 86f.

—, ANETS, 1969.

Purves, P. M., Nuzi Names, JAOS 58 (1938), 462—471.

—, MacRae, G., and Gelb, I. J., Nuzi Personal Names, 1943.

Rabinowitz, J. J., The Meaning of the Phrase מחר או יום אחרן in the Aramaic Papyri, JNES 14 (1955), 59f.

—, Semitic Elements in the Egyptian Adoption Papyrus Published by Gardiner, JNES 17 (1958), 145f.

Rad, G. von, History and the Patriarchs, ET 72 (1960/1961), 213—216.

—, Offene Fragen im Umkreis einer Theologie des Alten Testaments, TLZ 88 (1963), cols. 401—416.

—, Das erste Buch Mose, 1964[7].

Rainey, A. F., A Canaanite at Ugarit, IEJ 13 (1963), 43—45.

—, Ugarit and the Canaanites Again, IEJ 14 (1964), 101.

—, Family Relationships in Ugarit, Orientalia 34 (1965), 10—22.

Ranke, H., Early Babylonian Personal Names, Babylonian Expedition of the University of Pennsylvania, Series D, III 1905.

—, Die ägyptischen Personennamen, I 1935.

Rawlinson, H. C., On the Inscriptions of Assyria and Babylonia, JRAS 12 (1850), 401—483.

Redford, D. B., On the Chronology of the Egyptian Eighteenth Dynasty, JNES 25 (1966), 113—124.

—, A Study of the Biblical Story of Joseph, 1970.

Rhodokanakis, N., Studien zur Lexikographie und Grammatik des Altsüdarabischen, Sitzungsberichte der Akademie der Wissenschaften in Wien, I 1915.

Rienecker, F., Lexikon zur Bibel, 1960.

Ringgren, H., Israelite Religion, 1966.

Roeder, G., Les Temples Immergés de la Nubie Dehod bis B ab Kalabsche, I—III 1911.

Röllig, W., and Donner, H., Kanaanäische und aramäische Inschriften, I—III, 1966 to 1969².

—, Zur Datierung Zimri-Lims, XVe RAI, Les Congrès et Colloques de L'Université de Liège 42 (1967), 97—102.

—, Zur Typologie und Entstehung der babylonischen und assyrischen Königslisten, AOAT 1 (1969), 265—277.

Rössler, O., Das ältere ägyptische Umschreibungssystem für Fremdnamen und seine sprachwissenschaftlichen Lehren, Neue Afrikanistische Studien, Hamburger Beiträge zur Afrika-Kunde, 5 (1966), 218—229.

Ron, Z., Agricultural Terraces in the Judaean Mountains, IEJ 16 (1966), 33—49. 111—122.

Rossi, Fabretti, and Lanzone. Regio Museo di Torino, I—II 1882—1888.

Rothenberg, B., God's Wilderness, 1961.

Routh, M. J., Reliquiae Sacrae, II 1846.

Rowe, A., Topography and History of Beth-Shan, 1930.

—, Catalogue of Egyptian Scarabs, 1936.

Rowley, H. H., The Re-Discovery of the Old Testament, 1945.

—, Proceedings of the British Society of Old Testament Study, JBL 66 (1947), XXVII—XXXII.

—, Recent Discoveries and the Patriarchal Age, BJRL 32 (1949/1950), 44—79 (= The Servant of the Lord, 1952, 271—305).

—, From Joseph to Joshua, 1950.

—, The Servant of the Lord, 1952.

—, Worship in Ancient Israel, 1967.

Rowton, M., The Physical Environment and the Problem of the Nomads, RAI 15, 1967, 109—121.

Rutten, M., Un Lot de Lettres de Mananâ, RA 52 (1958), 208—225; 53 (1959), 77—96; 54 (1960), 19—40. 147—152.

Ryckmans, G., Les noms propres sudsémitique, Bibliotheque du Muséon II, parts 1—3 (1934—1935).

—, Inscriptions Safaïtique, 1950.

—, Les noms de Parenté en Safaïtique, RB 58 (1951), 377—392.

—, A Propos des Noms de Parenté en Safaïtique, RB 60 (1953), 524f.

Sa'ad, Y., A Bronze Age Tomb Group from Hablet El Amud, Silwan Village Lands, ADAJ 8—9 (1964), 77—80.

Saarisalo, A., New Kirkuk Documents Relative to Slaves, Studia Orientalia 4, 3, 1934.

Sachsse, E., Die Etymologie und älteste Aussprache des Namens ישראל, ZAW 34 (1914), 1—15.

Säve-Söderbergh, T., Ägypten und Nubien, 1941.
Saggs, H. W., Ur of the Chaldees, Iraq 22 (1960), 200—209.
Saller, S., Bab edh-Dhra, Studii Biblici Franciscani, Liber Annuus 15 (1964—1965), 137—219.
Sanders, J. A., ed., Near Eastern Archaeology in the Twentieth Century, Essays in Honor of N. Glueck, 1970.
San Nicolo, M., and Ungnad, A., Neubabylonische Rechts- und Verwaltungsurkunden, I 1935.
—, Due atti matrimoniali neobabilonesi, Aegyptus 27 (1947), 118—143.
Sayce, A. H., Ur of the Chaldees, ET 13 (1901/1902), 64—66.
Schachermeyr, F., Indogermanen und Orient, 1944.
Schäfer, H., and Lange, H. O., Grab- und Denksteine des Mittleren Reichs im Museum von Kairo, I, 1902.
Schaeffer, C. F. A., Les Fouilles de Minet-el-Beida et de Ras Shamra (Campagne du Printemps 1929), Syria 10 (1929), 285—297.
—, Les Fouilles de Minet-El-Beida et de Ras Shamra (troisieme Campagne, Printemps 1931), Syria 13 (1932), 1—27.
—, Les Fouilles de Minet-El-Beida et de Ras Shamra (Quatrième Campagne, Printemps 1932), Syria 14 (1933), 93—127.
—, Les Fouilles de Ras Shamra (Cinquième Campagne, Printemps 1933), Syria 15 (1934), 105—131.
—, Ugaritica, I 1939.
—, Stratigraphie Comparée, 1948.
—, Résumé des Résultats de la XXIIe Campagne de Fouilles à Ras Shamra-Ugarit, 1959, AAS 10 (1960), 133—158.
Scharff, A., Über einige fremdartige Darstellungen auf Siegelbildern aus dem späten Alten Reich und der ersten Zwischenzeit, ZÄS 67 (1931), 95—102.
—, Der historische Abschnitt der Lehre für König Merikarê, SBAW 8, 1936.
—, and Moortgat, A., Ägypten und Vorderasien im Altertum, 1950.
Scheil, V., Lettre Assyrienne de Kerkouk, Recueil de Travaux 31 (1909), 56—58.
—, Cylindres et Légendes Inédits, RA 13 (1916), 5—25.
—, Tablettes de Kerkouk, RA 15 (1918), 65ff.
Schenkel, W., Frühmittelägyptische Studien, BOS 13, 1962.
—, Zum Feudalismus der ersten Zwischenzeit Ägyptens, Orientalia 33 (1964), 263—266.
Schiffer, S., Die Aramäer, 1911.
Schneider, N., Aram und Aramäer in der Ur III Zeit, Bb 30 (1949), 109—111.
—, Herrschernamen als theophores Element bei Personennamen, ArOr 17, 2 (1949), 351—358.
—, Patriarchennamen in zeitgenössischen Keilschriftsurkunden, Bb 33 (1952), 516 bis 522.
Schofield, J. N., Some Archaeological Sites and the Old Testament: Nuzu, ET 66 (1955), 315—318.
—, Megiddo, in: Archaeology and OT Study, ed. by D. W. Thomas, 1967, 309—328.
Schorr, M., Altbabylonische Rechtsurkunden aus der Zeit der ersten babylonischen Dynastie. III. Heft SKAWW 165, 2, 1910.
—, Urkunden des altbabylonischen Zivil- und Prozeßrechts, VAB 8, 1, 1913.
Schott, S., Hieroglyphen, 1950.
Schrader, E., Die Keilinschriften und das Alte Testament, 1903^{3}.

Schroeder, O., Aus den keilinschriftlichen Sammlungen des Berliner Museums, ZA 34 (1922), 157—169.

Schunck, K., Benjamin, BZAW 86, 1963.

Schwartz, E., Eusebius, II, 13, 1919.

Seebass, H., Gen 15 26, ZAW 75 (1963), 317—319.

—, Der Erzvater Israel und die Einführung der Jahweverehrung in Kanaan, BZAW 98, 1966.

Seibert, P., Die Charakteristik, ÄgAb 17, 1967.

Seidl, E., Vom Erbrecht der alten Ägypter, ZDMG 107 (1957), 270—281.

Seif, M., Über die altbabylonischen Rechts- und Wirtschaftsurkunden aus Iščalî (Berlin Dissertation), 1938.

Selbie, J. A., Eber, HDB, I, 636f.

—, Terah, HDB, IV, 718.

Sellin, E., and Watzinger, C., Jericho. Die Ergebnisse der Ausgrabungen, 1913.

Selms, A. van, The Best Man and Bride — From Sumer to St. John with a new interpretation of Judges, Chapters 14 and 15, JNES 9 (1950), 65—75.

—, The Canaanites in the Book of Genesis, OTS 12 (1958), 182—213.

—, Marriage and Family Life in Ugaritic Literature, 1954.

Seters, J. van, A Date for the "Admonitions" in the Second Intermediate Period, JEA 50 (1964), 13—23.

—, The Hyksos, 1966.

—, The Problem of Childlessness in Near Eastern Law and the Patriarchs of Israel, JBL 87 (1968), 401—408.

—, Jacob's Marriages and Ancient Near East Customs: A Reexamination, HThR 62 (1969), 377—395.

Sethe, K., Die Ächtung feindlicher Fürsten, Völker und Dinge auf altägyptischen Tongefäßscherben des Mittleren Reiches, APAW, 1926.

—, Urkunden der 18. Dynastie, III, (Nachdruck von 1927^2 1961).

—, Urkunden des Alten Reichs, I 1933.

—, Historisch-biographische Urkunden des Mittleren Reiches I, Urkunden VII, 1935.

Shaffer, A., Kitru/kiterru: New Documentation for a Nuzi Legal Term, in: Studies presented to A. L. Oppenheim, 1964, 181ff.

Shipton, G. M., and Engberg, R. M., Notes on the Chalcolithic and Early Bronze Age Pottery of Megiddo, 1934.

—, Notes on the Megiddo Pottery of Strata VI—XX, 1938.

Shore, A. F., The Sale of the House of Senkhonsis Daughter of Phibis, JEA 54 (1968), 193—198.

Simmons, S. D., Early Old Babylonian Tablets from Harmal and Elsewhere, JCS 14 (1960), 23—32. 49—55. 75—87. 117—125.

Simons, J., Egyptian Topographical Lists, 1937.

—, The Table of Nations, OTS 10 (1954), 155—184.

Simpson, C. A., The Early Traditions of Israel, 1948.

Singer, Holmyard, and Hall, A History of Technology, 1965.

Skaist, A., The Authority of the Brother at Arrapha and Nuzi, JAOS 89 (1969), 10—17.

Skinner, J., Genesis, 1917.

—, A Critical and Exegetical Commentary on Genesis, 1930^2.

Smend, R., Die Erzählung des Hexateuch auf ihre Quellen untersucht, 1912.

Smith, H. S., Review of E. Lüddeckens' Aegyptische Eheverträge, and P. W. Westman's Marriage and Matrimonial Property in Ancient Egypt, JEA 48 (1962), 172—176.

Smith, M., The Present State of Old Testament Studies, JBL 88 (1969), 19—35.

Smith, S., Early History of Assyria to 1000 B. C., History of Babylonia and Assyria, III 1928.

—, What were the Teraphim ?, JTS 33 (1932), 33—36.

Smith, W. R., Kinship and Marriage in Early Arabia, 1903.

Smith, W. S., Interconnections in the Ancient Near East, 1965.

—, Influence of the Middle Kingdom of Egypt in Western Asia, Especially in Byblos, AJA 73 (1969), 277—281.

Snijders, L. A., Genesis XV. The Covenant with Abram, OTS 12 (1958), 261—279.

Soden, W. von, Das altbabylonische Briefarchiv von Mari, WO I, 3 (1948), 187—204.

—, Review of A. Borst: Der Turmbau von Babel, BiOr 16 (1959), 129—133.

—, Zur Einteilung der semitischen Sprachen, WZKM 56 (1960), 177—191.

—, Jahwe, Er ist, Er erweist sich, WO 3 (1966), 177—187.

Soggin, J. A., Ancient Biblical Traditions and Modern Archeological Discoveries, BA 23 (1960), 95—100.

Speiser, E. A., and Chiera, E., A New Factor in the History of the Ancient East, AASOR 6 (1926), 75—90.

—, and Chiera, E., Selected "Kirkuk" Documents, JAOS 47 (1927), 36—60.

—, and Chiera, E., A New Factor in the History of the Ancient East, AASOR 6 (1926), 75—92.

—, Preliminary Excavations at Tepe Gawra, AASOR 9 (1927—1928), 17—94.

—, A Letter of Sauššatar and the Date of the Kirkuk Tablets, JAOS 49 (1929), 269—275.

—, Mesopotamian Origins, 1930.

—, New Kirkuk Documents Relating to Family Laws, AASOR 10 (1930), 1—73.

—, Review of R. Pfeiffer, Excavations at Nuzi II, HSS IX, JAOS 52 (1932), 257—260.

—, New Kirkuk Documents Relating to Security Transactions, Part I, JAOS 52 (1932), 350—367; Part II, 53 (1933), 24—46.

—, Ethnic Movements in the Near East in the Second Millenium, AASOR 13 (1933), 13—54.

—, Notes to Recently Published Nuzi Texts, JAOS 55 (1935), 432—443.

—, 100 New Selected Nuzi Texts, AASOR 16 (1936), 1ff.

—, Excavations in NE Babylonia, BASOR 67 (1937), 2ff.

—, Mesopotamian Miscellanea, BASOR 68 (1937), 7ff.

—, Progress of the Joint Expedition to Mesopotamia, BASOR 70 (1938), 3ff.

—, The Nuzi Tablets Solve a Puzzle in the Books of Samuel, BASOR 72 (1938), 15—17.

—, Progress in the Study of the Hurrian Language, BASOR 74 (1939), 4ff.

—, Of Shoes and Shekels, BASOR 77 (1940), 15—20 (= OBS 151—159).

—, Introduction to Hurrian, AASOR 20 (1941).

—, An Intrusive Hurro-Hittite Myth, JAOS 62 (1942), 98—102.

—, Some Sources of Intellectual and Social Progress in the Ancient Near East, in: Studies in the History of Culture, dedicated to W. G. Leland, 1942, 51—62 (= OBS 517—533.

—, Hurrians and Subarians, JAOS 68 (1948), 1—13.

Speiser, E. A., Review of R. O'Callaghan, Aram Naharaim, JAOS 70 (1950), 307—309.
—, Review of S. Smith, The Statue of Idrimi, JAOS 71 (1951), 151f.
—, "Damascus" as Ša-imerišu, JAOS 71 (1951), 257f.
—, Review of Lacheman, HSS XIV, JAOS 72 (1952), 94f.
—, Comments on Recent Studies in Akkadian Grammar, JAOS 73 (1953), 129—138.
—, The Hurrian participation in the Civilization of Mesopotamia, Syria, and Palestine, Cahiers d'Histoire Mondiale 1 (1953), 311—327 (= OBS 244—269).
—, Early Law and Civilization, Canadian Bar Review 31 (1953), 863—877 (= OBS 534—555).
—, A Vivid Sidelight on the Machpelah Episode, Israel Life and Letters, I (1953), 56—59.
—, The Alalakh Tablets, JAOS 74 (1954), 18—25.
—, Nuzi or Nuzu, JAOS 75 (1955), 52—55.
—, Akkadian Documents from Ras Shamra, JAOS 75 (1955), 154—165.
—, I know not the Day of my Death, JBL 74 (1955), 252—256.
—, Ydwn, Gen 6 3, JBL 75 (1956), 126—129 (= OBS, 35—40).
—, Nuzi Marginalia, Orientalia 25 (1956), 1—23.
—, Word Plays on the Creation Epic's Version of the Founding of Babylon, Orientalia 25 (1956), 317—323 (= OBS 53—61).
—, The Biblical Idea of History in its Common Near Eastern Setting, IEJ 7 (1957), 201—216 (= OBS 187—210).
—, In Search of Nimrod, Eretz Israel 5 (1958), 32—36 (= OBS 41—52).
—, The Rivers of Paradise, in: Festschrift J. Friedrich, 473—485 (= OBS 23—34).
—, The Word SHR in Genesis, BASOR 164 (1961), 23—28.
—, Nuzi, IDB III, 573f.
—, Amorites and Canaanites. At the Dawn of Civilization, in: The World History of the Jewish People, I 1963, 162—169.
—, The Wife-Sister Motif in the Patriarchal Narratives, in: Biblical and Other Studies, ed. by A. Altmann, 15—28 (= OBS 62—82).
—, Background and Function of the Biblical Nasi, CBQ 25 (1963), 111—117.
—, Genesis, 1964.
—, Oriental and Biblical Studies, ed. by J. J. Finkelstein and M. Greenberg, 1967.

Speleers, L., Recueil des Inscriptions de l'Asie antérieure, 1925.

Sperber, A., Hebrew Based upon Greek and Latin Transliterations, HUCA 12/13 (1937/1938), 103—274.
—, Hebrew Based upon Biblical Passages in Parallel Transmission, HUCA 14 (1939), 153—249.
—, Biblical Exegesis: Prolegomena to a Commentary and Dictionary to the Bible, JBL 64 (1945), 39—140.
—, A Historical Grammar of Biblical Hebrew, 1966.

Spiegelberg, W., Der Siegeshymnus des Merneptah auf der Flinders Petrie-Stele, ZÄS 34 (1896), 1—25.
—, Eine Vermutung über den Ursprung des Namens יהוה, ZDMG 53 (1899), 633—643.
—, Aegyptologische Randglossen zum Alten Testament, 1904.
—, Ägyptische Verpfründungsverträge, SHAW 6, 1923.

Stählin, W., Auch darin hat die Bibel Recht, 1964.

Stamm, J. J., Die Akkadische Namengebung, MVÄG 44, 1939.
—, Der Name Isaac, in: Festschrift A. Schädelin, 1950, 33—38.

Starr, R. F. S., Notes from the Excavation at Nuzi, BASOR 38 (1930) 3—8.
—, Kirkuk Expedition, Fogg Art Museum Notes, II, 5 1930, 182—197.
—, Report from Our Expeditions in Iraq, BASOR 41 (1931), 24—27.
—, Nuzi, I—II 1939.
Steindorff, G., Israel in einer altägyptischen Inschrift, ZAW 16 (1896), 330—333.
Steuernagel, C., Die Einwanderung der israelitischen Stämme in Kanaan, 1901.
Stinespring, W. F., Review of J. Bright, Early Israel in Recent History Writing, JBL 76 (1957), 249.
Stock, H., Studien zur Geschichte und Archaeologie der 13. bis 17. Dynastie Ägyptens, ÄgF 12, 1942.
Stracmans, M., and Pirenne, J., Le testament à l'époque de l'Ancien Empire Egyptien, RIDA 1 (1954), 49—72.
Streck, M., Über die älteste Geschichte der Aramäer, mit besonderer Berücksichtigung der Verhältnisse in Babylonien und Assyrien, Klio 6 (1906), 185—235.
Strong, J., The Exhaustive Concordance of the Bible, 1963[25].
Struve, P., Mathematical Papyri in Moskow, 1930.
Stubbings, F. H., Mycenaean Pottery from the Levant, 1951.
Sutherland-Black, J., and Cheyne, T. K., Encyclopedia Biblica, I—IV 1899—1903.
Szemerényi, O., The Origin of the Name Lakedaimon, Glotta 38 (1960), 14—17.
Szlechter, E., Des droits successoraux dérivées de l'adoption en droit babylonien, RIDA 14 (1967), 79—106.

Tadmor, H., Historical Implications of the Correct Rendering of Akkadian dâku, JNES 17 (1958), 129—141.
—, The Southern Border of Aram, IEJ 12 (1962), 114—122.
Tadmor, M., Contacts between the ʿAmug and Syria-Palestine, IEJ 14 (1964), 253—269.
Tallqvist, K. L., Neubabylonisches Namenbuch (zu den Geschäftsurkunden aus der Zeit des šamaššumukîn bis Xerxes), Acta Societates Scientiorum Fennicae, Tom 32, 2, 1906.
—, Assyrian Personal Names, Acta Societatis Scientiorum Fennicae, Tom. 43, 1, 1918.
Tanner, R., Untersuchungen zur ehe- und erbrechtlichen Stellung der Frau im pharaonischen Ägypten, Klio, BAG 49 (1967), 5—37.
Théodoridès, A., Le Papyrus des Adoptions, RIDA[3] 12 (1965), 79—142.
—, Le "testament" de Naunakhte, RIDA[3] 13 (1966), 31—70.
—, A propos de la Loi dans l'Egypte pharaonique, RIDA[3] 14 (1967), 107—152.
—, Le Testament d'Imenkhârou, JEA 54 (1968), 149—154.
Thomas, D. W., ed., Archaeology and Old Testament Study, 1967.
Thompson, H. O., Tell el-Husn-Biblical Beth-Shan, BA 30 (1967), 110—135.
Thompson, R. Cambell, The Epic of Gilgamish, 1930.
Thompson, S., Motif-Index of Folk Literature, I—V 1966.
Thompson, Th. with D. Irvin, Some Legal Problems in the Book of Ruth, VT 18 (1968), 79—99.
—, Review of H. Schmid, Mose: Überlieferung und Geschichte, CBQ 31 (1969), 607f.
—, Review of W. F. Albright, Yahweh and the Gods of Canaan, CBQ 32 (1970), 251f.
—, The Dating of the Megiddo Temples in Strata XV—XIV, ZDPV 86 (1970), 38—49.
Thureau-Dangin, F., Une Inscription de Narâm-Sin, RA 8 (1911), 199—200.
—, Trois Contrats de Ras-Shamra, Syria 18 (1937), 245—255.

Tournay, R., Nouzi, DBS VI, col. 644—674.
—, Bulletin: Assyriologie, RB 68 (1961), 475.
Trawick, B. B., The Bible as Literature, 1963.
Tucker, G. M., The Legal Background of Genesis 23, JBL 85 (1966), 77—84.
Tufnell, O., Lachish IV. The Bronze Age, 1958.
—, and Ward, W. A., Relations between Byblos, Egypt and Mesopotamia at the End of the Third Millenium B. C., Syria 43 (1966), 165—241.
—, The Pottery from Royal Tombs I—III at Byblos, Berytus 18 (1969), 5—33.

Uchelen, N. A. van, Abraham de Hebreeër, 1964.
Unger, E., Aḫlamê, RLA I, 57f.
—, Arrapha, RLA I, 154a.
Unger, M. F., Some Comments on the Text of Genesis 15 2. 3, JBL 72 (1953), 49f.
—, Archaeology and the Old Testament, 1956.
—, Israel and the Aramaeans of Damascus, 1957.
Ungnad, A., VAS I, 1907.
—, Urkunden aus Dilbat, VAS VII, 1909.
—, Kohler, J., and Koschaker, P., Hammurabi's Gesetz, III—VI 1909—1923.
—, and Kohler, J., Assyrische Rechtsurkunden, 1903.
—, Die ältesten Völkerwanderungen Vorderasiens, 1923.
—, Das hurritische Fragment des Gilgamesch-Epos, ZA 35 (1924), 133—140.
—, and Nicolò, M. San, Neubabylonische Rechts- und Verwaltungsurkunden, I 1935.
—, Subartu, 1936.
Uphill, E. P., Pithom and Raamses: their Location and Significance, II, JNES 28 (1969), 15—39.

Vandier, J., and Clère, J. J., Textes de la Première Période Intermédiaire et de la XIeme Dynastie, BiÄg 19, 1948.
Vaux, R. de, La Palestine et la Transjordanie au IIe millénaire et les origines israélites, ZAW 56 (1938), 225—238.
—, Les Patriarches Hebreux et les Découvertes Modernes, RB 53 (1946), 321—348; 55 (1948), 321—347; 56 (1949), 5—36.
—, Les Institutions de l'Ancien Testament, I—II 1958.
—, Die hebräischen Patriarchen und die modernen Entdeckungen, 1959.
—, The Hebrew Patriarchs and History, ThD 12 (1964), 227—240.
—, Les Patriarches hébreux et l'histoire, RB 72 (1965), 5—28.
—, Die Patriarchenerzählungen und die Geschichte, 1965.
—, Palestine During the Neolithic and Chalcolithic Periods, CAH², fascicle 47, 1966.
—, Method in the Study of Early Hebrew History, in: The Bible in Modern Scholarship, ed. by J. Philip Hyatt, 1966, 15—29.
—, Review of C. Epstein, Palestinian Bichrome Ware, RB 74 (1967), 268—271.
—, Review of P. Lapp, Dhahr Mirzbaneh Tombs, RB 74 (1967), 471—474.
—, Les Hurrites de l'Histoire et les Horites de la Bible, RB 74 (1967), 481—503.
—, Bulletin: Archéologie palestinienne, RB 74 (1967), 471—474.
—, Tirzah, in: Archaeology and Old Testament Study, ed. by D. W. Thomas, 1967, 371—383.
—, Bible et Orient, 1967.
—, Téman, ville ou région d'Édom, RB 76 (1969), 379—385.
—, On Right and Wrong Uses of Archaeology, in: Glueck Festschrift, 1970, 64—80.

Vawter, B., A Path Through Genesis, 1965^2.
—, Response to A. S. Kapelrud's "The Role of the Cult in Old Israel", in: The Bible in Modern Scholarship, ed. by J. P. Hyatt, 1966, 57—64.
Vercoutter, J., La Nubie au sud d'Abou-Simbel, Journal des Savants (1963), 129—134.
—, Fouilles à Mirgissa, Rev. d'égyptol. 15 (1963), 69—75.
—, Deux mois de fouilles à Mirgissa en Nubie Soudanaise, Bulletin de la Societé d'Égyptologie 37/38 (1963), 28f.
—, Textes Exécratoires de Mirgissa, CRAI (1963), 97—102.
—, Collections égyptiennes et soudanaises de l'Institut de Papyrologie et d'Egyptologie de Lille, 1964.
—, Excavations at Mirgissa I, Kush 12 (1964), 61.
Vernier, E., Bijoux et Orfèvreries, II 1927.
Vila, A., Un dépot de textes envoûtement an Moyen Empire, Journal des Savants (1963), 135—160.
Vincent, A., La Religion des Judéo-Araméens d'Éléphantine, 1937.
Vincent, L. H., Les Fouilles Américaines de Beisan, RB 37 (1928), 123—138.
—, Les Pays Bibliques et l'Égypte à la Fin de la XIIe Dynastie Égyptienne, Vivre et Penser, RB 51 (1942), 187—212.
Virolleaux, Ch., Baghouz l'ancienne Corsote, 1948.
—, Les Nouvelles Tablettes de Ras Shamra (1948—1949), Syria 28 (1951), 22—56.
—, Les Nouvelles Tablettes Alphabétiques de Ras Shamra, Comptes Rendus, Academie des Inscriptions et Belles-Lettres, 1955.
—, Le Palais Royal d'Ugarit, V 1965.
Vogt, E., Ugaritica, Bb 37 (1956), 387.
Volten, A., Zwei altägyptische politische Schriften, Analecta Aegyptiaca 4, 1945.
Vries, S. J. de, Chronology of the OT, IDB II, 580—599.

Wade-Gery, H. T., The Poet of the Iliad, 1952.
Wagner, M., Beiträge zur Aramaismenfrage im alttestamentlichen Hebräisch, VTS 16 (1967), 355—371.
Wailly, F. El., Tell al-Fikhar, Sumer 23 (1967), ef.
Walcot, P., and Lambert, W. G., A New Babylonian Theogony and Hesiod, Kadmos 4 (1965), 64—72.
Walle, B. van de, Remarques paléographiques sur les textes de proscription de Berlin, in: G. Posener, Princes et Pays D'Asie et de Nubie, 1940, 99—109.
Wallis, G., Die Tradition von den drei Ahnvätern, ZAW 81 (1969), 18—40.
Ward, W. A., Comparative Studies in Egyptian and Ugaritic, JNES 20 (1961), 31—40.
—, Egypt and the East Mediterranean in the Early Second Millenium B. C., Orientalia 30 (1961), 22—45. 129—155.
—, Egypt and the East Mediterranean from Predynastic times to the end of the Old Kingdom, JESHO 6 (1963), 1—57.
—, Relations between Egypt and Mesopotamia from Prehistoric Times to the End of the Middle Kingdom, JESHO 7 (1964), 1—45. 121—135.
—, Cylinders and Scarabs from a LB Temple at Amman, ADAJ 8/9 (1964), 47—55.
—, and Tufnell, O., Relations between Byblos, Egypt, and Mesopotamia at the end of the Third Millenium B. C., Syria 43 (1966), 165—241.
—, The Nomarch Khnumhotep at Pelusium, JEA 55 (1969), 215f.

Waterman, L., Some Repercussions from Late Levitical Genealogical Accretions in P and the Chronicler, AJSL 58 (1941), 49—56.

Watson, P. J., The Chronology of North Syria and North Mesopotamia from 10,000 B. C. to 2000 B. C., in: Chronologies in Old World Archaeology, ed. by R. W. Ehrich, 1945.

Watzinger, C., and Sellin, E., Jericho. Die Ergebnisse der Ausgrabungen, 1913.

Weidmann, H., Die Patriarchen und ihre Religion im Licht der Forschung seit Julius Wellhausen, 1968.

Weidner, E. F., Die Könige von Assyrien, MVÄG 26 (1921), no. 2.

—, Der Königspalast von Ugarit, AfO 16, 1 (1952), 114—116.

Weill, R., L'installation des Israélites en Palestine et la Légende des Patriarches, RL'HR 87 (1923), 69—120; 88 (1923), 1—44.

—, Notes sur les noms Asiatiques des "Textes d'Exécration" Égyptiens du Moyen Empire, in: Mélanges Syriens offerts à R. Dussaud, 2 (1939), 947—958.

Weinheimer, H., Hebräer und Israeliten, ZAW 29 (1909), 275—280.

Weippert, M., Die Landnahme der israelitischen Stämme in der neueren wissenschaftlichen Diskussion, 1967.

—, Die Nomadenquelle, in: Galling Festschrift, 1970, 259—272.

—, Abraham der Hebräer? Bemerkungen zu W. F. Albrights Deutung der Väter Israels, Bb 52 (1971), 407—432.

Weir, C. J. M., Nuzi, in: Archaeology and Old Testament Study, ed. by D. W. Thomas, 1967.

Weiser, A., Abraham, RGG³, I, col. 68—71.

Welles, C. B., Manumission and Adoption, RIDA 3 (1949), 507—520.

Wellhausen, J., Skizzen und Vorarbeiten, III 1887.

—, Prolegomena zur Geschichte Israels, 1905.

Wenig, S., Die Frau im alten Ägypten, 1967.

Westermarck, E., The History of Human Marriage, 1901.

Wilcke, C., Zur Geschichte der Amurriter in der Ur III Zeit, WO 5 (1969), 1—31.

—, Drei Phasen des Niedergangs des Reiches von Ur III, ZA 60 (1970), 54—69.

Wilhelm, G., Untersuchungen zum Hurro-Akkadischen von Nuzi, AOAT 9 (1970).

Wilson, J. A., The Egyptian Middle Kingdom at Megiddo, AJSL 58 (1941), 225—236.

Winckler, H., Altorientalische Forschungen, I 1893.

—, 'Ur-Kasdim als Heimat Abrahams'. Altorientalische Forschungen, I 1893, 98—100.

—, Altorientalische Forschungen, IIte Reihe, II 1900.

—, and Zimmern, H., ed., Die Keilinschriften und das Alte Testament, 1903³.

—, Zur Genesis, Altorientalische Forschungen IIIte Reihe, III/1 1906.

Winlock, H., The Rise and Fall of the Middle Kingdom, 1947.

Wiseman, D. J., The Alalakh Tablets, Occasional Publication of the British Institute of Archaeology at Ankara, no. 2, 1953.

—, The Laws of Hammurabi Again, JSS 7 (1962), 161—172.

Wolf, W., Die Bewaffnung des altägyptischen Heeres, 1926.

—, Der Stand der Hyksosfrage, ZDMG 83 (1929), 67—79.

Woolley, C. L., and Lawrence, T. E., The Wilderness of Zin, PEFA (1914/1915).

—, Abraham, 1935.

—, and Hawkes, J., Prehistory and the Beginnings of Civilization, I, History of Mankind, 1963.

Wright, G. E., The Pottery of Palestine from the Earliest Times to the End of the Early Bronze Age, 1937.
—, The Chronology of Palestinian Pottery in Middle Bronze I, BASOR 71 (1938), 27—34.
—, and Grant, E., Ain Shems Excavations, IV—V 1938—1939.
—, The Literary and Historical Problem of Joshua 10 and Judges 1, JNES 5 (1946), 105—114.
—, The Study of the Old Testament, in: Protestant Thought in the Twentieth Century, ed. by A. S. Nash, 1951, 15—44.
—, The Old Testament Against its Environment, 1955.
—, The First Campaign at Tell Balâtah (Shechem), BASOR 144 (1956), 9—20.
—, The Westminster Historical Atlas to the Bible, 1957.
—, The Second Campaign at Tell Balâtah (Shechem), BASOR 148 (1957), 11—28.
—, Biblical Archaeology, 1957.
—, Bringing Old Testament Times to Life. The National Geographic Magazine 112 (1957), 833—864.
—, Biblische Archäologie, 1958 (German trans. of Biblical Archaeology).
—, Archaeology and Old Testament Studies, JBL 77 (1958), 39—51.
—, Modern Issues in Biblical Studies — History and the Patriarchs, ET 71 (1959/1960), 292—296.
—, Is Glueck's Aim to Prove that the Bible is True?, BAR 1 (1961), 14—21.
—, The Archaeology of Palestine, in: Albright Festschrift, 73—112.
—, ed., The Bible and the Ancient Near East, Essays in honor of W. F. Albright, 1961.
—, The Achievement of N. Glueck, BAR I (1961), 11—14.
—, Biblical Archaeology, 1962.
—, Cult and History, Interpretation 16 (1962), 3—20.
—, God who Acts, 1962.
—, History and Reality, in: The Old Testament and Christian Faith, ed. by B. W. Anderson, 1964, 176—199.
—, Shechem, in: Archaeology and Old Testament Study, ed. by D. W. Thomas, 1967, 355—370.
—, The Significance of Ai in the Third Millenium, B. C., in: Galling Festschrift, 1970, 299—319.
—, The Phenomenon of American Archaeology, in: Glueck Festschrift, 3—40.
—, Archaeological Method in Palestine — An American Interpretation, Erez Israel 9 (1969), 120—133.
—, The Archaeology of Palestine from the Neolithic through the Middle Bronze Age, JAOS 91 (1971), 276—293.
Wright, G. R. H., The Bronze Age Temple at Amman, ZAW 78 (1966), 351—357.
—, A Method of Excavation Common in Palestine, ZDPV 82 (1966), 113—124.
—, Tell el-Yehudiyah and the Glacis, ZDPV 84 (1968), 1—17.

Yadin, Y., The Earliest Record of Egypt's Military Penetration into Asia, IEJ 5 (1955), 1—16.
—, Hyksos Fortifications and the Battering Ram, BASOR 137 (1955), 23—32.
—, Excavations at Hazor, 1956, (preliminary communiqué) IEJ 7 (1957), 118—123.
—, Excavations at Hazor, 1958, IEJ 9 (1959), 74—88.

Yadin, Y., The Art of Warfare in Biblical Lands, 1963.
—, Hazor, in: Archaeology and Old Testament Study, ed. by D. W. Thomas, 1967, 245 bis 263.
Yaron, R., and Daube, D., Jacob's Reception by Laban, JSS 1 (1956), 60—62.
—, Redemption of Persons in the Ancient Near East, RIDA 6 (1959), 155—176.
—, On Divorce in Old Testament Times, RIDA 4 (1957), 117—128.
—, Introduction to the Law of the Aramaic Papyri, 1961.
—, Duabus sororibus coniunctio, RIDA 10 (1963), 115—136.
—, Matrimonial Mishaps at Eshnunna, JSS 8 (1963), 1—16.
—, The Rejected Bridegroom, Orientalia 34 (1965), 23—29.
—, The Middle Assyrian Laws and the Bible, Biblica 51 (1970), 549—557.
Yeivin, S., A New Egyptian Source for the History of Palestine and Syria, JPOS 14 (1934), 194—229.
—, Ya'qob'el, JEA 45 (1959), 16—18.
—, Early Contacts between Canaan and Egypt, IEJ 10 (1960), 193—203.

Zeuner, F. E., A History of Domesticated Animals, 1963.
Zimmern, H., and Winkler, H., ed., Die Keilinschriften und das Alte Testament, 1903³.

Indices

A. General Index

B. Index of Authors

C. Onomastic Index

1. Names in Transliteration

2. Names in Quadratic Script

D. Index of Nuzi Tablets

E. Index of Biblical Texts